The ASAM Criteria

Treatment Criteria for Addictive, Substance-Related,

and Co-Occurring Conditions

Third Edition

Published by:
The Change Companies®
5221 Sigstrom Drive
Carson City, NV 89706
Phone: (888) 889-8866
E-mail: <contact@changecompanies.net>
Website: www.changecompanies.net

The correct bibliographic citation for this book is Mee-Lee D, Shulman GD, Fishman MJ, Gastfriend
DR, Miller MM, eds. *The ASAM Criteria: Treatment Criteria for Addictive, Substance-Related, and
Co-Occurring Conditions.* 3rd ed. Carson City, NV: The Change Companies®; 2013.

ISBN-13: 978-1-61702-197-8

Library of Congress Control Number: 2013947771

10   9   8   7   6   5   4

For additional copies of this book, please contact 888-889-8866.

The ASAM Criteria

Treatment Criteria for Addictive, Substance-Related, and Co-Occurring Conditions

Third Edition

David Mee-Lee, MD
Chief Editor

Gerald D. Shulman, MA, FACATA
Marc J. Fishman, MD, FASAM
David R. Gastfriend, MD
Deputy Editors

Michael M. Miller, MD, FASAM
Managing Editor

Scott M. Provence, MA, MFA
Publication Editor

Table of Contents

About the Tabs

Readers can use the tabs in this book to quickly reference key components of the treatment process. Most tabs contain multiple chapters, which move sequentially through assessment, service planning, and level of care placement. Both tab and chapter titles are listed at the top of each page for further reference.

Table of Contents

LOC Placement

5

Emerging Understandings

---- **The ASAM Criteria Editors** ----

David Mee-Lee, MD
Chief Editor

Gerald D. Shulman, MA, FACATA
Marc J. Fishman, MD, FASAM
David R. Gastfriend, MD
Deputy Editors

Michael M. Miller, MD, FASAM
Managing Editor

Scott M. Provence, MA, MFA
Publication Editor

Lead Authors and Workgroup Members for *The ASAM Criteria*

Adolescent Criteria
Lead Author
Marc J. Fishman, MD, FASAM

The ASAM Criteria Software
Lead Author
David R. Gastfriend, MD

Withdrawal Management and Intoxication Management
Lead Author
George Kolodner, MD

Workgroup Members
Margaret Kotz, DO, FASAM
David M. Ockert, PhD

Level 0.5
Lead Authors
Ray Daugherty, BA
Frankie D. Lemus, MA, LMFT

Levels 1 and 2
Lead Author
Gerald D. Shulman, MA, FACATA

Level 3
Lead Author
Gerald D. Shulman, MA, FACATA

Workgroup Members
Ray Daugherty, BA
Karen Garrett, MA, CPLP, CAP, CPP, CMHP
Manuel Guantez, PsyD, LCADC
Patrice Muchowski, ScD, CADAC
Glenda J. Spencer, MS, LAC

Lead Authors and Workgroup Members for
The ASAM Criteria (continued)

Level 4
Lead Author
David Mee-Lee, MD

Opioid Treatment Services
Lead Author
Joel L. Millard, DSW, LCSW

Workgroup Members
Edwin A. Salsitz, MD, FASAM
George E. Stavros, MD

Special Populations
Chair
Gerald D. Shulman, MA, FACATA

Older Adults
Lead Author
Gerald D. Shulman, MA, FACATA

Parents or Prospective Parents Receiving Addiction Treatment Concurrently with their Children
Lead Author
Carleen Jimenez, MA, CMHC, ASUDC

Workgroup Members
Gerald D. Shulman, MA, FACATA

Persons in Safety Sensitive Occupations
Lead Author
Paul H. Earley, MD, FASAM

Persons in Criminal Justice Settings
Lead Author
Frankie D. Lemus, MA, LMFT

Workgroup Members
Robert M. Hooper, PhD, LGSW
Kevin Lowe, PhD
Stephen K. Valle, ScD, MBA, LADC I, CADAC
Vicky Westmoreland, LSAC, APC

Gambling Disorder
Lead Author
Gerald D. Shulman, MA, FACATA

Tobacco Use Disorder
Lead Authors
Susan Blank, MD, FAPA
Lori D. Karan, MD, FACP, FASAM

Workgroup Members
Michael V. Burke, EdD
Richard D. Hurt, MD
Michael M. Miller, MD, FASAM
Judith Prochaska, PhD, MPH
David Sachs, MD
Peter Selby, MBBS, CCFP, FCFP, FASAM
Michael Steinberg, MD, MPH
Ken Wassum
Jill M. Williams, MD

Co-Occurring Disorders
Lead Author
David Mee-Lee, MD

Workgroup Member
Kenneth Minkoff, MD

Cautionary Statement

for Use of *The ASAM Criteria*

The ASAM criteria do not purport to set a medical or legal standard of care and may not encompass all of the levels of service options that may be available in a changing health care field. Therefore, the ASAM criteria presented and discussed may not be wholly relevant to all levels and modalities of care (such as forensic treatment facilities, custodial care providers, or addiction treatment programs that address concomitant developmental disability disorders) or to external judgments, such as those made by legal or regulatory entities concerning the appropriateness of patient admission into various levels of care. The ASAM criteria are designed to serve as a resource for general, mental health, and addiction treatment clinicians and counselors, but are not intended to substitute for their independent clinical judgment based on the particular facts and circumstances presented by individual patients.

ASAM and the publisher, workgroup members, authors, and editors of *The ASAM Criteria: Treatment Criteria for Addictive, Substance-Related, and Co-Occurring Conditions* expressly disclaim that application of the ASAM criteria to any particular patient will result in the appropriate service plan and level of care. Furthermore, they expressly disclaim any and all responsibility for application of these criteria. They shall not be responsible for any action or omission by any person rendering or recommending treatment or otherwise making a patient placement decision or recommendation with respect to any particular patient. The content of this publication has been provided by authors, editors, workgroup members, and other contributing individuals, and does not necessarily represent the opinions of any organizations or affiliations with which these individuals are associated. There is no warranty that the information in *The ASAM Criteria* or *The ASAM Criteria Software* is free from all errors and omissions.

Preface

The ASAM Criteria text and *The ASAM Criteria Software* are clinical guides designed by the American Society of Addiction Medicine (ASAM) to improve assessment and outcomes-driven treatment and recovery services. It is also used to match patients to appropriate types and levels of care. In general, the purpose of *The ASAM Criteria* is to enhance the use of multidimensional assessments to develop patient-centered service plans and to guide clinicians, counselors, and care managers in making objective decisions about patient admission, continuing care, and transfer/discharge for various levels of care for addictive, substance-related, and co-occurring conditions. This publication is a companion to *The ASAM Criteria Software*, a standardized software version of the adult criteria for open-source release, funded by the U.S. Substance Abuse and Mental Health Services Administration (SAMHSA). The criteria contained within these pages are considered evolutionary in nature and are intended to encourage further patient matching and placement research. They reflect a clinical consensus of adult and adolescent addiction treatment specialists, developed through the incorporation of extensive field review comments.

The full name for this publication is *The ASAM Criteria: Treatment Criteria for Addictive, Substance-Related, and Co-Occurring Conditions.* A revision of the previous edition, titled *ASAM Patient Placement Criteria for the Treatment of Substance-Related Disorders, Second Edition-Revised (ASAM PPC-2R,* 2001), was referred to in many circles as "The ASAM PPC" (an abbreviation of *"Patient Placement Criteria"*), or, simply, "The ASAM." Earlier editions of this work described various levels of care, or intensities of service, for the treatment of addiction and other substance use disorders. The focus was on "placing" patients into a circumscribed "level of care," often operationally described as a "setting" or a "structured program of care." In the current edition,

The ASAM Criteria seeks to de-emphasize the notion of "placement" and to respond to advances in clinical knowledge, clinical practice, and public policy (including the enactment of health care reform in the form of the 2010 Patient Protection and Affordable Care Act).

The ASAM Criteria is intended as a stimulus for further research and discussion of the treatment and care of addiction and other substance-related and co-occurring conditions. The criteria contained within are necessarily general in their approach and are not intended as, nor should be used as, a standard of care for the treatment of any individual. The treatment of individual patients suffering from addiction and co-occurring conditions requires professional evaluation and the exercise of independent judgment on a case-by-case basis. So while *The ASAM Criteria* was designed to be as objective, measurable and quantifiable as possible, readers must also recognize that certain aspects of these criteria require subjective interpretation. In this regard, the assessment and treatment of substance-related disorders is no different from biomedical or psychiatric conditions in which diagnosis or assessment and treatment is a mix of objectively measured criteria and experientially based professional judgments.

A major emphasis of this revision is to provide a user-friendly guide to understanding the principles, processes, and procedures to implement and apply *The ASAM Criteria* to a variety of patient populations in a wide range of settings.

It is the hope of the editors and authors that *The ASAM Criteria* will continue to help increase access to care in the addiction, mental health, and general health care systems for all who suffer from addiction. The principles, concepts, and criteria of this text promote good stewardship of resources to allow people to receive all the care they need for successful recovery.

Acknowledgments

ASAM wishes to thank The Change Companies®' publication team who worked diligently with Publication Editor, Scott M. Provence, and ASAM Publications Manager and Managing Editor, Brendan McEntee, to design and craft an attractive, user-friendly manual. Key members include Jessica Fanaselle, Johanna Landis, Frankie D. Lemus, Jennifer Sande, and Brianna Sheck. In addition, ASAM wishes to acknowledge the valuable comments and recommendations of the members of the Coalition for National Clinical Criteria, the members of its subcommittees, and those participants who drafted material for and served as reviewers of *The ASAM Criteria*.

ASAM expresses special gratitude to those individuals who chaired the following drafting committees: Gerald D. Shulman, MA, FACATA, Chair, Workgroup on Residential, Outpatient, and Special Populations; George Kolodner, MD, Chair, Workgroup on Withdrawal Management; David Mee-Lee, MD, Chair, Workgroup on Co-Occurring Disorders and Medically Managed Inpatient Treatment; Marc J. Fishman, MD, FASAM, Chair, Workgroup on Adolescent Criteria; Joel L. Millard, DSW, LCSW, Chair, Workgroup on Opioid Treatment Services; Frankie D. Lemus, MA, LMFT, Chair, Workgroup on Persons in Criminal Justice Settings; Susan Blank, MD, and Lori D. Karan, MD, Co-Chairs, Workgroup on Tobacco Use Disorder.

This publication incorporates and supersedes the *Patient Placement Criteria for the Treatment of Psychoactive Substance Use Disorders*, April 1991; *Patient Placement Criteria for the Treatment of Substance-Related Disorders*, Second Edition, April 1996; and the *Patient Placement Criteria for the Treatment of Substance-Related Disorders, Second Edition–Revised*, April 2001; all published by the American Society of Addiction Medicine.

How to
Use This Book

Moving From Assessment Through Service Planning and Level of Care Placement

Among the guiding principles of *The ASAM Criteria* is the goal of helping move practitioners toward individualized, clinically driven, participant-directed, and outcome-informed treatment. This approach to care goes beyond treatment methods for addictive, substance-related, and co-occurring conditions that are driven by the patient's diagnosis (every patient gets the same treatment simply because they have a given diagnosis) or are program-driven (every patient gets the treatment that the program offers, just because that is what the program offers in its service continuum). This approach creates several distinct and unique steps and cycles in the services a patient participates in, which may need to be modified depending on the individual receiving care, but which represent a participant's journey through treatment: moving from assessment through service planning and level of care placement.*

In addiction treatment, the treatment itself should extend beyond simple resolution of observable physical, social, or mental health distress, to the achievement of overall healthier functioning and wellness, where the patient demonstrates a response to treatment through new insights, attitudes, and behaviors. Addiction treatment services have as their goal not simply stabilizing the patient's condition, but altering the course of the patient's disease toward wellness and recovery.

To that end, the treatment process outlined in *The ASAM Criteria* mirrors that of a clinically driven and participant-directed treatment process. After receiving a foundational grounding in

Although it may not be possible to always move step-by-step through a participant-focused treatment approach, the process illustrated in this book represents what ASAM's criteria are capable of in guiding the user of the criteria. *The ASAM Criteria* is organized to follow the steps toward participant-focused treatment, and while not all steps may be represented in these pages, readers will notice how **content is arranged to match a patient's journey from assessment through treatment.**

ASAM's criteria, readers will notice how sections of this book move from asking initial questions like "What does the patient want? Why now?" to "What life areas, or 'dimensions,' are most important to determining treatment priorities?" to "What specific services are needed, and what is the appropriate dose, intensity, frequency, and duration of those services?" all the way through "What is the progress and outcome of the treatment plan and placement decision?"

The following chapters of *The ASAM Criteria* focus on components of this broad view of treatment, detailing everything from the intake and multidimensional assessment process to priority-based service planning to intensity of services and appropriate level of care placement.

See page 15 for a description of the use of terms such as "patient," "participant," and "client."

The Tabs along the book's side provide quick-reference access to large content portions of the book. Abbreviated chapter or section titles, or other content information, are also listed here for ease of use.

In addition to facilitating content access, tabs 2, 3, and 4 represent key stages in the treatment process, showing how practitioners can move from assessment through service planning and level of care placement.

Tabs

1 History and Applications

2 Intake and Assessment

3 Service Planning and Placement

4 Level of Care Placement
- Withdrawal Management
- LOC Placement
- Special Populations

5 Emerging Understandings of Addiction

Key Stages in The ASAM Criteria Treatment Process

…ner levels of care, and their staff can help …ts access support services such as child …vocational training, and transportation. …ment interventions and modalities may also …d to be tailored to engage adolescents who …at varying levels of developmental maturity.

Intensive pharmacotherapy treatment …ervices, such as Opioid Treatment Programs …referred to in former years as "methadone maintenance treatment" (MMT) clinics, or as "Opioid Maintenance Therapy" (OMT)), can involve patients in intensive psychosocial interventions concurrently. Such programs, involving three to five or more contact days per week and at least nine hou…

here for two variations: Inte… Services (Level 2.1) and Par… (Level 2.5) programs.

Length of Service
The duration of treatment v… severity of the patient's illne… response to treatment.

Co-Occurring Mental and … Related Disorders
The services of a Level 2 trea… appropriate for patients with … tal and substance-related dis…

a Adolescent-Specific Content

Content accompanied by this symbol represents information and considerations relevant to adolescent populations.

…ddiction trea… …he intensive …ram. Suc… …services … …evel 2.1 c… …anced pr… …an includ… …erapists, …actice me… …) workin… …on clinic… …ors, nurse… …and physicians). All of these … are working in collaboration … clinicians and professionals w… trained and credentialed to w… complex cases (eg, addiction … ing in collaboration with othe… interdisciplinary team).

…those patien… …sion, Level 2… …ed with Level 3.1, Cli… …ntensity Residen- tial Trea… Dist… …e made among various sub- types of … 2 programs. Criteria are offered

a Adolescent-Specific Considerations: Withdrawal Manag…

Dimension 1 (Acute Intoxication and/or Withdrawal Potential) is the first of the six asses… sions to be evaluated in making treatment and placement decisions. The range of clinic… dimension has given rise to a range of withdrawal management levels of service. A pati… encing or at risk of an acute withdrawal syndrome should not be treated at Level 2.1. Fo… designation of Level 2.1-WM has not been used. However, it is important to recognize li… withdrawal symptoms (such as severe insomnia and vivid, disturbing dreams associated… withdrawal), which can be quite impairing, are appropriately addressed in a Level 2.1 se…

Each content page of *The ASAM Criteria* has been created with several tools to facilitate reader usability. Take a look at the page sample below for an example of how to navigate through this book.

Treatment Levels Within Level 2
Level 2.1: Intensive Outpatient Services

> **Pay attention to these section break indicators. Within certain chapters, breaks between sections may represent a new criteria set or a new population focus.**

...ient
...ization

...ne
...or her

...e-

...ram are
...ng men-
...e men-
...ces are
...or partial
...require
...ould be
...g capable
...aff for
...mental
...s, psychol-
...n nurses,
...oration
...fied and/
...ogists,
...specialists
...al health
...ecially
...the most
...sts, work-
...rs of the

...s (IOPs) generally
...ured programming
...hours for adoles-
...counseling and
...ated and mental
...s needs for psy-
...are addressed
...rral arrangements
...quires only mainte-
nance monitoring. (Services provided outside th...
primary program must be tightly coordinate...

There are occasions when the patient's
progress in the IOP no longer requires nine
hours per week of treatment for adults or six
hours per week for adolescents but he or she...
not yet made enough stable progress to be f...
transferred to a Level 1 program. In such cases,
less than nine hours per week for adults and six
hours per week for adolescents as a transition
step down in intensity should be considered as a
continuation of the IOP program for one or two
weeks. Such continuity allows for a smoother
transition to Level 1 to avoid exacerbation and
recurrence of signs and symptoms.

Intensive outpatient treatment differs from
partial hospitalization (Level 2.5) programs in
the intensity of clinical services that are directly
available. Specifically, most intensive outpatient
programs have less capacity to effectively treat

offered in any appropriate setting that meets
state licensure or certification criteria.

SUPPORT SYSTEMS
All Programs
In Level 2.1 programs, necessary sup-
p... ms include:

...psychiatric, labo-

> **Certain chapters of the book will use icons to highlight service characteristics within a level of care.**

by telephone 24 hours a day, 7 days a
week when the treatment program is not
in session.

c. Direct affiliation with (or close coordination
through referral to) more and less intensive levels of care and supportive housing
services.

Co-Occurring Enhanced Programs
In addition to the support systems described
here for co-occurring capable programs, Level
2.1 co-occurring enhanced programs offer

LEVEL 2.1 ❹

Using both the book and the software

This book and *The ASAM Criteria Software* are companion text and software application. This text delineates the dimensions, levels of care, and decision rules that comprise the ASAM criteria. *The ASAM Criteria Software* provides the approved structured interview to guide the adult assessment and calculate the complex decision tree to yield suggested levels of care. The text and the software should be used in tandem, the text to provide the clinical background and guidance as to the decision rules in the software, and the software to enable comprehensive, standardized evaluation. Effective, reliable treatment planning requires that both be used together. Note that services specifically tailored for adolescents are addressed throughout *The ASAM Criteria* but are not included in *The ASAM Criteria Software*.

...men-
...y in this
...experi-
...on, the
...ubacute
...rijuana

THEN AND NOW
1

The ASAM Criteria:
Then and Now

Historical Foundations

In the 1980s, addiction treatment providers were experiencing increasing pressure to explain and justify long lengths of stay in residential and inpatient programs, especially if they were fixed length of stay programs. Rather than simply fight such pressure politically, several organizations recognized the need to proactively offer clinically sound alternatives to the proprietary, variable, and sometimes idiosyncratic criteria used by payers who funded or managed the care.

Approximately 40 to 50 sets of criteria were being used by various insurers and utilization management firms in the private sector by the end of the 1980s. Many of them varied sharply in their guidance regarding assessment and placement, and some were even in direct contradiction to other criteria sets. This patchwork effort caused confusion where consensus was desperately needed. Some of the initiatives to reach consensus during this time laid the foundation on which *The ASAM Criteria* rests today.

Cleveland Criteria
Developed at the request of the Northern Ohio Chemical Dependency Treatment Directors Association, the "Cleveland Criteria" were designed by a team of consultants coordinated by the Chemical Abuse Treatment Outcome Registry (CATOR). Members of the steering committee that guided the project represented treatment programs and other interested organizations in northern Ohio. The authors of the Cleveland Criteria were Norman G. Hoffmann, PhD, James A. Halikas, MD, and David Mee-Lee, MD. As documented in the seminal 1990 report of the Institute of Medicine of the National Academy of Sciences, *Broadening the Base of Treatment for Alcohol Problems*, the Cleveland Criteria were a significant contribution to the addiction field and provided a springboard for treatment evaluation and assessment studies to follow.[1]

NAATP Criteria
In a parallel effort, a workgroup composed of providers and consultants, coordinated by Richard D. Weedman, MSW, FACATA, of Health care Network, Inc., used all criteria sets available at the time to produce the National Association of Addiction Treatment Providers' (NAATP) *Patient Placement Criteria*. These criteria were used by approximately 210 publicly and privately funded addiction treatment programs to enhance their internal utilization review and case management systems, as well as to guide their clinical decision-making processes.

NAATP-ASAM Collaboration
Progress made by these initial efforts eventually led to another project, in which NAATP and the American Society of Addiction Medicine

(ASAM) recruited a representative group of addiction experts to develop adult and adolescent criteria, based on the Cleveland Criteria and the NAATP Criteria. The project resulted in the identification and description of four levels of care, which were differentiated from each other by the following characteristics:

» Degree of direct medical management provided

» Structure, safety, and security provided

» Intensity of treatment services provided

This project also identified and described six assessment dimensions that could be used to differentiate patient needs for services across the four levels of care. The result of these efforts were compiled to create the *Patient Placement Criteria for the Treatment of Psychoactive Substance Use Disorders*, which was published by the American Society of Addiction Medicine in 1991.

Coalition for National Clinical Criteria

Recognizing the need to broaden stakeholder participation in developing patient placement criteria, ASAM convened a meeting of providers, payers, managed care professionals, and policymakers the same year its initial *Patient Placement Criteria* was published. Out of this session emerged a consensus that the field ought to work toward one national set of criteria that could be accepted by employers, purchasers, and providers of care, both in the public and private sector. This group helped identify the desirable characteristics of clinical criteria guidelines.

Group participants concluded that consensus criteria should be developed with input from all stakeholders, which were defined as (a) those who use criteria to make decisions about patient care, utilization review, and payment; and (b) those who suffer the consequences if such criteria are not used or are used inappropriately.

In November of 1992, ASAM again convened representatives of all stakeholder groups to build on the work of the first conference. At this meeting, an ad hoc entity called the "Coalition for National Clinical Criteria" was formed to continue the consensus-building process. The Coalition initially met annually and has continued its influence through a Steering Committee, comprised of major stakeholders who have either endorsed the use of the ASAM criteria and/or actively promote their use in care provision and care management. Workgroups composed of Steering Committee members and associated organizations served as drafters and field reviewers of the *ASAM PPC-2* (1996), *ASAM PPC-2R* (2001), and the current edition, *The ASAM Criteria.*

ASAM's Commitment to The ASAM Criteria

ASAM is committed to shepherding the ongoing development and application of its criteria. This book continues the mission entrusted to ASAM for a unified voice for clinically driven criteria that preserves access to care and resources for all who suffer from addiction.

Current and Future Directions

The point in history held by the current edition of *The ASAM Criteria* will no doubt be an interesting one. It is arguably quite appropriate for this edition to focus on addiction associated with substance use (as its subtitle claims), because, except for gambling disorder, there is not a clear evidence base regarding the true epidemiology of non-substance-associated addiction. In the future, however, one could envision *The ASAM Criteria*'s admission to levels of care as applicable to other cases of addiction. The current edition takes steps toward this with the inclusion of a section on gambling disorder, as articulated in the *DSM-5*[2], while other cases of addiction, such as "sex addiction," "Internet addiction," or "exercise addiction," still await a consensus on definitions, criteria, prevalence, and incidence that has yet to emerge.

During the years when the current edition of *The ASAM Criteria* was under development, ASAM published a groundbreaking definition of addiction,[3] describing addiction as involving a pathological pursuit of "reward and/or relief by substance use and other behaviors." But there has not been sufficient research done within the conceptual format of this new definition from ASAM to allow an understanding of which over-gamblers, which over-exercisers, or which over-eaters actually have addiction associated with such behaviors. Likewise, we do not yet know if others who seem to manifest a loss of control over certain behaviors or deficits in satiety when pursuing pleasure through various behaviors actually have the illness of addiction.

Looking toward the future, however, with better understanding of non-substance-related cases of addiction, it is likely that professionals in general health care settings, specialty mental health settings, and specialty addiction settings, will develop brief interventions and screening methodologies for these conditions as well. Regardless of its point in history, each edition of ASAM's criteria aims to encourage the addiction services field and all of health care to better understand how to best meet the needs of persons in distress, particularly when the vast majority of those needing addiction treatment are involved with general medical care services and are not yet—likely for reasons having to do with their readiness to change—engaged with any specialty services to address their needs.

Guiding Principles of *The ASAM Criteria*

Beginning with the first edition of ASAM's criteria, certain foundational concepts have continued through this edition and will no doubt serve as the foundation for any future developments. Similar to its predecessors, the following guiding principles serve as the basis for all content within *The ASAM Criteria*:

» Moving from one-dimensional to **multidimensional assessment**
» Moving from program-driven to **clinically driven and outcomes-driven treatment**
» Moving from fixed length of service to **variable length of service**
» Moving from a limited number of discrete levels of care to a **broad and flexible continuum of care**
» Identifying **adolescent-specific needs**
» **Clarifying the goals of treatment**
» **Moving away from using previous "treatment failure"** as an admission prerequisite
» Moving toward an **interdisciplinary, team approach to care**
» **Clarifying the role of the physician**
» **Focusing on treatment outcomes**
» Engaging with **"Informed Consent"**
» Clarifying **"Medical Necessity"**
» **Incorporating ASAM's definition of addiction**

Moving from one-dimensional to multidimensional assessment

The ASAM Criteria continues to encourage moving away from treatment based on diagnosis alone (ie, seeing a diagnosis as a sufficient justification for entering a certain modality or intensity of treatment) toward treatment that is holistic and able to address multiple needs. A diversity of clinical offerings and intensities reflects the diversity of patients who may have needs in a number of clinical and functional dimensions. The criteria's six assessment dimensions were specified in order to address this guiding principle. These dimensions are introduced in Chapter Three: Intake and Assessment.

Moving from program-driven to clinically driven and outcomes-driven treatment

Rather than focusing on "placement" in a program, often with a fixed length of stay, *The ASAM Criteria* supports individualized, person-centered treatment that is responsive to the patient's specific needs and progress in treatment.

Moving from fixed length of service to variable length of service

Outcomes research in addiction treatment has not yet provided a scientific basis for determining precise lengths of stay for optimum results. Thus, addiction treatment professionals recognize that length of stay must be individualized, based on the severity of the patient's illness and the patient's level of functioning at the point of service entry, as well as based on their response to treatment, progress, and outcomes. At the same time, research does show a positive correlation between longer participation in the continuum of care and better outcomes. While in the current edition, length of service is still presented as variable, based on patients' complex needs and outcomes, both sides of this discussion (fixed versus variable lengths of service) are raised within this edition in order to increase awareness of length-of-stay issues.

Moving from a limited number of discrete levels of care to a broad and flexible continuum of care

The criteria build on the original concept that levels of care represent intensities of service along a continuum, each of which may be provided in a variety of program types, including those that offer more than one level of care and that serve multiple populations. Treatment is delivered across a continuum of services that reflect the varying severity of illnesses treated and the intensity of services required.

Referral to a specific level of care must be based on a careful assessment of the patient with an alcohol, tobacco, and/or other substance use disorder, and/or a gambling disorder. A primary goal underlying the criteria presented here is for the patient to be placed in the most appropriate level of care. For both clinical and financial reasons, the preferable level of care is that which is the least intensive while still meeting treatment objectives and providing safety and security for the patient. Moreover, while the levels of care are presented as discrete ranks, in reality they represent benchmarks or points along a continuum of treatment services that could be harnessed in a variety of ways, depending on a patient's needs and responses. A patient may begin at a required level and move to a more or less intensive level of care, depending on his or her individual needs.

It is recognized that payments for services need to match this continuum of care and intensity of service. Many providers of addiction treatment offer only one or two of the many levels of service described in these criteria. In such situations, movement through levels might mean referring the patient out of the provider's own network of care. ASAM believes that an accurate and thorough description of both patient needs and treatment levels will further assist the treatment field to develop the appropriate continuum of specialty care necessary for effective treatment. While lack of reimbursement for some levels of care, or lack of availability of other levels of care, may render this impossible at present, the goal of *The ASAM Criteria* is to stimulate the development of efficient treatment services that can be made available to all patients.

Identifying adolescent-specific needs

Adolescents who use alcohol, tobacco, and/ or other drugs, or who manifest pathological patterns of gambling, differ significantly from adults who do the same. While substance use disorders in adolescents and adults may have common biopsychosocial elements of etiology, they are different in many aspects of their expression and treatment. Adolescence affords a unique opportunity to modify risk factors that are still active and not yet complete in their influence on development. Adolescents must be approached differently from adults because of differences in their stages of emotional, cognitive, physical, social, and moral development. Examples of these fundamental developmental issues include the extremely potent influences of the adolescent's interactions with family and peers, the expected immaturity of most adolescents' independent living skills, and the fact that some amount of testing limits is a normative developmental task of adolescence.

Most adolescents do not develop classic physical dependence or well-defined withdrawal symptoms (although the epidemic of youth opioid addiction is an exception), nor do they exhibit the physiological deterioration seen in many adults suffering from substance-related disorders, because of the shorter duration of their exposure to alcohol, tobacco, and/or other drugs. Nevertheless, they are vulnerable to the full range of emotional, behavioral, familial, and cognitive manifestations of addiction.

In fact, adolescents may be more susceptible than adults to the functionally impairing impact of the use of substances, even in the absence of physiological withdrawal. The progression from casual use to high severity substance use disorders can be more rapid in adolescents than in adults. Also, adolescents typically demonstrate a higher degree of co-occurring psychopathology, which may not remit with abstinence. These limitations severely inhibit the ability of adolescents to arrest their addiction and address essential developmental tasks without external assistance and supports.

Adolescents' use of substances frequently impairs their emotional and intellectual growth. Substance use can limit a young person's ability to complete the maturational tasks of adolescence, which involve personal relationships and social skills, identity formation, individuation, development of a full repertoire of coping skills, education, employment, and family role responsibilities. Because substance use alters the way in which individuals approach and experience interpersonal interactions, the substance-using adolescent's psychological and social development are compromised, as is the formation of a strong positive self-identity.

Younger adolescents have a very narrow view of the world, with little capacity to think of future implications of present actions; nevertheless, they may adopt a pseudomature ("streetwise") posture. Adolescents, especially those who live in a stressed family system, or those with limited intellectual development, may be delayed or impaired in acquiring abstract thinking. Thus, the physician or counselor who attempts to reason with an adolescent about the long-term health effects of substance use often does so with minimal impact because the adolescent is unable to appreciate such long-term consequences.

These and other developmental issues make adolescents particularly vulnerable. As a result, they typically require greater amounts of external assistance and support, both to protect them from the sequelae of substance use and to engage them in the recovery process. Adolescents usually have not yet acquired the

The ASAM Criteria distinguishes and highlights adult and **adolescent** treatment information, where appropriate. Within each level of care, for example, unique diagnostic and dimensional admission criteria are presented for both adults and adolescents. At the same time, this edition also takes steps to recognize the overlapping and congruent approaches to treatment these populations share.

skills for independent living, and, even without the impairments associated with substance use, they must rely heavily on the guidance of adults. In general, for a given degree of severity or functional impairment, adolescents require more intensive treatment than adults. This difference is reflected in clinical practice—and in the criteria—by a tendency to place adolescents in more intensive levels of care.

Clarifying the goals of treatment

Treatment that is tailored to the needs of the individual, guided by an individualized treatment plan, and developed in consultation with the patient, is helpful in establishing a therapeutic alliance and therefore contributing significantly to treatment outcomes. The individualized plan should be based on a comprehensive biopsychosocial assessment of the patient and, when possible, a comprehensive evaluation of the family as well.

Patient-centered care includes documentation showing where and how the treatment plan...

» Identifies problems or priorities, such as obstacles to recovery, or knowledge or skill deficits that inhibit achievement of the patient's overall reason for seeking treatment.

» Includes strengths, skills, and resources, such as coping strategies to deal with negative affects and stressors, successful exercise routines, medications that have been effective, positive social supports, and a strong connection to a source of spiritual support.

» States goals that guide realistic, measurable, achievable, and short-term resolution of priorities or reduction of the symptoms or problems.

» Lists methods or strategies that identify the personal actions of the patient and the treatment services to be provided by staff, the site of those services, staff responsible for delivering treatment, and a timetable for follow through with the treatment plan that promotes accountability.

» Is written so as to facilitate measurement of progress. As with other disease processes, length of service should be linked directly to the patient's response to treatment (for example, attainment of the treatment goals and degree of resolution regarding the identified clinical problems or priorities).

The goals of intervention and treatment (including safe and comfortable withdrawal management, motivational enhancement to identify the need for recovery, the attainment of skills to maintain abstinence, etc.) determine the methods, intensity, frequency, and types of services provided. The clinician's decision to prescribe a type of service, and subsequent discharge or transfer of a patient from a level of care, needs to be based on how that treatment and its duration will not only influence the resolution of the dysfunction, but also positively alter the prognosis for long-term recovery and outcome for that individual patient.

Thus, in addiction treatment, the treatment may extend beyond simple resolution of observable physical, social, or mental health distress to the achievement of overall healthier functioning and wellness. The patient demonstrates a response to treatment through new insights, attitudes, and behaviors. Addiction treatment services have as their goal not simply stabilizing the patient's condition but altering the course of the patient's disease toward wellness and recovery.

Moving away from using previous "treatment failure" as an admission prerequisite

Another concern that guided the development of this publication is the concept of "treatment failure." This term has been used by some reimbursement or managed care organizations as a prerequisite for approving admission to a more intensive level of care (for example, "failure" in outpatient treatment as a prerequisite for admission to inpatient treatment). In fact, the requirement that a person "fail first" in outpatient treatment before inpatient treatment is approved is no more rational than treating every patient

THEN AND NOW

1

in an inpatient program or using a fixed length of stay for all. It also does not recognize the obvious parallels between addictive disorders and other chronic diseases, such as diabetes or hypertension. For example, failure of outpatient treatment is not a prerequisite for acute inpatient admission for diabetic ketoacidosis or hypertensive crisis.

A "treatment failure" approach potentially puts the patient at risk because it delays a more appropriate level of treatment, and potentially increases health care costs, if restricting the appropriate level of treatment allows the addictive disorder to progress.

Moving toward an interdisciplinary, team approach to care

The ASAM Criteria maintains and builds on ASAM's previous efforts to respond to ongoing changes and needs within the special field of addiction treatment. It also recognizes that with health reform, more services to persons with addiction will be delivered outside of a separate (and separately funded) specialty treatment system for addiction and will be delivered inside of general medical and general behavioral health settings. Addiction care has always been built around services involving interdisciplinary teams of professionals, including and sometimes led by physicians. With health reform, addiction care as well as mental health care will increasingly be delivered by clinicians working in interdisciplinary teams of not only "addiction professionals" but also general medical care professionals.

The expansion of the Patient Centered Health Care Home model for delivering comprehensive, integrated care for patients and families—including "behavioral health care" (mental health and substance-related disorders care)— will mean that persons making decisions about how and where to offer treatment to persons with addiction and related conditions will need to envision new treatment models and settings. Such models and settings will be unfamiliar to many clinicians who have been practicing in, and who likely received their clinical training in, specialty settings for addiction care. They will need to incorporate new skills of greater

collaboration with other non-addiction treatment professionals, and inclusion of peers and peer supports.

The current edition of *The ASAM Criteria* recognizes that a broad trend in health care is for addiction and related disorders to be increasingly recognized and embraced by physicians— both general medical providers and physicians in a wide range of medical and surgical specialties, and an expanding number of physicians trained and certified (eg, by the American Board of Addiction Medicine and the American Board of Psychiatry and Neurology) as specialists in addiction care.

Clarifying the role of the physician

Due to their prevalence, substance use and addictive disorders are health conditions that have a significant impact. Physicians are an essential part of the health care delivery system for addiction, as well as for all acute and chronic medical and surgical conditions. Increasingly, teams of professionals are working in a coordinated fashion to deliver health care. While mental health care has been offered through interdisciplinary teams for decades, especially in public sector settings, general medical care is only recently developing models to involve a range of health, social services, rehabilitation, and other professionals to manage chronic diseases. The Patient Centered Health Care Home model is a prominent example of this.

In addiction care, non-physician providers have a long tradition of offering counseling services for persons with addiction. Nurses with special expertise, experience, and certification have been central to the care process and enhancing outcomes for persons needing management of withdrawal syndromes. Physicians—both general medical/psychiatric practitioners and addiction specialists—are important members of any health care team working with persons with addiction and substance-related conditions, but they have not been utilized as much as they might be. This is partly because the numbers of interested and well-trained physicians in addiction evaluation and management have been so sparse in comparison to the tens of millions of people who need addiction care. It is also due to the "non-medical" orientation of some treatment programs. Some policy advocates (notable among these would be The National Center on Addiction and Substance Abuse at Columbia University, CASAColumbia) have argued that the ideal for addiction care would be to offer it through the general medical system, comparable to the method of other chronic diseases (diabetes, heart disease, lung disease, cancer). In these situations, physicians make the definitive diagnosis and oversee the development and implementation of acute and ongoing care plans.

Providers such as physician assistants and nurse practitioners have a role, as do a range of non-physician professionals. While the addiction field broadly is not at this point yet, eventually the physician would be tasked with supervising and managing treatment protocols in which a team approach would provide integrated, person-centered care. This team would include psychologists, nurses, clinical social workers, case managers, peer specialists, and other licensed or certified behavioral health clinical staff, including licensed and certified addiction counselors. ASAM's criteria, since the first edition, has described not only various levels of care, but also the staffing necessary for care in various service intensities to be delivered appropriately to meet patient needs. Physicians are important in the differential diagnosis of the clinical presentations of persons with addiction and substance-related conditions. They help confirm the presence of intoxication, withdrawal, and general medical or psychiatric conditions or complications.

Physical and mental health evaluations within the scope of practice of psychologists, nurse practitioners, and others can be accomplished and complement what physicians can do. Both psychiatric and general medical triage can be performed by general medical physicians and psychiatrists. More specific diagnosis may require psychiatrists to consult with internists or adolescent medicine specialists, or for family physicians to consult with psychiatrists. In many cases, an addiction specialist physician—trained and then certified (eg, by the American Board

of Addiction Medicine or the American Board of Psychiatry and Neurology)—is needed to determine whether a psychiatric comorbidity is present. In complex clinical presentations, an addiction psychiatrist is best qualified to assess if the patient has a substance-induced disorder, an addiction or mental illness alone, or co-occurring mental and addictive disorders, and to then coordinate care accordingly. Moreover, pharmacotherapy for addiction can be managed by general medical physicians and general psychiatrists with significant knowledge of addiction care. However, in some cases, an addiction medicine physician or addiction psychiatrist is needed to manage more complex cases.

There are many patients with substance use and other addictive disorders, and many more with high-risk substance use and addictive behaviors, who could benefit from the care interventions described as Level 0.5, Early Intervention, in The ASAM Criteria. Such interventions include Screening, Brief Intervention, Referral, and Treatment (SBIRT); risk advice; and education. Because so few physicians have had special addiction training, this approach cannot be universally applied.

Efforts to ameliorate lack of physician training have included attempts to expand addiction training within medical schools. But the broadest effort to meet the needs of the population of patients or potential patients has focused on the involvement of other health care professionals in the direct treatment of addiction. There is no clear evidence on which member of the health care team is best suited to meet which specific patient needs. That is, we do not know if a patient with addictive illness, seen by a highly skilled social worker, psychologist, nurse, counselor, or generalist physician would have the same outcome if that patient were seen by a highly skilled addiction specialist physician instead. Research on provider-specific outcomes is scanty, and underscores a need for further study. Because of workforce, financial, and clinical needs, it is likely that a team approach is necessary to meet the needs of patients with high-risk substance use, addictive behaviors, and addiction illness.

Focusing on treatment outcomes

Increasingly, payments to practitioners and programs will be based not on the service provided, but on the outcomes achieved. Treatment services and reimbursement based on patient engagement and outcomes is consistent with trends in disease and illness management, especially when conducted in real-time during the treatment experience, as with the management of hypertension or diabetes. With these chronic illnesses, changes to the treatment plan are based on treatment outcomes and tracked by real-time measurement at every visit (eg, blood pressure or blood sugar levels are monitored to determine the success of the current treatment regimen). While there has been increased attention on evidence-based practices (EBP), more focus on patient engagement and outcome-driven services is still needed.

While EBPs contribute to positive outcomes in treatment, the quality of the therapeutic alliance and the degree to which hope for recovery is conveyed to the patient contribute even more to the outcome.[4,5,6,7,8,9]

Engaging with "Informed Consent"

Treatment adherence and outcomes are enhanced by patient collaboration and shared decision-making. To engage people in treatment and recovery, person-centered services encompass clear information to patients. Certain sections of *The ASAM Criteria* mention directly or draw upon the concept of "informed consent." Health care requires informed consent, indicating that the adult, adolescent, legal guardian, and/or family member has been made aware of the proposed modalities of treatment, the risks and benefits of such treatment, appropriate alternative treatment modalities, and the risks of treatment versus no treatment.

Clarifying "Medical Necessity"

Some sections of *The ASAM Criteria* may mention or draw upon the term of "medical necessity." This concept is central to judgments for third-party payers and managed care organizations to determine appropriateness of care. Because substance use, addictive, and mental disorders are biopsychosocial in etiology and

Adolescent-Specific Considerations: Informed Consent

Attention should be given to the special requirements for informed consent in the treatment of adolescents. Before a formal interview begins, certain "ground rules" must be explained to the adolescent and family, as they form the basis for the therapeutic alliance. For example, it should be made clear that all information gathered in the interview becomes part of the adolescent's permanent record and will be shared by treating physicians, social workers, therapists, and others. "Secrets" regarding substance use should be avoided. On the other hand, sensitivity to an adolescent's concerns about privacy and confidentiality is very important. The adolescent and parents have a right to refuse to answer any question, although openness and honesty are expected and strongly encouraged because they contribute to a more accurate diagnosis and formulation of an appropriate treatment plan.

Certain confidentiality standards are imposed by federal and possibly state law. For example, the provider may be required to inform the parent, guardian, and–under certain circumstances–the police or child protective agencies if a child or adolescent is engaged in behavior that is injurious or life threatening, or that demonstrates suicidal intent, or if a disclosure of physical or sexual abuse is made to the physician or other clinician, or if there is a strong suspicion of such abuse.

expression, treatment and care management are most effective if they, too, are biopsychosocial. The six assessment dimensions identified in *The ASAM Criteria* encompass all pertinent biopsychosocial aspects of addiction and mental health that determine the severity of the patient's illness and level of function.

For these reasons, *The ASAM Criteria* asserts that "medical necessity" should pertain to necessary care for biopsychosocial severity and is defined by the extent and severity of problems in all six multidimensional assessment areas of the patient. It should not be restricted to acute care and narrow medical concerns (such as severity of withdrawal risk as in Dimension 1); acuity of physical health needs (as in Dimension 2); or Dimension 3 psychiatric issues (such as imminent suicidality). Rather, "medical necessity" encompasses all six assessment dimensions so that a more holistic concept would be "necessity of care," "clinical necessity," or "clinical appropriateness."

Incorporating ASAM's definition of addiction

When it was first published in 1991, ASAM's *Patient Placement Criteria* was considered a guide for linking severity of illness to intensity of service, specifically when the health condition was a "Psychoactive Substance Use Disorder." This first edition was published only two years after ASAM adopted its current name as a national medical specialty society, the American Society of Addiction Medicine. At the time, bringing together physicians interested in treating alcoholism with physicians interested in treating opioid and other drug addiction, along with physicians interested in treating nicotine addiction, was revolutionary in its own way.

But still, the focus of this new society was on the prevention and treatment of, and medical education and research about, specific forms of "chemical dependency." Conditions such as "pathological gambling" were well known, but over the years ASAM repeatedly declined to redefine itself as an organization that would address "non-substance-related addiction" in its

policies, education, or advocacy activities. ASAM chose not to identify its mission as including "behavioral addiction."

Eventually, however, advancements in neuroscience helped ASAM member physicians and organizational leaders recognize the biomedical processes in the brain underlying the outward behavioral manifestations of persons with addiction. And in the first decade of the 21st century, ASAM set out to define "addiction" in a way that was consistent with both clinical wisdom and research discoveries. The result of this work, performed by a collection of ASAM volunteer members designated the Descriptive and Diagnostic Terminology Action Group (DDTAG), was two related documents: a "short version" definition of addiction (shown here), as well as a "long version" definition (available

ASAM DEFINITION OF ADDICTION "SHORT VERSION"[3]

Addiction is a primary, chronic disease of brain reward, motivation, memory, and related circuitry. Dysfunction in these circuits leads to characteristic biological, psychological, social, and spiritual manifestations. This is reflected in an individual pathologically pursuing reward and/or relief by substance use and other behaviors.

Addiction is characterized by inability to consistently abstain, impairment in behavioral control, craving, diminished recognition of significant problems with one's behaviors and interpersonal relationships, and a dysfunctional emotional response. Like other chronic diseases, addiction often involves cycles of relapse and remission. Without treatment or engagement in recovery activities, addiction is progressive and can result in disability or premature death.

THEN AND NOW
1

at http://www.asam.org/for-the-public/ definition-of-addiction), which serves as more of a description of the condition.[3] In April of 2011, these two versions were unanimously adopted as official ASAM statements.

Notice how the "short version" definition uses the singular term "addiction" to describe a condition that is "primary" and "chronic." So although this definition explains how compulsive, impulsive, or out-of-control substance use can be present, addiction can also involve impaired control over behaviors (such as gambling) that do not involve psychoactive substance use.

What's New in *The ASAM Criteria*

While relying on the same principles that have guided previous editions, *The ASAM Criteria* now expands on prior understanding and applications to serve a wider and more diverse population. This broader population includes people with addiction who are older adults, parents with children, and also those working in safety-sensitive occupations. The current edition also branches out to explore addiction services within criminal justice settings.

In addition, new information has been included to assist in applying *The ASAM Criteria* in managed care, in utilization management, and in the context of mental health and addiction parity and federal health care reform. Finally, additional sections have been added to this edition to respond to the request of users of the criteria—clinicians, care managers, and public and private sector payers—to make information more applicable to the "real world" in which providers deliver care and payers and third parties authorize and manage care.

Other key highlights of this new edition include, but are not limited to...

» **Synchronization with *The ASAM Criteria Software***, such that the definitions and specifications in this text for the dimensions, levels of care, and admissions decision rules serve as the reference manual for *The ASAM Criteria Software*, developed with the support of SAMHSA.

» **Combining adult and adolescent treatment information** in order to show overarching alignment with the guiding principles and applications of *The ASAM Criteria*. At the same time, *The ASAM Criteria* continues to distinguish between adult and adolescent populations, and presents separate diagnostic and dimensional admission criteria within each level of care.

» **Incorporation of the latest understanding of Co-Occurring Disorders Capability** (formerly termed Dual Diagnosis Capability), and what might better be termed "complexity capability," to acknowledge the range of service needs beyond just addiction and mental health treatment. The need for persons with substance

The ASAM Criteria Software is a standardized, computer-assisted implementation of the adult admission decision rules in this book to provide a direct mechanism for linking the addiction specialty care system with general medical systems in the era of three intersecting legislative initiatives in the U.S.: health care reform, parity, and health information technology. It does not address specialized treatment services for adolescents.

BRAND NEW CHAPTERS IN *THE ASAM CRITERIA*

Application to Adult Special Populations

» Older Adults

» Parents or Prospective Parents Receiving Addiction Treatment Concurrently with Their Children

» Persons in Safety-Sensitive Occupations

» Persons in Criminal Justice Settings

Emerging Understandings of Addiction

» Gambling Disorder

» Tobacco Use Disorder

use disorders to be assessed and treated for co-occurring infectious diseases is but one clear example of this concept. Programs and practitioners increasingly understand the need for trauma-informed care and primary health/behavioral health integration as core features of all addiction treatment programs.

As the treatment field has learned more about the complexities of the people we serve, it increasingly is becoming more trauma informed and responsive to the needs of people with co-occurring mental and substance use disorders. Services that are "co-occurring capable or enhanced" and "complexity capable" are described within this edition.

» **Inclusion of the conceptual framework of Recovery-Oriented Systems of Care** to facilitate understanding of addiction treatment

services within a recovery-oriented "chronic disease management" continuum, rather than as repeated and disconnected "acute episodes of treatment" for the acute complications of addiction; and/or repeated and disconnected readmissions to addiction or mental health programs that employ rigid lengths of stay into which patients are "placed."

» **Further expansion on the role of the physician.** The role of physicians within interdisciplinary teams, in various levels of care, deserves attention, which work-group members, authors, and editors have attempted to recognize and articulate. There are physicians working in more traditional medical practices (outpatient clinic settings described as Outpatient Services or Level 1 settings by *The ASAM Criteria)* and not necessarily in interdisciplinary teams. It is hoped that, in their own offices, they will increasingly meet patient needs through the use of pharmacotherapies as well as psychosocial therapies, as these are indicated in individual cases. More change is occurring in mental health settings where psychiatrists and other mental health clinicians are screening for and treating addiction, and are more open to co-occurring disorders treatment. ASAM is committed, through the publication of this and future editions of *The ASAM Criteria*, to be relevant to an ever-evolving health care service delivery landscape.

The "Staff" sections at the beginning of each treatment level of care in *The ASAM Criteria* indicate physician involvement. In the *ASAM PPC-2R* (2001), there was mention of physician involvement without noting whether the physician is an addiction specialist or simply any licensed physician. This was based, at least to some extent, upon the *status quo*, specifically the availability or lack of specially trained and certified physicians with respect to addiction treatment. Even if there were an unlimited availability of such treatment, economic considerations would still play a role in which one would want the least expensive alternative to obtain identical outcomes. In *The ASAM Criteria*, Third Edition, authors and editors have indicated where specialist and non-specialist physicians must be involved in services for addiction, which for most people is a lifelong illness.

This edition also has continued to describe "Medically Monitored," versus "Medically Managed," intensive addiction services (Level 3.7 vs. Level 4) but medical management can apply in outpatient care (Level 1 and Level 2) as well. Even when care is medically monitored (provided to the patient primarily by non-physicians as part of a team supervised by a physician), the physician will be in the position to offer service components that contribute to the care experience of the patient.

Federal agencies have made policy decisions to promote office-based (Level 1) care by generalist physicians as the prescribers. There has been insufficient research on the specific utilization of addiction specialist physicians compared with general medical or general psychiatric physicians in the Level 1 management of opioid addiction involving pharmacotherapy. In this edition of the criteria, authors and editors offer suggestions regarding the utilization of physicians in the care of patients in various levels of care, including suggestions on the utilization of physicians specifically trained and certified in the care of addiction. These suggestions have been generated via the expert consensus of the authors, field reviewers, and editors of *The ASAM Criteria*. The empirical validation of these suggestions awaits future analysis by competent and experienced health services researchers.

» **Updated diagnostic admission criteria for the levels of care** to be consistent with the American Psychiatric Association's 2013 publication of the *Diagnostic and Statistical Manual of Mental Disorders* (*DSM-5*).

» **A new section on gambling disorder** that is consistent with ASAM's definition of

addiction, asserting that the pathological pursuit of reward or relief can involve not just the use of psychoactive substances, but also the engagement in certain behaviors. The inclusion of a gambling disorder section also reflects shifts in the latest edition of the *Diagnostic and Statistical Manual of Mental Disorders* (*DSM-5*), which includes gambling disorder in the Substance Use and Addictive Disorders chapter.

» **A new section on tobacco use disorder** reflects a decision to address the treatment field's inconsistencies in, and even ambivalence about, viewing this condition as similar to alcohol and other substance use disorders.

» **An updated opioid treatment section** to incorporate new advances, named Opioid Treatment Services (addressing opioid antagonist pharmacotherapy in addition to opioid agonist pharmacotherapy).

Previous editions and supplements of ASAM's criteria have described care offered in what this edition is naming Opioid Treatment Programs (utilizing methadone to treat opioid use disorder in Level 1 and previously called Opioid Maintenance Therapy, OMT.) *The ASAM Criteria*, Third Edition, is the first edition to address the growing use of office-based opioid treatment, utilizing buprenorphine products to treat opioid addiction.

» **Updates to better assess, understand, and provide services for all six ASAM criteria dimensions** to reflect current science and research. This can be seen in Chapter 6: Addressing Withdrawal Management and Intoxication Management, and Appendix B: Special Considerations for Dimension 5 Criteria, for example.

» **Revised terminology** reflects contemporary usage and a strength-based, recovery-oriented, trauma-informed, and culturally competent approach. See Chapter 3: Intake and Assessment for more information.

» **Reformatted level of care numbers.** Listed in previous editions of the criteria using Roman numerals, levels of care have been reformatted using Arabic numbers.

» **A user-friendly format.** In the publication design and delivery of the content in this edition, much attention has been paid to make *The ASAM Criteria* book user-friendly so that information is more easily retrieved and cross-referenced.

New Terminology

*T*he ASAM Criteria uses new terminology and language in its attempt to embrace a broader view of the conditions addressed by health care professionals. Specifically, addiction care professionals may notice content and terminology addressing substance use disorders not covered in previous editions (eg, tobacco use disorder), other addictive disorders (eg, gambling disorder), and references to the definition of addiction adopted by ASAM in 2011. Other references to specific terminology revisions have been briefly explained below. For a more comprehensive list of terms used in this edition, consult the Glossary provided in Appendix C.

NEW TERMINOLOGY IN *THE ASAM CRITERIA*

» The individuals served in treatment are now most often referred to as **"individual," "person," "participant,"** or **"patient,"** and these are used interchangeably in this publication

» Book title and concept is now **"*The ASAM Criteria*"**

» Terms such as **"dual diagnosis"** and **"dual disorders"** are now described in the spectrum of **"co-occurring disorders or conditions"**

» **"Detoxification services"** are referred to in this edition as **"withdrawal management"**

» **"Opioid Maintenance Therapy (OMT)"** is now discussed as Opioid Treatment Programs (OTP) and Office-Based Opioid Treatment (OBOT) within **"Opioid Treatment Services (OTS)"**

» **"Level III.3: Clinically Managed Medium-Intensity Residential Treatment"** is now **"Level 3.3: Clinically Managed Population-Specific High-Intensity Residential Services"**

New Terminology Explained

See the following boxes for further explanations of some of the key terminology changes introduced in *The ASAM Criteria*, Third Edition.

"INDIVIDUAL," "PERSON," "PARTICIPANT," "PATIENT"

In addiction and mental health services, there is a wide variety of terminology used to describe the people served: patients, clients, consumers, participants, residents, persons, individuals, customers, etc. In *The ASAM Criteria*, various terms will be used at different times, depending on what seems to flow best in the context. "Individual," "person," "participant," and "patient" will be used most often. The use of the term "patient" implies the highest biopsychosocial values of the helping professions: to serve as the patient's agent and support, to care for the patient as we would want ourselves and our loved ones to be treated, healing where possible but always seeking to reduce suffering.

In order to limit complexity in terms, "client," "consumer," and "customer" will not be used. It should be noted, however, that regardless of the term given, *The ASAM Criteria* always supports and promotes a collaborative, participatory process of assessment and service planning. This approach is consistent with evidence-based practices and the outcomes research that finds the quality of the therapeutic alliance with the participant to have a significant impact on achieving effective outcomes, and that finds person-centered services to improve the adherence to treatment.

"THE ASAM CRITERIA"

The title of this 2013 edition is *The ASAM Criteria* with the subtitle, *Treatment Criteria for Addictive, Substance-Related, and Co-Occurring Conditions*. This is the third edition of ASAM's criteria. The 2001 edition was named *ASAM Patient Placement Criteria for the Treatment of Substance-Related Disorders, Second Edition-Revised (ASAM PPC-2R)*, which was seen as so long and complicated that many would say "Do you use the ASAM?" Suggested terminology for this edition is the following:

"**The** *ASAM Criteria*," to reinforce that these criteria are the official, accepted criteria of ASAM and not associated with any of the various state adaptations or interpretations also in existence. Also, *The ASAM Criteria*, Third Edition, now directly and specifically relates to and supports *The ASAM Criteria Software*, which is the only authorized implementation of these decision rules.

The new title broadens the reach of the criteria beyond "patients" and "placement" to speak to and encourage other non-medical disciplines to use *The ASAM Criteria*. It is this movement beyond "placement" which will challenge the perpetuated idea that placing people in programs is a primary and sufficient goal. The essential focus is on matching services to each patient's unique multidimensional needs. Placement is simply where this individualized treatment can efficiently and effectively be delivered. (See the arrangement of later sections which move from assessment through service planning and placement.)

The subtitle connotes that these criteria address conditions related to addiction and other substance-related disorders. However, not every person is suffering from the disease of addiction. Certain people may just need Early Intervention (Level 0.5) or Screening, Brief Intervention, Referral, and Treatment (SBIRT).

In addition, there are other health conditions that are not necessarily related to substance use or gambling, but that co-occur and need physical and/or mental health services. Some of these may be sub-diagnostic and therefore "conditions" rather than disorders. Thus the subtitle of *The ASAM Criteria* is intended to cover the broader range of conditions to help with integration into general health care (under health care reform) and into behavioral health with co-occurring disorders.

"CO-OCCURRING DISORDERS OR CONDITIONS"

The addiction and mental health fields have made progress on developing a consensus on terminology to describe individuals who are experiencing simultaneous mental health and substance use conditions. Terms previously in use include "dual diagnosis," "dual disorders," "mentally ill chemically addicted" (MICA), "chemically addicted mentally ill" (CAMI), "mentally ill substance abusers" (MISA), "mentally ill chemically dependent" (MICD), "co-occurring disorders," "coexisting disorders," "comorbid disorders," "concurrent disorders" (Canada), and "individuals with co-occurring psychiatric and substance symptomatology" (ICOPSS). Many of these terms are historical terms, no longer in routine use.

For the sake of consistency with national trends, *The ASAM Criteria* has adopted the term "co-occurring mental health and substance-related conditions and disorders." Throughout the text, the term "co-occurring disorders or conditions" refers to mental health and substance-related conditions, unless specifically otherwise stated. A more extensive discussion related to co-occurring disorders or conditions, including expanded definitions for terms such as "Co-Occurring Capability," "Co-Occurring Enhanced," and "Complexity Capability," can be found in the "Integrated Services" sections of Chapter 2.

"WITHDRAWAL MANAGEMENT"

This refers to the services required for Dimension 1: Acute Intoxication and/or Withdrawal Potential. Previously referred to as "detoxification services," *The ASAM Criteria*, Third Edition, more accurately describes services to assist a patient's withdrawal. The liver detoxifies, but clinicians manage withdrawal. If the person is intoxicated and not yet in withdrawal, the Dimension 1 services needed would be termed "Intoxication Management."

"OPIOID TREATMENT SERVICES"

In the *ASAM PPC-2R* (2001), a chapter titled "Opioid Maintenance Therapy" was focused solely on opioid agonist medications—methadone and LAAM (levo-alpha-acetylmethadol). LAAM is no longer used in the United States, and buprenorphine is now available as a pharmacological therapy for opioid addiction. In addition, previous editions of ASAM's criteria did not address opioid antagonist medications to treat opioid addiction, such as naltrexone (which has been available in an oral tablet form since the 1970s). The new title for this chapter, "Opioid Treatment Services," is intended to broaden the term to include all medications used to treat opioid use disorders and the psychosocial services that are offered concurrently with these pharmacotherapies.

Within this chapter, Opioid Treatment Programs (OTP) and Office-Based Opioid Treatment (OBOT) are explained.

"LEVEL 3.3: CLINICALLY MANAGED POPULATION-SPECIFIC HIGH-INTENSITY RESIDENTIAL SERVICES"

The adult level of care, Level 3.3, has been renamed and changed from its original description as "Clinically Managed Medium-Intensity Residential Treatment." Treatment is specific to persons with cognitive difficulties needing more specialized, individualized services. The cognitive impairments manifested in patients most appropriately treated in Level 3.3 services can be due to aging, traumatic brain injury, acute but lasting injury, or due to illness. Level 3.3 is described in more detail in Chapter 7.

Applications

Real World Considerations in Using *The ASAM Criteria*

While founded on the guiding principles and theory described earlier, authors and editors also have taken efforts to make sure *The ASAM Criteria* addresses issues that arise in today's "real world" of treatment. The following topics represent some of the steps this publication takes toward an integrated and holistic approach to care.

Clinical versus Reimbursement Considerations

The information presented in *The ASAM Criteria* has been developed to describe a wide range of levels and types of care for addiction and substance-related conditions. Not all of these services are available in all locations, nor do all payers and benefit plans cover them. Clinicians who make placement decisions are expected to amplify the criteria with their clinical judgment, their knowledge of the patient, and their knowledge of the available resources. *The ASAM Criteria* is not intended as a reimbursement guideline, but rather as a clinical guideline for making the most appropriate treatment and placement recommendation for an individual patient with a specific set of signs, symptoms, and behaviors. If the criteria only covered the levels of care commonly reimbursed by private insurance carriers and other funders, they would not address many of the resources of the public sector and, thus, would tacitly endorse limitations on a complete continuum of care. For more on how to work together with managed care and payers, see the Understanding How to Work Effectively with Managed Care and Health Care Reform section in Chapter Five.

The Concept of "Unbundling"

While the first edition of the *Patient Placement Criteria* "bundled" clinical services with environmental supports in fixed levels of care, there is increasing recognition that clinical services can be and often are provided separately from environmental supports. Indeed, many managed care companies and public treatment systems are suggesting that treatment modality and intensity be "unbundled" from the treatment setting.

Unbundling is a practice that allows any type of clinical service (such as psychiatric consultation, withdrawal management, etc.) to be delivered in any setting (such as a residential or outpatient service or a supportive living environment). With unbundling, the type and intensity of treatment is based on the patient's needs and not on limitations imposed by the treatment setting. The unbundling concept is thus designed to maximize individualized care and to encourage the delivery of requisite treatment in any clinically feasible setting.

As a first step toward unbundled criteria, the second edition of the *Patient Placement Criteria* incorporated criteria for five levels of withdrawal management as a clinical service separate from the environmental supports. The *PPC-2R*, and now *The ASAM Criteria*, continue with this unbundled concept. Without this approach, a clinician might bundle together an issue of homelessness with an issue of withdrawal management and decide the person must be placed in a hospital level of withdrawal care. But this patient may need only a supportive living environment in a safe 24-hour setting and Ambulatory Withdrawal Management without Extended

On-Site Monitoring (Level 1-WM) to adequately meet all of the assessed needs. Unbundling in this way allows for safe and cost-conscious care that makes for efficient use of resources and increases access to care where it is most needed.

Contrasting Adult and Adolescent Pharmacotherapy

The use of pharmacotherapy for addiction (alternatively described as medication assisted treatment, medication assisted recovery, relapse prevention medications, anti-addiction medication, etc.) is growing in adolescent treatment. Research demonstrating its effectiveness, understanding of its appropriate incorporation into standard treatment delivery models, and adoption by the field, all lag behind the corresponding progress in adult treatment. But nevertheless, its importance is growing, and it holds promise as an important addition to the tool chest.

In the area of opioid addiction, historically high levels of heroin use and an exploding epidemic of prescription opioid use have pushed the field to look for new methods and try to adapt adult models of care to more developmentally appropriate approaches for youth. While withdrawal management followed by recommendations for psychosocial treatment alone has been the rule, the field has increasingly started to adopt buprenorphine and extended release naltrexone as ongoing treatment options. Practitioners have been more reluctant to utilize methadone, perhaps more out of concern that the current specialty delivery system in the U.S. is not adolescent friendly, rather than out of critical examination of the independent properties of the medication itself. Tobacco use is another area where the field has made substantial advances with effective pharmacotherapy, but so far these tools have not had substantial demonstration of efficacy in adolescents. Compelling new work points to future advances in pharmacotherapy for marijuana addiction, which is particularly relevant to adolescents.

But many of the fundamental questions remain to be answered: How should these medications be adapted to adolescent use? What

Adolescent-Specific Considerations: Integrated Withdrawal Management

Withdrawal management services remain integrated into levels of care for adolescent patients. An integrated approach was judged better for adolescents, because severe physiological withdrawal is seen less often in this unique population. Therefore, in *The ASAM Criteria*, withdrawal management is presented in two separate ways: as an "unbundled" version for adults (found in Chapter 6: Addressing Withdrawal Management and Intoxication Management), and as adolescent-specific information within each level of care section.

are the appropriate criteria for patient selection? What is the appropriate duration of treatment? How should their use be integrated into standard psychosocial treatment? What about diversion risk for agonist agents? What are the interactions with level of care?

In general, the emerging knowledge about pharmacotherapy in adolescent treatment (gleaned from experience in treatment of opioid addiction where there has been the most work so far) suggests that medications are probably less potently effective than in adult patients, and that it is far too early to think of them as a dose-sparing "alternative" to current psychosocial treatments. In fact, it may turn out that much of their effectiveness derives from a synergy with psychosocial treatments. In general, like other treatment delivery, medication treatments for adolescents have required greater intensity of treatment and more intense levels of care to accomplish successfully than for adults. For example, it has so far proven difficult to sustain outpatient induction of buprenorphine for opioid addiction in youth, whereas this has become standard in adults, and while the field has reported some early successes in outpatient induction with extended release naltrexone in opioid addicts, this remains elusive in youth. The adolescent criteria speak to this issue by prescribing an inpatient (Level 3.7) level of care for medically monitored withdrawal when there is sufficient severity to warrant the use of pharmacotherapy for withdrawal management and/or induction onto relapse prevention medication. While much work remains to be done to inform future editions of the criteria, this current treatment matching guidance remains sound.

The ASAM Criteria and State Licensure or Certification

The ASAM Criteria contains descriptions of treatment programs at each level of care, including the setting, staffing, support systems, therapies, assessments, documentation, and treatment plan reviews typically found at that level. This information should be useful to providers who are preparing to serve a particular group of patients, as well as to clinicians who are making placement decisions. Nevertheless, these descriptions are intended to provide a more comprehensive understanding of each level of care; and are not intended to replace or supersede the relevant statutes, licensure, or certification requirements of any state or federal jurisdiction.

Placement Impediments and Dilemmas

In the real world, issues surrounding access, reimbursement, funding, resource allocation, and availability may affect the patient placement decision. In this edition, please see the added specific sections on special populations, working with managed care, and additions to existing sections for more information on dealing with real-world impediments and dilemmas.

Logistical Impediments

Logistical problems can arise anywhere, but they are often found in rural and underserved inner-city areas. When logistical considerations impede the matching of services to need, practitioners may have to work with the patient to identify creative solutions to address individualized needs and combine them with the care that is available.

Examples of logistical impediments can include housing, transportation, availability of a needed level of care, waiting lists, financial concerns, child care issues, job or school restrictions, and conflicting legal requirements.

A LOGISTICAL IMPEDIMENT: HOUSING

An outpatient service combined with unsupervised/minimally supervised housing may be an appropriate treatment intervention. In cities or towns, such a domiciliary option might be found in a group living situation (such as a sober homeless shelter, motel accommodations, a runaway shelter or crisis center for adolescents, or a faith-based temporary shelter).

In rural and other underserved areas, options may include: (a) the creation of a supervised housing situation by using unused treatment beds; (b) assertive community treatment models in which the treatment is brought to rural areas (such as Native American settings) and provided in weekend intensive models such as day treatment to both the identified patient and family members, utilizing as sites community resources such as churches; (c) using vans that are sent out to pick up individuals and bring them to a treatment site; (d) conducting counseling sessions on-site, using a van or motor home as an office or group therapy room; (e) telemedicine and telehealth services for physician assessments, therapy and pharmacotherapy, and other health counseling services; or (f) online individual and group treatment where treatment can be accessed from anywhere in the world with Internet access.

Need for a Safe Environment

When a patient lives in a recovery environment that is so toxic as to preclude effective recovery efforts (eg, victimization or exposure to people with active addiction) and a Level 1 or 2 outpatient service is indicated, the patient may need referral to a safe place to live while in treatment (that is, a domiciliary facility or, if necessary, a 24-hour supportive environment: a Level 3.1 facility.) However, even if a patient is safe in a residential setting, or in a combination of outpatient services with living support, careful attention to community reintegration is also important. Some patients ask to go far away for treatment, thinking that they will be separated from their neighborhood triggers. But upon discharge, they find themselves returning to the same drug-infested communities, making them at high risk for relapse. When patients are separated from their community, proactive planning is needed to link the patient to reliable professional and natural resources in their community where their long-term recovery efforts take place.

Interface with Mandated Treatment in the Criminal Justice System, with Child Protective Services, and for Persons in Safety-Sensitive Occupations

There has been an expansion of drug and mental health courts, diversion from incarceration, child protective services, professional health programs such as Physicians' Health Programs, and monitoring programs for pilots, nurses, and lawyers. Such programs pair services with contingencies to maintain a professional license, prevent the separation of, or reunify, parents and children, or facilitate early release from jail, etc. Effective outcomes require adequate durations of care and chronic disease management with close monitoring. See Chapter 8: Application to Adult Special Populations.

Mandated Level of Care or Length of Stay

In some cases, an individual is referred for treatment at a specific level of care and/or for a specific length of stay. For example, an offender in the criminal justice system may be given a choice of a prison term or fixed length of stay in a treatment center. Other examples include those convicted on multiple episodes of impaired driving who are required to complete fixed lengths of stay in jail and in treatment. Alleged abuse or neglect of children or older adults, involuntary commitment to outpatient mental health, inpatient mental health, or addiction treatment also serve as examples.

Such mandated or court-ordered referrals may not be based on clinical considerations and thus are inconsistent with an assessment-based and outcomes-driven placement decision. In such a case, the provider should make reasonable attempts to have the order amended to reflect the assessed clinical level or length of service. The criminal justice system is increasingly focused on effective outcomes of increased public safety and decreased legal recidivism and crime. Judges, attorneys, probation and parole officers, and others are aware of the expensive and ineffective phenomenon of the revolving door of mandated treatment, reoffending, sanctions, incarceration, and back to mandated treatment. In that context, there is increasing collaboration between criminal justice and treatment providers to focus on patients "doing treatment and change" rather than "doing time" in a mandated treatment level and length that is not assessment- and outcomes-driven. Similar awareness is increasing in child protective service agencies as well.

If the court order or other mandate cannot be amended, the individual may be continuing treatment at a level of care or for a length of stay more intensive than is clinically indicated. The patient's readiness for discharge or transfer and the staff's attempts to implement a clinically appropriate placement should be noted in the clinical record. The treatment plan should be updated in a manner that provides the patient with the opportunity to continue the recovery process in the mandated level of care, even though treatment could have been provided at a less intensive level of care.

Fidelity to the Spirit and Content of *The ASAM Criteria*

The considerations stated in the previous section have helped guide the development of this publication. Even still, other issues often persist in today's "real world" of treatment, suggesting that clinicians and programs still struggle with understanding the full intent of ASAM's criteria. These ongoing issues include:

» **Some programs still describe their services as a fixed length of stay program,** as evidenced by description of the program as a "Thirty-Day Inpatient Program or "24-session IOP." Or, if the program claims no fixed length of stay, check what participants say if you ask: "How long do you have to be here?" An answer involving fixed numbers of sessions or weeks reveals regression to a program-driven model.

Such programs also may reveal their length of stay rigidity through the language used. Wording like "extended residential" may refer to a fixed program, since length of stay should be decided by tracking severity, function, and progress, not by a predetermined decision that the patient needs a certain extended length of stay in a residential setting. Likewise, "graduating" and "completing a program" also reveal a focus on a fixed plan and program, rather than on functional improvement as the determinant of level of care and ongoing chronic-disease management (with certain episodes of care being offered with increased intensity for a relatively brief span of time) being what is needed for most patients with a substance-related or co-occurring disorder.

» **A misunderstanding of residential treatment.** In *The ASAM Criteria*, admission criteria for residential treatment encompass such severity and imminent danger that a 24-hour treatment setting is necessary. Yet, individuals are sometimes assessed as requiring

residential treatment and then placed on a waiting list. The patient may need a 24-hour living support, such as Level 3.1 plus some outpatient intensity of services (Levels 1, 2.1, or 2.5). By definition, it is a misunderstanding of residential treatment to place a person on a waiting list.

» **Funding limited to certain levels of care.** States and counties that fund only a few levels of care can discourage a seamless continuum of care. Licensure and contractual arrangements that keep levels of care in fixed programs can discourage or even forbid flexible overlapping of levels (eg, a public sector entity may contract only for Level 3.7-WM, which forces the program to staff for and document on every patient as if they are continually at a 3.7-WM severity). In fact, a patient may need that intensity of withdrawal management for only two days and could then be safely treated by seamlessly continuing in 3.2-WM or even overlapping 2-WM services within the structure of the withdrawal management facility.

» **Limited levels of withdrawal management.** Available levels of withdrawal management are often only Levels 4-WM or 3.7-WM, which drives up cost and allows only brief lengths of stay in high-intensity settings. This leads to rapid relapse when the patient has not had their acute withdrawal adequately managed. An ambulatory level of care for withdrawal management might be both more clinically appropriate and less costly. Full use of the five levels of withdrawal management as described in *The ASAM Criteria* would allow longer lengths of stay for the same or less resources. Underutilization of ambulatory withdrawal management and a continuum of withdrawal management levels are due partly to benefit management design that often puts medical withdrawal management in a general health benefit split out from the behavioral health benefit. It is also due

to provider and payer inexperience with ambulatory withdrawal management and hesitancy over risk management concerns.

Integrated Services: Integration of Addiction Treatment and Mental Health Treatment

Integration of Criteria for Co-Occurring Capability and Complexity Capability

When the *ASAM PPC-2R* was published in 2001, it significantly advanced the conceptual framework not only for the addiction field, but also for all of behavioral health. Recognizing that co-occurring mental health conditions are an "expectation, not an exception" in all settings[1], ASAM introduced the terms "Dual Diagnosis Capable" and "Dual Diagnosis Enhanced" into the behavioral health lexicon. The *ASAM PPC-2R* provided definitions for these terms and incorporated them into the *ASAM Patient Placement Criteria* throughout, stating the following as a vision of the future, as quoted from page 11 of the *ASAM PPC-2R* Preface:

"All individuals, programs and health systems that provide treatment for addictive disorders should be prepared to serve the needs of dual diagnosis patients, at least to the extent described here as Dual Diagnosis Capable."

"All health care delivery systems should be able to deliver the services needed by patients with co-occurring mental and substance-related disorders. Provider networks should include facilities that can deliver Dual Diagnosis Enhanced services at Levels I through IV, as described in the ASAM PPC-2R."

Recognizing that some in the addiction treatment field were not yet ready to establish "Dual Diagnosis Capability" as a core expectation, the original version of the *ASAM PPC-2R* defined the concept of addiction-only services (AOS). The expectation of the workgroup members who

drafted the *ASAM PPC-2R* was that this category of program or service would gradually disappear, as more clinicians and services paid routine attention to assessment and treatment of co-occurring mental health issues and conditions. Dual diagnosis capability in addiction treatment settings of any kind would then gradually become the norm.

Since the introduction of these terms over a decade ago, there has been substantial growth in the understanding of how to provide successful, integrated interventions to individuals with complex co-occurring conditions in all settings. There also has been substantial growth in the establishment of "dual diagnosis capability" in addiction treatment delivery systems nationwide (and, in fact, across the globe). This has been accompanied by a number of advances in the addiction treatment field, having been prompted by the introduction of the dual diagnosis capability concept in the *ASAM PPC-2R*. Such advancements include:

» The term "dual diagnosis capability" (and its companion "dual diagnosis enhanced") has expanded to be utilized in all types of behavioral health settings. Traditional "mental health only services" are expanding their capability to concurrently assess for and meet the needs of cases of a "dual diagnosis" or co-occurring mental disorder and substance-related disorder. Traditional "addiction-only services" are expanding their capabilities as well.

» Terminology in general has changed. It is far more common to use the term "Co-occurring

Capability" today, which represents in part the shifting focus toward holistic, person-centered services for "individuals with co-occurring conditions." Such individuals may need addiction and psychotropic medication; concurrent addiction, mental, and physical health services; individual, group, or family therapy; and a variety of other modalities delivered in an integrated fashion.

» Tools for assessing co-occurring capability at a treatment-provider-organization level have been developed to facilitate quality improvement activities for such organizations. Tools such as the DDCAT (Dual Diagnosis Capability in Addiction Treatment) or DDCMHT (Dual Diagnosis Capability in Mental Health Treatment)[2] and the COMPASS-EZ[3] have been utilized throughout the nation to support progress in this area. The Comprehensive Continuous Integrated System of Care (CCISC) model of system design developed by Minkoff & Cline[4,5] and cited by SAMHSA[1,6] has become recognized for leveraging a process by which all service providers and clinicians providing care become recovery-oriented and co-occurring capable. This is in order to better match available services to the expectation that individuals presenting for help will have complex needs (eg, trauma-informed or gender-specific services; concurrent nicotine, alcohol, and opioid withdrawal; etc.), and that such needs will be identified via multidimensional assessments and manageable via services with appropriately broad capabilities.

While there remains an emphasis on addiction treatment providers having the capacity to offer their patients a range of "evidence-based practices" (EBP)* the clinical and organizational understanding of how to implement co-occurring capability has expanded through both clinical research and health services research. Such research has investigated integrated service delivery for all types of populations, as well as "practice-based evidence" from the actual experiences of thousands of treatment organizations.

This has led to updated definitions and criteria for co-occurring capability (and co-occurring enhanced), compared to what was published in 2001 in the *ASAM PPC-2R*.[7,2] These updates include the following:

» There has been widespread understanding of the high prevalence of psychological trauma of all kinds in both men and women who present for services for their substance use disorder.[8] Psychological trauma, resulting from episodes of physical, sexual, or emotional abuse, and leading to frank cases of posttraumatic stress disorder (PTSD), is better understood as a clinical entity. Biomedical, neurochemical, and neurohumoral underpinnings of the mental health presentations of persons who have developed PTSD are also better understood. Advances in basic and clinical science and epidemiology regarding trauma, and translation of these findings into clinical settings, have resulted in the dissemination of trauma-informed care concepts into addiction treatment settings. These concepts are increasingly being integrated into all behavioral health settings, particularly those serving women, but also treating persons of any gender and age group. For this reason, trauma-informed care and co-occurring capability are often regarded as complementary approaches to enhancing the service capacity of treatment provider organizations and therefore better addressing the needs of people in specialty addiction and mental health treatment systems. As behavioral health care moves more into primary care settings, capabilities of delivering trauma-informed care and co-occurring capable care will become expectations of those delivery systems as well.

» Related to trauma-informed care, there has been increasing recognition of the need for gender-specific services and the evolution of family-focused programs. Such programs can

NREPP is SAMHSA's National Registry of Evidence-based Programs and Practices.

accommodate pregnant women and parents, usually women, with their children.

» Further, the emergence of health care reform has stimulated great attention to the importance of integration of primary health and behavioral health care. There have been seminal papers on the capacity of substance use disorder treatment programs to transform themselves into either becoming a "Health Care Home" or becoming a viable resource to partner with primary health providers in a continuum of services within a community Health Care Neighborhood.[9] More and more addiction and mental health treatment providers are becoming more intentional about addressing co-occurring primary health issues within their treatment continuum, just as Patient Centered Health Care Homes and Patient Centered Health Care Neighborhood entities are intentionally building capacity into their service portfolios and into their staff development and workforce development plans.

» Moreover, the concept of co-occurring capability has begun to expand on efforts to better integrate primary health care and behavioral health care. Appropriate tools and toolkits are being developed, such as the COMPASS PH/BH[3] and the DDCHCS (Dual Diagnosis Capability in Health Care Settings) and DDMICe (Dual Diagnosis Medically Integrated Care).[2]

» Finally, as recognition of the multiplicity of complex issues emerging in the behavioral health population becomes increasingly apparent, the term "Complexity Capability" has been introduced. This is a natural evolution of the early work of McLellan and others on addressing multiple problems along with addiction,[10] but it expands the range of issues addressed, within a recovery-oriented framework, to

permit much better positioning for all service provider entities to work with all the complex multidimensional needs of the individuals and families presenting for service.

Because of all of this progress, *The ASAM Criteria* is written with the sincere hope that it will assist the "traditional" specialty addiction treatment field to address co-occurring conditions. In the current edition, ASAM has incorporated the following updates relating to integrated services:

» Updated terminology regarding co-occurring conditions and co-occurring capability.

» Updated definitions and criteria for co-occurring capable and co-occurring enhanced.

» Elimination of a specific definition for addiction-only services within this edition of ASAM's criteria. Editors also omitted providing a specific definition for mental health only services, since mental health programs should also be capable of assessing and treating co-occurring conditions.

» Updated language reflecting inclusion of trauma-informed care as part of the routine design of treatment services.

» Updated language reflecting inclusion of primary health and behavioral health integration as part of the routine design of treatment services.

» Introduction of a definition of complexity capability as future guidance for the field.

Note as well that all of these changes are consistent with the conceptualization of the Recovery-Oriented System of Care that is introduced and discussed elsewhere in *The ASAM Criteria*.

APPLICATIONS

1

CO-OCCURRING CONDITION CATEGORIES

As the following text defining co-occurring conditions and the range of service categories illustrates, *The ASAM Criteria* enhances the ability to meet diverse patient needs by incorporating criteria that address the natural diversity of individuals who present for treatment with co-occurring conditions. This includes not only co-occurring substance use disorders and mental disorders, but also many individuals who present with co-occurring symptoms that are not associated with a formal mental health diagnosis. Individuals with such co-occurring conditions can be conceptualized as belonging to one of two general categories:

Moderate Severity Conditions

Such people may present with mood or anxiety symptoms and disorders of moderate severity (including suicidal thoughts without significant impulses, trauma-related flashbacks or anxiety, well-controlled schizophrenia or other psychotic disorders, and cases of acute exacerbation of bipolar affective disorder which is in the process of resolution); or with personality disorders of all types with moderate severity. These people may also present with psychiatric signs and symptoms that are not so severe as to meet the diagnostic threshold for a specific mental disorder. For example, a significant number of women (especially those in residential addiction treatment) have experienced trauma. Many of these women do not meet formal criteria for a mental disorder, yet they may experience significant mental health symptoms due to the trauma that complicates their treatment and recovery.

High Severity Conditions

Such people may present with schizophrenia-spectrum disorders associated with continuing significant symptomatology and/or disability at baseline, severe mood disorders including those with psychotic features and more intense bipolar-spectrum disorders, severe trauma-related or anxiety disorders, significant dissociative disorders, or severe personality disorders (such as fragile borderline conditions). These individuals have significant symptoms and impairments, even at baseline, but may still participate successfully in recovery-oriented services to address their substance use conditions if they are provided with the appropriate support.

Definitions within Addiction Treatment and Mental Health Treatment Integration

In the face of health care reform, there will be increasing emphasis on population health care and it will be important for all health professionals to understand the context of a changing general and behavioral health care context. To that end, the following definitions and health care systems issues are presented here. While the individual counselor, practitioner, general physician, or addiction specialist physician (addiction medicine physician or addiction psychiatrist) may not immediately see the relevance of these issues to their daily work, discussions of them are essential for moving the field forward.

Co-Occurring Conditions

An individual has co-occurring behavioral health conditions or issues if he or she has any combination of any mental health or any substance use or addictive behavior condition, even if the condition is not associated with a formal diagnosis. This has also been referred to as a "service definition of co-occurring disorders" meaning that such individuals require co-occurring disorders services even though they may not have formal diagnoses. This reflects "clinical realities and constraints and/ or programmatically meaningful descriptions of 'at-risk' populations targeted for prevention and early intervention."[11]

This definition of co-occurring conditions encompasses a wider population than just individuals who already have been diagnosed. It is particularly relevant from a service planning perspective for addiction treatment service providers, where many patients have clear symptomatology that needs to be addressed (eg, trauma histories, depression, suicidal thoughts, anxiety) even if the diagnosis may as yet be unclear. The addiction condition may also be broader than just substance use and may include gambling difficulties, over-exercising, Internet preoccupation, or over-eating. This may be true even if the diagnosis is yet unclear or has not reached the level of a formal diagnosis (eg, gambling disorder).

Co-Occurring Disorders

The term "co-occurring disorders" refers to "co-occurring substance-related and mental disorders" when "at least one disorder of each type can be established independent of the other and is not simply a cluster of symptoms resulting from [a single] disorder."[6]

Co-Occurring Capability

True for any type of program, and as defined by the mission and resources of that program, recovery-oriented co-occurring capability involves integrating at every level the concept that the next person "coming to the door" of the program is likely to have co-occurring conditions and needs. This approach emphasizes

that such people need to be welcomed for care, engaged with empathy and the hope of recovery, and provided what they need in a person-specific and integrated fashion. These steps will help such individuals make progress toward a happy, productive life.

Recovery oriented co-occurring capability necessitates that all care is welcoming and person-centered. This approach to service and care is attuned to people and families with diverse goals, strengths, histories, and cultures. Co-occurring capability involves looking at all aspects of program design and functioning in order to embed integrated policies, procedures, and practices in the operations of the program. This will make it easier and more routine for each clinician to deliver integrated care successfully.

For any type of addiction and mental health program, co-occurring capability can be achieved within existing program resources. It is not about associating a psychiatrist or hiring a mental health or addiction treatment specialist, so much as it is about designing all aspects of the program, the competencies of all staff, and the "recovery community" within the program as a whole, to help patients address co-occurring substance use and mental health, trauma, and (increasingly) general medical issues in the routine course of treatment. Progress toward co-occurring capability for addiction and mental health programs includes addressing the following indicators, through policy, procedure, practice improvement, and workforce development over time:

» Individuals with co-occurring mental health and addiction symptoms are welcome in the program and encouraged to discuss all issues in treatment to get help with managing mental health and addiction issues.

» Access to care barriers based on the presence of a psychiatric diagnosis or prescribed psychotropic medications are eliminated. In a mental health service, barriers based on current substance use are eliminated.

APPLICATIONS

❶

» Individuals are routinely screened for co-occurring substance use, addictive behavior, mental health, and trauma issues, and the results of screening inform assessment and intervention.

» Assessment and identification of existing substance use, addictive behavior, and mental health conditions is routinely incorporated into treatment planning.

» Mental health and addiction consultation is routinely available to the treatment team. The program develops partnerships with prescribers of psychotropic medications and addiction medications to facilitate organized communication between the treatment team and the prescribers. In mental health systems, there are partnerships with addiction treatment providers for consultation and coordinated addiction services, including pharmacological therapies.

» Ongoing education to patients about the medication that they are prescribed. Often, patients are provided with education but such information may need to be repeated due to issues such as the patient's condition, level of receptiveness, cognitive difficulties, etc.

» Mental health crisis intervention is readily available for patients who develop more acute mental health symptoms that cannot be safely managed in the program. In mental health settings, withdrawal management services are readily available for patients who develop pressing withdrawal management needs.

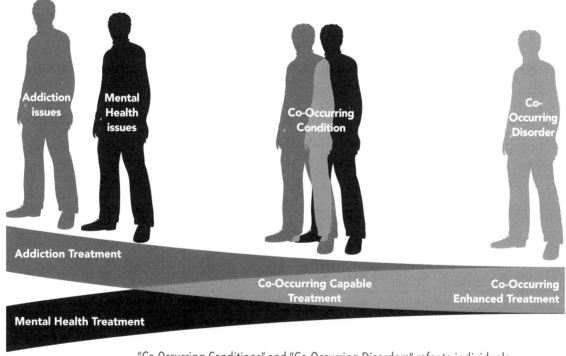

"Co-Occurring Conditions" and "Co-Occurring Disorders" refer to individuals.
"Co-Occurring Capable" and "Co-Occurring Enhanced" refer to types of programs.

Adolescent-Specific Considerations: Co-Occurring Disorders

It is increasingly recognized that comorbidity among adolescents with substance use disorders is the rule and not the exception. As in adults, the line between addiction treatment and mental health treatment is increasingly blurring, and the need for co-occurring enhanced, or combined behavioral health programming, is great. Although our evidence base for co-occurring treatment is limited compared to that for adults, it is growing. For example, there is mounting evidence that identifying and treating depression in substance-involved youth improves substance use outcomes, and vice versa. Another example is our growing awareness of the psychiatric sequelae of marijuana use in youth, and our growing clinical suspicions that these problems are much worse with synthetic cannabinoids ("K2," "spice," etc.). As more knowledge emerges, future editions of the criteria should incorporate it to support clinical decision making.

» Treatment plans include specific interventions to help patients manage their addiction and mental health symptoms, including, but not limited to, learning skills for taking medication as prescribed or coping with relapse triggers or impulses. Skill-based learning can be adapted to the cognitive/learning capacity of patients who may have cognitive or psychiatric disabilities.

» Treatment plans are stage-matched for multiple issues, recognizing that individuals may be in a different stage of change for their substance and addictive disorders issues and mental health issues.

» Group programming routinely includes education about substance use and addiction, as well as mental health symptoms and mental illnesses; and group therapy services facilitate conversation among patients to make it easier for the community to support individuals in the program who are struggling with co-occurring conditions.

» All staff, including addiction counselors, nurses, mental health clinicians, and residential aides, are supported and assisted to be "co-occurring competent", so that all staff work as an integrated team to help patients with multiple issues make progress toward their goals.

Co-occurring capable addiction treatment programs generally serve a diverse population. Some individuals in the program may have no mental health condition or trauma history. For those individuals, addiction-focused treatment is all that is necessary. Usually the majority of individuals, however, will have a range of mental health conditions, cognitive/learning issues, and/or trauma issues that should be screened for in a co-occurring capable program. Most of these individuals will have symptoms and impairments that are mild to moderate in acuity and/or severity.

The typical co-occurring capable addiction treatment program, at any level of care, will be able to manage a small percentage of individuals who have more serious psychiatric conditions (eg, a person with schizophrenia who is on disability, a person with a more severe personality disorder, etc.). The same is likely true for managing individuals who may intermittently have flare-ups of acute symptoms (eg, flashbacks or panic attacks), but do not need acute mental health treatment. Such patients are still interested in receiving addiction treatment and, with support, are capable of succeeding in the addiction program.

Similarly, co-occurring capable mental health programs may have individuals who have no substance use condition. It is not uncommon, however, for many individuals with mental health conditions to use substances in an unhealthy way, sometimes in an attempt to self-medicate mental health symptoms, and/or concurrently use alcohol, tobacco, and/or other drugs as part of a co-occurring substance use disorder.

Co-Occurring Enhanced

Co-occurring enhanced programs are "special programs" designed to routinely (as opposed to occasionally) deal with patients who have mental health or cognitive conditions that are more acute or associated with more serious disabilities.[12] Co-occurring enhanced programs should be clearly distinguished from programs that have made more progress in being co-occurring capable. At any level of care, co-occurring enhanced programs will have higher levels of staffing, smaller patient-to-staff ratios, and a generally greater mix of mental health specialty staff than a comparable co-occurring capable program. A mental health co-occurring enhanced service serves patients who have more acute addiction and withdrawal management needs, which can be managed by an enhanced program concurrently with the mental health services.

In *The ASAM Criteria*, for each level of care (except Level 0.5: Early Intervention), there is a brief description of the difference between routine **co-occurring capable** services and specialized **co-occurring enhanced** services at that level of care.

Comprehensive Continuous Integrated System of Care (CCISC)[4,5]

This term represents both a framework and a process for designing a whole system of care to address the complex needs of the individuals and families being served. In CCISC, all programs in the system engage in partnership with other programs, along with the leadership of the system and the individual and family stakeholders, to become welcoming, recovery-oriented, and (at minimum) co-occurring capable.

In addition, every person delivering and supporting care is engaged in a process to become welcoming, recovery-oriented, and co-occurring competent as well. Many systems are now also incorporating trauma-informed care as a routine feature of both program capability and clinician competency.

Complexity Capability

In the past decade, the concept of "co-occurring capability" has evolved to address more than just mental health and substance use issues. In real world general and behavioral health systems, individuals and families with multiple co-occurring needs are an expectation, not an exception. Individuals and families not only have substance use and mental health issues, they frequently have general medical issues, including HIV and other infectious disease issues, legal issues, trauma issues, housing issues, parenting issues, educational issues, vocational issues, and cognitive/learning issues. In addition, these individuals and families are culturally and linguistically diverse. In short, these are people and families who are characterized by "**complexity**," and they tend to have poorer outcomes and higher costs of care. In the general medical world, some patients who are high utilizers of service and those with poorer overall outcomes are those with "**multiple chronic conditions**." But even these conceptualizations often look only at multiple diagnosed medical/surgical conditions and do not address the range of psychosocial issues that can complicate people's lives. These psychosocial issues also complicate the provision of services and the successful results of care.

Instead of designing systems and programs to clearly welcome and prioritize such complex individuals and families experiencing high risk and poor outcomes, such people have historically been deemed "misfits" at every level. This realization has become a major driver for comprehensive system change. In order for systems with scarce resources to successfully address the needs of the individuals and families with complex co-occurring issues, it is not adequate to fund a few "special programs" to work around a fundamentally misdesigned system. There is a need for a process of organizing everything done at every level with every scarce resource to focus on the complex needs of the people and families seeking help. Patient Centered Health Care Homes have been conceptualized—and implemented—to recognize the multidimensional, biopsychosocial needs of patients and to address the complex needs of patients and families. Some systems have begun to use the terminology of "complexity capability" to reflect this broader perspective. Although *The ASAM Criteria* primarily uses the terminology co-occurring capability, its editors anticipate that over time this term may well be replaced with complexity capability.[3]

CO-OCCURRING CONDITIONS AND MATCHING SERVICES TO NEEDS

PATIENTS

SERVICES

Patients with co-occurring mental health needs of mild to moderate severity: Individuals who exhibit (1) sub-threshold diagnostic (ie, traits, symptoms) or (2) diagnosable but stable disorders (ie, bipolar disorder but adherent with and stable on lithium).

Co-Occurring Capable (COC): Primary focus on substance use disorders but capable of treating patients with sub-threshold or diagnosable but stable mental disorders. Psychiatric services available on-site or by consultation; at least some staff are competent to understand and identify signs and symptoms of acute psychiatric conditions.

For a co-occurring capable mental health program, the primary focus is on mental disorders but capable of treating patients with sub-threshold or diagnosable but stable substance use disorders. Addiction services are available on-site or by consultation with some staff competent to understand addiction.

Patients with co-occurring mental health needs of moderate to high severity: Individuals who exhibit moderate to severe diagnosable mental disorders, who are not stable, and who require mental health as well as addiction treatment concurrently.

Co-Occurring Enhanced (COE): All staff cross-trained in addiction and mental health and are competent to understand and identify signs and symptoms of acute psychiatric and substance use conditions and treat both unstable mental and substance use disorders concurrently. Treatment for both mental health and substance use disorders is integrated.

Patients with multiple co-occurring needs: Individuals and families not only have substance use and mental health issues, but frequently have general health, legal, trauma, housing, parenting, educational, vocational, and cognitive/learning issues. In addition, these individuals and families are culturally and linguistically diverse. In short, they are characterized by "complexity," and tend to have poorer outcomes and higher costs of care.

Complexity Capable (CC): Complex individuals and families have historically been deemed "misfits" at every level. This realization is a major driver for comprehensive system change. It is not adequate to fund a few "special programs" to work around a fundamentally misdesigned system. Patient Centered Health Care Homes have been conceptualized–and implemented–to recognize the multidimensional, biopsychosocial needs of patients and to address the complex needs of patients and families. "Complexity capability" reflects this broader perspective.

APPLICATIONS

1

Integrated Services: Integration of Addiction Treatment and General Health Treatment

Primary Health/Behavioral Health Integration

A major advance during the past decade has been the growth of capacity or capability to address mental health, substance use disorder, and general health issues in "integrated" settings. This approach facilitates participant engagement and improves outcomes while using resources more efficiently. Consequently, just as addiction programs have improved co-occurring capability (and thereby improved their ability to integrate attention to co-occurring issues within addiction settings), the same thing has been happening in other areas of the health care system as well. There are three major areas that are relevant to the continuum of addiction services:

» **Integration of substance use services into primary health care:** With the evolution of the concept of the Patient Centered Health Care Home (which, by definition, integrates behavioral health as a core feature of care), primary health settings (particularly those with a public health mission,

such as Federally Qualified Health Centers, or FQHCs) are integrating both substance use screening (as a part of overall health risk assessment) and basic motivational and skill-based interventions for substance use problems and early-stage/milder substance use disorders into core practice. Interventions such as Screening, Brief Intervention, Referral, and Treatment (SBIRT) are starting to be widely disseminated, and medical personnel (ie, physicians and nurses) are increasingly partnering with addiction counselors in general health care settings to promote earlier identification and intervention as a cost-effective approach to care. Addiction treatment services are recognized as an important specialty or tertiary care intervention that complements primary health interventions in a broad public health or population health approach to the widespread need to address substance use issues (including tobacco/nicotine addiction, as well as opioid misuse and addiction in the context of chronic pain) in society as a whole.

RELEVANT AREAS OF INTEGRATION

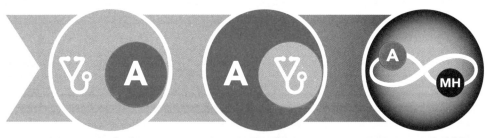

Integration of substance use services into primary health care

Integration of primary health into addiction treatment settings

Integration of addiction and mental health services in a variety of settings

Previous editions of ASAM's criteria foresaw these trends and provided a framework for including descriptions of these services within the overall ASAM criteria levels of care, characterizing these primary-care-based interventions as examples of Level 0.5 services. Thus, Level 0.5 encompasses specialty services for persons with hazardous, at-risk, or harmful substance use where there is not the severity to meet criteria for diagnosis of a substance use disorder. Level 0.5 also encompasses services offered to persons in non-specialty settings such as hospital emergency departments, primary care medical clinics (which may or may not be organized as Patient Centered Health Care Homes), or prenatal care. Such individuals may present along a continuum of intermittent risky use to more frequent at-risk use to harmful use to a mild case of diagnosable substance use disorder.

SERVICE LINKAGES & PARTNERSHIPS

In addition to the specific services that are provided within co-occurring capable and co-occurring enhanced programs, it is important for health care provider entities to develop a full array of service linkages and partnerships with the continuum of addiction, mental health, and general medical services available in their communities. These partnerships should be considered a priority and reinforced by regular meetings and collaborations, to facilitate all partners working together in the form of on-site consultation, interdisciplinary collaboration, and support. Specific policies and procedures enhance the linkage of services required by patients with co-occurring mental and substance-related disorders:

1. **Formal memoranda of understanding and cross-consultation/collaboration agreements** specify what is expected of each provider, as well as expectations for ongoing partnership in treatment planning, collaborative monitoring, and transfer to other aspects of care. An entity providing general medical services, for example, might be an entity designated as a Qualified Service Organization (QSO) for an addiction specialty services provider organization.

2. **Staff is trained** to facilitate admission procedures and negotiate common obstacles encountered by patients with complexity, as well as in identification of key persons to be contacted if problems should arise.

3. **The program has clear delineation of staff responsibility** for coordination with other service providers, whether through designated case managers, or through allocation of coordination responsibilities to members of the treatment team.

4. **Procedures are in place** for notification and collaboration in emergencies and/or in referral for acute treatment in another setting (involving a patient who is suicidal or hospitalized, or in severe withdrawal, for example).

5. **There are formal mechanisms for facilitating information sharing and releases of information**, while adhering to clearly spelled out confidentiality regulations. Training on policies and procedures to facilitate information sharing while protecting confidentiality is provided to all staff, including training on electronic health records.

» **Integration of primary health into addiction treatment settings:** As noted previously, some addiction treatment settings have begun to integrate general medical care services into the addiction treatment continuum. Examples include Opioid Treatment Programs (OTPs, so designated by their licensure as granted by federal and state regulatory agencies), which integrate assessment and treatment services for infectious diseases (Hepatitis C and HIV) acquired via injection drug use, into their core service offerings. Some writers describe this process as "reverse integration" to distinguish it from the integration of addiction services into general medical care settings. Some addiction services, which weave general medical care services into their core processes may function as an integrated Patient Centered Health Care Home for their patients who may have great difficulty accessing routine health care of any kind, and do so while they are participating in a continuum of co-occurring capable addiction services to promote their long-term recovery.[9] Others do not develop into a Patient Centered Health Care Home but can become part of a Patient Centered Health Care Neighborhood.

» **Integration of addiction and mental health services in a variety of settings:** Increasingly, mental health settings are becoming co-occurring capable and able to provide substance use screening, motivational interventions, and skill-based interventions for substance use disorders, integrated into mental health care for individuals and families with mental health conditions. This is also seen in publicly funded programs designed to meet the needs of those with severe and chronic mental illness. Community support programs originally designed to provide psychiatric care have sometimes evolved into providing care that is fully co-occurring capable. Beyond this, more and more behavioral health provider organizations are now offering integrated "one-stop shops," where the mental health and addiction services are organized into an integrated team approach, and the setting can provide appropriately matched co-occurring capable services for individuals with addiction only, mental illness only, and any combination thereof. Some of these settings are also integrating primary health services into the same setting. As *The ASAM Criteria* evolves, it will increasingly recognize the diversity and flexibility of the settings and arrangements, at any level of care, in which co-occurring capable addiction services are being provided.

The Standard Implementation of *The ASAM Criteria*

Without a standard implementation, ASAM's criteria are seriously vulnerable to subjective interpretation. This is a problem that is common in many aspects of health care, but it is even worse in a disease as multi-factorial and diverse along its time course as addiction. Therefore, when using *The ASAM Criteria,* two resources are essential: 1) *The ASAM Criteria* (this text), which provides the definitions and specifications for a common language, the dimensions, and the levels of care, and 2) *The ASAM Criteria Software,* which provides a computer-assisted structured interview

for the provider to use in direct patient assessment, and calculates the ASAM criteria level of care. The use of this book offers several advantages over idiosyncratic assessment to programs, payers, and public agencies. The software can further improve reliability and validity, while the book is the companion text to the software that elucidates the decision rules underlying the software's calculations.

The development of *The ASAM Criteria Software* and its validation is a process that has been ongoing for two decades and is still underway. The Substance Abuse and Mental Health Services Administration (SAMHSA) initiated development of a standard version for open-source release to the field in 2012, and began testing this free application in 2013. With the availability of this module for incorporation into the electronic health record (EHR) and practice management software, the addiction treatment field is finally able to adopt both the principles and practice of the ASAM criteria as a single, common standard for assessing patient needs, optimizing placement, determining medical necessity, and documenting the appropriateness of reimbursement.

Scientists began the crucial process of testing the ASAM criteria in the early 1990s to develop preeminent decision rules not simply through expert consensus, but through an international system of data gathering, quantitative analysis, and empirical feedback.[13]

In general, multidimensional assessment has been found to improve treatment planning.[14,15,16] The first scientific review of the criteria concluded that the ASAM dimensions would predict treatment success.[17] Numerous studies have shown that patient assessment using ASAM-like dimensions can generate both better clinical outcomes and lower costs.[18,19,17,20,21]

In the intervening decades, dozens of reports published in the peer-reviewed literature have been supported by over seven million dollars of U.S. government funding. Project funding came from the National Institute on Drug Abuse (NIDA) and the National Institute on Alcohol Abuse and Alcoholism (NIAAA), and the Center for Substance Abuse Treatment (CSAT) of the Substance Abuse and Mental Health Services Administration (SAMHSA). Consultation or training projects were funded by Aetna Behavioral Health, the Oklahoma Department of Mental Health and Substance Abuse Services, and the U.S. Veterans Administration. Additional studies were subsequently supported by the federal governments of Belgium and Norway. Research training fellowships have been funded by the World Health Organization and the government of Israel, and scientific review conferences have been conducted in Iceland and Switzerland.

Early Studies

In the earliest evaluation, counselors used a simple, one-page summary of the ASAM criteria, First Edition, in three Boston Target Cities Central Intakes.[22] Compared to conventional intake without criteria at treatment sites, patients who were referred to inpatient detoxification using PPC-guided assessment were 38% more likely to transition to continuing treatment within 30 days (as in outpatient care following detoxification) (odds ratio = 1.55, p<.005) and were significantly less likely to return for detoxification within 90 days (odds ratio = .57, p<.005). Thus, even a rough approximation of the ASAM criteria was associated with improved retention and outcome.

A pilot study by Morey[23] retrospectively applied an abbreviated PPC-1 algorithm to telephone survey data. The results showed a good degree of face validity and level of care utilization patterns that suggested a degree of concurrent validity (Morey, personal communication, 1996).

When the state of Kansas adopted the ASAM criteria, early reviews suggested a benefit of substantial cost savings (L. Sperling, personal communication, 1998). Subsequently, a large Kansas study (N=3,093) employed independent placement interviewers with an ASAM-oriented placement tool, and found that homelessness and unemployment were among the best predictors of residential placement, highlighting the importance of social needs as well as clinical dimensions.[24]

Another study of homeless adults (N=382) in need of addiction treatment found that, had the ASAM criteria been followed, 40.3% would have been recommended for Level II intensive outpatient/partial hospital care, whereas in reality, only 1.6% received it.[25] A prospective, naturalistic study compared the placement of 287 adults in Washington State with 240 adults in Oregon, where a statewide ASAM criteria training model was fully implemented. Results showed that in Oregon, with use of the ASAM criteria, patients had more individualized lengths of stay and were more likely to utilize the intensive outpatient level of care—the desired outcome.[26]

Finally, in managed care, where some had raised initial concerns that the ASAM criteria might favor costly residential placement,[27] a study of 250 patients at three Pennsylvania facilities showed that ASAM and managed care recommendations agreed in 85% of cases, and ASAM recommendations became the actual treatment in 93%, suggesting good convergence with cost-effective placement decision-making, and even a preference for the ASAM criteria in practice.[28]

Problems with Implementation

A retrospective study by McKay et al.[16] implemented only the psychosocial dimensions of ASAM's criteria in the first edition (ie, Dimensions 4, 5, and 6), with a degree of brevity that may have made the implementation less than adequate. The investigators found support for predictive validity for some aspects of dependence, but not others, suggesting the need for a comprehensive implementation. A comprehensive assessment tool, however, did not exist, making the ASAM criteria quite difficult to use both clinically and for research.[14]

The same problem arose in a 1998 West Virginia Office of Behavioral Health Services adaptation of the first edition. Even staff who received extensive training reported that "their ability to determine a patient's readiness for a particular level of care is made more difficult due to (a) long and often ambiguous text/format and (b) the lack of clear directions on the use of the cross-walks provided in these instruments."[29]

A recent study tried to evaluate two different automated ASAM-related software approaches, based on an enhanced Addiction Severity Index (ASI). Patients completing an intake ASI (N = 2,429) in 78 addiction treatment programs in Arkansas, New Hampshire, Rhode Island, and Utah were naturalistically given level of care assignments based on availability and clinical considerations. Two placement recommendations were independently calculated using either ASI summary score thresholds or an algorithm approximating the ASAM criteria. Using treatment completion and self-reported abstinence at six months post-dis-

charge as outcomes, both approaches showed evidence of predictive validity. Patients who were undertreated according to the matching calculations did consistently worse on both outcomes, and generally significantly so, but results were not as consistent with regard to overmatching.[30]

Comprehensive Implementation

To help deal with the complexity of the multidimensional branching logic of the ASAM criteria, Gastfriend et al. at the Massachusetts General Hospital and Harvard Medical School constructed the authorized implementation of the ASAM criteria, First Edition, as a comprehensive computerized interview.[31] This approach was definitive, with a comprehensive algorithm that calculated all 266 distinct decision rules as written. It utilized quantitative, research quality question items. Another benefit was the ability for counselors to use the computer in real time with the patient in the intake office. Finally, with this computerized method, different providers assessing the same patient had a good likelihood of arriving at the same level-of-care recommendation (ie, inter-rater reliability; intraclass correlation coefficient = 0.77, $p<0.01$),[32] comparing favorably with *DSM* diagnosis and severity ratings.[33,34,35]

Three Prospective Software Trials

Subsequently, three prospective studies tested this authorized, computer-assisted software. These studies varied in their methods and drew on three groups as patient samples: 1) public system Medicaid and uninsured patients, 2) insured patients and 3) veterans. The studies also used three different outcomes and timeframes of measurement: 1) acute no-show to treatment, 2) 90-day drinking outcomes, and 3) long-term hospital utilization.

State of Adoption

At this point, a considerable body of work exists on the ASAM criteria, including at least nine evaluations involving a total of 3,641 study patients. The six dimensions of ASAM's criteria have been endorsed by the U.S. Department of Health and Human Services.[41] Adoption has progressed, abetted by these data, to the point that a survey of all 50 U.S. State authorities conducted under the auspices of the National Association of State Alcohol/Drug Abuse Directors (NASADAD) found that 43 states (84%) required the use of standard patient-placement criteria.[42] Among the states that require patient placement criteria, approximately two-thirds require providers to use the ASAM criteria, and this percentage is growing. The U.S. Department of Defense has endorsed the ASAM criteria, and a national survey of Veterans Health Administration addiction program leaders reported that 48% were very familiar with the ASAM criteria.[43]

Return on Investment (ROI)

A key concern is that assessment time is costly and scarce, and assessment rigor poses a trade-

THREE PROSPECTIVE SOFTWARE TRIALS

TRIAL 1

The first prospective study, a multisite trial in three regions of Massachusetts, was a randomized, controlled trial in which 700 alcohol and/or drug dependent adults were randomly selected to receive Level 2 or 3 treatment, either matched or mismatched, according to the computer recommendation. Good concurrent validity was demonstrated between the ASAM criteria level of care (LOC) recommendations and other validated assessments such as the Addiction Severity Index.[36] Good predictive validity was also demonstrated for the ASAM criteria software, as patients who were mismatched to a lower level of care than was recommended by the computer ended up having significantly higher acute no-show rates.[14] In addition to these findings in the overall study cohort, the same findings were found in patient subgroups with high-frequency cocaine use[37] and with comorbid symptomatology. Interestingly, patients with comorbid symptomatology also had higher no-show rates when mismatched to a higher level of care than recommended,[38] in contrast to findings using the software approaches of Camilleri et al.[30] Thus, with a comprehensive software implementation of the ASAM criteria, patients have been found to have adverse outcomes both with undermatching and overmatching.

TRIAL 2

The second trial was a naturalistic, prospective study of 248 newly admitted, who were primarily alcohol-dependent, insured adults in New York City. Magura et al.[39] found that outpatients treated in a lower LOC than recommended by the ASAM software (eg, patient received Level 1, outpatient care, whereas Level 2, intensive outpatient care, was recommended) had substantially poorer alcohol-use outcomes than matched patients 90 days after admission. Also, overtreatment, according to the ASAM software, was not associated with improved outcome. Finally, despite ASAM criteria training and the benefits provided by the highly structured, computerized question sequence, counselor judgment alone did not generate as wide a treatment advantage as when treatment assignments also had the benefit of the computer algorithm scoring calculation.

TRIAL 3

The third trial was a naturalistic, prospective study of 95 U.S. male veterans in Bedford, Massachusetts, where the only treatment received was Level 3 residential care. Controlling for past year hospital bed days of utilization, this study looked at the number of hospital bed days over the next annualized period, following the index Level 3 treatment episode. According to the ASAM software at the beginning of this index episode of care, patients who were receiving Level 3 care and were appropriately matched to this level, or overmatched to this level (ie, needed only Level 2, but received Level 3) experienced fewer hospital bed days over the next year. Patients who were undermatched, however (ie, who were judged by the algorithm as needing Level 4 (ie, hospital) care but actually received only Level 3 care (residential rehabilitation), required nearly twice as many hospital bed days over the subsequent year as those who qualified for only Level 2 or 3 (residential care) (p<.05). This finding could not be explained by premorbid differential chronicity (p = n.s.).[40]

off with efficiency, particularly in understaffed treatment programs. When 95 ASAM physician members were surveyed about potential interest in an ASAM criteria software tool, the top five reasons for using such a program were: 1) if it standardizes assessment, 2) if it reduces time spent updating/negotiating with insurance companies, 3) if it generates outcome reports, 4) if it trains counselors, and 5) if it provides a program with certification as "ASAM PPC compliant."[44] In a case study of CRC Health, which operates 145 addiction clinics treating 30,000 people annually, CRC reported devoting 3-5 full-time equivalents at each center dedicated to utilization review, with approximately 20% of cases contested by payers and approximately 30% of physician time spent dealing with payers instead of patients. Even if administrative time is reduced only slightly, such software could yield a substantial ROI.

A nationally representative sampling of 175 U.S. programs found that the leading assessment tool in the U.S., the Addiction Severity Index (ASI), was collected in most cases because it was required by some administrative agency or organization, but it was rarely used for any clinical planning.[45] According to that survey, almost no program director considered any of the data that were collected with the ASI at assessment to be clinically or administratively useful. The ASAM criteria were considered valuable, however, because they offered justification to a managed care organization for a requested admission to a more intensive level of care.

In community implementation, ASAM criteria adoption has proven effective not only for improving patient outcomes, but also for organizational outcomes. For example, at the Addiction Resource Center at Mid-Coast Hospital in Bruns-

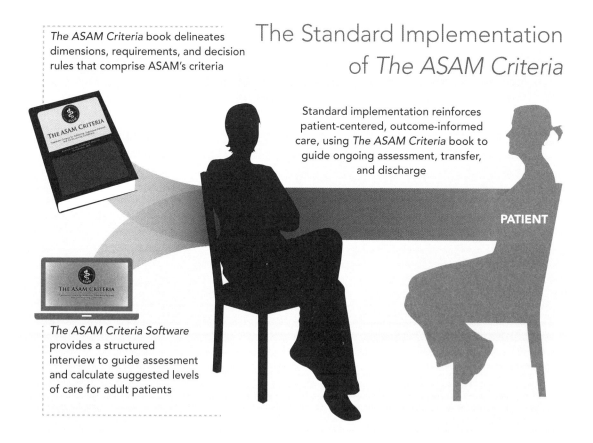

The Standard Implementation of *The ASAM Criteria*

The ASAM Criteria book delineates dimensions, requirements, and decision rules that comprise ASAM's criteria

Standard implementation reinforces patient-centered, outcome-informed care, using *The ASAM Criteria* book to guide ongoing assessment, transfer, and discharge

PATIENT

The ASAM Criteria Software provides a structured interview to guide assessment and calculate suggested levels of care for adult patients

wick, Maine, a key to achieving up to five-fold growth without jeopardizing fiscal stability was making the ASAM criteria their standard for assessment. "We made the ASAM criteria a staff competency…This took away all of the artificial triage filters we had before." The organization was thereby able to terminate redundant assessments, and rationally determine LOC.[46]

Managed care exerts strong pressure to adopt ASAM's criteria: a national survey of U.S. outpatient treatment programs found that a majority (57%) routinely use the ASAM criteria to place patients, and the more a program treated Medicaid or private managed care patients, the more likely it is to use the ASAM criteria. Accreditation is another factor associated with adoption.[47] Finally, a survey of 450 private addiction treatment agencies, conducted by the National Treatment Center, revealed that ASAM criteria adoption was associated with better program survival; programs that had not survived 24 months after an earlier survey were less likely to have adopted the ASAM criteria, and those that closed within six months of the initial survey had even lower adoption rates. ASAM criteria adoption may confer a possible competitive advantage with managed care providers.[48]

Given studies showing reliability, good concurrent validity, and predictive validity, the ASAM criteria appear to be clinically meaningful and suitable for research evaluation at a high level of scientific rigor. Although evidence confirms that patients who are both under-matched and overmatched exhibit worse outcomes, undoubtedly, much work still remains to be done. For example, the increased number of levels of care in the Second Edition-Revised (*PPC-2R*), and continued in *The ASAM Criteria*, Third Edition, and the sublevels for co-occurring capability and enhancement call for more research.

The field also needs a means of properly characterizing treatment programs to accurately determine whether a program delivers co-occurring capable or co-occurring enhanced care. McGovern et al. at Dartmouth Medical School created and validated the Dual Diagnosis Capability in Addiction Treatment (DDCAT) Index for this purpose, and found it to have acceptable psychometric properties (internal consistency, inter-rater agreement, kappa) and sensitivity to program change.[2]

INTAKE/ASSESSMENT

2

Intake and Assessment

The assessment and treatment process, as defined in ASAM's criteria, begins with intake and assessment, which includes a comprehensive biopsychosocial assessment and risk/severity rating, as well as an immediate need profile. Adults and adolescents involved with alcohol, tobacco, and/or other drugs or addictive behaviors require a comprehensive and multidimensional assessment to receive individualized, adaptable, and interdisciplinary care that incorporates inpatient as well as outpatient treatment and ongoing continuing care. In the course of an assessment, certain factors should be recognized and addressed for both adults and adolescents.

For adolescents specifically, these factors include more entrenched early stages of readiness to change (often precontemplation), accelerated progression of addiction in this age group, a marked prevalence of co-occurring disorders, polydrug involvement, and the challenges of habilitation as opposed to rehabilitation. This latter issue can apply also to young adults who have not previously learned skills for effective communication, impulse control, prosocial behavior, and interpersonal interactions. Thus, there is nothing to be rehabilitated because these are new skills and knowledge to be applied.

An assessment should include, wherever possible, collateral informants to augment, and clarify (and often correct) the history given by the patient. Key informants may be family members or significant others; adult friends or surrogate parent figures (for adolescents); school, work, and court officials; court-appointed special advocates; social service workers (especially when the adult or adolescent has been involved with the social service system); previous treatment providers; and past assessors. The greater the apparent severity of the patient's condition and impairment, based on past history or family history known at the onset of the assessment, the more comprehensive the assessment should be.

A comprehensive biopsychosocial assessment includes all of the following elements (in less severe cases, the assessment should at least involve screening of these elements, as through use of a multidimensional screening instrument). Each area of inquiry contributes to a comprehensive profile of the patient, which should be organized according to the six dimensions of the ASAM criteria.

a ▸ Adolescent-Specific Considerations

Adolescent assessments cannot rely on adult assessment methodologies, but must be augmented by developmentally appropriate, adolescent-specific elements.

» **History of the present episode**, including precipitating factors, current symptoms, and pertinent present risks

» **Family history**:
    Family alcohol, tobacco, and other drug use and addictive behavior history, including past treatment episodes
    Family social history, including profiles of parents (or guardians or other caregivers), siblings, home atmosphere, economic status, religious affiliation, cultural influences, leisure activities, monitoring and supervision, and relocations
    Religious, spiritual, or faith background and practice
    Family medical and psychiatric history

» Especially for adolescents and young adults, **developmental history**, including pregnancy and delivery, developmental milestones, and temperament

» **Alcohol, tobacco, and other drug use or addictive behavior history,** including onset and pattern of progression, past sequelae, and past treatment episodes including past successes and barriers to success

» **Personal/social history**:
    School or work history
    Peer relationships and friendships
    Leisure and recreational activities
    Sexual activity, including choice of partners, romantic relationships, sexual risk behaviors, relation of sexual activity to substance use and addictive behavior
    Physical or sexual abuse, or other maltreatment, either as victim or perpetrator
    Disruption of healthy social supports and problems in interpersonal relationships, which can also impact the development of resiliencies
    Military service, veteran status
    Religious, spiritual, and faith-based history

» **Legal history**, including past behaviors and their relation to substance use and addictive

BIOPSYCHOSOCIAL ASSESSMENT ELEMENTS

History of the present episode

Family history

Developmental history

Alcohol, tobacco, other drug use, addictive behavior history

Personal/social history

Legal history

Psychiatric history

Medical history

Spiritual history

Review of systems

Mental status examination

Physical examination

Formulation and diagnoses

Survey of assets, vulnerabilities, and supports

Treatment recommendations

behavior, arrests, adjudications, and details of current status

» **Psychiatric history**, including symptoms and their relation to substance use and addictive behavior, current and past diagnoses, treatments, and providers. The assessment should go beyond possible psychiatric pathology and also assess relevant psychological structures and processes, including belief systems (about oneself, one's substance use or involvement with other pathological sources or reward or relief); cognitive and affective distortions; patterns of attribution of life problems (eg, taking responsibility vs. projecting it onto others, accurately making links between substance use and life problems vs. denying the role of substances or addictive behaviors in causing life problems); patterns of internal vs. external locus of control; and other psychological processes which can impair perceptions and compromise the ability to deal with feelings, resulting in significant self-deception

» **Medical history**, including pertinent medical problems and treatment; emergency department visits, including those for substance-related problems, surgeries, and head injuries; present medications; allergies; and most recent medical evaluation

» **Spiritual history**, including one's sense of meaning, purpose, and values that guides attitudes, thinking, and behavior; and any distortions in a person's connection with self, with others, and with the transcendent (referred to as God by many, Higher Power by 12-Step groups, or higher consciousness by others); including the individual's history with religious affiliations and practices, and how those may relate to current or past spiritual practices

» **Review of systems**, including present and past medical and psychological symptoms

» **Mental status examination**, including memory assessment

» Focused **physical examination**, especially addressing physical manifestations of acute intoxication/withdrawal, and signs of any chronic illnesses

» **Formulation and diagnoses**

» **Survey of assets, vulnerabilities, and supports**

» **Treatment recommendations**

All of these assessment elements then contribute to a profile of the patient, organized by the six specific ASAM criteria assessment dimensions.

Diagnosis

In general, all patients accepted for the treatment of addiction should meet the diagnostic criteria for a substance-related and/or addictive disorder of the current edition of the *Diagnostic and Statistical Manual of Mental Disorders (DSM)* of the American Psychiatric Association or other standardized and widely accepted diagnostic criteria (eg, the most recent edition of the International Classification of Diseases, the ICD). Exceptions would be made for individuals who are not yet known to meet the full diagnostic criteria but whose symptoms are suggestive enough to warrant additional assessment. The diagnosis is likely to be more accurate after completing the multidimensional assessment, a description of which follows in the next section.

The content of the ASAM definition of addiction, part of which is as follows, should be considered as part of the formulation:

"Addiction is a primary, chronic disease of brain reward, motivation, memory, and related circuitry. Dysfunction in these circuits leads to

Characteristics of addiction from ASAM's definition of addiction

Inability to consistently **A**bstain

Impairment in **B**ehavioral control

Craving; or increased "hunger" for drugs or rewarding experiences

Diminished recognition of significant problems with one's behaviors and interpersonal relationships

A dysfunctional **E**motional response[1]

characteristic biological, psychological, social, and spiritual manifestations. This is reflected in an individual pathologically pursuing reward and/or relief by substance use and other behaviors.

Addiction is characterized by inability to consistently abstain, impairment in behavioral control, craving, diminished recognition of significant problems with one's behaviors and interpersonal relationships, and a dysfunctional emotional response. Like other chronic diseases, addiction often involves cycles of relapse and remission. Without treatment or engagement in recovery activities, addiction is progressive and can result in disability or premature death."[1]

Thus, any statement of the assessor's formulation of the case, or a diagnostic summary, would ideally reference the individual's manifestation of the acronym ABCDE (on page 41) referencing the characteristics from this definition.

Who can do an ASAM criteria assessment?

A credentialed counselor or clinician, a certified addiction registered nurse, a psychologist, or a physician may gather diagnostic and multidimensional assessment data relevant to the six ASAM criteria dimensions. However, interpretation of such information must be within the assessor's scope of practice. Consultation with the interdisciplinary team is required whenever the assessor is outside of his or her scope of practice and expertise. For example, a counselor can gather a history of recent substance use and past history of withdrawal but would need nursing or medical consultation to determine the severity of withdrawal and the matched level of withdrawal management.

Nurses, physicians, and psychologists should be knowledgeable regarding addiction and related disorders, the components of multidimensional assessment, mental status examination, and screening for co-occurring disorders; but should the training and experience of the professional align with these principles (and especially if the psychologist or generalist physician has received some special training and certification akin to the training received by addiction specialist clinicians), they should be able to conduct an assessment, especially if they use *The ASAM Criteria Software* to structure their interview. An addiction specialist physician, certified in addiction medicine or addiction psychiatry, is not necessary to conduct the assessment, but if intensive treatment is recommended (Level 2, 3, or 4), then review of the assessment findings by an addiction specialist physician is recommended.

THE IMPORTANCE OF STANDARDIZATION AND TRAINING

By standardizing criteria for assessment, treatment and continued care, ASAM helps providers communicate, both with their patients and with each other. However, standardized practice is only effective when clinicians, counselors and support staff are all properly educated in how to interpret and apply these criteria.

ASAM has worked to develop both in-person and online training courses for professionals at all levels. These training resources create fidelity to the principles and spirit that have guided the ASAM criteria for over 20 years. At the same time, they incorporate the newest science and practical applications from the field to ensure use of the ASAM criteria is ever-evolving.

For more information about resources and training materials, visit www.asamcriteria.org.

The Six Dimensions of Multidimensional Assessment

In its continued effort to move practitioners away from a one-dimensional, diagnosis-driven approach to treatment, ASAM uses six unique dimensions, which represent different life areas that together impact any and all assessment, service planning, and level of care placement decisions.

The ASAM Criteria structures multidimensional assessment around these six dimensions to provide a common language of holistic, biopsychosocial assessment and treatment across addiction treatment, physical health, and mental health services, which addresses as well the spiritual issues relevant in recovery.

AT A GLANCE: THE SIX DIMENSIONS OF MULTIDIMENSIONAL ASSESSMENT

ASAM's criteria uses six dimensions to create a holistic, biopsychosocial assessment of an individual to be used for service planning and treatment across all services and levels of care. The six dimensions are:

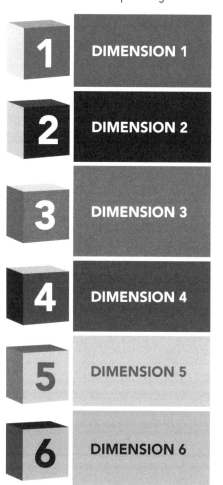

DIMENSION 1

Acute Intoxication and/or Withdrawal Potential

Exploring an individual's past and current experiences of substance use and withdrawal

DIMENSION 2

Biomedical Conditions and Complications

Exploring an individual's health history and current physical condition

DIMENSION 3

Emotional, Behavioral, or Cognitive Conditions and Complications

Exploring an individual's thoughts, emotions, and mental health issues

DIMENSION 4

Readiness to Change

Exploring an individual's readiness and interest in changing

DIMENSION 5

Relapse, Continued Use, or Continued Problem Potential

Exploring an individual's unique relationship with relapse or continued use or problems

DIMENSION 6

Recovery/Living Environment

Exploring an individual's recovery or living situation, and the surrounding people, places, and things

SIX DIMENSIONS ❷

The six assessment dimensions, briefly described here, are essentially the same as in earlier editions of ASAM's criteria, with slight modifications to apply to co-occurring mental health conditions that were initially described in *PPC-2R* (2001):

Dimension 1: Acute Intoxication and/or Withdrawal Potential

Dimension 1 assesses the need for stabilization of acute intoxication. When concerning withdrawal, this dimension assesses what type and intensity of withdrawal management services are needed. The goals of care in Dimension 1 can be summarized as follows:

1. To avoid the potentially hazardous consequences of abrupt discontinuation of use of alcohol, tobacco, and other drugs, by applying the criteria across a seamless continuum of five levels of withdrawal management services. This continuum of withdrawal management services should be used flexibly and in a clinically driven manner.

2. To engage and facilitate the patient to complete withdrawal management and link the patient to timely, continued general medical, addiction, or mental health treatment. Involvement in self/mutual help recovery or other community supports for recovery may also apply where appropriate. When withdrawal management services are more fully integrated into addiction treatment and general medical and mental health treatment settings, continuity of care and engagement into continuing care are improved.

3. To promote patient dignity and ease patient discomfort during the withdrawal process. This can be achieved by utilizing a seamless continuum of withdrawal management services. The patient is thus able to receive longer lengths of withdrawal

DIMENSION 1

ASSESSMENT CONSIDERATIONS INCLUDE

» What risk is associated with the patient's current level of acute intoxication?

» Are intoxication management services needed to address acute intoxication (eg, preventing drunk driving by holding a person's car keys until he or she is abstinent or in safety with family members; managing acute alcohol poisoning in an adolescent experimenting with rapid intake)?

» Is there significant risk of severe withdrawal symptoms, seizures, or other medical complications based on the patient's previous withdrawal history, as well as the amount, frequency, chronicity and recency of discontinuation of (or significant reduction in) alcohol, tobacco, or other drug use?

» Are there current signs of withdrawal?

» What scores are derived from use of standardized withdrawal rating scales?

» What are the patient's vital signs?

» Does the patient have sufficient supports to assist in ambulatory withdrawal management, if medically safe to consider?

SIX DIMENSIONS

2

support for the same or even less use of resources compared to when withdrawal management occurs exclusively or predominantly in high-intensity medically monitored or medically managed inpatient levels of care. The focus of withdrawal management in acute inpatient services is on the treatment or prevention of serious, life-threatening withdrawal symptoms or complications (eg, seizures, arrhythmias). Transfer to or direct admission to less intensive levels of withdrawal management care provides for more efficient withdrawal support and improved outcomes.

For patients who require a more intensive level of care because of conditions in other dimensions, it may be more expedient to carry out management of intoxication or withdrawal in that more intensive level of care. On the other hand, many patients who enter addiction treatment do not require formal withdrawal management. Nevertheless, all patients should be assessed upon initial presentation for services in Dimension 1.

Dimension 2: Biomedical Conditions and Complications

Dimension 2 assesses the need for physical health services, including whether there are needs for acute stabilization and/or ongoing disease management for a chronic physical health condition.

Dimension 3: Emotional, Behavioral, or Cognitive Conditions and Complications

Dimension 3 assesses the need for mental health services. If the emotional, behavioral, or cognitive signs and symptoms are part of addiction (eg, mood swings because the individual is using "uppers" and "downers"), then Dimension 3 needs may be safely addressed as part of addiction treatment. On the other hand, if mood swings relate to a concurrent bipolar disorder, then additional mental health services are warranted.

This dimension specifically references mental health conditions, including trauma-related issues and conditions such as posttraumatic stress, cognitive conditions and developmental disorders, and substance-related mental health conditions. Other terminology includes: mental illnesses, psychiatric conditions or disorders, psychological or emotional or behavioral issues or complications, changes in mental status, or transient neuropsychiatric complications. This edition of *The ASAM Criteria* will utilize "mental health conditions," "trauma-related conditions," and "cognitive conditions" as consistent terminology. Unless otherwise noted, the term "mental health conditions" will generally reference all three.

Spiritual aspects, related to what gives meaning and purpose to an individual and their appreciation of and connection to a higher power or a conception of the transcendent

DIMENSION 2

ASSESSMENT CONSIDERATIONS INCLUDE

» Are there current physical illnesses, other than withdrawal, that need to be addressed due to their risk or potential for treatment complications?

» Are there chronic conditions that need stabilization or ongoing disease management (eg, chronic pain needing pain management)?

» Is there a communicable disease present that could impact the well-being of other patients or staff?

» For female patients, is the patient pregnant? What is her pregnancy history, especially if she has opioid use disorder?

should be included as part of the clinical assessment of this dimension.

There are subdomains of assessment in Dimension 3 to address co-occurring mental health and substance-related conditions in more detail. See "Subdomain" in the Glossary for definitions.

It is important to note that, in assessing co-occurring disorders, 1) a mental health or substance-related disorder should be considered "secondary" (from a causation perspective) only if the course demonstrates that the "secondary" condition emerged subsequent to the "primary" condition, *and* 2) that the secondary condition resolved completely within a relatively short period of time (eg, 30 days) once the primary condition was stabilized. Note as well that when the two or more disorders co-occur and are concurrent, they all need to be addressed simultaneously as "primary" conditions in order to provide the most effective integrated and holistic care. Further, the terminology specifically encourages attention to co-occurring mental health "conditions" that may warrant intervention, even though it may be too early to be certain that criteria are met for a particular "mental disorder" diagnosis per the latest edition of the *Diagnostic and Statistical Manual of Mental Disorders*, published by the American Psychiatric Association.

ASSESSMENT CONSIDERATIONS INCLUDE

DIMENSION 3

» Are there current psychiatric illnesses or psychological, behavioral, emotional, or cognitive conditions that need to be addressed because they create risk or complicate treatment?

» Are there chronic conditions that need stabilization or ongoing treatment (eg, bipolar disorder or chronic anxiety)?

» Do any emotional, behavioral, or cognitive signs or symptoms appear to be an expected part of the addictive disorder, or do they appear to be autonomous?

» Even if connected to the addiction and subdiagnostic, are any emotional, behavioral, or cognitive signs or symptoms severe enough to warrant specific mental health treatment (eg, suicidal ideation and depression from "cocaine crash")?

» Is the patient able to manage the activities of daily living?

» Can he or she cope with any emotional, behavioral, or cognitive conditions?

SIX DIMENSIONS

②

RISK DOMAINS

A risk domain is an assessment subcategory within Dimension 3, as described below. These criteria sub-domains emphasize the broad functional impairments that are associated with both substance-related disorders and mental health problems. They were developed specifically for use with adolescent populations; however, they were incorporated into the Dimension 3 subdomains of the adult matrix as well.

DIMENSION 3

» **Dangerousness/Lethality**

This risk domain describes how impulsive an individual may be with regard to homicide, suicide, or other forms of harm to self or others and/or to property. The seriousness and immediacy of the individual's ideation, plans, and behavior—as well as his or her ability to act on such impulses—determine the patient's risk rating and the type and intensity of services he or she needs.

» **Interference with Addiction Recovery Efforts**

This risk domain describes the degree to which a patient is distracted from addiction recovery efforts by emotional, behavioral, and/or cognitive problems and, conversely, the degree to which a patient is able to focus on addiction recovery. For example, the person's depression or psychosis makes attendance at mutual help meetings sporadic. (Note that high risk and severe impairment in this domain do not, in themselves, require services in a Level 4 program.) For co-occurring capable and enhanced mental health programs, a similar domain could be called **Interference with Mental Health Recovery Efforts**, describing the degree to which a patient is distracted from mental health recovery efforts by addiction problems. For example, difficulties with psychotropic medication adherence due to frequent intoxication.

» **Social Functioning**

This risk domain describes the degree to which an individual's relationships (eg, coping with friends, significant others, or family; parental responsibilities; vocational or educational demands; and ability to meet personal responsibilities) are affected by his or her substance use and/or other emotional, behavioral, and cognitive problems. (Note that high risk and severe impairment in this domain do not, in themselves, require services in a Level 4 program.)

RISK DOMAINS

DIMENSION 3

» **Ability for Self-Care**

This risk domain describes the degree to which an individual's ability to perform activities of daily living (such as grooming and having appropriate food and shelter) are affected by his or her substance use and/or other emotional, behavioral, and cognitive problems. (Note that high risk and severe impairment in this domain do not, in themselves, require services in a Level 4 program.)

» **Course of Illness**

This risk domain employs the history of the patient's illness and response to treatment to interpret the patient's current signs, symptoms, and presentation, and to predict the patient's likely response to treatment. Thus, the domain assesses the interaction between the chronicity and acuity of the patient's current deficits. A high risk rating is warranted when the individual is assessed as at significant risk and vulnerability for dangerous consequences either because of severe, acute life-threatening symptoms, or because a history of such instability suggests that high-intensity services are needed to prevent dangerous consequences.

For example, a patient may present with medication adherence difficulties, having discontinued antipsychotic medication two days ago. If a patient is known to rapidly decompensate into acute psychosis when medication is stopped, his or her rating is high. However, if it is known that he or she slowly isolates without any rapid deterioration when medication is stopped, the risk rating would be lower. Another example could be the patient who has been depressed, socially withdrawn, staying in bed, and not bathing. If this has been a problem for six weeks, the risk rating is much higher than for a patient who has been chronically withdrawn and isolated for six years with a severe and chronic schizophrenic disorder.

SIX DIMENSIONS

2

Adolescent-Specific Considerations: Dimension 3

Cognitive abilities, as well as global or focal cognitive impairments, play a large role in an adolescent's functional capacity. These cognitive problems can interfere significantly with treatment and recovery, regardless of the type of impairment. They may be expressions of pre-existing conditions, such as borderline intellectual functioning, fetal alcohol effects, or learning disorders. They may be complications of substance use, such as marijuana-induced amnestic disorders. Cannabinoid-related cognitive impairment may also be attributable to use of synthetic cannabinoid molecules which may be more neurotoxic than herbal cannabis and which may not be detected by some urine drug testing processes. Or, they may be the cognitive impairment sometimes caused by methamphetamine or various synthetic/designer drugs, such as "ecstasy" or "molly" (MDMA, ie, 3,4-methylenedioxy-N-methamphetamine), or the mephedrone-related and pyrovalerone-related compounds (eg, MDPV) sold as "bath salts."

Dimension 3 also encompasses the broad consideration of developmental issues, including those reflected in the symptoms of various developmental disabilities (eg, features of autism spectrum disorder or other developmental disorders) or those reflected in the more generic, dimensional consideration of immaturity. To be most effective, treatment providers must adapt their methods and strategies to respond to adolescents' emotional, behavioral, and cognitive vulnerabilities and strengths, as well as a developmental perspective that evolves dynamically.

Dimension 4: Readiness to Change

Dimension 4 assesses the degree of need for motivational enhancement services to engage a person and begin a recovery process. This dimension reflects such stages of change models as Prochaska and DiClemente's Transtheoretical Model,[2,3] thus moving the criteria beyond the concepts of "denial" and "resistance to treatment."

Since most people who present for treatment are not necessarily ready to embrace full recovery, Dimension 4 emphasizes the need to engage and attract individuals to make changes in their thinking, emotions, and behavior. Thus, treatment approaches and intensity should be tailored to the assessed stage of change.

More recent work in this area has demonstrated that the concepts of "readiness to change" and "stage of change" are not person-specific, but problem- or issue-specific.

Patients can be at different stages of change for different issues. For example, an individual may be in an earlier stage of change regard-ing his or her addictive disorder, but in a more active stage of change regarding his or her general health issues, mental health conditions, and/or social issues. Certain people may recognize that they have difficulty controlling their alcohol use, but see no difficulty in their marijuana use. A patient may be concerned about an anxiety problem, but not recognize that she is struggling with a psychosis. Or a patient may be ready to deal with hypertension, but not be ready to lose weight or stop smoking. The lack of interest in addressing, or readiness to address, tobacco use along with other addictive substance use is such a common finding that an entire chapter of this edition of *The ASAM Criteria* addresses this issue.

Some individuals vocalize a cognitive awareness of the need to address a given aspect of their health condition or life circumstances. However, they may be ambivalent about seeking services, or following recommended "wrap-around services" to prevent

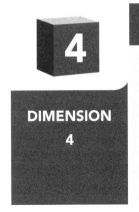

ASSESSMENT CONSIDERATIONS INCLUDE

DIMENSION 4

» How aware is the patient of the relationship between his or her alcohol, tobacco, or other drug use or behaviors involved in the pathological pursuit of reward or relief and his or her negative life consequences?

» How ready, willing, or able does the patient feel to make changes to his or her substance using or addictive behaviors?

» How much does the patient feel in control of his or her treatment service?

relapse and progression of their condition. Attention must be paid to these potentially different and co-occurring stages of readiness in order to sufficiently reduce the risk of relapse to the addictive disorder.

Understanding the variability of the "readiness to change" concept facilitates more accurate treatment engagement and matching, and emphasizes the importance of individualized stage-matched services. Individuals should not be clinically assessed as being at one stage of change and assigned to a stage-matched program as if the individual's readiness is one-dimensional and responsive to a standardized set of group activities. Further, it is clinically useful to note that assessment of stage of change is designated from the clinician's point of view as to what the individual needs to change and accept as a condition requiring treatment.

From the patient's point of view, if an individual is participating in a professionally conducted assessment, that person is manifesting motivation and readiness to change something, which has prompted him or her to appear at a clinical facility for an assessment. What they may be motivated to achieve and to change may be to stay out of jail or to get a family member, school official, employer, or a judge to leave them alone. They may be motivated to keep a child, a job, or a relationship. They may want to change their probation officer, their teacher, their supervisor, or their life partner.

All of these motivations can be expressed separate from wanting to change or addressing a substance use or addictive behavior. Thus, a patient's motivation may not be what the clinician thinks they should be motivated about. This is a Dimension 4 assessment and treatment issue, and not a reason to label the person as "unmotivated," "treatment-resistant," or "rejecting help." The goal of Dimension 4 services, in this case, will be to "attract" the participant into recovery, rather than to mandate services that do not match their readiness to change.

Because "readiness to change," occurs on a continuum (ie, stages of change), interventions should be stage-matched. It is the *degree* of readiness to change for any one issue or a set of issues that helps determine the setting for and intensity of motivating strategies needed, rather than determining the patient's eligibility for treatment itself. In summary, the assessment of severity and functioning in Dimension 4, and what intensity of services and level of care is recommended, are subject to interpretation, based on a wide list of issues: clinician and program ideology; clinician knowledge and skill in assessment of stage of change and engagement strategies; availability of a variety of motivational enhancement therapies and levels of service; and the degree of commitment to patient-centered, participatory treatment planning.

SIX DIMENSIONS

❷

Dimension 5: Relapse, Continued Use, or Continued Problem Potential

Dimension 5 assesses the need for relapse prevention services. If the person has not achieved a period of recovery from which to relapse, this dimension assesses the potential for continued use for substance use disorders, or continued problem potential to include attention to gambling and/or co-occurring mental health, trauma, and cognitive conditions that add to the patient's difficulty maintaining stability and making progress in recovery.

For example, a psychotic, paranoid individual who is fearful of being poisoned and thus fails to take his or her medications would be described as having a high "continued problem potential." This indicates that the patient is at high risk for becoming acutely psychotic and/or increasingly paranoid. Such a patient may also be at high risk of relapse to substance use if suffering from co-occurring disorders.

For addiction, Dimension 5 focuses on previous periods of sobriety or wellness and what worked to achieve this. Responses may include coping skills to deal with peer pressure or cravings to use substances, the ability to cope with protracted withdrawal, and the ability to tolerate negative affects and stress without recurrence of use or other addictive behaviors. The assignment of a level of care after a patient has relapsed should be made on the basis of both history and an assessment of current problems, and not merely history alone. It should not be automatically assumed that the patient requires a more intensive level of care than the one at which the relapse occurred.

DIMENSION 5

ASSESSMENT CONSIDERATIONS INCLUDE

» Is the patient in immediate danger of continued severe mental health distress and/or alcohol, tobacco, and/or other drug use?

» Does the patient have any recognition or understanding of, or skills in coping with, his or her addictive or co-occurring mental health disorder in order to prevent relapse, continued use, or continued problems such as suicidal behavior?

» Have addiction and/or psychotropic medications assisted in recovery before?

» What are the person's skills in coping with protracted withdrawal, cravings, or impulses?

» How well can the patient cope with negative affects, peer pressure, and stress without recurrence of addictive thinking and behavior?

» How severe are the problems and further distress that may continue or reappear if the patient is not successfully engaged in treatment and continues to use, gamble, or have mental health difficulties?

» How aware is the patient of relapse triggers and skills to control addiction impulses or impulses to harm self or others?

DIMENSION 5:
USING & DEFINING "RELAPSE"

Dimension 5 is better understood through expanded constructs offered to assist in assessment. There are four domains that are not inconsistent with earlier versions of Dimension 5 in previous editions of the ASAM criteria, but which offer a conceptually clearer sequence of factors that contribute to relapse potential. The sequence involves the historical phenomenon of relapse, the acute pharmacologic response to substance(s), second-order behavioral responsivity that may mediate the preceding factors, and third-order personality or learned responses that may modify the preceding factors (See Appendix B for more detail and discussion of relapse policies).

The term "relapse" has generally been assigned to the resumption of use once abstinent (See the Glossary for ASAM's definition of relapse). It may no longer be appropriate for ASAM to use the term in this manner as we describe an illness that has symptoms that can be suppressed through the use of antiaddiction medicines. Further discussion of the term relapse and the possible need to review terminology occurs in Appendix B. For the present, application of the term "relapse" might best describe resumption of active addiction after a period of "recovery" rather than abstinence (See definition of recovery in the Glossary).

Dimension 6: Recovery/Living Environment

Dimension 6 assesses the need for specific individualized family or significant other support and services. It also assesses the need for housing, financial, vocational, educational, legal, transportation, or child care services. At the Early Intervention level of care, Dimension 6 is titled "Living Environment" to reflect the fact that, at this level, an individual has not been assessed as meeting criteria for a diagnostic substance use disorder in need of treatment and recovery. At this level, the individual may need only education and advice on managing health risks. For all others who do meet diagnostic criteria, Dimension 6 is titled "Recovery Environment" to reflect that treatment should include consideration of how supportive a person's current or future environment is to recovery. Consideration is needed to explore and support an individual's cultural uniqueness as well as spirituality to ensure congruence with what pro-

vides meaning and purpose to the individual's life; and that a connection to the transcendent, Higher Power or the individual's own concept of God is supported.

Note that in this dimension as well, different aspects of the recovery environment may provide support for different co-occurring conditions. For example, an individual with addiction and a severe mental illness may have an excellent support system from a mental health case management team, but no participation in 12-Step recovery programs, or vice versa. Similarly, an individual may have excellent family support for continuing to take psychotropic or physical health medications, but those same family members may be actively drinking, or they may express strong philosophical objections to addiction pharmacotherapies. Assessment of Dimension 6 should recognize the importance of identifying recovery and environmental supports for each significant co-occurring condition.

ASSESSMENT CONSIDERATIONS INCLUDE

**DIMENSION
6**

» Do any family members, significant others, living situations, or school or work situations pose a threat to the person's safety or engagement in treatment?

» Does the individual have supportive friendships, financial resources, or educational or vocational resources that can increase the likelihood of successful recovery?

» Are there legal, vocational, regulatory (eg, professional licensure), social service agency, or criminal justice mandates that may enhance the person's motivation for engagement in treatment if indicated?

» Are there transportation, child care, housing, or employment issues that need to be clarified and addressed?

Adolescent-Specific Considerations: Structured, Protective Living Environments

There is an acute shortage of availability of services that provide recovery environment support for youth. These structured, protective living environments are often vital to support ongoing treatment that might be integrated into the living environment itself or, more commonly, coordinated with programming off-site. Frequently they serve the function of a supervised context where adolescents can sustain and rehearse therapeutic gains initiated at a more intensive level of care. This need for step-down, lower intensity residential care is perhaps even more vital in the continuum of care for youth than for adults because of their lack of independence and reliance on the support or partial support of caregiving adults.

For younger adolescents, these programs would typically be considered Level 3.1, often group homes or similar programs. For young adults, these programs also could be Level 3.1. But there is also a need for less intensive recovery housing programs, with more supervision than typical adult-style self-organized sober housing (eg, Oxford Houses), or adult-style recovery house boarding houses that have minimal supervision, but perhaps with less intensity than the typical Level 3.1, or halfway house.

But there are far too few of such programs available, either for adolescents or for young adults. Such programs have typically not been part of the benefits package for either commercial or public insurers. Halfway houses are frequently funded only within the adult criminal justice system. As block grant funding for addiction services increasingly transitions into broader insurance funding for treatment services, this is an area where residual block grant funding must expand and take up the slack, and an area where the typical insurance benefit package must be expanded in both the public and private sectors.

SPIRITUALITY

Since the publication of the first edition of the ASAM patient placement criteria, many have asked why there is not a Dimension 7 on spirituality. From the beginning, significant consideration was given to inclusion of spiritual parameters as they relate to treatment and placement criteria. Although spiritual concepts, ideas, and relationships are important for many people's recovery, they are difficult to define acceptably in objective, behavioral, and measurable terms. There is no literature or even clinical consensus on how the assessment of spirituality relates to a level of care determination, or to length of stay in a level of care, or even when to transfer or discharge a person based on progress in a spiritual dimension. Still, national accreditation organizations[4] expect that attention will be paid to spiritual concepts in professional treatment experiences, and ASAM has defined addiction as having "characteristic biological, psychological, social, and spiritual manifestations."[1] As spirituality is an integral part of many addiction treatment programs, it has been included descriptively, but specific criteria have not been written incorporating the role of spirituality in placement or treatment decisions explicitly. Continued exploration of this aspect of addiction and mental health problems is encouraged.

A person's spirituality can be integrated within assessment and service planning across all six dimensions, rather than being addressed in a separate dimension. By assessing if and when spirituality has been meaningful for the individual in any or all of the assessment dimensions, strengths, skills, and resources can be identified to be incorporated into the service plan. For example, in Dimension 6, a patient may get more support from his or her faith community than from other support groups like Alcoholics Anonymous or SMART Recovery®. In Dimension 3, a patient may be depressed and demoralized, but find comfort and relief from prayer, meditation, or connecting with a Higher Power. The same might be said for a patient with a Dimension 2 chronic pain syndrome or other health condition. In Dimension 4, a patient may find relief from undue guilt and self-blame through spirituality, and thus move past an early stage of readiness to change. Spiritual surrender can paradoxically empower people to stop fighting their condition and blaming themselves for having addiction or mental illness. These examples show how spirituality and spiritual practices may be as effective as, or at least complementary to, other treatment modalities.

A Multidimensional Risk Profile

Individuals with mental and substance use disorders can be viewed as suffering from biopsychosocial illnesses that, to varying degrees, have biological and medical, psychological and psychiatric, and sociocultural origins and clinical features. Treatment of these individuals is most effective and efficient when it addresses the individuals' specific biopsychosocial issues in a manner that will stabilize the acute episode, arrest further deterioration of function, and help promote ongoing recovery.

PRINCIPLES FOR ASSESSING RISK[5(p23)]

As a step toward consensus–or at least toward minimizing confusion about assessment of patients with co-occurring conditions–the following principles provide guidance for assessing an individual's severity and level of function, or what has been termed here as "risk."

Risk is **multidimensional** and **biopsychosocial**.	Addressing a particular patient's risk may require more than one treatment component (eg, stabilizing a psychosis or managing a patient's withdrawal while also addressing an unstable or dangerous living environment). Risk is mediated by protective factors as well. If a patient in withdrawal also has a stable living situation with a supportive family, for example, withdrawal risk is moderated by these protective factors and resources. Because risk is multidimensional, each of the criteria's six dimensions is assessed independently and receives its own risk rating. This allows assessors to then compare information of dimensional risk and integrate priority needs within a holistic treatment plan.
Risk relates to the patient's **history**.	For example, the patient whose withdrawal always results in seizures has different treatment needs than the patient whose withdrawal involves only mild symptoms of anxiety. Or the patient who in the past has acted on suicidal impulses by hanging has needs different from the patient who acted on suicidal impulses by superficially scratching a wrist. The patient's history also encompasses past successes so as to identify strengths, skills, and resources that can be harnessed in treatment planning (eg, identify what worked in previous successful withdrawal management episodes).
Risk is expressed in **current status**, answering the question, "How acute, unstable, and active is the patient's current clinical presentation?"	For example, a patient who develops elevated vital signs in response to discontinuation of alcohol use requires different treatment services from a calm patient who is not currently using alcohol, tobacco, and/or other drugs. Similarly, an actively psychotic patient who is hallucinating needs more intensive services than a patient who is chronically psychotic but currently stable. Current status also includes protective factors such as current stable living situation, supportive friends or family, and professional resources, such as a therapist or primary care physician.
Risk involves a **degree of change from baseline or premorbid functioning**.	For example, a previously outgoing and fully functioning individual who suddenly withdraws from social contact needs more intensive services than does an individual who is chronically withdrawn and barely able to function outside a supportive living environment.

"HISTORY" AND "HERE AND NOW"

Risk assessment must integrate the patient's history, current status, and changing situation. The patient's historical function and severity does not override the current status when assessing "here and now" severity and level of function. However, the "here and now" current status of an individual's severity and level of function does override the patient's history. For example, if a patient has a history of seizures upon alcohol withdrawal, this is a concern. However, if the patient has not been drinking or using any other addictive substances for a month and is currently not in withdrawal, the history does not define the patient's current risk. In reverse, however, if the patient is currently in severe withdrawal with imminent potential for withdrawal seizures, the "here and now" risk is very high, even without a history of previous severe withdrawal signs and symptoms.

If a patient has both a history of severe withdrawal and is now also currently in severe withdrawal, then the integration of both severe history and current severity elevates the person's risk even more. The same principles guide the current risk of a person with suicidal history versus current suicidal impulses. An impulsive history would not drive current risk if the patient is not suicidal "here and now." But current, strong impulses to harm oneself is high risk, even without previous history of suicidal thoughts or behavior. A history of impulsivity, as well as "here and now" suicidal thoughts and strong impulses, would elevate the current risk even more.

To optimize the use of treatment and financial resources, patient care must be strength-based and individualized rather than driven solely by the patient's diagnosis or the availability of certain levels of care or types of treatment programs. Diagnosis is a necessary, but not sufficient, determinant of service needs. Just as with patients who are diagnosed with cancer, hypertension, or diabetes, it is the severity of the patient's illness and the degree of the patient's impairment—not merely the diagnosis—that determine the patient's specific treatment needs and thus drive the treatment plan.[5(p23)]

Professionals working in the addiction and mental health fields have yet to achieve consensus on how to assess clinical risk. As a result, a variety of payer and provider criteria and decision rules have been developed for placing patients in treatment services and level of care settings. The ensuing confusion adversely affects communications among professionals, with patients and their families, and with care managers and payers. It also dissipates limited resources.

Establishing a Risk Rating System

There are many ways to determine the severity of a patient's needs. Some providers and organizations evaluate risk in each dimension using an indication of "low," "moderate," or "high." Previous editions of ASAM's criteria introduced a scale of 0-4. Within this spectrum, 0 indicates a patient's stability or no to very low risk within a dimension. On the opposite end of the spectrum, a rating of 4 indicates a severe or very high risk.

Establishing a rating system creates a standard method for assessing patient severity and level of function, therefore helping identify individual priorities and needs. It is important to note that a risk rating given at the time of initial assessment will likely change throughout a patient's treatment and continuing care. Continued reassessment is key when establishing a patient-directed and outcome-informed approach to care.

When *The ASAM Criteria* book is used in conjunction with *The ASAM Criteria Software*, the computer algorithm provides computer-assisted clinical decision support about risk without a need to focus on a rating system. Thus a rating system is more clinically useful if *The ASAM Criteria Software* is not yet being used and for case presentations of multidimensional, biopsychosocial patient data and for succinct ways to review and communicate about progress and outcomes.

Although any appropriate and effective rating system may be used in an assessment, *The ASAM Criteria* references the 0-4 risk rating system in the brief summary provided here.

Assessing Strengths, Skills, and Resources

While the six dimensions are assessed for needs and barriers to recovery, they also structure assessment of a person's strengths, skills, and resources. No matter what severity of risk rating a dimension may yield, applicable strengths, skills, and resources may exist as well. To draw these to the surface, it helps to explore with the patient any periods of success in which he

or she was able to cope with or better manage these risk-related issues.

For example, in Dimension 5, Relapse, Continued Use, or Continued Problem Potential, if an individual has been able to achieve recovery for nine months, a strengths-based approach would help identify what skills and resources the person utilized to achieve that good outcome. An assessor might pose questions like, "What were your friends and family like at that time? Were you active in a self/mutual help group(s) that was a helpful resource? Did you utilize a sponsor, coach, or mentor in such groups? What helped you to deal with cravings to use or cope with stress without using substances? Did you use complementary and alternative medicine approaches such as mindfulness meditation to assist with preventing relapse? Did you take a pharmacological therapy to assist with preventing relapse?"

For Dimension 3, Emotional, Behavioral, or Cognitive Conditions and Complications, a person may have had suicidal ideation, but

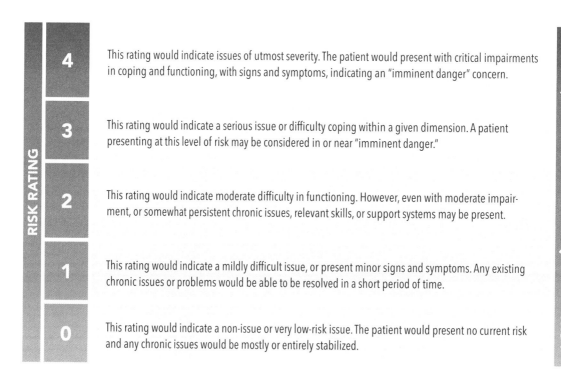

RISK RATING

4 — This rating would indicate issues of utmost severity. The patient would present with critical impairments in coping and functioning, with signs and symptoms, indicating an "imminent danger" concern.

3 — This rating would indicate a serious issue or difficulty coping within a given dimension. A patient presenting at this level of risk may be considered in or near "imminent danger."

2 — This rating would indicate moderate difficulty in functioning. However, even with moderate impairment, or somewhat persistent chronic issues, relevant skills, or support systems may be present.

1 — This rating would indicate a mildly difficult issue, or present minor signs and symptoms. Any existing chronic issues or problems would be able to be resolved in a short period of time.

0 — This rating would indicate a non-issue or very low-risk issue. The patient would present no current risk and any chronic issues would be mostly or entirely stabilized.

HIGH → / MODERATE → / ← LOW

WHAT THE PATIENT WANTS

The risks and needs, or strengths, skills, and resources, identified by a practitioner in a multidimensional assessment should not determine service planning alone. In addition to the rated severity of illness, practitioners must also cultivate an awareness of how these unique risks and needs, as well as the strengths, skills, and resources, function with regard to the patient's personal goals.

As stated in the introduction to Dimension 4, Readiness to Change, the patient who participates in a professionally conducted assessment is manifesting a motivation and readiness to change something. This personal motivation may be anything from staying out of jail to getting a family member, school official, employer, or judge to leave them alone. Other participants may want to keep a child, job (work or school), or relationship. Or they may want to change their probation officer, teacher, supervisor, or life partner.

These personal motivations may not match the needs assessed and identified by the clinician. However, the more that priority dimensions can be matched to or interpreted through the patient's personal goals, the more patient-centered and participatory the service plan and placement can be.

never acted on the impulses nor was committed to treatment. Appropriate strengths-based questions to ask may include, "What coping skills helped you resist impulses to harm yourself? Were there family or friends or a therapist who helped you contain your impulses? Was medication, exercise, or meditation helpful with your depression?" In Dimension 2, Biomedical Conditions and Complications, it is a strength to follow through with a commitment to do daily aerobic exercise, or to develop a diet or exercise regimen to prevent weight gain when addressing one's tobacco use disorder. In Dimension 6, Recovery/Living Environment, it is a resource to have even one family member who offers temporary living support, so long as the patient remains committed to treatment and recovery. Or, if a person has had a period of stable employment in the past, an assessor can explore what was working well and what skills and resources the person used during that period of vocational success.

Multidimensional assessment and severity of function ratings work best when individuals are first assessed in each dimension independently. Taking one dimension at a time and comparing relevant history information with here and now information ensures that risks and needs are assessed within the appropriate biopsychosocial boundaries. At the same time, it is also important to weigh each dimension-specific rating against its counterparts, thus evaluating how all six dimensions interact with and influence each other.[5(p14)]

DIMENSION INTERACTION

2

Determining Dimensional Interaction and Priorities

Interactions Across Dimensions in Assessing for Level of Care

There is considerable interaction across the six dimensions of the ASAM criteria. For example, significant problems with readiness to change (Dimension 4), coupled with a poor recovery environment (Dimension 6) or moderate problems with relapse or continued use (Dimension 5), may increase the risk of relapse. Another commonly seen combination involves problems in Dimension 2 (such as chronic pain that distracts the patient from the recovery process) coupled with problems in Dimensions 4, 5, or 6. The converse also is true. For example, problems with relapse potential (Dimension 5) may be offset by a high degree of readiness to change (Dimension 4) or a very supportive recovery environment (Dimension 6). The interaction of these factors may result in a lower level of severity than is seen in any dimension alone.

The lesson here is that assessments are most accurate when they take into account all of the factors that affect each individual's receptivity and ability to engage in treatment at a particular point in time. Being aware of cross-dimensional interactions, and the potential increase or decrease in overall risk they pose, can have a great effect on service planning and placement decisions.

The chart on pages 60-65 shows examples of history and current status a patient might present with in a given dimension. For each of the six dimensions, information is provided as to what cross-dimensional interaction might either increase or decrease the level of severity here.

Regardless of what risk rating system is used, any dimensional assessment that results in a moderate-intensity risk should be considered a priority, and therefore a focus for service planning and placement.

Determining Priority Needs

Appropriate and well-informed level of care placement can only occur after a sufficient multidimensional assessment and matching of needed services has been performed. Whether during an intake or follow-up assessment, all six dimensions are evaluated, both independently and interactively, to determine what risks and needs are most pressing for the patient in his or her current situation.

A severe risk rating, such as "high" risk, or a 4 in the 0-4 system, would indicate a case of "imminent danger," which would require immediate services (see subsection on Addressing Immediate Needs and Imminent Danger). Noting all of the risk ratings together will help highlight and determine any and all priority needs for the individual.

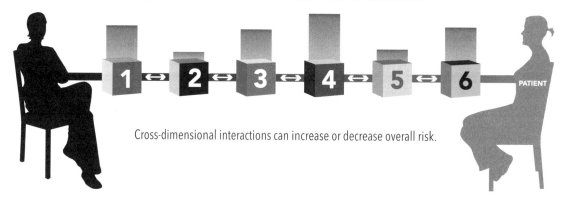

Cross-dimensional interactions can increase or decrease overall risk.

In addition to history and current status, interaction with other dimensions has the potential to increase or decrease severity for the dimension in question, as the following examples demonstrate.

DIMENSION 1: ACUTE INTOXICATION AND/OR WITHDRAWAL POTENTIAL[5(p15-16)]

DIMENSION INTERACTION ②

HISTORY	History of significant withdrawal symptoms (such as nausea and vomiting; sweats; tremors; seizures; tactile, auditory, and/or visual hallucinations; delirium tremens).
CURRENT STATUS	Current level of intoxication; current withdrawal signs and symptoms (nausea and vomiting; sweats; tremors; seizures; tactile, auditory, and/or visual hallucinations; delirium tremens, fever, anxiety, agitation, depression); quantity of drug used over a given period of time; frequency of use; time elapsed since last use (hours as well as days for substances with a short half-life); recent quantity used compared to capacity; pulse and blood pressure; CIWA-Ar score (for alcohol withdrawal); half-life of substances used; if multiple substances used, potential for drug interactions; ability to cope with withdrawal symptoms. Patients receiving opioid agonist therapy should be checked for drug interactions and possible dose adjustment.

DIMENSIONAL INTERACTIONS

SEVERITY INCREASE	**Dimension 2:** Withdrawal from sedative-hypnotics (eg, alcohol, barbiturates, benzodiazepines, other sedative hypnotics) complicated by impaired liver function, comorbid neurological conditions (eg, a seizure disorder) that could be exacerbated by autonomic nervous system hyperarousal, use or hazardous use of medications that potentiate the drug from which the patient is withdrawing, pregnancy. **Dimension 3:** Use or hazardous use of psychiatric medications that are metabolized in the liver, pregnancy, psychiatric disorganization that may affect patient adherence to withdrawal management regimen. **Dimension 4:** Lack of readiness to change affecting adherence to withdrawal management protocols or causing premature discharge from withdrawal management; lack of readiness to change affecting effectiveness of ambulatory withdrawal management (as by use of substances overnight or not returning for services the following day). **Dimension 5:** Continued use of alcohol, illicit drugs, or nonmedical use of prescription drugs. **Dimension 6:** Lack of a supportive recovery environment or transportation for ambulatory withdrawal management.
SEVERITY DECREASE	**Dimension 2:** Absence of a comorbid medical condition. **Dimension 3:** Absence of a comorbid psychiatric condition. **Dimension 4:** Readiness to change at a level that facilitates adherence to ambulatory withdrawal management services. **Dimension 5:** No continued use of alcohol, illicit drugs, or nonmedical use of prescription drugs. **Dimension 6:** A supportive recovery environment and transportation to ambulatory withdrawal management.

DIMENSION INTERACTION

DIMENSION 2: BIOMEDICAL CONDITIONS AND COMPLICATIONS[5(p16-17)]

HISTORY

History of hypertension; diabetes; gastrointestinal bleeding; advanced liver disease; esophageal varices, especially with a history of a major bleed; HIV/AIDS; hepatitis B or C; other autoimmune diseases; severe polyneuropathy; coronary artery disease; history of stroke combined with current use of cocaine; chronic pain disorder; history of use of volatile solvents.

CURRENT STATUS

Current hypertension, significantly abnormal blood sugar in a diabetic; G.I. bleeding; severe polyneuropathy; pregnancy, particularly with vaginal bleeding; need for regular medical treatment not provided by the addiction treatment provider (eg, kidney dialysis, chemotherapy, physical therapy); chronic pain disorder.

Any current comorbid medical problem that would preclude the ability to participate in treatment.

DIMENSIONAL INTERACTIONS

SEVERITY INCREASE

Dimension 1: Presence of comorbid medical conditions that could be exacerbated by withdrawal from sedative-hypnotics (eg, alcohol, barbiturates, benzodiazepines, other sedative hypnotics) with attendant autonomic nervous system hyperarousal (eg, hypertension complicated by withdrawal from alcohol), presence of medical conditions that could be exacerbated by withdrawal from stimulants (eg, cocaine, amphetamines).

Dimension 3: Presence of cognitive impairment sufficient to interfere with self-management of a chronic medical condition.

Dimension 4: Lack of readiness to change interfering with the management of a chronic medical condition.

Dimension 5: Continued use of hepatotoxic substances in the presence of liver damage; continued use of alcohol when contraindicated by the use of medications for medical conditions (eg, antiviral drugs); continued use of substances that interfere with the self-management of a chronic medical condition (eg, diabetes).

Dimension 6: Lack of child care or transportation for medical appointments; insufficient financial resources to purchase needed medications.

SEVERITY DECREASE

Dimension 1: No withdrawal-related problems.

Dimension 3: Cognitive impairment, if present, is not sufficient to interfere with self-management of a chronic medical condition.

Dimension 4: Stage of readiness to change is consistent with the management of a chronic medical condition.

Dimension 5: Absence of continued use of substances that would complicate a comorbid medical condition or interfere with self-management.

Dimension 6: Availability of child care or transportation for medical appointments; adequate finances or other mechanisms to purchase needed medications.

DIMENSION 3: EMOTIONAL, BEHAVIORAL, OR COGNITIVE CONDITIONS AND COMPLICATIONS[5(p18-19)]

HISTORY

Diagnosed mental disorder, with a history of psychiatric medication non-adherence or ineffectiveness; suicide attempts; family history of suicide; serious self-mutilation; hostile/aggressive acting out; poor impulse control; distractibility; history of ADHD; victimization history; subthreshold mental health problems (eg, anger management and impulse control problems but insufficient symptoms to meet diagnostic criteria for antisocial personality disorder).

CURRENT STATUS

Significant depression, mania, or anxiety; poor or tenuous reality contact; current suicidal/homicidal ideation with plan; poor coping skills; significantly impaired judgment; presence of ADHD interfering with attempts to effectively use treatment; diagnosed unstable mental disorder with current psychiatric medication non-adherence or lack of response; current unstable personality disorder; diagnostic subclinical mental disorder; feelings of guilt significant enough to paralyze recovery efforts.

DIMENSIONAL INTERACTIONS

SEVERITY INCREASE

Dimension 1: Alcohol withdrawal may destabilize psychiatric symptoms (eg, schizophrenic who has been drinking to "quiet the voices" or a person with bipolar illness who becomes non-adherent with prescribed mood stabilizer resulting in a return to substance use requiring withdrawal management).

Dimension 2: Pressure on coping skills to deal with medical condition (eg, anxiety about HIV disease or a comorbid chronic pain disorder).

Dimension 4: Lack of readiness to adhere to psychiatric medication directions.

Dimension 5: Continued use of substances that interfere with the effects of medications for mental health disorders (such as use of alcohol while taking SSRIs for depression).

Dimension 6: Stressors that increase pressure on coping skills; homelessness; lack of education; unemployment; lack of positive support system; recovery environment endemic with pressure to use substances or engage in antisocial/criminal behavior; problems with child care and transportation; lack of child care or transportation in general or for mental health treatment appointments; insufficient finances to purchase needed psychiatric medications.

SEVERITY DECREASE

Dimension 2: Absence of co-occurring medical conditions that can create emotional stress.

Dimension 4: Readiness to adhere to the psychiatric medication regimen.

Dimension 5: No use of any substance that could reduce the effects of medications for mental disorders (eg, use of alcohol while taking SSRIs for depression).

Dimension 6: A positive recovery environment; positive support system; absence of major stressors about health.

DIMENSION INTERACTION ❷

DIMENSION INTERACTION 2

DIMENSION 4: READINESS TO CHANGE[5(p19-20)]

HISTORY

Previous treatment history with positive or negative treatment outcomes; attitudes about treatment and self-help groups based on history; awareness of relationship between substance use and problems; history (positive or negative) with treatment or self-help recovery groups; demonstrated ability to adhere to treatment recommendations for other medical conditions (eg, hypertension, diabetes).

CURRENT STATUS

Level of current awareness of relationship between substance use and problems; stage of change in Prochaska and DiClemente's model (eg, precontemplation, contemplation, preparation, action, maintenance, relapse and recycling, termination); current drug craving; internal vs. external motivation; follow through (or lack of) on referral for assessment or treatment; ability to see value in recovery.

DIMENSIONAL INTERACTIONS

SEVERITY INCREASE

Dimension 2: Lack of success in managing other chronic illnesses (eg, hypertension, diet adherence for diabetic).

Dimension 3: History of or current non-adherence with prescribed psychiatric medications; low self-esteem; feelings of hopelessness; external locus of control; thought disorder or significant cognitive deficits that interfere with patient's ability to understand the connections between the substance use and resultant problems.

Dimension 5: Continued use in spite of serious adverse consequences.

Dimension 6: Lack of positive reinforcement for recovery in the patient's environment; seeing no value in recovery; not interested in changing because of negative environmental experience (eg, abusive parent who becomes abstinent but continues to abuse); absence of external pressures for recovery (eg, patient consistently enabled by family).

SEVERITY DECREASE

Dimension 2: History of adherence to a prescribed medication regimen or other treatment protocols; success in managing other chronic illnesses (such as hypertension).

Dimension 3: History of adherence to prescribed psychiatric medication regimen; current psychiatric medication adherence; hopefulness about recovery; at least a reasonable level of self-esteem.

Dimension 5: Cessation of use due to serious adverse consequences.

Dimension 6: Positive reinforcement in the recovery environment; patient perceives value in recovery; something of value in the recovery environment at stake with continued use (eg, employment, marriage, freedom, professional license); presence of external pressures for recovery (eg, family employing "tough love" with adolescent).

DIMENSION 5: RELAPSE, CONTINUED USE, OR CONTINUED PROBLEM POTENTIAL[5(p20-21)]

HISTORY

Past history of ability to remain abstinent; past relapse history; history of adherence with addiction medication (anti-craving or aversive medication).

CURRENT STATUS

Source of motivation (eg, internal vs. external); stage of readiness to change; current use, craving, and understanding that craving does not inevitably result in use; withdrawal; possession of relapse prevention strategies including identification of high-risk situations and triggers and a plan for responding to them without using; pharmacological responsivity (eg, positive reinforcement from use and/or negative withdrawal reinforcement).

DIMENSIONAL INTERACTIONS

SEVERITY INCREASE

Dimension 1: Current use of alcohol or other non-prescribed drugs; incomplete withdrawal from psychoactive substances.

Dimension 2: Presence of an acute medical problem (such as pancreatitis) that produces physical pain; a chronic pain disorder; a medical problem that distracts from recovery efforts.

Dimension 3: Presence of a comorbid, poorly managed mental disorder (eg, anxiety) or personality disorder (eg, impulsivity or poor anger management skills) traits that do not meet *DSM* diagnostic thresholds (ie, subclinical); external locus of control.

Dimension 4: Patient is not ready to change, or does not understand the connection between substance use and associated problems.

Dimension 6: Absence of a positive social support system; using or hazardous using social support system; perceiving no value in recovery; social support system encouraging high-risk use; support system oppositional/sabotaging; not interested in changing because of negative environmental experience (eg, abusive parent who becomes abstinent but continues to abuse); absence of external pressures for recovery (eg, patient consistently enabled by family); lack of high school education or GED; unemployed; lack of employment skills; ex-convict; homeless; unsafe housing (eg, being physically, emotionally, or sexually abused).

SEVERITY DECREASE

Dimension 1: Absence of craving associated with current use or withdrawal.

Dimension 2: Absence of pain associated with a medical disorder; absence of a medical problem creating distraction from recovery efforts.

Dimension 3: Absence of psychiatric comorbidity; presence of an internal locus of control.

Dimension 4: Patient is ready to change and understands the connection between substance use and associated problems.

Dimension 6: Presence of a positive social support system; perceived value in recovery; positive environmental recovery experiences; external pressures for recovery (eg, patient not enabled by family); high school education or GED; employed or with employment skills; safe place to live.

DIMENSION 6: RECOVERY/LIVING ENVIRONMENT[5(p22)]

HISTORY

Lack of experience with application skills for education or employment; ex-convict; lack of experience developing a positive social support system.

CURRENT STATUS

Lack of positive social support system; environment in which there is direct or indirect pressure to use (eg, all friends are users or dealers); opportunity so limited there is little advantage to recovery; illiteracy; lack of education (no high school diploma or GED); unemployed; lack of job skills, housing problems; child care problems; lack of adequate transportation; single parent status; lack of effective parenting skills.

DIMENSIONAL INTERACTIONS

SEVERITY INCREASE

Dimension 3: Presence of behaviors associated with a co-occurring mental disorder, which create environmental problems (eg, loss of housing due to atypical behavior associated with hallucinations in schizophrenia, loss of employment because of criminal behavior associated with antisocial personality disorder).

Dimension 4: Lack of readiness to change, resulting in poor decisions regarding the recovery environment (eg, electing to remain in an environment with pressures to use when other options exist).

Dimension 5: A recovery environment that accepts continued use or relapse.

SEVERITY DECREASE

Dimension 4: Readiness to change a nonsupportive recovery environment.

Dimension 5: A recovery environment that does not accept continued use or relapse.

Addressing Immediate Needs and Imminent Danger

Immediate Needs

All six assessment dimensions provide a structure for a timely, succinct, yet comprehensive review of any life area for which there is an acute need for immediate services for patient safety. The following questions can be administered in person or by telephone in five minutes or less to determine a patient's "immediate need profile" for all six dimensions. Practitioners work through the six dimensions, checking "yes" or "no" to these questions and obtaining from the patient just sufficient data to assess for immediate needs.

Also note that relevant treatment interventions are suggested for each dimension.

Imminent Danger

The concept of "imminent danger" often is used to describe problems in multiple areas, such as health, mental health, and substance use, that can lead to grave consequences to the individual patient, and possibly others. Such consequences may be the basis for the civil commitment of

IMMEDIATE NEED PROFILE

Work through the six dimensions, checking "yes" or "no" to these questions and obtaining from the patient just sufficient data to assess for immediate needs.

IMMEDIATE NEED PROFILE

DIMENSION 1: Acute Intoxication and/or Withdrawal Potential

a. Currently having severe, life-threatening, and/or similar withdrawal symptoms? ____No ____Yes

DIMENSION 2: Biomedical Conditions and Complications

a. Any current, severe physical health problems (eg, bleeding from mouth or rectum in past 24 hours; recent, unstable hypertension; recent, severe pain in chest, abdomen, head; significant problems in balance, gait, sensory, or motor abilities not related to intoxication)? ____No ____Yes

DIMENSION 3: Emotional, Behavioral, or Cognitive Conditions and Complications

a. Imminent danger of harming self or someone else (eg, suicidal ideation with intent, plan, and means to succeed; homicidal or violent ideation; impulses and uncertainty about ability to control impulses, with means to act on)? ____No ____Yes

b. Unable to function in activities of daily living or care for self with imminent, dangerous consequences (eg, unable to bathe, feed, groom, and care for self due to psychosis, organicity, or uncontrolled intoxication with threat to imminent safety of self or others as regards death or severe injury)? ____No ____Yes

DIMENSION 4: Readiness to Change

a. Does patient appear to need alcohol or other drug treatment/recovery and/or mental health treatment, but ambivalent or feels it unnecessary (eg, severe addiction, but patient feels controlled use still OK; psychotic, but blames a conspiracy)? ____No ____Yes

b. Patient has been coerced, mandated, or required to have assessment and/or treatment by mental health court or criminal justice system, health or social services, work or school, or family or significant other? ____No ____Yes

DIMENSION 5: Relapse, Continued Use, or Continued Problem Potential

a. Is patient currently under the influence and/or acutely psychotic, manic, suicidal? ____No ____Yes

b. Is patient likely to continue to use or have active, acute symptoms in an imminently dangerous manner, without immediate secure placement? ____No ____Yes

c. Is patient's most troubling presenting problem(s) that brings the patient for assessment dangerous to self or others? (See examples in Dimensions 1, 2, and 3) ____No ____Yes

DIMENSION 6: Recovery Environment

a. Are there any dangerous family; significant others; living, work, or school situations threatening patient's safety, immediate wellbeing, and/or sobriety (eg, living with a drug dealer; physically abused by partner or significant other; homeless in freezing temperatures)? ____No ____Yes

KEY

"Yes" answers to questions **1, 2, and/or 3 require** that the patient immediately receive medical or psychiatric care for evaluation of need for acute, inpatient care.

"Yes" answers to questions **4a and b, or 4b alone, require** the patient to be seen for assessment within 48 hours, and preferably earlier, for motivational strategies, unless patient is imminently likely to walk out and needs a more structured intervention.

For a "yes" answer to question **5a**, assess further for need for immediate intervention (eg, taking keys of car away; having a relative/friend pick patient up if severely intoxicated and unsafe; evaluate need for immediate psychiatric intervention).

"Yes" answers to questions **5b, 5c, and/or 6, without any "yes" answer in questions 1, 2, or 3, require** that the patient be referred to a safe or supervised environment (eg, shelter, alternative safe living environment, or residential or subacute care setting, depending on level of severity and impulsivity).

an individual to treatment, but even if there is no formal commitment process, the concept of "imminent danger" should be broad enough to support attending to patient safety in high-risk situations of any type.

Traditional concepts of imminent danger sometimes limit the definition of "high-risk situations" to suicidality, self-harm, violence, or acute medical risk. But in *The ASAM Criteria*, there are three components that broaden the concept of imminent danger beyond a narrower civil commitment definition of imminent danger (see the table below).

Here is an example of a person who is not considered in imminent danger because all three components are not met: The person may drive drunk or continue substance use (a), resulting in serious adverse consequences (b). But if this is just a possibility some months in the future, (c) is not met and the person is not in imminent danger in this context.

An example of imminent danger may be the imminent return to injection drug use in a person who has no demonstrated skills at drug refusal or establishing abstinence for themselves, (a) and (c). If such IV drug use worsens

a person's HIV or hepatitis C, this constitutes "danger," (b), even though this is outside of the traditional medical/surgical or acute psychiatric definitions of "dangerousness."

Another example of imminent danger may be the imminent return to substance use in a pregnant woman or a parent, (a) and (c), who has primary responsibility for the care of a young child, (b), may constitute "danger" and the need for intensive service interventions.

When a patient is in need of addiction care and, for instance, an external insurance reviewer or case manager probes only for the presence of imminent medical/surgical danger or imminent psychiatric danger, appropriate respect has not been paid to how lethal addiction can be, how dangerous ongoing substance use can be to an individual and persons in their immediate midst, or to systems of care designed to stabilize at-risk individuals and to help them establish abstinence so that they can constructively engage with ongoing substance use disorder care (see the subsection that addresses working with managed care, Chapter 5).

On one hand, the concept of imminent danger *does not* encompass the universe of possible adverse events that could happen at some distant point in the future (eg, intoxication with impulsive reckless driving under the influence, combative public intoxication behavior, or legal problems from forging prescriptions or embezzling money for drugs). The evaluation of imminent danger should be restricted to the three factors listed here. On the other hand, the interpretation of imminent danger should not be restricted to just acute suicidality, homicidality, or medical or psychiatric problems that create an immediate, catastrophic risk. In *The ASAM Criteria*, patients in imminent danger would need stabilization in a 24-hour treatment setting until no longer meeting the three components listed.

When assessing individuals who are in a controlled environment such as a jail or prison, imminent danger is assessed as it would be at the time of release and integration into the community, not as the person was at the time

THREE COMPONENTS OF IMMINENT DANGER

(a)	a strong probability that certain behaviors (such as continued alcohol, other drug use or addictive behavior relapse) will occur
(b)	the likelihood that such behaviors will present a significant risk of serious adverse consequences to the individual and/or others (as in reckless driving while intoxicated, or neglect of a child)
(c)	the likelihood that such adverse events will occur in the very near future, within hours and days, rather than weeks or months

prior to the incarceration. For example, a person may have demonstrated behaviors presenting a significant risk of serious consequences to the individual and/or others just before incarceration. However, if the individual, upon release, is now no longer exhibiting such behavior, nor is likely to be presenting it in the next few hours or days, then such a person is not in imminent danger simply because of his or her history prior to incarceration.

IMMINENT DANGER IN OUTPATIENT AND RESIDENTIAL LEVELS OF CARE

If an individual has problems in Dimensions 4 and 5 that require 24-hour supervision and treatment interventions (such as boundary setting), without which treatment services cannot be effectively delivered, and/or the individual is in imminent danger, then the mere addition of room and board in a domiciliary facility would be inadequate to meet the individual's needs. Such a patient needs placement in a residential program that offers clinical staff and services 24 hours a day in order to respond to the patient's issues involving imminent danger. Daily assessment of risk is conducted by appropriately licensed professionals and actively addressed as a primary focus of treatment.

If, instead of a Level 3 24-hour treatment service, Level 2.1 or 2:5 services can safely be combined with a domiciliary/supportive living component, there are a variety of ways in which domiciliary services can be provided. The living environment may be in the same facility as the treatment services or it may be in a separate facility. Patients may be housed at the treatment program or live at a crisis shelter, halfway house, or in another supportive living environment or Level 3.1 facility. If the clinical services are separated from the living environment, the relationship between the living environment and treatment services must be sufficiently direct to allow specific aspects of the individual treatment plan to be addressed in both facilities.

IMMINENT DANGER IN INPATIENT LEVELS OF CARE

If an individual has significant severity in Dimensions 1, 2, and/or 3, his or her imminent danger will usually require services in an inpatient setting rather than a residential level. Inpatient and residential services are two qualitatively different intensities of service. Both provide 24-hour support and structure for individuals who are not stable enough to effectively utilize outpatient services, no matter how intensive. Patients appropriate for both 24-hour service settings are presenting issues of imminent danger, defined as "high probability of significant risk in the near future," that exist in any of the six dimensions.

However, inpatient services differ from residential services in the need for access to and availability of 24-hour treatment for problems in Dimensions 1, 2, or 3 that require medical and/or nursing interventions. Individuals in residential services need access to and availability of 24-hour treatment for problems that exist in Dimensions 4, 5, or 6 and thereby require clinical rather than medical and/or nursing interventions.

Matching Multidimensional Severity

and Level of Function with Type and Intensity of Service

Matrices for Matching Risk and Severity with Type and Intensity of Services

A future directions "matrix" format was introduced in the *PPC-2R* (2001) to assist in guidelines and benchmarks for matching risk, severity of illness, and level of function with individualized service planning and intensity of service. While not a research-based tool field-tested for inter-rater reliability and predictive validity, many have used its face validity to more specifically match services to needs of individuals. *The ASAM Criteria* offers two matrices in this section (one for adult populations and one for adolescents) for matching multidimensional severity and level of function with type and intensity of service. In addition, substance-specific matrices are offered within Chapter 6, Addressing Withdrawal Management, for the unbundled levels of withdrawal management care.

All matrices in *The ASAM Criteria* correlate risk ratings and the types of services and modalities needed, and indicate the intensity of ser-

vices where the patient's needs can best be met. The goal is to promote improved assessment and treatment of patients with substance-related and/or co-occurring conditions by taking a more holistic, multidimensional approach that matches specific needs to services, rather than matching in a broader way to a level of care.

ASAM recognizes that current systems of financing care do not support such unbundling, which implies a patient-specific array of services and intensities of care. Matrices are not meant to replace the more detailed dimensional admission criteria offered in each level of care, or in *The ASAM Criteria Software*. Rather, they can:

a. help structure case presentations in care management and supervision to articulate a comprehensive and holistic multidimensional review of the patient

b.   prioritize which dimensions guide service planning and level of care placement

c.   assist those new to *The ASAM Criteria* to understand what data is relevant to each assessment dimension and how to rate severity and level of function for each dimension

Because there have not been validity or reliability studies with matrices, users should understand the piloting, field-testing nature of these and provide feedback and guidance accordingly.

These matrices are designed to be of assistance in the assessment of an individual, whether presenting to an addiction or mental health treatment service. By referring to them, practitioners can help all patients receive a similar quality of assessment and care, using criteria and guidelines that promote a common language of assessment and service planning within mental health and addiction treatment systems.

Matrix Components

Developing a multidimensional risk profile involves integrating biopsychosocial data from the patient's history and current status into a succinct summary. The matrices found in this section, as well as in Chapter 6, Addressing Withdrawal Management, facilitate this task by presenting descriptions in each of the criteria's six dimensions to use in determining the types of services/modalities and intensity of services needed.

For each assessment dimension, the risk description and rating suggest the severity of the patient's needs in that dimension. Each description of risk provides both a numerical rating and a narrative description of associated risk

LOCATING MATRICES IN *THE ASAM CRITERIA*

Matrix for Matching Adult Severity and Level of Function with Type and Intensity of Service	Page 73
Matrix for Matching Adolescent Severity and Level of Function with Type and Intensity of Service	Page 90
Withdrawal Management Matrices:	
Alcohol	Page 147
Sedative/Hypnotics	Page 155
Opioids	Page 162

in terms of signs and symptoms that indicate the individual's severity and level of function in a particular assessment dimension. The risk descriptions and ratings within each assessment dimension help staff determine the immediacy and scope of the service plan by guiding what types and modalities of service are needed.

The treatment priorities represented by the "Services and Modalities Needed" column suggest the specific types of treatment services/modalities the patient requires, as well as the intensity with which those services should be delivered to appropriately address the patient's

The process of assessing a risk rating for each assessment dimension is what underlies the specific clinical descriptions of risk and severity in the dimensional admission criteria for each level of care. These clinical descriptions of severity are what drive the decision rules in *The ASAM Criteria Software*. Thus, an understanding of matching risk and severity with intensity of service assists in using the dimensional admission criteria for each level of care, as well as in *The ASAM Criteria Software* application.

multidimensional service needs.

The matrices allow the intensity of clinical services to be "delinked" from the intensity of social and case management services, so as to promote the most efficient use of clinical care. It is at the point of developing the placement decision that these "unbundled" or "delinked" assessments must be reintegrated into a comprehensive treatment plan. As the treatment field develops and the array of treatment services, evidence-based practices, and modalities and settings expand, this will allow more specific matching of patient needs to type and intensity of service. The matrices and multidimensional risk profiles shown here, as well as in Chapter 6, Addressing Withdrawal Management, are offered in the hope that they will provide a basis for common understanding among mental health and addiction treatment professionals.

HOW TO USE THE MATRIX TO MATCH MULTIDIMENSIONAL RISK WITH TYPE AND INTENSITY OF SERVICE

STEP 1

Assess within and across all six dimensions to determine whether the patient has immediate needs related to imminent danger, as indicated by a risk rating of 4 in any of the six dimensions. The dimension with the highest risk rating determines the immediate service needs and placement decision. For example, if in Dimension 1, the patient has a risk rating of 4 due to severe withdrawal posing imminent risk of seizures and delirium tremens, then placement in Level 4-WM, Medically Managed Intensive Inpatient Withdrawal Management, is required. Further assessment of all six dimensions proceeds once placement has been achieved.

STEP 2

If the patient is not in imminent danger, determine the patient's risk rating in each of the six dimensions. For patients who have co-occurring disorders, assess Dimensions 4, 5, and 6 separately for the mental and substance use disorders. This assists in identifying differential mental health and addiction treatment service needs and helps determine the kind of co-occurring disorders program most likely to meet the patient's needs. Performing the actions within this step will allow practitioners to determine which dimensions indicate a clinically significant risk rating, and thus a priority for collaborative treatment focus.

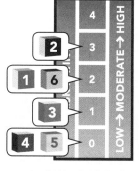

STEP 3

Identify the appropriate types of services and modalities needed for all dimensions with any clinically significant risk ratings. Not all dimensions may have sufficient severity to warrant service needs at the time of the assessment.

For example, a patient may have risk ratings of 0 in Dimensions 1 and 2 and need no withdrawal management or biomedical services. However, Dimensions 3 and 6 may have risk ratings of 2 and 3, respectively. The patient needs mental health and medication management and monitoring for the Dimension 3 depressive symptoms and rapidly deteriorating work functioning. For the Dimension 6 problems with a drinking, unsupportive spouse, the patient may need assertive assistance in coping with the living environment.

STEP 4

Use the multidimensional risk profile produced by the assessment in steps 2 and 3 to develop an initial treatment plan in the level of care determined by the dimensional admission criteria for each level of care in this book and/or *The ASAM Criteria Software*.

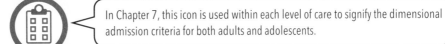

In Chapter 7, this icon is used within each level of care to signify the dimensional admission criteria for both adults and adolescents.

STEP 5

Make ongoing decisions about the patient's continued service needs by repeating steps 1 through 4. Keep in mind that movement into and through the continuum of care should be a fluid and flexible process that is driven by continuous monitoring of the patient's changing multidimensional risk profile. Use the guidelines of the continued service and transfer/discharge criteria to know when to maintain the level of care or to transfer to a more or less intensive level of care.

MATCHING RISK/SEVERITY

2

Matrix for Matching Adult Severity and Level of Function with Type and Intensity of Service

OVERVIEW OF MATRICES FOR MATCHING SEVERITY AND LEVEL OF FUNCTION WITH TYPE AND INTENSITY OF SERVICE

RISK RATING & DESCRIPTION Clinical descriptors of risk ratings 0 through 4	SERVICES & MODALITIES NEEDED Indicates which service(s) match the assessed risk rating
RISK RATING: 0 Indicates full functioning; no severity; no risk in this dimension.	Indicates no need for specific services in this dimension.
RISK RATING: 1-4 Indicates various levels of functioning and severity and the level of risk in this dimension.	Indicates the range of specific services needed in the treatment plan to match the patient's functioning and severity in this dimension.

NOTE: A higher number indicates a greater level of intensity.

4 **5** **6** You will note that for Dimensions 4, 5, and 6, there are risk ratings of **4a (No immediate action required)** and **4b (Immediate action required).** 4a refers to a patient who has high severity in that dimension, but has maintained this severity over time and is not in any immediate danger requiring secure placement and active interventions. For example, a person may have longstanding lack of interest and low readiness to change in Dimension 4. This does not place them in any immediate danger compared with another person who is equally not interested in recovery and does not believe they have a drinking problem. However, this second person demands the keys to their car and is planning to drive drunk, endangering themselves and others immediately. In the first patient, there is clearly low readiness to change but no immediate action is required (rating of 4a) versus an urgent need to take immediate action to prevent a severe accident with the second patient (rating of 4b).

Similarly, in Dimension 6, a person may be chronically homeless with no recovery supports, which indicates a severity of 4. However, since the person is well versed in survival on the streets as a homeless person, then help is needed, but not immediately. However, if the temperatures are well below freezing, and there is an immediate danger of freezing to death, then the severity rating would be 4b (Immediate action required in a shelter to prevent death), versus 4a, where recovery supports need to be developed, but no immediate danger is present and therefore no immediate action is required.

DIMENSION 1: ACUTE INTOXICATION AND/OR WITHDRAWAL POTENTIAL

RISK RATING & DESCRIPTION	SERVICES & MODALITIES NEEDED
RISK RATING: 0 The patient is fully functioning and demonstrates good ability to tolerate and cope with withdrawal discomfort. No signs or symptoms of intoxication or withdrawal are present, or signs or symptoms are resolving. For patients in Opioid Treatment Programs (OTP), the dose is well stabilized, with no opioid intoxication or withdrawal.	No immediate intoxication monitoring or management, or withdrawal management services are needed. The patient in OTP requires opioid agonist medications, such as methadone or buprenorphine.
RISK RATING: 1 The patient demonstrates adequate ability to tolerate and cope with withdrawal discomfort. Mild to moderate intoxication or signs and symptoms interfere with daily functioning, but do not pose an imminent danger to self or others. There is minimal risk of severe withdrawal (eg, as a continuation of withdrawal management at other levels of service, or in the presence of heavy alcohol or sedative-hypnotic use with minimal seizure risk). For patients in Opioid Treatment Programs (OTP), the dose is inadequately stabilized and the patient has mild symptoms of withdrawal, or occasional compensatory use of opioids or other drugs.	Low-intensity intoxication monitoring or management, or withdrawal management services are needed. For patients who require intensive mental health services (a Dimension 3 risk rating of 2 or higher), low-intensity withdrawal management can be provided in a mental health setting with ongoing case management to coordinate care. The patient in OTP requires dose adjustment, counseling services to assess and address readiness to change and relapse issues, and random urine testing.
RISK RATING: 2 The patient has some difficulty tolerating and coping with withdrawal discomfort. Intoxication may be severe, but responds to support and treatment sufficiently that the patient does not pose an imminent danger to self or others. Moderate signs and symptoms, with moderate risk of severe withdrawal (eg, as a continuation of withdrawal management at other levels of service, or in the presence of heavy alcohol or sedative-hypnotic use with minimal seizure risk, or many signs and symptoms of opioid or stimulant withdrawal). For patients in Opioid Treatment Programs (OTP), the dose is inadequately stabilized and the patient has moderate symptoms of withdrawal, or frequent compensatory use of opioids or other drugs.	Moderate-intensity intoxication monitoring or management, or withdrawal management services are needed. For patients who require partial hospital or more intensive mental health services (a Dimension 3 risk rating of 2 or higher), moderate-intensity withdrawal management can be provided in a mental health setting with ongoing case management to coordinate care. The patient in OTP requires dose adjustment, counseling services to assess and address readiness to change and relapse issues, and random urine testing.

DIMENSION 1: ACUTE INTOXICATION AND/OR WITHDRAWAL POTENTIAL (CONTINUED)

RISK RATING & DESCRIPTION	SERVICES & MODALITIES NEEDED
RISK RATING: 3 The patient demonstrates poor ability to tolerate and cope with withdrawal discomfort. Severe signs and symptoms of intoxication indicate that the patient may pose an imminent danger to self or others, and intoxication has not abated at less intensive levels of service. There are severe signs and symptoms of withdrawal, or risk of severe but manageable withdrawal; or withdrawal is worsening despite withdrawal management at a less intensive level of care (eg, as a continuation of withdrawal management at other levels of service, or in the presence of opioid withdrawal with cravings and impulsive behaviors). For patients in Opioid Treatment Programs (OTP), the dose is inadequately stabilized and the patient has severe symptoms of withdrawal, or frequent, significant, and ongoing compensatory use of opioids or other drugs.	Moderately high-intensity intoxication monitoring, management, or withdrawal management services are needed. Nursing and medical monitoring may be needed for more severe withdrawal. For patients who require medically monitored and nurse-managed mental health services (a Dimension 3 risk rating of 3 or higher), moderately high-intensity withdrawal management can be provided in a mental health setting with ongoing case management to coordinate care. The patient in OTP requires dose adjustment, counseling services to assess and address readiness to change and relapse issues, and random urine testing.
RISK RATING: 4 The patient is incapacitated, with severe signs and symptoms. Severe withdrawal presents danger, such as seizures. Continued use poses an imminent threat to life (eg, liver failure, GI bleeding, or fetal death). For patients in Opioid Treatment Programs (OTP), the dose is inadequately stabilized and the patient has repeated, significant concurrent use of opioids or other drugs. Such use is unresponsive to treatment interventions, dose adjustments, and increasing sanctions.	High-intensity intoxication monitoring or management, or withdrawal management services are needed, with monitoring and management more often than hourly. The patient in OTP requires dose adjustment, counseling services to assess readiness to change, and long-term outpatient withdrawal management from the OTP medication.

ADULT MATRIX

❷

DIMENSION 2: BIOMEDICAL CONDITIONS AND COMPLICATIONS

RISK RATING & DESCRIPTION	SERVICES & MODALITIES NEEDED
RISK RATING: 0 — The patient is fully functioning and demonstrates good ability to cope with physical discomfort. No biomedical signs or symptoms are present, or biomedical problems (such as hypertension or chronic pain) are stable.	No immediate biomedical services (except for long-term monitoring) are needed.
RISK RATING: 1 — The patient demonstrates adequate ability to tolerate and cope with physical discomfort. Mild to moderate signs or symptoms (such as mild to moderate pain) interfere with daily functioning.	Low-intensity biomedical services are needed, including case management to coordinate addiction and mental health care.
RISK RATING: 2 — The patient has some difficulty tolerating and coping with physical problems, and/or has other biomedical problems. These problems may interfere with recovery and mental health treatment. The patient neglects to care for serious biomedical problems. Acute, non-life-threatening medical signs and symptoms (such as acute episodes of chronic, distracting pain, or signs of malnutrition or electrolyte imbalance) are present.	Moderate-intensity biomedical services are needed, including case management to ensure further biomedical evaluation and treatment as part of the overall treatment plan. For patients with significant mental health impairments (a Dimension 3 risk rating of 2 or higher), case management may be needed to coordinate the patient's addiction, mental health, and biomedical care.
RISK RATING: 3 — The patient demonstrates poor ability to tolerate and cope with physical problems, and/or his or her general health condition is poor. The patient has serious medical problems, which he or she neglects during outpatient or intensive outpatient treatment. Severe medical problems (such as severe pain requiring medication, or brittle diabetes) are present but stable.	Moderately high-intensity biomedical services are needed, including medical and nursing monitoring to ensure stabilization. For patients with significant mental health impairments (a Dimension 3 risk rating of 2 or higher), case management may be needed to coordinate the patient's addiction, mental health, and biomedical care.
RISK RATING: 4 — The patient is incapacitated, with severe medical problems (such as extreme pain, uncontrolled diabetes, GI bleeding, or infection requiring IV antibiotics).	High-intensity biomedical services are needed for stabilization and medication management, including medical and nursing close observation and 24-hour management.

DIMENSION 3: EMOTIONAL, BEHAVIORAL, OR COGNITIVE CONDITIONS AND COMPLICATIONS

RISK RATING & DESCRIPTION	SERVICES & MODALITIES NEEDED

NOTE: Individuals need not match descriptions in all of the subdomains within any one risk rating.

RISK RATING: 0

The patient either has no mental health problems or has a diagnosed but stable mental disorder.

Dangerousness/Lethality: Good impulse control and coping skills.

Interference with Addiction Recovery Efforts: Ability to focus on recovery, identify appropriate supports and reach out for help.

Social Functioning: Full functioning in relationships with significant others, coworkers, friends, etc.

Ability for Self-Care: Full functioning, with good resources and skills to cope with emotional problems.

Course of Illness: No emotional or behavioral problems, or problems identified are stable (eg, depression that is stable and managed with antidepressants). No recent serious or high-risk vulnerability.

No immediate mental health services are needed.

RISK RATING: 1

The patient has a diagnosed mental disorder that requires intervention, but does not significantly interfere with addiction treatment.

Dangerousness/Lethality: Adequate impulse control and coping skills to deal with any thoughts of harm to self or others.

Interference with Addiction Recovery Efforts: Emotional concerns relate to negative consequences and effects of addiction. The patient is able to view these as part of addiction and recovery.

Low-intensity mental health services are needed, including case management to coordinate addiction and mental health care, medication monitoring, psychoeducation about mental disorders and psychotropic medications, self/mutual help, co-occurring disorders support, and recovery groups to deal with emotional aspects of recovery.

DIMENSION 3: EMOTIONAL, BEHAVIORAL, OR COGNITIVE CONDITIONS AND COMPLICATIONS (CONTINUED)

RISK RATING & DESCRIPTION	SERVICES & MODALITIES NEEDED
RISK RATING: 1 **Social Functioning:** Relationships or spheres of social functioning (as with significant others, friends, coworkers) are being impaired but not endangered by patient's substance use (eg, no imminent divorce, job loss, or coping in homeless situations). The patient is able to meet personal responsibilities and maintain stable, meaningful relationships despite the mild symptoms experienced (eg, mood or anxiety symptoms subthreshold for *DSM* diagnosis or, if meeting diagnostic criteria, patient is able to continue in essential roles). **Ability for Self-Care:** Adequate resources and skills to cope with emotional or behavioral problems. **Course of Illness:** Mild to moderate signs and symptoms (eg, dysphoria, relationship problems, work or school problems, or problems coping in the community) with good response to treatment in the past. Any past serious problems have a long period of stability (eg, serious depression and suicidal behavior 15 years ago) or past problems are chronic but not severe enough to pose any high-risk vulnerability (eg, superficial wrist scratching, but no previous hospitalization or life-threatening behavior).	Low-intensity mental health services are needed, including case management to coordinate addiction and mental health care, medication monitoring, psychoeducation about mental disorders and psychotropic medications, self/mutual help, co-occurring disorders support, and recovery groups to deal with emotional aspects of recovery.
RISK RATING: 2 Patients are of two types. The first exhibits this level of impairment only during acute decompensation. The second demonstrates this level of decompensation at baseline. This risk rating implies chronic mental illness, with symptoms and disability that cause significant interference with addiction treatment, but do not constitute an immediate threat to safety and do not prevent independent functioning. **Dangerousness/Lethality:** Suicidal ideation; violent impulses; significant history of suicidal or violent behavior requires more than routine monitoring. **Interference with Addiction Recovery Efforts:** Emotional, behavioral, or cognitive problems distract the patient from recovery efforts.	Moderate-intensity mental health services are needed, including case management to ensure monitoring and evaluation of emotional, behavioral, and cognitive status as part of the treatment plan; medication management and monitoring; and medical and nursing monitoring and management as needed. For acute decompensation patients, activities to address the substance use disorder may need to be postponed until the patient's mental health symptoms are more stable. For baseline patients, the patient's substance use disorder may be addressed in psychiatrically enhanced addiction services, staffed by mental health professionals with smaller caseloads. For patients with high risk ratings in Dimension 4, motivational enhancement therapies may be integrated into ongoing mental health services.

ADULT MATRIX

2

DIMENSION 3: EMOTIONAL, BEHAVIORAL, OR COGNITIVE CONDITIONS AND COMPLICATIONS (CONTINUED)

RISK RATING & DESCRIPTION	SERVICES & MODALITIES NEEDED
RISK RATING: 2 **Social Functioning:** Relationships or spheres of social functioning (as with significant others, friends, coworkers) are being impaired by substance use, but also are linked to a psychiatric disorder (eg, a patient with depression or anxiety disorder is unable to sleep or socialize). Symptoms are causing moderate difficulty in managing relationships with significant others; social, work, or school functioning; or coping in the community, but not to a degree that they pose a significant danger to self or others, or that the patient is unable to manage activities of daily living or basic responsibilities in the home, work, school, or community. **Ability for Self-Care:** Poor resources, with moderate or minimal skills to cope with emotional or behavioral problems. **Course of Illness:** Frequent and/or intensive symptoms (eg, frequent suicidal or homicidal ideation, vegetative signs, agitation or retardation, inconsistent impulse control), with a history that indicates significant problems that are not well stabilized (eg, psychotic episodes with frequent periods of decompensation). Acute or acute-on-chronic problems pose some risk of harm to self or others, but the patient is not imminently dangerous (eg, hallucinations and delusions invoke homicidal ideation, but the patient has no plan or means to harm others).	Moderate-intensity mental health services are needed, including case management to ensure monitoring and evaluation of emotional, behavioral, and cognitive status as part of the treatment plan, medication management and monitoring, and medical and nursing monitoring and management as needed. For acute decompensation patients, activities to address the substance use disorder may need to be postponed until the patient's mental health symptoms are more stable. For baseline patients, the patient's substance use disorder may be addressed in psychiatrically enhanced addiction services, staffed by mental health professionals with smaller caseloads. For patients with high risk ratings in Dimension 4, motivational enhancement therapies may be integrated into ongoing mental health services.
RISK RATING: 3 Patients are of two types. The first exhibits this level of impairment only during acute decompensation. The second demonstrates this level of decompensation at baseline. This risk rating is characterized by severe psychiatric symptomatology, disability, and impulsivity, but the patient has sufficient control that he or she does not require involuntary confinement. **Dangerousness/Lethality:** Frequent impulses to harm self or others, which are potentially destabilizing, but the patient is not imminently dangerous in a 24-hour setting.	Moderately high-intensity mental health services are needed, including daily monitoring and ready access to medical management, and medication management if symptoms become acute but not dangerous. Assertive case management and community outreach are needed for the severely and chronically mentally ill patient. Supportive living arrangements, with 24-hour supervision, are needed. For acute decompensation patients, activities to address the substance use disorder (other than withdrawal management and discharge planning) may need to be postponed until the patient's mental health symptoms are stabilized. For baseline patients, the patient's substance use disorder may be addressed in addiction treatment enhanced mental health services.

DIMENSION 3: EMOTIONAL, BEHAVIORAL, OR COGNITIVE CONDITIONS AND COMPLICATIONS (CONTINUED)

RISK RATING & DESCRIPTION	SERVICES & MODALITIES NEEDED

RISK RATING: 3

Interference with Addiction Recovery Efforts: Recovery efforts are negatively affected by the patient's emotional, behavioral, or cognitive problems in significant and distracting ways, up to and including inability to focus on recovery efforts.

Social Functioning: Risk in this domain does not influence type and intensity of services needed.

Ability for Self-Care: Insufficient or severe lack of capacity to cope with emotional or behavioral problems. Uncontrolled behavior, confusion, or disorientation, which limit the patient's capacity for self-care. Inadequate ability to manage the activities of daily living.

Course of Illness: Acute course of illness dominates the clinical presentation. Symptoms may involve impaired reality testing, communication, thought processes, judgment, or attention to personal hygiene. These symptoms significantly compromise the patient's ability to adjust his or her life in the community, or previous treatment has not achieved stabilization or complete remission of symptoms. The patient has limited ability to follow through with treatment recommendations, thus demonstrating risk of and vulnerability to dangerous consequences.

Moderately high-intensity mental health services are needed, including daily monitoring and ready access to medical management, and medication management if symptoms become acute but not dangerous. Assertive case management and community outreach are needed for the severely and chronically mentally ill patient. Supportive living arrangements, with 24-hour supervision, are needed.

For acute decompensation patients, activities to address the substance use disorder (other than withdrawal management and discharge planning) may need to be postponed until the patient's mental health symptoms are stabilized.

For baseline patients, the patient's substance use disorder may be addressed in addiction treatment enhanced mental health services.

RISK RATING: 4

Patients have severe psychiatric symptomatology, disability, and impulsivity, and require involuntary confinement.

Dangerousness/Lethality: Severe psychotic, mood, or personality disorder, which presents acute risk to the patient, such as immediate risk of suicide; psychosis with unpredictable, disorganized, or violent behavior; or gross neglect of self-care.

Interference with Addiction Recovery Efforts: Risk in this domain does not influence type and intensity of services needed.

Social Functioning: Risk in this domain does not influence type and intensity of services needed.

High-intensity mental health services are needed, including 24-hour medical and nursing monitoring and management, medication management, electroconvulsive therapy, or secure services, and close observation more often than hourly.

Appropriate addiction services (such as withdrawal management and motivational enhancement therapies) can be integrated into mental health services.

ADULT MATRIX

❷

ADULT MATRIX 2

DIMENSION 3: EMOTIONAL, BEHAVIORAL, OR COGNITIVE CONDITIONS AND COMPLICATIONS (CONTINUED)

RISK RATING & DESCRIPTION	SERVICES & MODALITIES NEEDED

RISK RATING: 4

Ability for Self-Care: Risk in this domain does not influence type and intensity of services needed.

Course of Illness: High risk and significant vulnerability for dangerous consequences. The patient exhibits severe and acute life-threatening symptoms (eg, dangerous or impulsive behavior or cognitive functioning) that pose imminent danger to self or others. Symptoms of psychosis include command hallucinations or paranoid delusions. History of instability is such that high-intensity services are needed to prevent dangerous consequences (eg, the patient is not responding to daily changes in medication at less intensive levels of service, with escalating psychosis).

High-intensity mental health services are needed, including 24-hour medical and nursing monitoring and management, medication management, ECT or secure services, and close observation more often than hourly.

Appropriate addiction services (such as withdrawal management and motivational enhancement therapies) can be integrated into mental health services.

NOTES ON DIMENSION 3

» Consider dangerousness and/or lethality, interference with addiction recovery efforts, social functioning, ability for self-care, and course of illness (history of present illness–the pattern of symptoms and response to treatment up to, and including, the present illness–and pattern of treatment response).

» Consider acute stabilization, medical management and monitoring, mental health consultation, and integration of mental health and addiction services, skills training, case management, medication management and monitoring, and systems intervention and coordination.

» Consider traditional addiction and mental health services, availability of addiction services coordinated with mental health services or mental health services coordinated with addiction treatment, integrated inpatient or outpatient co-occurring disorders services, assertive case management, and community outreach services.

DIMENSION 4: READINESS TO CHANGE

RISK RATING & DESCRIPTION	SERVICES & MODALITIES NEEDED
RISK RATING: 0 **Substance Use Disorders:** The patient is willingly engaged in treatment as a proactive, responsible participant, and is committed to changing his or her alcohol, tobacco, and/or other drug use. **Mental Disorders:** The patient is willingly engaged in treatment as a proactive, responsible participant, and is committed to changing his or her mental functioning and behavior.	No immediate engagement or motivational enhancement strategies or services are needed.
RISK RATING: 1 **Substance Use Disorders:** The patient is willing to enter treatment and to explore strategies for changing his or her substance use, but is ambivalent about the need for change. He or she is willing to explore the need for treatment and strategies to reduce or stop substance use (eg, the patient views his or her substance use problem as caused by depression or another psychiatric diagnosis). Or the patient is willing to change his or her substance use, but believes it will not be difficult to do so, or does not accept a full recovery treatment plan. **Mental Disorders:** The patient is willing to enter treatment and to explore strategies for changing his or her mental functioning, but is ambivalent about the need for change. He or she is willing to explore the need for treatment and strategies to deal with mental disorders. The patient's participation in mental health treatment is sufficient to avert mental decompensation (eg, a bipolar patient who is ambivalent about taking mood-stabilizing medications, but who generally follows through with treatment recommendations).	In any addiction/co-occurring disorders setting, low-intensity engagement or motivational strategies are needed. These include education about the illness(es), education of family and significant others, and legal, work, or school system reinforcement of the need for treatment. For patients with impairment in Dimension 3, motivational enhancement is integrated into continuing care management at any degree of intensity, as well as into specific treatment episodes.

ADULT MATRIX

2

DIMENSION 4: READINESS TO CHANGE (CONTINUED)

RISK RATING & DESCRIPTION	SERVICES & MODALITIES NEEDED

RISK RATING: 2

Substance Use Disorders: The patient is reluctant to agree to treatment for substance use problems. He or she is able to articulate the negative consequences of substance use, but has low commitment to change his or her use of alcohol or other drugs. The patient is assessed as having low readiness to change and is only passively involved in treatment, and is variably compliant with attendance at outpatient sessions or meetings of self/mutual help or other support groups.

Mental Disorders: The patient is reluctant to agree to treatment for mental disorders. He or she is able to articulate the negative consequences of his or her mental health problems, but has low commitment to therapy. The patient is assessed as having low readiness to change and is only passively involved in treatment (eg, is variable in follow through with use of psychotropic medications or attendance at therapy sessions).

Moderate-intensity engagement or motivational strategies are needed, with active support from family; significant others; legal, work, or school systems to set and follow through with clear, consistent limits and consequences. Assertive case management or assertive community treatment (ACT) may be needed.

For patients who face legal consequences, court-mandated treatment (as through drug court) may be indicated. For patients with Dimension 3 baseline risk ratings of 2 or higher, intensive care management may be required to integrate motivational enhancement therapies and continuing mental health care.

RISK RATING: 3

Substance Use Disorders: The patient exhibits inconsistent follow through and shows minimal awareness of his or her substance use disorder and need for treatment. He or she appears unaware of the need to change, and thus is unwilling or only partially able to follow through with treatment recommendations.

Mental Disorders: The patient exhibits inconsistent follow through and shows minimal awareness of his or her mental disorder and need for treatment. He or she appears unaware of the need to change, and thus is unwilling or only partially able to follow through with treatment recommendations.

Moderately high-intensity engagement or motivational enhancement strategies are needed to engage the patient in treatment. Effort should be focused on any available systems leverage (family, school, work, or legal system) to align incentives that promote treatment engagement and investment by the patient.

If opposition to treatment is caused by psychosis, intramuscular injections of a depot, slow-release antipsychotic medication, may be needed. Assertive case management or assertive community treatment (ACT) may be needed.

For patients with a Dimension 3 risk rating of 2 to 4, intensive case management or assertive community treatment (ACT) may be required.

DIMENSION 4: READINESS TO CHANGE (CONTINUED)

RISK RATING & DESCRIPTION	SERVICES & MODALITIES NEEDED
RISK RATING: 4A (No immediate action required)	**Substance Use Disorders:** The patient is unable to follow through, has little or no awareness of substance use problems and any associated negative consequences, knows very little about addiction, and sees no connection between his/her suffering and substance use. He or she is not imminently dangerous or unable to care for self, and is not willing to explore change regarding his or her illness and its implications (for example, he or she blames others for legal or family problems, and rejects treatment). **Mental Disorders:** The patient is unable to follow through, has little or no awareness of a mental disorder and any associated negative consequences, knows very little about mental illness, and sees no connection between his or her suffering and mental health problems. He or she is not imminently dangerous or unable to care for self, is not willing to explore change regarding his or her illness and its implications.	The patient needs high-intensity engagement or motivational strategies to try to engage him or her in treatment. Any available systems leverage (as through family, school, work, or the judicial system) should be used to align incentives to promote the patient's engagement and investment in treatment. Preferred strategies involve assertive community treatment (ACT) rather than intensive therapy aimed at "breaking through denial."
RISK RATING: 4B (Immediate action required)	**Substance Use Disorders:** The patient is unable to follow through with treatment recommendations. As a result, his or her behavior represents an imminent danger of harm to self or others, or he or she is unable to function independently and engage in self-care. For example, the patient repeatedly demonstrates inability to follow through with treatment, continues to use alcohol and/or other drugs, and to become violent, suicidal, or to drive dangerously. **Mental Disorders:** The patient is unable to follow through with treatment recommendations. As a result, his or her behavior represents an imminent danger of harm to self or others, or he or she is unable to function independently and engage in self-care. For example, the patient refuses all medications and is overtly psychotic, so that his or her judgment and impulse control is severely impaired.	The patient needs secure placement for stabilization while imminently dangerous. If treatment resistance is caused by psychosis, involuntary commitment and placement in a secure unit may be necessary. If treatment resistance is caused by severe, acute intoxication, close observation may be needed until the patient is less toxic.

ADULT MATRIX

❷

DIMENSION 5: RELAPSE, CONTINUED USE, OR CONTINUED PROBLEM POTENTIAL

RISK RATING & DESCRIPTION	SERVICES & MODALITIES NEEDED
RISK RATING: 0 **Substance Use Disorders:** The patient has no potential for further substance use problems, or has low relapse potential and good coping skills. **Mental Disorders:** The patient has no potential for further mental health problems, or has low potential and good coping skills.	No immediate relapse prevention services are needed. The patient may need self/mutual help or a non-professional support group.
RISK RATING: 1 **Substance Use Disorders:** The patient has minimal relapse potential, with some vulnerability, and has fair self-management and relapse prevention skills. **Mental Disorders:** The patient has minimal relapse potential, with some vulnerability, and has fair self-management and relapse prevention skills.	Low-intensity relapse prevention services are needed to reinforce coping skills until the patient is integrated into continuing care or a self/mutual help or non-professional group. Medication management may be needed (as with anti-craving, opioid agonist, or antipsychotic medications).
RISK RATING: 2 **Substance Use Disorders:** The patient has impaired recognition and understanding of substance use relapse issues, but is able to self-manage with prompting. **Mental Disorders:** The patient has impaired recognition and understanding of mental illness relapse issues, but is able to self-manage with prompting.	Moderate-intensity relapse prevention services are needed to monitor and strengthen the patient's coping skills. The patient also needs relapse prevention education and help with integration into self/mutual help and community support groups, assertive case management, and assertive community treatment (ACT). Medication management may be needed (as with anti-craving, opioid agonist, or antipsychotic medications). The patient may need addiction treatment coupled with continuing outpatient mental health and/or addiction care (routine or intensive). For patients with a Dimension 3 risk rating of 1 to 2, continuing coordinated and integrated mental health care is required while intensive addiction treatment is provided. For patients with a Dimension 3 risk rating of 2 or (especially) 3, intensive case management services may be required to coordinate and integrate addiction treatment into continuing mental health care.

DIMENSION 5: RELAPSE, CONTINUED USE, OR CONTINUED PROBLEM POTENTIAL (CONTINUED)

RISK RATING & DESCRIPTION

SERVICES & MODALITIES NEEDED

RISK RATING: 3

Substance Use Disorders: The patient has little recognition and understanding of substance use relapse issues, and has poor skills to cope with and interrupt addiction problems, or to avoid or limit relapse.

Mental Disorders: The patient has little recognition and understanding of mental illness relapse issues, and has poor skills to cope with and interrupt mental health problems, or to avoid or limit relapse.

Moderately high-intensity relapse prevention services are needed, including structured coping skills training, motivational strategies, and exploration of family and/or significant other's ability to align incentives to consolidate engagement in treatment, and possible assistance in finding a supportive living environment. The patient also needs assertive case management and assertive community treatment (ACT).

Medication management may be needed (as with anti-craving, opioid agonist, or antipsychotic medications).

The patient may need addiction treatment coupled with continuing outpatient mental health and/or addiction care (routine or intensive).

For patients with a Dimension 3 risk rating of 1 to 2, continuing coordinated and integrated addiction treatment and mental health care is required.

For patients with a Dimension 3 risk rating of 2 to 3 at baseline, assertive community treatment or other intensive case management services may be required.

RISK RATING: 4A

(No immediate action required)

Substance Use Disorders: Repeated treatment episodes have had little positive effect on the patient's functioning. He or she has no skills to cope with and interrupt addiction problems, or to prevent or limit relapse. However, the patient is not in imminent danger and is able to care for self (eg, the patient has undergone repeated withdrawal managements but is unable to cope with continued cravings to use).

Mental Disorders: Repeated treatment episodes have had little positive effect on the patient's functioning. He or she has no skills to cope with and interrupt mental health problems, or to prevent or limit relapse. However, the patient is not in imminent danger and is able to care for self (eg, the patient is severely and chronically mentally ill, with chronic dysfunction and inability to arrest psychotic episodes).

Exploration of systems incentives to consolidate the patient's engagement in treatment is required. The patient needs motivational strategies, structured coping skills, assertive case management and community outreach, assistance in finding supportive living arrangements, and assertive community treatment (ACT).

Medication management may be needed (as with anti-craving, opioid agonist, or antipsychotic medications).

The patient may need addiction treatment coupled with continuing outpatient mental health and/or addiction care (routine or intensive).

For patients with a Dimension 3 risk rating of 2 or higher, coordinated and integrated addiction treatment and mental health case management and/or assertive community treatment may be indicated.

DIMENSION 5: RELAPSE, CONTINUED USE, OR CONTINUED PROBLEM POTENTIAL (CONTINUED)

RISK RATING & DESCRIPTION

RISK RATING: 4B

(Immediate action required)

Substance Use Disorders: The patient has no skills to arrest the addictive disorder, or to prevent relapse to substance use. His or her continued addictive behavior places the patient and/or others in imminent danger (eg, a patient whose continued drug use leads to impulsive, psychotic, and aggressive behaviors).

Mental Disorders: The patient has no skills to arrest the mental illness, or to prevent relapse to mental health problems. His or her continued psychiatric disorder places the patient and/or others in imminent danger (eg, a patient whose depression and feelings of hopelessness cause strong impulses to slash his or her wrists, or who has paranoid delusions with command hallucinations to harm others).

SERVICES & MODALITIES NEEDED

The patient needs secure placement for stabilization while imminently dangerous. If the relapse and/or dangerousness is due to psychosis, placement in a secure unit and/or involuntary commitment may be necessary. If continued use is due to severe, acute intoxication, close observation may be needed until the patient is less toxic.

Medication management may be needed (as with anti-craving, opioid agonist, or antipsychotic medications).

When the patient is stabilized, a supportive living arrangement will be needed.

For patients with a Dimension 3 risk rating of 2 or higher at baseline, continuing mental health and addiction treatment with intensive case management also is required.

ADULT MATRIX

2

DIMENSION 6: RECOVERY/LIVING ENVIRONMENT

RISK RATING & DESCRIPTION	SERVICES & MODALITIES NEEDED
RISK RATING: 0	**Substance Use Disorders:** The patient has a supportive environment or is able to cope with poor supports. **Mental Disorders:** The patient has a supportive environment or is able to cope with poor supports.	No immediate supportive living or skills training services are needed.
RISK RATING: 1	**Substance Use Disorders:** The patient has passive support, or significant others are not interested in his or her addiction recovery, but he or she is not too distracted by this situation and is able to cope. **Mental Disorders:** The patient has passive support, or significant others are not interested in an improved mental health environment, but he or she is not too distracted by this situation and is able to cope.	The patient needs assistance in finding a supportive living environment or skills training, vocational training, child care, and transportation. For patients with a Dimension 3 risk rating of 1 or higher, coordination of mental health and addiction care may support functioning in the current recovery environment.
RISK RATING: 2	**Substance Use Disorders:** The patient's environment is not supportive of addiction recovery, but, with clinical structure, the patient is able to cope most of the time. **Mental Disorders:** The patient's environment is not supportive of good mental health, but, with clinical structure, the patient is able to cope most of the time.	The patient needs assistance in finding a supportive living environment or skills training, vocational training, child care, transportation, assertive case management, and assertive community treatment (ACT). The range of services needed depends on the interaction among Dimensions 3, 4, and 5. For example, a stabilized, depressed patient with alcohol use disorder who is ready for recovery and active in self/mutual help groups may need only individual or group counseling once a week, whereas a psychotic patient who is addicted to intravenous cocaine and who is not interested in recovery and has few skills to cope with craving may need more intensive services.
RISK RATING: 3	**Substance Use Disorders:** The patient's environment is not supportive of addiction recovery and he or she finds coping difficult, even with clinical structure. **Mental Disorders:** The patient's environment is not supportive of good mental health and he or she finds coping difficult, even with clinical structure.	The patient needs assertive assistance in finding a supportive living environment or skills training (depending on the patient's coping skills and impulse control), structured vocational rehabilitation, assertive case management and community outreach, and assertive community treatment (ACT). The range of services needed depends on the interaction among Dimensions 3, 4, and 5, as described in risk rating 2.

ADULT MATRIX ②

DIMENSION 6: RECOVERY/LIVING ENVIRONMENT (CONTINUED)

RISK RATING & DESCRIPTION	SERVICES & MODALITIES NEEDED
RISK RATING: 4A **(No immediate action required)**	**Substance Use Disorders:** The patient's environment is not supportive and is chronically hostile and toxic to addiction recovery or treatment progress (eg, the patient has many drug-using friends, or drugs are readily available in the home environment, or there are chronic lifestyle problems but not acute conditions). The patient is unable to cope with the negative effects of this environment on his or her recovery. **Mental Disorders:** The patient's environment is not supportive and is chronically hostile and toxic to good mental health (eg, the patient is homeless and unemployed and has chronic lifestyle problems but not acute conditions). The patient is unable to cope with the negative effects of this environment on his or her recovery.	The patient needs highly assertive assistance in finding a supportive living environment; or skills training and impulse control services; or need for protection, assertive case management and community outreach, and assertive community treatment (ACT). The range of services needed depends on the interaction among Dimensions 3, 4, and 5, as described in risk rating 2. For example, an alcoholic patient with alcohol use and panic disorder who is motivated for recovery may need Level 3.1 services, while a severely and chronically psychotic schizophrenic patient who drinks daily and lives on the street may need more ACT team contact than is available at Level 3.1.
RISK RATING: 4B **(Immediate action required)**	**Substance Use Disorders:** The patient's environment is not supportive and is actively hostile to addiction recovery, posing an immediate threat to the patient's safety and well-being (eg, the patient lives with a drug dealer who offers drugs daily). **Mental Disorders:** The patient's environment is not supportive or is actively hostile to a safe mental health environment, posing an immediate threat to the patient's safety and well-being (eg, the patient lives with a physically abusive, alcohol-using partner).	The patient needs immediate separation from a toxic environment and placement in a temporary supportive living environment. The range of services needed depends on the interaction among Dimensions 3, 4, and 5, as described in risk rating 2. For example, a psychotic patient who is not interested in recovery, or an impulsive heroin-addicted person may need a more intensive residential level for safety.

Matrix for Matching Adolescent Severity and Level of Function with Type and Intensity of Service

This matrix for matching severity and level of function with type and intensity of service needs is provided to help the field move from a program-driven system to assessment-driven services in the treatment and placement criteria for adolescents.

Before successfully moving through each developmental stage, the adolescent faces the complex nature of his/her involvement with family, school, work, and friends and the need to meet certain social, educational, and emotional requirements. Placing adolescents based on a diagnosis alone would not meet the more global biopsychosocial elements, which improve overall treatment outcomes for the adolescent patient.

For more information on how to use this matrix, see the introduction starting on page 69.

 DIMENSION 1: ACUTE INTOXICATION AND/OR WITHDRAWAL POTENTIAL

RISK RATING & DESCRIPTION		SERVICES & MODALITIES NEEDED
RISK RATING: 0	The patient is fully functioning and demonstrates good ability to tolerate and cope with withdrawal discomfort. No signs or symptoms of intoxication or withdrawal are present, or signs or symptoms are resolving.	No immediate intoxication monitoring or management, or withdrawal management services are needed.
RISK RATING: 1	The patient demonstrates adequate ability to tolerate and cope with withdrawal discomfort. Mild to moderate intoxication or signs and symptoms interfere with daily functioning, but do not pose an imminent danger to self or others. There is minimal risk of severe withdrawal (eg, as a continuation of withdrawal management at other levels of service, or in the presence of heavy alcohol or sedative-hypnotic use with minimal seizure risk).	Low-intensity intoxication monitoring or management, or withdrawal management services are needed.
RISK RATING: 2	The patient has some difficulty tolerating and coping with withdrawal discomfort. Intoxication may be severe, but responds to support and treatment sufficiently that the patient does not pose an imminent danger to self or others. There are moderate signs and symptoms, with moderate risk of severe withdrawal (eg, as a continuation of withdrawal management at other levels of service, or in the presence of heavy alcohol or sedative-hypnotic use with minimal seizure risk, or in the presence of many signs and symptoms of opioid or stimulant withdrawal, such as lethargy, agitation, or depression).	Moderate-intensity intoxication monitoring or management, or withdrawal management services are needed.

DIMENSION 1: ACUTE INTOXICATION AND/OR WITHDRAWAL POTENTIAL (CONTINUED)

RISK RATING & DESCRIPTION	SERVICES & MODALITIES NEEDED
RISK RATING: 3 The patient demonstrates poor ability to tolerate and cope with withdrawal discomfort. Severe signs and symptoms of intoxication indicate that the patient may pose an imminent danger to self or others, and intoxication has not abated at less intensive levels of care. There are severe signs and symptoms or risk of severe but manageable withdrawal, or withdrawal is worsening despite withdrawal management at a less intensive level of care (eg, as a continuation of withdrawal management at other levels of service, or in the presence of opioid withdrawal with cravings and impulsive behaviors). The patient may need opioid substitution therapy with titration.	Moderately high-intensity intoxication monitoring or management, or withdrawal management services are needed. Nursing and medical monitoring may be needed for more severe withdrawal.
RISK RATING: 4 The patient is incapacitated, with severe signs and symptoms. Severe withdrawal poses danger (eg, seizures). Continued use poses an imminent threat to life (as through liver failure, GI bleeding, or fetal death). Drug overdose or intoxication has compromised the patient's mental status, cardiac function, or other vital signs or functions.	High-intensity intoxication monitoring or management, or withdrawal management services are needed, with monitoring and management more often than hourly.

DIMENSION 2: BIOMEDICAL CONDITIONS AND COMPLICATIONS

RISK RATING & DESCRIPTION	SERVICES & MODALITIES NEEDED
RISK RATING: 0	The patient is fully functioning and demonstrates good ability to cope with physical discomfort. No biomedical signs or symptoms are present, or biomedical problems are stable (eg, stable asthma or stable juvenile arthritis).	No immediate biomedical services (except for long-term monitoring) are needed.
RISK RATING: 1	The patient demonstrates adequate ability to tolerate and cope with physical discomfort. Mild to moderate signs or symptoms (such as mild to moderate pain) interfere with daily functioning.	Low-intensity biomedical services are needed, including case management to ensure further biomedical evaluation and treatment as part of a treatment plan.
RISK RATING: 2	The patient has some difficulty tolerating and coping with physical problems and/or has other biomedical problems that may interfere with recovery and mental health treatment. The patient neglects to care for serious biomedical problems. Moderately severe biomedical conditions and problems (which require non-urgent attention) are active, but manageable with easily accessible off-site care.	Moderate-intensity biomedical services are needed, including case management to ensure further biomedical evaluation and treatment as part of a treatment plan.
RISK RATING: 3	The patient demonstrates poor ability to tolerate and cope with physical problems, or the patient's general health condition is poor. The patient has serious medical problems, which he or she neglects during outpatient or intensive outpatient treatment. Such problems are stable (eg, asthma or diabetes is complicated, or the patient is on a new treatment regimen).	Moderately high-intensity biomedical services are needed, including medical and nursing monitoring to ensure stabilization.
RISK RATING: 4	The patient is incapacitated, with severe medical problems (eg, extreme pain, uncontrolled diabetes, GI bleeding, or infection requiring IV antibiotics).	High-intensity biomedical services are needed for stabilization and medication management, including medical and nursing close observation and 24-hour management.

ADOLESCENT MATRIX

2

DIMENSION 3: EMOTIONAL, BEHAVIORAL, OR COGNITIVE CONDITIONS AND COMPLICATIONS

RISK RATING & DESCRIPTION	SERVICES & MODALITIES NEEDED

NOTE: Individuals need not match descriptions in all of the subdomains within any one risk rating.

RISK RATING: 0

Dangerousness/Lethality: The patient has good impulse control and coping skills.

Interference with Addiction Recovery Efforts: The patient is able to focus on recovery, identify appropriate supports, and reach out for help.

Social Functioning: The patient is fully functioning in relationships with significant others, school, work, and friends.

Ability for Self-Care: The patient is fully functioning, with good personal resources and skills to cope with emotional problems.

Course of Illness: The patient has no emotional or behavioral problems, or any problems identified are stable (eg, attention deficit hyperactivity disorder is stable and managed with medication). There is no recent serious or high-risk vulnerability.

No immediate mental health services are needed.

RISK RATING: 1

Dangerousness/Lethality: The patient has adequate impulse control and coping skills to deal with any thoughts of harm to self or others.

Interference with Addiction Recovery Efforts: The patient's emotional concerns relate to negative consequences and effects of addiction. He or she is able to view these as part of addiction and recovery.

Social Functioning: The patient's relationships or spheres of social functioning (significant others, friends, school, work) are being impaired but not endangered by the patient's substance use (for example, there is no imminent risk of expulsion from school or loss of job). The patient is able to meet personal responsibilities and maintain stable, meaningful relationships despite the mild symptoms experienced (eg, mood or anxiety symptoms are subthreshold for a *DSM* diagnosis or, if they meet diagnostic criteria, the patient is able to continue in essential roles).

Ability for Self-Care: The patient has adequate resources and skills to cope with emotional or behavioral problems.

Course of Illness: The patient has mild to moderate signs and symptoms (eg, dysphoria, relationship problems, work or school problems, or problems coping in the community), with good response to treatment in the past. Any past serious problems have a relatively long period of stability (eg, serious depression and suicidal behavior four years ago), or past problems are chronic but not severe enough to pose any high-risk vulnerability (eg, superficial wrist scratching, but no previous hospitalization or life-threatening behavior in a patient who has been able to contract for safety).

Low-intensity mental health services are needed, including case management to coordinate addiction and mental health care, medication monitoring, psychoeducation about mental disorders and psychotropic medications, and self/mutual help support groups to deal with the emotional aspects of recovery.

ADOLESCENT MATRIX

2

DIMENSION 3: EMOTIONAL, BEHAVIORAL, OR COGNITIVE CONDITIONS AND COMPLICATIONS (CONTINUED)

RISK RATING & DESCRIPTION

RISK RATING: 2

Dangerousness/Lethality: The patient has suicidal ideation or violent impulses (but without active behaviors or intent), which require more than routine outpatient monitoring.

Interference with Addiction Recovery Efforts: The patient's emotional, behavioral, or cognitive problems (eg, memory problems associated with marijuana use) distract from recovery efforts.

Social Functioning: The patient's relationships or spheres of social functioning (significant others, friends, school, work) are being impaired by substance use, and may be linked to a psychiatric disorder (for example, a patient with depression or anxiety disorder is unable to sleep or socialize). Symptoms are causing moderate difficulty in managing relationships with significant others, social, work, or school functioning, or coping in the community, but not to a degree that they pose a significant danger to self or others, or cause the patient to be unable to manage activities of daily living or basic responsibilities in the home, work, school, or community.

Ability for Self-Care: The patient has poor personal resources, with moderate or minimal skills to cope with emotional or behavioral problems.

Course of Illness: The patient has frequent and/or intense symptoms (for example, frequent outbursts of disruptive behavior; suicidal or homicidal ideation with ability to contract for safety; vegetative signs, agitation, or retardation; or inconsistent impulse control), with a history that indicates significant problems that are not well stabilized (eg, psychotic episodes with periods of decompensation). Acute problems pose some risk of harm to self or others, but the patient is not imminently dangerous (eg, hallucinations and delusions invoke homicidal ideation, but the patient has no plan or means to harm others).

SERVICES & MODALITIES NEEDED

Moderate-intensity mental health services are needed, including case management to ensure monitoring and evaluation of emotional, behavioral, and cognitive status as part of the treatment plan. Medication management and monitoring, and medical and nursing monitoring and management as needed.

Parents or guardians must be willing and able to supervise the adolescent while at home during treatment.

ADOLESCENT MATRIX

2

ADOLESCENT MATRIX
❷

DIMENSION 3: EMOTIONAL, BEHAVIORAL, OR COGNITIVE CONDITIONS AND COMPLICATIONS (CONTINUED)

RISK RATING & DESCRIPTION

RISK RATING: 3

Dangerousness/Lethality: The patient has frequent impulses to harm self or others, which are potentially destabilizing or chronic. However, the patient is not imminently dangerous in a 24-hour setting. For example, the patient has frequent suicidal ideation, but no plan, and can contract for safety at Level 3.5.

The patient is no longer experiencing command hallucinations and is responding to medication, but needs further stabilization at Level 3.7.

Interference with Addiction Recovery Efforts: Recovery efforts are negatively affected by the patient's emotional, behavioral, or cognitive problems in significant and distracting ways, up to and including inability to focus on recovery.

Social Functioning: The patient has significant functional impairment, with severe symptoms (eg, disorganized thinking, depression with significant vegetative signs, agitation or retardation, and poor impulse control). Such symptoms seriously impair the patient's ability to function in family, social, work, or school settings, and cannot be managed at a less intensive level of service, or (in chronic populations) to function in shelters, homeless and other community situations (for example, an adolescent has had multiple attempts at property damage when unsupervised, has personality traits that are not severe but do require consistent boundary setting, or has a history of runaway behavior that requires a 24-hour structured environment at Level 3.5).

Ability for Self-Care: The patient has insufficient or severe lack of capacity to cope with emotional or behavioral problems. His or her uncontrolled behavior, confusion, or disorientation limit the patient's capacity for self-care, leading to an inadequate ability to manage the activities of daily living.

Course of Illness: Acute course of illness dominates the clinical presentation, with symptoms involving impaired reality testing, communication, thought processes, judgment, or attention to personal hygiene, which significantly compromise the patient's ability to adjust to life in the community. Alternatively, interventions at previous treatment levels have not achieved stabilization or complete remission of symptoms. Patient has limited ability to follow through with treatment recommendations, thus demonstrating risk of and vulnerability to dangerous consequences.

SERVICES & MODALITIES NEEDED

Moderately high-intensity mental health services are needed, including daily monitoring and ready access to medical management, and medication management if symptoms become acute but not dangerous.

Discharge planning for intensive case management and community outreach are needed for the severely and chronically mentally ill patient. Supportive living arrangements are needed, with 24-hour supervision.

DIMENSION 3: EMOTIONAL, BEHAVIORAL, OR COGNITIVE CONDITIONS AND COMPLICATIONS (CONTINUED)

RISK RATING & DESCRIPTION

SERVICES & MODALITIES NEEDED

RISK RATING: 4

Dangerousness/Lethality: Severe psychotic, mood, or personality disorders present acute risk to the patient, such as immediate risk of suicide; psychosis with unpredictable, disorganized, or violent behavior; or gross neglect of self-care.

Interference with Addiction Recovery Efforts: The patient is unable to focus on addiction recovery due to severe overwhelming mental health problems or regression and psychiatric symptoms due to continued alcohol or other drug use.

Social Functioning: The patient is unable to cope with family, school, friends, or work due to overwhelming mental health problems (such as a thought disorder of acute onset that places self and others at risk). Or the patient is manic, exchanges sex for drugs, or engages in unsafe, sexually promiscuous behavior, and is unable to stop the behavior. Symptoms indicate that the patient is at risk of harming self or others, or has a seriously impaired ability to function in family, school, social, or work settings.

Ability for Self-Care: The patient has developed a life-threatening condition that requires medical management (such as a severe eating disorder with significant malnutrition).

Course of Illness: The patient is at high risk, with significant vulnerability to dangerous consequences. He or she exhibits severe and acute life-threatening symptoms (for example, dangerous or impulsive behavior or cognitive functioning) that pose imminent danger to self or others. These might include symptoms of psychosis, including command hallucinations or paranoid delusions. The patient's history of instability is such that high-intensity services are needed to prevent dangerous consequences (eg, the patient is not responding to daily changes in medication at less intensive levels of service, with escalating psychosis).

High-intensity mental health services are needed, including 24-hour medical and nursing monitoring and management, medication management, secure services, and close observation more often than hourly.

NOTES ON DIMENSION 3

- Consider dangerousness/lethality, interference with addiction recovery efforts, social functioning, ability for self-care, and course of illness (history of presenting illness–the pattern of symptoms and response to treatment up to, and including, the present illness–and the pattern of treatment response).

- Consider acute stabilization, medical management and monitoring, mental health consultation and integration of mental health and addiction services, skills training, multidimensional therapy (MDT), multisystemic therapy (MST), intensive in-home outreach, assertive community outreach services, or other approaches to case management that highly coordinate intensive therapies across multiple systems, medication management and monitoring, and systems intervention and coordination.

- Consider traditional addiction and mental health services, as well as availability of addiction services coordinated with mental health services, or mental health services coordinated with addiction treatment, integrated inpatient, or outpatient co-occurring disorders services.

DIMENSION 4: READINESS TO CHANGE

RISK RATING & DESCRIPTION

SERVICES & MODALITIES NEEDED

RISK RATING: 0

Substance Use Disorders: The patient is engaged in treatment as a proactive, responsible participant, and is committed to changing his or her alcohol and/or other drug use.

Mental Disorders: The patient is engaged in treatment as a proactive, responsible participant, and is committed to changing his or her mental functioning and behavior.

No immediate engagement or motivational enhancement strategies or services are needed.

RISK RATING: 1

Substance Use Disorders: The patient is willing to enter treatment and to explore strategies for changing his or her substance use, but is ambivalent about the need for change. He or she is willing to explore the need for treatment and strategies to reduce or stop substance use (eg, the patient views his or her substance use problem as caused by depression or another psychiatric diagnosis). Or the patient is willing to change his or her substance use, but believes it will not be difficult to do so, or will not accept full recovery treatment plans.

Mental Disorders: The patient is willing to enter treatment and to explore strategies for changing his or her mental functioning, but is ambivalent about the need for change. He or she is willing to explore the need for treatment and strategies to deal with mental disorders. The patient's participation in mental health treatment is sufficient to avert mental decompensation (eg, an adolescent who has attention deficit hyperactivity disorder is ambivalent about taking psychotropic medications, but generally follows through with treatment recommendations).

In any addiction or co-occurring disorders setting, low-intensity engagement or motivational strategies are needed. These include education about the illness(es), education of family and significant others, and reinforcement of the need for treatment by the legal, work, or school systems.

For patients with impairment in Dimension 3, motivational enhancement is integrated into continuing care management at any degree of intensity, as well as into specific treatment episodes.

RISK RATING: 2

Substance Use Disorders: The patient is reluctant to agree to treatment for substance use problems. He or she is able to articulate the negative consequences of substance use, but has a low level of commitment to change his or her use of alcohol or other drugs. The patient is assessed as having minimal readiness to change and is only passively involved in treatment. The patient is variably compliant with attendance at outpatient sessions or meetings of self/mutual help or other support groups.

Moderate-intensity engagement or motivational strategies are needed, with active support from family, significant others, legal, work, or school systems to set and follow through with clear, consistent limits and consequences.

Multidimensional therapy (MDT), multisystemic therapy (MST), intensive in-home outreach, assertive community outreach services, or other approaches to case management that highly coordinate intensive therapies across multiple systems may be needed.

(See next page for additional information.)

DIMENSION 4: READINESS TO CHANGE (CONTINUED)

RISK RATING & DESCRIPTION	SERVICES & MODALITIES NEEDED
RISK RATING: 2	**Mental Disorders:** The patient is reluctant to agree to treatment for mental disorders. He or she is able to articulate the negative consequences of his or her mental health problems, but has low commitment to treatment. The patient is assessed as having minimal readiness to change and is only passively involved in treatment (eg, the patient is variable in follow-through with use of psychotropic medications or attendance at therapy sessions).	Moderate-intensity engagement or motivational strategies are needed, with active support from family, significant others, legal, work, or school systems to set and follow through with clear, consistent limits and consequences. Multidimensional therapy (MDT), multisystemic therapy (MST), intensive in-home outreach, assertive community outreach services, or other approaches to case management that highly coordinate intensive therapies across multiple systems may be needed. For patients who face legal consequences, court-mandated treatment (as through drug court) may be indicated. For patients with Dimension 3 baseline risk ratings of 2 or higher, intensive case management may be required to integrate motivational enhancement therapies and continuing mental health care.

RISK RATING	RISK RATING & DESCRIPTION	SERVICES & MODALITIES NEEDED
RISK RATING: 2	**Mental Disorders:** The patient is reluctant to agree to treatment for mental disorders. He or she is able to articulate the negative consequences of his or her mental health problems, but has low commitment to treatment. The patient is assessed as having minimal readiness to change and is only passively involved in treatment (eg, the patient is variable in follow-through with use of psychotropic medications or attendance at therapy sessions).	Moderate-intensity engagement or motivational strategies are needed, with active support from family, significant others, legal, work, or school systems to set and follow through with clear, consistent limits and consequences. Multidimensional therapy (MDT), multisystemic therapy (MST), intensive in-home outreach, assertive community outreach services, or other approaches to case management that highly coordinate intensive therapies across multiple systems may be needed. For patients who face legal consequences, court-mandated treatment (as through drug court) may be indicated. For patients with Dimension 3 baseline risk ratings of 2 or higher, intensive case management may be required to integrate motivational enhancement therapies and continuing mental health care.
RISK RATING: 3	**Substance Use Disorders:** The patient exhibits inconsistent follow through, and shows minimal awareness of his or her substance use disorder and need for treatment. He or she appears unaware of the need to change, and is unwilling or only partially able to follow through with treatment recommendations. **Mental Disorders:** The patient exhibits inconsistent follow through and shows minimal awareness of his or her mental disorder and need for treatment. He or she appears unaware of the need to change, and thus is unwilling or only partially able to follow through with treatment recommendations.	Moderately high-intensity engagement or motivational enhancement strategies are needed to engage the patient in treatment. Effort should be focused on any available systems leverage (family, school, work, or legal system) to align incentives that promote treatment engagement and investment by the patient. If treatment reluctance is directly related to refractory ADHD or social anxiety disorder, multidimensional therapy (MDT), multisystemic therapy (MST), intensive in-home outreach, assertive community outreach services, or other approaches to case management that highly coordinate intensive therapies across multiple systems may be needed. For patients with a Dimension 3 risk rating of 2 to 3, the following may be needed: increased medical management, multidimensional therapy (MDT), multisystemic therapy (MST), intensive in-home outreach, assertive community outreach services, or other approaches to case management that highly coordinate intensive therapies across multiple systems.
RISK RATING: 4A (No immediate action required)	**Substance Use Disorders:** The patient is unable to follow through, has little or no awareness of substance use problems and any associated negative consequences, knows very little about addiction, and sees no connection between his/her suffering and substance use. He or she is not imminently dangerous to or unable to care for self and is not willing to explore change regarding his or her illness and its implications (for example, he or she blames others for legal or family problems, and rejects treatment).	High-intensity engagement or motivational strategies to try to engage the patient as a participant in treatment may be needed. Work with any systems leverage available (family, school, work, legal) to align incentives that promote treatment engagement and investment of patient. Any engagement and motivational strategies are practical multidimensional therapy or multisystemic interventions to develop leverage, rather than intensive therapy techniques aimed at "breaking through denial."

ADOLESCENT MATRIX

2

DIMENSION 4: READINESS TO CHANGE (CONTINUED)

ADOLESCENT MATRIX

2

RISK RATING & DESCRIPTION	SERVICES & MODALITIES NEEDED

RISK RATING: 4A

(No immediate action required)

Mental Disorders: The patient is unable to follow through, has little or no awareness of a mental disorder and any associated negative consequences, knows very little about mental illness, and sees no connection between his or her suffering and mental health problems. He or she is not imminently dangerous to or unable to care for self, is not willing to explore change regarding his or her illness and its implications.

High-intensity engagement or motivational strategies to try to engage the patient as a participant in treatment may be needed. Work with any systems leverage available (family, school, work, legal) to align incentives that promote treatment engagement and investment of patient.

Any engagement and motivational strategies are practical multidimensional therapy or multisystemic interventions to develop leverage, rather than intensive therapy techniques aimed at "breaking through denial."

RISK RATING: 4B

(Immediate action required)

Substance Use Disorders: The patient is unable to follow through with treatment recommendations. As a result, his or her behavior represents an imminent danger of harm to self or others, or he or she is unable to function independently and engage in self-care. For example, the patient repeatedly demonstrates inability to follow through with treatment, and continues to use alcohol and/or other drugs, becomes violent or suicidal, or acts impulsively in runaway behavior.

Mental Disorders: The patient is unable to follow through with treatment recommendations. As a result, his or her behavior poses an imminent danger of harm to self or others, or he or she is unable to function independently and engage in self-care. For example, the patient refuses all medications and is overtly psychotic, so that his or her judgment and impulse control is severely impaired.

The patient needs secure placement for stabilization while imminently dangerous. If treatment resistance is caused by psychosis, involuntary commitment and placement in a secure unit may be necessary.

If treatment resistance is caused by severe, acute intoxication, close observation may be needed until the patient is less toxic.

DIMENSION 5: RELAPSE, CONTINUED USE, OR CONTINUED PROBLEM POTENTIAL

RISK RATING & DESCRIPTION

SERVICES & MODALITIES NEEDED

RISK RATING: 0

Substance Use Disorders: The patient has no potential for further substance use problems, or is at minimal risk of relapse and has good coping skills.

Mental Disorders: The patient is not at risk of further mental health problems, or has low risk and good coping skills.

No immediate relapse prevention services are needed. The patient may need self/mutual help or a non-professional support group.

RISK RATING: 1

Substance Use Disorders: The patient has minimal relapse potential, with some vulnerability, and has fair self-management and relapse prevention skills.

Mental Disorders: The patient has minimal relapse potential, with some vulnerability, and has fair self-management and relapse prevention skills.

Low-intensity relapse prevention services are needed to reinforce coping skills until the patient is integrated into continuing care or a self/mutual help or non-professional group.

RISK RATING: 2

Substance Use Disorders: The patient has impaired recognition and understanding of substance use relapse issues, but is able to self-manage with prompting.

Mental Disorders: The patient has impaired recognition and understanding of mental illness relapse issues, but is able to self-manage with prompting.

Moderate-intensity relapse prevention services are needed to monitor and strengthen the patient's coping skills. The patient also needs relapse prevention education and help with integration into self/mutual help and community support groups. Multidimensional therapy (MDT), multisystemic therapy (MST), intensive in-home outreach, assertive community outreach services, or other approaches to case management that highly coordinate intensive therapies across multiple systems may be needed.

Medication management may be needed (such as anti-craving, antidepressants, mood stabilizers, or antipsychotic medications).

The patient may need addiction treatment coupled with continuing outpatient mental health and/or addiction care (routine or intensive).

For patients with a Dimension 3 risk rating of 1 to 2, continuing coordinated and integrated mental health care is required while intensive addiction treatment is provided.

For patients with a Dimension 3 risk rating of 2 or (especially) 3, intensive case management services may be required to coordinate and integrate addiction treatment into continuing mental health care.

RISK RATING: 3

Substance Use Disorders: The patient has little recognition and understanding of substance use relapse issues, and has poor skills to cope with and interrupt addiction problems, or to avoid or limit relapse.

Moderately high-intensity relapse prevention services are needed, including structured coping skills training, motivational strategies, and exploration of family and/or significant others' ability to align incentives to consolidate engagement in treatment. Possible assistance in finding a supportive living environment may be needed.

(See next page for additional information.)

ADOLESCENT MATRIX

❷

DIMENSION 5: RELAPSE, CONTINUED USE, OR CONTINUED PROBLEM POTENTIAL (CONTINUED)

RISK RATING & DESCRIPTION	SERVICES & MODALITIES NEEDED
RISK RATING: 3 **Mental Disorders:** The patient has little recognition and understanding of mental illness relapse issues, and has poor skills to cope with and interrupt mental health problems, or to avoid or limit relapse.	Moderately high-intensity relapse prevention services are needed, including structured coping skills training, motivational strategies, and exploration of family and/or significant others' ability to align incentives to consolidate engagement in treatment. Possible assistance in finding a supportive living environment may be needed. The patient also may need multidimensional therapy (MDT), multisystemic therapy (MST), intensive in-home outreach, assertive community outreach services, or other approaches to case management that tightly coordinate intensive therapies across multiple systems. Medication management may be needed (such as anti-craving, antidepressants, mood stabilizers, or antipsychotic medications). The patient may need addiction treatment coupled with continuing outpatient mental health and/or addiction care (routine or intensive). For patients with a Dimension 3 risk rating of 1 to 2, continuing coordinated and integrated addiction treatment and mental health care is required.
RISK RATING: 4A **(No immediate action required)** **Substance Use Disorders:** Repeated treatment episodes have had little positive effect on the patient's functioning. He or she has no skills to cope with and interrupt addiction problems, or to prevent or limit relapse (for example, the patient has undergone repeated episodes of addiction treatment, but is unable to cope with continued cravings to use). However, the patient is not in imminent danger and is able to care for self. **Mental Disorders:** Repeated treatment episodes have had little positive effect on the patient's functioning. He or she has no skills to cope with and interrupt mental health problems, or to prevent or limit relapse (for example, the patient is severely and chronically mentally ill, with chronic dysfunction and inability to arrest psychotic episodes). However, the patient is not in imminent danger and is able to care for self.	Exploration of systems incentives to consolidate the patient's engagement in treatment is required. The patient needs motivational strategies, structured coping skills, assistance in finding supportive living arrangements, multidimensional therapy (MDT), multisystemic therapy (MST), intensive in-home outreach, assertive community outreach services, or other approaches to case management that highly coordinate intensive therapies across multiple systems. Medication management may be needed (such as anti-craving, antidepressants, mood stabilizers, or antipsychotic medications). The patient may need addiction treatment coupled with continuing outpatient mental health and/or addiction care (routine or intensive). For patients with a Dimension 3 risk rating of 2 or higher, coordinated and integrated addiction treatment and mental health case management, and/or multidimensional therapy (MDT), multisystemic therapy (MST), intensive in-home outreach, assertive community outreach services, or other approaches to case management that highly coordinate intensive therapies across multiple systems may be indicated.

DIMENSION 5: RELAPSE, CONTINUED USE, OR CONTINUED PROBLEM POTENTIAL (CONTINUED)

RISK RATING & DESCRIPTION	SERVICES & MODALITIES NEEDED

RISK RATING: 4B

(Immediate action required)

Substance Use Disorders: The patient has no skills to arrest the addictive disorder, or to prevent relapse to substance use. His or her continued addictive behavior places the patient and/or others in imminent danger (eg, the patient's continued drug use leads to impulsive, psychotic, and aggressive behaviors).

Mental Disorders: The patient has no skills to arrest the mental illness, or to prevent relapse to mental health problems. His or her continued psychiatric disorder places the patient and/or others in imminent danger (eg, the patient's depression and feelings of hopelessness cause strong impulses to slash his or her wrists, or his or her paranoid delusions are accompanied by command hallucinations to harm others).

The patient needs secure placement for stabilization while imminently dangerous. If the relapse and/or dangerousness is due to psychosis, placement in a secure unit and/or involuntary commitment may be necessary. If continued use is due to severe, acute intoxication, close observation may be needed until the patient is less toxic.

Medication management may be needed (such as anti-craving, antidepressants, mood stabilizers, or antipsychotic medications).

When the patient is stabilized, a supportive living arrangement will be needed.

For patients with a Dimension 3 risk rating of 2 or higher at baseline, continuing mental health and addiction treatment with intensive case management also is required.

ADOLESCENT MATRIX

2

DIMENSION 6: RECOVERY/LIVING ENVIRONMENT

RISK RATING & DESCRIPTION	SERVICES & MODALITIES NEEDED
RISK RATING: 0 **Substance Use Disorders:** The patient has a supportive environment or is able to cope with poor supports. **Mental Disorders:** The patient has a supportive environment or is able to cope with poor supports.	No immediate supportive living or skills training services are needed.
RISK RATING: 1 **Substance Use Disorders:** The patient has passive support, or significant others are not interested in his or her addiction recovery, but he or she is not too distracted by this situation to be able to cope. **Mental Disorders:** The patient has passive support or significant others are not interested in an improved mental health environment, but he or she is not too distracted by this situation to be able to cope.	The patient needs assistance in finding a supportive living environment or skills training, support at school, vocational training, and transportation. For patients with a Dimension 3 risk rating of 1 or higher, coordination of mental health and addiction care may support functioning in the current recovery environment.
RISK RATING: 2 **Substance Use Disorders:** The patient's environment is not supportive of addiction recovery, but, with clinical structure, the patient is able to cope most of the time. **Mental Disorders:** The patient's environment is not supportive of good mental health, but, with clinical structure, the patient is able to cope most of the time.	The patient needs assistance in finding a supportive living environment or skills training, support at school, vocational training, and transportation. Multidimensional therapy (MDT), multisystemic therapy (MST), intensive in-home outreach, assertive community outreach services, or other approaches to case management that highly coordinate intensive therapies across multiple systems may be needed. The range of services needed depends on the interaction among Dimensions 3, 4, and 5. For example, an adolescent who has had one treatment episode for alcohol addiction is stable, back in school, ready for recovery, and active in self/mutual help groups may need only individual or group counseling once a week. However, for example, an adolescent who has had several treatment episodes, is involved with juvenile justice and gangs, is actively using ecstasy and heroin, is not motivated for recovery, and has few skills to cope with cravings may need more intensive services.
RISK RATING: 3 **Substance Use Disorders:** The patient's environment is not supportive of addiction recovery, and he or she finds coping difficult, even with clinical structure. **Mental Disorders:** The patient's environment is not supportive of good mental health, and he or she finds coping difficult, even with clinical structure.	The patient needs assertive assistance in finding a supportive living environment or skills training (depending on the patient's coping skills and impulse control), structured vocational rehabilitation, multidimensional therapy (MDT), multisystemic therapy (MST), intensive in-home outreach, assertive community outreach services, or other approaches to case management that highly coordinate intensive therapies across multiple systems. The range of services needed depends on the interaction among Dimensions 3, 4, and 5, as described in risk rating 2.

DIMENSION 6: RECOVERY/LIVING ENVIRONMENT (CONTINUED)

RISK RATING & DESCRIPTION		SERVICES & MODALITIES NEEDED
RISK RATING: 4A (No immediate action required)	**Substance Use Disorders:** The patient's environment is not supportive, and is chronically hostile and toxic to addiction recovery or treatment progress (for example, the patient has many drug-using friends, drugs are readily available in the home environment, or there are chronic lifestyle problems but not acute conditions). The patient is unable to cope with the negative effects of such an environment on his or her recovery. **Mental Disorders:** The patient's environment is not supportive, and is chronically hostile and toxic to good mental health (for example, there is chronic parental neglect, along with caretaking and adult supervision problems, but not acute conditions). The patient is unable to cope with the negative effects of this environment on his or her recovery.	The patient needs highly assertive assistance in finding a supportive living environment or skills training and impulse control services. Or there is a need for protection, multidimensional therapy (MDT), multisystemic therapy (MST), intensive in-home outreach, assertive community outreach services, or other approaches to case management that highly coordinate intensive therapies across multiple systems. The range of services needed depends on the interaction among Dimensions 3, 4, and 5, as described in risk rating 2. For example, an adolescent dependent on marijuana with chronic parental neglect but who is motivated for recovery may need Level 3.1 services. However, a gang-involved, juvenile justice-involved, highly impulsive adolescent who drinks daily and lacks parental supervision and adult caretaking may need multidimensional therapy (MDT), multisystemic therapy (MST), intensive in-home outreach, assertive community outreach services, or other approaches to case management that highly coordinate intensive therapies across multiple systems. These services may not be available at Level 3.1.
RISK RATING: 4B (Immediate action required)	**Substance Use Disorders:** The patient's environment is not supportive, and is actively hostile to addiction recovery, posing an immediate threat to the patient's safety and well-being (for example, the patient lives with a parent who is a drug dealer and who offers drugs daily). **Mental Disorders:** The patient's environment is not supportive, or is actively hostile, to a safe mental health environment, posing an immediate threat to the patient's safety and well-being (for example, the patient lives with a physically abusive parent or adult caretaker).	The patient needs immediate separation from a toxic environment and placement in a temporary supportive living environment. The range of services needed depends on the interaction among Dimensions 3, 4, and 5, as described in risk rating 2. For example, a psychotic patient who is not motivated for recovery, or an impulsive risk-taking adolescent with frequent cocaine use, may need a more intensive residential level for safety.

PLANNING/PLACEMENT

3

Service Planning and Placement

Understanding and Determining Level of Care Placement

Performing a multidimensional assessment that explores risks and needs, as well as strengths, skills, and resources, will help identify any immediate needs and also lead to dimension-specific risk ratings. Based on these ratings, priority dimensions then can be defined in collaboration with the patient. Once these initial steps have been completed, the next step in *The ASAM Criteria* process is to explore service planning and placement. Concepts pertaining to placement are best understood when placement is expressed within a flexible, seamless continuum, marked by five broad levels of service, as described here.

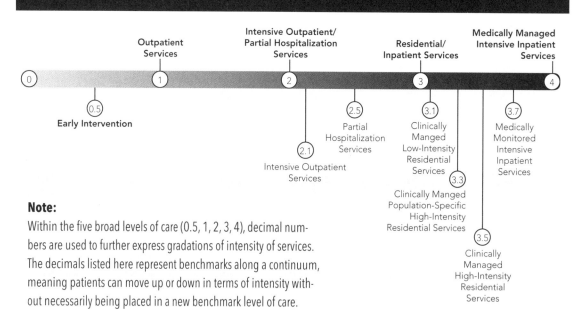

REFLECTING A CONTINUUM OF CARE

Outpatient Services — 1

Intensive Outpatient/ Partial Hospitalization Services — 2

Residential/ Inpatient Services — 3

Medically Managed Intensive Inpatient Services — 4

0

0.5 Early Intervention

2.1 Intensive Outpatient Services

2.5 Partial Hospitalization Services

3.1 Clinically Manged Low-Intensity Residential Services

3.3 Clinically Manged Population-Specific High-Intensity Residential Services

3.5 Clinically Managed High-Intensity Residential Services

3.7 Medically Monitored Intensive Inpatient Services

Note:

Within the five broad levels of care (0.5, 1, 2, 3, 4), decimal numbers are used to further express gradations of intensity of services. The decimals listed here represent benchmarks along a continuum, meaning patients can move up or down in terms of intensity without necessarily being placed in a new benchmark level of care.

Introduction to the Levels of Service

Similar to earlier editions, *The ASAM Criteria* describes treatment as a continuum marked by four broad levels of service and an early intervention level. Since the First Edition of the criteria (1991), Roman numerals have been used to identify each level of care. But in the 21st century, when technology allows for immediate electronic dissemination of information worldwide, Roman numerals are especially limiting. Thus, with this edition, regular Arabic numerals will be used to describe all levels of care (Levels 0.5 through 4).

LEVEL OF CARE	(a) ADOLESCENT TITLE	ADULT TITLE	DESCRIPTION
0.5	Early Intervention	Early Intervention	Assessment and education for at-risk individuals who do not meet diagnostic criteria for substance use disorder
1	Outpatient Services	Outpatient Services	Less than 9 hours of service/week (adults); less than 6 hours/week (adolescents) for recovery or motivational enhancement therapies/strategies
2.1	Intensive Outpatient Services	Intensive Outpatient Services	9 or more hours of service/week (adults); 6 or more hours/week (adolescents) to treat multidimensional instability
2.5	Partial Hospitalization Services	Partial Hospitalization Services	20 or more hours of service/week for multidimensional instability not requiring 24-hour care
3.1	Clinically Managed Low-Intensity Residential Services	Clinically Managed Low-Intensity Residential Services	24-hour structure with available trained personnel; at least 5 hours of clinical service/week
3.3	*This level of care not designated for adolescent populations	Clinically Managed Population-Specific High-Intensity Residential Services	24-hour care with trained counselors to stabilize multidimensional imminent danger. Less intense milieu and group treatment for those with cognitive or other impairments unable to use full active milieu or therapeutic community
3.5	Clinically Managed Medium-Intensity Residential Services	Clinically Managed High-Intensity Residential Services	24-hour care with trained counselors to stabilize multidimensional imminent danger and prepare for outpatient treatment. Able to tolerate and use full active milieu or therapeutic community
3.7	Medically Monitored High-Intensity Inpatient Services	Medically Monitored Intensive Inpatient Services	24-hour nursing care with physician availability for significant problems in Dimensions 1, 2, or 3. 16 hour/day counselor ability
4	Medically Managed Intensive Inpatient Services	Medically Managed Intensive Inpatient Services	24-hour nursing care and daily physician care for severe, unstable problems in Dimensions 1, 2, or 3. Counseling available to engage patient in treatment
OTP (LEVEL 1)	*OTPs not specified here for adolescent populations, though information may be found in discussion of adult services	Opioid Treatment Program (Level 1)	Daily or several times weekly opioid agonist medication and counseling available to maintain multidimensional stability for those with severe opioid use disorder

LEVEL OF WITHDRAWAL MANAGEMENT FOR ADULTS	LEVEL	DESCRIPTION
Ambulatory Withdrawal Management without Extended On-Site Monitoring	1-WM	Mild withdrawal with daily or less than daily outpatient supervision; likely to complete withdrawal management and to continue treatment or recovery
Ambulatory Withdrawal Management with Extended On-Site Monitoring	2-WM	Moderate withdrawal with all day withdrawal management support and supervision; at night, has supportive family or living situation; likely to complete withdrawal management
Clinically Managed Residential Withdrawal Management	3.2-WM	Moderate withdrawal, but needs 24-hour support to complete withdrawal management and increase likelihood of continuing treatment or recovery
Medically Monitored Inpatient Withdrawal Management	3.7-WM	Severe withdrawal and needs 24-hour nursing care and physician visits as necessary; unlikely to complete withdrawal management without medical, nursing monitoring
Medically Managed Intensive Inpatient Withdrawal Management	4-WM	Severe, unstable withdrawal and needs 24-hour nursing care and daily physician visits to modify withdrawal management regimen and manage medical instability

NOTE: There are no unbundled withdrawal management services for adolescents.

These levels of care provide the field with a nomenclature for describing the continuum of recovery-oriented addiction services.

Within the five broad levels of care, decimal numbers are used to further express gradations of intensity (including Levels 2.1, 2.5, 3.1, 3.3 [for adults only], 3.5, and 3.7). For example, a 2.1 level of care provides a benchmark for intensity at the minimum description of Level 2 care. This structure hopefully allows for improved precision of description of the intensity of services and better inter-rater reliability by focusing on five broad levels of service.

Conventional program design, licensing standards, benefit plan design, payment, and reimbursement have maintained usually strict separation of levels of care. With innovative overlapping of levels to create a seamless continuum of flexible services and levels of care,

access to care and efficiency and effectiveness of services can be greatly improved. For example, *The ASAM Criteria* describes a continuum of five levels of withdrawal management in the adult criteria.

Often only one or two levels of withdrawal management are funded and delivered, and these are usually the most intensive and expensive levels (Level 3.7-WM or Level 4-WM). As a result, waiting lists are not uncommon and staffing patterns, withdrawal management protocols, and progress note documentation all match intensive levels of withdrawal management.

Clinical reality, however, demonstrates that many patients either do not need to begin withdrawal management in the most intensive level of care, or could be moved sooner to less intensive levels of withdrawal management through the five levels of withdrawal management. The use of a flexible, overlapping continuum of care can allow for patients to receive a longer length of withdrawal management care and support with the same or even less resource utilization than would be expended in a few days of care at the most intensive level of hospital-based withdrawal management.

Similar outcomes-driven movement through a flexible and seamless continuum of levels of care could realize the same improved access to efficient and effective services, if licensing, payment, and benefit design practices would allow, permit, and encourage outcomes-driven placement into the most appropriate levels of care.

TWELVE-STEP, MUTUAL HELP, AND SELF-HELP RECOVERY GROUPS

Recovery groups such as Alcoholics Anonymous, Narcotics Anonymous, Dual Recovery Anonymous, Gamblers Anonymous, or SMART Recovery® do not constitute formal treatment programs. Clinicians see the value of such groups in their presence as a lifelong support system, and believe that an individual's chances of a successful outcome are significantly enhanced by involvement in recovery groups. Because of the importance of these fellowships, most providers integrate the philosophy of 12-Step recovery groups into the treatment services themselves. Thus, participation in mutual or self-help groups may be an important element of all levels of care.

As valuable as they are, however, these groups do not constitute a treatment level. Rather, it is best to consider them "self problem-identification, help-seeking options" and adjunctive sources of social support, especially for patients with unsupportive recovery environments. To refer an individual to self/mutual help groups without ongoing formal care based solely on cost considerations is analogous to referring a person with diabetes to a diabetes support group rather than to the care of a physician. On the other hand, there are situations in which a person may be evaluated for addiction and their use or behavior is high risk, but subdiagnostic, not warranting formal treatment. He or she may be referred to a 12-Step recovery or other mutual help or self-help group to raise consciousness about the harmful potential of substance use or gambling behavior.

 ### Adolescent-Specific Approaches to Treatment

At every level of care, program services for adolescents should be designed to meet their developmental and other special needs. Adaptations of adult treatment models often fall short. Ideally, the treatment environment should be physically separate from that of adult patients. Strategies to engage adolescents, channel their energy, hold their attention, and retain them in treatment are especially critical. Treatment must address the nuances of adolescent experience, including cognitive, emotional, physical, psychological, social, and moral development, in addition to involvement with alcohol and other drugs.

Given the current understanding of substance use disorders as having a chronic, long-term, remitting and relapsing course, it should be expected that effective treatment should match this chronic course. In fact, treatment should be regarded as a dynamic, longitudinal process, rather than as a discrete episode of care. While it may encompass one or several acute episodes, it also must endure over the long term. A now outdated approach viewed discrete time-limited episodes of program enrollment as adequate "doses" of treatment. In that view, any further care, also typically time-limited, was regarded as

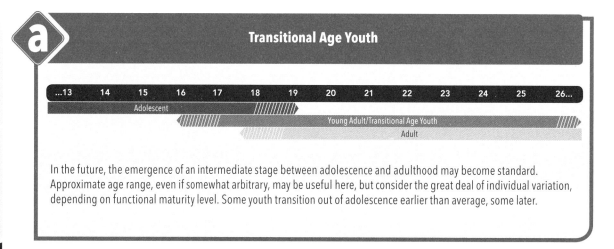

a Transitional Age Youth

In the future, the emergence of an intermediate stage between adolescence and adulthood may become standard. Approximate age range, even if somewhat arbitrary, may be useful here, but consider the great deal of individual variation, depending on functional maturity level. Some youth transition out of adolescence earlier than average, some later.

"aftercare" rather than ongoing care—as though the active part of treatment had ended.

The current view of addiction as a chronic disorder supports a stance of therapeutic optimism and an attitude of persistence toward the treatment-refractory patient. It also reinforces the need for chronic attention and vigilance in response to a chronic vulnerability, even in the improved patient. This view is not incompatible with the common experience that a subset of adolescents may respond to more time-limited interventions and seem to "grow out of" their difficulties with developmental maturation.

Transitional Age Youth

The definition of adolescence is better understood as a matter of a dimensional developmental stage, rather than a categorical cutoff of chronological age. Some youth transition out of adolescence into more adult-like functioning earlier than average, some later. On the other hand, it is useful to have some approximate age range in mind for practical purposes, even if somewhat arbitrary. Also, age range definitions may be written into local regulatory language. In general, most regulatory definitions encompass the ranges of 13-18 or 13-21, with some local variation. From a clinical perspective, these ranges should be viewed flexibly. Although payers may sometimes choose to apply a definition based on a rigid application of an age cutoff, such as age 18, there are many cases where individual variation and the functional

immaturity of a particular patient dictates that the adolescent criteria would be more appropriately applied to a 20 or 21 year old than the adult criteria.

Additionally, there is another whole set of issues that distinguish an intermediate group of young people – young adults or transitional age youth. These are a group of older, maturing adolescents and younger "twentysomethings" who have a foot in both worlds, adolescence and adulthood, and are making a messy, inexact transition. The age range might roughly be considered 17-26, with a great deal of individual variation, depending on functional maturity level. They often are simultaneously emerging into independence while still relying in large part on the support of parents or other caregiving adults.

The mixed features of both adolescence and adulthood for transition age youth require a special approach. Some providers have begun to develop specialized programming for this group and its unique clinical needs. Eventually, the separation of a third category of developmental programming may become standard. The tensions inherent in their transition often require a balancing act, especially between emerging independence and persistent dependence. For example, issues of confidentiality versus open sharing of information with parents/caregivers are common. Other common issues include financial support, shared living environments with parents, extension of standard insurance coverage under parental policies until age 26 with the Affordable Care Act. These tensions and the dynamic interplay between youth and parents is dramatized in the caricatured quotes: "I'm old enough to take care of myself…" versus "You may think you're all grown up, but as long as you're living under my roof…"

From the point of view of ASAM's criteria and treatment matching, it is likely that these in-between young adults need services and service doses somewhere in between adolescents and adults. For example, for a given problem, they may need more intensity than the typical adult, but less than the typical adolescent. Future editions of *The ASAM Criteria* may need to explore specialized considerations for transition age youth in greater detail, and may even consider a third set of criteria for this group of patients with special assets, vulnerabilities, and needs.

Progress Through the Levels of Service

As the patient moves through treatment in any level of service, his or her progress in all six dimensions should be formally assessed at regular intervals relevant to the patient's severity of illness and level of function, and the intensity of service and level of care. While there is not empirical data to inform what "regular intervals" should mean for each level of care, clinical experience suggests the guidelines shown in the box below.

In outpatient (OP) settings, progress in all of the relevant assessment dimensions should be formally assessed about every six sessions. For example, if a person were being seen once a week in Level 1, then that would be a formal review about every six weeks. If the patient were in Level 2.1, intensive outpatient treatment three times a week, then there would be a review at the two-week mark. If the person were coming daily to a partial hospital, Level 2.5 program, there would be a review after one week.

For acute care settings, the instability and rapid changes of a more acutely ill person may necessitate reviewing the treatment plan daily and even more than once daily—at every shift change—if very unstable. Residential levels should formally review progress once a week and more often if the person is quite unstable.

The ASAM criteria multidimensional assessment helps ensure comprehensive treatment. In the process of patient assessment, certain problems and priorities are identified as justifying admission to a particular level of care. The resolution of those problems and priorities determines when a patient can be treated at a different level of care or discharged from treatment. The appearance of new problems may require services that can be effectively provided at the same level of care, or that require a more or less intensive level of care.

As the patient's response to treatment is assessed, new priorities for recovery are identified. The intensity of the strategies of the treatment plan helps determine the most efficient and effective level of service that can safely provide the care articulated in the individualized treatment plan. Patients may, however, worsen or fail to improve in a given level of care or with a given type of program within a level of care or service. At such time, changing the level of care or changing the program should be based upon a reassessment of the treatment plan with modifications to achieve a better therapeutic response.

In cases where some extenuating circumstances must be considered, further justification and presentation of rationale should substantiate the level of care or type of service chosen.

③

Linkages Between Levels of Care

Issues regarding continuity of care, continuing care, and longitudinal follow-up are critical for all patient populations. But such issues are especially important for adolescents because they are so dynamic in their developmental changes and needs. Long-term relationships with patients and families, with the expectation of accommodating dropping in and dropping out, with changing needs over time, should be standard. While the fantasy notion that patients should be expected to be "fixed" after a discrete episode of care (for example, residential rehab) is both common and absurd in all ages, it is even more common for youth, who are too often assumed to have "learned their lesson" or "grown out of it." Episodes of care at different levels of care should be seamlessly linked. This can be achieved by role induction (preparing people for treatment by informing them about the rationale of treatment, the treatment process, and their part in therapy), coordination, communication, warm hand-offs, assertive outreach, and overlapping levels of care. Future editions of *The ASAM Criteria* will address standard approaches for these linkages in greater detail.

Exceptions to the Admission Criteria and Level of Care Placement

In making treatment placement decisions, there are circumstances when it is appropriate practice to not follow the placement decision of the admission criteria. While the admission criteria for each level of care are intended to be as specific as possible, unique clinical presentations or extenuating circumstances may dictate some flexibility in application of the criteria to ensure the safety and welfare of the patient.

These exceptions to the placement level defined by the dimensional admission criteria relate to three important factors:

1. **Lack of availability of appropriate, criteria-selected care.** The reality of limited availability of services continues to be a major problem for a variety of reasons. An indicated level of care may not exist or be accessible in a given community. While accessibility is a common problem in rural areas, it is an issue in many urban areas as well. Funding limitations and other resource constraints also are barriers to the availability of a level of care. Even logistical issues such as waiting lists can render a level of care unavailable. Moreover, the variations in programs within a given level of care sometimes mean that specific treatment services are not available even if an available setting meets the broader criteria.

   In general, when the criteria designate a treatment placement that is not available, a strategy must be crafted that gives the patient the needed services in another placement or combination of placements. The paramount objective should be safety and effectiveness, which usually requires opting for a program of greater intensity than the placement criteria indicate.

2. **Poor outcomes at a given level of care warrant a reassessment of the treatment plan with a view to modify the treatment approach.** Such situations may require transfer to a specialized program at the same level of care or to a more intensive or less intensive level of care to achieve a better therapeutic response.

3. **State laws regulating the practice of medicine or licensure of a facility requiring criteria different from the admission criteria of *The ASAM Criteria*.**

Stabilization Outside of *The ASAM Criteria* Continuum of Care

Some patients have mental health symptoms of sufficient acuity that they may require immediate stabilization of their psychiatric symptoms. Once stabilized, they can be engaged in ongoing care at any level, including ongoing addiction treatment and recovery programming, if indicated. Depending on the severity of their symptoms, such patients may require referral to medical and/or psychiatric services outside the levels of care for addiction services that are described in *The ASAM Criteria.*

Once acute medical/psychiatric stabilization has been achieved, the initial placement for substance use/addiction treatment services should reflect an assessment of the patient's status in all six ASAM criteria dimensions. The principle here is that the highest severity problem (particularly those in Dimensions 1, 2, or 3) should determine the patient's initial entry point into the treatment continuum. Subsequent resolution of the acute problem creates an opportunity to transfer the patient to a less intensive level of care. Addressing the individual's recovery needs thus may involve a sequence of services across several levels of care (involving transfer from low intensity services to more intensive levels of care if clinically necessary; or in the reverse direction, as a patient progresses and needs less intensive services).

For example, a patient who is assessed in Dimension 2 as dangerously hypertensive will need medically managed stabilization in a Level 4 inpatient general hospital. When the individual's Dimension 2 biomedical condition has been stabilized, they can then be transferred to a Level 1 program for continuing care of the addictive disorder. As is demonstrated in the discussions of the various levels of care, and has been learned more and more over the past decade through use of ASAM's criteria in various service intensity settings, the best "match" for ongoing attention to a substance use disorder may occur, for many individuals, in a primary health setting or in a mental health setting, rather than in an addiction treatment setting *per se.* This approach leverages more resources across the whole population to address the wide array of individuals with substance use disorders. It also helps the addiction treatment continuum focus its resources on those individuals with addiction and other complex needs who will be best matched for the types of specialty services provided in those settings.

PLANNING/PLACEMENT ③

Brief Descriptions of Levels of Care

Level 0.5: Early Intervention

Professional services for early intervention were included as a level of care (Level 0.5) in earlier editions, and continue to appear in *The ASAM Criteria.* Early intervention constitutes a service for specific individuals who, for a known reason, are at risk of developing substance-related problems, or a service for those for whom there is not yet sufficient information to document a diagnosable substance use disorder. Level 0.5 services may include Screening, Brief Intervention, Referral, and Treatment (SBIRT) that occurs in a primary care, school, mental health, or some other non-addiction treatment setting.

Where the Level 0.5 service is a Driving Under the Influence (DUI) or Driving While Intoxicated (DWI) program, the length of service is often determined by program rules and law, and completion of the program may be a prerequisite for reinstitution of driving privileges.

If the assessment of such an individual indicates a need for more intensive treatment than Level 0.5 services, there are three possible options:

1. If the individual is in imminent danger (see the section on Addressing Immediate Needs and Imminent Danger in Chapter 3), he or she should be transferred to a clinically appropriate level of care. In the case of impaired driving programs, this may preclude completion of the mandated DUI or DWI program.

2. If the individual is not in imminent danger but does require outpatient treatment (in a Level 1 or Level 2 service), the person should be linked to the relevant level of care. In the case of a DUI/DWI program, an attempt should be made to facilitate

such services within the programming of the Level 0.5 agency. This may be done by adding sufficient individual and/or group sessions to the person's service plan to meet the required intensity of service.

3. In the case of a DUI/DWI program, adding services may not be possible. If the individual can safely and appropriately wait to enter formal treatment until after the Level 0.5 program is completed, linkage to a more intensive level of care should then be arranged.

Level 1: Outpatient Services

Level 1 encompasses organized services that may be delivered in a wide variety of settings. Addiction, mental health, or general health care treatment personnel provide professionally directed screening, evaluation, treatment, and ongoing recovery and disease management services. Such services are provided in regularly scheduled sessions and follow a defined set of policies and procedures or medical protocols.

Services can include medication management services for addiction offered by primary care physicians or other general medical professionals, by general psychiatrists or other mental health professionals with prescribing authority, or by addiction specialist physicians or other trained and credentialed addiction care professionals. Services can also include counseling and psychosocial therapies for substance related and co-occurring disorders offered by professionals who specialize in addiction care or by other health care and mental health professionals.

Level 1 outpatient services are designed to treat the individual's level of clinical severity and function. They can help individuals achieve permanent changes in their alcohol-, tobacco-, and/ or other drug-using behavior, other behaviors that involve the pathological pursuit of reward or relief, and in their mental and physical health functioning. To accomplish this, Level 1 services must address major lifestyle, attitudinal, and behavioral issues that have the potential to undermine the goal of wellness and recovery or inhibit the individual's ability to cope with

major life tasks without the non-medical use of alcohol, tobacco, or other drugs, a pathological involvement with gambling, or with other addictive behaviors.

Keep in mind the Level 1 admission criteria were expanded in the *PPC-2R* (2001) to promote greater access to care for individuals with more complex challenges, such as those who have co-occurring health conditions, mental health conditions (including trauma), cognitive disabilities, and for individuals in earlier stages of readiness to address addiction and mental health issues. Such individuals are often mandated into treatment and, in previous eras, only had access to care if they agreed to extensive periods of intensive and often residential levels of care.

Knowledge and application of psychosocial therapies, such as cognitive-behavioral therapy, 12-step facilitation, motivational interviewing, motivational enhancement therapy, solution-focused therapy, and stages of change work have greatly increased. These have created more options for those who, in bygone decades, would have been turned away from addiction care as being "not ready for treatment" or "in denial." They would have been viewed as in need of coerced intensive treatment, sometimes in long length of stay residential services, until they demonstrated that they were sufficiently "motivated for recovery." Level 1 now is seen as appropriate for individuals who are assessed as having high severity in Dimension 4 (not manifesting much interest or internal motivation for recovery) but not high severity in other dimensions.

Level 1 services can be particularly effective for individuals with co-occurring conditions in a variety of health or mental health settings, who can be engaged in receiving help for one issue (eg, depression, hepatitis C, avoiding incarceration, or even focusing on keeping their children, a job, a relationship, or staying in school), while receiving integrated motivational interventions to move through the stages of change for their co-occurring substance use, or mental or physical health issues. The expansion of the use of Level 1 thus can enhance access to care and facilitate earlier engagement of patients in treatment, thereby allowing better utilization of resources and improving the effectiveness of recovery efforts.

Level 1 services include not only a point of entry into initiating treatment and recovery for a substance-related disorder, but also an alternative to entering the treatment continuum at an inappropriately more intensive level of service. Level 1 services are the backbone of ongoing care for addiction and related conditions: the psychosocial counseling and/or medication management that follows stabilization of an acute phase of addiction, which is often established at a more intensive level of care.

For those persons with addiction who have a chronic disease with a characteristic pattern of relapse and remission, Level 1 encompasses relapse prevention and ongoing coping skills services offered over time to individuals and affected family members. Moreover, in other areas of health care (oncology, cardiology, etc.) it is considered appropriate to arrange periodic monitoring visits to assess the state of remission for a condition prone to recurrence. In addiction care, this has been seen in ongoing management for persons working in safety-sensitive occupations (eg, health professionals). Such professionals may be required by a licensure board to have quarterly visits, even while in remission (and especially to confirm the state of remission, using laboratory data to support periodic clinical contacts).

Level 1 addiction services are appropriate for any patient after an episode of intensive addiction care (Level 2, 3, or 4). In the future, the use of periodic monitoring via drug testing of all patients may become more commonplace in Level 1 treatment planning. Chronic disease management should be the foundation of care planning for persons who engage in treatment services at more intensive levels of care. In every instance, such patients should be linked to Level 1 care at the appropriate point in time to continue their engagement in recovery activities beyond the intensive treatment experience.

Level 2: Intensive Outpatient/Partial Hospitalization Services

Level 2 encompasses services that are capable of meeting the complex needs of people with addiction and co-occurring conditions. It is an organized outpatient service that delivers treatment services during the day, before or after work or school, in the evening, and/or on weekends. For appropriately selected patients, such programs provide essential education and treatment components while allowing patients to apply their newly acquired skills within "real world" environments. Programs have the capacity to arrange for medical and psychiatric consultation, psychopharmacological consultation, addiction medication management, and 24-hour crisis services, if those services are not already designed to be components of the Level 2 service.

Level 2 programs provide comprehensive biopsychosocial assessments and individualized service plans, and can address multiple co-occurring issues, including formulation of problem or need statements, measurable treatment goals and specific strategies and methods—all developed in collaboration with the patient. Such programs should have active affiliations with other levels of addiction care, ideally seamlessly integrated, and their staff can help patients access recovery support services such as child care, vocational training, and transportation. Level 2 programs can offer direct physician services for physical exams and mental status exams. They also can collaborate with general medical or mental health service providers. Through coordinated care, patients can have their general medical or mental health needs assessed or concurrently managed while the patient is participating in the Level 2 service for their substance-related disorder.

Level 2 encompasses two levels of intensity:
Level 2.1: Intensive Outpatient (IOP) Services
Level 2.5: Partial Hospitalization (PHP) Services

Level 3: Residential/Inpatient Services

Level 3 encompasses residential services that are described as co-occurring capable, co-occurring enhanced, and complexity capable services (see definitions provided in Chapter 2), which are staffed by designated addiction treatment, mental health, and general medical personnel who provide a range of services in a 24-hour treatment setting. Such services adhere to defined sets of policies and procedures. They are housed in permanent facilities where patients can reside safely, and are staffed 24 hours a day to provide whatever clinical services are necessary. Mutual and self-help group meetings generally are available on-site.

Level 3 encompasses four different levels of intensity:

RENAMED LEVEL 3.3

In this edition, Level 3.3 has been renamed and changed from its original description as "Clinically Managed Medium-Intensity Residential Treatment." Level 3.3 was always intended to be a setting to meet the needs of people with cognitive difficulties, who could not make use of the more intensive Level 3.5 milieu, hence its previous name of "medium" intensity. However, some understandably misinterpreted Level 3.3 to be a step-down residential level, when it is intended to be qualitatively different from the other levels of care within Level 3. Thus, treatment is specific to persons with cognitive difficulties needing more specialized individualized services. The cognitive impairments manifested in patients most appropriately treated in Level 3.3 services can be due to aging, traumatic brain injury, acute but lasting injury, or due to illness.

The rationale for naming this level of care is not that patients in Level 3.3 are at "less severe" risk than those in Level 3.5 or 3.7. Rather, the decimal point relates to the intensity of services. Since patients with cognitive difficulties cannot tolerate or make use of the full intensity of Level 3.5 and need a slower pace and lower intensity of services, the designation of 3.3 is assigned.

Level 3.1: Clinically Managed Low-Intensity Residential Services

Level 3.3: Clinically Managed Population-Specific High-Intensity Residential Services (not designated for adolescent populations)

Level 3.5: Clinically Managed High-Intensity Residential Services (Adult Criteria)

Level 3.5: Clinically Managed Medium-Intensity Residential Services (Adolescent Criteria)

Level 3.7: Medically Monitored Intensive Inpatient Services (Adult Criteria)

Level 3.7: Medically Monitored High-Intensity Inpatient Services (Adolescent Criteria)

The defining characteristic of all Level 3 programs is that they serve individuals who need safe and stable living environments in order to stabilize their level of function and develop their recovery skills. Individuals are transferred to less intensive levels of care at the point that they have established sufficient skills to safely continue treatment without the immediate risk of relapse, continued use, or other continued problems, and are no longer in imminent danger of harm to themselves or others. Level 3 programs promote continuity of care and community reintegration through seamless and overlapping intensities of outpatient services.

Level 4: Medically Managed Intensive Inpatient Services

Level 4 programs provide 24-hour medically directed evaluation, care, and treatment of substance-related and co-occurring conditions in an acute care inpatient setting. They are staffed by designated addiction-credentialed physicians as well as other mental and general health- and addiction-credentialed clinicians. Such services are delivered under a defined set of policies and procedures and have permanent facilities that include inpatient beds. Some Level 4 programs integrate Level 4 treatment for substance use disorders with Level 4-WM withdrawal management services.

Adolescent-Specific Approaches to Sublevels of Care

Criteria sublevels are somewhat unique for adolescent populations. Moreover, there are unique intentions for certain sublevel designations. For example, sublevel 3.1 for adolescents (a group home or halfway house) is intended to convey a somewhat greater intensity of services and staffing than would a similar sublevel 3.1 program for adults. This difference reflects adolescents' greater need for supervision.

Similarly, the definition of Intensive Outpatient Services refers to a minimum of 6 hours of treatment per week for adolescents, as compared to 9 hours per week for adults. This difference reflects the developmental and attentional capacities of adolescents, for whom 6 hours of treatment (generally delivered in two sessions of 3 hours each, or three sessions of 2 hours each) falls more closely within the spectrum of Level 2 intensive outpatient services than of Level 1 outpatient services. This difference in hours in the adolescent criteria by no means implies that 6 hours is automatically sufficient or that 9 (or more) hours is excessive. Rather, it implies a range and continuum. Some programs, for example, offer 3-hour sessions two to five times per week, depending on need.

For adolescents, Level 3.5 is defined as "Clinically Managed *Medium*-intensity Residential Treatment", describing a variety of settings that provide 24-hour active monitoring and treatment, but relatively limited medical or nursing services. Adolescent populations do not define Level 3.3 because the adolescent Level 3.5 encompasses the range of adolescent treatment settings commonly employed, and the distinction between Levels 3.3 and 3.5 within this population does not have sufficient specificity in adolescent treatment to merit the added complexity of an additional level.

An adolescent Level 3.5 setting also includes subacute or step-down programs that follow stabilization at a more intensive residential setting, therapeutic community (TC) model programs, therapeutic group homes, and programs that emphasize a psychoeducational or psychosocial rehabilitation/habilitation model (in contrast to a medical model) for refractory Dimension 3 conditions such as conduct disorder, developmental difficulties, or personality vulnerabilities. While many Level 3.5 programs are freestanding, many others are provided as an internal step-down or lesser intensity track within a Level 3.7 program.

Adolescent Level 3.7 settings are defined as "Medically Monitored High-Intensity Inpatient Treatment." This describes a variety of settings that offer 24-hour active monitoring and treatment, with available medical or nursing services. Adolescent Level 3.7 also is distinguished by and often indicated for the overall high intensity of the program and treatment milieu. An adolescent patient may need Level 3.7 services for the intensity that draws on the overall staffing pattern, including the availability of various professional services to the program as a whole, and not only for specific medical or nursing services provided directly to the patient. The terms "residential" and "inpatient" are used to describe Level 3.7 programs because they often are used interchangeably in the field, whereas for Level 4 the term "inpatient" is used exclusively to denote the intensity associated with an acute hospital setting.

PLANNING/PLACEMENT

3

Level 4 programs provide co-occurring capable, co-occurring enhanced, and complexity capable care to patients whose physical, mental, and/or substance-related conditions are so severe that they require primary biomedical, addiction, or psychiatric care, along with an inpatient level of nursing and other care. Treatment is provided 24 hours a day, and the full resources of a general acute care hospital or psychiatric hospital are available. The treatment is specific to substance-related conditions. However, the skills of the interdisciplinary team and the availability of support services allow the integrated treatment of any co-occurring physical health and mental health conditions that need to be addressed. Examples include inpatient programs for co-occurring psychiatric, addiction, and related disorders staffed by a certified and/or licensed addiction psychiatrist as attending physician/medical director, or by a certified and/or licensed addiction medicine physician working conjointly with a certified and/or licensed adult or child and adolescent psychiatrist. Another example would be inpatient programs for spine injury or traumatic brain injury patients, staffed by a certified and/or licensed addiction specialist physician working conjointly with a certified and/or licensed physiatrist or neurologist, any of whom could serve as attending physician and/or medical director.

Opioid Treatment Services

Opioid Treatment Services (OTS) is an umbrella term that encompasses a variety of pharmacological and non-pharmacological treatment modalities, including the therapeutic use of specialized opioid agonist medications, such as methadone and buprenorphine, and opioid antagonist medications, such as naltrexone. OTS using opioid agonist medications are best conceptualized as services that can be provided with appropriate collaborations at many levels of care, depending on the patient's status in Dimensions 1 through 6. Adjunctive non-pharmacological psychosocial interventions are essential and may be provided in a Level 1 Outpatient Opioid Treatment Program (OTP); in Office-Based Opioid Treatment (OBOT) with buprenorphine, buprenorphine/naloxone, or naltrexone; or through coordination with other addiction and mental health treatment providers.

This section has been broadened beyond what was previously named Opioid Maintenance Therapy (OMT), which is now addressed as Level 1, Outpatient Opioid Treatment Program (OTP) within OTS.

The ASAM Criteria Software

Technology is poised to dramatically advance ASAM's criteria. Following Gastfriend et al.'s *PPC-1*-based computerized algorithm at Massachusetts General Hospital, a newer, *PPC-2R* software product was authorized by ASAM. This ASAM software was designed to implement every admission decision rule of the *PPC-2R* text, to be user-friendly, and to serve as the authorized, standard model for international implementation. After being translated into Norwegian and introduced across Norway, this software received high satisfaction ratings from both patients and counselors. In Uzbekistan, translated into both Uzbek and Russian, use of the ASAM criteria software reportedly would have increased individualization of placements.[1] Using Dutch and French translations, 201 Belgian patients who received matched or higher levels of care had significantly better 30-day global outcomes than patients who were mismatched to a lower level of care than recommended.[2]

The ASAM Criteria Software presents the opportunity, for the first time, to permit both providers and researchers throughout the field to speak the same language, and arrive at the same level of care determinations. The software includes an additional feature of confidential data uploads to an ASAM-authorized central data repository, which is facilitating aggregate analyses of patient placements, service utilizations, and clinical outcomes. This repository has two simultaneous benefits for the field. It will permit treatment programs to understand their utilization patterns and needs. At the same time, the data repository will offer research centers a precise, objective look at the validity of *The ASAM Criteria.* An ongoing field trial process is underway, reporting back to the National Coalition on Patient Placement Criteria and permitting ongoing improvement of the ASAM criteria. The result is that patients will benefit not only from the art of addiction medicine (ie, ASAM's expert consensus) but also from the science as well – driven by quantitative, empirical data.

The ASAM Criteria: Using both the book and the software

The ASAM Criteria book and *The ASAM Criteria Software* are companion text and software application. This text delineates the dimensions, requirements, and decision rules that comprise ASAM's criteria. The software provides the approved structured interview to guide the assessment and calculate the complex decision tree to yield suggested levels of care. The text and the software should be used in tandem, the text to provide the clinical background and guidance as to the decision rules in the software, and the software to enable comprehensive, standardized evaluation. Effective, reliable treatment planning for adults is enhanced by using the book and software together.

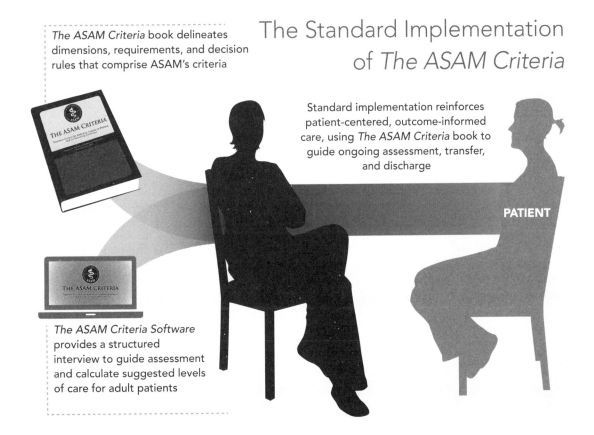

The ASAM Criteria book delineates dimensions, requirements, and decision rules that comprise ASAM's criteria

The ASAM Criteria Software provides a structured interview to guide assessment and calculate suggested levels of care for adult patients

The Standard Implementation of *The ASAM Criteria*

Standard implementation reinforces patient-centered, outcome-informed care, using *The ASAM Criteria* book to guide ongoing assessment, transfer, and discharge

PATIENT

PLANNING/PLACEMENT

3

Within this book, *The ASAM Criteria Software* is introduced here to show where it might be most effectively applied within the treatment process: as part of the comprehensive multi-dimensional assessment, performed with the knowledge and background provided in this book, in order to arrive at an appropriate level of care.

The standardized assessment built into the software covers all six ASAM dimensions. It leads to a recommended level of care placement using thousands of computer algorithm decision points that automatically rate severity and matches this severity of illness and level of function to the ASAM criteria level of care. The steps this book has described so far – ones of moving from assessment to service planning and level of care placement – are important to understand for clinical practice, whether or not one is currently using *The ASAM Criteria Software*. This book provides the conceptual framework and specific decision rules that drive the software, which then calculates standardized assessment and level of care placement suggestions.

Understanding How to Work Effectively with Managed Care and Health Care Reform

As increasing numbers of managed care companies, utilization management entities, and providers of care use *The ASAM Criteria* to guide level of care decisions, the opportunity for differences in interpretation and implementation also increases. With health care reform likely to significantly increase the number of patients who can now access addiction treatment, placement and treatment criteria will assume an even greater role in efficient and effective use of health care resources. In fact, the provision in the Affordable Care Act of 2010 that allows young adults to be covered under a parent's health plan has already resulted in significant increases in the number of young adults, without their own coverage and sometimes without their own jobs, to present to addiction service providers with a need for care.

Other implications of health care reform are referenced throughout this edition of *The ASAM Criteria*. However, as more focus is placed on health care cost containment and "bending the cost curve" (meaning decreasing the rate of increase in health care costs), it is increasingly incumbent on all parties (clinicians, provider organizations, care managers, and payers) to manage care with clinical and fiscal integrity.

Unless and until everyone is using common instrumentation with *The ASAM Criteria Software*, which allows all parties to use standardized instrumentation to implement *The ASAM Criteria*, conflicts will continue. This section provides some principles and guidance on how to improve communication and resolve conflicts over care management and placement issues. Essentially, all practitioners, counselors, clinicians, payers, and funders should be "managing care" to help preserve resources. With universal implementation of *The ASAM Criteria* continuum of care, access to care can be broadened, and resources used more efficiently and effectively to increase the length of treatment and improve outcomes.[3] This can be achieved in the following ways:

1. In discussions over authorization for an initial level of care, and in subsequent reauthorizations, patient information and clinical assessments by the treatment team

This section provides some principles and guidance on how to improve communication and resolve conflicts over care management and placement issues.

should encompass factual, biopsycho-social data. Providers should not resort to a selective skewing of clinical data to present either a more or less severe clinical picture of the patient than objective clinical data presents. Nor should they engage in maneuverings or bargaining negotiations with external utilization managers or peer-to-peer reviewers (eg, "I would like four weeks of treatment, but will you give me at least two weeks?"). Providers can feel compelled to focus on the most severe aspects of a person's health and treatment

WORKING WITH MANAGED CARE

1. In discussions over authorization for an initial level of care, and in subsequent reauthorizations, patient information and clinical assessments by the treatment team should encompass factual, biopsychosocial data.

2. A case presentation format can be used by the provider to concisely review the biopsychosocial data following the multidimensional assessment format of *The ASAM Criteria*.

3. Sequentially move through the decisional flow provided in this section to match assessment and treatment/placement assignment to guide the clinical discussion.

4. If either participant in the utilization management dialogue disagrees with the other, identify the specific area of disagreement.

5. If still no agreement or consensus is reached, providers must then activate appeal or grievance procedures.

history in order to impress the care manager of the need for treatment. In contrast, managed care reviewers can minimize this information and negotiate for fewer days or sessions than requested, and/or a less intensive level of care as an opening gambit in the utilization review conversation. Both parties should focus on an objective review of the facts and avoid posturing.

Thus, a provider needs to explain what problems and priorities in which dimensions require services, the "dose" and intensity of which can only safely be delivered in the particular level of care for which authorization of payment is sought. If the provider cannot explain specific patient information and service planning data, then authorization will likely be denied. Conversely, a care manager or utilization reviewer, if disagreeing with the level of care requested, needs to explain what problems and priorities in which dimensions require services, the "dose" and intensity of which can quite safely be delivered in a different level of care from the one for which authorization of payment was sought. If the care manager or utilization reviewer cannot explain their decision-making with patient-specific data, then the provider's request for level of care should be authorized since there is no objective clinical data or criteria to justify denial of services. (See the decisional flow chart in this section that guides clinicians and care managers through this process.)

2. A case presentation format (see sample displayed on page 125) can be used by the provider to concisely review the biopsychosocial data following the multidimensional assessment format of *The ASAM Criteria*. Focusing the discussion through preparation can result in less than five minutes required to review pertinent history and "here and now" information. In reviewing the facts to "make the case" for the level of care that

is proposed to meet the patient's needs, the intensity of service being requested for authorization should derive from the severity of illness and not on pre-assumed notions, philosophical positions, or the treatment levels available in the service portfolio of the provider organization. Use the structure built into the ASAM criteria dimensions to organize clinical data.

3. Sequentially move through the decisional flow provided in this section to match assessment and treatment/placement assignment to guide the clinical discussion. This can help identify where the points of disagreement may lie between clinicians requesting authorization and care managers initially denying such authorization. Does the difference of opinion relate to severity-of-illness rating? Which dimension of illness is considered the priority in treatment? What services are needed? What dose, frequency, and intensity of services and placement level is being proposed?

4. If either participant in the utilization management dialogue disagrees with the other, identify the specific area of disagreement. This may relate to any number of issues, including:
    The data discussed
    Alternative ways to understand/interpret the clinical data
    The severity rating and rationale
    The priority dimension or focus of treatment
    The service needed
    The dose and intensity of services

Discussion of these concerns may result in a final, collaborative decision about placement level. The final level of care is where the matching "dose" and intensity of services can be provided in the least intensive, but safe, level of care or site of care. (See decisional flow chart.)

The ASAM Criteria provides criteria that call for the least intensive level that is safe. But if on initial assessment, it is determined that the patient has such severity of illness that treatment in a less intensive level of care has already been determined to have a poor outcome; and/or the current assessment indicates that the patient's current instability and severity is such that treatment is not likely to be feasible or successful, then there are criteria that require the patient to be directly admitted to whatever level of care is safe and effective, regardless of whether it is the least intensive or not. The ASAM criteria does not support "treatment failure" criteria as a prerequisite for admission to any level of care.

5. If still no agreement or consensus is reached, providers must then activate appeal or grievance procedures.

Providers should understand exactly how the utilization management process occurs. The case manager from the external utilization management entity usually speaks not with a direct clinician but with an internal utilization management case manager from the provider entity. If there is no agreement at this level of review, the provider can (and should) request a "peer-to-peer" review, generally involving a physician employed or contracted by the managed care firm, and the attending physician representing the provider organization (clinic or treatment center).

The utilization management process is not where the "decision" is made about authorization, however. The initial case manager and the peer-to-peer reviewer only make recommendations to the managed care firm. An employee (often a medical director) at the utilization management firm then makes the decision. This is the decision which, if adverse to the clinical recommendations of the treatment team, can be "appealed" by the provider organization. This appeal can, upon the request of the service provider entity, be an "expedited appeal." Even if the "expedited appeal" is not successful, a "for-

PLANNING/PLACEMENT

3

mal appeal" can be requested (which may not be carried out until after discharge from a given care encounter).

Clinical Vignettes

Use of *The ASAM Criteria* in treatment planning involves much more than simply a decision about level of care. The assessment dimensions and the broad continuum of care surveyed by the ASAM criteria dimensions provide an opportunity to focus treatment consistent with a disease management approach that is individualized, patient centered, and recovery oriented. The following vignettes, which represent segments of comprehensive assessments, are designed to illustrate some of the more common problems encountered in determining severity of illness, developing treatment plans, and making placement decisions. Each vignette illustrates an initial response, a discussion, and a revised response.

CLINICAL VIGNETTES

CASE 1: MR. A

Mr. A is a 58-year-old male who meets diagnostic criteria for alcohol use disorder, severe. In terms of Dimension 1, he is currently in mild withdrawal from alcohol (CIWA-Ar score of 7) with a history of no more than moderate severity withdrawal. However, he stopped drinking only two hours ago after three months of five to six drinks per day. Mr. A is hypertensive by history, it is not well controlled with medication even when sober, and current blood pressure is 140/100. Severity in Dimensions 3 through 6 is low because he has no significant mental health needs (Dim. 3), he is interested in treatment (Dim. 4), and while he has been drinking for three months, he has now stopped and is able to use previous relapse prevention skills and supports in his environment to prevent immediate return to drinking (Dims. 5 and 6).

INITIAL RESPONSE

Based on only mild withdrawal severity in Dimension 1, Mr. A is referred for Level 1-WM, Ambulatory Withdrawal Management without Extended On-Site Monitoring. For his Dimension 2 problem, he is referred back to his primary care physician for review of his hypertension.

DISCUSSION

Given that Mr. A is withdrawing from alcohol, a sedative drug, the resultant autonomic arousal will create an increase in blood pressure. His current blood pressure reading is only two hours since his last drink and insufficient time has elapsed for the full withdrawal syndrome to develop. It can be assumed that the autonomic arousal could markedly increase his blood pressure and, because his baseline blood pressure is already elevated, the interaction between Dimension 1 and 2 increases his overall severity.

REVISED RESPONSE

Because of the high severity resulting from the interaction between Dimensions 1 and 2, Mr. A should be treated in Level 3.7-WM, Medically Monitored Inpatient Withdrawal Management service. An alternative might be referral to a Level 2-WM, Ambulatory Withdrawal Management with Extended On-Site Monitoring if Mr. A enters treatment early in the week and could be observed for a number of days; or if the Level 2-WM service operates seven days a week.

CASE 2: MS. P

A 16-year-old female is brought to the emergency department of an acute care hospital with a report that, in the course of an argument with her parents, she has thrown a chair. Her parents suspect drug intoxication is a significant contributing factor. They report that she has been staying out unusually late at night and mixing with "the wrong crowd." They also report a great deal of family discord, anger, and frustration, particularly directed by the young woman toward her father. Ms. P has no history of psychiatric or addiction treatment.

The parents both are present in the emergency department, although Ms. P is brought in by the police after her mother called for help. An emergency physician and a nurse from the psychiatric unit jointly evaluate Ms. P; they agree that she needs to be hospitalized in light of the animosity at home, her violent behavior, and the possibility that she is using an unknown drug.

Following the ASAM criteria assessment dimensions, they organize the clinical information as follows:

Dimension 1: Acute Intoxication and/or Withdrawal Potential: Although she was intoxicated at the time of the chair-throwing incident, Ms. P no longer is intoxicated and has not been using alcohol or other drugs in sufficient quantities or for a long enough period of time to suggest the possibility of a withdrawal syndrome.

Dimension 2: Biomedical Conditions and Complications: Ms. P is not taking any medications, is physically healthy, and has no current complaints.

Dimension 3: Emotional, Behavioral, or Cognitive Conditions and Complications: Ms. P has complex problems with anger management, as evidenced by the chair-throwing incident, but is not impulsive at present if separated from her parents, especially her father.

Dimension 4: Readiness to Change: Ms. P is willing to talk to a therapist, blames her parents for being overbearing and not trusting her, and agrees to come to treatment, but does not want to be at home with her father.

Dimension 5: Relapse, Continued Use, or Continued Problem Potential: The team concludes that Ms. P is likely to engage in drug use if released. They believe that, if she returns home immediately, there may be a recurrence of the fighting and, possibly, violence.

Dimension 6: Recovery Environment: Ms. P's parents are frustrated and angry as well. They are mistrustful of their daughter and want her hospitalized to provide a break in the family fighting.

INITIAL RESPONSE

Based on Ms. P's recent history of violent acting out, the emergency physician and the psychiatric nurse recommend that she be admitted to the hospital's psychiatric unit, at least for the night.

DISCUSSION

Ms. P's acting out occurred when she was intoxicated, but she is no longer under the influence. The major conflict appears to be a family issue, particularly between Ms. P and her father. There is no indication of a severe or imminently dangerous biomedical, emotional, behavioral, or cognitive problem that requires the resources of a medically managed intensive inpatient setting.

REVISED RESPONSE

The initial goal is to separate Ms. P from her father, which might be done by arranging for Ms. P to stay with a relative or family friend overnight, or by having Ms. P and her mother stay at a motel for the night. Based on the available information, Ms. P's behavior and conflict with her parents may reflect normal adolescent struggles rather than psychopathology. To address this, outpatient family counseling should be considered. Given the information available, there is also nothing indicating that Ms. P suffers from a diagnosable substance use disorder.

In crisis or mandated treatment situations, clinicians often come under pressure from family or referral agencies to provide a certain level of care. However, when the essential information is organized according to the ASAM criteria dimensions, the patient's real severity and needs are more easily identified. This leads to a more appropriate clinical plan and avoids wasteful use of resources by focusing on the services needed to meet the patient's individual needs.

PLANNING/PLACEMENT

Decisional Flow to Match Assessment and Treatment/Placement Assignment

To guide clinical evaluation and discussion, sequentially move through the following decisional flow to match assessment and treatment/placement assignment. If disagreement occurs with another member of the treatment team or a care manager or utilization reviewer, work through this flow to identify which steps there is clinical agreement on and which steps are in question.

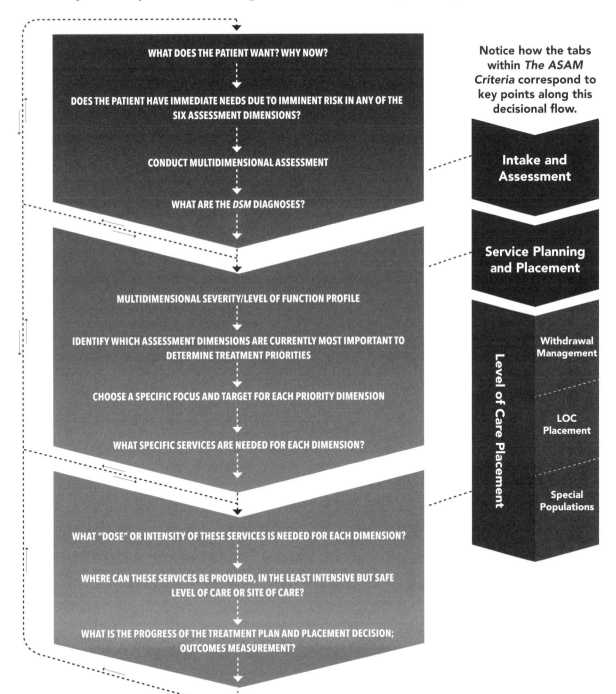

WHAT DOES THE PATIENT WANT? WHY NOW?

DOES THE PATIENT HAVE IMMEDIATE NEEDS DUE TO IMMINENT RISK IN ANY OF THE SIX ASSESSMENT DIMENSIONS?

CONDUCT MULTIDIMENSIONAL ASSESSMENT

WHAT ARE THE *DSM* DIAGNOSES?

MULTIDIMENSIONAL SEVERITY/LEVEL OF FUNCTION PROFILE

IDENTIFY WHICH ASSESSMENT DIMENSIONS ARE CURRENTLY MOST IMPORTANT TO DETERMINE TREATMENT PRIORITIES

CHOOSE A SPECIFIC FOCUS AND TARGET FOR EACH PRIORITY DIMENSION

WHAT SPECIFIC SERVICES ARE NEEDED FOR EACH DIMENSION?

WHAT "DOSE" OR INTENSITY OF THESE SERVICES IS NEEDED FOR EACH DIMENSION?

WHERE CAN THESE SERVICES BE PROVIDED, IN THE LEAST INTENSIVE BUT SAFE LEVEL OF CARE OR SITE OF CARE?

WHAT IS THE PROGRESS OF THE TREATMENT PLAN AND PLACEMENT DECISION; OUTCOMES MEASUREMENT?

Notice how the tabs within *The ASAM Criteria* correspond to key points along this decisional flow.

Intake and Assessment

Service Planning and Placement

Level of Care Placement

Withdrawal Management

LOC Placement

Special Populations

PLANNING/PLACEMENT

③

CASE PRESENTATION FORMAT

This case presentation format can be used by the provider to concisely review the biopsychosocial data following the multidimensional assessment format of *The ASAM Criteria*.

Case Presentation Format

Before presenting the case, please state why you chose the case and what you want to get from the discussion (eg, authorization of care, supervisory assistance, success story of an effective outcome, etc.). _____

_____

I. Identifying patient background data

Name _____

Age _____

Ethnicity and gender identification _____

Marital status _____

Employment status _____

Referral source _____

Date entered treatment or appeared for an assessment _____

Level of service patient entered treatment
(IF THIS CASE PRESENTATION IS A TREATMENT PLAN REVIEW) _____

Current level of service
(IF THIS CASE PRESENTATION IS A TREATMENT PLAN REVIEW) _____

DSM diagnoses _____

_____

Stated or identified motivation for treatment (What is the most important thing the patient wants you to help them with?)

_____

II. Current dimensional rating of severity and level of function using high, medium, or low severity; or 0 to 4 ratings

First state how severe you think each assessment ASAM criteria dimension is and why. Give a brief explanation for each rating. Focus on brief relevant history information and relevant here and now information. If a review of a current patient's progress, note whether it has changed since the patient entered treatment and why or why not.

1. _____
2. _____
3. _____
4. _____
5. _____
6. _____

III. What problem(s) with high and medium severity ratings are of greatest concern at this time?

Specificity of the problem or priority _____

Specificity of the strategies/interventions (consider strengths, skills, and resources) _____

_____

Efficiency of the intervention (least intensive, but safe, level of service) _____

_____

In an era of health care reform, it is the responsibility of all (counselors, clinicians, administrators, payers, funders, and care managers) to "manage care" and use scarce resources as efficiently and effectively as possible. Such stewardship of resources can help increase access to care and lengths of stay in the continuum of services and thus improve outcomes.

Gathering Data to Promote Systems Change

In the application of the ASAM criteria there frequently are times that a level of care or service is not available, not funded, or not easily accessed. Other systems issues impact the ability for patients to receive the clinically assessed service or level of care. Policy, payment, and systems issues cannot change quickly. However, as a first step toward reframing frustrating situations into systems change, each incident of inefficient or inadequate meeting of a patient's needs can be a data point that sets the foundation for strategic planning and change.

A method for efficiently gathering data as it happens in daily care of patients can help provide hope and direction for change. The options for "Reason for Difference" and the "Anticipated Outcomes if Service Cannot Be Provided" should be individualized to reflect local people and systems issues. The following are provided as common examples of people and systems issues.

DATA GATHERING TO PROMOTE SYSTEMS CHANGE

Level of Care/Service Indicated

Insert the ASAM criteria level number that offers the most efficient and effective level of care/service that can provide the service intensity needed to address the patient's current functioning/severity, eg, Level 2.1-WM or 3.2-WM; and/or the service needed, eg, shelter, housing, vocational training, transportation, or language interpreter.

Level of Care/Service Received - ASAM Criteria Level Number

If the most efficient and effective level or service is not utilized, insert the level of care or service available and actually received, and circle the Reason for Difference between Indicated and Received Level or Service below.

Reason for Difference Between Indicated and Received Level or Service

Circle only one number:

1. Service not available
2. Provider judgment
3. Patient preference
4. Patient is on waiting list for appropriate level
5. Service available, but no payment source

6. Geographic accessibility
7. Family responsibility
8. Language
9. Not applicable
10. Not listed (specify):

Anticipated Outcomes If Service Cannot Be Provided

Circle only one number:

1. Admitted to acute care setting
2. Discharged to street
3. Continued stay in acute care facility

4. Incarcerated
5. Patient will dropout until next crisis
6. Not listed (specify):

Addressing Withdrawal Management

and Intoxication Management

The ASAM Criteria describes various levels of care for withdrawal management for adults as if these services were offered separately from whatever services a patient may need to manage their addiction (substance use disorder). In many cases, services for withdrawal management and services for addiction management are offered concurrently, by the same staff, in the same treatment setting, in an integrated manner. But in making decisions about the clinical necessity of offering specific interventions to address intoxication or withdrawal, *The ASAM Criteria* "unbundles" services (at least conceptually) and examines the features of a patient's clinical presentation which may indicate specific interventions for "detoxification" – now termed "withdrawal management."

The widely used general term of "detoxification" can involve management of intoxication episodes and withdrawal episodes. Adults, at various points in time, may be in need of intoxication management and may be in need of withdrawal management, in addition to management of their substance use disorder. Adolescents are more frequently in need of management for intoxication episodes than management for withdrawal syndromes.

NOTE

This section presents withdrawal management information for adult patient populations. By contrast, withdrawal management information for adolescent patients is found within the appropriate level of care.

The process of withdrawal management includes not only attenuation of the physiological and psychological features of withdrawal, but also interrupting the momentum of habitual compulsive use in persons with addiction. Thus, a person admitted for withdrawal management is also receiving professional services that can serve to "break the cycle" of use and enable the patient to establish the first day(s) of abstinence and to be evaluated for the need for further care. The time spent in withdrawal manage-ment is a time of critical importance for initial engagement in addiction management services when treatment for a diagnosed substance use disorder or gambling disorder is indicated. Because of the force of the momentum of habitual compulsive use and the difficulties inherent in overcoming it (even when there is no clear physiological withdrawal syndrome *per se*), this phase of treatment often requires a greater intensity of services to establish initial treatment engagement and patient role induction.

Adolescent-Specific Considerations: Integrated Withdrawal Management Approach

The approach to management of intoxication and withdrawal for adolescent populations is unique. The authors of *The ASAM Criteria* believe a more integrated approach is preferable for adolescents, because severe physiological withdrawal is seen less often in adolescents than in adults. Therefore, the provision of adolescent withdrawal management as an "unbundled" or stand-alone service is less common and less needed. In this publication, withdrawal management information for adolescent patients appears in the description of each level of care (Levels 1, 2, 3, 4) for management of the adolescent's substance use disorder itself. Nevertheless, withdrawal syndromes do occur at times in adolescents and should not be overlooked. In cases where physiological withdrawal is present and its management is necessary, services are ideally provided in the same setting where adolescents are receiving substance use disorder care because of the developmental issues involved in the care of adolescents.

Events occurring during withdrawal management are particularly critical to the success of treatment for adolescents because it is difficult, if not impossible, for an adolescent to engage or participate in treatment while he or she is caught up in a cycle of intoxication and recovery from intoxication.

Introduction to Withdrawal Management

When a person's substance use disorder has progressed to the point that physical dependence has developed, withdrawal management becomes the first (but not the sole) priority in treatment planning. The onset of a physical withdrawal syndrome, uncomfortable and potentially dangerous, arguably provides an unparalleled opportunity to engage a patient in what will hopefully be sustained recovery.

Because current withdrawal management protocols can relieve withdrawal symptoms so quickly and effectively, counseling and therapy focused on initiation or resumption of recovery *can be instituted at the same time as withdrawal management*, rather than being delayed.

Although withdrawal management has historically been considered an inpatient procedure, current medication protocols now allow all

GOAL OF THIS SECTION

The goal of this section is to help determine the most effective, least intensive setting in which

1. The withdrawal syndrome can be managed safely and comfortably

2. The adult patient can be engaged in continued treatment that will lead to a sustained recovery from addiction

but the most severe withdrawal syndromes to be managed effectively on an ambulatory basis.[1,2,3,4] One great advantage of the ambulatory setting is that the simultaneous engagement in ongoing recovery treatment is much more feasible than when the withdrawal is managed in a general hospital where other addiction-specific services are not offered.

Continuing withdrawal support at less intensive levels of withdrawal management is critical because persisting discomforts from post-acute withdrawal can lead patients to return to substance use. Furthermore, for patients with long-term, high-dose benzodiazepine use, there may also be the continued risk of seizures.

Health maintenance and population health management, especially under recent health reforms, require that health care providers attend not only to stabilizing and resolving acute symptoms, but also to minimizing the potential for readmission to intensive levels of service, such as re-hospitalizations. For withdrawal management services, this means respect for the chronic disease nature of addiction as well as assuring secure care transitions to ongoing post-withdrawal services to meet the patient's particular addiction, general medical, and mental health treatment needs.

Put another way, a "successful detox" encounter involves more than acute management of withdrawal. It involves engagement in services to address the accompanying addiction process and thus reduce the likelihood of "readmission for detox." Integrated systems of care which are accountable (financially and otherwise) for health outcomes will be highly motivated to use the withdrawal management encounter as an opportunity to identify cases of addiction that need to be treated and otherwise may have escaped identification.

WITHDRAWAL
MANAGEMENT

4

CHANGES IN DIMENSION 1 CRITERIA FROM *PPC-2R* (2001)

CONTENT

The term "detoxification" has been changed from prior editions of the ASAM criteria, as these services are more accurately described as "intoxication management" and "withdrawal management," to contrast them with the "addiction management" services described in all other chapters in *The ASAM Criteria*.

This edition expands the severity range of withdrawal syndromes that can be safely and appropriately managed on an outpatient basis.

The risk rating assessment format is used in the first part of this chapter to help understand how to link severity, function, and service needs, across all six assessment dimensions to treatment plans and level of care decisions.

In this edition, the assessment discussion is organized by each class of substance. While ASAM views addiction as a unitary condition, withdrawal syndromes are separate from each other depending on the pharmacological class of the substance the individual may be withdrawing from, and interventions differ accordingly.

The first part of this chapter provides guidance in withdrawal management. It is designed to help users understand the clinical thinking underlying the full, detailed decision rules, which follow in the second part of this chapter. It is the detailed decision rules that comprise the algebra contained in *The ASAM Criteria Software*. The detailed decision rules are necessarily complex, but they are internal to the design of the software and not visible to users of the criteria or its accompanying software. The first part of this chapter provides the conceptual model for understanding clinical processes of care when patients experience acute withdrawal and are particularly useful to professionals who are not yet using *The ASAM Criteria Software* in their day-to-day work.

FORMAT

In an effort to make this complex material readable, the first part of this chapter presents content in a mostly narrative, summary format, while in the second part, the chapter provides the detailed tabular decision rules.

In the first part, the dimensional admission criteria have been separated out by substance class because of their complexity and the need to address the differences in managing withdrawal syndromes from different substances.

In the second part, the dimensional admission criteria for Dimension 1, beginning on page 165, organized by substance class, have been retained in tabular format to convey how severity compares across the five levels of withdrawal management. These tables of detailed admission criteria decision rules illustrate how medical necessity for withdrawal management is determined in *The ASAM Criteria Software*.

WITHDRAWAL MANAGEMENT

4

Treatment Levels and Comparison of Withdrawal Management Services

*T*he *ASAM Criteria* matches a patient's severity of illness along Dimension 1 with five intensities of withdrawal management service: Level 1-WM, Level 2-WM, Level 3.2-WM, Level 3.7-WM, and Level 4-WM. The qualifier "WM" designates a withdrawal management service within the broad division (such as Level 3.2-WM, Clinically Managed Residential Withdrawal Management services or Social Setting Withdrawal Management).

In the adult criteria, a particular withdrawal management service can be provided separately ("unbundled") from other treatment services. When such services are provided separately, a sufficiently comprehensive biopsychosocial screening assessment and linkage to addiction management services is essential to avoid the circumstance in which patients revolve through acute care facilities in repeated cycles of acute stabilization and relapse (the "revolving door syndrome").

For withdrawal management provided in conjunction with treatment for co-occurring conditions identified in the comprehensive biopsycho-social screening assessment, *The ASAM Criteria* calls for the patient to be placed in the level of care appropriate to the most acute problem.

While *The ASAM Criteria* describes five levels of withdrawal management, staffing at any given level may be structured to provide a range of intensities of service. For example, withdrawal management of some patients can be carried out in the office (Level 1-WM) or in more structured outpatient settings (Level 2-WM) without the use of beds or intensive nursing monitoring. Intensive medical monitoring is required for Level 2-WM because the patients are at risk rating scores of 2 and 3, indicating moderate to significant risk in withdrawal. Other patients may need to be monitored for a period of time before an appropriate determination can be made. (Such monitoring can, at times, be carried out in what is technically considered an outpatient setting, but may require an even more structured service, such as a "23-hour observation bed.") Some withdrawal management programs that are described as Level 3 may have

SERVICE CHARACTERISTIC CATEGORIES

In *The ASAM Criteria*, the following categories of service characteristics will deliver example and appropriate information for each withdrawal management level of care:

 Examples of Service Delivery and Settings

 Support Systems

 Staff

 Therapies

 Assessment/Treatment Plan Review

 Documentation

 Diagnostic Admission Criteria

 Dimensional Admission Criteria

the capacity for more or less intensive medical monitoring of withdrawal management. For example, Level 3.2-WM social setting withdrawal management may provide only minimal medical monitoring, while a Level 3.7-WM withdrawal management service includes significant medical monitoring.

The number of hours allocated to other treatment services (eg, recovery counseling) at Level 1 and Level 2 is separate from, and does not include, those to be allocated for withdrawal management in an ambulatory setting. Hence the intensity of withdrawal management services need not match the intensity of other treatment services in Level 1 or Level 2.

DIAGNOSTIC ADMISSION CRITERIA
The same diagnostic criteria apply to **all** levels of withdrawal management (WM)

care, with two exceptions. All patients who are appropriately placed in any level (1-WM through 4-WM) of withdrawal management meet the diagnostic criteria for substance withdrawal disorder of the current *Diagnostic and Statistical Manual of Mental Disorders* of the American Psychiatric Association or other standardized and widely accepted criteria, as well as the dimensional criteria for admission.

The only exceptions, however, are that in the case of Levels 1-WM and 2-WM, for patients whose presenting alcohol or other drug history is inadequate to substantiate such a diagnosis, information provided by collateral parties (such as family members or a legal guardian) can indicate a high probability of such a diagnosis, subject to confirmation by further evaluation.

Level 1-WM: Ambulatory Withdrawal Management without Extended On-Site Monitoring

Level 1-WM withdrawal management is an organized outpatient service, which may be delivered in an office setting, a health care or addiction treatment facility, or in a patient's home by trained clinicians who provide medically supervised evaluation, withdrawal management, and referral services according to a predetermined schedule. Services are provided in regularly scheduled sessions and should be delivered under a defined set of policies and procedures or medical protocols.

EXAMPLES OF SERVICE DELIVERY
Physician's office or home health care agency.

SUPPORT SYSTEMS
In Level 1-WM withdrawal management, support systems feature the following:

a. Availability of specialized psychological and psychiatric consultation and

supervision for biomedical, emotional, behavioral, and cognitive problems as indicated.

b. Ability to obtain a comprehensive medical history and physical examination of the patient at admission.

c. Affiliation with other levels of care, including other levels of specialty addiction treatment, for additional problems identified through a comprehensive biopsychosocial assessment.

d. Ability to conduct and/or arrange for appropriate laboratory and toxicology tests, which can be point-of-care testing.

e. 24-hour access to emergency medical consultation services should such services become indicated.

f. Ability to provide or assist in accessing transportation services for patients who lack safe transportation.

STAFF

Level 1-WM withdrawal management services are staffed by physicians and nurses, who are essential to this type of service, although they need not be present in the treatment setting at all times. (In states where physician assistants or nurse practitioners are licensed as physician extenders, they may perform the duties designated for a physician under collaborative agreements or other requirements of the medical practice act in the given jurisdiction.)

Because Level 1-WM withdrawal management is conducted on an outpatient basis, it is important for medical and nursing personnel to be readily available to evaluate and confirm that withdrawal management in the less supervised setting is relatively safe. (These services are distinguished from Level 3.2-WM services.) Physicians do not need to be certified as addiction specialist physicians and nurses do not need to be certified as addiction nurses, but training and experience in assessing and managing intoxication and withdrawal states is, of course, necessary.

The services of counselors, psychologists, and social workers may be available through the withdrawal management service, or may be accessed through affiliation with other entities providing Level 1 services.

All clinicians who assess and treat patients are able to obtain and interpret information regarding the needs of these persons, and are knowledgeable about the biopsychosocial dimensions of alcohol, tobacco, and other substance use disorders. Such knowledge includes the signs and symptoms of alcohol and other drug intoxication and withdrawal, as well as the appropriate treatment and monitoring of those conditions and how to facilitate the individual's entry into ongoing care.

THERAPIES

Therapies offered by Level 1-WM withdrawal management services include individual assessment, medication or non-medication methods of withdrawal management, patient education, non-pharmacological clinical support, involvement of family members or significant others in the withdrawal management process, and discharge or transfer planning, including referral for counseling and involvement in community recovery support groups.

Therapies also include physician and/or nurse monitoring, assessment, and management of signs and symptoms of intoxication and withdrawal.

ASSESSMENT/TREATMENT PLAN REVIEW

In Level 1-WM withdrawal management programs, elements of the assessment and treatment plan review include:

a. An addiction-focused history, obtained as part of the initial assessment and conducted by or reviewed by a physician during the admission process.

b. A physical examination by a physician, physician assistant, or nurse practitioner, performed within a reasonable time frame as part of the initial assessment.

c. Sufficient biopsychosocial screening assessments to determine the level of care in which the person should be placed and for the individualized care plan to address treatment priorities identified in Dimensions 2 through 6.

d. An individualized treatment plan, including problem identification in Dimensions 2 through 6 and development of treatment goals and measurable treatment objectives, as well as activities designed to meet those objectives as they apply to the management of the withdrawal syndrome.

e. Daily assessment of progress during withdrawal management and any

WITHDRAWAL MANAGEMENT

4

treatment changes (or less frequent, if the severity of withdrawal is sufficiently mild or stable).

f.   Transfer/discharge planning, beginning at the point of admission to Level 1-WM services.

g.   Referral and linking arrangements for counseling, medical, psychiatric, and continuing care.

DOCUMENTATION

Documentation standards of Level 1-WM services include progress notes in the patient record that clearly reflect implementation of the treatment plan and the patient's response to treatment, as well as subsequent amendments to the plan.

Withdrawal rating scale tables and flow sheets (which may include tabulation of vital signs) are used as needed.

Length of Service/Continued Service and Discharge Criteria

The patient continues in Level 1-WM withdrawal management services until:

1. Withdrawal signs and symptoms are sufficiently resolved that he or she can participate in self-directed recovery or ongoing treatment without the need for further medical or nursing withdrawal management monitoring; or,

2. The patient's signs and symptoms of withdrawal have failed to respond to treatment, and have intensified such that transfer to a more intensive level of withdrawal management service is indicated; or,

3. The patient is unable to complete withdrawal management at Level 1-WM, despite an adequate trial. For example, he or she is experiencing intense craving and evidences insufficient coping skills to prevent continued alcohol, tobacco, and/or other drug use concurrent with the withdrawal management medication, indicating a need for more intensive services (such as addition of a supportive living environment).

WITHDRAWAL MANAGEMENT

4

Level 2-WM: Ambulatory Withdrawal Management with Extended On-Site Monitoring

Level 2-WM withdrawal management is an organized service, which may be delivered in an office setting, a general health care or mental health care facility, or an addiction treatment facility by medical and nursing professionals who provide evaluation, withdrawal management, and referral services. Services are provided in regularly scheduled sessions and under a defined set of physician-approved policies and physician-monitored procedures or clinical protocols.

EXAMPLES OF SERVICE DELIVERY

Day hospital service.

SUPPORT SYSTEMS

In Level 2-WM withdrawal management, support systems feature:

a.   Availability of specialized clinical consultation and supervision for biomedical, emotional, behavioral, and cognitive problems.

b.   Ability to obtain a comprehensive medical history and physical examination of the patient at admission.

c. Access to psychological and psychiatric consultation.

d. Affiliation with other levels of care, including other levels of specialty addiction treatment, as well as general and psychiatric services for additional problems identified through a comprehensive biopsychosocial assessment.

e. Ability to conduct and/or arrange for appropriate laboratory and toxicology tests, which can be point-of-care testing.

f. 24-hour access to emergency medical consultation services, should such services become indicated.

g. Ability to provide or assist in accessing transportation services for patients who lack safe transportation.

STAFF

Level 2-WM withdrawal management programs are staffed by physicians and nurses, although they need not be present at all times. (In states where physician assistants or nurse practitioners are licensed as physician extenders, they may perform the duties designated for a physician under collaborative agreements or other requirements of the medical practice act in the given jurisdiction.)

Because Level 2-WM withdrawal management is conducted on an outpatient basis, it is important for medical and nursing personnel to be readily available to evaluate and confirm that withdrawal management in the less supervised setting is safe. Physicians do not need to be certified as addiction specialist physicians and nurses do not need to be certified as addiction nurses, but training and experience in assessing and managing intoxication and withdrawal states is necessary.

The services of counselors, psychologists, and social workers may be available through the withdrawal management service or may be accessed through affiliation with entities providing other Level 2 services.

All clinicians who assess and treat patients are able to obtain and interpret information regarding the needs of these persons, and are knowledgeable about the biopsychosocial dimensions of alcohol and other drug addiction. Such knowledge includes the signs and symptoms of alcohol and other drug intoxication and withdrawal, as well as the appropriate treatment and monitoring of those conditions and how to facilitate entry into ongoing care.

THERAPIES

Therapies offered by Level 2-WM withdrawal management programs include individual assessment, medication or non-medication methods of withdrawal management, patient education, non-pharmacological clinical support, involvement of family members or significant others in the withdrawal management process, and discharge or transfer planning, including referral for counseling and involvement in community recovery support groups.

Therapies also include physician and/or nurse monitoring, assessment, and management of signs and symptoms of intoxication and withdrawal.

ASSESSMENT/TREATMENT PLAN REVIEW

In Level 2-WM withdrawal management services, elements of the assessment and treatment plan review include:

a. An addiction-focused history, obtained as part of the initial assessment and reviewed by a physician during the admission process.

b. A physical examination by a physician, physician assistant, or nurse practitioner within a reasonable time frame as part of the initial assessment.

c. Sufficient biopsychosocial screening assessments to determine the level of care in which the patient should be placed for the individualized care plan to address treatment priorities identified in Dimensions 2 through 6.

d. An individualized treatment plan, including problem identification in Dimensions 2 through 6 and development of treatment goals and measurable treatment objectives and activities designed to meet those objectives as they apply to the management of the withdrawal syndrome.

e. Daily assessment of progress during withdrawal management and any treatment changes.

f. Discharge/transfer planning, beginning at admission.

g. Referral arrangements, made as needed.

h. Serial medical assessments, using appropriate measures of withdrawal.

DOCUMENTATION
Documentation standards of Level 2-WM services include progress notes in the patient record that clearly reflect implementation of the treatment plan and the patient's response to treatment, as well as subsequent amendments to the plan.

Withdrawal rating scale tables and flow sheets (which may include tabulation of vital signs) are used as needed.

Length of Service/Continued Service and Discharge Criteria
The patient continues in Level 2-WM withdrawal management services until:

1. Withdrawal signs and symptoms are sufficiently resolved that he or she can be safely managed at a less intensive level of care; or,

2. The patient's signs and symptoms of withdrawal have failed to respond to treatment and have intensified (as confirmed by higher scores on the CIWA-Ar or other comparable standardized scoring system), such that transfer to a more intensive level of withdrawal management service is indicated; or,

3. The patient is unable to complete withdrawal management at Level 2-WM, despite an adequate trial. For example, he or she is experiencing intense craving and has insufficient coping skills to prevent continued alcohol or other drug use, indicating a need for more intensive services.

Level 3-WM: Residential/Inpatient Withdrawal Management

Criteria are provided for two types of Level 3 Withdrawal Management programs: Level 3.2-WM (Clinically Managed Residential Withdrawal Management) and Level 3.7-WM (Medically Monitored Inpatient Withdrawal Management). The "residential" level of care has, in the past, been synonymous with rehabilitation services, whereas withdrawal management services and the "inpatient" level of care have been synonymous with acute inpatient hospital care. With the increased availability and utilization

of Medically Monitored Inpatient Withdrawal Management services, the terms "residential" and "inpatient" are being used more broadly to contrast ambulatory ("outpatient") withdrawal management with non-ambulatory ("residential" or "inpatient") withdrawal management services. The difference between these two types of Level 3-WM programs is the intensity of clinical services, particularly as demonstrated by the degree of involvement of medical and nursing professionals.

WITHDRAWAL MANAGEMENT

4

Level 3.2-WM: Clinically Managed Residential Withdrawal Management

Level 3.2-WM Clinically Managed Residential Withdrawal Management (sometimes referred to as "social setting detoxification" or "social detox.") is an organized service that may be delivered by appropriately trained staff, who provide 24-hour supervision, observation, and support for patients who are intoxicated or experiencing withdrawal. This level is characterized by its emphasis on peer and social support rather than medical and nursing care. This level provides care for patients whose intoxication/ withdrawal signs and symptoms are sufficiently severe to require 24-hour structure and support; however, the full resources of a Level 3.7-WM, Medically Monitored Inpatient Withdrawal Management service are not necessary.

Some programs are staffed to supervise self-administered medications for the management of withdrawal. All programs at this level rely on established clinical protocols to identify patients who are in need of medical services beyond the capacity of the facility and to transfer such patients to more appropriate levels of care.

EXAMPLES OF SERVICE DELIVERY
Social setting withdrawal management program.

SUPPORT SYSTEMS
In Level 3.2-WM withdrawal management, support systems feature:

a.   Availability of specialized clinical consultation and supervision for biomedical, emotional, behavioral, and cognitive problems.

b.   Since Level 3.2-WM is managed by clinicians, not medical or nursing staff, protocols are in place should a patient's condition deteriorate and appear to need medical or nursing interventions.

These protocols are used to determine the nature of the medical or nursing interventions that may be required. Protocols include under what conditions nursing and physician care is warranted and/or when transfer to a medically monitored facility or an acute care hospital is necessary. The protocols are developed and supported by a physician knowledgeable in addiction medicine.

c.   Affiliation with other levels of care.

d.   Ability to arrange for appropriate laboratory and toxicology tests.

STAFF
Level 3.2-WM social withdrawal management programs are staffed by appropriately credentialed personnel who are trained and competent to implement physician-approved protocols for patient observation and supervision, determination of appropriate level of care, and facilitation of the patient's transition to continuing care.

Level 3.2-WM social withdrawal management is a clinically managed withdrawal management service designed explicitly to safely assist patients through withdrawal without the need for ready on-site access to medical and nursing personnel.

Medical evaluation and consultation is available 24 hours a day, in accordance with treatment/transfer practice protocols and guidelines.

All clinicians who assess and treat patients are able to obtain and interpret information regarding the needs of these patients. Such knowledge includes the signs and symptoms of alcohol and other drug intoxication and withdrawal, as well as the appropriate treatment and monitoring of those conditions and how to facilitate entry into ongoing care.

Facilities that supervise self-administered

medications have appropriately licensed or credentialed staff and policies and procedures in accordance with state and federal law.

Staff assures that patients are taking medications according to physician prescription and legal requirements.

THERAPIES

Therapies offered by Level 3.2-WM withdrawal management programs include daily clinical services to assess and address the needs of each patient. Such clinical services may include appropriate medical services, individual and group therapies, and withdrawal support.

The following therapies are provided as clinically necessary, depending on the patient's progress through withdrawal management and his or her assessed needs in Dimensions 2 through 6:

a. A range of cognitive, behavioral, medical, mental health, and other therapies are administered to the patient on an individual or group basis. These are designed to enhance the patient's understanding of addiction, the completion of the withdrawal management process, and referral to an appropriate level of care for continuing treatment.

b. Interdisciplinary individualized assessment and treatment.

c. Health education services.

d. Services to families and significant others.

ASSESSMENT/TREATMENT PLAN REVIEW

In Level 3.2-WM withdrawal management programs, elements of the assessment and treatment plan review include:

a. An addiction-focused history, obtained as part of the initial assessment and reviewed with a physician during the admission process.

b. A physical examination by a physician, physician assistant, or nurse practitioner as part of the initial assessment, if self-administered withdrawal management medications are to be used.

c. Sufficient biopsychosocial screening assessments to determine the level of care in which the patient should be placed and for the individualized care plan to address treatment priorities identified in Dimensions 2 through 6.

d. An individualized treatment plan, including problem identification in Dimensions 2 through 6 and development of treatment goals and measurable treatment objectives and activities designed to meet those objectives.

e. Daily assessment of patient progress through withdrawal management and any treatment changes.

f. Discharge/transfer planning, beginning at admission.

g. Referral arrangements, made as needed.

DOCUMENTATION

Documentation standards of Level 3.2-WM programs include progress notes in the patient record that clearly reflect implementation of the treatment plan and the patient's response to treatment, as well as subsequent amendments to the plan.

Withdrawal rating scale tables and flow sheets (which may include tabulation of vital signs) are used as needed.

Length of Service/Continued Service and Discharge Criteria

The patient continues in a Level 3.2-WM withdrawal management program until:

1. Withdrawal signs and symptoms are sufficiently resolved that he or she can be safely managed at a less intensive level of care; or,

WITHDRAWAL MANAGEMENT

④

2. The patient's signs and symptoms of withdrawal have failed to respond to treatment and have intensified (as confirmed by higher scores on the CIWA-Ar or other comparable standardized scoring system), such that transfer to a more intensive level of withdrawal management service is indicated; or,

3. The patient is unable to complete withdrawal management at Level 3.2-WM, despite an adequate trial. For example, he or she is experiencing increasing depression and suicidal impulses complicating cocaine withdrawal and indicating the need for transfer to a more intensive level of care or the addition of other clinical services (such as intensive counseling).

Level 3.7-WM: Medically Monitored Inpatient Withdrawal Management

Level 3.7-WM: Medically Monitored Inpatient Withdrawal Management is an organized service delivered by medical and nursing professionals, which provides for 24-hour evaluation and withdrawal management in a permanent facility with inpatient beds. Services are delivered under a defined set of physician-approved policies and physician-monitored procedures or clinical protocols.

This level provides care to patients whose withdrawal signs and symptoms are sufficiently severe to require 24-hour inpatient care. It sometimes is provided by overlapping with Level 4-WM services (as a "step-down" service) in a specialty unit of an acute care general or psychiatric hospital. Twenty-four hour observation, monitoring, and treatment are available. However, the full resources of an acute care general hospital or a medically managed intensive inpatient treatment program are not necessary.

EXAMPLES OF SERVICE DELIVERY
Freestanding withdrawal management center.

SUPPORT SYSTEMS
In Level 3.7-WM withdrawal management support systems feature:

a. Availability of specialized clinical consultation and supervision for biomedical, emotional, behavioral, and cognitive problems.

b. Availability of medical nursing care and observation as warranted, based on clinical judgment.

c. Direct affiliation with other levels of care.

d. Ability to conduct or arrange for appropriate laboratory and toxicology tests.

STAFF
Level 3.7-WM withdrawal management programs are staffed by physicians, who are available 24 hours a day by telephone. (In states where physician assistants or nurse practitioners are licensed as physician extenders, they may perform the duties designated for a physician under collaborative agreements or other requirements of the medical practice act in the given jurisdiction.)

A physician is available to assess the patient within 24 hours of admission (or earlier, if medically necessary), and is available to provide on-site monitoring of care and further evaluation on a daily basis.

A registered nurse or other licensed and credentialed nurse is available to conduct a nursing assessment on admission.

A nurse is responsible for overseeing the monitoring of the patient's progress and medication administration on an hourly basis, if needed.

Appropriately licensed and credentialed staff is available to administer medications in accordance with physician orders. The level of nursing care is appropriate to the severity of patient needs.

Licensed, certified, or registered clinicians provide a planned regimen of 24-hour, professionally directed evaluation, care, and treatment services for patients and their families.

An interdisciplinary team of appropriately trained clinicians (such as physicians, nurses, counselors, social workers, and psychologists) is available to assess and treat the patient and to obtain and interpret information regarding the patient's needs. The number and disciplines of team members are appropriate to the range and severity of the patient's problems.

THERAPIES

Therapies offered by Level 3.7-WM withdrawal management programs include daily clinical services to assess and address the needs of each patient. Such clinical services may include appropriate medical services, individual and group therapies, and withdrawal support.

Hourly nurse monitoring of the patient's progress and medication administration are available, if needed.

The following therapies are provided as clinically necessary, depending on the patient's progress through withdrawal management and the assessed needs in Dimensions 2 through 6:

a. A range of cognitive, behavioral, medical, mental health, and other therapies are administered to the patient on an individual or group basis. These are designed to enhance the patient's understanding of addiction, the completion of the withdrawal management process, and referral to an appropriate level of care for continuing treatment.

b. Multidisciplinary individualized assessment and treatment.

c. Health education services.

d. Services to families and significant others.

ASSESSMENT/TREATMENT PLAN REVIEW

In Level 3.7-WM withdrawal management programs, elements of the assessment and treatment plan review include:

a. An addiction-focused history, obtained as part of the initial assessment and reviewed by a physician during the admission process.

b. A physical examination by a physician, physician assistant, or nurse practitioner within 24 hours of admission and appropriate laboratory and toxicology tests. If Level 3.7-WM withdrawal management services are step-down services from Level 4-WM, records of a physical examination within the preceding 7 days are evaluated by a physician within 24 hours of admission.

c. Sufficient biopsychosocial screening assessments to determine the level of care in which the patient should be placed and for the individualized care plan to address treatment priorities identified in Dimensions 2 through 6.

d. An individualized treatment plan, including problem identification in Dimensions 2 through 6 and development of treatment goals and measurable treatment objectives and activities designed to meet those objectives.

e. Daily assessment of patient progress through withdrawal management and any treatment changes.

WITHDRAWAL MANAGEMENT

4

f. Discharge/transfer planning, beginning at admission.

g. Referral arrangements, made as needed.

DOCUMENTATION

Documentation standards of Level 3.7-WM programs include progress notes in the patient record that clearly reflect implementation of the treatment plan and the patient's response to treatment, as well as subsequent amendments to the plan.

Withdrawal rating scale tables and flow sheets (which may include tabulation of vital signs) are used as needed.

Length of Service/Continued Service and Discharge Criteria

The patient continues in a Level 3.7-WM withdrawal management program until withdrawal signs and symptoms are sufficiently resolved that he or she can be safely managed at a less intensive level of care; or, alternatively, the patient's signs and symptoms of withdrawal have failed to respond to treatment and have intensified (as confirmed by higher scores on the CIWA-Ar or other comparable standardized scoring system), such that transfer to a Level 4-WM intensive level of withdrawal management service is indicated.

Level 4-WM: Medically Managed Intensive Inpatient Withdrawal Management

Level 4-WM withdrawal management is an organized service delivered by medical and nursing professionals that provides for 24-hour medically directed evaluation and withdrawal management in an acute care inpatient setting. Services are delivered under a defined set of physician-approved policies and physician-managed procedures or medical protocols.

This level provides care to patients whose withdrawal signs and symptoms are sufficiently severe to require primary medical and nursing care services. Twenty-four hour observation, monitoring, and treatment are available. Although Level 4-WM is specifically designed for acute medical withdrawal management, it also is important to assess the patient and develop a care plan for any treatment priorities identified in Dimensions 2 through 6.

EXAMPLES OF SERVICE DELIVERY

Acute care or psychiatric hospital inpatient unit.

SUPPORT SYSTEMS

In Level 4-WM withdrawal management, support systems feature:

a. Availability of specialized medical consultation.

b. Full medical acute care services.

c. Intensive care, as needed.

STAFF

Level 4-WM withdrawal management programs are staffed by physicians, who are available 24 hours a day as active members of an interdisciplinary team of appropriately trained professionals, and who medically manage the care of the patient. (In states where physician assistants or nurse practitioners are licensed as physician extenders, they may perform the duties designated for a physician under collaborative agreements or other requirements of the medical practice act in the given jurisdiction.)

A registered nurse or other licensed and credentialed nurse is available for primary nursing care and observation 24 hours per day.

Facility-approved addiction counselors or licensed, certified, or registered addiction clinicians are available 8 hours per day to administer planned interventions according to the assessed needs of the patient.

An interdisciplinary team of appropriately trained clinicians (such as physicians, nurses, counselors, social workers, and psychologists) is available to assess and treat the patient with a substance use disorder, or an addicted patient with a concomitant acute biomedical, emotional, or behavioral disorder.

THERAPIES

Therapies offered by Level 4-WM withdrawal management programs include highly individualized biomedical, emotional, behavioral, and addiction treatment. This includes the management of all concomitant biomedical, emotional, behavioral, and cognitive conditions in the context of addiction treatment. (The extent to which concomitant conditions can be treated depends on the capabilities of the particular Level 4-WM setting.)

Hourly or more frequent nurse monitoring is available, if needed.

The following therapies are provided as clinically necessary, depending on the patient's progress through withdrawal management and the assessed needs in Dimensions 2 through 6:

a. A range of cognitive, behavioral, medical, mental health and other therapies. These are designed to enhance the patient's understanding of addiction, the completion of the withdrawal management process and referral to an appropriate level of care for continuing treatment. For the patient with a severe comorbid psychiatric disorder, psychiatric interventions complement addiction treatment. For the patient with a severe comorbid biomedical disorder, biomedical interventions complement addiction treatment.

b. Health education services.

c. Services to families and significant others.

ASSESSMENT/TREATMENT PLAN REVIEW

In Level 4-WM withdrawal management programs, elements of the assessment and treatment plan review include:

a. A comprehensive nursing assessment, performed at admission.

b. Approval of the admission by a physician.

c. A comprehensive history and physical examination performed within 12 hours of admission, accompanied by appropriate laboratory and toxicology tests.

d. An addiction-focused history, obtained as part of the initial assessment and reviewed by a physician during the admission process.

e. Sufficient biopsychosocial screening assessments to determine placement, and for the individualized care plan to address treatment priorities identified in Dimensions 2 through 6.

f. Discharge/transfer planning, beginning at admission.

g. Referral arrangements, made as needed.

h. An individualized treatment plan, including problem identification in Dimensions 2 through 6 and development of treatment goals and measurable treatment objectives and activities designed to meet those objectives.

i. Daily assessment of patient progress through withdrawal management and any treatment changes.

DOCUMENTATION

Documentation standards of Level 4-WM programs include progress notes in the patient record that clearly reflect implementation of the treatment plan and the patient's response to treatment, as well as subsequent amendments to the plan.

Withdrawal rating scale tables and flow sheets (which may include tabulation of vital signs) are used as needed.

Length of Service/Continued Service and Discharge Criteria

The patient continues in a Level 4-WM withdrawal management program until withdrawal signs and symptoms are sufficiently resolved that he or she can be safely managed at a less intensive level of care.

Dimensional Admission and Treatment Considerations

The dimensional admission criteria and treatment considerations for each withdrawal management level of care have been separated out from the preceding descriptions because of their central position and complexity. Additionally, offering these considerations within a matrix format allows readers to better understand both the differences in risk rating and service needs, as well as the differences between substances.

In this section, you will find tables for understanding assessment and severity of withdrawal, and matrices for matching severity of withdrawal with the intensity of withdrawal management and level of care.

RISK ASSESSMENT MATRIX FORMAT: Using a Risk Assessment Format to Make Treatment Decisions

This section uses a risk assessment format as the basic framework to help clinicians assess

1   TABLE 1: SAMPLE ASSESSMENT OF A PATIENT IN DIMENSION 1[5(p25)]

Nature of the Problem

- Alcohol withdrawal

Severity of the Problem

- Significant (risk rating of 3)

Services Required

- Withdrawal management

Modalities and Dose

- Medical assessment for management of withdrawal – Immediately
- Supportive group counseling – Daily
- Medical management of withdrawal, including pharmacologic therapies – Daily
- Intensive monitoring of progress – Multiple times per day

Placement Considerations

Level 3.7-WM may be most appropriate for the patient's needs in Dimension 1. Alternatively, the patient may be placed at Level 2-WM, if available as a daily medically monitored service, and if adequate overnight support can be provided by the patient's family. Note that other dimensional needs may modify the placement.

and manage withdrawal. It also assists in understanding the concepts that drive the ASAM criteria decision rules. A similar format also appears in the section on "Matrices for Matching Risk and Severity with Intensity of Services." A more elaborate version of this format also can be found in the *ASAM PPC: Supplement on Pharmacotherapies for Alcohol Use Disorders.*

When it comes to assessment, treatment planning, and placement of the individual needing withdrawal management, the matrix provides the conceptual sequence and visual organization that underlie the dimensional admission criteria, which conclude this chapter and are found in other sections of this publication. The matrix format helps the user first identify areas of concern and then select appropriate interventions as components of a comprehensive treatment plan. In this chapter, the matrices use a multitiered format to first highlight initial

TABLE 2: EXAMPLES OF DIMENSIONAL INTERACTIONS THAT CAN INCREASE OR DECREASE SEVERITY AND RISK[5(pp15-16)]

 INTERACTIONS WITH DIMENSION 1: ACUTE INTOXICATION AND/OR WITHDRAWAL POTENTIAL

SEVERITY INCREASE

Dimension 2: Impaired liver function, comorbid neurological conditions (eg, a seizure disorder) that could be exacerbated by autonomic nervous system hyperarousal, pregnancy.

Dimension 3: Use or misuse of psychiatric medications that are metabolized in the liver, psychiatric disorganization that may affect patient adherence to withdrawal management regimen.

Dimension 4: Lack of readiness to change affecting adherence to withdrawal management protocols or causing premature discharge from withdrawal management, lack of readiness to change affecting effectiveness of ambulatory withdrawal management (as by use of substances overnight or not returning for services the following day).

Dimension 5: Continued use of alcohol, illicit drugs, or non-medical use of prescription drugs.

Dimension 6: Lack of a supportive recovery environment or transportation for ambulatory withdrawal management.

SEVERITY DECREASE

Dimension 2: Absence of a comorbid medical condition.

Dimension 3: Absence of a comorbid psychiatric condition.

Dimension 4: Readiness to change at a level that facilitates adherence to ambulatory withdrawal management services.

Dimension 5: No continued use of alcohol, illicit drugs, or non-medical use of prescription drugs.

Dimension 6: A supportive recovery environment and transportation to ambulatory withdrawal management.

WITHDRAWAL MANAGEMENT

4

assessment and reassessment, determine the type and modality of services needed, and then determine the appropriate level of care. This provides a brief and intuitive sense of how the detailed decision rules in *The ASAM Criteria* and *The ASAM Criteria Software* operate.

Each matrix is first separated by risk rating, as assigned by the prioritized problems. These ratings range from 0 (no or stable problem), to 1 (minimal risk), 2 (moderate risk), 3 (significant risk), or 4 (severe risk).[5(p24)] Potential evidence for an initial assessment or reassessment is shown side by side. Then, services to match that risk level are provided, followed by the modalities, level of care, and setting for delivering the services needed.

The primary goal of the matrix in this section is to illustrate the holistic, multidimensional ASAM criteria approach, which first matches the patient's needs to specific treatment services and only then to broad levels of withdrawal management care.

Once a risk rating has been determined, the risk assessment matrix suggests the patient's service needs in each level of care. The matrix approach requires a comprehensive assessment of the patient's strengths and problems in each of the six dimensions.[5(pp23-24)] Once a problem list is created, it is prioritized by severity (for example, Dimension 2, advanced liver disease in a patient with severe alcohol use disorder), risk (as in Dimension 3, suicidal thought with high lethality), or interference (reflected in Dimension 6, lack of child care or transportation for a patient who appears to be a likely candidate for an outpatient level of care).

The emphasis on services and modalities of care is consistent with a continuing emphasis on "unbundling" of services. Each dimension is initially considered separately from the other dimensions to allow for independent assessment of all areas of potential concern. Table 1 gives an example of this process in Dimension 1.[5(p24)]

The next step is to perform a similar assessment of the patient in each of the other Dimensions, as well as for interdimensional interactions.[5(p25)] Table 2 shows how other dimensions may increase or decrease severity within Dimension 1.

Variable Withdrawal Risk by Substance
ALCOHOL

Alcohol use leads to physical dependence in a minority of people with alcohol use disorder, but the widespread use of alcohol makes alcohol withdrawal syndrome (AWS) the most commonly seen withdrawal syndrome. Careful monitoring is required because of the possibility of grand mal seizures or alcohol withdrawal delirium.

Screening for the Possibility of a Withdrawal Syndrome and Predicting Severity

Although early intervention can prevent the development of a severe syndrome, there is little consensus about the best way to predict that a severe syndrome will in fact develop. Some of the factors making prediction difficult are:

» The number of days of daily drinking to create physical dependence has not been reliably determined.

» Patients sometimes do not accurately report the time of last drink, will minimize a past history of withdrawal symptoms, or may be amnestic for their experience with alcohol withdrawal delirium. These problems can be reduced if:

   Additional information from collateral sources can be obtained

   Blood alcohol level is measured

» The AWS is a changing condition, intensifying gradually over a period of 6 to 24 hours after the last drink, usually peaking at 36 hours, and then diminishing over 1 to 2 days. A given symptom has different significance depending on when in this process the patient is initially evaluated.

The possibility that an AWS will develop must be considered if the patient reports daily heavy drinking, especially if it begins early in the day, with no abstinence in the preceding 48 hours.

In order to help make decisions about appropriate levels of care, attempts have been made to develop severity prediction tools that are objective, measurable, and reliable. Although none of these have yet been validated, the following guidelines may be useful[6]:

» If the score on any of the withdrawal scales (such as the Clinical Institute Withdrawal Assessment-Alcohol Revised or CIWA-Ar – see Appendix A) is low over the first 24 hours, there is little or no risk of severe withdrawal.

» The following **individual** factors have been **most frequently associated** with more severe withdrawal syndromes. The presence of **multiple** factors is of **higher** predictive value[7]:

A past history of seizures or delirium tremens
Frequent sleep disturbances or nightmares in the previous week
The presence of sweating, tremor, or a pulse over 100 while the blood alcohol level is over .10 mg%
Serum chloride under 96 mmol/l
Severe somatic disease, particularly infection

» Factors that have **not** been useful predictors are: amount of daily drinking, duration of heavy drinking, age, or gender.

The CIWA-Ar scale can be a useful tool, but it has only been validated for tracking the withdrawal management process – not for making level of care decisions. Because it does not take into account the influence of the other five ASAM criteria dimensions, it should only be used as part of the decision making process and not as a stand-alone determinant for level of care decisions. Studies have documented its misapplication[8,9,10] when the elevated CIWA-Ar score is in fact due to a delirium with an etiology other than AWS, resulting in the actual disorder going untreated. Unrelated to the CIWA-Ar, these studies also documented a pattern of incorrectly assuming that a patient is being dishonest in denying recent drinking, resulting in unnecessary treatment for withdrawal management being given.

Recommendation

The risk matrix strategy on page 147 illustrates the theory and concepts underlying *The ASAM Criteria* decision rules. This matrix explains the clinical thought process to move from assessment of withdrawal risk to service matching and level of care for those not yet using *The ASAM Criteria Software.*

STRATEGY FOR APPLYING THE RISK MATRIX IN WITHDRAWAL MANAGEMENT

STEP 1 — Assess the patient in terms of ASAM criteria Dimensions 1 through 6 to determine the risk rating.

STEP 2 — Use the risk rating matrix on the following pages to suggest the least intensive level of care.

STEP 3 — For risk ratings of 2 or higher:

a) Strive for immediate reduction and ultimate elimination of AWS by using a symptom-triggered protocol with long half-life benzodiazepines. Medication should not be withheld while the patient is still experiencing withdrawal symptoms, even for scores of CIWA-Ar < 10.

b) Reassess the patient hourly during the first several hours to confirm that the level of care, as well as the medication dosage, are appropriate. If this frequent reassessment is not done, the result may be under-medication and the otherwise preventable escalation to a more severe AWS.

STEP 4 — Begin the rest of the addiction recovery treatment process concurrently as cognitive status permits, rather than delaying it until the patient's withdrawal management is completed.

STEP 5 — As the withdrawal syndrome resolves, quickly move the patient to a less intensive level of care. Conversely, move the patient to a more intensive level of care if the withdrawal symptoms do not respond to treatment.

RISK RATING MATRIX — ALCOHOL[5(p46)]

RISK RATING 0 — MINIMAL OR NO RISK

DESCRIPTION

A risk rating of 0 in Dimension 1 indicates that the patient is fully functioning and demonstrates good ability to tolerate and cope with the discomfort of withdrawal.

INITIAL ASSESSMENT

The patient with a risk rating of 0 evidences no observable signs or symptoms of intoxication or withdrawal, or minor signs or symptoms are resolving and the patient is fully functioning and demonstrates good ability to tolerate and cope with any withdrawal discomfort.

SERVICE NEEDS

A risk rating of 0 in Dimension 1 indicates that no immediate intoxication monitoring or management, or withdrawal management services are needed. It does not affect the overall placement decision.

TREATMENT INTERVENTIONS

At this level of risk, there is no need to initiate new professional services specifically for problems in Dimension 1. However, the patient may be receiving (and should continue to receive) maintenance treatment with anti-addiction medications, such as those for alcohol dependence or opioid addiction (OTP), as well as continuing care counseling, and these should be continued.

LEVEL OF CARE & SETTING

For the patient with a risk rating of 0 in Dimension 1, the determination of level of care or setting is guided by the risk rating in other dimensions.

WITHDRAWAL MANAGEMENT

RISK RATING MATRIX — ALCOHOL[5(pp47-48)]

RISK RATING 1 — MILD RISK

INITIAL ASSESSMENT

The patient with a risk rating of 1 might have mild anxiety, sweating, and insomnia, but no tremor (which is generally associated with a CIWA-Ar score of less than 10). In addition:

a) The patient is not withdrawing from other substances.

b) If the patient previously stopped drinking within the past year, he or she did not experience a severe withdrawal syndrome.

c) He or she is fully coherent and able to comprehend instructions.

d) The patient has no more than mild active medical problems, or any that exist are stable.

e) There are no symptoms of a co-occurring psychiatric disorder or such symptoms are mild, reflecting a low level of severity, or are stable as the result of treatment.

f) The patient has a high level of commitment to the withdrawal management process and is very cooperative with treatment interventions.

g) The patient demonstrates a clear understanding of treatment instructions and has the resources to carry them out. Reliability is demonstrated by the patient's willingness to accept recommendations for treatment and responsiveness to treatment interventions.

h) The patient has family or friends who are supportive of the withdrawal management process and can assist in providing transportation and a safe place to stay. Or, if such supports are absent, the patient demonstrates an ability to obtain transportation (other than driving himself or herself) and access to safe and appropriate housing.

REASSESSMENT

On reassessment after initiation of treatment, the patient with a risk rating of 1 evidences one of the following:

(1) The patient's symptoms are improving as a result of the medical and psychosocial interventions, but sufficient residual symptoms persist to justify a continued risk rating of 1;

or

(2) The patient's withdrawal symptoms initially were compatible with a risk rating of 0, but have intensified;

or

(3) The patient's withdrawal symptoms initially were compatible with a risk rating of 2 (or higher) and have improved sufficiently in response to treatment to warrant a reduction to a risk rating of 1.

SERVICE NEEDS

A risk rating of 1 indicates a need for professional services, such as low-intensity intoxication monitoring or management, or withdrawal management services, specifically to address problems in Dimension 1.

Immediate service needs include baseline measurement of blood alcohol level. If positive, serial measurements should be conducted until the level is 0. Urine drug testing should be conducted to detect the presence of substances in addition to alcohol.

TREATMENT INTERVENTIONS

A long-acting benzodiazepine should be given. Effects should be monitored through the use of the CIWA-Ar or equivalent instrument. Doses should be repeated, preferably daily, using a symptom-triggered protocol. Alternatively, a time-driven protocol with a symptom-driven override/rescue protocol can be used.

Anticonvulsants are sometimes used for mild to moderate withdrawal symptoms. For ambulatory withdrawal management, they offer the advantages of causing minimal sedation and not being subject to abuse.

A limited amount of medication should be prescribed or dispensed, sufficient to last until the next visit (ideally, the next day). The benzodiazepine medication should be adjusted at subsequent visits on a tapering schedule and discontinued entirely within a total treatment period of 3 to 5 days (longer in the case of additional withdrawal management from long-acting sedative/hypnotics).

Chronic abstinence symptoms beyond the period of acute withdrawal should not be treated with benzodiazepines because of the danger of cross-addiction.

The patient should be offered immediate access to, and simultaneous participation in, an addiction counseling program or other suitable psychosocial intervention.

Transportation to return the patient to his or her home and overnight supervision should be arranged.

LEVEL OF CARE & SETTING

A risk rating of 1 in Dimension 1 indicates the need for Level 1-WM Ambulatory Withdrawal Management without Extended On-Site Monitoring, if the patient has sufficient supports (such as family) to provide monitoring of symptoms.

If such supports are absent, the patient should be placed in a Level 2-WM withdrawal management program. Clinical services may be delivered in a primary care, addiction treatment, or mental health setting.

If family or other supports are not adequate or the patient meets residential criteria in other dimensions, then a Level 3.2-WM (Clinically Managed Residential Withdrawal Management) program with concurrent medical services equivalent to Level 1-WM may be appropriate.

If the patient requires intensive mental health services (with a risk rating of 2 or higher in Dimension 3), low-intensity withdrawal management can be provided in a mental health setting, with ongoing case management to coordinate care.

WITHDRAWAL MANAGEMENT

4

RISK RATING MATRIX — ALCOHOL[5(pp48-50)]

RISK RATING 2 — MODERATE RISK

INITIAL ASSESSMENT

The patient with a risk rating of 2 might evidence one of the following:

(1) Moderate anxiety, sweating, and insomnia, as well as a mild tremor, indicating a moderate risk of severe withdrawal (which is generally associated with a CIWA-Ar score of 10 to 18). He or she is not withdrawing from a substance other than alcohol, and is fully coherent and able to comprehend instructions. In addition:

a) If the patient previously stopped drinking within the past year, he or she did not experience a severe withdrawal syndrome.

b) The patient has no significant active medical problems, or any that exist are stable. Any current physical symptoms such as nausea or vomiting are no more than moderate in intensity.

c) Any symptoms of a co-occurring psychiatric disorder are mild, reflecting a low level of severity, or are stable as the result of treatment.

d) The patient has a high level of commitment to the withdrawal management process and is very cooperative.

e) The patient (or his or her significant support person) demonstrates a clear understanding of treatment instructions and the resources to carry them out. Reliability is demonstrated by the patient's willingness to accept recommendations for treatment and responsiveness to treatment interventions.

f) The patient has family or friends who are at least minimally supportive of the withdrawal management process and can assist in providing transportation and a safe place to stay. Or, if such supports are absent, the patient demonstrates an ability to obtain transportation (other than driving himself or herself) and access to safe and appropriate housing.

or

(2) The patient might exhibit moderate anxiety, sweating, and insomnia, but no tremor. He or she is not withdrawing from a substance other than alcohol, and is fully coherent and able to comprehend instructions. The patient otherwise would have had a risk rating of 1, but evidences one or more of the following problems, which pose a significant impediment to withdrawal management at a less intensive level of care:

a) The patient's past attempts to stop drinking were marked by severe withdrawal.

b) The patient has moderate, active, and potentially destabilizing medical problems.

c) Symptoms of a co-occurring psychiatric disorder are active, reflecting a moderate level of severity that is likely to complicate the withdrawal management.

d) The patient does not have a high level of commitment to the withdrawal management process and his or her level of cooperation and reliability are questionable.

e) The patient's likelihood of imminent relapse is high.

f) The patient's family or friends are not supportive of or oppose the withdrawal management process and will not assist in providing transportation and a safe place to stay. The patient appears unable to obtain transportation (other than driving himself or herself) and access to safe and appropriate housing.

REASSESSMENT

On reassessment after initiation of treatment, the patient with a risk rating of 2 evidences one of the following:

(1) The patient's symptoms are improving as a result of the medical and psychosocial interventions, but sufficient residual symptoms persist to justify a continued risk rating of 2;

or

(2) The patient's withdrawal symptoms initially were compatible with a risk rating of 1 and have intensified despite appropriate treatment;

or

(3) The patient's withdrawal symptoms initially were compatible with risk rating 3 and have improved sufficiently in response to treatment to warrant a reduction to a risk rating of 2.

WITHDRAWAL MANAGEMENT

4

RISK RATING MATRIX — ALCOHOL[5(pp48-50)]

RISK RATING 2 — MODERATE RISK

SERVICE NEEDS

A risk rating of 2 in Dimension 1 indicates the need for moderate-intensity intoxication monitoring or management, or withdrawal management services.

TREATMENT INTERVENTIONS

A long-acting benzodiazepine medication should be given. Medication effects should be monitored – preferably several times per day, in accordance with the severity and course of withdrawal symptoms – through the use of the CIWA-Ar or an equivalent instrument. Doses should be repeated, with the capacity for dosing multiple times per day, using a symptom-triggered protocol. Alternatively, a time-driven protocol with a symptom-driven override/rescue protocol can be used.

Anticonvulsants may be used as alternatives for mild to moderate withdrawal symptoms. For ambulatory withdrawal management, these medications offer the advantages of causing minimal sedation and not being subject to abuse.

A limited amount of medication should be prescribed or dispensed, sufficient to last until the next visit (ideally, the next day). The benzodiazepine medication should be adjusted at subsequent visits on a tapering schedule and discontinued entirely within a total treatment period of 3 to 5 days [by definition, a risk rating of 2 does not involve withdrawal from other substances.].

Chronic abstinence symptoms beyond the period of acute withdrawal should not be treated with benzodiazepines because of the danger of cross-addiction.

The patient should be offered immediate access to, and simultaneous participation in, an addiction counseling program or other suitable psychosocial intervention.

Transportation to return the patient to his or her home and overnight supervision should be arranged.

LEVEL OF CARE & SETTING

The patient with a risk rating of 2 in Dimension 1 should be placed in a Level 2-WM Ambulatory Withdrawal Management with Extended On-Site Monitoring program.

If family, transportation, or other supports are not adequate to enable the success of a Level 2-WM program or the patient meets residential criteria in other dimensions, then residential treatment supports should be added. If available, a Level 3.2-WM (Clinically Managed Residential Withdrawal Management) program with concurrent medical services equivalent to Level 2-WM should be considered.

If the patient requires partial hospitalization or more intensive mental health services (ie, a risk rating of 2 or 3 or higher in Dimension 3), moderate intensity withdrawal management can be provided in a properly equipped mental health setting with ongoing case management to coordinate care.

WITHDRAWAL MANAGEMENT

4

RISK RATING MATRIX — ALCOHOL[5(pp51-52)]

RISK RATING 3 — SIGNIFICANT RISK

INITIAL ASSESSMENT

The patient with a risk rating of 3 might evidence one of the following:

(1) Significant anxiety and a moderate to severe tremor (generally associated with a CIWA-Ar score of 19 or more). The patient also may be withdrawing from substances other than alcohol. However, he or she is fully coherent and able to comprehend instructions;

or

(2) The patient has moderate anxiety, sweating, and insomnia, as well as a mild tremor (generally associated with a CIWA-Ar score of 19 or more); he or she is not withdrawing from a substance other than alcohol; and is fully coherent and able to comprehend instructions.

The patient would otherwise have had a risk rating of 2, except that he or she evidences one or more of the following problems, which pose a significant impediment to withdrawal management at a less intensive level of care:

    a) The patient's past attempts to stop drinking were marked by severe withdrawal symptoms.

    b) The patient has moderate to severe active and potentially destabilizing medical problems.

    c) Symptoms of a co-occurring psychiatric disorder are moderate to severe.

    d) The patient does not have a high level of commitment to the withdrawal management process and his or her level of cooperation and reliability is questionable.

    e) The patient is at significant risk of imminent relapse.

    f) The patient's family or friends are not supportive of or oppose the withdrawal management process and will not assist in providing transportation and a safe place to stay. The patient appears unable to obtain transportation (other than driving himself or herself) and access to safe and appropriate housing.

REASSESSMENT

On reassessment after initiation of treatment, the patient with a risk rating of 3 evidences one of the following:

(1) The patient's symptoms are improving as a result of the medical and psychosocial interventions, but sufficient residual symptoms persist to justify a continued risk rating of 3;

or

(2) The patient's withdrawal symptoms, although initially compatible with a risk rating of 2, have intensified despite appropriate treatment;

or

(3) The patient's withdrawal symptoms, while initially compatible with a risk rating of 4, have improved sufficiently in response to treatment to warrant a reduction to a risk rating of 3.

WITHDRAWAL MANAGEMENT

4

RISK RATING MATRIX — ALCOHOL[5(pp51-52)]

RISK RATING 3 — SIGNIFICANT RISK

SERVICE NEEDS

A risk rating of 3 in Dimension 1 indicates a need for moderately high-intensity intoxication monitoring or management, or withdrawal management services. Nursing and medical care is essential.

TREATMENT INTERVENTIONS

A long-acting benzodiazepine medication should be given. Medication effects should be monitored very frequently (at least several times a day, or hourly if needed in the presence of severe tremor or elevated vital signs) through the use of the CIWA-Ar or equivalent instrument. Doses should be repeated, using a symptom-triggered protocol. Alternatively, a time-driven protocol with a symptom-driven override/rescue protocol can be used.

If the patient is in an ambulatory setting, a limited amount of medication should be prescribed or dispensed, sufficient to last until the next day. Patients should have access to on-call medical personnel between scheduled assessments in case of worsening symptoms.

The benzodiazepine medication should be adjusted at subsequent visits on a tapering schedule and discontinued entirely within a total treatment period of 3 to 5 days (longer if the patient also is being withdrawn from long-acting sedative-hypnotics).

Chronic abstinence symptoms beyond the period of acute withdrawal should not be treated with benzodiazepines because of the danger of cross-addiction.

The patient should be offered immediate access to, and simultaneous participation in, a rehabilitation program or other suitable psychosocial interventions.

Transportation to return the patient to his or her home and overnight supervision should be arranged. Alternatively, residential support may be indicated if there is a significant likelihood that the patient will not complete withdrawal management or enter into continuing addiction treatment.

LEVEL OF CARE & SETTING

The patient with a risk rating of 3 in Dimension 1 should be placed in a Level 2-WM (Ambulatory Withdrawal Management with Extended On-Site Monitoring) or Level 3.7-WM (Medically Monitored Inpatient Withdrawal Management) program. However, Level 2-WM is not appropriate if certain symptoms (such as agitation or severe tremor) are persistently present at the close of the day's program service hours despite having received multiple doses of medication, because such a patient needs 24-hour medical monitoring.

Level 2-WM also is not appropriate if assessment items 2d or 2f (see initial assessment on previous page) exist, unless Level 2-WM can be combined with a supportive living arrangement.

Alternatively, the patient may be placed in a Level 3.7-WM Medically Monitored Inpatient Withdrawal Management program. Such a program may be located in an addiction treatment or mental health setting.

If the patient requires medically monitored or clinically managed mental health services (with a risk rating of 3 or higher in Dimension 3), moderately high-intensity withdrawal management can be provided in a mental health setting with ongoing case management to coordinate care.

WITHDRAWAL MANAGEMENT

④

RISK RATING MATRIX — ALCOHOL[5(pp52-53)]

RISK RATING 4 — SEVERE RISK

INITIAL ASSESSMENT

The patient with a risk rating of 4 might evidence one of the following:

(1) The patient has clouding of the sensorium or confusion, or new onset of hallucinations, or has experienced a seizure, or is not able to fully comprehend instructions (which is generally associated with a CIWA-Ar score of 19 or greater);

or

(2) The patient has severe anxiety and a moderate to severe tremor. He or she also may be concurrently withdrawing from a substance other than alcohol. The patient would otherwise have had a risk rating of 3, except that he or she evidences one or more of the following problems, which pose a major impediment to withdrawal management at a less intensive level of care:

  a) The patient's past attempts to stop drinking were marked by seizures or delirium tremens.

  b) The patient has severe destabilizing medical problems or biomedical conditions that pose substantial risk of serious consequences during withdrawal.

  c) Symptoms of a co-occurring psychiatric disorder are severe.

  d) The patient is not cooperative or reliable, to an extent that places him or her at imminent risk of harm.

  e) The patient requires medical monitoring more frequently than hourly.

REASSESSMENT

On reassessment after initiation of treatment, the patient with a risk rating of 4 evidences one of the following:

(1) The patient's symptoms are currently improving as a result of the medical and psychosocial interventions, but sufficient residual symptoms persist to justify a continued risk rating of 4;

or

(2) The patient's withdrawal symptoms, although initially compatible with a risk rating of 3, have intensified despite appropriate treatment.

SERVICE NEEDS

A risk rating of 4 in Dimension 1 indicates a need for high-intensity intoxication monitoring or management, or withdrawal management services, with medical monitoring and management more often than hourly.

TREATMENT INTERVENTIONS

Benzodiazepine medication should be administered. Short- or long-acting agents may be appropriate, depending on the circumstances (for example, short-acting and non-hepatically metabolized agents such as oxazepam or lorazepam are preferable in the presence of hepatic insufficiency).

Parenteral hydration as well as other appropriate supportive medications should be available.

The patient should be closely monitored (at least several times a day, or hourly in the presence of delirium or substantial elevation of vital signs) through the use of the CIWA-Ar or equivalent instrument. The dose should be repeated, using a symptom-triggered protocol. Alternatively, a time-driven protocol with a symptom-driven override/rescue protocol can be used.

As soon as he or she is medically stable, the patient should be offered immediate access to, and simultaneous participation in, a rehabilitation program or other suitable psychosocial interventions.

LEVEL OF CARE & SETTING

The patient with a risk rating of 4 should be placed in a Level 4-WM Medically Managed Intensive Inpatient Withdrawal Management program, which is an organized hospital addiction service. In the absence of such a service, an organized medical or psychiatric service in a hospital under the direction of an addiction medicine specialist may be used.

If the patient requires medically monitored and nurse-managed mental health services (with a risk rating of 3 or higher in Dimension 3), moderately high-intensity withdrawal management can be provided in a mental health setting with ongoing case management to coordinate care.

WITHDRAWAL MANAGEMENT

4

SUMMARY OF RISK ASSESSMENT MATRIX FOR ALCOHOL

RISK RATING	WITHDRAWAL MANAGEMENT SERVICE NEEDS & INTERVENTIONS	LEVEL OF CARE & SETTING
0 (MINIMAL/ NONE)	None	None
1 (MILD)	**Service Needs** » Daily monitoring » Measurement of blood alcohol level, urine screen for drugs **Treatment Interventions** » Prescription or dispensing of long-acting benzodiazepines	1-WM, 3.2-WM
2 (MODERATE)	**Service Needs** » Hourly monitoring until improvement begins, then every 2 to 3 hours **Treatment Interventions** » Implementation of symptom-triggered withdrawal management protocol using long-acting benzodiazepines	2-WM
3 (SIGNIFICANT)	**Service Needs** » Hourly monitoring until improvement begins, then every 2 to 3 hours **Treatment Interventions** » Implementation of symptom-triggered withdrawal management protocol using long-acting benzodiazepines	2-WM, 3.7-WM
4 (SEVERE)	**Service Needs** » 24-hour monitoring – every 30 to 60 minutes until improvement begins, then every 2 hours **Treatment Interventions** » Implementation of symptom-triggered withdrawal management protocol using long-acting benzodiazepines	4-WM

Variable Withdrawal Risk by Substance
SEDATIVE/HYPNOTICS

The withdrawal syndrome from sedative/hypnotics resembles the alcohol withdrawal syndrome but the individual symptoms are more variable. In addition to differences between individuals, a variety of substances with different elimination half-lives are included in this substance category.

Screening for the Possibility of a Withdrawal Syndrome and Predicting Severity

Screening and predicting are more difficult for this category than for alcohol because:

» For a given individual, the symptoms of sedative/hypnotic withdrawal tend to fluctuate more than do symptoms of alcohol withdrawal

» Tremor and measurable signs may not accompany the patient's symptoms

» There is no consensus regarding validated severity scales

» The simultaneous re-emergence of underlying anxiety and insomnia can resemble the withdrawal symptoms

Guidelines for patterns of sedative/hypnotic use that are predictive of a withdrawal syndrome are[11]:

» Therapeutic ("low") dose use for at least 4 to 6 months

» "High" dose (two to three times the upper limit of recommended therapeutic dose) use for more than 2 to 3 months

Time frames for the withdrawal syndromes from sedative/hypnotics have been best defined for benzodiazepines[12]:

» Short acting:
  Onset: Within 24 hours of cessation
  Peak severity: 1 to 5 days
  Duration: 7 to 21 days

» Long acting:
  Onset: Within 5 days of cessation
  Peak severity: 1 to 9 days
  Duration: 10 to 28 days

Recommendation

As for alcohol withdrawal, begin with an assessment of all 6 assessment dimensions of the ASAM criteria to determine the patient's risk rating and institute treatment as soon as possible at the appropriate level of care. When treatment is provided in an ambulatory setting, give the patient only a small supply of detoxifying or tapering medication, sufficient until each next visit.

RISK RATING MATRIX — SEDATIVE/HYPNOTICS

RISK RATING 0 — MINIMAL OR NO RISK

DESCRIPTION

A risk rating of 0 in Dimension 1 indicates that the patient is fully functioning and demonstrates good ability to tolerate and cope with the discomfort of withdrawal.

INITIAL ASSESSMENT

The patient with a risk rating of 0 evidences no observable signs or symptoms of intoxication or withdrawal, or minor signs or symptoms are resolving and the patient is fully functioning and demonstrates good ability to tolerate and cope with any withdrawal discomfort.

SERVICE NEEDS

A risk rating of 0 in Dimension 1 indicates that no immediate intoxication monitoring or management, or withdrawal management services are needed. It does not affect the overall placement decision.

TREATMENT INTERVENTIONS

At this level of risk, there is no need to initiate new professional services specifically for problems in Dimension 1.

LEVEL OF CARE & SETTING

For the patient with a risk rating of 0 in Dimension 1, the determination of level of care or setting is guided by the risk rating in other dimensions.

RISK RATING MATRIX — SEDATIVE/HYPNOTICS

RISK RATING 1 — MILD RISK

INITIAL ASSESSMENT

The patient with a risk rating of 1 might evidence mild anxiety and insomnia. In addition:

a) The patient is not withdrawing from other substances.

b) If the patient previously stopped using sedative/hypnotics within the past year, he or she did not experience a severe withdrawal syndrome.

c) He or she is fully coherent and able to comprehend instructions.

d) The patient has no more than mild active medical problems, or any that exist (such as hypertension, diabetes, or hepatitis) are stable.

e) There are no symptoms of a co-occurring psychiatric disorder (such as a mood, anxiety, or attention deficit disorder) or such symptoms are mild, reflecting a low level of severity, or are stable as the result of treatment.

f) The patient has a high level of commitment to the withdrawal management process and is very cooperative with treatment interventions.

g) The patient demonstrates a clear understanding of treatment instructions and has the resources to carry them out. Reliability is demonstrated by the patient's willingness to accept recommendations for treatment and responsiveness to treatment interventions.

h) The patient has family or friends who are supportive of the withdrawal management process and can assist in providing transportation and a safe place to stay. Or, if such supports are absent, the patient demonstrates an ability to obtain transportation (other than driving himself or herself) and access to safe and appropriate housing.

REASSESSMENT

On reassessment after initiation of treatment, the patient with a risk rating of 1 evidences one of the following:

(1) The patient's symptoms are improving as a result of the medical and psychosocial interventions, but sufficient residual symptoms persist to justify a continued risk rating of 1;

or

(2) The patient's withdrawal symptoms initially were compatible with a risk rating of 0, but have intensified;

or

(3) The patient's withdrawal symptoms initially were compatible with a risk rating of 2 (or higher) and have improved sufficiently in response to treatment to warrant a reduction to a risk rating of 1.

SERVICE NEEDS

A risk rating of 1 indicates a need for professional services, such as low-intensity intoxication monitoring or management, or withdrawal management services, specifically to address problems in Dimension 1.

Immediate service needs include baseline measurement of blood alcohol level. If positive, serial measurements should be conducted until the level is zero. Urine drug testing should be conducted to detect the presence of other addictive substances.

TREATMENT INTERVENTIONS

Phenobarbital or a long-acting benzodiazepine should be given. Doses should be repeated, preferably daily, using a symptom-triggered or time-driven protocol with a symptom-driven override/rescue protocol.

Adjunctive anticonvulsants are sometimes used.

A limited amount of medication should be prescribed or dispensed, sufficient to last until the next visit (ideally, the next day). The medication should be adjusted at subsequent visits on a tapering schedule and discontinued entirely within a total treatment period of 2 to 8 weeks.

Low doses of non-addicting sleep medications may be useful for chronic insomnia.

The patient should be offered immediate access to, and simultaneous participation in, an addiction counseling program or other suitable psychosocial intervention.

Transportation to return the patient to his or her home and overnight supervision should be arranged.

LEVEL OF CARE & SETTING

A risk rating of 1 in Dimension 1 indicates the need for Level 1-WM Ambulatory Withdrawal Management without Extended On-Site Monitoring, if the patient has sufficient supports (such as family) to provide monitoring of symptoms.

If such supports are absent, the patient should be placed in a Level 2-WM withdrawal management program. Clinical services may be delivered in a primary care, addiction treatment, or mental health setting.

If family or other supports are not adequate or the patient meets residential criteria in other dimensions, then a Level 3.2-WM (Clinically Managed Residential Withdrawal Management) program with concurrent medical services equivalent to Level 1-WM may be appropriate.

If the patient requires intensive mental health services (with a risk rating of 2 or higher in Dimension 3), low-intensity withdrawal management can be provided in a mental health setting, with ongoing case management to coordinate care.

RISK RATING MATRIX — SEDATIVE/HYPNOTICS

RISK RATING 2 — MODERATE RISK

A risk rating of 2 in Dimension 1 indicates that the patient is experiencing moderate difficulty in tolerating and coping with the discomfort of withdrawal.

Alternatively, the patient's level of intoxication or withdrawal may be severe, but it responds to support and treatment sufficiently that the patient does not pose an imminent danger to self or others.

INITIAL ASSESSMENT

The patient with a risk rating of 2 evidences one of the following:

(1) The patient has moderate anxiety and insomnia, and possibly physical signs of withdrawal, eg, mild tremor, indicating a moderate risk of severe withdrawal. He or she is not withdrawing from a substance other than sedative/hypnotics, and is fully coherent and able to comprehend instructions. In addition:

a) If the patient previously stopped using sedative/hypnotics within the past year, he or she did not experience a severe withdrawal syndrome.

b) The patient has no significant active medical problems, or any that exist are stable. Any current physical symptoms such as nausea or vomiting are no more than moderate in intensity.

c) Any symptoms of a co-occurring psychiatric disorder are mild, reflecting a low level of severity, or are stable as the result of treatment.

d) The patient has a high level of commitment to the withdrawal management process and is very cooperative.

e) The patient (or his or her significant support person) demonstrates a clear understanding of treatment instructions and has the resources to carry them out. Reliability is demonstrated by the patient's willingness to accept recommendations for treatment and responsiveness to treatment interventions.

f) The patient has family or friends who are at least minimally supportive of the withdrawal management process and can assist in providing transportation and a safe place to stay. Or, if such supports are absent, the patient demonstrates an ability to obtain transportation (other than driving himself or herself) and access to safe and appropriate housing.

or

(2) The patient exhibits mild anxiety and insomnia without physical signs of withdrawal, eg, tremor. He or she is not withdrawing from a substance other than sedative/hypnotics, and is fully coherent and able to comprehend instructions. The patient otherwise would have had a risk rating of 1, but evidences one or more of the following problems, which pose a significant impediment to withdrawal management at a less intensive level of care:

a) The patient's past attempts to stop using sedative/hypnotics were marked by severe withdrawal symptoms.

b) The patient has moderate, active, and potentially destabilizing medical problems.

c) Symptoms of a co-occurring psychiatric disorder are active, reflecting a moderate level of severity that is likely to complicate the withdrawal management.

d) The patient does not have a high level of commitment to the withdrawal management process and his or her level of cooperation and reliability are questionable. For example, the patient has a recent history of withdrawal management at less intensive levels of care that were marked by inability to complete withdrawal management or to enter into continuing addiction treatment, and the patient lacks sufficient skills to complete withdrawal management

e) The patient's likelihood of imminent relapse is high.

f) The patient's family or friends are not supportive of or oppose the withdrawal management process and will not assist in providing transportation and a safe place to stay. The patient appears unable to obtain transportation (other than driving himself or herself) and access to safe and appropriate housing.

REASSESSMENT

On reassessment after initiation of treatment, the patient with a risk rating of 2 evidences one of the following:

(1) The patient's symptoms are improving as a result of the medical and psychosocial interventions, but sufficient residual symptoms persist to justify a continued risk rating of 2;

or

(2) The patient's withdrawal symptoms initially were compatible with a risk rating of 1 and have intensified despite appropriate treatment;

or

(3) The patient's withdrawal symptoms initially were compatible with risk rating 3 and have improved sufficiently in response to treatment to warrant a reduction to a risk rating of 2.

WITHDRAWAL MANAGEMENT

4

RISK RATING MATRIX — SEDATIVE/HYPNOTICS

RISK RATING 2 — MODERATE RISK

SERVICE NEEDS

A risk rating of 2 in Dimension 1 indicates the need for moderate-intensity intoxication monitoring or management, or withdrawal management services.

TREATMENT INTERVENTIONS

Phenobarbital or a long-acting benzodiazepine should be given. Doses should be repeated, preferably daily, using a symptom-triggered or time-driven protocol with a symptom-driven override/rescue protocol.

Adjunctive anticonvulsants are sometimes used.

A limited amount of medication should be prescribed or dispensed, sufficient to last until the next visit (ideally, the next day). The medication should be adjusted at subsequent visits on a tapering schedule and discontinued entirely within a total treatment period of 2 to 8 weeks.

Low doses of non-addicting sleep medications may be useful for chronic insomnia.

The patient should be offered immediate access to, and simultaneous participation in, an addiction counseling program or other suitable psychosocial intervention.

Transportation should be arranged to return the patient to his or her home and overnight supervision.

LEVEL OF CARE & SETTING

The patient with a risk rating of 2 in Dimension 1 should be placed in a Level 2-WM Ambulatory Withdrawal Management with Extended On-Site Monitoring program. Such a program may be located in an addiction treatment or mental health setting.

If family, transportation, or other supports are not adequate to enable the success of a Level 2-WM program or the patient meets residential criteria in other dimensions, then residential treatment supports should be added. If available, a Level 3.2-WM (Clinically Managed Residential Withdrawal Management) program with concurrent medical services equivalent to Level 2-WM should be considered.

If the patient requires partial hospitalization or more intensive mental health services (ie, a risk rating of 2 or 3 or higher in Dimension 3), moderate intensity withdrawal management can be provided in a properly equipped mental health setting with ongoing case management to coordinate care.

WITHDRAWAL MANAGEMENT

4

RISK RATING MATRIX — SEDATIVE/HYPNOTICS

RISK RATING 3 — SIGNIFICANT RISK

A risk rating of 3 in Dimension 1 indicates that the patient has significant signs and symptoms of withdrawal, or is at risk for significant but manageable withdrawal; or withdrawal is worsening despite withdrawal management at a less intensive level of care.

INITIAL ASSESSMENT

The patient with a risk rating of 3 might evidence one of the following:

(1) The patient has significant anxiety and a moderate to severe tremor. The patient also may be withdrawing from substances other than sedative/hypnotics. However, he or she is fully coherent and able to comprehend instructions;

or

(2) The patient has moderate anxiety and insomnia, as well as possibly a mild tremor. He or she is not withdrawing from a substance other than sedative/hypnotics, and is fully coherent and able to comprehend instructions.

The patient would otherwise have had a risk rating of 2, except that he or she evidences one or more of the following problems, which pose a significant impediment to withdrawal management at a less intensive level of care:

a) The patient's past attempts to stop using sedative/hypnotics were marked by severe withdrawal symptoms.

b) The patient has moderate to severe active and potentially destabilizing medical problems.

c) Symptoms of a co-occurring psychiatric disorder are moderate to severe.

d) The patient does not have a high level of commitment to the withdrawal management process and his or her level of cooperation and reliability are questionable. For example, the patient has a recent history of withdrawal management at less intensive levels of care that were marked by inability to complete withdrawal management or to enter into continuing addiction treatment, and the patient lacks sufficient skills to complete withdrawal management.

e) The patient is at significant risk of imminent relapse.

f) The patient's family or friends are not supportive of or oppose the withdrawal management process and will not assist in providing transportation and a safe place to stay. The patient appears unable to obtain transportation (other than driving himself or herself) and access to safe and appropriate housing.

REASSESSMENT

On reassessment after initiation of treatment, the patient with a risk rating of 3 evidences one of the following:

(1) The patient's symptoms are improving as a result of the medical and psychosocial interventions, but sufficient residual symptoms persist to justify a continued risk rating of 3;

or

(2) The patient's withdrawal symptoms, although initially compatible with a risk rating of 2, have intensified despite appropriate treatment;

or

(3) The patient's withdrawal symptoms, while initially compatible with a risk rating of 4, have improved sufficiently in response to treatment to warrant a reduction to a risk rating of 3.

WITHDRAWAL MANAGEMENT

4

RISK RATING MATRIX — SEDATIVE/HYPNOTICS

RISK RATING 3 — SIGNIFICANT RISK

SERVICE NEEDS

A risk rating of 3 in Dimension 1 indicates a need for moderately high-intensity intoxication monitoring or management, or withdrawal management services. Nursing and medical care is essential.

TREATMENT INTERVENTIONS

Phenobarbital or a long-acting benzodiazepine should be given. Doses should be repeated, preferably daily, using a symptom-triggered or time-driven protocol with a symptom-driven override/rescue protocol.

Adjunctive anticonvulsants are sometimes used.

A limited amount of medication should be prescribed or dispensed, sufficient to last until the next visit (ideally, the next day). The medication should be adjusted at subsequent visits on a tapering schedule and discontinued entirely within a total treatment period of 2 to 8 weeks.

Low doses of non-addicting sleep medications may be useful for chronic insomnia.

The patient should be offered immediate access to, and simultaneous participation in, an addiction counseling program or other suitable psychosocial intervention.

Transportation should be arranged to return the patient to his or her home and overnight supervision.

LEVEL OF CARE & SETTING

The patient with a risk rating of 3 in Dimension 1 should be placed in a Level 2-WM (Ambulatory Withdrawal Management with Extended On-Site Monitoring) or Level 3.7-WM (Medically Monitored Inpatient Withdrawal management) program. However, Level 2-WM is not appropriate if certain symptoms (such as agitation or severe tremor) are persistently present at the close of the day's program service hours, because such a patient needs 24-hour medical monitoring.

Level 2-WM also is not appropriate if assessment items 2d or 2f (see initial assessment on previous page) exist, unless Level 2-WM can be combined with a supportive living arrangement.

Alternatively, the patient may be placed in a Level 3.7-WM Medically Monitored Inpatient Withdrawal Management program. Such a program may be located in an addiction treatment or mental health setting.

If the patient requires medically monitored or clinically managed mental health services (with a risk rating of 3 or higher in Dimension 3), moderately high-intensity withdrawal management can be provided in a mental health setting with ongoing case management to coordinate care.

WITHDRAWAL MANAGEMENT

4

RISK RATING MATRIX — SEDATIVE/HYPNOTICS

RISK RATING 4 — SEVERE RISK

A risk rating of 4 in Dimension 1 indicates that the patient is incapacitated, with severe signs and symptoms of withdrawal. Such a patient is in imminent danger from either the continued use of sedative/hypnotics or the abrupt discontinuation of use.

INITIAL ASSESSMENT

The patient with a risk rating of 4 might evidence one of the following:

(1) The patient has clouding of the sensorium or confusion, or new onset of hallucinations, or has experienced a seizure, or is not able to fully comprehend instructions.
or

(2) The patient has severe anxiety and a moderate to severe tremor. He or she also may be withdrawing from a substance other than sedative/hypnotics. The patient would otherwise have had a risk rating of 3, except that he or she evidences one or more of the following problems, which pose a major impediment to withdrawal management at a less intensive level of care:

a) The patient's past attempts to stop using sedative/hypnotics were marked by seizures or delirium tremens.

b) The patient has severe destabilizing medical problems.

c) Symptoms of a co-occurring psychiatric disorder are severe.

d) The patient is not cooperative or reliable, to an extent that places him or her at imminent risk of harm.

e) The patient requires medical monitoring for more than 5 hours a day.

REASSESSMENT

On reassessment after initiation of treatment, the patient with a risk rating of 4 evidences one of the following:

(1) The patient's symptoms are currently improving as a result of the medical and psychosocial interventions, but sufficient residual symptoms persist to justify a continued risk rating of 4;
or

(2) The patient's withdrawal symptoms, although initially compatible with a risk rating of 3, have intensified despite appropriate treatment.

SERVICE NEEDS

A risk rating of 4 in Dimension 1 indicates a need for high-intensity intoxication monitoring or management, or withdrawal management services, with medical monitoring and management more often than hourly.

TREATMENT INTERVENTIONS

Phenobarbital or a long-acting benzodiazepine should be given. Adjunctive anticonvulsants are sometimes used.

The patient should be closely monitored (at least several times a day, or hourly in the presence of delirium or substantial elevation of vital signs). The dose should be repeated, using a symptom-triggered or time-driven protocol with a symptom-driven override/rescue protocol in place.

As soon as he or she is medically stable, the patient should be offered immediate access to, and simultaneous participation in, a rehabilitation program or other suitable psychosocial interventions.

LEVEL OF CARE & SETTING

The patient with a risk rating of 4 should be placed in a Level 4-WM Medically Managed Intensive Inpatient Withdrawal Management program, which is an organized hospital addiction service. In the absence of such a service, an organized medical or psychiatric service in a hospital under the direction of an addiction medicine specialist may be used.

If the patient requires medically monitored and nurse-managed mental health services (with a risk rating of 3 or higher in Dimension 3), moderately high-intensity withdrawal management can be provided in a mental health setting with ongoing case management to coordinate care.

Variable Withdrawal Risk by Substance
OPIOIDS

Opioid withdrawal can be intensely uncomfortable. Although they are not life threatening, the symptoms can be so severe and chronic that, if not properly treated, relapse is highly likely.

Screening for the Possibility of a Withdrawal Syndrome and Predicting Severity

Patients with opioid use disorder experience withdrawal frequently and are therefore usually familiar with the timing and early symptoms of withdrawal. The particular symptoms vary between individuals but tend to evolve in a predictable way for a given individual. Therefore, consulting with the patient about their individual pattern, in combination with noting vital sign and pupillary diameter, will usually result in an accurate estimate of when treatment is needed.

RISK ASSESSMENT MATRIX FOR OPIOID WITHDRAWAL SYNDROME

RISK RATING	WITHDRAWAL MANAGEMENT SERVICE NEEDS & INTERVENTIONS	LEVEL OF CARE & SETTING
0 (MINIMAL/NONE)	A risk rating of 0 in Dimension 1 indicates that the patient is fully functioning and demonstrates good ability to tolerate and cope with the discomfort of withdrawal. **Service Needs** A risk rating of 0 in Dimension 1 indicates that no immediate intoxication monitoring or management, or withdrawal management services are needed. It does not affect the overall placement decision. **Treatment Interventions** At this level of risk, there is no need to initiate new professional services specifically for problems in Dimension 1.	For the patient with a risk rating of 0 in Dimension 1, the determination of level of care or setting is guided by the risk rating in other dimensions.
1 (MILD)	Occasional yawning, slight pupillary dilation, rhinorrhea, chills, mild anxiety. **Service Needs** • Daily monitoring. • Measurement of blood alcohol level. Urine screen for drugs. **Treatment Interventions** • Implementation of symptom-triggered withdrawal management protocol using long-acting opioids or non-opioid medications.	1-WM 3.2-WM
2 (MODERATE)	Frequent yawning, mild piloerection, abdominal cramps, nausea, loose stools, body aches, mild elevation of blood pressure or pulse, moderate sweating, anxiety, tremulousness, restlessness, irritability. **Service Needs** • Hourly monitoring until improvement begins, then every 2 to 3 hours. **Treatment Interventions** • Implementation of symptom-triggered withdrawal management protocol using long-acting opioids or non-opioid medications.	2-WM
3 (SIGNIFICANT)	Vomiting, diarrhea, observable tremor, mild fever, moderate elevation of blood pressure or pulse Significant anxiety, sweating, restlessness, body aches, pupillary dilation, piloerection. **Service Needs** • Hourly monitoring until improvement begins, then every 2 to 3 hours. **Treatment Interventions** • Implementation of symptom-triggered withdrawal management protocol using long-acting opioids or non-opioid medications.	2-WM 3.7-WM
4 (SEVERE)	Debilitating vomiting and diarrhea, agitation, gross tremor, fever, severe elevation of blood pressure or pulse. **Service Needs** • 24-hour monitoring – hourly or more frequent until improvement begins, then every 2 to 3 hours. **Treatment Interventions** • Implementation of symptom-triggered withdrawal management protocols using long-acting opioids or non-opioid medications.	4-WM

WITHDRAWAL MANAGEMENT

The time course of the withdrawal syndrome is determined by the half-life of the substance.[12] Withdrawal symptoms from short-acting drugs, such as heroin, can begin within 4 to 6 hours, peak within 36 to 72 hours, and last for 7 to 14 days. In addition, a protracted abstinence syndrome may last for a period of months. For methadone, symptoms may take up to 36 hours to begin, peak in 10 to 14 days, and may persist for 6 months or more.

Recommendation

The recommendations for management of opioid withdrawal parallel those for sedative/hypnotics. The intensity and rapid onset of the withdrawal symptoms, however, generally require a more aggressive medication protocol to prevent the patient's discomfort from leading to dropping out of treatment.

Variable Withdrawal Risk by Substance
TOBACCO

Tobacco creates the most commonly encountered withdrawal syndrome which is one reason for the high relapse rate for this substance. The medical risk of this syndrome, however, is sufficiently low that it can be managed in a Level 1-WM setting, unless there are sufficient complications in the other five criteria dimensions to make a more intensive level of care necessary. Also see the section on tobacco use disorder in Chapter 9.

Variable Withdrawal Risk by Substance
MARIJUANA

The existence of a marijuana withdrawal syndrome has only recently been documented.[14] Consequently, the role of withdrawal in precipitating relapse as well as the use of detoxifying medications is not well researched. The medical risk of this syndrome is sufficiently low that it can be managed in a Level 1-WM setting, unless there are sufficient complications in the other five criteria dimensions to make a more intensive level of care necessary.

Variable Withdrawal Risk by Substance
STIMULANTS (AND DISSOCIATIVE ANESTHETICS)

The clinical management of problems associated with these substances revolves more around intoxication than withdrawal. Psychotic reactions and acute medical complications require treatment and level of care decisions that parallel management of these symptoms when substance use is not involved. Withdrawal symptoms from these substances are generally self-limited and respond to general supportive psychosocial measures without the need for specific treatment. When depression is of suicidal intensity, clinical management is the same as when not substance induced.

WITHDRAWAL MANAGEMENT

4

Withdrawal Syndromes Involving More Than One Class of Substances

Patients who have become physically dependent on two classes of substances may require a more intensive level of care than with only one substance. This is not, however, invariably the case. An individual assessment of the degree of physical dependence on each substance, as well as the status of the other five criteria dimensions, is essential before a level of care decision is made.

Alcohol and benzodiazepines

These can be managed simultaneously through the use of phenobarbital or a long-acting benzodiazepine.

Opioids and benzodiazepines

One option is to treat these simultaneously, but determining which one is creating the withdrawal anxiety can sometimes be difficult. An easier option is to separate these, first stabilizing the opioid withdrawal before initiating the benzodiazepine withdrawal management protocol.

Opioids and alcohol

These can be treated simultaneously. Benzodiazepines can be used with non-opioid medications and opioid agonists, but caution should be exercised because they gradually lift the "ceiling effect" on respiratory depression from buprenorphine.

Withdrawal Management Decision Rules in *The ASAM Criteria Software*

Comparison of Withdrawal Management Services Across Treatment Levels

While the preceding section provided a narrative and visual explanation of the thought process behind the ASAM criteria, the following section of this chapter provides the detailed decision rules incorporated in *The ASAM Criteria Software* for withdrawal management. Keep in mind, however, that the myriad conditions and clinical circumstances patients experience during intoxication and withdrawal are exceedingly complex. The rules that follow are embedded in *The ASAM Criteria Software*, which assists in the assessment and treatment of Dimension 1 withdrawal management.

Similar to the previous section, these dimensional admission criteria decision rules have been separated by substance for better understanding and ease of use.

WITHDRAWAL MANAGEMENT

4

DIMENSIONAL ADMISSION CRITERIA DECISION RULES

SPECIFICATIONS FOR APPROPRIATE PLACEMENT

LEVEL 1-WM
Ambulatory Withdrawal Management without Extended On-Site Monitoring

The patient is experiencing at least mild signs and symptoms of withdrawal, or there is evidence (based on history of substance intake; age; gender; previous withdrawal history; present symptoms; physical condition; and/or emotional, behavioral, or cognitive condition) that withdrawal is imminent.

The patient is assessed as being at minimal risk of severe withdrawal syndrome and can be safely managed at this level.

LEVEL 2-WM
Ambulatory Withdrawal Management with Extended On-Site Monitoring

The patient is experiencing signs and symptoms of withdrawal, or there is evidence (based on history of substance intake; age; gender; previous withdrawal history; present symptoms; physical condition; and/or emotional, behavioral, or cognitive condition) that withdrawal is imminent.

The patient is assessed as being at moderate risk of severe withdrawal syndrome outside the program setting; is free of severe physical and psychiatric complications; and would safely respond to several hours of monitoring, medication, and treatment.

LEVEL 3.2-WM
Clinically Managed Residential Withdrawal Management

The patient is experiencing signs and symptoms of withdrawal, or there is evidence (based on history of substance intake; age; gender; previous withdrawal history; present symptoms; physical condition; and/or emotional, behavioral, or cognitive condition) that withdrawal is imminent.

The patient is assessed as not being at risk of severe withdrawal syndrome, and moderate withdrawal is safely manageable at this level of service.

LEVEL 3.7-WM
Medically Monitored Inpatient Withdrawal Management

The patient is experiencing signs and symptoms of severe withdrawal, or there is evidence (based on history of substance intake; age; gender; previous withdrawal history; present symptoms; physical condition; and/or emotional, behavioral, or cognitive condition) that a severe withdrawal syndrome is imminent.

The severe withdrawal syndrome is assessed as manageable at this level of service.

LEVEL 4-WM
Medically Managed Intensive Inpatient Withdrawal Management

The patient is experiencing signs and symptoms of severe withdrawal, or there is evidence (based on history of substance intake; age; gender; previous withdrawal history; present symptoms; physical condition; and/or emotional, behavioral, or cognitive condition) that a severe withdrawal syndrome is imminent.

ALCOHOL

Examples include, but are not limited to the following:

1-WM

- The presence of mild to moderate symptoms of withdrawal, with a CIWA-Ar score of less than 10, or the equivalent for a comparable standardized scoring system.

2-WM

- A CIWA-Ar score of 10 to 25, or the equivalent for a comparable standardized scoring system.

3.2-WM

- The patient is intoxicated or is withdrawing from alcohol and the CIWA-Ar score is less than 8 at admission, and monitoring is available to assure that it remains less than 8, or the equivalent for a comparable standardized scoring system.

3.7-WM

- The patient is withdrawing from alcohol, the CIWA-Ar score is 19 or greater (or the equivalent for a standardized scoring system) by the end of the period of outpatient monitoring available in Level 2-WM.
- Alcohol <u>and</u> sedative/hypnotics: The patient has marked lethargy or hypersomnolence due to intoxication with alcohol or other drugs, and a history of severe withdrawal syndrome, or the patient's altered level of consciousness has not stabilized at the end of the period of outpatient monitoring available at Level 2-WM.

4-WM

- The patient is withdrawing from alcohol, and the CIWA-Ar score is 19 or greater (or the equivalent for a comparable standardized scoring system), and the patient requires monitoring more often than hourly; requires intravenous medication or infusions; or requires close behavioral monitoring because of high levels of agitation, confusion, or extremes of vital signs.
- Alcohol <u>and</u> sedative/hypnotics: The patient is experiencing seizures; delirium tremens; or severe, chronic hallucinations.

WITHDRAWAL MANAGEMENT

④

SEDATIVE/HYPNOTICS   Examples include, but are not limited to the following:

WITHDRAWAL MANAGEMENT

4

1-WM

- Any recent use is confined to therapeutic levels and is not complicated by daily use of alcohol or other mind-altering drugs known to produce a significant withdrawal syndrome.
- There is a reliable history that the patient is withdrawing from therapeutic doses of sedative/hypnotics, but there is no evidence of other alcohol or drug dependence. Withdrawal symptoms have responded to, or are likely to respond to, substitute doses of sedative/hypnotics in the therapeutic range within 2 hours.

2-WM

- There is a reliable history that the patient is withdrawing from sedative/hypnotics and withdrawal symptoms have responded to, or are likely to respond to, substitute doses of sedative/hypnotics within the observable hours of the program.
- The patient has ingested sedative/hypnotics in excess of therapeutic levels daily for at least 4 weeks, but the risk of seizures, hallucinations, dissociation, or severe affective disorder during unobserved periods outside the program is assessed as minimal. Close hourly monitoring is available, if needed. There is no accompanying chronic mental or physical disorder that poses a danger to the patient during withdrawal.
- The patient has ingested sedative/hypnotics at not more than therapeutic levels daily for at least 6 months, in combination with daily alcohol use or regular use of another mind-altering drug known to have its own dangerous withdrawal syndrome. Nonetheless, the risk of seizures, hallucinations, dissociation, or severe affective symptoms outside the program is minimal.

3.2-WM

3.7-WM

- The patient has ingested sedative/hypnotics at more than therapeutic levels daily for more than 4 weeks and is not responsive to appropriate recent efforts to maintain the dose at therapeutic levels.
- The patient has ingested sedative/hypnotics at more than therapeutic levels daily for more than 4 weeks, in combination with daily alcohol use or regular use of another mind-altering drug known to pose a severe risk of withdrawal. Signs and symptoms of withdrawal are of moderate severity, and the patient cannot be stabilized by the end of the period of outpatient monitoring available at Level 2-WM.
- Alcohol <u>and</u> sedative/hypnotics: The patient has marked lethargy or hypersomnolence due to intoxication with alcohol or other drugs, and a history of severe withdrawal syndrome, or the patient's altered level of consciousness has not stabilized at the end of the period of outpatient monitoring available at Level 2-WM.

4-WM

- Alcohol <u>and</u> sedative/hypnotics: The patient is experiencing seizures; delirium tremens; or severe, chronic hallucinations.
- The patient has ingested sedative/hypnotics at more than therapeutic levels daily for more than 4 weeks, and the patient has an accompanying acute mental or physical disorder that is complicating withdrawal.
- The patient has ingested sedative/hypnotics daily for at least 6 months, in combination with daily alcohol use or regular use of another mind-altering drug known to pose a severe withdrawal syndrome, and the patient has an accompanying acute mental or physical disorder that is complicating withdrawal.

OPIOIDS

Examples include, but are not limited to the following:

1-WM

- For withdrawal management not using opioid agonist medication: Either the patient's use of high-potency opioids (such as injectable or smoked forms) has not been daily for more than 2 weeks preceding admission or the use of opioids is near the therapeutically recommended level.
- For withdrawal management using opioid agonist medication, such as methadone or other appropriate opioids: Either the patient is being withdrawn gradually from opioid agonist medication or the patient is being treated for mild opioid withdrawal symptoms.

2-WM

- For withdrawal management not using opioid agonist medication: The abstinence syndrome—as indicated by vital signs and evidence of physical discomfort or craving—can be stabilized by the end of each day's monitoring, so that the patient can manage such symptoms at home with appropriate supervision.
- For withdrawal management using opioid agonist medication, such as methadone or other appropriate opioids: The withdrawal signs and symptoms are of such severity or instability that extended monitoring is required to determine the appropriate dosage.

3.2-WM

- Withdrawal signs and symptoms are distressing but do not require medication for reasonable withdrawal discomfort, and the patient is impulsive and lacks skills needed to prevent immediate continued drug use.

3.7-WM

- For withdrawal management not using opioid agonist medication: The patient has used opioids daily for more than 2 weeks and has a history of inability to complete withdrawal as an outpatient or without medication in a Level 3.2-WM service.
- Antagonist medication is to be used in withdrawal in a brief but intensive withdrawal management (as in multiday pharmacological induction onto naltrexone).

4-WM

- The patient is experiencing a severe opioid withdrawal syndrome that has not been stabilized or managed at a less intensive level of service.

WITHDRAWAL MANAGEMENT

4

WITHDRAWAL MANAGEMENT

4

STIMULANTS

Examples include, but are not limited to the following:

1-WM
- The patient is withdrawing from stimulants and is experiencing some lethargy, agitation, paranoia, mild psychotic symptoms, or depression, but he or she has good impulse control.

2-WM
- The patient is withdrawing from stimulants and is experiencing significant lethargy, agitation, paranoia, psychotic symptoms, or depression, and requires extended outpatient monitoring to determine impulse control and readiness for Level 1-WM ambulatory withdrawal management services or the need for Level 3.2-WM withdrawal management services.

3.2-WM
- The patient has marked lethargy, hypersomnolence, paranoia, or mild psychotic symptoms due to stimulant withdrawal, and these are still present beyond a period of outpatient monitoring available in Level 2-WM services.

3.7-WM
- The patient has marked lethargy, hypersomnolence, agitation, paranoia, depression, or mild psychotic symptoms due to stimulant withdrawal, and has poor impulse control and/or coping skills to prevent immediate continued drug use.

4-WM
- Intoxication or withdrawal signs and symptoms require psychiatric or medical monitoring more frequently than hourly (because of psychotic, impulsive behavior or depressive suicidality).

NICOTINE
Examples include, but are not limited to the following:

1-WM
- The patient is withdrawing from nicotine and is experiencing withdrawal symptoms that require either nicotine replacement therapies or non-nicotine agents for symptomatic treatment.

2-WM

3.2-WM

3.7-WM

4-WM

ALL SUBSTANCES
Examples include, but are not limited to the following:

1-WM

2-WM

3.2-WM

3.7-WM

4-WM
- There is recent (within 24 hours) serious head trauma or loss of consciousness, with chronic mental status or neurological changes resulting in the need to closely observe the patient at least hourly.
- Drug overdose or intoxication has compromised the patient's mental status, cardiac function, or other vital signs or functions.
- The patient has a significant acute biomedical disorder that poses substantial risk of serious or life-threatening consequences during withdrawal (such as significant hypertension or esophageal varices).

WITHDRAWAL MANAGEMENT

4

DIMENSIONAL ADMISSION CRITERIA DECISION RULES (CONTINUED)

WITHDRAWAL MANAGEMENT

❹

SPECIFICATIONS FOR APPROPRIATE PLACEMENT

LEVEL 1-WM Ambulatory Withdrawal Management without Extended On-Site Monitoring	**IN ADDITION** to specifications shown on the preceding pages	The patient has withdrawal symptoms but is at minimal risk of severe withdrawal syndrome and is assessed as likely to complete needed withdrawal management and to enter into continued treatment or self-help recovery, as evidenced by meeting **[1]** or **[2]** or **[3]**:
LEVEL 2-WM Ambulatory Withdrawal Management with Extended On-Site Monitoring	**IN ADDITION** to specifications shown on the preceding pages	The patient is assessed as likely to complete withdrawal management and to enter into continued treatment or self-help recovery, as evidenced by meeting **[1]** and either **[2]** or **[3]** or **[4]**:
LEVEL 3.2-WM Clinically Managed Residential Withdrawal Management	**IN ADDITION** to specifications shown on the preceding pages	The patient is assessed as not requiring medication, but requires this level of service to complete withdrawal management and enter into continued treatment or self-help recovery because of inadequate home supervision or support structure, as evidenced by meeting **[1]** or **[2]** or **[3]**:
LEVEL 3.7-WM Medically Monitored Inpatient Withdrawal Management	**ALTERNATIVELY** to the specifications shown on the preceding pages	There is a strong likelihood that the patient (who requires medication) will not complete withdrawal management at another level of care and enter into continuing treatment or self-help recovery, as evidenced (for example), by **any** of **[1]** or **[2]** or **[3]**:
LEVEL 4-WM Medically Managed Intensive Inpatient Withdrawal Management	**ALTERNATIVELY** to the specifications shown on the preceding pages	Level 4 is the only available level of care that can provide the medical support and comfort care needed by the patient, as evidenced by **[1]** or **[2]**:

1-WM

[1] The patient has an adequate understanding of ambulatory withdrawal management and has expressed commitment to enter such a program; **or**

[2] The patient has adequate support services to ensure commitment to completion of withdrawal management and entry into ongoing treatment or recovery; **or**

[3] The patient is willing to accept a recommendation for treatment (for example, to begin disulfiram, naltrexone, or other medication once withdrawal has been managed, or to attend outpatient sessions or self-help groups).

2-WM

[1] The patient or support persons clearly understand instructions for care and are able to follow instructions; **and**

[2] The patient has an adequate understanding of ambulatory withdrawal management and has expressed commitment to enter such a program; **or**

[3] The patient has adequate support services to ensure commitment to completion of withdrawal management and entry into ongoing treatment or recovery; **or**

[4] The patient evidences willingness to accept a recommendation for treatment once withdrawal has been managed (for example, to attend outpatient sessions or self-help groups).

3.2-WM

[1] The patient's recovery environment is not supportive of withdrawal management and entry into treatment, and the patient does not have sufficient coping skills to safely deal with the problems in the recovery environment; **or**

[2] The patient has a recent history of withdrawal management at less intensive levels of service that is marked by inability to complete withdrawal management or to enter into continuing addiction treatment, and the patient continues to have insufficient skills to complete withdrawal management; **or**

[3] The patient recently has demonstrated an inability to complete withdrawal management at a less intensive level of service, as by continued use of other-than-prescribed drugs or other mind-altering substances.

3.7-WM

[1] The patient requires medication and has a recent history of withdrawal management at a less intensive level of care, marked by past and current inability to complete withdrawal management and enter into continuing addiction treatment. The patient continues to have insufficient skills or supports to complete withdrawal management; **or**

[2] The patient has a recent history of withdrawal management at less intensive levels of service that is marked by inability to complete withdrawal management or to enter into continuing addiction treatment, and the patient continues to have insufficient skills to complete withdrawal management; **or**

[3] The patient has a comorbid physical, emotional, behavioral, or cognitive condition (such as chronic pain with active exacerbation or posttraumatic stress disorder with brief dissociative episodes) that is manageable in a Level 3.7-WM setting but which increases the clinical severity of the withdrawal and complicates withdrawal management.

4-WM

[1] A withdrawal management regimen or a patient's response to that regimen that requires monitoring or intervention more frequently than hourly; **or**

[2] The patient's need for withdrawal management or stabilization while pregnant, until she can be safely treated in a less intensive level of care. For example, the patient does not require medical management (as in the case of a patient who is soon to have the pregnancy terminated), or she no longer is bleeding or leaking amniotic fluid, or an unstable fetal heartbeat has improved.

WITHDRAWAL MANAGEMENT

❹

DIMENSIONAL ADMISSION CRITERIA DECISION RULES (CONTINUED)

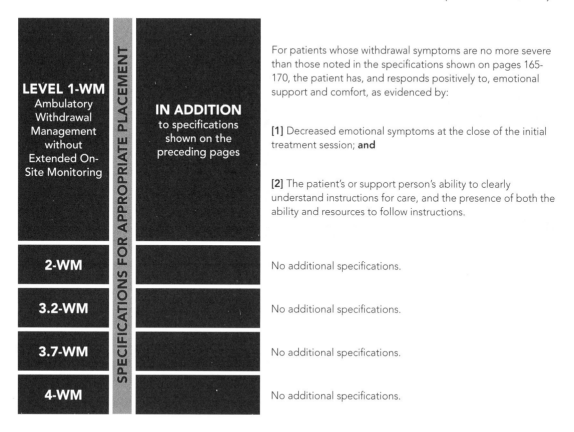

LEVEL 1-WM
Ambulatory Withdrawal Management without Extended On-Site Monitoring

SPECIFICATIONS FOR APPROPRIATE PLACEMENT

IN ADDITION to specifications shown on the preceding pages

For patients whose withdrawal symptoms are no more severe than those noted in the specifications shown on pages 165-170, the patient has, and responds positively to, emotional support and comfort, as evidenced by:

[1] Decreased emotional symptoms at the close of the initial treatment session; **and**

[2] The patient's or support person's ability to clearly understand instructions for care, and the presence of both the ability and resources to follow instructions.

2-WM — No additional specifications.

3.2-WM — No additional specifications.

3.7-WM — No additional specifications.

4-WM — No additional specifications.

WITHDRAWAL MANAGEMENT

4

Level of Care Placement

While many see level of care placement as an initial step in the treatment process, it is only after first determining priority dimensions (through a comprehensive assessment), diagnoses, and dose and intensities needed that practitioners of the ASAM criteria then move to consider a level of care placement.

Two "crosswalks" have been provided here to show how assessment information gained from the criteria's six dimensions can be applied to each level of care. One crosswalk considers adult patients and one considers adolescent patients.

Note that these adult and adolescent overviews of the admission criteria are approximate summaries, used to illustrate the principal concepts and structure of the criteria. The full set of criteria should be noted and this brief overview is not intended to replace the use of the comprehensive admission criteria provided in each level of care.

SERVICE CHARACTERISTIC CATEGORIES

As in other chapters of *The ASAM Criteria*, the following categories of service characteristics will deliver example and appropriate information for each level of care:

 Examples of Service Delivery and Settings

 Support Systems

 Staff

 Therapies

 Assessment/Treatment Plan Review

 Documentation

In addition, each level of care will articulate a separate, color-coded set of criteria for both adult and adolescent populations in the following categories:

 Diagnostic Admission Criteria

Dimensional Admission Criteria

LOC PLACEMENT

4

Adult Levels of Care	**DIMENSION 1** Acute Intoxication and/or Withdrawal Potential	**DIMENSION 2** Biomedical Conditions and Complications	**DIMENSION 3** Emotional, Behavioral, or Cognitive Conditions and Complications
LEVEL 0.5 Early Intervention	No withdrawal risk	None or very stable	None or very stable
OTP - LEVEL 1 Opioid Treatment Program	Physiologically dependent on opioids and requires OTP to prevent withdrawal	None or manageable with outpatient medical monitoring	None or manageable in an outpatient structured environment
LEVEL 1 Outpatient Services	Not experiencing significant withdrawal, or at minimal risk of severe withdrawal. Manageable at Level 1-WM (See withdrawal management criteria)	None or very stable, or is receiving concurrent medical monitoring	None or very stable, or is receiving concurrent mental health monitoring
LEVEL 2.1 Intensive Outpatient Services	Minimal risk of severe withdrawal, manageable at Level 2-WM (See withdrawal management criteria)	None or not a distraction from treatment. Such problems are manageable at Level 2.1	Mild severity, with potential to distract from recovery; needs monitoring
LEVEL 2.5 Partial Hospitalization Services	Moderate risk of severe withdrawal manageable at Level 2-WM (See withdrawal management criteria)	None or not sufficient to distract from treatment. Such problems are manageable at Level 2.5	Mild to moderate severity, with potential to distract from recovery; needs stabilization
LEVEL 3.1 Clinically Managed Low-Intensity Residential Services	No withdrawal risk, or minimal or stable withdrawal. Concurrently receiving Level 1-WM (minimal) or Level 2-WM (moderate) services (See withdrawal management criteria)	None or stable, or receiving concurrent medical monitoring	None or minimal; not distracting to recovery. If stable, a co-occurring capable program is appropriate. If not, a co-occurring enhanced program is required
LEVEL 3.3 Clinically Managed Population-Specific High-Intensity Residential Services	At minimal risk of severe withdrawal. If withdrawal is present, manageable at Level 3.2-WM (See withdrawal management criteria)	None or stable, or receiving concurrent medical monitoring	Mild to moderate severity; needs structure to focus on recovery. Treatment should be designed to address significant cognitive deficits. If stable, a co-occurring capable program is appropriate. If not, a co-occurring enhanced program is required
LEVEL 3.5 Clinically Managed High-Intensity Residential Services	At minimal risk of severe withdrawal. If withdrawal is present, manageable at Level 3.2-WM (See withdrawal management criteria)	None or stable, or receiving concurrent medical monitoring	Demonstrates repeated inability to control impulses, or unstable and dangerous signs/symptoms require stabilization. Other functional deficits require stabilization and a 24-hour setting to prepare for community integration and continuing care. A co-occurring enhanced setting is required for those with severe and chronic mental illness
LEVEL 3.7 Medically Monitored Intensive Inpatient Services	At high risk of withdrawal, but manageable at Level 3.7-WM and does not require the full resources of a licensed hospital (See withdrawal management criteria)	Requires 24-hour medical monitoring but not intensive treatment	Moderate severity; needs a 24-hour structured setting. If the patient has a co-occurring mental disorder, requires concurrent mental health services in a medically monitored setting
LEVEL 4 Medically Managed Intensive Inpatient Services	At high risk of withdrawal and requires Level 4-WM and the full resources of a licensed hospital (See withdrawal management criteria)	Requires 24-hour medical and nursing care and the full resources of a licensed hospital	Because of severe and unstable problems, requires 24-hour psychiatric care with concomitant addiction treatment (co-occurring enhanced)

ADULT CROSSWALK

4

DIMENSION 4 Readiness to Change	DIMENSION 5 Relapse, Continued Use, or Continued Problem Potential	DIMENSION 6 Recovery/Living Environment
Willing to explore how current alcohol, tobacco, other drug, or medication use, and/or high-risk behaviors may affect personal goals	Needs an understanding of, or skills to change, current alcohol, tobacco, other drug, or medication use patterns, and/or high risk behavior	Social support system or significant others increase the risk of personal conflict about alcohol, tobacco, and/or other drug use
Ready to change the negative effects of opioid use, but is not ready for total abstinence from illicit prescription or non-prescription drug use	At high risk of relapse or continued use without OTP and structured therapy to promote treatment progress	Recovery environment is supportive and/or the patient has skills to cope
Ready for recovery but needs motivating and monitoring strategies to strengthen readiness. Or needs ongoing monitoring and disease management. Or high severity in this dimension but not in other dimensions. Needs Level 1 motivational enhancement strategies	Able to maintain abstinence or control use and/or addictive behaviors and pursue recovery or motivational goals with minimal support	Recovery environment is supportive and/or the patient has skills to cope
Has variable engagement in treatment, ambivalence, or a lack of awareness of the substance use or mental health problem, and requires a structured program several times a week to promote progress through the stages of change	Intensification of addiction or mental health symptoms indicate a high likelihood of relapse or continued use or continued problems without close monitoring and support several times a week	Recovery environment is not supportive, but with structure and support, the patient can cope
Has poor engagement in treatment, significant ambivalence, or a lack of awareness of the substance use or mental health problem, requiring a near-daily structured program or intensive engagement services to promote progress through the stages of change	Intensification of addiction or mental health symptoms, despite active participation in a Level 1 or 2.1 program, indicates a high likelihood of relapse or continued use or continued problems without near-daily monitoring and support	Recovery environment is not supportive, but with structure and support and relief from the home environment, the patient can cope
Open to recovery, but needs a structured environment to maintain therapeutic gains	Understands relapse but needs structure to maintain therapeutic gains	Environment is dangerous, but recovery is achievable if Level 3.1 24-hour structure is available
Has little awareness and needs interventions available only at Level 3.3 to engage and stay in treatment. If there is high severity in Dimension 4 but not in any other dimension, motivational enhancement strategies should be provided in Level 1	Has little awareness and needs interventions available only at Level 3.3 to prevent continued use, with imminent dangerous consequences, because of cognitive deficits or comparable dysfunction	Environment is dangerous and patient needs 24-hour structure to learn to cope
Has marked difficulty with, or opposition to, treatment, with dangerous consequences. If there is high severity in Dimension 4 but not in any other dimension, motivational enhancement strategies should be provided in Level 1	Has no recognition of the skills needed to prevent continued use, with imminently dangerous consequences	Environment is dangerous and the patient lacks skills to cope outside of a highly structured 24-hour setting
Low interest in treatment and impulse control is poor, despite negative consequences; needs motivating strategies only safely available in a 24-hour structured setting. If there is high severity in Dimension 4 but not in any other dimension, motivational enhancement strategies should be provided in Level 1	Unable to control use, with imminently dangerous consequences, despite active participation at less intensive levels of care	Environment is dangerous and the patient lacks skills to cope outside of a highly structured 24-hour setting
Problems in this dimension do not qualify the patient for Level 4 services. If the patient's only severity is in Dimension 4, 5, and/or 6 without high severity in Dimensions 1, 2, and/or 3, then the patient does not qualify for Level 4	Problems in this dimension do not qualify the patient for Level 4 services. See further explanation in Dimension 4	Problems in this dimension do not qualify the patient for Level 4 services. See further explanation in Dimension 4

ADULT CROSSWALK

4

NOTE: THIS OVERVIEW OF THE ADULT ADMISSION CRITERIA IS AN APPROXIMATE SUMMARY TO ILLUSTRATE THE PRINCIPAL CONCEPTS AND STRUCTURE OF THE CRITERIA. THIS BRIEF OVERVIEW IS NOT INTENDED TO REPLACE THE USE OF THE COMPREHENSIVE ADMISSION CRITERIA.

Adolescent Levels of Care	DIMENSION 1 Acute Intoxication and/or Withdrawal Potential	DIMENSION 2 Biomedical Conditions and Complications	DIMENSION 3 Emotional, Behavioral, or Cognitive Conditions and Complications A) Dangerousness/Lethality, B) Interference with Addiction and/or Mental Health Recovery Efforts, C) Social Functioning, D) Ability for Self-Care, E) Course of Illness
LEVEL 0.5 Early Intervention	No withdrawal risk	None or very stable	None or very stable. Any Dimension 3 issues are being addressed through concurrent mental health services and do not interfere with early intervention addiction treatment services
LEVEL 1 Outpatient Services	No withdrawal risk	None or very stable, or is receiving concurrent medical monitoring	The adolescent's status in Dimension 3 is characterized by all of the following: A) The adolescent is not at risk of harm, B) There is minimal interference, C) Minimal to mild impairment, D) The adolescent is experiencing minimal current difficulties with activities of daily living, but there is significant risk of deterioration, E) The adolescent is at minimal imminent risk, which predicts a need for some monitoring or interventions
LEVEL 2.1 Intensive Outpatient Services	Experiencing minimal withdrawal, or is at risk of withdrawal	None or stable, or distracting from treatment at a less intensive level of care. Such problems are manageable at Level 2.1	The adolescent's status in Dimension 3 features one or more of the following: A) The adolescent is at low risk of harm, and he or she is safe between sessions, B) Mild interference requires the intensity of this level of care to support treatment engagement, C) Mild to moderate impairment, but can sustain responsibilities, D) The adolescent is experiencing mild to moderate difficulties with activities of daily living, and requires frequent monitoring or interventions, E) The adolescent's history (combined with the present situation) predicts the need for frequent monitoring or interventions
LEVEL 2.5 Partial Hospitalization Services	Experiencing mild withdrawal, or is at risk of withdrawal	None or stable, or distracting from treatment at a less intensive level of care. Such problems are manageable at Level 2.5	The adolescent's status in Dimension 3 features one or more of the following: A) The adolescent is at low risk of harm, and he or she is safe overnight, B) Moderate interference requires the intensity of this level of care to support treatment engagement, C) Moderate impairment, but can sustain responsibilities, D) The adolescent is experiencing moderate difficulties with activities of daily living and requires near-daily monitoring or interventions, E) The adolescent's history (combined with the present situation) predicts the need for near-daily monitoring or interventions
LEVEL 3.1 Clinically Managed Low-Intensity Residential Services	The adolescent's state of withdrawal (or risk of withdrawal) is being managed concurrently at another level of care	None or stable, or receiving concurrent medical monitoring as needed	The adolescent's status in Dimension 3 is characterized by one or more of the following: A) The adolescent needs a stable living environment for safety, B) Moderate interference requiring limited 24-hour supervision to support treatment engagement, C) Moderate impairment needing limited 24-hour supervision to sustain responsibilities, D) Moderate difficulties with activities of daily living requiring limited 24-hour supervision and frequent prompting, E) The adolescent's history (combined with the present situation) predicts instability without limited 24-hour supervision
LEVEL 3.5 Clinically Managed Medium-Intensity Residential Services	Adolescent is experiencing mild to moderate withdrawal (or is at risk of withdrawal), but does not need pharmacological management or frequent medical or nursing monitoring	None or stable, or receiving concurrent medical monitoring as needed	The adolescent's status in Dimension 3 features one or more of the following: A) Moderate but stable risk of harm, thus needing medium-intensity 24-hour monitoring or treatment for safety, B) Moderate to severe interference requiring medium-intensity residential treatment to support engagement, C) Moderate to severe impairment that cannot be managed at a less intensive level of care, D) Moderate to severe difficulties with activities of daily living requiring 24-hour supervision and medium-intensity staff assistance, E) The adolescent's history (combined with the present situation) predicts destabilization without medium-intensity residential treatment
LEVEL 3.7 Medically Monitored High-Intensity Inpatient Services	Adolescent is experiencing moderate to severe withdrawal (or is at risk of withdrawal), but this is manageable at Level 3.7	Requires 24-hour medical monitoring, but not intensive treatment	The adolescent's status in Dimension 3 features one or more of the following: A) Moderate risk of harm needing high-intensity 24-hour monitoring or treatment, or secure placement, for safety, B) Severe interference requiring high-intensity residential treatment to support engagement, C) Severe impairment that cannot be managed at a less intensive level of care, D) Severe difficulties with activities of daily living requiring 24-hour supervision and high-intensity staff assistance, E) The adolescent's history (combined with the present situation) predicts destabilization without high-intensity residential treatment
LEVEL 4 Medically Managed Intensive Inpatient Services	Adolescent is experiencing severe withdrawal (or is at risk of withdrawal) and requires intensive active medical management	Requires 24-hour medical and nursing care and the full resources of a licensed hospital	The adolescent's status in Dimension 3 features one or more of the following: A) The adolescent is at severe risk of harm, B) Very severe, almost overwhelming interference renders the adolescent incapable of participating in treatment at a less intensive level of care, C) Very severe, dangerous impairment requiring frequent medical and nursing interventions, D) Very severe difficulties with activities of daily living requiring frequent medical and nursing interventions, E) The adolescent's history (combined with the present situation) predicts destabilization without inpatient medical management

DIMENSION 4 Readiness to Change	DIMENSION 5 Relapse, Continued Use, or Continued Problem Potential	DIMENSION 6 Recovery/Living Environment
Willing to explore how current alcohol, tobacco, medication, other drug use, and/or high-risk behaviors may affect achievement of personal goals	Needs an understanding of, or skills to change, current alcohol, tobacco, other drug, or medication use patterns, and/or high-risk behaviors	Adolescent's risk of initiation of or progression in substance use and/or high-risk behaviors is increased by substance use or values about use. High-risk behaviors of family, peers, or others in the adolescent's social support system
Willing to engage in treatment, and is at least contemplating change, but needs motivating and monitoring strategies	Able to maintain abstinence or control use and pursue recovery or motivational goals with minimal support	Family and environment can support recovery with limited assistance
Requires close monitoring and support several times a week to promote progress through the stages of change because of variable treatment engagement, or no interest in getting assistance	Significant risk of relapse or continued use, or continued problems and deterioration in level of functioning. Has poor prevention skills and needs close monitoring and support	Adolescent's environment is impeding his or her recovery, and adolescent requires close monitoring and support to overcome that barrier
Requires a near-daily structured program to promote progress through the stages of change because of little treatment engagement or escalating use and impairment, or no awareness of the role of alcohol, tobacco, and/or other drugs play in his or her present problems	High risk of relapse or continued use, or continued problems and deterioration in level of functioning. Has minimal prevention skills and needs near-daily monitoring and support	Adolescent's environment renders recovery unlikely without near-daily monitoring and support, or frequent relief from his or her home environment
Open to recovery, but needs limited 24-hour supervision to promote or sustain progress	Understands the potential for continued use and/or has emerging recovery skills, but needs supervision to reinforce recovery and relapse prevention skills, limit exposure to substances and/or environmental triggers, or maintain therapeutic gains	Environment poses a risk to his or her recovery, so that he or she requires alternative residential secure placement or support
The adolescent needs intensive motivating strategies in a 24-hour structured program to address minimal engagement in, or opposition to, treatment, or to address his or her lack of recognition of current severe impairment	Unable to control use and/or behaviors and avoid serious impairment without a 24-hour structured program. He or she is unable to overcome environmental triggers or cravings, has insufficient supervision between encounters at a less intensive level of care, or has high chronicity and/or poor response to treatment	Environment is dangerous to his or her recovery, so that he or she requires residential treatment to promote recovery goals, or for protection
The adolescent needs motivating strategies in a 24-hour medically monitored program due to no treatment engagement associated with a biomedical, emotional, or behavioral condition; or because he or she actively opposes treatment, requiring secure placement to remain safe; or because he or she needs high-intensity case management to create linkages that would support outpatient treatment	Unable to interrupt high-severity or high-frequency pattern of use and/or behaviors and avoid dangerous consequences without high-intensity 24-hour interventions (because of an emotional, behavioral, or cognitive condition; severe impulse control problems; withdrawal symptoms; and the like)	Environment is dangerous to his or her recovery, and he or she requires residential treatment to promote recovery goals or for protection, and to help him or her establish a successful transition to a less intensive level of care
Problems in this dimension do not qualify the patient for Level 4 services. If the patient's only severity is in Dimension 4, 5, and/or 6 without high severity in Dimensions 1, 2, and/or 3, then the patient does not qualify for Level 4	Problems in this dimension do not qualify the patient for Level 4 services. If the patient's only severity is in Dimension 4, 5, and/or 6 without high severity in Dimensions 1, 2, and/or 3, then the patient does not qualify for Level 4	Problems in this dimension do not qualify the patient for Level 4 services. If the patient's only severity is in Dimension 4, 5, and/or 6 without high severity in Dimensions 1, 2, and/or 3, then the patient does not qualify for Level 4

ADOLESCENT CROSSWALK ④

NOTE: THIS OVERVIEW OF THE ADOLESCENT ADMISSION CRITERIA IS AN APPROXIMATE SUMMARY TO ILLUSTRATE THE PRINCIPAL CONCEPTS AND STRUCTURE OF THE CRITERIA. THIS BRIEF OVERVIEW IS NOT INTENDED TO REPLACE THE USE OF THE COMPREHENSIVE ADMISSION CRITERIA.

Level 0.5
Early Intervention

Early intervention is an organized service that may be delivered in a wide variety of settings. Early intervention services are designed to explore and address problems or risk factors that appear to be related to substance use and addictive behavior, and to help the individual recognize the harmful consequences of high-risk substance use and/or addictive behavior.

Level 0.5 constitutes a service for specific individuals who, for a specific reason, are at risk of developing substance-related or addictive behavior problems, or those for whom there is not yet sufficient information to document a substance use or addictive disorder. Level 0.5 is consistent with "Indicated Prevention," as described by the National Institute on Drug Abuse. It is also synonymous with the public health description of "Secondary Prevention."[1]

Early intervention also encompasses services offered to persons in non-specialty settings, such as hospital emergency departments, or primary care medical clinics (which may or may not be organized as Patient Centered Health Care Homes). In these settings, the presentation may be substance use that is beginning to cause some harmful effects and/or high-risk use. Level 0.5 services in such settings take the form of Screening, Brief Intervention, and Referral to Treatment (SBIRT).

SBIRT attempts to intervene early with non-addicted people, and to identify those who do have a substance use or addictive disorder and need linking to formal treatment. SBIRT is commonly delivered in emergency rooms, trauma centers, and other primary care settings. It can also include multi-hour interventions occurring over a few days or a few weeks, as is common in impaired driving interventions or in SBIRT's Brief Intervention of one to five short motivational sessions, designed to encourage and promote healthy behaviors and focusing on increasing insight and awareness.

Where Level 0.5 is delivered as an impaired driving program (eg, Driving Under the Influence (DUI), Driving While Intoxicated (DWI), Operating a Motor Vehicle while Intoxicated (OMVI)), the length of service may be mandated and determined by program and regulatory rules. Completion of the program may be a prerequisite to reinstitution of driving privileges.

Prior to admission, a diagnostic assessment should be performed in conjunction with a comprehensive multidimensional assessment to determine whether the person meets the diagnostic admission criteria of Level 0.5, which requires that a person does not meet diagnostic criteria of a substance use disorder. If new information is identified through the reassessment process that indicates an actual substance use disorder and the need for treatment, there are three possible options:

a. If the individual is in imminent danger, he or she should be transferred to a clinically appropriate level of care, even if that precludes completion of the mandated impaired driving program.

b. If the individual is not in imminent danger but does require formalized treatment services, an attempt should be made to facilitate such treatment with the services of the Level 0.5 program. These services can be provided concurrently, if possible.

c. If the individual can wait to enter formal treatment until after the Level 0.5 program is completed, transfer to the appropriate level of care should be arranged as soon as possible after the Level 0.5 program is completed.

LEVEL 0.5

4

Length of Service

Length of service at Level 0.5 varies according to the following:

a. an individual's ability to comprehend the information provided and use that information to make behavior changes and avoid problems related to substance use;

b. the appearance of new problems that require treatment at another level of care; or

c. regulatory mandated length of service. Length will vary from as little as 15-60 minutes in SBIRT to several weeks as in impaired driving programs.

EXAMPLES OF SERVICE DELIVERY

Level 0.5 program services encompass one-to-one counseling with at-risk individuals, motivational interventions, and educational programs for groups such as DUI (Driving Under the Influence) offenders, family members of those in treatment, and other populations with increased risk. Additional services may include those provided in Employee Assistance Programs (EAP); drug-free workplace initiatives; community-based correctional settings; student assistance and school programs; community mental health clinics; and Screening, Brief Intervention, and Referral to Treatment (SBIRT). Level 0.5 services may also be delivered in hospital emergency departments or primary care medical clinics.

SETTING

Level 0.5 programming may be offered in any appropriate setting, including clinical offices or permanent facilities, schools, work sites, community centers, emergency rooms, primary care settings, or an individual's home.

SUPPORT SYSTEMS

At Level 0.5, necessary support systems include:

a. Referral for and linking to ongoing treatment of substance use or addictive disorders treatment if a person is found to meet diagnostic criteria for addiction.

b. Referral for medical, psychological, or psychiatric services, including assessment.

c. Referral for community social services.

An adolescent's family may be referred for any of these services as well.

STAFF

Level 0.5 programs are staffed by trained personnel who are knowledgeable about the biopsychosocial dimensions of substance use and addictive disorders; the recognition of addictive and substance-related disorders; alcohol, tobacco, and other drug education; motivational counseling; adolescent development (if working with adolescents); and the legal and personal consequences of high-risk substance use and/or addictive behavior.

Physicians, especially primary care physicians and emergency medicine physicians, may be directly involved in Screening and Brief Intervention (SBI) activities with persons with high-risk drinking, drugging, non-medical use of prescription drugs, and/or high-risk addictive behaviors. Addiction specialist physicians usually are not involved in direct service provision of SBI or SBI with Referral to Treatment (SBIRT), but often are influential in clinical teams, designing and overseeing SBIRT activities carried out by other staff.

Certified and/or licensed addiction counselors can be involved with screening and especially brief intervention activities, but often generalist health care professionals (such as social workers, bedside nurses, and health educators) staff SBI activities instead of certified and/or licensed addiction counselors. Educational programs designed to reduce or eliminate at-risk substance use (eg, those targeted for DUI offenders or persons identified through drug-free workplace programs) generally are staffed by certified and/or licensed addiction counselors, social workers, or health educators, and not by physicians.

LEVEL 0.5 ❹

Interventions

Interventions offered at Level 0.5 may involve individual, group, or family counseling, SBIRT services, as well as planned educational experiences focused on helping the individual recognize and avoid harmful or high-risk substance use and/or addictive behavior.

ASSESSMENT

At Level 0.5, screening to rule in or rule out substance-related or addictive disorders and sufficient assessment of the dimensional risk and severity of need is performed prior to services, and may continue throughout the process of delivering services.

DOCUMENTATION

Documentation standards for Level 0.5 programs include progress notes in the individual's record that clearly indicate assessment findings, attendance, and significant clinical events, particularly those that require further assessment and referral.

ADULT DIAGNOSTIC ADMISSION CRITERIA

The individual who is an appropriate candidate for Level 0.5 services evidences problems and risk factors that appear to be related to substance use or addictive behavior. However, the individual may not meet the diagnostic criteria for a substance use or addictive disorder, as defined in the current *Diagnostic and Statistical Manual of Mental Disorders* (*DSM*) of the American Psychiatric Association or other standardized and widely accepted criteria, or there is currently insufficient information to perform a diagnostic assessment.

ADULT DIMENSIONAL ADMISSION CRITERIA

The individual who is appropriately cared for at Level 0.5 meets at least **one** of the specifications in Dimensions 4, 5, or 6. Any identifiable problems in Dimensions 1, 2, or 3 are stable or are being addressed through appropriate outpatient medical or mental health services.

1 **DIMENSION 1:** Acute Intoxication and/or Withdrawal Potential	See separate withdrawal management chapter for how to approach "unbundled" withdrawal management for adults.
2 **DIMENSION 2:** Biomedical Conditions and Complications	The individual's biomedical conditions and problems, if any, are stable or are being actively addressed, and thus will not interfere with therapeutic interventions.
3 **DIMENSION 3:** Emotional, Behavioral, or Cognitive Conditions and Complications	The individual's emotional, behavioral, or cognitive conditions and complications, if any, are being addressed through appropriate mental health services, and thus will not interfere with therapeutic interventions.
4 **DIMENSION 4:** Readiness to Change	The individual expresses willingness to gain an understanding of how his or her current addictive behavior and/or use of alcohol, tobacco, and/or other drugs may be harmful or impair his or her ability to meet responsibilities and achieve personal goals. This could also include those individuals who are ambivalent about exploring how their current behavior or use of alcohol and other drugs may be harmful or impairing, or those whose motivation is to achieve some goal other than the modification of their substance use behaviors (eg, having their driving privileges restored).

LEVEL 0.5

④

ADULT DIMENSIONAL ADMISSION CRITERIA (CONTINUED)

DIMENSION 5:
Relapse, Continued Use, or Continued Problem Potential

The individual's status in Dimension 5 is characterized by (a) *or* (b):

a. The individual does not understand the need to alter his or her current behavior or pattern of use of alcohol, tobacco, and/or other drugs to prevent harm that may be related to such use or behavior;

or

b. The individual needs to acquire specific skills needed to change his or her current pattern of use or behavior.

DIMENSION 6:
Living Environment

The individual's status in Dimension 6 is characterized by at least (a) *or* (b) *or* (c) *or* (d):

a. The individual's social support system is composed primarily of persons whose substance use or addictive behavior patterns prevent them from meeting social, work, school, or family obligations;

or

b. The individual's family member(s) currently is/are addictively using alcohol or other drugs (or has/have done so in the past), thereby heightening the individual's risk for a substance use disorder;

or

c. The individual's significant other expresses values concerning addictive behavior and/or alcohol or other drug use that create serious conflict for the individual;

or

d. The individual's significant other condones or encourages high-risk addictive behavior and/or use of alcohol or other drugs.

ADOLESCENT DIAGNOSTIC ADMISSION CRITERIA

The adolescent who is an appropriate candidate for Level 0.5 services evidences problems and risk factors that appear to be related to substance use or addictive behavior. However, the individual may not meet the diagnostic criteria for substance use or addictive disorder, as defined in the current *Diagnostic and Statistical Manual of Mental Disorders* (*DSM*) of the American Psychiatric Association or other standardized and widely accepted criteria, or there is currently insufficient information to perform a diagnostic assessment.

ADOLESCENT DIMENSIONAL ADMISSION CRITERIA

The adolescent who is appropriately cared for at Level 0.5 meets at least **one** of the specifications in Dimensions 4, 5, or 6. Any identifiable problems in Dimensions 1, 2, or 3 are stable or are being addressed through appropriate outpatient medical or mental health services.

DIMENSION 1:
Acute Intoxication and/or Withdrawal Potential

The adolescent who is an appropriate candidate for Level 0.5 services shows no signs of acute or subacute withdrawal, or risk of acute withdrawal.

DIMENSION 2:
Biomedical Conditions and Complications

The adolescent's biomedical conditions and problems, if any, are stable or are being actively addressed, and thus will not interfere with therapeutic interventions.

DIMENSION 3:
Emotional, Behavioral, or Cognitive Conditions and Complications

The adolescent's emotional, behavioral, or cognitive conditions and complications, if any, are being addressed through appropriate mental health services, and thus will not interfere with therapeutic interventions.

DIMENSION 4:
Readiness to Change

The adolescent expresses willingness to gain an understanding of how his or her current addictive behavior and/or use of alcohol, tobacco, and/or other drugs may be harmful or impair his or her ability to meet responsibilities and achieve personal goals. This could also include those individuals who are ambivalent about exploring how their current behavior or use of alcohol and other drugs may be harmful or impairing, or those whose motivation is to achieve some goal other than the modification of their substance use behaviors (eg, having their driving privileges restored).

DIMENSION 5:
Relapse, Continued Use, or Continued Problem Potential

The adolescent's status in Dimension 5 is characterized by (a) **or** (b):

a. The adolescent does not understand the need to alter his or her current behavior or pattern of use of alcohol, tobacco, and/or other drugs to prevent harm that may be related to such use or behavior;

or

b. The adolescent needs to acquire specific skills needed to change his or her current pattern of use or behavior.

DIMENSION 6:
Living Environment

The adolescent's status in Dimension 6 is characterized by at least (a) **or** (b) **or** (c) **or** (d):

a. The adolescent's social support system is composed primarily of persons whose substance use or addictive behavior patterns prevent him or her from meeting social, work, school, or family obligations;

or

b. The adolescent's family member(s) currently is/are addictively using alcohol or other drugs (or has/have done so in the past), thereby heightening the adolescent's risk for a substance use disorder;

or

c. A significant member of the adolescent's support system expresses values concerning addictive behavior and/or alcohol or other drug use that create serious conflict for the individual;

or

d. A significant member of the adolescent's support system condones or encourages high-risk addictive behavior and/or use of alcohol or other drugs.

LEVEL 0.5

4

Level 1
Outpatient Services

Level 1 encompasses organized outpatient treatment services, which may be delivered in a wide variety of settings. In Level 1 services, addiction, mental health treatment, or general health care personnel, including addiction-credentialed physicians, provide professionally directed screening, evaluation, treatment, and ongoing recovery and disease management services. Such services are provided in regularly scheduled sessions of (usually) fewer than nine contact hours a week for adults and fewer than six hours for adolescents. The services follow a defined set of policies and procedures or clinical protocols.

Level 1 services are tailored to each patient's level of clinical severity and function and are designed to help the patient achieve changes in his or her alcohol, tobacco, and/or other drug use or addictive behaviors. Treatment thus must address major lifestyle, attitudinal, and behavioral issues that have the potential to undermine the goals of treatment or to impair the individual's ability to cope with major life tasks without the addictive use of alcohol, tobacco, and/or other drugs and/or other addictive behaviors, such as gambling.

Level 1 Outpatient Services criteria promote greater access to care for:

a. Patients with co-occurring substance use and physical and mental health conditions.

b. Individuals not interested in recovery who are mandated into treatment, and others who previously only had access to care if they agreed to intensive periods of primary treatment.

c. Individuals in early stages of readiness to change. Knowledge and application of therapies such as motivational interviewing, motivational enhancement therapy, cognitive-behavioral therapy, solution-focused therapy, and stages of change work have greatly increased. This has created more options for those who before would have been turned away as "not ready for treatment" or "in denial" and thus in need of coerced, more intensive treatment to "break through denial."

d. Patients in early recovery who need education about addiction and person-centered treatment.

e. Patients in ongoing recovery who need monitoring and continuing disease management.

Level 1 services are appropriate in several different situations:

a. Level 1 may be the initial level of care for a patient whose severity of illness and level of function warrants this intensity of treatment. Such a patient should be able to complete professionally directed addiction and/or mental health treatment at this level, thus using only one level of care, unless (1) an unanticipated event causes a change in his or her level of functioning, leading to a reassessment of the appropriateness of this level of care, or (2) there is recurring evidence of the patient's inability to use this level of care (such as repeated episodes of drinking or non-medical drug use or other addictive disorders such as gambling even after the treatment plan has been reviewed and revised).

b. Level 1 may represent a "step down" from a more intensive level of care for a patient whose progress warrants such a

LEVEL 1   ④

transfer, assuming that he or she meets the criteria for placement in Level 1.

c. Level 1 may be used for a patient who is in the early stages of change and who is not yet ready to commit to full recovery (Dimension 4 issues). For such a patient, placement in a more intensive level of care is apt to lead to increased conflict, passive compliance, or even leaving treatment.

d. Level 1 may be used for patients as a direct admission if a co-occurring condition is stable and monitored whether or not they have responded to more intensive services.

Adolescent-Specific Considerations: Level 1

Especially at Level 1, ongoing active treatment often is required simply to sustain an adolescent's therapeutic gains. The much-needed maintenance phase of treatment often is long term (sometimes even indefinite) and too often is overlooked. Treatment successes such as a period of abstinence or improvement in function sometimes are misinterpreted as indicating that treatment is completed. In fact, maintenance strategies such as relapse prevention and strengthening protective factors are critical components of treatment. Even simple ongoing monitoring (such as checking on parental supervision, scrutinizing school performance or peer relationships, reviewing warning signs of recurrence of affective disorder, and the like) is a desirable goal of active outpatient treatment.

Withdrawal Management

Dimension 1 (Acute Intoxication and/or Withdrawal Potential) is the first of the six assessment dimensions to be evaluated in making treatment and placement decisions. The range of clinical severity in this dimension has given rise to a range of withdrawal management levels. Patients who are experiencing or are at risk of an acute withdrawal syndrome should not be treated at Level 1. For this reason, the designation "Level 1-WM" has not been used.

As used here, withdrawal management refers not only to the attenuation of the physiological and psychological features of withdrawal syndromes, but also to the process of interrupting the momentum of habitual compulsive use in adolescents who are diagnosed with high-severity substance use disorder. Because of the force of this momentum, and the inherent difficulties in overcoming it even when there is no clear withdrawal syndrome *per se*, this phase of treatment frequently requires a greater intensity of services initially in order to establish treatment engagement and patient role induction. This is, of course, critical to the course of treatment because it is impossible to engage an adolescent in treatment while he or she is caught up in a cycle of frequent intoxication and recovery from intoxication. Although the process of interrupting a pattern of high-frequency use may reasonably be attempted at Level 1, such efforts often are unsuccessful. In such circumstances, it is safer to place the adolescent at a more intensive level of care.

LEVEL 1
4

e. For patients who have achieved stability in recovery, Level 1 is used for ongoing monitoring and disease management indefinitely as is done with other chronic diseases such as hypertension, diabetes, and asthma.

Level 1 has always been appropriate for people who recognize their substance use or other addictive disorder and are committed to recovery. But it is also appropriate for individuals who are assessed as having high severity in Dimension 4 (that is, not manifesting much interest in or internal motivation for recovery) but not severe in the other dimensions. The use of motivational services in Level 1 avoids placing people at a more intensive level of care, which may only serve to increase their disinterest in changing and create discord in both their treatment and the treatment milieu. Thus, Level 1 enhances access to care and facilitates earlier engagement of patients in treatment. If this approach proves successful, the patient may no longer require a more intensive level of service, or may be able to better use such services.

Interventions to secure patient engagement can be provided by a range of professionals, from a certified and/or licensed addiction counselor to a nurse (either certified and/or licensed in addiction care or trained/certified and/or licensed as mental health specialist) to a generalist physician or an addiction specialist physician.

Length of Service
The duration of treatment varies with the severity of the individual's illness and his or her response to treatment.

Co-Occurring Mental and Substance-Related Disorders
Level 1 services are appropriate for patients with co-occurring mental and substance use disorders *if:*

a. The patient's disorders are of *moderate severity* and have responded to more intensive treatment services. The

mental disorders have resolved to an extent that addiction treatment services are assessed as potentially beneficial. However, ongoing monitoring of the patient's mental status is required;

or

b. The patient's disorders are of *high severity* and are chronic, but have stabilized to such an extent that integrated mental health and addiction treatment services are assessed as potentially beneficial. Patients who have severe and chronic mental disorders may not have been able to achieve sobriety or to maintain abstinence for a significant period of time (months) in the past; nevertheless, they are appropriately placed at Level 1 because they need engagement strategies and intensive case management.

Staff for such interventions can include general mental health clinicians (therapists, counselors, psychologists, advanced practice mental health nurses, general psychiatrists), general addiction clinicians (licensed and/or certified counselors, nurses, psychologists, and physicians, all of whom, as addiction specialists, should have general skills in the assessment and management of co-occurring conditions); and professionals specially trained and credentialed to work with the most complex cases (eg, certified and/or licensed addiction psychiatrists). These services may be provided by a member of the Level 1 staff or by referral to a licensed professional to work with the mental health issue in an integrated manner with the addiction professional as he or she provides addiction treatment.

EXAMPLES OF SERVICE DELIVERY
All Programs
Level 1 services may be delivered in office practices, health clinics, school-based health clinics, primary care clinics, addiction programs, mental health clinics, and child and adolescent behavioral health clinics.

SETTING
All Programs
Level 1 services may be offered in any appropriate setting that meets state licensure or certification criteria.

SUPPORT SYSTEMS
All Programs
In Level 1 services, necessary support systems include:

a. Medical, psychiatric, psychological, laboratory, and toxicology services, which are available on-site or through consultation or referral. Medical and psychiatric consultation is available within 24 hours by telephone or, if in person, within a time frame appropriate to the severity and urgency of the consultation requested.

b. Direct affiliation with (or close coordination through referral to) more intensive levels of care and medication management.

c. Emergency services available by telephone 24 hours a day, 7 days a week.

Co-Occurring Enhanced Programs
In addition to the support systems listed above, which encompass those offered by Level 1 co-occurring capable programs, Level 1 co-occurring enhanced programs offer ongoing intensive case management for highly crisis-prone (and often homeless) individuals with co-occurring disorders. Such services are delivered by cross-trained interdisciplinary staff through mobile outreach and engagement-oriented psychiatric and addictive disorders programming.

STAFF
All Programs
Level 1 services are staffed by appropriately credentialed and/or licensed treatment professionals (including addiction-credentialed physicians, counselors, psychologists, social workers, and others) who assess and treat substance-related, mental, and addictive disorders. Generalist physicians can be involved in Level 1 care, as described here. Staff is able to obtain and interpret information regarding the patient's biopsychosocial needs, and are knowledgeable about the biopsychosocial dimensions of alcohol, tobacco, and other drug and addictive disorders, including assessment of the patient's stage of readiness to change.

Program staff is capable of monitoring stabilized mental health problems and recognizing any instability of patients with co-occurring mental health conditions.

Certified and/or licensed addiction counselors offer much of the counseling in Level 1 services, but medication management (pharmacotherapy) services are generally Level 1 services and require the involvement of a licensed independent practitioner with prescribing authority as granted by state-based professional licensing boards. Physicians and physician assistants/advanced registered nurse practitioners are the most common prescribers, but office-based nurses (not Master's-prepared advanced practice nurses) often are involved with medication management in support of phy-

Adolescent-Specific Considerations: Staff

In addition to the specifications for staff for all services, staff should be knowledgeable about adolescent development and experienced in working with and engaging adolescents.

sicians. They provide patient education about medications and optimize patient adherence and treatment retention with outpatient medication management.

Addiction specialist physicians provide Level 1 services for medication management or integrated psychosocial services/medication management in referral from generalist physicians, mental health professionals, or certified and/or licensed addiction counselors when the complexity of the case or problematic previous treatment response warrant the involvement of the most highly skilled clinician available.

Assessment services provided to outpatients are, by definition, Level 1 services. When co-occurring mental health or general medical conditions (eg, pain syndromes, sleep disorders, infectious diseases) are present, assessment services for both diagnostic and treatment planning purposes may require the most highly skilled clinician available. Or such co-occurring conditions may require collaboration between credentialed and/or licensed mental health or addiction professionals, eg, an addiction specialist physician. In the absence of an addiction specialist physician, a prescribing physician or physician extender may be used in consultation with an addiction specialist physician.

Co-Occurring Enhanced Programs

Staff of Level 1 co-occurring enhanced programs include credentialed mental health trained personnel who are able to assess, monitor, and manage the types of severe and chronic mental disorders seen in a Level 1 setting, as well as other psychiatric disorders that are mildly unstable. Such staff is knowledgeable about the management of co-occurring mental and substance-related disorders, including assessment of the patient's stage of readiness to change and engagement of patients who have co-occurring mental disorders.

THERAPIES
All Programs

Therapies offered in Level 1 involve skilled treatment services, which may include individual and group counseling, motivational enhancement, family therapy, educational groups, occupational and recreational therapy, psychotherapy, addiction pharmacotherapy, or other therapies. Such services are provided in an amount, frequency, and intensity appropriate to the patient's multidimensional severity and level of function. Motivational enhancement and engagement strategies are used in preference to confrontational approaches. For patients with mental health conditions, the issues of psychotropic medication, mental health treatment, and their relationship to substance use and addictive disorders are addressed as the need arises.

Co-Occurring Enhanced Programs

In addition to the therapies described above, Level 1 co-occurring enhanced programs offer therapies to actively address, monitor, and manage psychotropic medication, mental health treatment, and the interaction with substance-related and addictive disorders. There may be close coordination with intensive case management and assertive community treatment for patients who have severe and chronic mental illnesses. This can include addiction medicine physicians, but more often involves certified addiction psychiatrists.

Integrated Addiction/General Medical Care Services

With trends to integrate addiction services with primary medical care and other general medical care services, eg, in Patient Centered Health Care Homes and Patient Centered Health Care Neighborhoods, more addiction care will be delivered outside of stand-alone specialty clinics or service provider organizations designed to treat persons with addiction and a variety of substance-related disorders. Specialty addiction services can become part of a Patient Centered Health Care Neighborhood where planned efforts are made to integrate the care experience for the patient even if service locations are multiple; but addiction services can also be completely integrated into Community Health Centers and Patient Centered Health Care Homes. Health care reform initiatives will likely increase trends in the direction of integration, but integration activities have been expanding in recent years even prior to the policy reforms seen in federal health care reform legislation.

ASSESSMENT/TREATMENT PLAN REVIEW
All Programs

In Level 1, the assessment and treatment plan review include:

a. An individual biopsychosocial assessment of each patient, which includes a comprehensive substance use and addictive disorders history obtained as part of the initial assessment and reviewed by a physician, if necessary. A physical examination may be performed within a reasonable time, as determined by the patient's medical condition. Such determinations are made according to established protocols, which include reliance on the patient's personal physician whenever possible. They are based on the staff's capabilities and the severity of the patient's symptoms, and are approved by a physician. (In states where physician assistants or nurse practitioners are under physician supervision and are licensed as physician extenders, they may perform the duties designated here for a physician.)

b. An individualized treatment plan, which involves problems, needs, strengths, skills, and priority formulation. Short-term, measurable treatment goals and preferences are articulated along with activities designed to achieve those goals. The plan is developed in collaboration with the patient and reflects the patient's personal goals. Treatment plan reviews are conducted at specified times, as noted in the plan, or more frequently as determined by the appropriate credentialed professional.

c. Monitoring, including biomarkers and/or toxicology testing.

Co-Occurring Enhanced Programs

In addition to the assessment and treatment plan review activities just described, which encompass co-occurring capable programs, Level 1 co-occurring enhanced programs provide a review of the patient's recent psychiatric history and a mental status examination. If necessary, the review is conducted by a psychiatrist. A comprehensive psychiatric history and examination, and a psychodiagnostic assessment are performed within a reasonable time, as determined by the patient's psychiatric condition.

Level 1 co-occurring enhanced programs also provide active reassessment of the patient's mental status and follow through with mental health treatment and psychotropic medication at each visit. Patients in need of co-occurring capable services also may require the kinds of assessment and treatment plan reviews offered by co-occurring enhanced programs, but at a reduced level of frequency and comprehensiveness, because their mental health problems are more stable.

DOCUMENTATION
All Programs

Documentation standards for Level 1 programs include individualized progress notes in the patient's record that clearly reflect implementation of the treatment plan and the patient's response to therapeutic interventions for all disorders treated, as well as subsequent amendments to the plan.

Co-Occurring Programs

In addition to the information just described, Level 1 co-occurring capable and co-occurring enhanced programs document the patient's mental health problems, the relationship between the patient's mental and substance-related and addictive disorders, and the patient's current level of mental functioning.

LEVEL 1
4

ADULT DIAGNOSTIC ADMISSION CRITERIA

The patient who is appropriately placed in a Level 1 program is assessed as meeting the diagnostic criteria for a substance use, substance-induced, and/or other addictive disorder as defined in the current *Diagnostic and Statistical Manual of Mental Disorders* (*DSM*) of the American Psychiatric Association or other standardized and widely accepted criteria, as well as the dimensional criteria for admission.

If the patient's presenting alcohol, tobacco, and/or other drug use or addictive behavior history is inadequate to substantiate such a diagnosis, the probability of such a diagnosis may be determined from information appropriately submitted or obtained from collateral parties (such as family members, legal guardians, and significant others) when there is valid authorization to obtain this information.

Co-Occurring Capable Programs

At Level 1, some patients have co-occurring mental disorders that meet the stability criteria for a co-occurring capable program. Other patients have difficulties in mood, behavior, or cognition as the result of other psychiatric or substance-induced disorders, or the patient's emotional, behavioral, or cognitive symptoms are troublesome but not sufficient to meet the criteria for a diagnosed mental disorder.

Co-Occurring Enhanced Programs

In contrast to the diagnostic criteria described above for co-occurring capable programs, the patient who is identified as in need of Level 1 co-occurring enhanced program services is assessed as meeting the diagnostic criteria for a mental disorder as well as a substance use or induced disorder, as defined in the current *Diagnostic and Statistical Manual of Mental Disorders* (*DSM*) of the American Psychiatric Association or other standardized and widely accepted criteria, as well as the dimensional criteria for admission.

If the patient's presenting history is inadequate to substantiate such a diagnosis, the probability of such a diagnosis may be determined from information submitted by collateral parties (such as family members, legal guardians, and significant others).

LEVEL 1

4

ADULT DIMENSIONAL ADMISSION CRITERIA

All Services

The patient who is appropriately admitted to Level 1 is assessed as meeting specifications in **all** of the following six dimensions.

1

DIMENSION 1:
Acute Intoxication and/or
Withdrawal Potential

All Programs

The patient has no signs or symptoms of withdrawal, or his or her withdrawal needs can be safely managed in a Level 1 setting. See separate withdrawal management chapter for how to approach "unbundled" withdrawal management for adults.

2

DIMENSION 2:
Biomedical Conditions and
Complications

All Programs

The patient's status in Dimension 2 is characterized by biomedical conditions and problems, if any, that are sufficiently stable to permit participation in outpatient treatment. Examples include uncomplicated pregnancy or asymptomatic HIV disease.

All Programs

The patient's status in Dimension 3 is characterized by (a) **or** (b); **and** both (c) **and** (d):

    a. The patient has no symptoms of a co-occurring mental disorder, or any symptoms are mild, stable, fully related to a substance use or other addictive disorder, and do not interfere with the patient's ability to focus on addiction treatment issues;
        or

    b. The patient's psychiatric symptoms (such as anxiety, guilt, or thought disorders) are mild, mostly stable, and primarily related to either a substance use or other addictive disorder, or to a co-occurring cognitive, emotional, or behavioral condition. Mental health monitoring is needed to maintain stable mood, cognition, and behavior. For example, fluctuations in mood only recently stabilized with medication, substance-induced depression that is resolving but still significant, or a patient with schizophrenic disorder recently released from the hospital;
        and

    c. The patient's mental status does not preclude his or her ability to: (1) understand the information presented and (2) participate in treatment planning and the treatment process;
        and

    d. The patient is assessed as not posing a risk of harm to self or others and is not vulnerable to victimization by another.

3

DIMENSION 3:
Emotional, Behavioral, or
Cognitive Conditions and
Complications

Co-Occurring Enhanced Programs

In addition to the above criteria, the patient's status in Dimension 3 is characterized by either (a); **or** all of (b) **and** (c) **and** (d):

    a. The patient has a severe and chronic mental illness that impairs his or her ability to follow through consistently with mental health appointments and psychotropic medication. However, the patient has the ability to access services such as assertive community treatment and intensive case management or supportive living designed to help the patient remain engaged in treatment;
        or

    b. The patient has a severe and chronic mental disorder or other emotional, behavioral, or cognitive problems, or substance-induced disorder;
        and

    c. The patient's mental health functioning is such that he or she has impaired ability to: (1) understand the information presented, and (2) participate in treatment planning and the treatment process. Mental health management is required to stabilize mood, cognition, and behavior;
        and

    d. The patient is assessed as not posing a risk of harm to self or others and is not vulnerable to victimization by another.

4   LEVEL 1

ADULT DIMENSIONAL ADMISSION CRITERIA (CONTINUED)

4 **DIMENSION 4:**
Readiness to Change

All Programs

The patient's status in Dimension 4 is characterized by (a); **and** one of (b) **or** (c) **or** (d):

a. The patient expresses willingness to participate in treatment planning and to attend all scheduled activities mutually agreed upon in the treatment plan;
and

b. The patient acknowledges that he or she has a substance-related or other addictive disorder and/or mental health problem and wants help to change;
or

c. The patient is ambivalent about a substance-related or other addictive disorder and/or mental health condition. He or she requires monitoring and motivating strategies, but not a structured milieu program. For example: (a) the patient has sufficient awareness and recognition of a substance use or addictive disorder and/or mental health problems to allow engagement and follow through with attendance at intermittent treatment sessions as scheduled; (b) The patient acknowledges that he or she has a substance-related and/or mental health problem but is ambivalent about change. He or she is invested in avoiding negative consequences and is in need of monitoring and motivating strategies to engage in treatment and progress through stages of change;
or

d. The patient may not recognize that he or she has a substance-related or other addictive disorder and/or mental health problem. For example, he or she is more invested in avoiding a negative consequence than in the recovery effort. Such a patient may require monitoring and motivating strategies to engage in treatment and to progress through stages of change.

5 **DIMENSION 5:**
Relapse, Continued Use, or Continued Problem Potential

All Programs

In Dimension 5, the patient is assessed as able to achieve or maintain abstinence and related recovery goals. Or the patient is able to achieve awareness of a substance or other addiction problem and related motivational enhancement goals, only with support and scheduled therapeutic contact. This is to assist him or her in dealing with issues that include (but are not limited to) concern or ambivalence about preoccupation with alcohol, tobacco, and/or other drug use; other addictive behavior; cravings to use or gamble; peer pressure; and lifestyle and attitude changes.

Co-Occurring Programs

In addition to the above criteria for all programs, the patient is assessed as able to achieve or maintain mental health functioning and related goals only with support and scheduled therapeutic contact to assist him or her in dealing with issues that include (but are not limited to) impulses to harm self or others and difficulty in coping with his or her affects, impulses, or cognition.

While such impulses and difficulty in coping may apply to patients in both co-occurring capable and co-occurring enhanced programs, patients in need of co-occurring enhanced program services are more unstable and require the outreach and support of assertive community treatment and intensive case management to maintain their mental health function. For example, such a patient may be unable to reliably keep mental health appointments because of instability in cognition, behavior, or mood.

LEVEL 1 ④

ADULT DIMENSIONAL ADMISSION CRITERIA (CONTINUED)

DIMENSION 6:
Recovery Environment

All Programs

The patient's status in Dimension 6 is characterized by (a) *or* (b) *or* (c):

a. The patient's psychosocial environment is sufficiently supportive that outpatient treatment is feasible (for example, significant others are in agreement with the recovery effort; there is a supportive work environment or legal coercion; adequate transportation to the program is available; and support meeting locations and non-alcohol/drug-centered work are near the home environment and accessible);
or

b. The patient does not have an adequate primary or social support system, but he or she has demonstrated motivation and willingness to obtain such a support system;
or

c. The patient's family, guardian, or significant others are supportive but require professional interventions to improve the patient's chance of treatment success and recovery. Such interventions may involve assistance in limit-setting, communication skills, a reduction in rescuing behaviors, and the like.

Co-Occurring Enhanced Programs

In addition to the above criteria, the patient's status in Dimension 6 is characterized by (a) *or* (b) *or* (c):

a. The patient does not have an adequate primary or social support system and has mild impairment in his or her ability to obtain a support system. For example, mood, cognition, and impulse control fluctuate and distract the patient from focusing on treatment tasks;
or

b. The family, guardian, or significant others require active family therapy or systems interventions to improve the patient's chances of treatment success and recovery. These may include family enmeshment issues, significant guilt or anxiety, or passivity or disengaged aloofness or neglect;
or

c. The patient's status in Dimension 6 is characterized by *all* of the following: (1) the patient has a severe and chronic mental disorder or an emotional, behavioral, or cognitive condition, and (2) the patient does not have an adequate family or social support system, and (3) the patient is chronically impaired, but not in imminent danger, and has limited ability to establish a supportive recovery environment. However, he or she does have access to intensive outreach and case management services that can provide structure and allow him or her to work toward stabilizing both the substance use or other addictive disorder and mental disorders.

LEVEL 1
4

ADOLESCENT DIAGNOSTIC ADMISSION CRITERIA

The adolescent who is appropriately placed in a Level 1 program is assessed as meeting the diagnostic criteria for a substance use, substance-induced, and/or other addictive disorder as defined in the current *Diagnostic and Statistical Manual of Mental Disorders* (*DSM*) of the American Psychiatric Association or other standardized and widely accepted criteria, as well as the dimensional criteria for admission.

If the adolescent's presenting alcohol, tobacco, and/or other drug use or addictive behavior history is inadequate to substantiate such a diagnosis, the probability of such a diagnosis may be determined from information appropriately submitted or obtained from collateral parties (such as family members, legal guardians, and significant others) when there is valid authorization to obtain this information.

ADOLESCENT DIMENSIONAL ADMISSION CRITERIA

The adolescent who is appropriately admitted to Level 1 is assessed as meeting specifications in *all* of the following six dimensions.

DIMENSION 1:
Acute Intoxication and/or Withdrawal Potential

The adolescent has no signs or symptoms of withdrawal, or his or her withdrawal needs can be safely managed in a Level 1 setting.

The adolescent who is appropriately placed in a Level 1 program is not experiencing acute or subacute withdrawal from alcohol or other drugs, and is not at risk of acute withdrawal; *or*

If the adolescent is experiencing very mild withdrawal, the symptoms consist of no more than lingering but improving sleep disturbance.

Nicotine: Nicotine withdrawal is the exception to the previous statement, as it may be marked by more severe symptoms. However, these can be managed in a Level 1 setting. Nicotine withdrawal symptoms may require either nicotine replacement therapy or non-nicotine pharmacological agents for symptomatic treatment.

NOTE: If the adolescent is presenting for treatment after recently experiencing an episode of acute withdrawal without treatment (as opposed to stepping down from a more intensive level of care following a good response to treatment), it is safer to err on the side of greater intensity of services in making a placement. For example, a Level 2.1 setting may be indicated if the adolescent is doing poorly or if there are indicators for that level of care in other dimensions.

DIMENSION 2:
Biomedical Conditions and Complications

The adolescent's status in Dimension 2 is characterized by biomedical conditions and problems, if any, that are sufficiently stable to permit participation in outpatient treatment. Examples include uncomplicated pregnancy or asymptomatic HIV disease.

DIMENSION 3:
Emotional, Behavioral, or Cognitive Conditions and Complications

The adolescent's status in Dimension 3 is characterized by *all* of the following:

a. **Dangerousness/Lethality:** The adolescent is assessed as not posing a risk of harm to self or others. He or she has adequate impulse control to deal with any thoughts of harm to self or others.

LEVEL 1 4

ADOLESCENT DIMENSIONAL ADMISSION CRITERIA (CONTINUED)

3

DIMENSION 3:
Emotional, Behavioral, or Cognitive Conditions and Complications

b. **Interference with Addiction Recovery Efforts:** The adolescent's emotional concerns relate to negative consequences and effects of addiction, and he or she is able to view them as part of addiction and recovery. Emotional, behavioral, or cognitive symptoms, if present, appear to be related to substance-related problems rather than to a co-occurring psychiatric, emotional, or behavioral condition. If they *are* related to such a condition, appropriate additional psychiatric services are provided concurrent with the Level 1 treatment. The adolescent's mental status does not preclude his or her ability to: (1) understand the materials presented (that is, his or her cognitive abilities are appropriate to the treatment modality and materials used); and (2) participate in the treatment process.

c. **Social Functioning:** Relationships or spheres of social functioning (as with family, friends, and peers at school and work) are impaired but not endangered by substance use (for example, there is no imminent break-up of family, expulsion from home, or imminent failure at school). The adolescent is able to meet personal responsibilities and to maintain stable, meaningful relationships despite the mild symptoms experienced (such as mood swings without aggression or threats of danger, or in-school suspension for lateness but no suspensions for truancy).

d. **Ability for Self-Care:** The adolescent has adequate resources and skills to cope with emotional, behavioral, or cognitive problems, with some assistance. He or she has the support of a stable environment and is able to manage the activities of daily living (feeding, personal hygiene, grooming, and the like).

e. **Course of Illness:** The adolescent has only mild signs and symptoms. Any acute problems (such as severe depression, suicidality, aggression, or dangerous delinquent behaviors) have been well stabilized, and chronic problems are not serious enough to pose a high risk of vulnerability (such as chronic and stable low-lethality self-injurious behavior, chronic depression without significant impairment or increase in severity, or chronic stable threats without risk of aggression).

LEVEL 1

4

DIMENSION 4:
Readiness to Change

The adolescent's status in Dimension 4 is characterized by (a) *and* one of (b) *or* (c) *or* (d):

a. The adolescent expresses willingness to participate in treatment planning and to attend all scheduled activities mutually agreed upon in the treatment plan;
and

b. The adolescent acknowledges that he or she has a substance-related or other addictive disorder and/or mental health problem and wants help to change, but is ambivalent about recovery efforts and requires monitoring and motivating strategies;
or

c. The adolescent is ambivalent about a substance-related or other addictive disorder and/or mental health condition. He or she requires monitoring and motivating strategies, but not a structured milieu program. For example: (a) the adolescent has sufficient awareness and recognition of a substance use or addictive disorder and/or mental health problems to allow engagement and follow through with attendance at intermittent treatment sessions as scheduled; (b) The adolescent acknowledges that he or she has a substance-related and/or mental health problem but is ambivalent about change. He or she is invested in avoiding negative consequences and is in need of monitoring and motivating strategies to engage in treatment and progress through stages of change;
or

d. The adolescent may not recognize that he or she has a substance-related or other addictive disorder and/or mental health problem. For example, he or she is more invested in avoiding a negative consequence than in the recovery effort. Such an adolescent may require monitoring and motivating strategies to engage in treatment and to progress through the stages of change.

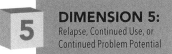

ADOLESCENT DIMENSIONAL ADMISSION CRITERIA (CONTINUED)

DIMENSION 5:
Relapse, Continued Use, or Continued Problem Potential

In Dimension 5, the adolescent is assessed as able to achieve or maintain abstinence and related recovery goals. Or the adolescent is able to achieve awareness of a substance or other addiction problem and related motivational enhancement goals, only with support and scheduled therapeutic contact. This is to assist him or her in dealing with issues that include (but are not limited to) concern or ambivalence about preoccupation with alcohol, tobacco, and/or other drug use; other addictive behavior; cravings to use or gamble; peer pressure; and lifestyle and attitude changes.

DIMENSION 6:
Recovery Environment

The adolescent's status in Dimension 6 is characterized by (a) *or* (b) *or* (c):

a. The adolescent's psychosocial environment is sufficiently supportive that outpatient treatment is feasible (for example, significant others are in agreement with the recovery effort; there is a supportive work environment or legal coercion; adequate transportation to the program is available; and support meeting locations and non-alcohol/drug-centered work are near the home environment and accessible);
or
b. The adolescent does not have an adequate primary or social support system, but he or she has demonstrated motivation and willingness to obtain such a support system;
or
c. The adolescent's family, guardian, or significant others are supportive but require professional interventions to improve the adolescent's chance of treatment success and recovery. Such interventions may involve assistance in limit-setting, communication skills, a reduction in rescuing behaviors, and the like.

Level 2
Intensive Outpatient/Partial Hospitalization Services

Level 2 encompasses intensive outpatient treatment services, which may be delivered in a wide variety of outpatient or partial hospitalization settings. Distinctions are made among various subtypes of Level 2 programs. Criteria are offered here for two variations: Intensive Outpatient (Level 2.1) and Partial Hospitalization (Level 2.5) programs.

Level 2 treatment services can be delivered during the day, before or after work or school, in the evening, or on weekends. For appropriately selected patients, such programs provide essential addiction education and treatment components while allowing patients to apply their newly acquired skills within "real world" environments. Beyond the essential services, many

Level 2 programs have the capacity to effectively treat patients who have complex co-occurring mental and substance-related conditions. Programs also have the capacity to arrange for medical and psychiatric consultation, psychopharmacological consultation, medication management, and 24-hour crisis services.

Level 2 programs can provide comprehensive biopsychosocial assessments and individualized treatment plans, including formulation of problem needs, strengths, skills, and priority formulation and articulation of short-term, measurable treatment goals and preferences, and activities designed to achieve those goals—all developed in consultation with the patient. Such programs typically have active affiliations

LEVEL 2

with other levels of care, and their staff can help patients access support services such as child care, vocational training, and transportation. Treatment interventions and modalities may also need to be tailored to engage adolescents who are at varying levels of developmental maturity.

Intensive pharmacotherapy treatment services, such as Opioid Treatment Programs (referred to in former years as "methadone maintenance treatment" (MMT) clinics, or as "Opioid Maintenance Therapy" (OMT)), can involve patients in intensive psychosocial interventions concurrently. Such programs, involving three to five or more contact days per week and at least nine hours of counseling per week, would also classify as Level 2 addiction services for adults. The pharmacotherapy treatment services are separate from the nine hours of counseling services.

Some programs also can provide overnight housing for patients who have problems related to family environment or transportation but who do not need the supervision or 24-hour access to services afforded by a Level 3 program. Such structured day and evening treatment programs unbundle actual clinical treatment from "around-the-clock" supervised living environments that include overnight housing. For those patients who do need 24-hour supervision, Level 2 programs can be combined with Level 3.1, Clinically Managed Low-Intensity Residential Treatment.

Distinctions are made among various subtypes of Level 2 programs. Criteria are offered here for two variations: Intensive Outpatient Services (Level 2.1) and Partial Hospitalization (Level 2.5) programs.

Length of Service
The duration of treatment varies with the severity of the patient's illness and his or her response to treatment.

Co-Occurring Mental and Substance-Related Disorders
The services of a Level 2 treatment program are appropriate for patients with co-occurring mental and substance-related disorders if the mental health and addiction treatment services are integrated into the intensive outpatient or partial hospitalization program. Such patients require active mental health services, which should be delivered through Level 2.1 co-occurring capable or co-occurring enhanced programs. Staff for such interventions can include general mental health clinicians (therapists, counselors, psychologists, advanced practice mental health nurses, general psychiatrists) working in collaboration with general addiction clinicians (certified and/or licensed counselors, nurses, psychologists, and physicians). All of these addiction specialists are working in collaboration with mental health clinicians and professionals who are specially trained and credentialed to work with the most complex cases (eg, addiction psychiatrists, working in collaboration with other members of the interdisciplinary team).

Adolescent-Specific Considerations: Withdrawal Management

Dimension 1 (Acute Intoxication and/or Withdrawal Potential) is the first of the six assessment dimensions to be evaluated in making treatment and placement decisions. The range of clinical severity in this dimension has given rise to a range of withdrawal management levels of service. A patient who is experiencing or at risk of an acute withdrawal syndrome should not be treated at Level 2.1. For this reason, the designation of Level 2.1-WM has not been used. However, it is important to recognize lingering subacute withdrawal symptoms (such as severe insomnia and vivid, disturbing dreams associated with marijuana withdrawal), which can be quite impairing, are appropriately addressed in a Level 2.1 setting.

LEVEL 2

4

Treatment Levels Within Level 2
Level 2.1: Intensive Outpatient Services

Intensive outpatient programs (IOPs) generally provide 9-19 hours of structured programming per week for adults and 6-19 hours for adolescents, consisting primarily of counseling and education about addiction-related and mental health problems. The patient's needs for psychiatric and medical services are addressed through consultation and referral arrangements if the patient is stable and requires only maintenance monitoring. (Services provided outside the primary program must be tightly coordinated.)

There are occasions when the patient's progress in the IOP no longer requires nine hours per week of treatment for adults or six hours per week for adolescents but he or she has not yet made enough stable progress to be fully transferred to a Level 1 program. In such cases, less than nine hours per week for adults and six hours per week for adolescents as a transition step down in intensity should be considered as a continuation of the IOP program for one or two weeks. Such continuity allows for a smoother transition to Level 1 to avoid exacerbation and recurrence of signs and symptoms.

Intensive outpatient treatment differs from partial hospitalization (Level 2.5) programs in the intensity of clinical services that are directly available. Specifically, most intensive outpatient programs have less capacity to effectively treat patients who have substantial unstable medical and psychiatric problems than do partial hospitalization programs.

EXAMPLES OF SERVICE DELIVERY
All Programs
Examples of Level 2.1 programs are after-school, day or evening, and/or weekend intensive outpatient programs.

SETTING
All Programs
Level 2.1 program services may be offered in any appropriate setting that meets state licensure or certification criteria.

SUPPORT SYSTEMS
All Programs
In Level 2.1 programs, necessary support systems include:

a. Medical, psychological, psychiatric, laboratory, and toxicology services, which are available through consultation or referral. Psychiatric and other medical consultation is available within 24 hours by telephone and within 72 hours in person.

b. Emergency services, which are available by telephone 24 hours a day, 7 days a week when the treatment program is not in session.

c. Direct affiliation with (or close coordination through referral to) more and less intensive levels of care and supportive housing services.

Co-Occurring Enhanced Programs
In addition to the support systems described here for co-occurring capable programs, Level 2.1 co-occurring enhanced programs offer psychiatric services appropriate to the patient's mental health condition. Such services are available by telephone and on site, or closely coordinated off site, within a shorter time than in a co-occurring capable program.

STAFF
All Programs
Level 2.1 programs are staffed by an interdisciplinary team of appropriately credentialed addiction treatment professionals, including counselors, psychologists, social workers, and addiction-credentialed physicians

LEVEL 2.1

4

who assess and treat substance use and other addictive disorders. Physicians treating patients in this level should have specialty training and/or experience in addiction medicine or addiction psychiatry, and if treating adolescents, experience with adolescent medicine. Program staff is able to obtain and interpret information regarding the patient's biopsychosocial needs. Generalist physicians may be involved in providing general medical evaluations (physical exams) and concurrent/integrated general medical care (eg, services for hepatitis, HIV disease, tuberculosis, or other co-occurring infectious diseases) during the provision of Level 2 addiction care.

Some, if not all, program staff should have sufficient cross-training to understand the signs and symptoms of mental disorders, and to understand and be able to explain the uses of psychotropic medications and their interactions with substance use and other addictive disorders.

Co-Occurring Enhanced Programs

In addition to the staff capabilities listed here, which encompass those of co-occurring capable programs, Level 2.1 co-occurring enhanced programs are staffed by appropriately credentialed mental health professionals, who assess and treat co-occurring mental disorders.

Clinical leadership and oversight may be offered by an addiction specialist physician. But at a minimum, capacity to consult with an addiction psychiatrist should be available. Some Level 2.1 services are specifically designed to be "co-occurring" programs in distinction from addiction specialty services. All should have some degree of co-occurring capability.

THERAPIES
All Programs

Therapies offered by Level 2.1 programs include:

a. A minimum of 9 hours per week for adults and 6 hours per week for adolescents of skilled treatment services. Such services may include individual and group counseling, medication management, family therapy, educational groups, occupational and recreational therapy, and other therapies. Services are provided in amounts, frequencies, and intensities appropriate to the objectives of the treatment plan.

In cases in which the patient is not yet fully stable to safely transfer to a Level 1 program that is not associated with the treatment agency, the patient's treatment for Level 1 services may be continued within the current Level 2.1 program.

b. Family therapy, which involves family members, guardians, or significant other(s) in the assessment, treatment, and continuing care of the patient.

c. A planned format of therapies, delivered on an individual and group basis and adapted to the patient's developmental stage and comprehension level.

d. Motivational interviewing, enhancement, and engagement strategies,

LEVEL 2.1

a Adolescent-Specific Considerations: Staff

In addition to the specifications for staff for all services, staff should be knowledgeable about adolescent development and experienced in engaging and working with adolescents. Clinical staff who assess and treat adolescents are able to recognize the need for specialty evaluation and treatment for intoxication or withdrawal and are able to arrange for such evaluation or treatment in a timely manner.

which are used in preference to confrontational approaches.

Co-Occurring Programs

The therapies previously described typically are offered by co-occurring capable programs to patients with co-occurring addictive and mental disorders who are able to tolerate and benefit from a planned program of therapies.

Other patients (especially those who are severely and chronically mentally ill) may not be able to benefit from a full program of therapies and thus may require co-occurring enhanced program services that constitute the defined intensity of hours in Level 2.1. Such services may involve intensive case management, assertive community treatment, medication management, and psychotherapy.

ASSESSMENT/TREATMENT PLAN REVIEW
All Programs

In Level 2.1 programs, the assessment and treatment plan review include:

a. An individual biopsychosocial assessment of each patient, which includes a comprehensive substance use and addictive behaviors history obtained as part of the initial assessment and reviewed by a physician, if necessary. A physical examination may be performed within a reasonable time, as determined by the patient's medical condition. Such determinations are made according to established protocols, which include reliance on the patient's personal physician whenever possible. They are based on the staff's capabilities and the severity of the patient's symptoms, and are approved by a physician. (In states where physician assistants or nurse practitioners are under physician supervision and are licensed as physician extenders, they may perform the duties designated here for a physician.)

b. An individualized treatment plan, which involves problems, needs, strengths, skills, and priority formulation and articulation of short-term, measurable treatment goals and preferences and activities designed to achieve those goals. The plan is developed in collaboration with the patient and reflects the patient's personal goals. Treatment plan reviews are conducted at specified times, as noted in the plan, or more frequently as determined by the appropriate credentialed professional.

c. Monitoring, including biomarkers and/or toxicology testing.

Treatment plan reviews are conducted at specified times, as noted in the treatment plan.

Co-Occurring Enhanced Programs

In addition to the activities described above for co-occurring capable programs, Level 2.1 co-occurring enhanced programs provide a review of the patient's recent psychiatric history and a mental status examination (which are reviewed by a psychiatrist, if necessary). A comprehensive psychiatric history and examination and a psychodiagnostic assessment are performed within a reasonable time frame, as determined by the patient's psychiatric condition.

Adolescent-Specific Considerations: Assessment and Treatment Planning

Information for assessment and treatment planning may be obtained from a parent, guardian, or other important resource (such as a teacher or probation officer).

LEVEL 2.1   ④

DOCUMENTATION
All Programs

Documentation standards for Level 2.1 programs include individualized progress notes in the patient's record that clearly reflect implementation of the treatment plan and the patient's response to therapeutic interventions for all disorders treated, as well as subsequent amendments to the plan.

Co-Occurring Programs

In addition to the documentation standards described here, Level 2.1 co-occurring capable and co-occurring enhanced programs document the patient's mental health problems, the relationship between the mental and substance-related disorders, and the patient's current level of mental functioning.

ADULT DIAGNOSTIC ADMISSION CRITERIA
All Programs

The patient who is appropriately placed in a Level 2.1 program is assessed as meeting the diagnostic criteria for a substance use and/or other addictive disorder as defined in the current *Diagnostic and Statistical Manual of Mental Disorders* (*DSM*) of the American Psychiatric Association or other standardized and widely accepted criteria, as well as the dimensional criteria for admission.

If the patient's presenting alcohol and/or other drug use and other addictive behavior history is inadequate to substantiate such a diagnosis, the probability of such a diagnosis may be determined from information submitted by collateral parties (such as family members, legal guardians, and significant others).

Co-Occurring Enhanced Programs

The patient in need of Level 2.1 co-occurring enhanced program services is assessed as meeting the diagnostic criteria for a mental disorder as well as a substance use disorder, as defined in the current *Diagnostic and Statistical Manual of Mental Disorders* (*DSM*) of the American Psychiatric Association or other standardized and widely accepted criteria, as well as the dimensional criteria for admission.

If the patient's presenting history is inadequate to substantiate such a diagnosis, the probability of such a diagnosis may be determined from information submitted by collateral parties (such as family members, legal guardians, and significant others).

ADULT DIMENSIONAL ADMISSION CRITERIA

All Programs

Direct admission to a Level 2.1 program is advisable for the patient who meets specifications in Dimension 2 (if any biomedical conditions or problems exist) **and** in Dimension 3 (if any emotional, behavioral, or cognitive conditions or problems exist), as well as in at least **one** of Dimensions 4, 5, or 6.

Transfer to a Level 2.1 program is advisable for the patient who

a. has met the essential treatment objectives at a more intensive level of care

   and

b. requires the intensity of services provided at Level 2.1 in at least one of Dimensions 4, 5, or 6.

A patient also may be transferred to Level 2.1 from a Level 1 program when the services provided at Level 1 have proved insufficient to address the patient's needs or when Level 1 services have consisted of motivational interventions to prepare the patient for participation in a more intensive level of service, for which he or she now meets the admission criteria.

DIMENSION 1:
Acute Intoxication and/or Withdrawal Potential

All Programs

The patient has no signs or symptoms of withdrawal, or his or her withdrawal needs can be safely managed in a Level 2.1 setting. See separate withdrawal management chapter for how to approach "unbundled" withdrawal management for adults.

DIMENSION 2:
Biomedical Conditions and Complications

All Programs

In Dimension 2, the patient's biomedical conditions and problems, if any, are stable or are being addressed concurrently and thus will not interfere with treatment. Examples include mild pregnancy-related hypertension, asthma, hypertension, or diabetes.

DIMENSION 3:
Emotional, Behavioral, or Cognitive Conditions and Complications

All Programs

Problems in Dimension 3 are not necessary for admission to a Level 2.1 program. However, if any of the Dimension 3 conditions are present, the patient must be admitted to either a co-occurring capable or co-occurring enhanced program, depending on the patient's level of function, stability, and degree of impairment in this dimension.

Co-Occurring Capable Programs

The patient's status in Dimension 3 is characterized by (a) **or** (b):

a. The patient engages in abuse of family members or significant others, and requires intensive outpatient treatment to reduce the risk of further deterioration;

   or

b. The patient has a diagnosed emotional, behavioral, or cognitive disorder that requires intensive outpatient monitoring to minimize distractions from his or her treatment or recovery.

Co-Occurring Enhanced Programs

The patient's status in Dimension 3 is characterized by (a) **or** (b) **or** (c):

a. The patient has a diagnosed emotional, behavioral, or cognitive disorder that requires management because the patient's history suggests a high potential for distraction from treatment; such a disorder requires stabilization concurrent with addiction treatment (for example, an unstable borderline personality disorder, compulsive personality disorder, unstable anxiety, or mood disorder);

   or

LEVEL 2.1

4

ADULT DIMENSIONAL ADMISSION CRITERIA (CONTINUED)

DIMENSION 3:
Emotional, Behavioral, or Cognitive Conditions and Complications

b. The patient is assessed as at mild risk of behaviors endangering self, others, or property (for example, he or she has suicidal or homicidal thoughts but no active plan);
or
c. The patient is at significant risk of victimization by another. However, the risk is not severe enough to require 24-hour supervision (for example, the patient has sufficient coping skills to maintain safety through attendance at treatment sessions at least 9 or more hours per week).

All Programs

The patient's status in Dimension 4 is characterized by (a) *or* (b):

a. The patient requires structured therapy and a programmatic milieu to promote treatment progress and recovery because motivational interventions at another level of care have failed. Such interventions are not feasible or are not likely to succeed in a Level 1 program;
or
b. The patient's perspective inhibits his or her ability to make behavioral changes without repeated, structured, clinically directed motivational interventions. (For example, the patient attributes his or her alcohol or other drug and mental health problems to other persons or external events rather than to an addictive or mental disorder.) Such interventions are not feasible or are not likely to succeed in a Level 1 program. However, the patient's willingness to participate in treatment and to explore his or her level of awareness and readiness to change suggest that treatment at Level 2.1 can be effective.

DIMENSION 4:
Readiness to Change

Co-Occurring Enhanced Programs

The patient's status in Dimension 4 is characterized by meeting criteria for all programs and (a); *and* one of (b) *or* (c):

a. The patient is reluctant to agree to treatment and is ambivalent about his or her commitment to change a co-occurring mental health problem;
and
b. The patient is assessed as requiring intensive services to improve his or her awareness of the need to change. The patient has such limited awareness of or commitment to change that he or she cannot maintain an adequate level of functioning without Level 2.1 services. For example, the patient continues to experience mild to moderate depression, anxiety, or mood swings, and is inconsistent in taking medication, keeping appointments, and completing mental health assignments;
or
c. The patient's follow through in treatment is so poor or inconsistent that Level 1 services are not succeeding or are not feasible.

ADULT DIMENSIONAL ADMISSION CRITERIA (CONTINUED)

DIMENSION 5:
Relapse, Continued Use, or
Continued Problem Potential

All Programs
The patient's status in Dimension 5 is characterized by (a) *or* (b):

    a. Although the patient has been an active participant at a less intensive level of care, he or she is experiencing an intensification of symptoms of the substance-related disorder (such as difficulty postponing immediate gratification and related drug-seeking behavior) and his or her level of functioning is deteriorating despite modification of the treatment plan;
    or

    b. There is a high likelihood that the patient will continue to use or relapse to use of alcohol and/or other drugs or gambling without close outpatient monitoring and structured therapeutic services, as indicated by his or her lack of awareness of relapse triggers, difficulty in coping, or in postponing immediate gratification or ambivalence toward treatment. The patient has unsuccessfully attempted treatment at a less intensive level of care, or such treatment is adjudged insufficient to stabilize the patient's condition so that direct admission to Level 2.1 is indicated.

Co-Occurring Enhanced Programs
The patient's status in Dimension 5 is characterized by psychiatric symptoms that pose a moderate risk of relapse to the alcohol, other drug, or other addictive or psychiatric disorder.

Such a patient has impaired recognition or understanding of–and difficulty in managing–relapse issues, and requires Level 2.1 co-occurring enhanced program services to maintain an adequate level of functioning. For example, the patient may have chronic difficulty in controlling his or her anger, with impulses to damage property, or the patient continues to increase his or her medication dose beyond the prescribed level in an attempt to control continued symptoms of anxiety or panic.

DIMENSION 6:
Recovery Environment

All Programs
The patient's status in Dimension 6 is characterized by (a) *or* (b):

    a. Continued exposure to the patient's current school, work, or living environment will render recovery unlikely. The patient lacks the resources or skills necessary to maintain an adequate level of functioning without the services of a Level 2.1 program;
    or

    b. The patient lacks social contacts, has unsupportive social contacts that jeopardize recovery, or has few friends or peers who do not use alcohol or other drugs. He or she also lacks the resources or skills necessary to maintain an adequate level of functioning without Level 2.1 services.

Co-Occurring Enhanced Programs
The patient's status in Dimension 6 is characterized by a living, working, social, and/or community environment that is not supportive of good mental functioning. The patient has insufficient resources and skills to deal with this situation.

For example, the patient is unable to cope with continuing stresses caused by hostile family members with addiction, and he or she evidences increasing depression and anxiety. The support and structure of a Level 2.1 co-occurring enhanced program provide sufficient stability to prevent further deterioration.

LEVEL 2.1 ④

ADOLESCENT DIAGNOSTIC ADMISSION CRITERIA

The adolescent who is appropriately placed in a Level 2.1 program is assessed as meeting the diagnostic criteria for a substance use and/or other addictive disorder as defined in the current *Diagnostic and Statistical Manual of Mental Disorders* (*DSM*) of the American Psychiatric Association or other standardized and widely accepted criteria, as well as the dimensional criteria for admission.

If the adolescent's presenting alcohol and/or other drug use and other addictive behavior history is inadequate to substantiate such a diagnosis, the probability of such a diagnosis may be determined from information submitted by collateral parties (such as family members, legal guardians, and significant others).

  ## ADOLESCENT DIMENSIONAL ADMISSION CRITERIA

Direct admission to a Level 2.1 program is advisable for the adolescent who meets the stability specifications in Dimension 1 (if any withdrawal problems exist) **and** Dimension 2 (if any biomedical conditions or problems exist) and the severity specifications in at least **one** of Dimensions 3, 4, 5, and 6.

Transfer to a Level 2.1 program is appropriate for the adolescent who has met the objectives of treatment in a more intensive level of care **and** who requires the intensity of service provided at Level 2.1 in at least **one** dimension.

An adolescent also may be transferred to Level 2.1 from a Level 1 program when the services provided at that level have proven insufficient to address his or her needs or when Level 1 services have consisted of motivational interventions to prepare the adolescent for participation in a more intensive level of care for which he or she now meets criteria. (The adolescent may be transferred to the next higher intensity level of care if the indicated level is not available in the immediate geographic area.)

DIMENSION 1:
Acute Intoxication and/or Withdrawal Potential

The adolescent who is appropriately placed in a Level 2.1 program is not experiencing or at risk of acute withdrawal. At most, the adolescent's symptoms consist of subacute withdrawal marked by minimal symptoms that are diminishing (as during the first several weeks of abstinence following a period of more severe acute withdrawal).

The adolescent is likely to attend, engage, and participate in treatment, as evidenced by his or her meeting the following criteria:

a. The adolescent is able to tolerate mild subacute withdrawal symptoms.

b. He or she has made a commitment to sustain treatment and to follow treatment recommendations.

c. The adolescent has external supports (family and/or court) that promote engagement in treatment.

NOTE: If the adolescent presents for treatment after recently experiencing an episode of acute withdrawal without treatment (as opposed to stepping down from a more intensive level of care following a good response), it is safer to err on the side of greater intensity of services when making a placement decision. For example, a Level 2.5 setting may be indicated if the adolescent is doing poorly or if there are indications in other dimensions that he or she would benefit from that level of care.

LEVEL 2.1

2

DIMENSION 2:
Biomedical Conditions and Complications

In Dimension 2, the adolescent's biomedical conditions and problems, if any, are stable or are being addressed concurrently and thus will not interfere with treatment. Examples include mild pregnancy-related hypertension, asthma, hypertension, or diabetes.

or

The adolescent's biomedical conditions and problems are severe enough to distract from recovery and treatment at a less intensive level of care, but will not interfere with recovery at Level 2.1. The biomedical conditions and problems are being addressed concurrently by a medical treatment provider.

3

DIMENSION 3:
Emotional, Behavioral, or Cognitive Conditions and Complications

The adolescent's status in Dimension 3 is characterized by at least *one* of the following:

a. **Dangerousness/Lethality:** The adolescent is at mild risk of behaviors endangering self, others, or property (for example, he or she has suicidal or homicidal thoughts, but no active plan), and requires frequent monitoring to assure that there is a reasonable likelihood of safety between IOP sessions. However, his or her condition is not so severe as to require daily supervision.

b. **Interference with Addiction Recovery Efforts:** The adolescent's recovery efforts are negatively affected by an emotional, behavioral, or cognitive problem, which causes mild interference with, and requires increased intensity to support, treatment participation and/or adherence. For example, the adolescent requires frequent repetition of treatment materials because of memory impairment associated with marijuana use.

c. **Social Functioning:** The adolescent's symptoms are causing mild to moderate difficulty in social functioning (involving family, friends, school, or work), but not to such a degree that he or she is unable to manage the activities of daily living or to fulfill responsibilities at home, school, work, or community. For example, the adolescent's problems may involve significantly worsening school performance or in-school detentions, a circle of friends that has narrowed to predominantly drug users, or loss of interest in most activities other than drug use.

d. **Ability for Self-Care:** The adolescent is experiencing mild to moderate impairment in ability to manage the activities of daily living, and thus requires frequent monitoring and treatment interventions. Problems may involve poor hygiene secondary to exacerbation of a chronic mental illness, poor self-care, or lack of independent living skills in an older adolescent who is transitioning to adulthood, or in a younger adolescent who lacks adequate family supports.

e. **Course of Illness:** The adolescent's history and present situation suggest that an emotional, behavioral, or cognitive condition would become unstable without frequent monitoring and maintenance. For example, he or she may require frequent prompting and monitoring of medication adherence (in an adolescent with a history of medication non-adherence) or frequent prompting and monitoring of behavioral adherence (in an adolescent with a conduct disorder or other serious pattern of delinquent behavior).

LEVEL 2.1

4

ADOLESCENT DIMENSIONAL ADMISSION CRITERIA (CONTINUED)

DIMENSION 4:
Readiness to Change

The adolescent's status in Dimension 4 is characterized by (a) *or* (b):

a. The adolescent requires structured therapy and a programmatic milieu to promote progress through the stages of change, as evidenced by behaviors such as the following: (1) the adolescent is verbally compliant, but does not demonstrate consistent behaviors; (2) the adolescent is only passively involved in treatment; or (3) the adolescent demonstrates variable adherence with attendance at outpatient sessions or self or mutual help meetings or support groups. Such interventions are not feasible or are not likely to succeed in a Level 1 service;
or

b. The adolescent's perspective inhibits his or her ability to make progress through the stages of change. For example, he or she has unrealistic expectations that the alcohol or other drug problem will resolve quickly and with little or no effort, or does not recognize the need for continued assistance. The adolescent thus requires structured therapy and a programmatic milieu. Such interventions are not feasible or are not likely to succeed in a Level 1 service.

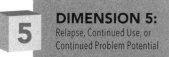

DIMENSION 5:
Relapse, Continued Use, or
Continued Problem Potential

The adolescent's status in Dimension 5 is characterized by (a) *or* (b):

a. Although the adolescent has been an active participant at a less intensive level of care, he or she is experiencing an intensification of symptoms of the substance-related disorder (such as difficulty postponing immediate gratification and related drug-seeking behavior) and his or her level of functioning is deteriorating despite modification of the treatment plan;
or

b. There is a high likelihood that the adolescent will continue to use or relapse to use of alcohol and/or other drugs or gambling without close outpatient monitoring and structured therapeutic services, as indicated by his or her lack of awareness of relapse triggers, difficulty in coping, or in postponing immediate gratification or ambivalence toward treatment. The adolescent has unsuccessfully attempted treatment at a less intensive level of care, or such treatment is adjudged insufficient to stabilize the adolescent's condition so that direct admission to Level 2.1 is indicated.

DIMENSION 6:
Recovery Environment

The adolescent's status in Dimension 6 is characterized by (a) *or* (b) *or* (c):

a. Continued exposure to the adolescent's current school, work, or living environment will render recovery unlikely. The adolescent lacks the resources or skills necessary to maintain an adequate level of functioning without the services of a Level 2.1 program;
or

b. The adolescent lacks social contacts, has unsupportive social contacts that jeopardize recovery, or has few friends or peers who do not use alcohol or other drugs. He or she also lacks the resources or skills necessary to maintain an adequate level of functioning without Level 2.1 services.
or

c. In addition to the characteristics for all programs, a third option is that the adolescent's family or caretakers are supportive of recovery, but family conflicts and related family dysfunction impede the adolescent's ability to learn the skills necessary to achieve and maintain abstinence.

NOTE: The adolescent may require Level 2.1 services in addition to an out-of-home placement (for example, at Level 3.1 or the equivalent, such as a group home or a non-treatment residential setting such as a detention program). If his or her present environment is supportive of recovery but does not provide sufficient addiction-specific services to foster and sustain recovery goals, the adolescent's needs in Dimension 6 may be met through an out-of-home placement, while other dimensional criteria would indicate the need for care in a Level 2.1 program.

Level 2.5
Partial Hospitalization Services

Partial hospitalization programs (PHP), known in some areas as "day treatment," generally feature 20 or more hours of clinically intensive programming per week, as specified in the patient's treatment plan. Level 2.5 partial hospitalization programs typically have direct access to psychiatric, medical, and laboratory services, and thus are better able than Level 2.1 programs to meet needs identified in Dimensions 1, 2, and 3, which warrant daily monitoring or management but which can be appropriately addressed in a structured outpatient setting.

For adolescents, partial hospitalization often occurs during school hours; such programs typically have access to educational services for their adolescent patients. Programs that do not provide educational services should coordinate with a school system in order to assess and meet their adolescent patients' educational needs.

Patients who meet Level 2.1 criteria in Dimensions 4, 5, or 6 and who otherwise would be placed in a Level 2.1 program may be considered for placement in a Level 2.5 program if the patient resides in a facility that provides 24-hour support and structure and that limits access to alcohol and other drugs, such as a correctional facility or other licensed health care facility or a supervised living situation.

EXAMPLES OF SERVICE DELIVERY
All Programs

Examples of Level 2.5 programs are day treatment or partial hospital programs.

SETTING
All Programs

Level 2.5 program services may be offered in any appropriate setting that meets state licensure or certification criteria.

SUPPORT SYSTEMS
All Programs

In Level 2.5 programs, necessary support systems include:

a. Medical, psychological, psychiatric, laboratory, and toxicology services, which are available through consultation or referral. Psychiatric and other medical consultation is available within 8 hours by telephone and within 48 hours in person.

b. Emergency services, which are available by telephone 24 hours a day, 7 days a week when the treatment program is not in session.

c. Direct affiliation with (or close coordination through referral to) more and less intensive levels of care and supportive housing services.

Co-Occurring Enhanced Programs

In addition to the support systems just described for co-occurring capable programs, Level 2.5 co-occurring enhanced programs offer psychiatric services appropriate to the patient's mental health condition. Such services are available by telephone and on site, or closely coordinated off site, within a shorter time than in a co-occurring capable program.

Clinical leadership and oversight may be offered by a certified addiction medicine physician with at least the capacity to consult with an addiction psychiatrist. Some Level 2.5 services are specifically designed to be "co-occurring disorders" programs in distinction from addiction specialty services.

LEVEL 2.5 ④

a ▸ Adolescent-Specific Considerations: Support Systems

In Level 2.5 adolescent programs, necessary support services include:

a. Medical, psychological, psychiatric, laboratory, and toxicology, educational, occupational, and other services needed by adolescents are available through consultation or referral. Medical and psychiatric consultation is available within 8 hours by telephone and within 48 hours face-to-face (depending on the urgency of the situation) through on-site services, referral to off-site services, or transfer to another level of care.

b. Emergency services, which are available by telephone 24 hours a day, 7 days a week when the program is not in session.

c. Direct affiliation with more and less intensive levels of care.

Adolescent Level 2.5-WM support systems should also feature:

a. Availability of specialized clinical consultation and supervision for biomedical, emotional, cognitive, or behavioral problems related to intoxication or withdrawal management.

b. Protocols used to determine the nature of the medical monitoring and/or interventions required (including the need for nursing or physician care and/or transfer to a more intensive level of care) are developed and supported by a physician who is knowledgeable in addiction medicine.

STAFF
All Programs

Level 2.5 programs are staffed by an interdisciplinary team of appropriately credentialed addiction treatment professionals, including counselors, psychologists, social workers, and addiction-credentialed physicians, who assess and treat substance-related or other addictive disorders. Physicians treating patients in this level should have specialty training and/or experience in addiction medicine or addiction psychiatry and, if treating adolescents, experience with adolescent medicine. Program staff is able to obtain and interpret information regarding the patient's biopsychosocial needs.

Some, if not all, program staff should have sufficient cross-training to understand the signs and symptoms of mental disorders, and to understand and be able to explain the uses of psychotropic medications and their interactions with substance-related disorders.

Co-Occurring Enhanced Programs

In addition to the staff capabilities just listed, which encompass those of co-occurring capable programs, Level 2.5 co-occurring enhanced programs are staffed by appropriately credentialed mental health professionals, who assess and treat co-occurring mental disorders.

Clinical leadership and oversight may be offered by a certified and/or licensed addiction psychiatrist. Some Level 2.5 services are specifically designed to be "co-occurring" programs in distinction from addiction specialty services.

Co-occurring enhanced programs also provide ongoing intensive case management for highly crisis-prone (and often homeless) patients with co-occurring disorders. Such case management is delivered by cross-trained, interdisciplinary staff through mobile outreach, and involves engagement-oriented addiction treatment and psychiatric programming.

LEVEL 2.5 — 4

Adolescent-Specific Considerations: Staff

In addition to the specifications for staff for all services, staff should be knowledgeable about adolescent development and experienced in engaging and working with adolescents. Clinical staff who assess and treat adolescents are able to recognize the need for specialty evaluation and treatment for intoxication or withdrawal and are able to arrange for such evaluation or treatment in a timely manner.

Enhanced Programs (including adolescent Level 2.5-WM Withdrawal Management)

Appropriately licensed and credentialed staff are available to administer and/or monitor medications and to provide individual or group education about the medications and their use. The intensity of nursing care is appropriate to the services provided.

While most withdrawal management in Level 2 occurs in Level 2.5-WM, if a Level 2.1 program provides withdrawal management services to adolescents, it must offer:

a. Appropriately trained personnel who are competent to implement physician-approved protocols for patient observation, supervision, treatment (including the use of over-the-counter medications for symptomatic relief), and determination of the appropriate level of care.

b. Nursing and/or medical evaluation and consultation, which are available 24 hours a day to monitor the safety and outcome of withdrawal management efforts, in accordance with practice guidelines for patient treatment or transfer.

c. Clinicians who assess and treat adolescents are able to obtain and interpret information regarding the signs and symptoms of intoxication and withdrawal, as well as the appropriate treatment and monitoring of those conditions and the best way to facilitate the adolescent's transition to ongoing care.

LEVEL 2.5 ④

THERAPIES
All Programs

Therapies offered by Level 2.5 programs include:

a. A minimum of 20 hours per week of skilled treatment services. Services may include individual and group counseling, medication management, family therapy, educational groups, occupational and recreational therapy, and other therapies. These are provided in the amounts, frequencies, and intensities appropriate to the objectives of the treatment plan.

b. Family therapy, which involves family members, guardians, or significant other(s) in the assessment, treatment, and continuing care of the patient.

c. A planned format of therapies, delivered on an individual and group basis and adapted to the patient's developmental stage and comprehension level.

d. Motivational enhancement and engagement strategies, which are preferred over confrontational approaches.

a Adolescent-Specific Considerations: Therapies

In addition to the therapies described for all programs, educational services are provided (when not available through other resources), which are designed to maintain the educational and intellectual development of the patient and, when indicated, to provide opportunities to remedy deficits in the adolescent's education.

Clinical services are provided to assess and address the adolescent's withdrawal status and treatment needs. Such clinical services may include nursing and medical monitoring or treatment, use of over-the-counter medications for symptomatic relief, individual or group therapies specific to withdrawal, and withdrawal support.

Co-Occurring Programs

The therapies just described typically are offered by Level 2.5 co-occurring capable programs to patients with co-occurring addictive and mental disorders who are able to tolerate and benefit from a planned program of therapies.

Other patients (especially those who have severe and chronic mental illness) may not be able to benefit from a full program of therapies and thus may require co-occurring enhanced program services that constitute the defined intensity of hours in Level 2.5. Such services may involve intensive case management, assertive community treatment, medication management, and psychotherapy.

ASSESSMENT/TREATMENT PLAN REVIEW
All Programs

In Level 2.5 programs, the assessment and treatment plan review include:

a. A biopsychosocial assessment which includes a comprehensive substance use and addictive behaviors history, obtained as part of the initial assessment and reviewed by a physician, if necessary. A physical examination may be performed within a reasonable time, as determined by the patient's medical condition. Such

a Adolescent-Specific Considerations: Assessment and Treatment Planning

Information for assessment and treatment planning may be obtained from a parent, guardian, or other important resource (such as a teacher or probation officer).

Elements of the assessment and treatment plan review should also include:

a. An initial withdrawal assessment, including a medical evaluation at admission (or medical review of an evaluation performed within the 48 hours preceding admission, or within 7 days preceding admission for a patient who is stepping down from a residential setting).

b. Ongoing withdrawal monitoring assessments, performed several times a week.

c. Ongoing screening for medical and nursing needs, with medical and nursing evaluation available through consultation or referral.

determinations are made according to established protocols, which include reliance on the patient's personal physician whenever possible. The determination is based on the staff's capabilities and the severity of the patient's symptoms, and is approved by a physician. (In states where physician assistants or nurse practitioners are under physician supervision and are licensed as physician extenders, they may perform the duties designated here for a physician.)

b. An individualized treatment plan, which involves problems, needs, strengths, skills, and priority formulation and articulation of short-term, measurable treatment goals, preferences, and activities designed to achieve those goals. The plan is developed in collaboration with the patient and reflects the patient's personal goals. Treatment plan reviews are conducted at specified times, as noted in the treatment plan.

Co-Occurring Enhanced Programs
In addition to the activities just described, which encompass co-occurring capable programs,

Level 2.5 co-occurring enhanced programs provide a review of the patient's recent psychiatric history and a mental status examination (which are reviewed by a psychiatrist, if necessary). A comprehensive psychiatric history and examination and a psychodiagnostic assessment are performed within a reasonable time frame, as determined by the patient's psychiatric condition.

DOCUMENTATION
All Programs
Documentation standards for Level 2.5 programs include individualized progress notes in the patient's record that clearly reflect implementation of the treatment plan and the patient's response to therapeutic interventions for all disorders treated, as well as subsequent amendments to the plan.

Co-Occurring Programs
In addition to the documentation standards previously described, Level 2.5 co-occurring capable and co-occurring enhanced programs document the patient's mental health problems, the relationship between the mental and substance-related disorders, and the patient's current level of mental functioning.

ADULT DIAGNOSTIC ADMISSION CRITERIA
All Services
The patient who is appropriately placed in a Level 2.5 program is assessed as meeting the diagnostic criteria for a substance use and/or other addictive disorder as defined in the current *Diagnostic and Statistical Manual of Mental Disorders (DSM)* of the American Psychiatric Association or other standardized and widely accepted criteria, as well as the dimensional criteria for admission.

If the patient's presenting substance use or gambling history is inadequate to substantiate such a diagnosis, the probability of such a diagnosis may be determined from information submitted by collateral parties (such as family members, legal guardians, and significant others).

Co-Occurring Enhanced Programs
The patient in need of Level 2.5 co-occurring enhanced program services is assessed as meeting the diagnostic criteria for a mental disorder as well as a substance use or addictive disorder, as defined in the current *Diagnostic and Statistical Manual of Mental Disorders (DSM)* of the American Psychiatric Association or other standardized and widely accepted criteria, as well as the dimensional criteria for admission.

If the patient's presenting history is inadequate to substantiate such a diagnosis, the probability of such a diagnosis may be determined from information submitted by collateral parties (such as family members, legal guardians, and significant others).

ADULT DIMENSIONAL ADMISSION CRITERIA

All Programs

Direct admission to a Level 2.5 program is advisable for the patient who meets specifications in Dimension 2 (if any biomedical conditions or problems exist) **and** in Dimension 3 (if any emotional, behavioral, or cognitive conditions or problems exist), as well as in at least **one** of Dimensions 4, 5, or 6.

Transfer to a Level 2.5 program is advisable for the patient who

    a. has met essential treatment objectives at a more intensive level of care

       and

    b. requires the intensity of services provided at Level 2.5 in at least **one** dimension.

A patient also may be transferred to Level 2.5 from a Level 1 or Level 2.1 program when the services provided at the less intensive level have proved insufficient to address the patient's needs, or when those services have consisted of motivational interventions to prepare the patient for participation in a more intensive level of service, for which he or she now meets the admission criteria.

DIMENSION 1:
Acute Intoxication and/or Withdrawal Potential

All Programs

The patient has no signs or symptoms of withdrawal, or his or her withdrawal needs can be safely managed in a Level 2.5 setting. See separate withdrawal management chapter for how to approach "unbundled" withdrawal management for adults.

DIMENSION 2:
Biomedical Conditions and Complications

All Programs

In Dimension 2, the patient's biomedical conditions and problems, if any, are not sufficient to interfere with treatment, but are severe enough to distract from recovery efforts. Examples include unstable hypertension or asthma requiring medication adjustment or chronic back pain that distracts from recovery efforts.

Such problems require medical monitoring and/or medical management, which can be provided by a Level 2.5 program either directly or through an arrangement with another treatment provider.

All Programs

Problems in Dimension 3 are not necessary for admission to a Level 2.5 program. However, if any of the Dimension 3 conditions are present, the patient must be admitted to either a co-occurring capable or co-occurring enhanced program, depending on the patient's level of function, stability, and degree of impairment in this dimension.

The severity of the patient's problems in Dimension 3 may require partial hospitalization or a similar supportive living environment in conjunction with a Level 3.1 program. On the other hand, if the patient receives adequate support from his or her family or significant other(s), a Level 2.5 program may suffice.

DIMENSION 3:
Emotional, Behavioral, or Cognitive Conditions and Complications

Co-Occurring Capable Programs

The patient's status in Dimension 3 is characterized by a history of mild to moderate psychiatric decompensation (marked by paranoia or mild psychotic symptoms) on discontinuation of the drug use. Such decompensation may occur and requires monitoring to permit early intervention.

Co-Occurring Enhanced Programs

The patient's status in Dimension 3 is characterized by (a) **or** (b) **or** (c):

    a. The patient evidences current inability to maintain behavioral stability over a 48-hour period (as evidenced by distractibility, negative emotions, or generalized anxiety that significantly affects his or her daily functioning);

       or

    b. The patient has a history of moderate psychiatric decompensation (marked by severe, non-suicidal depression) on discontinuation of the drug of abuse. Such decompensation is currently observable;

LEVEL 2.5

ADULT DIMENSIONAL ADMISSION CRITERIA (CONTINUED)

DIMENSION 3:
Emotional, Behavioral, or Cognitive Conditions and Complications

or

c. The patient is at mild to moderate risk of behaviors endangering self, others, or property, and is at imminent risk of relapse, with dangerous emotional, behavioral, or cognitive consequences, in the absence of Level 2.5 structured services. For example, the patient does not have sufficient internal coping skills to maintain safety to self, others, or property without the consistent structure achieved through attendance at treatment sessions daily, or at least 20 hours per week.

All Programs

The patient's status in Dimension 4 is characterized by (a) *or* (b):

a. The patient requires structured therapy and a programmatic milieu to promote treatment progress and recovery because motivational interventions at another level of care have failed. Such interventions are not feasible or are not likely to succeed in a Level 2.1 program;
or

b. The patient's perspective and lack of impulse control inhibit his or her ability to make behavioral changes without repeated, structured, clinically directed motivational interventions. (For example, the patient has unrealistic expectations that his or her alcohol, other drug, or mental health problem will resolve quickly, with little or no effort, or the patient experiences frequent impulses to harm himself or herself. He or she is willing to reach out but lacks ability to ask for help.) Such interventions are not feasible or are not likely to succeed in a Level 1 or Level 2.1 program. However, the patient's willingness to participate in treatment and to explore his or her level of awareness and readiness to change suggest that treatment at Level 2.5 can be effective.

DIMENSION 4:
Readiness to Change

Co-Occurring Enhanced Programs

The patient's status in Dimension 4 is characterized by (a); *and* one of (b) *or* (c):

a. The patient has little awareness of his or her co-occurring mental disorder;
and

b. The patient is assessed as requiring more intensive engagement, community, or case management services than are available at Level 2.1 in order to maintain an adequate level of functioning (for example, the patient experiences frequent impulses to harm himself or herself, with poor commitment to reach out for help);
or

c. The patient's follow through in treatment is so poor or inconsistent that Level 2.1 services are not succeeding or are not feasible.

All Programs

The patient's status in Dimension 5 is characterized by (a) *or* (b):

a. Although the patient has been an active participant at a less intensive level of care, he or she is experiencing an intensification of symptoms of the substance-related disorder (such as difficulty postponing immediate gratification and related drug-seeking behavior) and his or her level of functioning is deteriorating despite modification of the treatment plan;
or

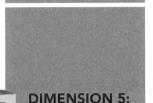

DIMENSION 5:
Relapse, Continued Use, or Continued Problem Potential

b. There is a high likelihood that the patient will continue to use or relapse to use of substances or gambling without close outpatient monitoring and structured therapeutic services, as indicated by his or her lack of awareness of relapse triggers, difficulty in coping or postponing immediate gratification, or ambivalence toward treatment. The patient has unsuccessfully attempted treatment at a less intensive level of care, or such treatment is adjudged insufficient to stabilize the patient's condition so that direct admission to Level 2.5 is indicated.

LEVEL 2.5

ADULT DIMENSIONAL ADMISSION CRITERIA (CONTINUED)

DIMENSION 5:
Relapse, Continued Use, or Continued Problem Potential

Co-Occurring Enhanced Programs

The patient's status in Dimension 5 is characterized by psychiatric symptoms that pose a high risk of relapse to the substance or psychiatric disorder.

Such a patient has impaired recognition or understanding of relapse issues, and inadequate skills in coping with and interrupting mental disorders and/or avoiding or limiting relapse. Such a patient's follow through in treatment is so inadequate or inconsistent, and his or her relapse problems are escalating to such a degree, that treatment at Level 2.1 is not succeeding or not feasible.

For example, the patient may continue to inflict superficial wounds on himself or herself and have continuing suicidal ideation and impulses. However, he or she has no specific suicide plan and agrees to reach out for help if seriously suicidal. Or the patient's continuing substance-induced psychotic symptoms are resolving, but difficulties in controlling his or her substance use exacerbate the psychotic symptoms.

All Programs

The patient's status in Dimension 6 is characterized by (a) *or* (b):

a. Continued exposure to the patient's current school, work, or living environment will render recovery unlikely. The patient lacks the resources or skills necessary to maintain an adequate level of functioning without the services of a Level 2.5 program;
   or
b. Family members and/or significant other(s) who live with the patient are not supportive of his or her recovery goals, or are passively opposed to his or her treatment. The patient requires the intermittent structure of Level 2.5 treatment services and relief from the home environment in order to remain focused on recovery, but may live at home because there is no active opposition to, or sabotaging of, his or her recovery efforts.

DIMENSION 6:
Recovery Environment

Co-Occurring Enhanced Programs

The patient's status in Dimension 6 is characterized by a living, working, social, and/or community environment that is not supportive of good mental functioning. The patient has such limited resources and skills to deal with this situation that treatment is not succeeding or not feasible.

For example, the patient is unable to cope with continuing stresses caused by homelessness, unemployment, and isolation, and evidences increasing depression and hopelessness. The support and intermittent structure of a Level 2.5 co-occurring enhanced program provide sufficient stability to prevent further deterioration.

ADOLESCENT DIAGNOSTIC ADMISSION CRITERIA

The adolescent who is appropriately placed in a Level 2.5 program is assessed as meeting the diagnostic criteria for a substance use and/or other addictive disorder as defined in the current *Diagnostic and Statistical Manual of Mental Disorders* (DSM) of the American Psychiatric Association or other standardized and widely accepted criteria, as well as the dimensional criteria for admission.

If the adolescent's presenting substance use or gambling history is inadequate to substantiate such a diagnosis, the probability of such a diagnosis may be determined from information submitted by collateral parties (such as family members, legal guardians, and significant others).

LEVEL 2.5

ADOLESCENT DIMENSIONAL ADMISSION CRITERIA

Direct admission to a Level 2.5 program is advisable for the adolescent who meets the stability specifications in Dimension 1 (if any withdrawal problems exist) **and** Dimension 2 (if any biomedical conditions or problems exist) and the severity specifications in **one** of Dimensions 3, 4, 5, and 6.

Transfer to a Level 2.5 program is appropriate for the adolescent who has met the objectives of treatment in a more intensive level of care **and** who requires the intensity of service provided at Level 2.5 in at least **one** dimension.

An adolescent also may be transferred to Level 2.5 from a Level 1 or 2.1 program when the services provided at those levels have proven insufficient to address his or her needs or when Level 1 or 2.1 services have consisted of motivational interventions to prepare the adolescent for participation in a more intensive level of care for which he or she now meets criteria. (The adolescent may be transferred to the next higher level of care if the indicated level is not available in the immediate geographic area.)

DIMENSION 1:
Acute Intoxication and/or Withdrawal Potential

The adolescent who is appropriately placed in a Level 2.5 program is experiencing acute or subacute withdrawal, marked by mild symptoms that are diminishing (as during the first several weeks of abstinence following a period of more severe acute withdrawal).

Withdrawal rating scale tables and flow sheets (which may include tabulation of vital signs) are used as needed.

The adolescent is likely to attend, engage, and participate in treatment, as evidenced by meeting the following criteria:

a. The adolescent is able to tolerate mild withdrawal symptoms.

b. He or she has made a commitment to sustain treatment and to follow treatment recommendations.

c. The adolescent has external supports (as from family and/or court) that promote treatment engagement.

Drug-specific examples follow:

a. **Alcohol:** Mild withdrawal; no need for sedative/hypnotic substitution therapy; no hyperdynamic state; CIWA-Ar score of ≤6; no significant history of regular morning drinking; the adolescent's symptoms are stabilized and he or she is comfortable by the end of each day's active treatment or monitoring.

b. **Sedative/hypnotics:** Mild withdrawal; the adolescent may have a history of near-daily sedative/hypnotic use, but no cross-dependence on other substances; no disturbance of vital signs; no unstable complicating exacerbation of affective disturbance; no need for sedative/hypnotic substitution therapy; the adolescent's symptoms are stabilized, and he or she is comfortable by the end of each day's active treatment or monitoring.

c. **Opiates:** Mild withdrawal; the adolescent may need over-the-counter medications for symptomatic relief, but does not need prescription medications or opiate agonist substitution therapy; he or she is comfortable by the end of each day's active treatment or monitoring. The adolescent has sufficient impulse control, coping skills, and/or supports to prevent immediate continued use beyond the active treatment day.

d. **Stimulants:** Mild to moderate withdrawal (for example, involving depression, lethargy, or agitation), so that the adolescent is likely to need frequent contact and/or higher intensity services to tolerate symptoms, engage in treatment, and bolster external supports. The adolescent has sufficient impulse control, coping skills, and/or supports to prevent immediate continued use beyond the active treatment day.

e. **Inhalants:** Mild subacute intoxication (involving cognitive impairment, lethargy, agitation, and depression), such that the adolescent is likely to need frequent contact and/or higher intensity services to tolerate symptoms, engage in treatment, and bolster external supports. The adolescent has sufficient impulse control, coping skills, and/or supports to prevent immediate continued use beyond the active treatment day.

LEVEL 2.5

4

ADOLESCENT DIMENSIONAL ADMISSION CRITERIA (CONTINUED)

DIMENSION 1:
Acute Intoxication and/or
Withdrawal Potential

f. **Marijuana:** Moderate withdrawal (involving irritability, general malaise, inner agitation, and sleep disturbance) or sustained subacute intoxication (involving cognitive disorganization, memory impairment, and executive dysfunction), such that the adolescent is likely to need frequent contact and/or higher intensity services to tolerate symptoms, engage in treatment, and bolster external supports.

g. **Hallucinogens:** Mild chronic intoxication (involving mild perceptual distortion, mild suspiciousness, or mild affective instability). The adolescent has sufficient compensatory coping skills to support engagement in treatment.

DIMENSION 2:
Biomedical Conditions and
Complications

The adolescent's biomedical conditions and problems are severe enough to distract from recovery and treatment at a less intensive level of care, but will not interfere with recovery at Level 2.5. Examples include unstable diabetes or asthma requiring medication adjustment, or physical disabilities that distract from recovery efforts.

Such problems require medical monitoring and/or medical management, which can be provided by a Level 2.5 program either directly or through an arrangement with another treatment provider.

The adolescent's status in Dimension 3 is characterized by at least *one* of the following:

a. **Dangerousness/Lethality:** The adolescent is at mild risk of behaviors endangering self, others, or property (for example, he or she has suicidal or homicidal thoughts, but no active plan), and requires frequent monitoring to assure that there is a reasonable likelihood of safety between PHP sessions. However, his or her condition is not so severe as to require 24-hour supervision.

b. **Interference with Addiction Recovery Efforts:** The adolescent's recovery efforts are negatively affected by an emotional, behavioral, or cognitive problem, which causes moderate interference with, and requires increased intensity to support, treatment participation and/or adherence. For example, cognitive impairment or significant attention deficit hyperactivity disorder prevents achievement of recovery tasks or goals.

c. **Social Functioning:** The adolescent's symptoms are causing mild to moderate difficulty in social functioning (involving family, friends, school, or work), but not to such a degree that the adolescent is unable to manage the activities of daily living or to fulfill responsibilities at home, school, work, or community. For example, the adolescent's problems may involve recent arrests or legal charges, or non-adherence with probation, progressive school suspensions or truancy, risk of failing the school year, regular intoxication at school or work, involvement in drug trafficking, or a pattern of intentional property damage.

Alternatively, the adolescent may be transitioning back to the community as a step down from an institutionalized setting.

DIMENSION 3:
Emotional, Behavioral, or
Cognitive Conditions and
Complications

d. **Ability for Self-Care:** The adolescent is experiencing moderate impairment in ability to manage the activities of daily living, and thus requires near-daily monitoring and treatment interventions. Problems may involve disorganization and inability to manage the demands of daily self-scheduling, a progressive pattern of promiscuous or unprotected sexual contacts, or poor vocational or prevocational skills that require habilitation and training provided in the program.

e. **Course of Illness:** The adolescent's history and present situation suggest that an emotional, behavioral, or cognitive condition would become unstable without daily or near-daily monitoring and maintenance. For example, signs of imminent relapse may indicate a need for near-daily monitoring of an adolescent with attention deficit hyperactivity disorder and a history of disorganization that becomes unmanageable in school with substance use; or an initial lapse indicates a need for near-daily monitoring in an adolescent whose conduct disorder worsens dangerously within the context of progressive use.

ADOLESCENT DIMENSIONAL ADMISSION CRITERIA (CONTINUED)

DIMENSION 4:
Readiness to Change

The adolescent's status in Dimension 4 is characterized by (a) *or* (b):

a. The adolescent requires structured therapy and a programmatic milieu to promote treatment progress and recovery because motivational interventions at another level of care have failed. Such interventions are not feasible or are not likely to succeed in a Level 2.1 program; *or*

b. The adolescent's perspective and lack of impulse control inhibit his or her ability to make behavioral changes without repeated, structured, clinically directed motivational interventions. (For example, the adolescent has unrealistic expectations that his or her alcohol, other drug, or mental health problem will resolve quickly, with little or no effort, or the adolescent experiences frequent impulses to harm himself or herself. He or she is willing to reach out but lacks the ability to ask for help.) Such interventions are not feasible or are not likely to succeed in a Level 1 or Level 2.1 program. However, the adolescent's willingness to participate in treatment and to explore his or her level of awareness and readiness to change suggest that treatment at Level 2.5 can be effective.

DIMENSION 5:
Relapse, Continued Use, or Continued Problem Potential

The adolescent's status in Dimension 5 is characterized by (a) *or* (b):

a. The adolescent is at high risk of relapse or continued use without almost daily outpatient monitoring and structured therapeutic services (as indicated, for example, by susceptibility to relapse triggers, a pattern of frequent or progressive lapses, inability to overcome the momentum of a pattern of habitual use, difficulty in overcoming a pattern of impulsive behaviors, or ambivalence about or disinterest in treatment). Also, treatment at a less intensive level of care has been attempted or given serious consideration and been judged insufficient to stabilize the adolescent's condition; *or*

b. The adolescent demonstrates impaired recognition and understanding of relapse or continued use issues. He or she has such poor skills in coping with and interrupting substance use problems, and avoiding or limiting relapse, that the near-daily structure afforded by a Level 2.5 program is needed to prevent or arrest significant deterioration in function.

DIMENSION 6:
Recovery Environment

The adolescent's status in Dimension 6 is characterized by (a) *or* (b) *or* (c):

a. Continued exposure to the adolescent's current school, work, or living environment will render recovery unlikely. The adolescent lacks the resources or skills necessary to maintain an adequate level of functioning without the services of a Level 2.5 program; *or*

b. Family members and/or significant other(s) who live with the adolescent are not supportive of his or her recovery goals, or are passively opposed to his or her treatment. The adolescent requires the intermittent structure of Level 2.5 treatment services and relief from the home environment in order to remain focused on recovery, but may live at home because there is no active opposition to, or sabotaging of, his or her recovery efforts; *or*

c. The adolescent lacks social contacts, or has high-risk social contacts that jeopardize recovery, or has few friends or peers who do not use alcohol or other drugs. He or she also has insufficient (or severely limited) resources or skills necessary to maintain an adequate level of functioning without the services of a Level 2.5 program, but is capable of maintaining an adequate level of functioning between sessions.

The adolescent may require Level 2.5 services in addition to an out-of-home placement (for example, at Level 3.1 or the equivalent, such as a group home or a non-treatment residential setting such as a detention program). If his or her present environment is supportive of recovery but does not provide sufficient addiction-specific services to foster and sustain recovery goals, the adolescent's needs in Dimension 6 may be met through an out-of-home placement, while other dimensional criteria would indicate the need for care in a Level 2.5 program.

LEVEL 2.5

4

Level 3
Residential/Inpatient Services

Level 3 programs offer organized treatment services that feature a planned and structured regimen of care in a 24-hour residential setting. Treatment services adhere to defined policies, procedures, and clinical protocols. They are housed in, or affiliated with, permanent facilities where patients can reside safely. (One of the purposes of these programs is to demonstrate aspects of a positive recovery environment.) They are staffed 24 hours a day. Mutual/self-help group meetings, while not clinical services, usually are available on-site.

All Level 3 programs serve individuals who, because of specific functional limitations, need safe and stable living environments and 24-hour care. This is needed to develop, practice, and/or demonstrate the recovery skills necessary so that patients do not immediately relapse or continue to use or gamble in an imminently dangerous manner upon transfer to a less intensive level of care. Such services are community-based rather than hospital-based services, although they might be housed in a hospital. The living environments may be housed in the same facility as the treatment services, or they may be in separate facilities that are affiliated

with the treatment provider. In the latter situation, the relationship between the living environment and the treatment provider must be sufficiently close to allow specific aspects of the individual treatment plan to be addressed in both facilities.

The sublevels within Level 3 exist on a continuum ranging from the least intensive residential services to the most intensive medically monitored intensive inpatient services. Sublevels of Level 3 programs, however, are not distinguished by the number of hours of services. Indeed, Level 3 always has consisted of a range of intensities of service. All Level 3 sublevels have 24-hour staff, but Level 3.1 is qualitatively different in that it is a 24-hour supportive living environment whereas the other sublevels are 24-hour treatment settings. The intent is not to create discrete sublevels of care within Level 3, but rather to create a range of intensities, with each designated sublevel (such as Level 3.5) suggesting a particular *point* within that range. When a program provides Level 3 services that exceed the intensity usually ascribed to that level, or can appropriately treat an individual who has a more severe illness than usually is

LEVEL 3 BENCHMARK SERVICES

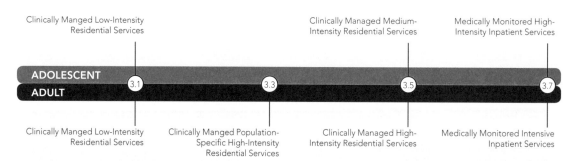

Clinically Manged Low-Intensity Residential Services

Clinically Managed Medium-Intensity Residential Services

Medically Monitored High-Intensity Inpatient Services

ADOLESCENT

3.1   3.3   3.5   3.7

ADULT

Clinically Manged Low-Intensity Residential Services

Clinically Manged Population-Specific High-Intensity Residential Services

Clinically Managed High-Intensity Residential Services

Medically Monitored Intensive Inpatient Services

addressed at that level, it should be considered an *enhanced service.*

Differences between Level 3 programs may be based partially on intensity (eg, Level 3.1 requires a minimum of 5 hours of treatment per week compared to Level 3.5 which provides 24-hour services and supports). However, the defining differences between these levels of care are the functional limitations of the patients and the services provided to respond to those limitations. The goal is to provide a flexible system with overlapping levels of care making transition between levels of care as seamless as possible. For example, for those patients who are homeless but are not in imminent danger, and would normally require the intensity of services of a Level 3.5, Level 2.5, Partial Hospitalization services, can be provided in conjunction with supportive living options which address the homelessness issue or in conjunction with Level 3.1.

The term "clinically managed" is used to describe Level 3.1 through 3.5 programs and places emphasis on the therapeutic milieu. Individuals who are appropriately placed in the clinically managed levels of care have minimal problems with intoxication or withdrawal (Dimension 1) and few biomedical complications (Dimension 2), so on-site physician services are not required. Such individuals may have relatively stable problems in emotional, behavioral, and cognitive conditions (Dimension 3), meeting the diagnostic criteria of the *Diagnostic and Statistical Manual of Mental Disorders* (*DSM*) of the American Psychiatric Association. Many also have significant limitations in the areas of readiness to change (Dimension 4), relapse, continued use, or continued problem potential (Dimension 5), or recovery environment (Dimension 6). Therefore, they are in need of interventions directed by appropriately trained and credentialed addiction treatment staff. Such individuals also need case management services to facilitate their reintegration into the larger community.

Length of Service
The duration of treatment always depends on individual progress and outcome. Because treatment plans should be individualized, lengths of stay should be flexible and individualized to meet the needs of each patient. While the duration of treatment varies with the severity of an individual's illness and his or her response to treatment, the length of service in clinically managed Level 3 programs tends to be longer than in the more intensive medically monitored and medically managed levels of care.

The ASAM Criteria promotes a flexible, outcomes-based approach that takes into account the actual progress and dynamic needs of the unique individual. Programs that have predetermined minimum lengths of stay or overall program lengths of stay that must be achieved in order for a patient to "complete treatment" or "graduate" are inconsistent with an individualized and outcomes-driven system of care.

Some individuals enter Level 3 programs under a court order that specifies their length of stay. However, treatment professionals have a responsibility to make admission, continued service, and discharge decisions based on their own clinical evaluation of an individual's assessed needs and treatment progress. Thus, if a patient has improved sufficiently to warrant discharge or transfer, the treatment professional has a responsibility to contact the appropriate court and seek to have the court order amended. (See also "Mandated Level of Care or Length of Stay" in the Real World Considerations in Using *The ASAM Criteria* section of Chapter 2.)

There is little data and knowledge on the dose-response relationship for residential treatment, and further research is needed to clarify these matters. As more evidence emerges, we may be able to make more informed decisions about predicting typical lengths of service in advance. Nevertheless, there may be certain threshold lengths of stay that are associated with specific therapeutic gains. In particular, the needs of juvenile justice-involved adolescents in public-sector programs that use coercive treatment engagement methods (such as a court order or probationary mandate) may be best served by more predictable, though not rigid, lengths of stay. Clinicians and the courts must collaborate closely to assure that the interests of each patient are assessed and met.

LEVEL 3 ④

Individuals are transferred to less intensive levels of care at the point that they have established sufficient skills to safely continue treatment without the immediate risk of relapse, continued use, or other continued problems, and are no longer in imminent danger of harm to themselves or others.

Longer exposure to treatment interventions is necessary for certain patients to acquire basic living skills and to master the application of coping and recovery skills. Such patients require the intensity and duration of treatment found in a Level 3.5 program to accomplish some of the tasks of habilitation in a temporary "home" that can imprint the features of a recovery environment. Level 3 programs promote continuity of care and community reintegration through seamless and overlapping intensities of outpatient services.

In general, length of service is subject to increasing pressures by payers, and may be restricted by funding constraints, making access to higher doses of residential treatment less accessible.

Adolescent-Specific Considerations: Withdrawal Management

Dimension 1 (Acute Intoxication and/or Withdrawal Potential) is the first of the six assessment dimensions to be evaluated in making treatment and placement decisions. The range of clinical severity in this dimension has given rise to a range of withdrawal management levels of service.

As used here, withdrawal management refers not only to the attenuation of the physiological and psychological features of withdrawal syndromes, but also to the process of interrupting the momentum of habitual compulsive use in adolescents diagnosed with high-severity substance use disorder. Because of the force of this momentum, and the inherent difficulties in overcoming it even when there is no clear withdrawal syndrome *per se*, this phase of treatment frequently requires a greater intensity of services initially in order to establish treatment engagement and patient role induction. This is, of course, critical to the course of treatment because it is impossible to engage the adolescent in treatment while he/she is caught up in the cycle of frequent intoxication and recovery from intoxication.

Criteria are provided for two types of Level 3 residential/inpatient withdrawal management programs: Level 3.5-WM and Level 3.7-WM. The difference between these two levels of withdrawal management is the intensity of clinical services, particularly as demonstrated by the degree of involvement of medical and nursing professionals.

Level 3.5-WM: Withdrawal Management provided within a Level 3.5 program is an organized service that is delivered by appropriately trained staff, who provide 24-hour supervision, observation, and support for the adolescent who is intoxicated or experiencing mild withdrawal. Clinically managed residential withdrawal management is characterized by its emphasis on staff, peer, and social support.

Level 3.5-WM programs care for adolescents whose intoxication/withdrawal signs and symptoms are significant enough to warrant 24-hour structure and support. However, the medical and nursing services and other resources of a Level 3.7-WM medically monitored inpatient withdrawal management program are not present.

Adolescent-Specific Considerations: Withdrawal Management (continued)

Level 3.5-WM (continued): Some clinically managed residential withdrawal management programs are staffed to supervise self-administered over-the-counter medications for the management of withdrawal. All programs at this level rely on established clinical protocols to identify adolescents who are in need of medical services beyond the capability of the program and to transfer such patients to a more appropriate facility.

Level 3.7-WM: Medically monitored inpatient withdrawal management is an organized service delivered by medical and nursing professionals, who provide 24-hour medically supervised evaluation and withdrawal management in a permanent facility with inpatient beds. Services are delivered under a defined set of physician-approved policies and physician-monitored procedures or clinical protocols.

Placement in a Level 3.7-WM program is appropriate for the adolescent whose withdrawal signs and symptoms are moderate to severe and thus require 24-hour inpatient care. Services may be provided in a specialty unit or track within a Level 3.7 program. Alternatively, they may involve overlapping the Level 3.7 care with Level 4-WM (as a step-down service) in a specialty unit of an acute care general or psychiatric hospital where 24-hour observation, monitoring, and treatment are available. In either case, the full resources of an acute care general hospital or a medically managed intensive inpatient treatment program are not required.

Level 3.1: Clinically Managed Low-Intensity Residential Services

Level 3.1 programs offer at least 5 hours per week of low-intensity treatment of substance-related disorders (or as specified by state licensure requirements). Treatment is characterized by services such as individual, group, and family therapy; medication management; and psychoeducation. These services facilitate the application of recovery skills, relapse prevention, and emotional coping strategies. They promote personal responsibility and reintegration of the individual into the network systems of work, education, and family life. Mutual/self-help meetings are available on-site, or easily accessible in the local community.

When the clinical services and recovery residence components are provided together, Level 3.1 programs often are considered appropriate for individuals who need time and structure to practice and integrate their recovery and coping skills in a residential, supportive environment.

The residential component of Level 3.1 programs also can be combined with intensive (Level 2.1) outpatient services for individuals whose living situations or recovery environments are incompatible with their recovery goals, if they otherwise meet the dimensional admission criteria for intensive outpatient care.

The functional limitations found in populations typically treated at Level 3.1 include problems in the application of recovery skills, self-efficacy, or lack of connection to the community systems of work, education, or family life. In a setting that provides 24-hour structure and support, residents have an opportunity to develop and practice their interpersonal and group living skills, strengthen their recovery skills, reintegrate

LEVEL 3.1

④

LEVEL 3.1 COMPONENTS

CLINICAL SERVICES COMPONENT

The clinical component of Level 3.1 provides for weekly clinical services of an intensity determined by the patient's clinical need and/or state licensing requirements. These are usually outpatient services, but no less than 5 hours per week. In Level 3.1, the treatment services are focused on improving the individual's readiness to change (Dimension 4) and/or functioning and coping skills in Dimensions 5 and 6. Services may include individual, group, and family therapy; medication management and medication education; mental health evaluation and treatment; vocational rehabilitation and job placement; and either introductory or remedial life skills workshops.

RECOVERY RESIDENCE COMPONENT

The other component of care is a structured recovery residence environment, staffed 24 hours a day, which provides sufficient stability to prevent or minimize relapse or continued use and continued problem potential (Dimension 5). Interpersonal and group living skills generally are promoted through the use of community or house meetings of residents and staff. The emphasis on community within the residence facilitates social bonding and cohesion among recovering persons, reinforces recovery concepts and norms, and introduces patients to the larger local recovery community and the recovery-oriented resources it provides.

into the community and family, and begin or resume employment or academic pursuits.

Level 3.1 programs also can meet the needs of individuals who may not yet acknowledge that they have a substance use or other addictive problem. Such individuals may be living in a recovery environment that is too toxic to permit treatment on an outpatient basis. They therefore may need to be removed from an unsupportive living environment in order to minimize their continued alcohol, other drug use, and/or addictive behavior. Because these individuals are at an early stage of readiness to change ("precontemplation" in Prochaska and DiClemente's stages of change model), they may need monitoring and motivating strategies to prevent deterioration, engage them in treatment and facilitate their progress through the stages of change to recovery. They are appropriately placed in a Level 3.1 supportive environment while receiving "discovery, dropout prevention" services, as opposed to "recovery, relapse prevention" services. "Discovery, dropout prevention" services are aimed at patients who have not yet determined that they have an addiction problem or who are currently not interested in addressing it, and for whom "recovery" services would be unsuitable. An important focus of treatment is thus engagement and attracting people into continuing treatment. (Because continued use of substances in a "discovery" population likely will be more common than in a

"recovery" population, consideration should be given to the problems inherent in housing the two populations together.)

Intoxication and withdrawal require separate consideration. Intoxication or withdrawal in an individual who is placed in a Level 3.1 program usually represents an isolated relapse associated with problems in applying recovery skills (Dimension 5). If the intoxication or withdrawal is associated with limitations in problem recognition or understanding (Dimension 4), the individual is appropriately placed in a Level 3.1 program only if Level 1 or 2 motivational and engagement services are being provided concurrently.

Treatment at Level 3.1 sometimes is warranted as a substitute for or supplement to deficits in the patient's recovery environment, such as a chaotic home situation; drug-using family or significant others, caretakers, or siblings; or a lack of daily structured activity (such as school or work). In other cases, an extended period in Level 3.1 treatment is needed to sustain and further therapeutic gains made at more intensive levels of care because of the patient's functional deficits (including developmental immaturity, co-occurring conditions, greater than average susceptibility to peer influence or significant others, or lack of impulse control). Many patients evidence a combination of these vulnerabilities.

The length of stay in a clinically managed Level 3.1 program tends to be longer than in the more intensive residential levels of care. Longer exposure to monitoring, supervision, and low-intensity treatment interventions is necessary for patients to practice basic living skills and to master the application of coping and recovery skills. In some situations, there may initially be no effective substitute for residential secure placement and support as reliable protection from the toxic influences of substance exposure, problematic or substance-infested environments, or the cultures of substance-involved and antisocial behaviors. But upon admission, a focus of treatment planning is on plans for community re-integration and transition to less intensive levels of residential and treatment support and services.

Level 3.1 is not intended to describe or include sober houses, boarding houses, or group homes where treatment services are not provided.

EXAMPLES OF SERVICE DELIVERY
All Programs
An example of a Level 3.1 program is a halfway house, group home, or other supportive living environment (SLE) with 24-hour staff and close integration with clinical services.

SETTING
All Programs
Level 3.1 program services may be offered in a (usually) freestanding, appropriately licensed facility located in a community setting.

SUPPORT SYSTEMS
All Programs
In Level 3.1 programs, necessary support systems include:

a. Telephone or in-person consultation with a physician and emergency services, available 24 hours a day, 7 days a week.

b. Direct affiliations with other levels of care, or close coordination through referral to more and less intensive levels of care and other services (such as intensive outpatient treatment, vocational assessment and placement, literacy training and adult education).

c. Ability to arrange for needed procedures (including indicated laboratory and toxicology tests) as appropriate to the severity and urgency of the patient's condition.

d. Ability to arrange for pharmacotherapy for psychiatric or anti-addiction medications.

e. Direct affiliations with other levels of care or close coordination through referral to more and less intensive levels of care and other services (such as sheltered workshops, literacy training, and adult education).

Co-Occurring Enhanced Programs
In addition to the support systems just described, Level 3.1 co-occurring enhanced programs offer appropriate psychiatric services, including medication evaluation and laboratory services. Such services are provided on-site or closely coordinated off-site, as appropriate to the severity and urgency of the patient's mental condition.

STAFF
All Programs
Level 3.1 programs are staffed by:

a. Allied health professional staff, such as counselor aides or group living workers, who are available on-site 24 hours a day or as required by licensing regulations.

b. Clinical staff who are knowledgeable about the biological and psychosocial dimensions of substance use disorders and their treatment, and are able to identify the signs and symptoms of acute psychiatric conditions, including psychiatric decompensation.

c. A team comprised of appropriately trained and credentialed medical, addiction, and mental health professionals.

Physicians, advanced registered nurse practitioners, and physician assistants are not involved in direct service provision as staff at this level of care. However, as this level of care is addiction care, an addiction physician should review admission decisions to confirm clinical necessity of services. Patients admitted to this level of care should have been seen in Level 1 or 2 services prior to admission to this level of care even in the past for multidimensional assessment and differential diagnosis.

Biomedical Enhanced Services

Biomedical enhanced services are delivered by appropriately credentialed medical staff, physicians, advanced registered nurse practitioners, and physician assistants who are available to assess and treat co-occurring biomedical disorders and to monitor the patient's administration of medications in accordance with a physician's prescription.

The intensity of nursing care and observation is sufficient to meet the patient's needs.

Co-Occurring Enhanced Programs

In addition to the staff listed above, Level 3.1 co-occurring enhanced programs are staffed by appropriately credentialed mental health professionals, who are able to assess and treat co-occurring disorders with the capacity to involve addiction-trained psychiatrists.

Some (if not all) of the addiction treatment professionals should have sufficient cross-training in addiction and mental health to understand the signs and symptoms of mental disorders, and to understand and be able to explain to the patient the purposes of psychotropic medications and their interactions with substance use.

The intensity of nursing care and observation is sufficient to meet the patient's needs.

THERAPIES
All Programs

Therapies offered by Level 3.1 programs include:

a. Services designed to improve the patient's ability to structure and organize the tasks of daily living and recovery, such as personal responsibility, personal appearance, and punctuality.

b. Planned clinical program activities (constituting at least 5 hours per week of professionally directed treatment) to stabilize and maintain the stability of the patient's substance use disorder symptoms, and to help him or her develop and apply recovery skills. Activities may include relapse prevention, exploring interpersonal choices, and development of a social network supportive of recovery.

c. Addiction pharmacotherapy.

d. Random drug screening to monitor and reinforce treatment gains, as appropriate to the patient's individual treatment plan.

e. Motivational enhancement and engagement strategies appropriate to the patient's stage of readiness to change, which are used in preference to confrontational approaches.

f. Counseling and clinical monitoring to support successful initial involvement or reinvolvement in regular, productive daily activity (such as work or school) and, as indicated, successful

LEVEL 3.1

4

Adolescent-Specific Considerations: Staff

In addition to the specifications for staff for all services, staff should be knowledgeable about adolescent development and experienced in engaging and working with adolescents. Experience in adolescent medicine is ideal.

NOTE

The therapies described here encompass Level 3.1 co-occurring capable program services for patients who are able to tolerate and benefit from a planned program of therapies. Other patients–especially those who have severe and chronic mental illness–may not be able to benefit from such a program. Once stabilized, such patients will require planning for and integration into intensive case management, medication management, and/or psychotherapy.

reintegration into family living. Health education services also are provided.

g. Regular monitoring of the patient's medication adherence.

h. Recovery support services.

i. Services for the patient's family and significant others, as appropriate.

j. Opportunities for the patient to be introduced to the potential benefits of addiction pharmacotherapies as a tool to manage his or her addictive disorder.

Co-Occurring Enhanced Programs

In addition to the therapies described above, Level 3.1 co-occurring enhanced programs offer planned clinical activities (either directly or through affiliated providers) that are designed to stabilize the patient's mental health problems and psychiatric symptoms and to maintain such stabilization.

The goals of therapy apply to both the substance use or addictive disorder and any co-occurring mental disorder.

Specific attention is given to medication education and management and to motivational and engagement strategies, which are used in preference to confrontational approaches.

ASSESSMENT/TREATMENT PLAN REVIEW
All Programs

In Level 3.1 programs, the assessment and treatment plan review include:

a. An individualized, comprehensive biopsychosocial assessment of the patient's

substance use disorder, conducted or updated by staff who are knowledgeable about addiction treatment, to confirm the appropriateness of placement at Level 3.1 and to help guide the individualized treatment planning process.

b. An individualized treatment plan, which involves problems, needs, strengths, skills, priority formulation, and articulation of short-term, measurable treatment goals, preferences, and activities designed to achieve those goals. The plan is developed in collaboration with the patient and reflects the patient's personal goals.

c. A biopsychosocial assessment, treatment plan, and updates that reflect the patient's clinical progress.

d. A physical examination, performed within a reasonable time, as defined in the program's policy and procedure manual, and as determined by the patient's medical condition.

The treatment plan reflects case management conducted by on-site staff; coordination of related addiction treatment, health care, mental health, and social, vocational, or housing services (provided concurrently); and the integration of services at this and other levels of care.

Co-Occurring Enhanced Programs

In addition to the assessment and treatment plan review activities just described, Level 3.1 co-occurring enhanced programs provide a review of the patient's recent psychiatric history and mental status examination. (If necessary, this review is conducted by a psychiatrist.) A comprehensive psychiatric history, examination, and psychodiagnostic assessment are performed within a reasonable time, as determined by the patient's needs.

Level 3.1 co-occurring enhanced programs (either directly or through affiliation with another program) also provide active reassessment of the patient's mental status, at a frequency determined by the urgency of the patient's psychiatric problems, and follow through with mental health treatment and psychotropic medications. **NOTE:** Certain patients may need the kinds of assessment and treatment services described here for co-occurring enhanced, but at a reduced level of frequency and comprehensiveness to match the greater stability of the patient's mental health problems. For such patients, placement in a co-occurring capable program may be appropriate.

DOCUMENTATION
All Programs
Documentation standards for Level 3.1 programs include individualized progress notes in the patient's record that clearly reflect implementation of the treatment plan and the patient's response to therapeutic interventions for all disorders treated, as well as subsequent amendments to the plan.

Treatment plan reviews are conducted at specified times and recorded in the treatment plan.

Co-Occurring Enhanced Programs
In addition to the information just described, Level 3.1 co-occurring enhanced programs document the patient's mental health problems, the relationship between the mental and substance use and addictive disorders, and the patient's current level of mental functioning.

ADULT DIAGNOSTIC ADMISSION CRITERIA
All Programs
The patient who is appropriately placed in a Level 3.1 program meets the diagnostic criteria for a moderate or severe substance use and/or addictive disorder, as defined in the current *Diagnostic and Statistical Manual of Mental Disorders* (*DSM*) of the American Psychiatric Association or other standardized and widely accepted criteria, as well as the dimensional criteria for admission.

If the patient's presenting history is inadequate to substantiate such a diagnosis, the probability of such a diagnosis may be determined from information submitted by collateral parties (such as family members, legal guardians, and significant others).

NOTE: Patients in Level 3.1 co-occurring capable programs may have co-occurring mental disorders that meet the stability criteria for placement in a co-occurring capable program; or difficulties with mood, behavior, or cognition related to a substance use, other addictive, or mental disorder; or emotional, behavioral, or cognitive symptoms that are troublesome but do not meet the *DSM* criteria for a mental disorder.

Co-Occurring Enhanced Programs

The patient who is appropriately admitted to a Level 3.1 co-occurring enhanced program meets the diagnostic criteria for a mental disorder as well as a moderate or severe substance use and/or addictive disorder, as defined in the current *Diagnostic and Statistical Manual of Mental Disorders* (*DSM*) of the American Psychiatric Association or other standardized and widely accepted criteria, as well as the dimensional criteria for admission.

If the patient's presenting history is inadequate to substantiate such a diagnosis, the probability of such a diagnosis may be determined from information submitted by collateral parties (such as family members, legal guardians, and significant others).

LEVEL 3.1

4

ADULT DIMENSIONAL ADMISSION CRITERIA

All Programs
The adult patient who is appropriately admitted to a Level 3.1 program meets specifications in *each* of the six dimensions.

DIMENSION 1:
Acute Intoxication and/or Withdrawal Potential

All Programs
The patient has no signs or symptoms of withdrawal, or his or her withdrawal needs can be safely managed in a Level 3.1 setting. See separate withdrawal management chapter for how to approach "unbundled" withdrawal management for adults.

DIMENSION 2:
Biomedical Conditions and Complications

All Programs
The patient's status in Dimension 2 is characterized by *one* of the following:
   a. Biomedical problems, if any, are stable and do not require medical or nurse monitoring, and the patient is capable of self-administering any prescribed medications;
      or
   b. A current biomedical condition is not severe enough to warrant inpatient treatment but is sufficient to distract from treatment or recovery efforts. The problem requires medical monitoring, which can be provided by the program or through an established arrangement with another provider.

Biomedical Enhanced Services
The patient who has a biomedical problem that requires a degree of staff attention (such as monitoring of medications or assistance with mobility) that is not available in other Level 3.1 programs is in need of biomedical enhanced services.

DIMENSION 3:
Emotional, Behavioral, or Cognitive Conditions and Complications

All Programs
The patient may not have any significant problems in this dimension. However, if *any* of the Dimension 3 conditions are present, the patient must be admitted to a co-occurring capable or co-occurring enhanced program (depending on his or her level of function, stability, and degree of impairment).

Co-Occurring Capable Programs
The patient's status in Dimension 3 is characterized by (a); *and* one of (b) *or* (c) *or* (d) *or* (e):
   a. The patient's mental status (including emotional stability and cognitive functioning) is assessed as sufficiently stable to allow the patient to participate in the therapeutic interventions provided at this level of care and to benefit from treatment.
      and
   b. The patient's psychiatric condition is stable, and he or she is assessed as having minimal problems in this area, as evidenced by *both* of the following: (1) the patient's thought disorder, anxiety, guilt, and/or depression may be related to substance use problems or to a stable co-occurring emotional, behavioral, or cognitive condition, with imminent likelihood of relapse with dangerous consequences outside of a structured environment. For mandated patients, examples of "dangerous consequences" may be the imminent loss of their children, imminent years of impending imprisonment, etc. as consequences of relapse, and (2) the patient is assessed as not posing a risk to self or others;
      or
   c. The patient's symptoms and functional limitations, when considered in the context of his or her home environment, are sufficiently severe that he or she is assessed as not likely to maintain mental stability and/or abstinence if treatment is provided in a nonresidential setting. Functional limitations may include—but are not limited to—residual psychiatric symptoms, chronic addictive disorder, history of criminality, marginal intellectual ability, limited educational achievement, poor vocational skills, inadequate anger management skills, and the sequelae of physical, sexual, or emotional trauma. These limitations may be complicated by problems in Dimensions 2 through 6;
      or

LEVEL 3.1

4

ADULT DIMENSIONAL ADMISSION CRITERIA (CONTINUED)

d. The patient demonstrates (through distractibility, negative emotions, or generalized anxiety) an inability to maintain stable behavior over a 24-hour period without the structure and support of a 24-hour setting;
      or
   e. The patient's co-occurring psychiatric, emotional, behavioral, or cognitive conditions are being addressed concurrently through appropriate psychiatric services.

Co-Occurring Enhanced Programs
The patient's status in Dimension 3 is characterized by one of (a) *or* (b); *and* (c):
   a. The patient has a diagnosed emotional, behavioral, or cognitive disorder that requires monitoring of medications or assessment of psychiatric symptoms or behavioral management techniques, because the patient's history suggests that these disorders are likely to distract him or her from treatment efforts;
      or
   b. The patient needs monitoring of psychiatric symptoms concurrent with addiction treatment (as may occur in a patient with borderline or compulsive personality disorder, anxiety or mood disorder, or chronic schizophrenic disorder in addition to a stabilizing substance use or other addictive disorder);
      and
   c. The patient is assessed as able to safely access the community for work, education, and other community resources.

NOTE: Such a patient may be receiving specific co-occurring services in a Level 2.1 or 2.5 program, or be receiving Level 1 outpatient services with intensive case management.

DIMENSION 3:
Emotional, Behavioral, or Cognitive Conditions and Complications

All Programs
The patient's status in Dimension 4 is characterized by at least *one* of the following:
   a. The patient acknowledges the existence of a psychiatric condition and/or substance use problem. He or she recognizes specific negative consequences and dysfunctional behaviors and their effect on his or her desire to change. He or she is sufficiently ready to change and cooperative enough to respond to treatment at Level 3.1;
      or
   b. The patient is assessed as appropriately placed at Level 1 or 2 and is receiving Level 3.1 services concurrently. The patient may be at an early stage of readiness to change and thus in need of engagement and motivational strategies;
      or
   c. The patient requires a 24-hour structured milieu to promote treatment progress and recovery, because motivating interventions have failed in the past and such interventions are assessed as not likely to succeed in an outpatient setting;
      or
   d. The patient's perspective impairs his or her ability to make behavior changes without the support of a structured environment. For example, the patient attributes his or her alcohol, other drug, or mental health problem to other persons or external events, rather than to a substance use or mental disorder. Interventions are assessed as not likely to succeed in an outpatient setting.

DIMENSION 4:
Readiness to Change

Co-Occurring Enhanced Programs
The patient's status in Dimension 4 is characterized by ambivalence in his or her commitment to change a co-occurring mental health problem.

(See following page for additional information.)

LEVEL 3.1

ADULT DIMENSIONAL ADMISSION CRITERIA (CONTINUED)

DIMENSION 4:
Readiness to Change

Similarly, the patient is appropriately placed in a Level 3.1 co-occurring enhanced program when he or she is not consistently able to follow through with treatment, or demonstrates minimal awareness of a problem, or is unaware of the need to change. Such a patient requires active interventions with family, significant others, and other external systems to create leverage and align incentives so as to promote engagement in treatment.

All Programs
The patient's status in Dimension 5 is characterized by at least *one* of the following:

a. The patient demonstrates limited coping skills to address relapse triggers and urges and/or deteriorating mental functioning. He or she thus is in imminent danger of relapse, with dangerous emotional, behavioral, or cognitive consequences, and needs 24-hour structure to help him or her apply recovery and coping skills;
   or

b. The patient understands his or her addiction and/or mental disorder but is at risk of relapse in a less structured level of care because he or she is unable to consistently address either or both;
   or

c. The patient needs staff support to maintain engagement in his or her recovery program while transitioning to life in the community;
   or

d. The patient is at high risk of substance use, addictive behavior, or deteriorated mental functioning, with dangerous emotional, behavioral, or cognitive consequences, in the absence of close 24-hour structured support (as evidenced, for example, by lack of awareness of relapse triggers, difficulty in postponing immediate gratification, or ambivalence toward or low interest in treatment), and these issues are being addressed concurrently in a Level 2 program.

DIMENSION 5:
Relapse, Continued Use, or
Continued Problem Potential

Co-Occurring Enhanced Programs
The patient's status in Dimension 5 is characterized by psychiatric symptoms that pose a moderate risk of relapse to a substance use or mental disorder. Such a patient demonstrates limited ability to apply relapse prevention skills, as well as deteriorating psychiatric functioning, which increases his or her risk of serious consequences and requires the types of services and 24-hour structure of a Level 3.1 co-occurring enhanced program in order to maintain an adequate level of functioning. For example, the patient demonstrates deteriorating functioning during outpatient treatment or while in a halfway house that does not provide co-occurring enhanced services.

The patient who is receiving concurrent Level 2 and Level 3.1 services requires case management to coordinate the services across levels of care. Case management and collaboration across levels of care may be needed to manage anticraving, psychotropic, or opioid agonist medications. For example, the patient may have only recently developed the ability to control his or her anger and impulses to damage property. Or the patient may have only recently become adherent in taking psychotropic medications as prescribed and is not increasing the dose to control continuing symptoms of anxiety or panic.

Preparation for transfer of the patient to a less intensive level of care and/or reentry into the community requires case management and staff exploration of supportive living environments, separately from their therapeutic work with the patient.

All Programs
The patient's status in Dimension 6 is characterized by one of (a); *and* one of (b) *or* (c) *or* (d) *or* (e) *or* (f):

DIMENSION 6:
Recovery Environment

a. The patient is able to cope, for limited periods of time, outside the 24-hour structure of a Level 3.1 program in order to pursue clinical, vocational, educational, and community activities;

ADULT DIMENSIONAL ADMISSION CRITERIA (CONTINUED)

DIMENSION 6:
Recovery Environment

and

b. The patient has been living in an environment that is characterized by a moderately high risk of initiation or repetition of physical, sexual, or emotional abuse, or substance use so endemic that the patient is assessed as being unable to achieve or maintain recovery at a less intensive level of care;

or

c. The patient lacks social contacts or has high-risk social contacts that jeopardize his or her recovery, or the patient's social network is characterized by significant social isolation and withdrawal. The patient's social network includes many friends who are regular users of alcohol or other drugs or regular gamblers, leading recovery goals to be assessed as unachievable outside of a 24-hour supportive setting;

or

d. The patient's social network involves living in an environment that is so highly invested in alcohol or other drug use that the patient's recovery goals are assessed as unachievable;

or

e. Continued exposure to the patient's school, work, or living environment makes recovery unlikely, and the patient has insufficient resources and skills to maintain an adequate level of functioning outside of a 24-hour supportive environment;

or

f. The patient is in danger of victimization by another and thus requires 24-hour supervision.

Co-Occurring Enhanced Programs

The patient's status in Dimension 6 is characterized by severe and chronic mental illness. He or she may be too ill to benefit from skills training to learn to cope with problems in the recovery environment. Such a patient requires planning for assertive community treatment, intensive case management, or other community outreach and support services.

The patient's living, working, social, and/or community environment is not supportive of good mental health functioning. He or she has insufficient resources and skills to deal with this situation. For example, the patient may be unable to cope with the continuing stress of homelessness, or hostile or addicted family members, and thus exhibits increasing anxiety and depression. Such a patient needs the support and structure of a Level 3.1 co-occurring enhanced program to achieve stabilization and prevent further deterioration.

ADOLESCENT DIAGNOSTIC ADMISSION CRITERIA

The adolescent who is appropriately placed in a Level 3.1 program meets the diagnostic criteria for a moderate or severe substance use and/or addictive disorder, as defined in the current *Diagnostic and Statistical Manual of Mental Disorders* (*DSM*) of the American Psychiatric Association or other standardized and widely accepted criteria, as well as the dimensional criteria for admission.

If the adolescent's presenting history is inadequate to substantiate such a diagnosis, the probability of such a diagnosis may be determined from information submitted by collateral parties (such as family members, legal guardians, and significant others).

ADOLESCENT DIMENSIONAL ADMISSION CRITERIA

The adolescent who is appropriately placed in a Level 3.1 program meets specifications in at least **two** of the six dimensions.

DIMENSION 1:
Acute Intoxication and/or Withdrawal Potential

The adolescent's status in Dimension 1 is characterized by problems with intoxication or withdrawal (if any) that are being managed through concurrent placement at another level of care for withdrawal management (typically Level 1, Level 2.1, or Level 2.5).

If residential placement in a Level 3.1 program is being used to support withdrawal management at a non-residential level of care, then the adolescent is considered to have met specifications in Dimension 1.

DIMENSION 2:
Biomedical Conditions and Complications

The adolescent's status in Dimension 2 is characterized by **one** of the following:

a. Biomedical conditions distract from recovery efforts and require limited residential supervision to ensure their adequate treatment or to provide support to overcome the distraction. Adequate nursing or medical monitoring can be provided through an arrangement with another provider. The adolescent is capable of self-administering any prescribed medications or procedures, with available supervision;
   or
b. Continued substance use would place the adolescent at risk of serious damage to his or her physical health because of a biomedical condition (such as pregnancy or HIV) or an imminently dangerous pattern of high-risk use (such as continued use of shared injection apparatus). Adequate nursing or medical monitoring for biomedical conditions can be provided through an arrangement with another provider. The adolescent is capable of self-administering any prescribed medications or procedures, with available supervision.

Biomedical Enhanced Services
The adolescent who has a biomedical problem that requires a degree of staff attention (such as monitoring of medications or assistance with mobility) that is not available in other Level 3.1 programs is in need of biomedical enhanced services.

DIMENSION 3:
Emotional, Behavioral, or Cognitive Conditions and Complications

The adolescent's status in Dimension 3 is characterized by at least **one** of the following (requiring 24-hour supervision):

a. **Dangerousness/Lethality:** The adolescent is at risk of dangerous consequences because of the lack of a stable living environment (for example, exposure to the elements, risk of assault, risk of prostitution, and the like). He or she needs a stable residential setting for protection.
b. **Interference with Addiction Recovery Efforts:** The adolescent needs a stable living environment to promote a sustained focus on recovery tasks (for example, recovery efforts are hindered by the adolescent's preoccupying worries about shelter).
c. **Social Functioning:** The adolescent's emotional, behavioral, or cognitive problem results in moderate impairment in social functioning. He or she therefore needs limited 24-hour supervision, which can be provided by program staff or in combination with a Level 1 or Level 2 program. This might involve protection from antisocial peer influences in a motivated adolescent, reinforcement of improving behavior self-management techniques, support of increasingly independent functions (such as school or work), and the like.
d. **Ability for Self-Care:** The adolescent has moderate impairment in his or her ability to manage the activities of daily living and thus needs limited 24-hour supervision, which can be provided by program staff or through coordination with a Level 1 or Level 2 program. The adolescent's impairments might require the provision of food and shelter, prompting for self-care, or supervised self-administration of medications.

LEVEL 3.1　④

a ADOLESCENT DIMENSIONAL ADMISSION CRITERIA (CONTINUED)

The adolescent who is appropriately placed in a Level 3.1 program meets specifications in at least **two** of the six dimensions.

DIMENSION 3:
Emotional, Behavioral, or Cognitive Conditions and Complications

e. **Course of Illness:** The adolescent's history and present situation suggest that an emotional, behavioral, or cognitive condition would become unstable without 24-hour supervision (for example, an adolescent who experiences rapid, dangerous exacerbation if he or she misses a few doses of medicine or if he or she has even a minor relapse to substance use).
   or

f. The adolescent's emotional, behavioral, or cognitive condition suggests the need for low-intensity and/or longer-term reinforcement and practice of recovery skills in a controlled environment.

DIMENSION 4:
Readiness to Change

The adolescent's status in Dimension 4 is characterized by at least **one** of the following:

a. The adolescent acknowledges the existence of a psychiatric condition and/or substance use problem. He or she recognizes specific negative consequences and dysfunctional behaviors and their effect on his or her desire to change. He or she is sufficiently ready to change and cooperative enough to respond to treatment at Level 3.1;
   or

b. The adolescent is assessed as appropriately placed at Level 1 or 2 and is receiving Level 3.1 services concurrently. The adolescent may be at an early stage of readiness to change and thus in need of engagement and motivational strategies;
   or

c. The adolescent requires a 24-hour structured milieu to promote treatment progress and recovery, because motivating interventions have failed in the past and such interventions are assessed as not likely to succeed in an outpatient setting;
   or

d. The adolescent's perspective impairs his or her ability to make behavior changes without the support of a structured environment. For example, the adolescent attributes his or her alcohol, other drug, or mental health problem to other persons or external events, rather than to a substance use or mental disorder. Interventions are assessed as not likely to succeed in an outpatient setting.

DIMENSION 5:
Relapse, Continued Use, or Continued Problem Potential

The adolescent's status in Dimension 5 is characterized by at least **one** of the following:

a. The adolescent demonstrates limited coping skills to address relapse triggers and urges and/or deteriorating mental functioning. He or she thus is in imminent danger of relapse, with dangerous emotional, behavioral, or cognitive consequences, and needs 24-hour structure to help him or her apply recovery and coping skills;
   or

b. The adolescent understands his or her addiction and/or mental disorder but is at risk of relapse in a less structured level of care because he or she is unable to consistently address either or both;
   or

LEVEL 3.1
4

ADOLESCENT DIMENSIONAL ADMISSION CRITERIA (CONTINUED)

The adolescent who is appropriately placed in a Level 3.1 program meets specifications in at least **two** of the six dimensions.

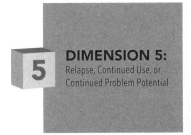

DIMENSION 5:
Relapse, Continued Use, or Continued Problem Potential

c. The adolescent needs staff support to maintain engagement in his or her recovery program while transitioning to life in the community;
or
d. The adolescent is at high risk of substance use, addictive behavior, or deteriorated mental functioning, with dangerous emotional, behavioral, or cognitive consequences, in the absence of close 24-hour structured support (as evidenced, for example, by lack of awareness of relapse triggers, difficulty in postponing immediate gratification or ambivalence toward or low interest in treatment), and these issues are being addressed concurrently in a Level 2 program.

DIMENSION 6:
Recovery Environment

The adolescent's status in Dimension 6 is characterized by at least **one** of the following:

a. The adolescent has been living in an environment in which there is a high risk of neglect, or initiation or repetition of physical, sexual, or severe emotional abuse, such that the adolescent is assessed as being unable to achieve or maintain recovery without residential secure placement;
or
b. The adolescent has a family or other household member who has an active substance use disorder, or substance use is endemic in his or her home environment or broader social network, so that recovery goals are assessed as unachievable without residential secure placement;
or
c. The adolescent's home environment or social network is too chaotic or ineffective to support or sustain treatment goals, so that recovery is assessed as unachievable without residential support. For example, the adolescent's family reinforces antisocial norms and values, or the family cannot sustain treatment engagement or school attendance, or the family is experiencing significant social isolation or withdrawal;
or
d. Logistical impediments (such as distance from a treatment facility, mobility limitations, lack of transportation, and the like) preclude participation in treatment at a less intensive level of care.

LEVEL 3.3 ④

Level 3.3: Clinically Managed Population-Specific High-Intensity Residential Services (Adult Criteria Only)

Level 3.3 programs provide a structured recovery environment in combination with high-intensity clinical services provided in a manner to meet the functional limitations of patients to support recovery from substance-related disorders.

For the typical patient in a Level 3.3 program, the effects of the substance use or other addictive disorder or a co-occurring disorder resulting in cognitive impairment on the individual's life are so significant, and the resulting level of impairment so great, that outpatient motivational and/or relapse prevention strategies are not feasible or effective. Similarly, the patient's cognitive limitations make it unlikely that he or she could benefit from other levels of residential care.

The functional limitations seen in individuals who are appropriately placed at Level 3.3 are primarily cognitive and can be either temporary or permanent. They may result in problems in interpersonal relationships, emotional coping skills, or comprehension. For example, temporary limitations may be seen in the individual who suffers from an organic brain syndrome as a result of his or her substance use and who requires treatment that is slower paced, more concrete, and more repetitive until his or her cognitive impairment subsides.

When assessment indicates that such an individual no longer is cognitively impaired, he or she can be transferred to another level of care (such as a Level 3.5 program) or a less intensive level of care (such as a Level 1, 2.1, 2.5 or 3.1 program), based on a reassessment of his or her severity of illness and rehabilitative needs. (Transfer to a Level 3.7 or more intensive level of care would not be considered except in the presence of unstable or acute medical or psychiatric problems that require medical and nursing care.)

By contrast, the individual who suffers from chronic brain syndrome, or the older adult who has age and substance-related cognitive limitations, or the individual who has experienced a traumatic brain injury, or the patient with developmental disabilities would continue to receive treatment in a Level 3.3 program. For such an individual, the effects of the addictive disorder or co-occurring condition are so significant, and the level of his or her impairment so great, that outpatient or other levels of residential care would not be feasible or effective.

Some individuals have such severe limitations in interpersonal and coping skills that the treatment process is one of habilitation rather than rehabilitation. Treatment of such individuals is directed toward overcoming their lack of awareness of, or ambivalence about, the effects of substance-related problems or addiction on their lives, as well as enhancing their readiness to change. Treatment also is focused on preventing relapse, continued problems, and/or continued use, and promoting the eventual reintegration of the individual into the community. In every case, the individual should be involved in planning continuing care to support recovery and improve his or her functioning.

Level 3.3 programs generally are considered to deliver high-intensity services, which may be provided in a deliberately repetitive fash-

ion to address the special needs of individuals for whom a Level 3.3 program is considered medically necessary. Such individuals often are elderly, cognitively impaired, or developmentally delayed, or are those for whom the chronicity and intensity of the primary disease process requires a program that allows sufficient time to integrate the lessons and experiences of treatment into their daily lives. Typically, they need a slower pace of treatment because of mental health problems or reduced cognitive functioning (Dimension 3), or because of the chronicity of their illness (Dimensions 4 and 5). They also may be homeless, although homelessness is not, in itself, a sufficient indication for admission to a Level 3.3 program.

Where treatment staff have been specially trained and adequate nursing supervision is available, Level 3.3 programs are able to address the needs of patients with certain medical problems as well. These include patients whose biomedical conditions otherwise would meet medical necessity criteria for placement in a nursing home or other medically staffed facility. For such persons, their general medical condition (Dimension 2 comorbidity) provides the justification for admission to a Level 3.3 program.

Reintegration of patients in a Level 3.3 program into the community requires case management activities directed toward networking patients into community-based ancil-

NOTE

Adolescent-specific considerations are not included in Level 3.3 programming because the types of programs described in Level 3.5 encompass the range of settings in which adolescent treatment is provided, and the distinction between Level 3.3 and Level 3.5 does not have sufficient specificity in adolescent treatment to merit the added complexity of adolescent-specific considerations.

LEVEL 3.3

4

lary or "wrap-around" services such as housing, vocational services, or transportation assistance so that they are able to attend mutual/self-help meetings or vocational activities after discharge.

EXAMPLES OF SERVICE DELIVERY
All Programs

An example of a Level 3.3 program is a therapeutic rehabilitation facility or a traumatic brain injury program.

SETTING
All Programs

Level 3.3 program services may be offered in a (usually) freestanding, appropriately licensed facility located in a community setting or a specialty unit within a licensed health care facility.

SUPPORT SYSTEMS
All Programs

In Level 3.3 programs, necessary support systems include:

a. Telephone or in-person consultation with a physician, or a physician assistant or nurse practitioner in states where they are licensed as physician extenders and may perform the duties designated here for a physician; and emergency services, available 24 hours a day, 7 days a week.

b. Direct affiliations with other easily accessible levels of care or close coordination through referral to more and less intensive levels of care and other services (such as supported employment, literacy training, and adult education).

c. Medical, psychiatric, psychological, laboratory, and toxicology services, available through consultation or referral, as appropriate to the severity and urgency of the patient's condition.

Co-Occurring Enhanced Programs

In addition to the support systems described here, Level 3.3 co-occurring enhanced programs offer psychiatric services, medication evaluation, and laboratory services. Such services are available by telephone within 8 hours and on-site or closely coordinated off-site within 24 hours, as appropriate to the severity and urgency of the patient's mental condition.

STAFF
All Programs

Level 3.3 programs are staffed by:

a. Physicians or physician extenders, and appropriately credentialed mental health professionals.

b. Allied health professional staff, such as counselor aides or group living workers, on-site 24 hours a day or as required by licensing regulations. One or more clinicians with competence in the treatment of substance use disorders are available on-site or by telephone 24 hours a day.

c. Clinical staff knowledgeable about the biological and psychosocial dimensions of substance use and mental disorders and their treatment, and able to identify the signs and symptoms of acute psychiatric conditions, including psychiatric decompensation. Staff have specialized training in behavior management techniques.

Biomedical Enhanced Services

Biomedical enhanced services are delivered by appropriately credentialed medical staff, who are available to assess and treat co-occurring biomedical disorders and to monitor the patient's administration of medications in accordance with a physician's prescription.

The intensity of nursing care and observation is sufficient to meet the patient's needs.

Co-Occurring Enhanced Programs

In addition to the staff listed above, Level 3.3 co-occurring enhanced programs are staffed by appropriately credentialed psychiatrists and men-

LEVEL 3.3

4

tal health professionals, who are able to assess and treat co-occurring mental disorders and who have specialized training in behavior management techniques.

Some (if not all) of the addiction treatment professionals should have sufficient cross-training to understand the signs and symptoms of mental disorders, and to understand and be able to explain to the patient the purposes of psychotropic medications and their interactions with substance use.

The intensity of nursing care and observation is sufficient to meet the patient's needs.

THERAPIES
All Programs

Therapies offered by Level 3.3 programs include:

a. Daily clinical services to improve the patient's ability to structure and organize the tasks of daily living and recovery, such as personal responsibility, personal appearance, and punctuality. Family services are provided. Such services are designed to accommodate the cognitive limitations frequently seen in this population.

b. Planned clinical program activities designed to stabilize and maintain the stability of the patient's addiction symptoms and to help him or her develop and apply recovery skills. Activities may include relapse prevention, guidance on the choices a patient makes about interpersonal and social relationships, and development of a social network supportive of recovery.

c. Random drug screening to monitor progress and reinforce treatment gains, as appropriate to the patient's individual treatment plan.

d. A range of cognitive, behavioral, and other therapies administered on an individual and group basis, medication

education and management, educational groups, and occupational or recreational activities, adapted to the patient's developmental stage and level of comprehension.

For patients with significant cognitive deficits (such as chronic brain syndrome, mental retardation, or traumatic brain injury), therapies are delivered in a manner that is slower paced, more concrete, and more repetitive.

e. Counseling and clinical monitoring to assist the patient with successful initial involvement or reinvolvement in regular, productive daily activity (such as work or school) and, as indicated, successful reintegration into family living. Health education services are provided.

f. Regular monitoring of the patient's adherence in taking any prescribed medications.

g. Daily scheduled professional addiction and mental health treatment services, designed to develop and apply recovery skills. These may include relapse prevention, exploring interpersonal choices, and development of a social network supportive of recovery from the psychiatric and/or addictive disorder. Such services also may include medical services; nursing services; individual and group counseling; family therapy; educational groups; occupational and recreational therapies; art, music, or movement therapies; physical therapy; and vocational rehabilitation activities.

h. Clinical and didactic motivational interventions appropriate to the patient's stage of readiness to change, designed to facilitate the patient's understanding of the relationship between his or her substance use disorder and attendant life issues.

LEVEL 3.3
4

i. Services for the patient's family and significant others.

Co-Occurring Enhanced Programs

In addition to the therapies just described, Level 3.3 co-occurring enhanced programs offer planned clinical activities designed to stabilize the patient's mental health problems and psychiatric symptoms, and to maintain such stabilization.

The goals of therapy apply to both the substance use disorder and any co-occurring mental disorder.

Specific attention is given to medication education and management and to motivational and engagement strategies, which are used in preference to confrontational approaches. **NOTE:** The therapies just described encompass Level 3.3 co-occurring capable program services for patients who are able to tolerate and benefit from a planned program of therapies. Other patients, especially those who have severe and chronic mental illness, may not be able to benefit from such a program. Once stabilized, such patients will require planning for and integration into intensive case management, medication management, and/or psychotherapy.

ASSESSMENT/TREATMENT PLAN REVIEW
All Programs

In Level 3.3 programs, the assessment and treatment plan review include:

a. An individualized, comprehensive bio-psychosocial assessment of the patient's substance use or addictive disorder, conducted or updated by staff who are knowledgeable about addiction treatment, to confirm the appropriateness of placement at Level 3.3 and to help guide the individualized treatment planning process.

b. An individualized treatment plan, which includes problem formulation and articulation of short-term, measurable treatment goals and activities designed to achieve those goals. The plan is developed in collaboration with the patient and reflects the patient's personal goals.

c. A biopsychosocial assessment, treatment plan, and updates that reflect the patient's clinical progress, as reviewed by an interdisciplinary treatment team.

d. A physical examination, performed within a reasonable time, as determined by the patient's medical condition.

e. Ongoing transition/continuing care planning.

The treatment plan reflects case management conducted by on-site staff; coordination of related addiction treatment, health care, mental health, and social, vocational, or housing services (provided concurrently); and the integration of services at this and other levels of care.

Co-Occurring Enhanced Programs

In addition to the assessment and treatment plan review activities described above, Level 3.3 co-occurring enhanced programs provide a review of the patient's recent psychiatric history and mental status examination. (If necessary, this review is conducted by a psychiatrist.) A comprehensive psychiatric history, examination, and psychodiagnostic assessment are performed within a reasonable time, as determined by the patient's needs.

Level 3.3 co-occurring enhanced programs also provide active reassessments of the patient's mental status, at a frequency determined by the urgency of the patient's psychiatric problems, and follow through with mental health treatment and psychotropic medications. **NOTE:** Certain patients may need the kinds of assessment and treatment services described here for co-occurring enhanced programs, but at a reduced level of frequency and comprehensiveness to match the greater stability of the patient's mental health problems. For such patients, placement in a co-occurring capable program may be appropriate.

LEVEL 3.3 ④

DOCUMENTATION
All Programs

Documentation standards for Level 3.3 programs include individualized progress notes in the patient's record that clearly reflect implementation of the treatment plan and the patient's response to therapeutic interventions for all disorders treated, as well as subsequent amendments to the plan.

Treatment plan reviews are conducted at specified times and recorded in the treatment plan.

Co-Occurring Enhanced Programs

In addition to the information just described, Level 3.3 co-occurring enhanced programs document the patient's mental health problems, the relationship between the mental and substance use or addictive disorders, and the patient's current level of mental functioning.

ADULT DIAGNOSTIC ADMISSION CRITERIA

All Programs

The patient who is appropriately placed in a Level 3.3 program meets the diagnostic criteria for a moderate or severe substance use and/or addictive disorder, as defined in the current *Diagnostic and Statistical Manual of Mental Disorders* (*DSM*) of the American Psychiatric Association or other standardized and widely accepted criteria, as well as the dimensional criteria for admission.

If the patient's presenting history is inadequate to substantiate such a diagnosis, the probability of such a diagnosis may be determined from information submitted by collateral parties (such as family members, legal guardians, and significant others).

NOTE: Patients in Level 3.3 co-occurring capable programs may have co-occurring mental disorders that meet the stability criteria for placement in a co-occurring capable program; or difficulties with mood, behavior, or cognition related to a substance use, other addictive, or mental disorder; or emotional, behavioral, or cognitive symptoms that are troublesome but do not meet the *DSM* criteria for a mental disorder.

Co-Occurring Enhanced Programs

The patient who is appropriately admitted to a Level 3.3 co-occurring enhanced program meets the diagnostic criteria for a mental disorder as well as a moderate or severe substance use and/or addictive disorder, as defined in the current *Diagnostic and Statistical Manual of Mental Disorders* (*DSM*) of the American Psychiatric Association or other standardized and widely accepted criteria, as well as the dimensional criteria for admission.

If the patient's presenting history is inadequate to substantiate such a diagnosis, the probability of such a diagnosis may be determined from information submitted by collateral parties (such as family members, legal guardians, and significant others).

ADULT DIMENSIONAL ADMISSION CRITERIA

All Programs

The patient who is appropriately admitted to a Level 3.3 program meets specifications in **each** of the six dimensions.

DIMENSION 1:
Acute Intoxication and/or
Withdrawal Potential

All Programs

The patient has no signs or symptoms of withdrawal, or his or her withdrawal needs can be safely managed in a Level 3.3 setting. See separate withdrawal management chapter for how to approach "unbundled" withdrawal management for adults.

DIMENSION 2:
Biomedical Conditions and
Complications

All Programs

The patient's status in Dimension 2 is characterized by **one** of the following:

a. Biomedical problems, if any, are stable and do not require medical or nurse monitoring, and the patient is capable of self-administering any prescribed medications;

 or

b. A current biomedical condition is not severe enough to warrant inpatient treatment but is sufficient to distract from treatment or recovery efforts. The problem requires medical monitoring, which can be provided by the program or through an established arrangement with another provider.

Biomedical Enhanced Services

The patient who has a biomedical problem that requires a degree of staff attention (such as monitoring of medications or assistance with mobility) that is not available in other Level 3.3 programs is in need of biomedical enhanced services.

DIMENSION 3:
Emotional, Behavioral, or
Cognitive Conditions and
Complications

All Programs

If any of the Dimension 3 conditions are present, the patient must be admitted to either a co-occurring capable or a co-occurring enhanced program (depending on his or her level of function, stability, and degree of impairment).

Co-Occurring Capable Programs

The patient's status in Dimension 3 is characterized by (a); **and** one of (b) **or** (c) **or** (d):

a. The patient's mental status (including emotional stability and cognitive functioning) is assessed as sufficiently stable to permit the patient to participate in the therapeutic interventions provided at this level of care and to benefit from treatment;

 and

b. The patient's psychiatric condition is stabilizing, but he or she is assessed as in need of a 24-hour structured environment, as evidenced by **one** of the following: (1) depression or other emotional, behavioral, or cognitive conditions significantly interfere with activities of daily living and recovery; or (2) the patient exhibits violent or disruptive behavior when intoxicated and is assessed as posing a danger to self or others; or (3) the patient exhibits stress behaviors related to recent or threatened losses in work, family, or social arenas, such that activities of daily living are significantly impaired and the patient requires a secure environment to focus on the substance use or mental health problem; or (4) concomitant personality disorders are of such severity that the accompanying dysfunctional behaviors require continuing structured interventions;

 or

c. The patient's symptoms and functional limitations, when considered in the context of his or her home environment, are assessed as sufficiently severe that the patient is not likely to maintain mental stability and/or abstinence if treatment is provided in a non-residential setting. Functional limitations may include, but are not limited to, cognitive impairment, developmental disability, manifest chronicity and intensity of the primary addictive disease process, residual psychiatric symptoms, cognitive deficits resulting from traumatic brain injury, limited educational achievement, poor vocational skills, inadequate anger management skills, and other equivalent indications that services need to be presented at a pace that is slower and/or more repetitive and concrete than is found at other levels of care. These deficits may be complicated by problems in Dimensions 2 through 6;

ADULT DIMENSIONAL ADMISSION CRITERIA (CONTINUED)

or

d. The patient is at mild risk of behaviors endangering self, others, or property, and is in imminent danger of relapse (with dangerous emotional, behavioral, or cognitive consequences or serious life consequences, such as imminent criminality, ie, extensive and recurrent patterns of criminal behavior such as robbery, DUI, child neglect, assault, etc.) without the 24-hour support and structure of a Level 3.3 program.

Co-Occurring Enhanced Programs

The patient's status in Dimension 3 is characterized by (a) *or* (b):

a. The patient has a diagnosed emotional, behavioral, or cognitive disorder that requires active management (involving monitoring of medications or assessment of psychiatric symptoms or behavioral management techniques, for example). Such disorders complicate treatment of the patient's substance use or substance-induced disorder and require differential diagnosis. The patient thus is in need of stabilization of psychiatric symptoms concurrent with addiction treatment (examples include a patient with unstable borderline or compulsive personality disorder or unstable anxiety or mood disorder, in addition to his or her substance use or substance-induced disorder).

Because cognitive deficits are commonly seen in patients treated at Level 3.3, such patients may require treatment that is delivered at a slower pace or in a more concrete or repetitive fashion;

or

b. The patient is assessed as at mild to moderate risk of behaviors endangering self, others, or property (for example, he or she has suicidal or homicidal thoughts, but lacks an active plan).

NOTE: The patient who has a severe and chronic mental disorder may manifest inadequate skills to manage the activities of daily living, poor social functioning, disorganized thinking, and/or periods of confusion, disorientation, or impaired reality testing. The patient's dysfunction is so severe that 24-hour structure is required to provide sufficient stabilization so that the patient can safely survive at a less intensive level of care.

During the stabilization period, expectations for the patient's involvement in group, community, and activities therapy are limited. A more highly individualized regimen of individual, group, and activities involvement may be required.

All Programs

The patient's status in Dimension 4 is characterized by at least *one* of the following:

a. Because of the intensity and chronicity of the addictive disorder or the patient's cognitive limitations, he or she has little awareness of the need for continuing care or the existence of his or her substance use or mental health problem and need for treatment, and thus has limited readiness to change;

or

b. Despite experiencing serious consequences or effects of the addictive disorder or mental health problem, the patient has marked difficulty in understanding the relationship between his or her substance use, addiction, mental health, or life problems, and impaired coping skills and level of functioning;

or

c. The patient's continued substance use poses a danger of harm to self or others, and he or she demonstrates no awareness of the need to address the severity of his or her addiction or psychiatric problem or does not recognize the need for treatment. However, assessment indicates that treatment interventions available at Level 3.3 may increase the patient's degree of readiness to change;

or

DIMENSION 3:
Emotional, Behavioral, or Cognitive Conditions and Complications

3

DIMENSION 4:
Readiness to Change

4

LEVEL 3.3

ADULT DIMENSIONAL ADMISSION CRITERIA (CONTINUED)

DIMENSION 4:
Readiness to Change

d. The patient's perspective impairs his or her ability to make behavior changes without repeated, structured, clinically directed motivational interventions, delivered in a 24-hour milieu. For example, because of cognitive deficits, the patient attributes his or her alcohol and/or other drug, or mental health problem to other persons or external events, rather than to a substance use or mental disorder. Interventions in an outpatient setting are assessed as not feasible or not likely to succeed.

Co-Occurring Enhanced Programs

The patient's status in Dimension 4 is characterized by ambivalence in his or her commitment to change and reluctance to engage in activities necessary to address a co-occurring mental health problem. For example, such a patient does not understand the need for antipsychotic medications, so that his or her medication adherence is inconsistent.

Similarly, the patient is appropriately placed in a Level 3.3 co-occurring enhanced program when he or she is not consistently able to follow through with treatment, or demonstrates minimal awareness of a problem, or is unaware of the need to change. Such a patient requires active interventions with family, significant others, and other external systems to create leverage and align incentives so as to promote engagement in treatment.

DIMENSION 5:
Relapse, Continued Use, or
Continued Problem Potential

All Programs

The patient's status in Dimension 5 is characterized by at least **one** of the following:

a. The patient does not recognize relapse triggers and has little awareness of the need for continuing care. Because of the intensity or chronicity of the patient's addictive disorder or the chronicity of the mental health problem or cognitive limitations, he or she is in imminent danger of continued substance use or mental health problems, with dangerous emotional, behavioral, or cognitive consequences. The patient thus needs 24-hour monitoring and structure to assist in the application of recovery and coping skills, as well as active staff interventions to prevent relapse;
or

b. The patient is experiencing an intensification of symptoms of his or her substance use disorder (such as difficulty in postponing immediate gratification and related drug-seeking behavior) or mental disorder (for example, increasing suicidal thoughts or impulses without a plan), and his or her level of functioning is deteriorating despite an amendment of the treatment plan;
or

c. The patient's cognitive impairment has limited his or her ability to identify and cope with relapse triggers and high-risk situations. He or she requires relapse prevention activities that are delivered at a slower pace, more concretely, and more repetitively, in a setting that provides 24-hour structure and support to prevent imminent dangerous consequences;
or

d. Despite recent, active participation in treatment at a less intensive level of care, the patient continues to use alcohol and/or other drugs or to continue other addictive behavior or to deteriorate psychiatrically, with imminent serious consequences. For mandated patients, serious consequences may be criminal and addictive behavior of such instability that the patient demonstrates imminent risk to public safety. There is a high risk of continued substance use, addictive behavior, or mental deterioration without close 24-hour monitoring and structured treatment.

Co-Occurring Enhanced Programs

The patient's status in Dimension 5 is characterized by psychiatric symptoms that pose a moderate risk of relapse to a substance use or mental disorder. Such a patient demonstrates limited ability to apply relapse prevention skills, as well as poor skills in coping with mental disorders and/or avoiding or limiting relapse, with imminent serious consequences. For example, the patient continues to engage in behaviors that pose a risk of relapse (such as non-adherence with the medication regimen or spending time in places where drugs are

ADULT DIMENSIONAL ADMISSION CRITERIA (CONTINUED)

being sold or used) because he or she has cognitive deficits that prevent understanding of the relationship between those behaviors and relapse to substance use or mental disorders. The presence of these relapse issues requires the types of services and 24-hour structure of a Level 3.3 co-occurring enhanced program.

Case management and collaboration across levels of care may be needed to manage anti-craving, psychotropic, or opioid agonist medications. For example, because of significant cognitive deficits, the patient may have difficulty in managing the activities of daily living without 24-hour interventions, and thus require preparation for placement in a group home in order to support his or her continued recovery from a substance use disorder or mental health problem. (Such a group home may involve supervised living for persons with cognitive deficits such as developmental disabilities or those who have severe and chronic mental illness.)

Preparation for transfer of the patient to a less intensive level of care, a different type of service in the community, and/or reentry into the community requires case management and staff exploration of supportive living environments, separately from their therapeutic work with the patient.

DIMENSION 5:
Relapse, Continued Use, or
Continued Problem Potential

DIMENSION 6:
Recovery Environment

All Programs

The patient's status in Dimension 6 is characterized by at least **one** of the following:

  a. The patient has been living in an environment that is characterized by a moderately high risk of initiation or repetition of physical, sexual, or emotional abuse, or substance use so endemic that the patient is assessed as being unable to achieve or maintain recovery at a less intensive level of care;

  or

  b. The patient is in significant danger of victimization and thus requires 24-hour supervision. For example, the patient has sustained a traumatic brain injury, as a result of which he or she is vulnerable to victimization when using psychoactive substances;

  or

  c. The patient's social network includes regular users of alcohol or other drugs, such that recovery goals are assessed as unachievable at a less intensive level of care;

  or

  d. The patient's social network involves living with an individual who is a regular user, addicted user, or dealer of alcohol or other drugs, or the patient's living environment is so highly invested in alcohol or other drug use that his or her recovery goals are assessed as unachievable;

  or

  e. Because of cognitive limitations, the patient is in danger of victimization by another and thus requires 24-hour supervision;

  or

  f. The patient is unable to cope, for even limited periods of time, outside the 24-hour structure of a Level 3.3 program. He or she needs staff monitoring to assure his or her safety and well-being.

Co-Occurring Enhanced Programs

The patient's status in Dimension 6 is characterized by severe and chronic mental illness. He or she may be too ill to benefit from skills training to learn to cope with problems in the recovery environment. Such a patient requires planning for assertive community treatment, intensive case management, or other community outreach and support services.

The patient's living, working, social, and/or community environment is not supportive of good mental health functioning. He or she has insufficient resources and skills to deal with this situation. For example, the patient may be unable to cope with the continuing stress of decreased cognitive functioning, or hostile family members with alcohol use disorder, and thus exhibits increasing anxiety and depression. Such a patient needs the support and structure of a Level 3.3 co-occurring enhanced program to achieve stabilization and prevent further deterioration.

LEVEL 3.3

4

Level 3.5
Clinically Managed High-Intensity Residential Services (Adult Criteria)

Level 3.5
Clinically Managed Medium-Intensity Residential Services (Adolescent Criteria)

Level 3.5 programs are designed to serve individuals who, because of specific functional limitations, need safe and stable living environments in order to develop and/or demonstrate sufficient recovery skills so that they do not immediately relapse or continue to use in an imminently dangerous manner upon transfer to a less intensive level of care. Level 3.5 assists individuals whose addiction is currently so out of control that they need a 24-hour supportive treatment environment to initiate or continue a recovery process that has failed to progress. Their multidimensional needs are of such severity that they cannot safely be treated in less intensive levels of care.

Many patients treated in Level 3.5 have significant social and psychological problems. For these patients, Level 3.5 programs are characterized by their reliance on the treatment community as a therapeutic agent. The goals of treatment in these programs are to promote abstinence from substance use, arrest other addictive and antisocial behaviors, and effect change in participants' lifestyles, attitudes, and values. This philosophy views substance-related and other addictive problems as disorders of the whole person that are reflected in problems with conduct, attitudes, moods, values, and emotional management. Frequent defining characteristics of these patients are found in their emotional, behavioral, and cognitive conditions (Dimension 3) and their living environments (Dimension 6).

Individuals who are placed in a Level 3.5 program typically have multiple limitations, which may include substance use and addictive disorders, criminal activity, psychological problems, impaired functioning, and disaffiliation from mainstream values. Their mental disorders may involve serious and chronic mental disorders (such as schizophrenia, bipolar disorders, and major depression) and personality disorders (such as borderline, narcissistic, and antisocial personality disorders).

Such individuals generally can be characterized as having chaotic, non-supportive, and often abusive interpersonal relationships; extensive treatment or criminal justice histories; limited work histories and educational experiences; and antisocial value systems. These limitations require comprehensive, multifaceted treatment that can address all of the patient's interrelated problems. For such patients, standard rehabilitation methods are inadequate.

These are patients who have never developed adequate coping skills and for whom the mere cessation of alcohol and/or other drug use or addictive behavior does not result in reemergence of previous coping skills. These patients stand in contrast to those who have developed adequate coping skills, usually before the onset of their addiction, and for whom addiction has impeded the application of those skills. Effective treatment approaches for some are primarily *habilitative* rather than *rehabilitative* in focus, addressing the patient's educational and voca-

LEVEL 3.5

tional limitations, as well as his or her socially dysfunctional behavior, until the patient can be stabilized and is appropriately transferred to a less intensive level of care.

Patients may present with the sequelae of physical, sexual, or emotional trauma. Chronic use of psychoactive substances also may have impaired their judgment, at least temporarily, leaving them vulnerable to relapse, continued problems, or continued use outside of a structured environment.

Other functional limitations in patients appropriately placed at this level of care include a constellation of past criminal or antisocial behaviors, with a risk of continued criminal behavior, an extensive history of treatment and/or criminal justice involvement, limited education, little or no work history, limited vocational skills, poor social skills, inadequate anger management skills, extreme impulsivity, emotional immaturity, and/or an antisocial value system.

For such patients, treatment is directed toward ameliorating their limitations through targeted interventions. For example, treatment may be focused on reducing the risk of relapse, reinforcing prosocial behaviors, and assisting with healthy reintegration into the community. This treatment is accomplished by providing specialty modalities and skills training while the patient is in a safe and structured environment, thus providing an opportunity for continued

improvement. Because treatment plans are individualized, fixed lengths of stay are inappropriate. The intensity and duration of clinical and habilitative or rehabilitative services, rather than medical services, are the defining characteristics of Level 3.5 programs.

Some patients may meet *DSM* diagnostic criteria for a co-occurring personality disorder (such as antisocial personality disorder) or another mental disorder (such as attention deficit hyperactivity disorder). Other patients may not meet diagnostic criteria and exhibit subthreshold Dimension 3 problems. Examples include impulsivity, deficient anger management skills, hostile and violent acting out, antagonism to limits and authority, hyperactivity, and distractibility. When treatment of these limitations cannot be implemented safely and successfully on an outpatient basis, placement in a Level 3.5 program should be considered.

Dimension 6 problems that may lead to placement in a Level 3.5 program include a living environment in which substance use, crime, and unemployment are endemic. These social influences may represent a sense of hopelessness or an acceptance of deviance as normative (in such an environment, the threat of incarceration is not a source of motivation because it is a common occurrence). Recovery may be perceived by the patient as providing a lesser

NOTE

Treatment in a Level 3.5 program is tailored to the patient's level of readiness to change. For some patients, "discovery" (becoming aware for the first time of the nature of their substance use or addictive disorder and/or mental health condition) may be an appropriate treatment plan. For others, they may need to focus on maintaining abstinence and preventing relapse to alcohol and/or other drug use or addictive behavior, as well as to antisocial behavior. Yet other patients may require treatment to develop a sense of personal responsibility and positive character change.

return for the effort (for example, the patient may not associate recovery from an addiction with outcomes such as vocational and housing opportunities). Some patients may have had no experience in a living environment that is conducive to healthy psychosocial development. Their entire social network may be composed of others who are involved in addictive disorders and/or criminal behaviors.

Patients may be appropriately placed in a Level 3.5 program as direct admissions or as transfers from a Level 3.7 or Level 4 program when their problems in Dimensions 1, 2, and 3 no longer warrant the availability of 24-hour medical or nursing interventions, but problems in Dimensions 4, 5, and 6 are sufficiently severe to exclude outpatient treatment as a viable option. Patients also may be transferred to a Level 3.5 program from less intensive levels of care.

When offered to patients who are being transferred from a Level 3.7 program, the services of a Level 3.5 program may be provided by a separate treatment program in the patient's home area. But Level 3.5 may also be provided by continued care in the program at which they received their Level 3.7 treatment, thus providing continuity of care.

The duration of treatment always depends on an individual's progress in acquiring basic living skills. How long a person stays in a 24-hour treatment setting depends on his or her ability to apply and demonstrate coping and recovery skills, such that he or she doesn't immediately relapse or continue to use in an imminently dangerous manner upon transfer to a less intensive level of care.

It is not intended in *The ASAM Criteria* that all, or even the majority of social and psychological problems will be resolved in the Level 3.5 treatment stay. Such complex and often lifelong challenges will need an ongoing treatment process to enhance wellness and recov-

ery. Thus, the treatment in Level 3.5 is best viewed as just one part of a person's treatment and recovery process seamlessly integrated into a flexible continuum of services. Treatment may begin in an outpatient setting, but require transfer to Level 3.5 if an individual is not progressing and faces imminent danger if not in a supportive 24-hour treatment setting.

An individual may need direct admission to Level 3.5 because the assessment indicates that the patient's multidimensional assessment is of such severity and functioning that outpatient treatment is not safe or feasible. Admission to Level 3.5 is indicated to further assess severity and function and treat priorities so there is not a continuation or recurrence of imminently dangerous addiction signs and symptoms. The focus of Level 3.5 is on stabilization of dangerous addiction signs and symptoms, initiation or restoration of a recovery process, and preparation for ongoing recovery in the broad continuum of care of the ASAM criteria. At the point that the patient is not likely to immediately relapse or continue to use in an imminently dangerous manner, transfer to another level of care to continue the recovery process is indicated.

Although the therapeutic community is widely identified as an example of a Level 3.5 program, other types of programs also fall within Level 3.5. For example, a Level 3.5 program may represent a "step down" for patients of a Level 3.7 program if their complications in Dimensions 1, 2, or 3 no longer require subacute medical services. However, the patient's problems in Dimensions 4, 5, and 6 warrant 24-hour structure and clinical services to facilitate initial recovery. (One way of conceptualizing this level of service is as a Level 3.7 program without the intensive medical and nursing component.)

Where treatment staff have been specially trained and adequate nursing supervision is available, Level 3.5 programs are able to

LEVEL 3.5

Adolescent-Specific Considerations: Level 3.5

For adolescents, critical treatment interventions that require intensity and persistence over extended periods of time, such as modeling prosocial patterns of behavior and adaptive patterns of emotional responsiveness, have sometimes been likened to surrogate or remedial parenting. Just as important can be the induction into a healthy peer group, with the formation of a group identity that emphasizes recovery and overcoming adversity.

The adolescent who is appropriately placed in Level 3.5 care typically has impaired functioning across a broad range of psychosocial domains. These impairments may be expressed as disruptive behaviors, delinquency and juvenile justice involvement, educational difficulties, family conflicts and chaotic home situations, developmental immaturity, and psychological problems.

Such an adolescent may have a variety of psychological or psychiatric problems. Particularly suitable for Level 3.5 treatments are the entrenched patterns of maladaptive behavior, extremes of temperament, and developmental or cognitive abnormalities related to mental health symptoms or disorders. Examples of co-occurring disorders that often require extended treatment at Level 3.5 are conduct disorder and oppositional defiant disorder, as well as the chronic patterns of disruptive behavior that may be associated with other disorders even after they have responded to acute treatment. Level 3.5 programs frequently work with aspects of adolescent temperament–including impulsive, extroverted, dramatic, antisocial, thrill-seeking, or other personality traits–that may otherwise have the potential to solidify as components of emerging personality disorders.

Even adolescents who are not diagnosed with psychiatric disorders (either because they do not meet full diagnostic criteria, or because they have not yet had a formal psychiatric evaluation) may have problems in Dimension 3 that render treatment ineffective at less intensive levels of care. Examples include hyperactivity or distractibility without a diagnosis of attention deficit hyperactivity disorder (ADHD), explosive temper and anger management problems, resistance to limits and authority, patterns of hostility or aggression, impulse control problems, cognitive limitations, and learning difficulties. Difficulties with interpersonal relationships (including poor conflict resolution abilities, fighting, social inhibition or withdrawal, and high-risk or indiscriminate sexual activity) frequently are targets of treatment. When treatment in the context of these problems cannot be implemented successfully on an outpatient basis, placement in a Level 3.5 program should be considered.

Level 3.5 also is appropriate for the adolescent whose problems include delinquency and juvenile justice involvement. In fact, this level of care often is warranted for adolescents who have the constellation of

LEVEL 3.5

4

difficulties associated with severe conduct problems, a progressive history of illegal behaviors, a pattern of emerging criminality, or an incipient antisocial value system. In this context, treatment must proceed in a contained, safe, and structured environment to allow teaching and practicing of prosocial behaviors and to facilitate healthy reintegration into the community. One of the key purposes of Level 3.5 treatment for this set of problems is assessment and monitoring of safety, with particular attention to issues of potential safety outside of the contained setting. Goals of treatment include overcoming oppositionality through a combination of confrontation, motivational enhancement, and supportive limit setting; anger management and acquisition of conflict resolution skills; values clarification and moral habilitation; character molding and education; development of effective behavioral contingency strategies; establishment of a reliable response to external structure; and the internalization of structure through self-regulation skills.

Some Level 3.5 programs specialize in the care of adolescents who are involved in the juvenile justice system. In fact, many programs actually are part of, or closely affiliated with, the juvenile justice system (including drug courts) or are located within juvenile justice facilities. Other programs may have a specific track for juvenile justice involved adolescents within the program; while some make no special distinction and integrate their care into the overall program.

Problems in Dimension 6 that would warrant placement in a Level 3.5 program include a chaotic home environment in which substance use, illegal behaviors, abuse, neglect, or lack of supervision are prominent, or a broader community in which substance use and crime are endemic. These social influences may represent a sense of hopelessness or an acceptance of deviance as normative. There may not be readily apparent role models for the rewards of abstinence. Many adolescents have a social network composed primarily or even exclusively of family or peers who are involved in substance use or criminal behaviors. Some adolescents may have had no experience of a living environment conducive to healthy psychosocial development.

The length of stay in a clinically managed Level 3.5 program as in all levels of care is based on the patient's severity of illness, level of function, and progress in treatment. Predetermined minimum lengths of stay or overall program lengths of stay that must be achieved in order for a patient to "complete treatment" or "graduate" are inconsistent with an individualized and outcomes-driven system of care. Upon admission, a focus of treatment planning is on plans for community reintegration and transition to less intensive levels of care. Such transfer is determined by when the patient has achieved a level of stability with sufficient skills to safely continue treatment without the immediate risk of relapse, continued use, or other continued problems, and are no longer in imminent danger of harm to themselves or others.

LEVEL 3.5

4

address the needs of individuals who have relatively severe biomedical problems (Dimension 2). For example, some patients may require daily medical monitoring or administration of prescription medications. A number of Level 3.5 programs offer a full range of medical services.

EXAMPLES OF SERVICE DELIVERY
All Programs

Examples of Level 3.5 programs are a therapeutic community of variable length of stay with appropriately clinically trained staff; or a residential treatment center.

SETTING
All Programs

Level 3.5 program services may be offered in a (usually) freestanding, appropriately licensed facility located in a community setting or a specialty unit within a licensed health care facility. Some Level 3.5 programs are offered in prisons or secure community settings for those inmates released from prison as a step down.

SUPPORT SYSTEMS
All Programs

In Level 3.5 programs, necessary support systems include:

a. Telephone or in-person consultation with a physician, or a physician assistant or nurse practitioner in states where they are licensed as physician extenders and may perform the duties designated here for a physician; emergency services, available 24 hours a day, 7 days a week.

b. Direct affiliations with other levels of care or close coordination through referral to more and less intensive levels of care and other services (such as vocational assessment and training, literacy training, and adult education).

c. Arranged medical, psychiatric, psychological, laboratory, and toxicology services, as appropriate to the severity and urgency of the patient's condition.

Co-Occurring Enhanced Programs

In addition to the support systems just described, Level 3.5 co-occurring enhanced programs offer psychiatric services, medication evaluation, and laboratory services. Such services are available by telephone within 8 hours and on-site or closely coordinated off-site within 24 hours, as appropriate to the severity and urgency of the patient's mental condition.

Adolescent-Specific Considerations: Support Systems

In Level 3.5 adolescent programs, necessary support systems include:

a. Availability of emergency consultation with a physician (by telephone or in person) and emergency services.

b. Ability to arrange for appropriate medical procedures, including indicated laboratory and toxicology testing.

c. Ability to arrange for appropriate medical and psychiatric treatment through consultation, referral to off-site concurrent treatment services, or transfer to another level of care.

d. Direct affiliation with other levels of care.

Adolescent-Specific Considerations: Support Systems (continued)

In Level 3.5-WM programs, support systems should also feature:

a. Availability of specialized clinical consultation and supervision for biomedical and emotional/behavioral problems related to intoxication and withdrawal management.

b. Protocols used to determine the nature of the medical monitoring and other interventions required (including nursing and physician care and/or transfer to a medically monitored facility or an acute care hospital) are developed and supported by a physician knowledgeable in addiction medicine.

STAFF
All Programs
Level 3.5 programs are staffed by:

a. Licensed or credentialed clinical staff such as addiction counselors, social workers, and licensed professional counselors (LPCs) who work with the allied health professional staff in an interdisciplinary team approach.

b. Allied health professional staff, such as counselor aides or group living workers, on-site 24 hours a day or as required by licensing regulations. One or more clinicians with competence in the treatment of substance use disorders are available on-site or by telephone 24 hours a day.

c. Clinical staff knowledgeable about the biological and psychosocial dimensions

Adolescent-Specific Considerations: Staff

When a Level 3.5-WM program provides withdrawal management services to adolescents (typically without on-site access to medical and nursing personnel), it must provide (in addition to the staff and therapies listed here):

a. Clinicians who are able to obtain and interpret information regarding the signs and symptoms of intoxication and withdrawal, as well as the appropriate monitoring and treatment of those conditions and how to facilitate entry into ongoing care; and

b. Appropriately trained staff who are competent to implement physician-approved protocols for patient observation, supervision, treatment (including over-the-counter medications for symptomatic relief), determination of the appropriate level of care, and facilitation of the patient's transition to continuing care; and

c. Access, as needed, to medical evaluation and consultation, which are available 24 hours a day to monitor the safety and outcome of withdrawal management in this setting, in accordance with treatment/transfer practice guidelines.

LEVEL 3.5 ④

of substance use and mental health disorders and their treatment. They are able to identify the signs and symptoms of acute psychiatric conditions, including psychiatric decompensation. Staff have specialized training in behavior management techniques.

Biomedical Enhanced Services

Biomedical enhanced services are delivered by appropriately credentialed medical staff, who are available to assess and treat co-occurring biomedical disorders and to monitor the patient's administration of medications in accordance with a physician's prescription.

The intensity of nursing care and observation is sufficient to meet the patient's needs.

Co-Occurring Enhanced Programs

In addition to the staff listed above, Level 3.5 co-occurring enhanced programs are staffed by appropriately credentialed mental health professionals, including addiction psychiatrists who are able to assess and treat co-occurring mental disorders and who have specialized training in behavior management techniques.

Some (if not all) of the addiction treatment professionals should have sufficient cross-training to understand the signs and symptoms of co-occurring mental disorders, and to understand and be able to explain to the patient the purposes of psychotropic medications and their interactions with substance use.

The intensity of nursing care and observation is sufficient to meet the patient's needs.

THERAPIES
All Programs

Therapies offered by Level 3.5 programs include:

a. Daily clinical services to improve the patient's ability to structure and organize the tasks of daily living and recovery (such as personal responsibility, personal appearance, and punctuality), and to develop and practice prosocial behaviors.

b. Planned clinical program activities to stabilize and maintain stabilization of the patient's addiction symptoms, and to help him or her develop and apply recovery skills. Activities may include relapse prevention, exploring interpersonal choices, and development of a social network supportive of recovery.

c. Counseling and clinical monitoring to promote successful initial involvement or reinvolvement in regular, productive daily activity, such as work or school and, as indicated, successful reintegration into family living.

d. Random drug screening to shape behavior and reinforce treatment gains, as appropriate to the patient's individual treatment plan.

e. A range of evidence-based cognitive, behavioral, and other therapies administered on an individual and group basis, medication education and management, addiction pharmacotherapy, educational skill building groups, and occupational or recreational activities, adapted to the patient's developmental stage and level of comprehension, understanding, and physical abilities.

f. Motivational enhancement and engagement strategies appropriate to the patient's stage of readiness and desire to change. Motivational therapies and other evidence-based practices are used in preference to confrontational strategies.

g. Counseling and clinical interventions to facilitate teaching the patient the skills needed for productive daily activity (such as work or school) and, as indicated, successful reintegration into family living. Health education services also are provided.

LEVEL 3.5

h. Monitoring of the patient's adherence in taking any prescribed medications, and/or any permitted over-the-counter (OTC) medications or supplements.

i. Planned clinical activities to enhance the patient's understanding of his or her substance use and/or mental disorders.

j. Daily scheduled professional services, including interdisciplinary assessments and treatment, designed to develop and apply recovery skills. Such services may include relapse prevention, exploring interpersonal choices, and development of a social network supportive of recovery. Such services also may include medical services; nursing services; individual and group counseling; psychotherapy; family therapy; educational and skill building groups; occupational and recreational therapies; art, music, or movement therapies; physical therapy; and vocational rehabilitation activities.

k. Planned community reinforcement designed to foster prosocial values and milieu or community living skills.

l. Services for the patient's family and significant others.

Co-Occurring Enhanced Programs

In addition to the therapies just described, Level 3.5 co-occurring enhanced programs offer planned clinical activities designed to stabilize the patient's mental health problems and psychiatric symptoms, and to maintain such stabilization.

The goals of therapy apply to both the substance use disorder and any co-occurring mental disorder.

Specific attention is given to medication education and management and to motivational and engagement strategies, which are used in preference to non-evidence-based practices. **NOTE:** The therapies described here encompass Level 3.5 co-occurring capable program services for patients who are able to tolerate and benefit from a planned program of therapies. Other patients—especially those with severe and chronic mental illness—may not be able to benefit from such a program. Once stabilized, such patients will require planning for and integration into intensive case management, medication management, and/or psychotherapy.

ASSESSMENT/TREATMENT PLAN REVIEW
All Programs

In Level 3.5 programs, the assessment and treatment plan review include:

a. An individualized, comprehensive biopsychosocial assessment of the patient's substance use or addictive disorder,

Adolescent-specific Considerations: Therapies

In addition to the therapies detailed above for all programs, educational services are provided in accordance with local regulations (typically on-site) and are designed to maintain the educational and intellectual development of the adolescent and, when indicated, to provide opportunities to remedy deficits in the educational level of adolescents who have fallen behind because of their involvement with alcohol and other drugs.

Trained clinicians provide daily clinical services to assess and address the adolescent's withdrawal status and service needs. Such clinical services may include nursing or medical monitoring, use of medications to alleviate symptoms, individual or group therapy specific to withdrawal, and withdrawal support.

conducted or updated by staff who are knowledgeable about addiction treatment. This assessment is used to confirm the appropriateness of placement at Level 3.5, and to help guide the individualized treatment planning process, which is focused on the patient's strengths, needs, abilities, preferences, and desired goals.

b. An individualized treatment plan, which includes problem formulation and articulation of short-term, measurable treatment goals and activities designed to achieve those goals. The plan is developed in collaboration with the patient and reflects the patient's personal goals, while considering the capabilities and resources available to achieve the patient's personal goals.

c. A biopsychosocial assessment, treatment plan, and updates that reflect the patient's clinical progress, as reviewed by an interdisciplinary treatment team in collaboration with the patient.

d. A physical examination, performed within a reasonable time, as determined by the patient's medical condition consistent with facility policy or legal requirements.

The treatment plan reflects case management conducted by on-site staff; coordination of related addiction treatment, health care, mental health, social, vocational, or housing services (provided concurrently); and the integration of services at this and other levels of care.

Co-Occurring Enhanced Programs

In addition to the assessment and treatment plan review activities described above, Level 3.5 co-occurring enhanced programs provide a review of the patient's recent psychiatric history and mental status examination. (If necessary, this review is conducted by a psychiatrist.) A comprehensive psychiatric history and examination and psychodiagnostic assessment are performed within a reasonable time, as determined by the patient's needs.

Level 3.5 co-occurring enhanced programs also provide active reassessments of the patient's mental status, at a frequency determined by the urgency of the patient's psychiatric symptoms, and follow through with mental health treatment and psychotropic medications as indicated. **NOTE:** Certain patients may need the kinds of assessment and treatment services described here for co-occurring enhanced, but at a reduced level of frequency and comprehensiveness to match the greater stability of their mental health symptoms. For such patients, placement in a co-occurring capable program may be appropriate.

Adolescent-Specific Considerations: Assessment and Treatment Planning

Elements of the assessment and treatment plan review should also include:

a. An initial withdrawal assessment, including a medical evaluation and referral within the 48 hours preceding admission (or if a step down from another residential setting, within 7 days preceding admission).

b. Daily withdrawal monitoring assessments.

c. Ongoing screening for medical and nursing needs, with such medical and nursing services available as needed through consultation or referral.

DOCUMENTATION
All Programs

Documentation standards for Level 3.5 programs include individualized progress notes in the patient's record that clearly reflect implementation of the treatment plan and the patient's response to therapeutic interventions for all disorders treated, as well as subsequent amendments to the plan.

Treatment plan reviews are conducted at specified times and recorded in the treatment plan.

Co-Occurring Enhanced Programs

In addition to the information just described, Level 3.5 co-occurring enhanced programs document the patient's mental health status, the relationship between the mental and substance use disorders, and the patient's current level of mental functioning.

ADULT DIAGNOSTIC ADMISSION CRITERIA
All Programs

The patient who is appropriately placed in a Level 3.5 program meets the diagnostic criteria for a substance use and/or addictive disorder of moderate to high severity as defined in the current *Diagnostic and Statistical Manual of Mental Disorders* (*DSM*) of the American Psychiatric Association or other standardized and widely accepted criteria, as well as the dimensional criteria for admission. If the patient's presenting history is inadequate to substantiate such a diagnosis, the probability of such a diagnosis may be determined from information submitted by collateral parties (such as family members, legal guardians, and significant others).

NOTE: Patients in Level 3.5 co-occurring disorders programs may have co-occurring mental disorders that meet the stability criteria for placement in a co-occurring capable program; or difficulties with mood, behavior, or cognition related to a substance use or mental disorder; or emotional, behavioral, or cognitive symptoms that are problematic but do not meet the *DSM* criteria for a mental disorder.

Co-Occurring Enhanced Programs

The patient who is appropriately admitted to a Level 3.5 co-occurring enhanced program meets the diagnostic criteria for a mental disorder as well as a substance use or addictive disorder, as defined in the current *Diagnostic and Statistical Manual of Mental Disorders* (*DSM*) of the American Psychiatric Association or other standardized and widely accepted criteria, as well as the dimensional criteria for admission.

If the patient's presenting history is inadequate to substantiate such a diagnosis, the probability of such a diagnosis may be determined from information submitted by collateral parties (such as family members, legal guardians, and significant others).

ADULT DIMENSIONAL ADMISSION CRITERIA
All Programs

The adult patient who is appropriately admitted to a Level 3.5 program meets specifications in *each* of the six dimensions.

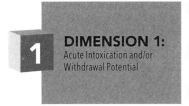

DIMENSION 1:
Acute Intoxication and/or Withdrawal Potential

All Programs

The patient has no signs or symptoms of withdrawal, or his or her withdrawal needs can be safely managed in a Level 3.5 setting. See separate withdrawal management chapter for how to approach "unbundled" withdrawal management for adults.

NOTE: A patient who is being transferred from a Level 3.7 program should not require medically managed or monitored withdrawal management services.

ADULT DIMENSIONAL ADMISSION CRITERIA (CONTINUED)

DIMENSION 2:
Biomedical Conditions and
Complications

All Programs

The patient's status in Dimension 2 is characterized by **one** of the following:

a. Biomedical problems, if any, are stable and do not require 24-hour medical or nurse monitoring, and the patient is capable of self-administering any prescribed medications;
or

b. A current biomedical condition is not severe enough to warrant inpatient treatment but is sufficient to distract from treatment or recovery efforts. The problem requires medical monitoring, which can be provided by the program or through an established arrangement with another provider.

Biomedical Enhanced Services

The patient is in need of biomedical enhanced services if he or she has a biomedical problem that requires a degree of staff attention (such as monitoring of adherence to medications or assistance with mobility) that is not available in other Level 3.5 programs.

All Programs

If any of the Dimension 3 conditions are present, the patient must be admitted to a co-occurring capable or co-occurring enhanced program (depending on his or her level of function, stability, and degree of impairment).

Co-Occurring Capable Programs

The patient's status in Dimension 3 is characterized by (a); **and** one of (b) **or** (c) **or** (d) **or** (e) **or** (f):

a. The patient's mental status (including emotional stability and cognitive functioning) is assessed as sufficiently stable to permit the patient to participate in the therapeutic interventions provided at this level of care and to benefit from treatment.
and

DIMENSION 3:
Emotional, Behavioral, or
Cognitive Conditions and
Complications

b. The patient's psychiatric condition is stabilizing. However, despite his or her best efforts, the patient is unable to control his or her use of alcohol, tobacco, and/or other drugs and/or antisocial behaviors, with attendant probability of imminent danger. The resulting level of dysfunction is so severe that it precludes the patient's participation in a less structured and intensive level of care;
or

c. The patient demonstrates repeated inability to control his or her impulses to use alcohol and/or other drugs and/or to engage in antisocial behavior, and is in imminent danger of relapse, with attendant likelihood of harm to self, others, or property. The resulting level of dysfunction is of such severity that it precludes participation in treatment in the absence of the 24-hour support and structure of a Level 3.5 program;
or

d. The patient demonstrates antisocial behavior patterns (as evidenced by criminal activity) that have led or could lead to significant criminal justice problems, lack of concern for others, and extreme lack of regard for authority (expressed through distrust, conflict, or opposition), and which prevents movement toward positive change and precludes participation in a less structured and intensive level of care;
or

ADULT DIMENSIONAL ADMISSION CRITERIA (CONTINUED)

DIMENSION 3:
Emotional, Behavioral, or Cognitive Conditions and Complications

e. The patient has significant functional deficits, which are likely to respond to staff interventions. These symptoms and deficits, when considered in the context of his or her home environment, are sufficiently severe that the patient is not likely to maintain mental stability and/or abstinence if treatment is provided in a non-residential setting. The functional deficits are of a pervasive nature, requiring treatment that is primarily habilitative in focus; they do not require medical monitoring or management. They may include—but are not limited to—residual psychiatric symptoms, chronic addictive disorder, history of criminality, marginal intellectual ability, limited educational achievement, poor vocational skills, inadequate anger management skills, poor impulse control, and the sequelae of physical, sexual, or emotional trauma. These deficits may be complicated by problems in Dimensions 2 through 6;
   or

f. The patient's concomitant personality disorders (eg, antisocial personality disorder with verbal aggressive behavior requiring consistent limit-setting) are of such severity that the accompanying dysfunctional behaviors provide opportunities to promote continuous boundary setting interventions.

Co-Occurring Enhanced Programs

The patient's status in Dimension 3 is characterized by a range of psychiatric symptoms that require active monitoring, such as low anger management skills. These are assessed as posing a risk of harm to self or others if the patient is not contained in a 24-hour structured environment.

Although such patients do not require specialized psychiatric nursing and close observation, they do need monitoring and interventions by mental health staff to limit and de-escalate their behaviors, develop a therapeutic alliance, and process events that trigger symptomatology and identify and utilize appropriate coping techniques and medical interventions or relaxation. A 24-hour milieu is sufficient to contain such impulses in most cases, but enhanced staff and therapeutic interventions are required to manage unpredictable losses of impulse control.

The treatment regimen should be strengths-based and focused on rapid formal feedback regarding change of treatment plan, process, and outcomes in treatment, while avoiding highly confrontational strategies or strong affect that are intended to induce submissive behavior.

All Programs

The patient's status in Dimension 4 is characterized by at least *one* of the following:

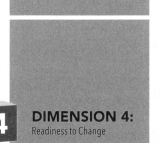

DIMENSION 4:
Readiness to Change

a. Because of the intensity and chronicity of the addictive disorder or the patient's mental health problems, he or she has limited insight and little awareness of the need for continuing care or the existence of his or her substance use or mental health problem and need for treatment, and thus has limited readiness to change;
   or

b. Despite experiencing serious consequences or effects of the addictive disorder or mental health problem, the patient has marked difficulty in understanding the relationship between his or her substance use, addiction, mental health, or life problems and his or her impaired coping skills and level of functioning, often blaming others for his or her addiction problems;
   or

LEVEL 3.5 ④

ADULT DIMENSIONAL ADMISSION CRITERIA (CONTINUED)

DIMENSION 4:
Readiness to Change

c. The patient demonstrates passive or active opposition to addressing the severity of his or her mental or addiction problem, or does not recognize the need for treatment. Such continued substance use or inability to follow through with mental health treatment poses a danger of harm to self or others. However, assessment indicates that treatment interventions available at Level 3.5 may increase the patient's degree of readiness to change;
   or

d. The patient requires structured therapy and a 24-hour programmatic milieu to promote treatment progress and recovery, because motivational interventions have not succeeded at less intensive levels of care and such interventions are assessed as not likely to succeed at a less intensive level of care;
   or

e. The patient's perspective impairs his or her ability to make behavior changes without repeated, structured, clinically directed motivational interventions, which will enable him/her to develop insight into the role he or she plays in his or her substance use and/or mental condition, and empower him/her to make behavioral changes which can only be delivered in a 24-hour milieu;
   or

f. Despite recognition of a substance use or addictive behavior problem and understanding of the relationship between his or her substance use, addiction, and life problems, the patient expresses little to no interest in changing. Because of the intensity or chronicity of the patient's addictive disorder and high-risk criminogenic needs, he or she is in imminent danger of continued substance use or addictive behavior. This poses imminent serious life consequences (ie, imminent risk to public safety or imminent abuse or neglect of children) and/or a continued pattern of risk of harm to others (ie, extensive pattern of assaults, burglaries, DUI) while under the influence of substances;
   or

g. The patient attributes his or her alcohol, drug, addictive, or mental health problem to other persons or external events, rather than to a substance use or addictive or mental disorder. The patient requires clinical directed motivation interventions that will enable him or her to develop insight into the role he/she plays in his or her health condition, and empower him or her to make behavioral changes. Interventions are adjudged as not feasible or unlikely succeed at a less intensive level of care.

Co-Occurring Enhanced Programs

The patient's status in Dimension 4 is characterized by a lack of commitment to change and reluctance to engage in activities necessary to address a co-occurring mental health problem. For example, the patient does not understand the need for antidepressant or antimania medications, and so does not adhere to a medication regimen.

Similarly, the patient is appropriately placed in a Level 3.5 co-occurring enhanced program if he or she is not consistently able to follow through with treatment, or demonstrates minimal awareness of a problem, or is unaware of the need to change. Such a patient requires active interventions with family, significant others, and other external systems to create leverage and align incentives so as to promote engagement in treatment.

LEVEL 3.5

ADULT DIMENSIONAL ADMISSION CRITERIA (CONTINUED)

DIMENSION 5:
Relapse, Continued Use, or
Continued Problem Potential

All Programs

The patient's status in Dimension 5 is characterized by at least **one** of the following:

a. The patient does not recognize relapse triggers and lacks insight into the benefits of continuing care, and is therefore not committed to treatment. His or her continued substance use poses an imminent danger of harm to self or others in the absence of 24-hour monitoring and structured support;

or

b. The patient's psychiatric condition is stabilizing. However, despite his or her best efforts, the patient is unable to control his or her use of alcohol, other drugs, and/or antisocial behaviors, with attendant probability of harm to self or others. The patient has limited ability to interrupt the relapse process or continued use, or to use peer supports when at risk for relapse to his or her addiction or mental disorder. His or her continued substance use poses an imminent danger of harm to self or others in the absence of 24-hour monitoring and structured support;

or

c. The patient is experiencing psychiatric or addiction symptoms such as drug craving, insufficient ability to postpone immediate gratification, and other drug-seeking behaviors. This situation poses an imminent danger of harm to self or others in the absence of close 24-hour monitoring and structured support. The introduction of psychopharmacologic support is indicated to decrease psychiatric or addictive symptoms, such as cravings, that will enable the patient to delay immediate gratification and reinforce positive recovery behaviors;

or

d. The patient is in imminent danger of relapse or continued use, with dangerous emotional, behavioral, or cognitive consequences, as a result of a crisis situation;

or

e. Despite recent, active participation in treatment at a less intensive level of care, the patient continues to use alcohol or other drugs, or to deteriorate psychiatrically, with imminent serious consequences, and is at high risk of continued substance use or mental deterioration in the absence of close 24-hour monitoring and structured treatment;

or

f. The patient demonstrates a lifetime history of repeated incarceration with a pattern of relapse to substances and uninterrupted use outside of incarceration, with imminent risk of relapse to addiction or mental health problems and recidivism to criminal behavior (for example, extensive and recurrent pattern of crimes such as burglary, assault, robbery, DUI). This poses imminent risk of harm to self or others. The patient's imminent danger of relapse is accompanied by an uninterrupted cycle of relapse-reoffending-incarceration-release-relapse without the opportunity for treatment. The patient requires 24-hour monitoring and structure to assist in the initiation and application of recovery and coping skills.

Co-Occurring Enhanced Programs

The patient's status in Dimension 5 is characterized by psychiatric symptoms that pose a moderate to high risk of relapse to a substance use or mental disorder. Such a patient demonstrates limited ability to apply relapse prevention skills, as well as inadequate skills in coping with mental disorders and/or avoiding or limiting relapse, with imminent serious consequences.

For example, the patient continues to engage repetitively and compulsively in behaviors that pose a risk of relapse (such as antisocial behavior or criminal activity, or spending time in places where antisocial behavior is the attraction) because of an inability to understand the relationship between those behaviors and relapse to substance use or mental disorders or criminal activity. The presence of these relapse issues requires the intensity and types of services and 24-hour structure of a Level 3.5 co-occurring enhanced program.

ADULT DIMENSIONAL ADMISSION CRITERIA (CONTINUED)

DIMENSION 5:
Relapse, Continued Use, or Continued Problem Potential

Case management and collaboration across levels of care may be needed to manage anti-craving, psychotropic, or opioid agonist medications. For example, because of an external locus of control, the patient may have difficulty resisting pressures to use psychoactive substances. He or she may continue involvement or become reinvolved with peers who are engaged in antisocial and/or criminal behaviors, and thus requires some type of group living situation that provides ongoing structure and support. (Such a group home may be a supervised living arrangement for ex-offenders.)

Discharge planning includes preparation for transfer of the patient to a less intensive level of care, a different type of service in the community, and/or reentry into the community. This requires case management and staff exploration of supportive living environments, separate from their therapeutic work with the patient.

All Programs

The patient's status in Dimension 6 is characterized by at least **one** of the following:

a. The patient has been living in an environment that is characterized by a moderately high risk of neglect; initiation or repetition of physical, sexual, or emotional abuse; or substance use so endemic that the patient is assessed as being unable to achieve or maintain recovery at a less intensive level of care;
   or

b. The patient's social network includes regular users of alcohol, tobacco, and/or other drugs, such that recovery goals are assessed as unachievable at a less intensive level of care;
   or

c. The patient's social network is characterized by significant social isolation or withdrawal, such that recovery goals are assessed as inconsistently unachievable at a less intensive level of care;
   or

d. The patient's social network involves living with an individual who is a regular user, addicted user or dealer of alcohol or other drugs, or the patient's living environment is so highly invested in alcohol and/or other drug use that his or her recovery goals are assessed as unachievable;
   or

e. The patient is unable to cope, for even limited periods of time, outside of 24-hour care. He or she needs staff monitoring to learn to cope with Dimension 6 problems before being transferred safely to a less intensive setting.

DIMENSION 6:
Recovery Environment

Co-Occurring Enhanced Programs

The patient's status in Dimension 6 is characterized by severe and chronic mental illness. He or she may be too ill to benefit from skills training to learn to cope with problems in the recovery environment. Such a patient requires planning for assertive community treatment, intensive case management, or other community outreach and support services.

Such a patient's living, working, social, and/or community environment is not supportive of good mental health functioning. He or she has insufficient resources and skills to deal with this situation. For example, the patient may be unable to cope with the continuing stress of peer pressure to be involved in criminal behavior, or threats by former criminal associates, or hostile family members with alcohol use disorder, and thus exhibits increasing anxiety and depression. Such a patient needs the support and structure of a Level 3.5 co-occurring enhanced program to achieve stabilization and prevent further deterioration.

LEVEL 3.5

4

ADOLESCENT DIAGNOSTIC ADMISSION CRITERIA

The adolescent who is appropriately placed in a Level 3.5 program meets the diagnostic criteria for a substance use and/or addictive disorder of moderate to high severity as defined in the current *Diagnostic and Statistical Manual of Mental Disorders* (*DSM*) of the American Psychiatric Association or other standardized and widely accepted criteria, as well as the dimensional criteria for admission.

If the adolescent's presenting history is inadequate to substantiate such a diagnosis, the probability of such a diagnosis may be determined from information submitted by collateral parties (such as family members, legal guardians, and significant others).

ADOLESCENT DIMENSIONAL ADMISSION CRITERIA

The adolescent who is appropriately placed in a Level 3.5 program meets specifications in at least **two** of Dimensions 1 through 6.

DIMENSION 1:
Acute Intoxication and/or Withdrawal Potential

The adolescent's status in Dimension 1 is characterized by the following:

The adolescent is at risk of or experiencing acute or subacute intoxication or withdrawal, with mild to moderate symptoms. He or she needs secure placement and increased treatment intensity (without frequent access to medical or nursing services) to support engagement in treatment, ability to tolerate withdrawal, and prevention of immediate continued use. Alternatively, the adolescent has a history of failure in treatment at the same or a less intensive level of care.

Problems with intoxication or withdrawal are manageable at this level of care.

Withdrawal rating scale tables and flow sheets (which may include tabulation of vital signs) are used as needed.

Drug-specific examples follow:

a. **Alcohol:** Mild acute withdrawal or moderate subacute withdrawal, with symptoms that require 24-hour support, extended monitoring, and non-pharmacological management; no abnormal vital signs; no need for sedative/hypnotic substitution withdrawal management; a CIWA -Ar score of <8; no significant history of regular morning drinking.
b. **Sedative/hypnotics:** Mild to moderate withdrawal, with symptoms that require 24-hour support and extended monitoring; may have a recent history of low-level daily sedative/hypnotic use, but no cross-dependence on other substances; may have a need for extended agonist substitution therapy, but only with a stable taper regimen in the context of a step down from a more intensive level of care, where the regimen has been titrated and established; no abnormal vital signs; no unstable complicating exacerbation of affective disorder.
c. **Opiates:** Mild to moderate withdrawal, with symptoms requiring 24-hour support and extended monitoring and non-pharmacological or over-the-counter medication for symptomatic relief; no need for prescription pharmacological treatments or agonist substitution therapy.

LEVEL 3.5 ④

ADOLESCENT DIMENSIONAL ADMISSION CRITERIA (CONTINUED)

The adolescent who is appropriately placed in a Level 3.5 program meets specifications in at least **two** of Dimensions 1 through 6.

DIMENSION 1:
Acute Intoxication and/or Withdrawal Potential

With the high craving states typical of opioid withdrawal, the adolescent may require 24-hour secure placement and increased intensity of treatment because of lack of sufficient impulse control, coping skills, or supports to prevent immediate continued use.

d. **Stimulants:** Mild to moderate to severe withdrawal (involving lethargy, apathy, agitation, depression, suspiciousness, fearfulness, or hypervigilance) of sufficient intensity that the patient needs 24-hour secure placement and increased intensity of treatment to support the ability to tolerate symptoms, support treatment engagement, and bolster external supports.

With the high craving states typical of stimulant withdrawal, the adolescent may require 24-hour secure placement and increased intensity of treatment because of lack of sufficient impulse control, coping skills, or supports to prevent immediate continued use.

e. **Inhalants:** Moderate subacute intoxication (involving cognitive impairment, lethargy, agitation, and depression) of sufficient intensity that the patient needs 24-hour secure placement and increased treatment intensity to support the ability to tolerate symptoms, support engagement in treatment, and bolster external supports.

f. **Marijuana:** Moderate to severe withdrawal symptoms (involving irritability, general malaise, inner agitation, severe sleep disturbance, and severe craving) or sustained susceptibility, subacute intoxication states (involving cognitive disorganization, memory impairment, executive dysfunction, and the like), such that the patient needs 24-hour secure placement and increased treatment intensity to support the adolescent's ability to tolerate symptoms, support engagement in treatment, and bolster external supports. The patient may be using or likely to use marijuana in order to relieve withdrawal from other substances, and may need secure placement to prevent immediate continued use.

g. **Hallucinogens:** Moderate to severe chronic intoxication (involving perceptual distortion, moderate non-delusional suspiciousness, moderate affective instability, and the like), which requires 24-hour secure placement and increased intensity of treatment to support the adolescent's ability to tolerate symptoms, support engagement in treatment, and bolster external supports.

DIMENSION 2:
Biomedical Conditions and Complications

The adolescent's status in Dimension 2 is characterized by **one** of the following:

a. Biomedical conditions distract from recovery efforts and require residential supervision (that is unavailable at a less intensive level of care) to ensure their adequate treatment, or they require medium-intensity residential treatment to provide support to overcome the distraction. Adequate nursing or medical monitoring can be provided through an arrangement with another provider. The adolescent is capable of self-administering any prescribed medications or procedures, with available supervision.

or

b. Continued substance use would place the adolescent at risk of serious damage to his or her physical health because of a biomedical condition (such as pregnancy or HIV) or an imminently dangerous pattern of high-risk use (such as continued use of shared injection apparatus). Adequate nursing or medical monitoring for biomedical conditions can be provided through an arrangement with another provider. The adolescent is capable of self-administering any prescribed medications or procedures, with available supervision.

Biomedical Enhanced Services
The adolescent is in need of biomedical enhanced services if he or she has a biomedical problem that requires a degree of staff attention (such as monitoring of adherence to medications or assistance with mobility) that is not available in other Level 3.5 programs.

4
LEVEL 3.5

a ADOLESCENT DIMENSIONAL ADMISSION CRITERIA (CONTINUED)

The adolescent who is appropriately placed in a Level 3.5 program meets specifications in at least **two** of Dimensions 1 through 6.

DIMENSION 3:
Emotional, Behavioral, or Cognitive Conditions and Complications

The adolescent's status in Dimension 3 is characterized by at least **one** of the following (requiring 24-hour supervision and a medium-intensity therapeutic milieu):

a. **Dangerousness/Lethality:** The adolescent is at moderate but stable risk of imminent harm to self or others, and needs medium-intensity 24-hour monitoring and/or treatment for protection and safety. However, he or she does not require access to medical or nursing services.

b. **Interference with Addiction Recovery Efforts:** The adolescent's recovery efforts are negatively affected by his or her emotional, behavioral, or cognitive problems in significant and distracting ways. He or she requires 24-hour structured therapy and/or a programmatic milieu to promote sustained focus on recovery tasks because of active symptoms.

c. **Social Functioning:** The adolescent has significant impairments, with moderate to severe symptoms (such as poor impulse control, disorganization, and the like). These seriously impair his or her ability to function in family, social, school, or work settings, and cannot be managed at a less intensive level of care. This might involve, for example, a recent history of high-risk runaway behavior, inability to resist antisocial peer influences, a need for consistent boundaries unavailable in the home environment, or inability to sustain school attendance, and the like.

d. **Ability for Self-Care:** The adolescent has moderate impairment in his or her ability to manage the activities of daily living and thus requires 24-hour supervision and staff assistance, which can be provided by the program. The adolescent's impairments may involve a need for intensive modeling and reinforcement of personal grooming and hygiene, a pattern of continuing indiscriminate or unprotected sexual contacts in an adolescent with a history of sexually transmitted diseases, moderate dilapidation and self-neglect in the context of advanced alcohol or drug dependence, a need for intensive teaching of personal safety techniques in an adolescent who has suffered physical or sexual assault, and the like.

e. **Course of Illness:** The adolescent's history and present situation suggest that an emotional, behavioral, or cognitive condition would become unstable without 24-hour supervision and a medium-intensity structured programmatic milieu. These may involve, for example, an adolescent whose substance use has been associated with a dangerous pattern of criminal or delinquent behaviors and who needs monitoring to assess safety and the likelihood of successful treatment on an outpatient basis before being returned to the community following release from a juvenile justice setting, or an adolescent with a recent lapse or relapse, whose history suggests that this is likely to result in disruptive behavior that will impede participation in treatment at a less intensive level of care, and the like.

DIMENSION 4:
Readiness to Change

The adolescent's status in Dimension 4 is characterized by at least **one** of the following:

a. Because of the intensity and chronicity of the addictive disorder or the adolescent's mental health problems, he or she has limited insight into and little awareness of the need for continuing care or the existence of his or her substance use or mental health problem and need for treatment, and thus has limited readiness to change;
or

b. Despite experiencing serious consequences or effects of the addictive disorder or mental health problem, the adolescent has marked difficulty in understanding the relationship between his or her substance use, addiction, mental health, or life problems and his or her impaired coping skills and level of functioning, often blaming others for his or her addiction problems;
or

LEVEL 3.5

4

a ADOLESCENT DIMENSIONAL ADMISSION CRITERIA (CONTINUED)

The adolescent who is appropriately placed in a Level 3.5 program meets specifications in at least **two** of Dimensions 1 through 6.

DIMENSION 4:
Readiness to Change

c. The adolescent demonstrates passive or active opposition to addressing the severity of his or her mental health problem or addiction, or does not recognize the need for treatment. Such continued substance use or inability to follow through with mental health treatment poses a danger of harm to self or others. However, assessment indicates that treatment interventions available at Level 3.5 may increase the patient's degree of readiness to change; *or*

d. The adolescent requires structured therapy and a 24-hour programmatic milieu to promote treatment progress and recovery, because motivational interventions have not succeeded at less intensive levels of care and such interventions are assessed as not likely to succeed at a less intensive level of care; *or*

e. The adolescent's perspective impairs his or her ability to make behavior changes without repeated, structured, clinically directed motivational interventions, which will enable him/her to develop insight into the role he or she plays in his or her substance use and/or mental condition, and empower him/her to make behavioral changes, which can only be delivered in a 24-hour milieu; *or*

f. Despite recognition of a substance use or addictive behavior problem and understanding of the relationship between his or her substance use, addiction, and life problems, the patient expresses little to no interest in changing. Because of the intensity or chronicity of the adolescent's addictive disorder and high-risk criminogenic needs, he or she is in imminent danger of continued substance use or addictive behavior. This poses imminent serious life consequences (ie, imminent risk to public safety or imminent abuse or neglect of children) and/or a continued pattern of risk of harm to others (ie, extensive pattern of assaults, burglaries) while under the influence of substances; *or*

g. The adolescent attributes his or her alcohol, drug, addictive, or mental health problem to other persons or external events, rather than to a substance use or addictive or mental disorder. The adolescent requires clinical, directed motivation interventions that will enable him or her to develop insight into the role he/she plays in his or her health condition, and empower him or her to make behavioral changes. Interventions are adjudged as not feasible or unlikely succeed at a less intensive level of care.

DIMENSION 5:
Relapse, Continued Use, or Continued Problem Potential

The adolescent's status in Dimension 5 is characterized by at least **one** of the following:

a. The adolescent does not recognize relapse triggers and lacks insight into the benefits of continuing care, and is therefore not committed to treatment. His or her continued substance use poses an imminent danger of harm to self or others in the absence of 24-hour monitoring and structured support; *or*

b. The adolescent's psychiatric condition is stabilizing. However, despite his or her best efforts, the adolescent is unable to control his or her use of alcohol, other drugs, and/or antisocial behaviors, with attendant probability of harm to self or others. The adolescent has limited ability to interrupt the relapse process or continued use, or to use peer supports when at risk for relapse to his or her addiction or mental disorder. His or her continued substance use poses an imminent danger of harm to self or others in the absence of 24-hour monitoring and structured support; *or*

LEVEL 3.5

④

ADOLESCENT DIMENSIONAL ADMISSION CRITERIA (CONTINUED)

The adolescent who is appropriately placed in a Level 3.5 program meets specifications in at least **two** of Dimensions 1 through 6.

DIMENSION 5:
Relapse, Continued Use, or Continued Problem Potential

c. The adolescent is experiencing psychiatric or addiction symptoms such as drug craving, insufficient ability to postpone immediate gratification, and other drug-seeking behaviors. This situation poses an imminent danger of harm to self or others in the absence of close 24-hour monitoring and structured support. The introduction of psychopharmacologic support is indicated to decrease psychiatric or addictive symptoms, such as cravings, that will enable the patient to delay immediate gratification and reinforce positive recovery behaviors;
or

d. The adolescent is in imminent danger of relapse or continued use, with dangerous emotional, behavioral, or cognitive consequences, as a result of a crisis situation;
or

e. Despite recent, active participation in treatment at a less intensive level of care, the adolescent continues to use alcohol or other drugs, or to deteriorate psychiatrically, with imminent serious consequences, and is at high risk of continued substance use or mental deterioration in the absence of close 24-hour monitoring and structured treatment;
or

f. The adolescent demonstrates a lifetime history of repeated incarceration with a pattern of relapse to substances and uninterrupted use outside of incarceration, with imminent risk of relapse to addiction or mental health problems and recidivism to criminal behavior (for example, extensive and recurrent pattern of crimes such as burglary, assault, robbery). This poses imminent risk of harm to self or others. The adolescent's imminent danger of relapse is accompanied by an uninterrupted cycle of relapse-reoffending-incarceration-release-relapse without the opportunity for treatment. The adolescent requires 24-hour monitoring and structure to assist in the initiation and application of recovery and coping skills.

DIMENSION 6:
Recovery Environment

The adolescent's status in Dimension 6 is characterized by at least **one** of the following:

a. The adolescent has been living in an environment in which there is a high risk of neglect, or initiation or repetition of physical, sexual, or severe, emotional abuse, such that the patient is assessed as being unable to achieve or maintain recovery without residential treatment.
or

b. The adolescent has a family or other household member who has an active substance use disorder, or substance use is endemic in his or her home environment or broader social network, so that recovery goals are assessed as unachievable without residential treatment.
or

c. The adolescent's home environment or social network is too chaotic or ineffective to support or sustain treatment goals, so that recovery is assessed as unachievable without residential treatment. For example, the adolescent's family reinforces antisocial norms and values, or the family cannot sustain treatment engagement or school attendance, or the family is experiencing significant social isolation or withdrawal.
or

d. Logistical impediments (such as distance from a treatment facility, mobility limitations, lack of transportation, and the like) preclude participation in treatment at a less intensive level of care.

LEVEL 3.5 ④

Level 3.7
Medically Monitored Intensive Inpatient Services (Adult Criteria)

Level 3.7
Medically Monitored High-Intensity Inpatient Services (Adolescent Criteria)

Level 3.7 programs provide a planned and structured regimen of 24-hour professionally directed evaluation, observation, medical monitoring, and addiction treatment in an inpatient setting. They feature permanent facilities, including inpatient beds, and function under a defined set of policies, procedures, and clini-

cal protocols. They are appropriate for patients whose subacute biomedical and emotional, behavioral, or cognitive problems are so severe that they require inpatient treatment, but who do not need the full resources of an acute care general hospital or a medically managed inpatient treatment program.

Adolescent-Specific Considerations: Level 3.7

For adolescents, problems in Dimension 3 probably are the most common reason for admission to Level 3.7 programs. Such problems include co-occurring psychiatric disorders (such as depressive disorders, bipolar disorders, and attention deficit hyperactivity disorder) or symptoms (such as hypomania, severe lability, mood dysregulation, disorganization or impulsiveness, or aggressive behaviors). Because mental health symptoms exist on a continuum of severity, specific problems may fall short of the criteria for diagnoses of specific disorders but still require treatment in a Level 3.7 program. For example, an adolescent's high level of inattention and distractibility may significantly interfere with his or her addiction recovery efforts, but not warrant a diagnosis of ADHD. An adolescent's behavioral symptom of disruptive behavior may require the high intensity staffing found in a Level 3.7 program, but not warrant a diagnosis of a co-occurring mental disorder.

For an adolescent, treatment at Level 3.7 often is necessary simply to orient the adolescent to the structure of daily life, according to other organizing principles than "getting high" and "being high." Initial abstinence through confinement in a Level 3.7 program provides many adolescents who have addiction syndromes with a much-needed reintroduction to their own patterns of emotional and cognitive experience without a nearly constant cloud of intoxication.

The services of a Level 3.7 program are designed to meet the needs of patients who have functional limitations in Dimensions 1, 2, and/or 3. For example, a patient may present with moderate to severe Dimension 1 problems, such as withdrawal risk. Dimension 2 problems could include such comorbid medical problems as poorly controlled asthma, hypertension, or diabetes, or a co-occurring chronic pain disorder that interferes with the patient's ability to engage in a recovery program. Dimension 3 problems would include either a diagnosable comorbid mental disorder or symptoms of such a disorder that are subthreshold and not severe enough to meet diagnostic criteria, but that do interfere with or distract from recovery efforts (for example, anxiety or hypomanic behavior), and thus require the availability of 24-hour nursing and medical interventions.

Because physical and mental health problems exist on a continuum of severity, problems that exist in Dimensions 2 or 3 may fall short of reaching the threshold to meet diagnostic criteria, but still require treatment in a Level 3.7 program. For example, a patient's high level of anxiety distracts him or her from recovery efforts, but falls short of the *DSM* criteria required to meet the diagnosis for an anxiety disorder.

Requirements for admission to a Level 3.7 program indicate that at least one of the two specifications must be in Dimensions 1, 2, or 3. Individuals whose major problems are in Dimensions 4, 5, or 6 are better served by admission to a clinically managed residential program, or by combining an intensive outpatient program or partial hospitalization with a housing or domiciliary/supportive living component.

The care provided in Level 3.7 programs is delivered by an interdisciplinary staff of appropriately credentialed treatment professionals, including addiction-credentialed physicians. The primary focus of treatment is specific to substance-related disorders. The skills of the interdisciplinary team and the availability of support services also can accommodate withdrawal management and/or intensive inpatient treatment of addiction, and/or integrated treatment of co-occurring subacute biomedical and/or emotional, behavioral, or cognitive conditions.

Individuals who have a greater severity of illness in Dimension 1 (withdrawal), Dimension 2 (biomedical conditions), or Dimension 3 (emotional, behavioral, or cognitive complications) require use of more intensive staffing patterns and support services. For example, patients undergoing medical withdrawal management or with co-occurring medical conditions typically require more intensive medical and nursing care than do other patients in a Level 3.7 program.

EXAMPLES OF SERVICE DELIVERY

An example of a Level 3.7 adult program is an inpatient treatment center within the context of an acute care hospital or acute psychiatric unit, or a separate, more intensive unit of a freestanding Level 3.5 residential facility. An example of a Level 3.7 adolescent program is an inpatient or medical model residential treatment program (intermediate care facility or residential treatment center).

SETTING

Level 3.7 program services may be offered in a (usually) freestanding, appropriately licensed facility located in a community setting, or a specialty unit in a general or psychiatric hospital or other licensed health care facility.

SUPPORT SYSTEMS
All Programs

In Level 3.7 programs, necessary support systems include:

a. Physician monitoring, nursing care, and observation are available. A physician is available to assess the patient in person within 24 hours of admission and thereafter as medically necessary. (In states where physician assistants or nurse practitioners are licensed to provide such services, they may perform the duties designated here for a physician.)

A registered nurse conducts an alcohol or other drug-focused nursing

267 ◀ Tab 4: Level of Care Placement ◀ Chapter 7: Level of Care Placement

⬥ a ⬥ Adolescent-Specific Considerations: Support Systems

In Level 3.7 adolescent programs, necessary support systems include:

a. Physician monitoring and nursing care and observation, available as needed, based on clinical judgment. A physician is available to assess the adolescent in person within 24 hours of admission and thereafter as medically necessary. (In states where physician assistants or nurse practitioners are licensed as physician extenders, they may perform the duties designated here for a physician.) An appropriately trained and licensed nurse conducts an alcohol or other drug-focused nursing assessment at the time of admission and is responsible for monitoring the patient's progress and for medication administration.
b. Additional medical specialty consultation, psychological, laboratory, and toxicology services are available through consultation or referral.
c. Direct affiliation with other levels of care.

In Level 3.7-WM programs, support systems feature availability of specialized clinical consultation and supervision for biomedical, emotional, or behavioral problems related to intoxication and withdrawal management.

LEVEL 3.7 ❹

assessment at the time of admission. An appropriately credentialed and licensed nurse is responsible for monitoring the patient's progress and for medication administration.

b. Additional medical specialty consultation, psychological, laboratory, and toxicology services are available on-site, through consultation or referral.

c. Coordination of necessary services or other levels of care are available through direct affiliation or referral processes (such as step down services for continuing care and/or medical follow-up services).

d. Psychiatric services are available on-site, through consultation or referral when a presenting issue could be attended to at a later time. Such services are available within 8 hours by telephone or 24 hours in person.

Co-Occurring Enhanced Programs

In addition to the support systems described above, Level 3.7 co-occurring enhanced programs offer appropriate psychiatric services, medication evaluation, and laboratory services.

A psychiatrist assesses the patient within 4 hours of admission by telephone and within 24 hours following admission in person, or sooner, as appropriate to the patient's behavioral health condition, and thereafter as medically necessary (the services of another physician may be required for biomedical concerns). A registered nurse or licensed mental health clinician conducts a behavioral health-focused assessment at the time of admission. If not done by an RN, a separate nursing assessment must be done. A registered nurse is responsible for monitoring the patient's progress and administering or monitoring the patient's self-administration of psychotropic medications.

STAFF
All Programs
Level 3.7 programs are staffed by:

a. An interdisciplinary staff (including physicians, nurses, addiction counselors, and behavioral health specialists), who are able to assess and treat the patient and to obtain and interpret information regarding the patient's psychiatric and substance use or addictive disorders.

b. Clinical staff knowledgeable about the biological and psychosocial dimensions of addiction and other behavioral health disorders, and with specialized training in behavior management techniques and evidence-based practices. The staff is able to provide a planned regimen of 24-hour professionally directed evaluation, care, and treatment services (including administration of prescribed medications).

c. A licensed physician to oversee the treatment process and assure the quality of care. Physicians perform physical examinations for all patients admitted to this level of care. Many states require that the physician serving as medical director for a Level 3.7 treatment program be a certified addiction medicine physician or addiction psychiatrist. These physicians have specialty training and/or experience in addiction medicine or addiction psychiatry and if treating adolescents, experience with adolescent medicine. Many patients in this level of care receive addiction pharmacotherapy, integrated with psychosocial therapies. The provider of such care can be a physician assistant or other licensed independent practitioner with prescribing authority, but should be knowledgeable about addiction treatment, especially pharmacotherapies.

Biomedical Enhanced Services

Biomedical enhanced services are delivered by appropriately credentialed medical staff, who are available to assess and treat co-occurring biomedical disorders, and to monitor the patient's administration of medications in accordance with a physician's prescription.

The intensity of nursing care and observation is sufficient to meet the patient's needs. Biomedical enhanced Level 3.7 programs are usually staffed by a certified addiction specialist physician, often with additional certification in a general medical specialty.

Co-Occurring Enhanced Programs

In addition to the staff listed here, Level 3.7 co-occurring enhanced programs are staffed by addiction psychiatrists and appropriately credentialed behavioral health professionals,

LEVEL 3.7

4

Adolescent-Specific Considerations: Staff

In addition to the specifications for staff for all services, staff should be knowledgeable about adolescent development and experienced in engaging and working with adolescents. Experience in adolescent medicine is ideal.

When a Level 3.7 program provides withdrawal management services to adolescents, it must provide (in addition to the staff and therapies listed above) a physician who is routinely available by telephone 24 hours a day. In states where physician assistants or nurse practitioners are licensed as physician extenders, they may perform the duties designated for a physician.

who are able to assess and treat co-occurring psychiatric disorders and who have specialized training in behavior management techniques and evidence-based practices. Co-occurring enhanced Level 3.7 programs are ideally staffed by a certified addiction specialist physician along with a general psychiatrist, or by a physician certified as an addiction psychiatrist.

Some (if not all) of the addiction treatment professionals should have sufficient cross-training to understand the signs and symptoms of psychiatric disorders and to understand and explain to the patient the purposes of psychotropic medications and their interactions with substance use.

The intensity of nursing care and observation is sufficient to meet the patient's needs.

THERAPIES
All Programs

Therapies offered by Level 3.7 programs include:

a. Daily clinical services (provided by an interdisciplinary treatment team) to assess and address the patient's individual needs. Clinical services may involve appropriate medical and nursing services, individual, group, family, and activity services.

b. Planned clinical program activities to stabilize the acute addictive and/or psychiatric symptoms. Activities may include pharmacological, cognitive-behavioral, and other therapies administered to the patient on an individual and/or group basis. Such activities are adapted to the patient's level of comprehension.

c. Counseling and clinical monitoring to promote successful initial involvement or reinvolvement in, and skill building for, regular, productive daily activity, such as work or school and, as indicated, successful reintegration into family living.

d. Random drug screening to monitor drug use and reinforce treatment gains, as appropriate to the patient's individual treatment plan.

e. Regular monitoring of the patient's adherence in taking any prescribed medications.

f. Planned clinical program activities, designed to enhance the patient's understanding of his or her substance use and/or mental disorder.

g. Health education services associated with the course of addiction and other potential health-related risk factors as appropriate (for example: HIV, hepatitis C, sexually transmitted diseases).

h. Evidence-based practices, such as motivational enhancement strategies and interventions appropriate to the patient's stage of readiness to change, designed to facilitate the patient's understanding of the relationship between his or her substance use disorder and attendant life issues.

i. Daily treatment services to manage acute symptoms of the patient's biomedical, substance use, or mental disorder.

j. Services for the patient's family and significant others.

Co-Occurring Enhanced Programs

In addition to the therapies described above, Level 3.7 co-occurring enhanced programs offer planned clinical activities designed to promote stabilization of the patient's behavioral health needs and psychiatric symptoms, and to promote such stabilization.

The goals of therapy apply to both the substance use disorder and any co-occurring mental health disorder.

Specific attention is given to medication education and management, to motivational

Adolescent-Specific Considerations: Therapies

In addition to the therapies listed here for all programs, educational services are provided in accordance with local regulations (typically on-site) and are designed to maintain the educational and intellectual development of the adolescent and, when indicated, to provide opportunities to remedy deficits in the educational level of adolescents who have fallen behind because of their involvement with alcohol and other drugs.

An interdisciplinary team provides daily clinical services to assess and address the adolescent's withdrawal status and service needs. Such clinical services may include nursing or medical monitoring, pharmacologic therapies as needed, individual or group therapy specific to withdrawal, and withdrawal support.

Frequent nurse monitoring of the adolescent's progress in withdrawal management and medication administration is available, if needed.

and engagement strategies and other evidence-based practices, which are used in preference to confrontational approaches. **NOTE:** The therapies previously described encompass Level 3.7 co-occurring enhanced program services for patients who are able to tolerate and benefit from a planned program of therapies. Other patients—especially those with severe and chronic mental illness—may not be able to benefit from such a program until further stabilized. Once stabilized, the patient and staff will plan for appropriate services to maintain stabilization, such as intensive case management, medication management, psychotherapy, and ongoing addiction treatment.

ASSESSMENT/TREATMENT PLAN REVIEW
All Programs

In Level 3.7 programs, the assessment and treatment plan review include:

a. A physical examination, performed by a physician within 24 hours of admission, or a review and update by a facility physician within 24 hours of admission of the record of a physical examination conducted no more than 7 days prior to admission.

b. A comprehensive nursing assessment, performed at the time of admission.

c. An individualized, comprehensive biopsychosocial assessment of the patient's substance use disorder and co-occurring disorder, conducted or updated by staff who are knowledgeable about addiction treatment, to confirm the appropriateness of placement at Level 3.7 and to guide the individualized treatment planning process.

d. An individualized treatment plan, which includes problem formulation and articulation of short-term, measurable treatment goals, and activities designed to achieve those goals. The plan is developed in collaboration with the patient, reflects the patient's personal goals, and incorporates the patient's strengths. The treatment plan also reflects case management conducted

> ### a Adolescent-Specific Considerations: Assessment and Treatment Planning
>
> Elements of the assessment and treatment plan review should also include:
>
> a. An initial withdrawal assessment within 24 hours of admission, or earlier if clinically warranted.
> b. Daily nursing withdrawal monitoring assessments and continuous availability of nursing evaluation.
> c. Daily availability of medical evaluation, with continuous on-call coverage.

by on-site staff; coordination of related addiction treatment, health care, mental health, social, vocational, or housing services (provided concurrently); and the integration of services at this and other levels of care.

Co-Occurring Enhanced Programs

In addition to the assessment and treatment plan review activities just described, Level 3.7 co-occurring enhanced programs provide a review of the patient's recent psychiatric history and mental status examination. (If necessary, this review is conducted by a psychiatrist.) A comprehensive examination and psychodiagnostic assessment are performed within a reasonable time, as determined by the patient's needs and progress in treatment.

Level 3.7 co-occurring enhanced programs also provide active reassessments of the patient's mental status, at a frequency determined by the urgency of the patient's psychiatric condition. The treatment plan will be adjusted accordingly. The patient's history of follow through with behavioral health treatment and adherence with psychotropic medications is also assessed and addressed in the treatment plan.

Level 3.7 co-occurring enhanced programs are able to provide a psychiatric assessment, to be performed within 24 hours of admission.

NOTE: Certain patients may need the kinds of assessment and treatment services described here for co-occurring enhanced programs, but at a reduced level of frequency and comprehensiveness to match the greater stability of the patient's mental health problems. For such patients, placement in a co-occurring capable program may be appropriate.

DOCUMENTATION
All Programs

Documentation standards for Level 3.7 programs include individualized progress notes in the patient's record that clearly reflect implementation of the treatment plan, and the patient's response to therapeutic interventions for all disorders treated, as well as subsequent amendments to the plan.

Treatment plan reviews are conducted and recorded in the treatment plan and updated at a frequency relevant to the patient's level of stability and severity of illness.

Co-Occurring Enhanced Programs

In addition to the information described above, Level 3.7 co-occurring enhanced programs document the patient's mental health problems, the relationship between the mental and substance use disorders, and the patient's overall assessment of functioning and mental status.

LEVEL 3.7
4

ADULT DIAGNOSTIC ADMISSION CRITERIA

All Programs

The patient who is appropriately placed in a Level 3.7 program meets the diagnostic criteria for a moderate or severe substance use or addictive disorder, as defined in the current *Diagnostic and Statistical Manual of Mental Disorders* (*DSM*) of the American Psychiatric Association or other standardized and widely accepted criteria, as well as the dimensional criteria for admission.

If the patient's presenting history is conflicting or inadequate to substantiate such a diagnosis, the probability of such a diagnosis may be determined from information provided by collateral parties (such as family members, legal guardians, and significant others).

NOTE: Patients in Level 3.7 co-occurring capable programs may have co-occurring mental disorders that meet the stability criteria for placement in a co-occurring capable program; or difficulties with mood, behavior, or cognition related to a substance use or mental disorder; or emotional, behavioral, or cognitive symptoms that interfere with overall functioning but do not meet the *DSM* criteria for a mental disorder.

Co-Occurring Enhanced Programs

The patient who is appropriately admitted to a Level 3.7 co-occurring enhanced program meets the diagnostic criteria for a mental disorder as well as a substance use or addictive disorder, as defined in the current *Diagnostic and Statistical Manual of Mental Disorders* (*DSM*) of the American Psychiatric Association or other standardized and widely accepted criteria, as well as the dimensional criteria for admission.

If the patient's presenting history is conflicting or inadequate to substantiate such a diagnosis, the probability of such a diagnosis may be determined from information obtained by collateral parties (such as family members, legal guardians, and significant others).

ADULT DIMENSIONAL ADMISSION CRITERIA

All Programs
The patient who is appropriately admitted to a Level 3.7 program meets specifications in at least **two** of the six dimensions, at least **one** of which is in Dimension 1, 2, or 3.

DIMENSION 1:
Acute Intoxication and/or
Withdrawal Potential

All Programs
See separate withdrawal management chapter for how to approach "unbundled" withdrawal management for adults.

All Programs
The patient's status in Dimension 2 is characterized by **one** of the following:
   a. The interaction of the patient's biomedical condition and continued alcohol and/or other drug use places the patient at significant risk of serious damage to physical health or concomitant biomedical conditions (such as pregnancy with vaginal bleeding or ruptured membranes, unstable diabetes, etc.);
   or
   b. A current biomedical condition requires 24-hour nursing and medical monitoring or active treatment, but not the full resources of an acute care hospital.

DIMENSION 2:
Biomedical Conditions and
Complications

Biomedical Enhanced Services
The patient who has a biomedical problem that requires a degree of staff attention (such as monitoring of medications or assistance with mobility) or staff intervention (such as changes in medication) that is not available in other Level 3.7 programs is in need of biomedical enhanced services.

LEVEL 3.7 ④

ADULT DIMENSIONAL ADMISSION CRITERIA (CONTINUED)

All Programs

The patient who is appropriately admitted to a Level 3.7 program meets specifications in at least **two** of the six dimensions, at least **one** of which is in Dimension 1, 2, or 3.

DIMENSION 3:
Emotional, Behavioral, or Cognitive Conditions and Complications

3

LEVEL 3.7

4

All Programs

Problems in Dimension 3 are not necessary for admission to a Level 3.7 program. However, if any of the Dimension 3 conditions are present, the patient must be admitted to a co-occurring capable or co-occurring enhanced program (depending on his or her level of function, stability, and degree of impairment).

Co-Occurring Capable Programs

The patient's status in Dimension 3 is characterized by at least **one** of the following:

a. The patient's psychiatric condition is unstable and presents with symptoms (which may include compulsive behaviors, suicidal or homicidal ideation with a recent history of attempts but no specific plan, or hallucinations and delusions without acute risk to self or others) that are interfering with abstinence, recovery, and stability to such a degree that the patient needs a structured 24-hour, medically monitored (but not medically managed) environment to address recovery efforts;

or

b. The patient exhibits stress behaviors associated with recent or threatened losses in work, family, or social domains; or there is a reemergence of feelings and memories of trauma and loss once the patient achieves abstinence, to a degree that his or her ability to manage the activities of daily living is significantly impaired. The patient thus requires a secure, medically monitored environment in which to address self-care problems (such as those associated with eating, sleeplessness, or personal hygiene) and to focus on his or her substance use or behavioral health problems;

or

c. The patient has significant functional limitations that require active psychiatric monitoring. They may include—but are not limited to—problems with activities of daily living; problems with self-care, lethality, or dangerousness; and problems with social functioning. These limitations may be complicated by problems in Dimensions 2 through 6;

or

d. The patient is at moderate risk of behaviors endangering self, others, or property, likely to result in imminent incarceration or loss of custody of children, and/or is in imminent danger of relapse (with dangerous emotional, behavioral, or cognitive consequences) without the 24-hour support and structure of a Level 3.7 program;

or

e. The patient is actively intoxicated, with resulting violent or disruptive behavior that poses imminent danger to self or others. Such a patient may, on further evaluation, belong in Level 4-WM withdrawal management or an acute observational setting if assessed as not safe in a Level 3.7 service;

or

f. The patient is psychiatrically unstable or has cognitive limitations that require stabilization but not medical management.

Co-Occurring Enhanced Programs

The patient's status in Dimension 3 is characterized by at least **one** of the following:

a. The patient has a history of moderate psychiatric decompensation (which may involve paranoia; moderate psychotic symptoms; or severe, depressed mood, but not actively suicidal); or such symptoms occur during discontinuation of addictive drugs or when experiencing post-acute withdrawal symptoms, and such decompensation is present;

ADULT DIMENSIONAL ADMISSION CRITERIA (CONTINUED)

All Programs

The patient who is appropriately admitted to a Level 3.7 program meets specifications in at least ***two*** of the six dimensions, at least ***one*** of which is in Dimension 1, 2, or 3.

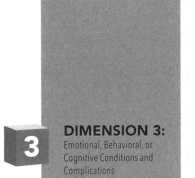

DIMENSION 3:
Emotional, Behavioral, or Cognitive Conditions and Complications

or

b. The patient is assessed as at moderate to high risk of behaviors endangering self, others or property, or is in imminent danger of relapse (with dangerous emotional, behavioral, or cognitive consequences) without 24-hour structure and support and medically monitored treatment. For example, without medically monitored inpatient treatment, the patient does not have sufficient coping skills to avoid harm to self, others, or property because of co-occurring mania;

or

c. The patient is severely depressed, with suicidal urges and a plan. However, he or she is able to reach out for help as needed and does not require a one-on-one suicide watch;

or

d. The patient has a co-occurring psychiatric disorder (such as anxiety, distractibility, or depression) that is interfering with his or her addiction treatment or ability to participate in a less intensive level of care, and thus requires stabilization with psychotropic medications;

or

e. The patient has a co-occurring psychiatric disorder of moderate to high severity that is marginally and tenuously stable and requires care to prevent further decompensation. The patient thus requires co-occurring enhanced services and is best served in an addiction treatment program with integrated mental health services, or in a mental health program with integrated addiction treatment services.

All Programs

The patient's status in Dimension 4 is characterized by at least ***one*** of the following:

a. Despite experiencing serious consequences or effects of the addictive disorder and/or behavioral health problem, the patient does not accept or relate the addictive disorder to the severity of the presenting problem;

or

b. The patient is in need of intensive motivating strategies, activities, and processes available only in a 24-hour structured, medically monitored setting;

or

c. The patient needs ongoing 24-hour psychiatric monitoring to assure follow through with the treatment regimen, and to deal with issues such as ambivalence about adherence to psychiatric medications and a recovery program.

DIMENSION 4:
Readiness to Change

Co-Occurring Enhanced Programs

The patient's status in Dimension 4 is characterized by no commitment to change and no interest in engaging in activities necessary to address a co-occurring psychiatric disorder. For example, the patient with bipolar disorder prefers his or her manic state over what feels like depression when stabilized, and thus does not adhere to a regimen of mood-stabilizing medications.

Similarly, the patient is not consistently able to follow through with treatment, or demonstrates minimal awareness of a problem, or is unaware of the need to change behaviors related to behavioral or health problems. Such an individual requires active interventions with family, significant others, and/or other external systems to create leverage and align incentives so as to promote engagement in treatment, and is appropriately placed in a Level 3.7 co-occurring enhanced program.

ADULT DIMENSIONAL ADMISSION CRITERIA (CONTINUED)

All Programs

The patient who is appropriately admitted to a Level 3.7 program meets specifications in at least **two** of the six dimensions, at least **one** of which is in Dimension 1, 2, or 3.

DIMENSION 5:
Relapse, Continued Use, or Continued Problem Potential

All Programs

The patient's status in Dimension 5 is characterized by at least **one** of the following:

a. The patient is experiencing an acute psychiatric or substance use crisis, marked by intensification of symptoms of his or her addictive or mental disorder (such as poor impulse control, drug seeking behavior, or increasing severity of anxiety or depressive symptoms). This situation poses a serious risk of harm to self or others in the absence of 24-hour monitoring and structured support;

or

b. The patient is experiencing an escalation of relapse behaviors and/or reemergence of acute symptoms, which places the patient at serious risk to self or others in the absence of the type of 24-hour monitoring and structured support found in a medically monitored setting (for example, Driving Under the Influence (DUI), or not taking life-sustaining medications);

or

c. The modality or intensity of treatment protocols to address relapse require that the patient receive care in a Level 3.7 program (such as initiating or restarting medications for medical or psychiatric conditions, an acute stress disorder, or the processing of a traumatic event) to safely and effectively initiate antagonist therapy (such as naltrexone for severe opioid use disorder), or agonist therapy (such as methadone or buprenorphine for severe opioid use disorder).

Co-Occurring Enhanced Programs

The patient's status in Dimension 5 is characterized by psychiatric symptoms that pose a moderate to high risk of relapse to a substance use or mental disorder. Such a patient demonstrates limited ability to apply relapse prevention skills, as well as demonstrating poor skills in coping with psychiatric disorders and/or avoiding or limiting relapse, with imminent serious consequences.

The patient's follow through in treatment is limited or inconsistent, and his or her relapse problems are escalating to such a degree that treatment at a less intensive level of care is not succeeding or not feasible.

For example, the patient continues to evidence self-harm behaviors or suicidal ideation or impulses with a plan to commit suicide, but agrees to reach out if seriously suicidal, and is assessed as capable of enough internal control to do so. Or the patient's continuing substance-induced mood states or psychotic symptoms are resolving, but his or her difficulties in remaining abstinent and craving for use are exacerbating his or her psychiatric symptoms.

DIMENSION 6:
Recovery Environment

All Programs

The patient's status in Dimension 6 is characterized by at least **one** of the following:

a. The patient requires continuous medical monitoring while addressing his or her substance use and/or psychiatric symptoms because his or her current living situation is characterized by a high risk of initiation or repetition of physical, sexual, or emotional abuse, or active substance use, such that the patient is assessed as being unable to achieve or maintain recovery at a less intensive level of care. For example, the patient is involved in an abusive relationship with an actively using significant other;

ADULT DIMENSIONAL ADMISSION CRITERIA (CONTINUED)

All Programs
The patient who is appropriately admitted to a Level 3.7 program meets specifications in at least **two** of the six dimensions, at least **one** of which is in Dimension 1, 2, or 3.

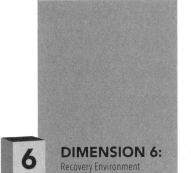

or

b. Family members or significant others living with the patient are not supportive of his or her recovery goals and are actively sabotaging treatment, or their behavior jeopardizes recovery efforts. This situation requires structured treatment services and relief from the home environment in order for the patient to focus on recovery;

or

c. The patient is unable to cope, for even limited periods of time, outside of 24-hour care. The patient needs staff monitoring to learn to cope with Dimension 6 problems before he or she can be transferred safely to a less intensive setting.

DIMENSION 6:
Recovery Environment

Co-Occurring Enhanced Programs
The patient's status in Dimension 6 is characterized by severe psychiatric symptoms. He or she may be too compromised to benefit from skills training to learn to cope with problems in the recovery environment. Such a patient requires planning for assertive community treatment, intensive case management, or other community outreach and support services.

Such a patient's living, working, social, and/or community environment is not supportive of addiction and/or psychiatric recovery. He or she has insufficient resources and skills to deal with this situation. For example, the patient may be unable to cope with a hostile family member with alcohol use disorder, and thus exhibits increasing anxiety and depression. Such a patient needs the support and structure of a Level 3.7 co-occurring enhanced program to achieve stabilization and prevent further decompensation.

ADOLESCENT DIAGNOSTIC ADMISSION CRITERIA

The adolescent who is appropriately placed in a Level 3.7 program meets the diagnostic criteria for a moderate or severe substance use or addictive disorder, as defined in the current *Diagnostic and Statistical Manual of Mental Disorders* (*DSM*) of the American Psychiatric Association or other standardized and widely accepted criteria, as well as the dimensional criteria for admission.

If the adolescent's presenting history is conflicting or inadequate to substantiate such a diagnosis, the probability of such a diagnosis may be determined from information provided by collateral parties (such as family members, legal guardians, and significant others).

ADOLESCENT DIMENSIONAL ADMISSION CRITERIA

The adolescent who is appropriately admitted to a Level 3.7 program meets specifications in **two** of the six dimensions, at least **one** of which is in Dimension 1, 2, or 3.

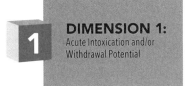

DIMENSION 1:
Acute Intoxication and/or Withdrawal Potential

The adolescent's status in Dimension 1 is characterized by the following:

The adolescent is experiencing or at risk of acute or subacute intoxication or withdrawal, with moderate to severe signs and symptoms. He or she needs 24-hour treatment services, including the availability of active medical and nursing monitoring to manage withdrawal, support engagement in treatment, and prevent immediate continued use. Alternatively, the adolescent has a history of failure in treatment at the same or a less intensive level of care.

LEVEL 3.7 ④

ADOLESCENT DIMENSIONAL ADMISSION CRITERIA (CONTINUED)

The adolescent who is appropriately admitted to a Level 3.7 program meets specifications in **two** of the six dimensions, at least **one** of which is in Dimension 1, 2, or 3.

DIMENSION 1:
Acute Intoxication and/or
Withdrawal Potential

Problems with intoxication or withdrawal are manageable at this level of care.

Withdrawal rating scale tables and flow sheets (which may include tabulation of vital signs) are used as needed.

Drug-specific examples follow:

    a. **Alcohol:** Moderate withdrawal, with significant symptoms that require access to nursing and medical monitoring. The patient may have a history of daily drinking or drinking to self-medicate withdrawal, or regular morning drinking. He or she may require sedative/hypnotic substitution therapy, but typically this can be managed with a standing taper without the need for extensive titration.

    b. **Sedative/hypnotics:** Moderate withdrawal, with significant symptoms that require access to nursing and medical monitoring. The adolescent may be cross-dependent on other substances and may require withdrawal management with tapering substitute agonist therapy and/or pharmacological management of symptoms.

    c. **Opiates:** Moderate to severe withdrawal, usually in the context of daily opiate use. The patient requires access to nursing and medical monitoring, may require use of prescription medications or agonist substitution therapy, and may need monitoring for induction of antagonist therapy (as with naltrexone). Severe craving states or affective instability typical of withdrawal may require high-intensity 24-hour treatment to support engagement.

    d. **Stimulants:** Severe withdrawal (involving sustained affective or behavioral disturbances or mild psychotic symptoms), which requires access to nursing and medical monitoring. Severe craving states or affective instability typical of withdrawal may require high-intensity 24-hour treatment to support engagement.

    e. **Inhalants:** Severe subacute intoxication (involving mild delirium or other serious cognitive impairment, lethargy, agitation, and depression) of sufficient intensity that the patient requires access to nursing and medical monitoring.

    f. **Marijuana:** Severe sustained intoxication (involving mild psychosis, coarse cognitive disorganization, agitation, and the like), which requires access to nursing and medical monitoring.

    g. **Hallucinogens:** Severe chronic intoxication (involving mild delirium, mild psychosis, agitation, moderate to severe affective instability, cognitive disorganization, and the like), which requires access to nursing and medical monitoring.

DIMENSION 2:
Biomedical Conditions and
Complications

The adolescent's status in Dimension 2 is characterized by **one** of the following:

    a. The interaction of the adolescent's biomedical condition and continued alcohol and/or other drug use places the adolescent at significant risk of serious damage to physical health or concomitant biomedical conditions (such as pregnancy with vaginal bleeding or ruptured membranes, unstable diabetes or asthma, etc.);

    or

    b. A current biomedical condition requires 24-hour nursing and medical monitoring or active treatment, but not the full resources of an acute care hospital.

Biomedical Enhanced Services

The adolescent who has a biomedical problem that requires a degree of staff attention (such as monitoring of medications or assistance with mobility) or staff intervention (such as changes in medication) that is not available in other Level 3.7 programs is in need of biomedical enhanced services.

LEVEL 3.7

4

ADOLESCENT DIMENSIONAL ADMISSION CRITERIA (CONTINUED)

The adolescent who is appropriately admitted to a Level 3.7 program meets specifications in **two** of the six dimensions, at least **one** of which is in Dimension 1, 2, or 3.

DIMENSION 3:
Emotional, Behavioral, or Cognitive Conditions and Complications

The adolescent's status in Dimension 3 is characterized by at least **one** of the following (requiring 24-hour supervision and a high-intensity therapeutic milieu, with access to nursing and medical monitoring and treatment):

a. **Dangerousness/Lethality:** The adolescent is at moderate (and possibly unpredictable) risk of imminent harm to self or others and needs 24-hour monitoring and/or treatment in a high-intensity programmatic milieu and/or enforced secure placement for safety.

b. **Interference with Addiction Recovery Efforts:** The adolescent's recovery efforts are negatively affected by his or her emotional, behavioral, or cognitive problems in significant and distracting ways. He or she requires 24-hour structured therapy and/or a high-intensity programmatic milieu to stabilize unstable emotional or behavioral problems (as through ongoing medical or nursing evaluation, behavior modification, titration of medications, and the like).

c. **Social Functioning:** The adolescent has significant impairments, with severe symptoms (such as poor impulse control, disorganization, and the like), which seriously impair his or her ability to function in family, social, school, or work settings and which cannot be managed at a less intensive level of care. These might involve a recent history of aggressive or severely disruptive behavior, severe inability to manage peer conflict, a recurrent or chronic pattern of runaway behavior requiring enforced confinement, and the like.

d. **Ability for Self-Care:** The adolescent has a significant lack of personal resources and moderate to severe impairment in ability to manage the activities of daily living. He or she thus needs 24-hour supervision and significant staff assistance, including access to nursing or medical services. The adolescent's impairments may involve progressive and severe dilapidation and self-neglect in the context of advanced substance use disorder, the need for observation after eating to prevent self-induced vomiting, the need for intensive reinforcement of medication adherence, the need for intensive modeling of adequate self-care during pregnancy, the need for intensive training for self-care in a cognitively impaired patient, and the like.

e. **Course of Illness:** The adolescent's history and present situation suggest that an emotional, behavioral, or cognitive condition would become unstable without 24-hour supervision and a high-intensity structured programmatic milieu, with access to nursing or medical monitoring or treatment. These may be required to treat an adolescent who, for example, requires secure placement or enforced abstinence for reinstatement or titration of a pharmacological treatment regimen; or an adolescent whose substance use has been associated with a dangerous pattern of aggressive/violent behaviors and who needs monitoring to assess safety and likelihood of outpatient treatment success before returning to the community following release from a juvenile justice setting; or an adolescent who requires intensive monitoring or treatment because ongoing substance use prevents adequate or safe treatment or diagnostic clarification for an emotional, behavioral, or cognitive condition that may or may not be substance-induced; or an adolescent whose history suggests rapid escalation of dangerousness/lethality when using alcohol or drugs and who is in relapse or at imminent risk of relapse.

DIMENSION 4:
Readiness to Change

The adolescent's status in Dimension 4 is characterized by at least **one** of the following:

a. Despite experiencing serious consequences or effects of the addictive disorder and/or behavioral health problem, the adolescent does not accept or relate the addictive disorder to the severity of the presenting problem;

ADOLESCENT DIMENSIONAL ADMISSION CRITERIA (CONTINUED)

The adolescent who is appropriately admitted to a Level 3.7 program meets specifications in **two** of the six dimensions, at least **one** of which is in Dimension 1, 2, or 3.

DIMENSION 4:
Readiness to Change

or

b. The adolescent is in need of intensive motivating strategies, activities, and processes available only in a 24-hour structured, medically monitored setting;

or

c. The adolescent needs ongoing 24-hour psychiatric monitoring to assure follow through with the treatment regimen, and to deal with issues such as ambivalence about adherence to psychiatric medications and a recovery program.

The adolescent's status in Dimension 5 is characterized by at least **one** of the following:

a. The adolescent is experiencing an acute psychiatric or substance use crisis, marked by intensification of symptoms of his or her addictive or mental disorder (such as poor impulse control, drug seeking behavior, or increasing severity of anxiety or depressive symptoms). This situation poses a serious risk of harm to self or others in the absence of 24-hour monitoring and structured support;

or

b. The adolescent is experiencing an escalation of relapse behaviors and/or reemergence of acute symptoms, which places the patient at serious risk to self or others in the absence of the type of 24-hour monitoring and structured support found in a medically monitored setting (for example, not taking life-sustaining medications; or the adolescent has severe and chronic problems with impulse control that require stabilization through high-intensity medical and nursing interventions; or he or she has issues with intoxication or withdrawal that require stabilization in a medically monitored setting; or there is a likelihood of self-medication of recurrent symptoms of a mood disorder, which require stabilization in a medically monitored setting). Treatment at a less intensive level of care has been attempted or given serious consideration.

or

c. The modality or intensity of treatment protocols to address relapse require that the patient receive care in a Level 3.7 program (such as initiating or restarting medications for medical or psychiatric conditions, an acute stress disorder, or the processing of a traumatic event; to safely and effectively initiate antagonist therapy (such as naltrexone for severe opioid use disorder), or agonist therapy (such as methadone or buprenorphine for severe opioid use disorder).

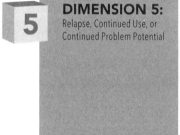

DIMENSION 5:
Relapse, Continued Use, or
Continued Problem Potential

LEVEL 3.7

The adolescent's status in Dimension 6 is characterized by **one** of the following:

a. The adolescent has been living in an environment in which supports that might otherwise have enabled treatment at a less intensive level of care are unavailable. For example, the family undermines the adolescent's treatment, or is unable to sustain treatment attendance at a less intensive level of care, or family members have active substance use disorders and/or facilitate access to alcohol or other drugs, or the home environment is dangerously chaotic or abusive, or the family is unable to adequately supervise medications, or the family is unable to adequately implement a needed behavior management plan. Level 3.7 care thus is needed to effect a change in the home environment so as to establish a successful transition to a less intensive level of care.

or

b. Logistical impediments (such as distance from a treatment facility, mobility limitations, lack of transportation, and the like) preclude participation in treatment at a less intensive level of care, and Level 3.7 care is necessary to establish a successful transition to a less intensive level of care.

DIMENSION 6:
Recovery Environment

Level 4
Medically Managed Intensive Inpatient Services

Level 4, Medically Managed Intensive Inpatient Services is an organized service delivered in an acute care inpatient setting. It is appropriate for patients whose acute biomedical, emotional, behavioral, and cognitive problems are so severe that they require primary medical and nursing care.

Level 4 program services are delivered by an interdisciplinary staff of addiction-credentialed physicians and other appropriately credentialed treatment professionals. Such a program encompasses a regimen of medically directed evaluation and treatment services, provided in a 24-hour treatment setting, under a defined set of policies, procedures, and individualized clinical protocols.

By definition, Level 4 medically managed services are managed by a physician who is responsible for diagnosis, treatment, and treatment plan decisions in collaboration with the patient. Those decisions encompass whether and when to admit the patient, con-

Adolescent-Specific Considerations: Withdrawal Management

Dimension 1 (Acute Intoxication and/or Withdrawal Potential) is the first of the six assessment dimensions to be evaluated in making treatment and placement decisions. The range of clinical severity in this dimension has given rise to a range of withdrawal management levels of service.

As used here, withdrawal management refers not only to the attenuation of the physiological and psychological features of withdrawal syndromes, but also to the process of interrupting the momentum of habitual compulsive use in adolescents diagnosed with high-severity substance use disorder. Because of the force of this momentum, and the inherent difficulties in overcoming it even when there is no clear withdrawal syndrome *per se,* this phase of treatment frequently requires a greater intensity of services initially in order to establish treatment engagement and patient role induction. This is, of course, critical to the course of treatment because it is impossible to engage the adolescent in treatment while he or she is caught up in the cycle of frequent intoxication and recovery from intoxication.

Level 4-WM services are delivered under a defined set of physician-approved policies and physician-managed procedures or medical protocols. This level is appropriate for the adolescent whose withdrawal signs and symptoms are so severe that he or she needs primary medical and nursing care services, including 24-hour observation, monitoring, and treatment.

The treatment is specific to acute medical withdrawal management. However, the call for a multidisciplinary team and the availability of support services emphasize the importance of assessing and developing a care plan for any treatment priorities identified in Dimensions 2 through 6.

LEVEL 4

tinue a patient in care, and when to transfer or discharge the patient from this level of care. As Level 4 offers specialty addiction services, the physician staffing such services is usually an addiction specialist physician.

Treatment is provided 24 hours a day in a permanent facility with inpatient beds. The full resources of a general acute care or psychiatric hospital are available. Although treatment is specific to substance use and other addictive disorders, the skills of the interdisciplinary team and the availability of support services, including medical consultation services, allow the joint treatment of any co-occurring biomedical conditions and mental disorders that need to be addressed.

Length of Service

The duration of treatment varies with the severity of the patient's illness and his or her response to treatment.

Co-Occurring Mental and Substance-Related Disorders

The services of a Level 4 program are appropriate for patients who have severe, unstable mental and substance use disorders, which at times may be complicated by significant medical issues. Such disorders typically require a range of medical, nursing, and other clinical interventions that can be delivered safely only in a 24-hour medically managed setting. They may include:

a. Co-occurring severe substance-related and mental disorders, such as an acutely suicidal patient who also is acutely in need of medical withdrawal management.

b. Severe intoxication or withdrawal problems or other severe biomedical conditions that occur simultaneously with more stabilized mental health problems.

c. Severe mental health problems that co-occur with more stabilized addiction conditions.

Because Level 4 program services are the most intensive in the continuum of care, their principal focus is the stabilization of the patient and preparation for his or her transfer to a less intensive setting for continuing care.

EXAMPLES OF SERVICE DELIVERY
All Programs

Level 4 programs typically are housed in three types of settings: an acute care general hospital, an acute psychiatric hospital or psychiatric unit within an acute care general hospital, and a licensed addiction treatment specialty hospital with acute care medical and nursing staff.

SETTING
All Programs

Level 4 program services may be offered in any appropriately licensed acute care setting that offers addiction treatment services in concert with intensive biomedical and/or psychiatric services.

Such a program must offer medically directed acute withdrawal management and related treatment designed to alleviate acute emotional, behavioral, cognitive, and/or biomedical distress resulting from, or co-occurring with, a patient's use of alcohol, tobacco, and/or other drugs. The program may provide emergency life support care and treatment—either directly, or through transfer of the patient to another service within the facility, or to another medical facility equipped to provide such care.

Patients who meet the criteria for Dimension 1 may be admitted to a Level 4 program in an acute care general hospital, a psychiatric hospital, or an addiction specialty hospital. Those who meet criteria in Dimension 2 would be admitted to a Level 4 program in an acute care general hospital or an addiction specialty hospital. Those who meet the criteria in Dimension 3 may be admitted to a Level 4 program in a psychiatric specialty hospital or a psychiatric specialty unit in a general hospital.

SUPPORT SYSTEMS
All Programs

In Level 4, necessary support systems

Adolescent-Specific Considerations: Setting

Level 4-WM withdrawal management services may be offered in any appropriately licensed acute care setting that is able to provide medically directed acute withdrawal management and related treatment aimed at alleviating acute emotional, behavioral, or biomedical distress resulting from the adolescent's use of alcohol or other drugs.

At least three types of settings provide this level of care:

a. An acute care general hospital.

b. An acute care psychiatric hospital with ready access to the full resources of an acute care general hospital, or a psychiatric unit in an acute care general hospital.

c. An appropriately licensed addiction specialty hospital with acute care medical and nursing staff and life-support equipment, or an acute care addiction treatment unit in an acute care general hospital.

include a full range of acute care services, specialty consultation, and intensive care.

STAFF
All Programs
Level 4 programs are staffed by:

a. An interdisciplinary team of appropriately credentialed clinical staff (including addiction-credentialed physicians, nurse practitioners, physician assistants, nurses, counselors, psychologists, and social workers) who assess and treat patients with severe substance use disorders, or addicted patients with concomitant acute biomedical, emotional, or behavioral disorders. Staff are knowledgeable about the biopsychosocial dimensions of addiction as well as biomedical, emotional, behavioral, and cognitive disorders. If Level 4 is a specialty addiction service, the physician staffing a Level 4 service is frequently an addiction specialist physician. If Level 4 is an acute psychiatric facility, the physician is ideally an addiction specialist psychiatrist.

b. A team of appropriately trained and credentialed professionals who provide medical management by physicians 24 hours a day, primary nursing care and observation 24 hours a day, and professional counseling services 16 hours a day.

c. Facility-approved addiction counselors or licensed, certified, or registered addiction clinicians who administer planned interventions according to the assessed needs of the patient.

Some, if not all, program staff should have sufficient cross-training to understand the signs and symptoms of mental disorders and to understand and explain the uses of psychotropic medications and their interactions with substance-related disorders.

Co-Occurring Enhanced Programs
In addition to the staff just listed, which encompass co-occurring capable programs, Level 4 co-occurring enhanced programs are staffed by appropriately credentialed mental health professionals, who assess and treat the patient's

LEVEL 4 ④

co-occurring mental disorders. Such staff is knowledgeable about the biological and psycho-social dimensions of psychiatric disorders and their treatment. The staff includes cross-trained and appropriately credentialed addiction and mental health professionals. Level 4 co-occurring or complexity capable programs are ideally led by a certified addiction psychiatrist. Because currently there are insufficient numbers of certified addiction psychiatrists, other leadership possibilities may involve an addiction specialist physician working in collaboration with a psychiatrist consultant; a board-certified psychiatrist working in collaboration with an addiction specialist physician; or an addiction specialist physician who has had further training in psychiatry but is not a board-certified psychiatrist.

 THERAPIES
All Programs
Therapies offered by Level 4 programs include:

a. An individualized array of treatment services for substance use disorders, as well as any concurrent biomedical, emotional, behavioral, or cognitive problems, delivered by an interdisciplinary treatment team.

b. Cognitive, behavioral, motivational, pharmacologic, and other therapies provided on an individual or group basis, depending on the patient's needs. For

the patient who has a severe biomedical disorder, physical health interventions are available to supplement addiction treatment. For the patient who has stable psychiatric symptoms, Level 4 co-occurring capable programs offer individualized treatment activities designed to monitor the patient's mental health, and to address the interaction of the mental health problems and substance use disorders.

c. Health education services.

d. Planned clinical interventions that are designed to enhance the patient's understanding and acceptance of his or her addiction illness.

e. Services for the patient's family, guardian, or significant other(s).

Because the length of stay in a Level 4 program typically is sufficient only to stabilize the patient's acute signs and symptoms, a primary focus of the treatment plan is case management and coordination of care to ensure a smooth transition to continuing treatment at another level of care.

Co-Occurring Enhanced Programs
In addition to the therapies described above, Level 4 co-occurring enhanced programs offer individualized treatment activities designed to

 Adolescent-Specific Considerations: Therapies

Level 4-WM withdrawal management is provided by an interdisciplinary team offering daily clinical services to assess the adolescent patient's withdrawal status and provide treatment as needed. Clinical services involve medical management (including pharmacological treatments, as appropriate) and individual and/or group therapy specific to withdrawal and withdrawal support. Frequent nurse monitoring of the adolescent's progress in withdrawal management is available. Medication administration is available as needed.

stabilize the patient's active psychiatric symptoms. Specific attention is given to medication evaluation and management. Treatment features motivational and engagement strategies, which are used in preference to confrontational approaches.

ASSESSMENT/TREATMENT PLAN REVIEW
All Programs

In Level 4 programs, the assessment and treatment plan review include:

a. A comprehensive nursing assessment, conducted at the time of admission.

b. Physician approval of the admission.

c. A comprehensive history and physical examination, performed by a physician within 12 hours of admission.

d. A comprehensive biopsychosocial assessment, begun at the time of admission.

e. An individualized treatment plan, which includes problem formulation and articulation of short-term, measurable treatment goals and activities designed to achieve those goals. The plan is developed in collaboration with the patient and reflects the patient's personal goals. Treatment plan reviews are conducted at specified times, as noted in the treatment plan.

Co-Occurring Capable Programs

In addition to the assessment and treatment plan activities just described, Level 4 co-occurring capable programs offer skilled assessment and monitoring of the patient's co-occurring mental disorder. However, the primary focus of these programs is the assessment, stabilization, and treatment of the patient's substance-induced intoxication, withdrawal, or biomedical problem(s), rather than the more stable co-occurring mental health problem(s).

Co-Occurring Enhanced Programs

In addition to the assessment and treatment plan activities previously described, staff of Level 4 co-occurring enhanced programs give equal attention to the patient's co-occurring mental disorder. Because acute stabilization usually occurs in a Level 4 program that is focused on the patient's most acute problem, any acute substance-induced psychiatric disorder or co-occurring mental disorder is appropriately addressed at this level of care.

Level 4 co-occurring enhanced programs offer assessment and treatment planning for all aspects of a patient's addiction and mental health needs.

LEVEL 4 ④

 Adolescent-Specific Considerations: Assessment and Treatment Planning

In addition to the assessment and treatment plan activities described here for all programs, an educational assessment should be performed to assist in the design of an appropriate educational program.

Elements of the Level 4-WM assessment and treatment plan review should also include:

a. An initial withdrawal assessment by a physician or nurse, conducted at the time of admission.
b. Daily assessment of the adolescent's withdrawal symptoms and progress during withdrawal management, as well as any amendments to the treatment plan.

DOCUMENTATION

All Programs

Documentation standards for Level 4 programs include individualized progress notes in each patient's record for every shift. Such notes clearly reflect implementation of the treatment plan and the patient's response to therapeutic interventions for all disorders treated, as well as subsequent amendments to the plan.

The focus of documentation is the degree of stabilization of the patient's substance-related disorder and any concurrent biomedical, emotional, behavioral, or cognitive problem(s). Documentation also focuses on the elements of the treatment plan that are related to case management and coordination of care to ensure a smooth transition to continuing service or another level of care.

ADULT DIAGNOSTIC ADMISSION CRITERIA

All Programs

The patient who is appropriately placed in a Level 4 program is assessed as meeting the diagnostic criteria for a substance use or substance-induced disorder, as defined in the current Diagnostic and Statistical Manual of Mental Disorders (DSM) of the American Psychiatric Association or other standardized and widely accepted criteria, as well as the dimensional criteria for admission.

If the patient's presenting alcohol or other drug use history is inadequate to substantiate such a diagnosis, the probability of such a diagnosis may be determined from information submitted by collateral parties (such as family members, legal guardians, and significant others).

Co-Occurring Capable Programs

Some patients have co-occurring mental disorders that meet stability criteria for admission to a co-occurring capable program. Other patients may have difficulties with mood, behavior, or cognition as the result of other psychiatric or substance-induced disorders, or the patient's emotional, behavioral, or cognitive symptoms may be troublesome but not sufficient to meet the criteria for a diagnosed mental disorder.

Co-Occurring Enhanced Programs

In contrast to the diagnostic criteria described above for co-occurring capable programs, the patient who is appropriately placed in a Level 4 co-occurring enhanced program is assessed as meeting the diagnostic criteria for a mental disorder as well as a substance use or substance-induced disorder, as defined in the current Diagnostic and Statistical Manual of Mental Disorders (DSM) of the American Psychiatric Association or other standardized and widely accepted criteria, as well as the dimensional criteria for admission.

If the patient's presenting history is inadequate to substantiate such a diagnosis, the probability of such a diagnosis may be determined from information submitted by collateral parties (such as family members, legal guardians, and significant others).

LEVEL 4

ADULT DIMENSIONAL ADMISSION CRITERIA

All Programs

The patient who is appropriately admitted to a Level 4 program meets specifications in at least **one** of Dimensions 1, 2, or 3.

DIMENSION 1:
Acute Intoxication and/or Withdrawal Potential

All Programs

See separate withdrawal management chapter for how to approach "unbundled" withdrawal management for adults.

DIMENSION 2:
Biomedical Conditions and Complications

All Programs

The patient's status in Dimension 2 is characterized by at least **one** of the following:

a. Biomedical complications of the addictive disorder require medical management and skilled nursing care;

or

b. A concurrent biomedical illness or pregnancy requires stabilization and daily medical management, with daily primary nursing interventions;

or

c. The patient has a concurrent biomedical condition(s) (including pregnancy) in which continued alcohol or other drug use presents an imminent danger to life or severe danger to health;

or

d. The patient is experiencing recurrent or multiple seizures;

or

e. The patient is experiencing a disulfiram-alcohol reaction;

or

f. The patient has life-threatening symptoms (such as stupor or convulsions) that are related to use of alcohol, tobacco, and/or other drugs;

or

g. The patient's alcohol, tobacco, and/or other drug use is gravely complicating or exacerbating a previously diagnosed medical condition;

or

h. Changes in the patient's medical status, such as significant worsening of a medical condition, make abstinence imperative;

or

i. Significant improvement in a previously unstable medical condition allows the patient to respond to addiction treatment;

or

j. The patient has (an)other biomedical problem(s) that requires 24-hour observation and evaluation.

DIMENSION 3:
Emotional, Behavioral, or Cognitive Conditions and Complications

All Programs

The patient whose status in Dimension 3 is characterized by stabilized emotional, behavioral, or cognitive conditions is appropriately assessed as in need of Level 4 co-occurring capable program services.

On the other hand, if the patient's symptoms in Dimension 3 are so severe as to require admission to a Level 4 program, then only a co-occurring enhanced program is sufficient to meet the patient's needs.

LEVEL 4

4

ADULT DIMENSIONAL ADMISSION CRITERIA (CONTINUED)

All Programs
The patient who is appropriately admitted to a Level 4 program meets specifications in at least **one** of Dimensions 1, 2, or 3.

DIMENSION 3:
Emotional, Behavioral, or Cognitive Conditions and Complications

Co-Occurring Enhanced Programs
For admission to a Level 4 co-occurring enhanced program, the patient's status in Dimension 3 is characterized by at least **one** of the following:

    a. Emotional, behavioral, or cognitive complications of the patient's addictive disorder require psychiatric management and skilled nursing care;
       or

    b. A concurrent emotional, behavioral, or cognitive illness requires stabilization, daily psychiatric management, and primary nursing interventions;
       or

    c. The patient's uncontrolled behavior poses an imminent danger to self or others;
       or

    d. The patient's mental confusion or fluctuating orientation poses an imminent danger to self or others (for example, severe self-care problems, violence, or suicide);
       or

    e. A concurrent serious emotional, behavioral, or cognitive disorder complicates the treatment of addiction and requires differential diagnosis and treatment;
       or

    f. The patient's extreme depression poses an imminent risk to his or her safety;
       or

    g. Impairment of the patient's thought processes or abstract thinking, limitations in his or her ability to conceptualize, and impairment in the patient's ability to manage the activities of daily living pose an imminent risk to his or her safety;
       or

    h. The patient's continued alcohol, tobacco, and/or drug use is causing grave complications or exacerbation of a previously diagnosed psychiatric, emotional, or behavioral condition;
       or

    i. The patient is experiencing altered mental status, with or without delirium, as manifested by: (1) disorientation to self, or (2) alcoholic hallucinosis, or (3) toxic psychosis.

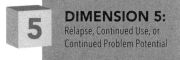

DIMENSION 4:
Readiness to Change

All Programs
Only a patient who meets criteria in Dimensions 1, 2, or 3 is appropriately placed in a Level 4 program. Problems in Dimension 4 alone are not sufficient for placement at Level 4.

DIMENSION 5:
Relapse, Continued Use, or Continued Problem Potential

All Programs
Only a patient who meets criteria in Dimensions 1, 2, or 3 is appropriately placed in a Level 4 program. Problems in Dimension 5 alone are not sufficient for placement at Level 4.

DIMENSION 6:
Recovery Environment

All Programs
Only a patient who meets criteria in Dimensions 1, 2, or 3 is appropriately placed in a Level 4 program. Problems in Dimension 6 alone are not sufficient for placement at Level 4.

LEVEL 4

ADOLESCENT DIAGNOSTIC ADMISSION CRITERIA

The adolescent who is appropriately placed in a Level 4 program is assessed as meeting the diagnostic criteria for a substance use or substance-induced disorder, as defined in the current *Diagnostic and Statistical Manual of Mental Disorders* (*DSM*) of the American Psychiatric Association or other standardized and widely accepted criteria, as well as the dimensional criteria for admission.

If the adolescent's presenting alcohol or drug use history is inadequate to substantiate such a diagnosis, the probability of such a diagnosis may be determined from information submitted by collateral parties (such as family members, legal guardians, and significant others).

ADOLESCENT DIMENSIONAL ADMISSION CRITERIA

The adolescent who is appropriately admitted to a Level 4 program meets specifications in at least **one** of Dimensions 1, 2, or 3.

DIMENSION 1:
Acute Intoxication and/or Withdrawal Potential

The adolescent's status in Dimension 1 is characterized by at least **one** of the following:
a. The adolescent who is appropriately placed in a Level 4 program is experiencing acute withdrawal, with severe signs or symptoms, and is at risk for complications that require 24-hour intensive medical services. Such complications may involve delirium, hallucinosis, seizures, high morbidity medical complications, pregnancy, severe agitation, psychosis, unremitting suicide risk, and the like;
   or
b. There is recent (within 24 hours) serious head trauma or loss of consciousness, with chronic mental status or neurological changes, resulting in the need to closely observe the adolescent at least hourly;
   or
c. Drug overdose or intoxication has compromised the adolescent's mental status, cardiac function, or other vital signs or functions;
   or
d. The adolescent has a significant acute biomedical disorder that poses substantial risk of serious or life-threatening consequences during withdrawal (such as significant hypertension or esophageal varices).

Withdrawal rating scale tables and flow sheets (which may include tabulation of vital signs) are used as needed.

DIMENSION 2:
Biomedical Conditions And Complications

The adolescent's status in Dimension 2 is characterized by at least **one** of the following:
a. Biomedical complications of the addictive disorder require medical management and skilled nursing care;
   or
b. A concurrent biomedical illness or pregnancy requires stabilization and daily medical management, with daily primary nursing interventions;
   or
c. The adolescent has a concurrent biomedical condition(s) (including pregnancy) in which continued alcohol or other drug use presents an imminent danger to life or severe danger to health;
   or

LEVEL 4

a ADOLESCENT DIMENSIONAL ADMISSION CRITERIA (CONTINUED)

The adolescent who is appropriately admitted to a Level 4 program meets specifications in at least *one* of Dimensions 1, 2, or 3.

DIMENSION 2:
Biomedical Conditions and Complications

d. The adolescent's alcohol, tobacco, and/or other drug use is gravely complicating or exacerbating a previously diagnosed medical condition;
or

e. Changes in the adolescent's medical status, such as significant worsening of a medical condition, make abstinence imperative;
or

f. Significant improvement in a previously unstable medical condition allows the adolescent to respond to addiction treatment;
or

g. The adolescent has (an)other biomedical problem(s) that requires 24-hour observation and evaluation.

DIMENSION 3:
Emotional, Behavioral, or Cognitive Conditions and Complications

The adolescent's status in Dimension 3 is characterized by at least *one* of the following:

a. **Dangerousness/Lethality:** The adolescent presents an imminent risk of suicidal, homicidal, or other violent behavior, or is at risk of a psychosis with unpredictable, disorganized, or agitated behavior that endangers self or others. Such a patient may require a locked unit.

b. **Interference with Addiction Recovery Efforts:** The adolescent is unable to focus on recovery tasks because of unstable, overwhelming psychiatric problems (for example, a patient with schizophrenia who has gravely regressed to a lower level of functioning, or a bipolar youth who is manic, or a juvenile diabetic whose uncontrolled glucose levels are causing his or her confusion).

c. **Social Functioning:** The adolescent is unable to cope with family, school, work, or friends, or has severely impaired ability to function in family, social, work, or school settings because of an overwhelming mental health problem (such as a thought disorder or severe mood lability that places the patient at risk).

d. **Ability for Self-Care:** The adolescent has insufficient resources and skills to maintain an adequate level of functioning and requires daily medical and nursing care (for example, an adolescent with head injury, mental retardation, severe depression, eating disorder, and severe cachexia).

e. **Course of Illness:** The adolescent's history and present situation suggest that, in the absence of medical management, the patient's emotional, behavioral, or cognitive condition will become unstable. The unfolding course of the adolescent's illness, with ensuing changes in symptoms or mental status, is likely to lead to imminently dangerous consequences. (Examples include an adolescent in relapse who has a history of severe psychosis with intoxication, or an adolescent who requires withdrawal management and has become acutely suicidal during past attempts at withdrawal, or an adolescent who is experiencing a recurrence of severe depression and who has had a dangerous relapse to alcohol or drug use, with attendant high-severity, high-risk behaviors and episodes of depression in the past.)

DIMENSION 4:
Readiness to Change

Only an adolescent who meets criteria in Dimensions 1, 2, or 3 is appropriately placed in a Level 4 program. Problems in Dimension 4 alone are not sufficient for placement at Level 4.

DIMENSION 5:
Relapse, Continued Use, or Continued Problem Potential

Only an adolescent who meets criteria in Dimensions 1, 2, or 3 is appropriately placed in a Level 4 program. Problems in Dimension 5 alone are not sufficient for placement at Level 4.

LEVEL 4

ADOLESCENT DIMENSIONAL ADMISSION CRITERIA (CONTINUED)

The adolescent who is appropriately admitted to a Level 4 program meets specifications in at least *one* of Dimensions 1, 2, or 3.

6 **DIMENSION 6:**
Recovery Environment

Only an adolescent who meets criteria in Dimensions 1, 2, or 3 is appropriately placed in a Level 4 program. Problems in Dimension 6 alone are not sufficient for placement at Level 4.

Opioid Treatment Services (OTS)

"Opioid Treatment Services" is an umbrella term that encompasses a variety of pharmacological and nonpharmacological treatment modalities. This term is intended to broaden understandings of opioid treatments to include all medications used to treat opioid use disorders and the psychosocial services that are offered concurrently with these pharmacotherapies. Pharmacological agents include opioid agonist medications such as methadone and buprenorphine, and opioid antagonist medications such as naltrexone.

Agonist and Antagonist Medications

Opioid agonist medications pharmacologically occupy opioid receptors in the body. They thereby relieve withdrawal symptoms and reduce or extinguish cravings for opioids. The result is a continuously maintained physiological/neurochemical state in which the therapeutic agent does not produce euphoria, intoxication, or withdrawal symptoms. This allows the patient to function free of the major physiological components of their opioid use disorder.

Opioid antagonist medications pharmacologically occupy opioid receptors in the body, but do not activate the receptors. This effectively blocks the receptor, preventing the brain from responding to opioids. The result is that further use of opioids does not produce reinforcing euphoria or intoxication. When using opioid treatment medications, collaboration with other providers and accessing statewide prescription monitoring programs is highly recommended, given the dangerous drug interactions that are possible.

Agonist, partial agonist, or antagonist medications used in the treatment of opioid use disorder should be prescribed in the context of psychosocial supports and interventions to manage the patient's addiction.

In office-based opioid treatment (OBOT) services and in the prescribing of opioid antagonist medications, it is a clinical judgment of the physician whether to use medications as part of a care plan of "Medication-Assisted Treatment" (MAT)—in addition to the psychosocial therapy services described elsewhere in *The ASAM Criteria* for the care of the patient with a substance use or co-occurring disorder. Currently, there is no established and recognized practice guideline on patient selection for pharmacotherapy interventions for opioid use disorder, or to guide

OTS **4**

Specific program characteristics and criteria for opioid treatment programs (OTP) using methadone and/or buprenorphine are presented here as a Level 1 service because an outpatient setting is the context in which opioid agonist medications are most commonly offered. Patients receiving Level 2 and 3 substance use and co-occurring disorders care can be referred to, or otherwise be concurrently enrolled in, OTP or OBOT services, and patients in Levels 2, 3, and 4 care can be prescribed buprenorphine while receiving psychosocial services in the level of addiction care most appropriate given their severity of illness and their assets and resiliencies.

patient selection for the use of antagonist vs. partial agonist vs. full agonist agents.

Integrated Care

Based on the patient-centered multidimensional assessment and the patient's recovery goals, these therapies may also need to address co-occurring issues (mental disorders, infectious diseases, and other co-occurring illnesses). Some individuals may require psychotropic medications to achieve full recovery. Other patients for whom Opioid Treatment Services are indicated may have a co-occurring chronic pain condition requiring integration of pain management services with indicated addiction management services.

Integrated concurrent care for the patient's various conditions is recommended where possible, in lieu of sequential care. However, co-occurring expertise may not be available in all OTS programs. When this is the case, it is important to note that Opioid Treatment Services using opioid agonist and antagonist medications can be provided with appropriate collaborations across different settings and at many levels of care, depending on the patient-centered assessment findings in Dimensions 1 through 6, and the patient's recovery-oriented goals. It is important to remember that when agonist therapies are provided, all of the standards set out in 42 CFR 8.12[1], along with individual state and local regulations must be met regardless of the level of care or the physical setting of treatment services.

Opioid Antagonist Medication

Opioid antagonist therapies involve medications that are not covered under the Controlled Substances Act, so no special regulations or

> Opioid Treatment Services using opioid agonist and antagonist medications can be provided with appropriate collaborations across different settings and at many levels of care, depending on the patient-centered assessment findings in Dimensions 1 through 6, and the patient's recovery-oriented goals.

authorizations are required of the prescribing practitioner or the treatment agency where such a professional with prescribing privileges works. An addiction specialist physician prescribes these non-controlled substances in the course of general medical or mental health practice.

Treatment with naltrexone also is designed to address the patient's need to achieve changes in his or her level of function, including elimination of the use of any drugs that could compromise recovery. To accomplish such change, the patient-centered treatment plan will address major lifestyle, attitudinal, and behavioral issues that have the potential to undermine the patient's recovery-oriented goals and inhibit his or her ability to cope with major life tasks. No regulatory structures are tied to physicians' involvement in the prescribing of oral naltrexone or the administering of sustained-release naltrexone intramuscular injections.

Since the use of naltrexone tablets or sustained-release injectable naltrexone for the treatment of opioid use disorders does not require a waiver, there is no limit on the number of patients that can be under treatment at a given point in time.

Two Models for Opioid Agonist Medication: OTPs and OBOTs

Health services which provide patients with authorizations for opioid agonists fall under two federally authorized models. Opioid treatment programs (OTPs) are heavily regulated by federal agencies and involve the direct administration of medications on a daily basis without the prescribing of medications; even "take-home" supplies originate at the "dispensing window" of the OTP and do not involve prescriptions taken to a retail outpatient pharmacy. OTPs – known in past years to many as "Methadone Maintenance Treatment" (MMT) clinics or "Opioid Maintenance Therapy" (OMT) – also are under strict state regulations that usually reflect federal regulations.

The other model is the office-based opioid treatment (OBOT) model, in which physicians in private practices or a number of types of public sector clinics can be authorized to prescribe

TWO MODELS FOR OPIOID AGONIST MEDICATION

OPIOID TREATMENT PROGRAMS (OTPs)

Heavily regulated by federal agencies and involve the direct administration of medications on a daily basis without prescribing of medications; even "take-home" supplies originate at the "dispensing window" of the OTP and do not involve prescriptions taken to an outpatient dispensing pharmacy. OTPs – known in past years to many as "Methadone Maintenance Treatment" (MMT) clinics or "Opioid Maintenance Therapy" (OMT) – also are under strict state regulations that usually reflect federal regulations.

OFFICE-BASED OPIOID TREATMENT (OBOT)

Physicians in private practices or a number of types of public sector clinics can be authorized to prescribe outpatient supplies of the partial opioid agonist buprenorphine (though OTPs can administer or dispense buprenorphine products as well). There is no regulation *per se* of the clinic sites where physicians prescribing OBOT practice. It is the practice of the individual physician which is regulated by federal regulations addressing office-based treatment.

outpatient supplies of the partial opioid agonist buprenorphine (though OTPs can administer or dispense buprenorphine products as well). There is no regulation *per se* of the clinic sites where physicians prescribing OBOT practice. It is the practice of the individual physician which is regulated by federal regulations addressing office-based treatment.

There are important psychosocial components to the services offered in the OTP and OBOT models. OTP services include a highly structured environment in which daily attendance at the treatment facility is required (at least until later in a patient's treatment course). Such services should also offer patient-centered addiction counseling and mental health therapy to address the emotional/psychological and behavioral components of the patient's opioid use disorder. In order to receive permission to prescribe under the OBOT model, the physician must demonstrate the existence of referral relationships with the capacity to refer to psychosocial counseling for the patient's addiction, including individual, group, and family therapy in Level 1 care, or more intensive addiction treatment in Levels 2, 3, or 4, based on clinical necessity.

Of significance in the provision of buprenorphine through OTPs is the federal rule change regarding unsupervised use of buprenorphine products ("take-home" doses of medication). (For more detail, see the reference information provided for this chapter.)[1]

Brief Description of Office-Based Opioid Treatment (OBOT)

OBOT utilizing buprenorphine may only be prescribed by certified, waivered physicians in a variety of practice settings. The "waiver" is an exception to the 1914 Harrison Act, which forbids physicians from prescribing opioids to treat opioid addiction or withdrawal. With OBOT the buprenorphine or buprenorphine/naloxone is prescribed and generally obtained from a retail outpatient pharmacy or, depending on local regulations, may be purchased from a pharmaceutical distributor. Some physicians choose to dispense the medications from their office setting depending on applicable regulations.

Physicians must take an 8-hour training course to receive their waiver to prescribe buprenorphine for an opioid use disorder. The training is approved by the Center for Substance Abuse Treatment and may be taken online. Once credits are approved and submitted to the Drug Enforcement Administration (DEA), the DEA issues an additional controlled substances prescriber registration number to the physician (current law does not allow physician assistants, nurse practitioners, or other non-physicians with prescribing authority in their state to receive a waiver).

There is a 30-patient limit per prescriber during the first year after the physician has been granted the waiver, and at the request of the physician, a 100-patient limit can be authorized by the DEA after the first year. The physician needs to maintain a log of all current patients, which should include dosage, start date, number of doses authorized, and other data (such as the run-out date for the last authorized prescription), and a notation if the patient is no longer under the physician's care.

When a patient leaves a physician's OBOT program, another patient may be added to the roster, as long as the number of current active prescriptions does not exceed the 30 or 100 patient limit. This numerical "cap" is applied to the prescriber and applies to all patients receiving prescriptions at all practice locations where the waivered physician may happen to see patients.

Since nurse practitioners and physician assistants are not permitted to prescribe buprenorphine for treatment of substance use disorders, and are not eligible for the waiver, the prescribing physician must see the patient and write the prescription at each visit. The DEA is authorized to audit physicians' OBOT programs, and will generally call to set up an appointment but may arrive unexpectedly.

In all OBOT paradigms, psychosocial interventions, in addition to medication management, are strongly recommended in the Center for Substance Abuse Treatment (CSAT) Treatment Improvement Protocol (TIP) Numbers 40[2] and 43.[3]

Brief Description of Opioid Treatment Programs (OTPs)

An opioid treatment program utilizing methadone or buprenorphine formulations is an organized, ambulatory, addiction treatment service for patients with an opioid use disorder. It is delivered by a team of personnel trained in the treatment of opioid use disorder, which includes, at a minimum, physicians, nurses, licensed or certified addiction counselors, and mental health therapists who provide patient-centered and recovery-oriented individualized treatment, case management, and health education (including education about HIV, tuberculosis, hepatitis C, and sexually transmitted diseases).

The nature of the services provided, including dose, level of care, length of service, and frequency of visits, is determined by the physician and based on the patient's goals and clinical needs. Federally mandated program components include regularly scheduled psychosocial treatment sessions, random urine drug tests, and scheduled medication visits within a program structure.

An opioid treatment program is operated under a defined set of policies and procedures, including admission, discharge, and continued service criteria stipulated by federal regulations (42 CFR 8.12) and individual state regulations.

Treatment with methadone or buprenorphine is designed to address the patient's need to achieve changes in his or her level of function, including elimination of the use of any drugs that could compromise recovery. To accomplish such change, the patient-centered treatment plan will address major lifestyle, attitudinal, and behavioral issues that have the potential to undermine the patient's recovery-oriented goals and inhibit his or her ability to cope with major life tasks.

Length of Service

Duration of treatment varies with the severity of the patient's illness and his or her response to treatment and desire to continue treatment. For some patients, treatment will be indefinite, even lifelong. Most studies have shown high rates of relapse to opioid use when participation in opioid treatment programs is discontinued.

Characteristics and Criteria for Admission: Opioid Treatment Program

EXAMPLES OF SERVICE DELIVERY
Examples of an Opioid Treatment Program (OTP) include methadone and/or buprenorphine therapy provided in a Level 1 outpatient treatment setting. These are sometimes variously called methadone treatment programs, narcotic treatment programs, and methadone maintenance clinics, but all must meet the criteria identified in 42 CFR 8. The OTP treatment focus will generally include ongoing treatment as well as time-limited withdrawal management services.

SETTING

OTP services may be offered in any licensed program with the necessary and appropriate licenses, certifications, and accreditations. OTP services typically are provided in permanent, freestanding clinics, community mental health centers, community health centers, hospital medication units or satellite clinics, and mobile units attached to a permanent clinic site. It may also be accomplished in an inpatient setting.

SUPPORT SYSTEMS

Currently in OTPs, both methadone and buprenorphine can only be dispensed and administered, not prescribed.

In OTPs, necessary support systems include:

a. Linkage with or access to psychological, medical, and psychiatric consultation.

b. Access to emergency medical and psychiatric care through affiliations with more intensive levels of care.

c. Access to evaluation and ongoing primary medical care.

d. Ability to conduct or arrange for appropriate laboratory and toxicology tests.

e. Availability of physicians to evaluate, order, and monitor use of methadone or buprenorphine, and of pharmacists and nurses to dispense and administer methadone or buprenorphine.

STAFF

Staff of opioid treatment programs includes:

a. An interdisciplinary team of personnel trained in the treatment of opioid use disorder, including a medical director, counselors, and the professional staff delineated in (b). The team can include social workers, professional counselors, and licensed psychologists, as needed.

Team members must be knowledgeable in the assessment, interpretation, and treatment of the biopsychosocial dimensions of alcohol or other substance use disorders. They receive supervision appropriate to their level of training and experience.

b. A physician or his/her appropriately licensed supervisee, who is available during medication dispensing and clinic operating hours, either in person or by telephone. Unlike OBOTs using buprenorphine products, OTPs can utilize physician assistants and nurse practitioners as prescribers.

THERAPIES

Therapies offered in opioid treatment programs include:

a. Individualized, patient-centered assessment and treatment.

b. Assessing, ordering, administering, reassessing, and regulating medication and dose levels appropriate to the individual; supervising withdrawal management from opioid analgesics, including methadone or buprenorphine; overseeing and facilitating access to appropriate treatment. Medication for other physical and mental health disorders is provided as needed either on-site or through collaboration with other providers. Since no regulations are attached to the prescribing of the non-controlled substance naltrexone, this medication is offered to patients in many other clinical settings.

c. Monitored drug testing, to be done a minimum of 8 times a year.

d. A range of cognitive, behavioral, and other substance use disorder-focused therapies, reflecting a variety of treatment approaches, provided to the patient on an individual, group, or family basis.

e. Case management, including medical monitoring and coordination of on- and off-site treatment services, provided as needed. Case managers also assure the provision of, or referral to, educational and vocational counseling, treatment of psychiatric illness, child care, parenting skills development, primary health care, and other adjunct services, as needed.

f. Psychoeducation, including HIV/AIDS education, and other health education services.

ASSESSMENT/TREATMENT PLAN REVIEW

In opioid treatment programs, the assessment and treatment plan review include:

a. A comprehensive medical history, physical examination, and laboratory tests, provided or obtained in accordance with federal regulations. The tests must be done prior to the time of admission and reviewed by a physician as soon as possible, but no later than 14 days after admission [42 CFR 8.12(f)].

b. An individual biopsychosocial assessment.

c. An appropriate regimen of methadone or buprenorphine (as required by CSAT regulation), at a dose established by a physician or his/her appropriately licensed supervisee at the time of admission and monitored carefully until the patient is stable and an adequate dose has been established. The dose then is reviewed as indicated by the patient's course of treatment.

d. Continuing evaluation and referral for care of any serious biomedical problems.

e. An individualized, patient-centered, and recovery-focused treatment plan, including problem formulation and articulation of short-term, measurable treatment goals and activities designed to achieve those goals. The plan is patient-centered and therefore developed in collaboration with the patient and reflective of the patient's personal goals for recovery. Treatment plan reviews are conducted at specified times, as noted in the plan.

DOCUMENTATION

Documentation standards of opioid treatment programs (OTPs) include individualized progress notes in each patient's record for every service. Such notes clearly reflect implementation of the treatment plan and the patient's response to therapeutic interventions for all disorders treated, as well as subsequent amendments to the plan.

Because of special recordkeeping requirements for OTPs, records also should include documentation of each dose of methadone or buprenorphine administered, with a copy of the physician's or his or her appropriately licensed supervisee's order for methadone. At present, only physicians can order or prescribe buprenorphine.

Opioid Treatment Services, to provide the patient with oral or monthly-injectable naltrexone, must meet comparable standards for patient evaluation, management, and monitoring processes. Documentation for prescribing of opioid antagonist medications follows the identical documentation requirements as any other Level 1 substance use and co-occurring disorders care.

Opioid Antagonist Medication

Documentation for OBOT follows the identical documentation requirements as any other Level 1 substance use and co-occurring disorders care, except for the additional "patient log" documentation requirements for buprenorphine patients that are incumbent upon any "waivered physician" as described in the Brief Description of Office-Based Opioid Treatment.

DIAGNOSTIC ADMISSION CRITERIA

The patient who is appropriately placed in an opioid treatment program is assessed as meeting the diagnostic criteria for severe opioid use disorder, as defined in the current *Diagnostic and Statistical Manual of Mental Disorders* (*DSM*) or other standardized and widely accepted criteria, aside from those exceptions listed in 42 CFR 8.12.

If the patient's drug use history is inadequate to substantiate such a diagnosis, the probability of such a diagnosis may be determined from information submitted by other health care professionals and programs and collateral parties (such as family members, legal guardians, or significant others).

Individuals who are admitted to treatment with methadone or buprenorphine must demonstrate specific objective and subjective signs of opioid use disorder, as defined in 42 CFR 8.12.

OPIOID TREATMENT PROGRAM DIMENSIONAL ADMISSION CRITERIA

The patient who is appropriately placed in an opioid treatment program is assessed as meeting the required specifications in Dimensions 1 through 6.

DIMENSION 1:
Acute Intoxication and/or Withdrawal Potential

In Dimension 1, the patient meets specifications as indicated in 42 CFR 8.12 (e).

Patient admission criteria

1. **Maintenance treatment**

An OTP shall maintain current procedures designed to ensure that patients are admitted to maintenance treatment by qualified personnel who have determined, using accepted medical criteria such as those listed in the *Diagnostic and Statistical Manual of Mental Disorders* (*DSM*), that the person is currently addicted to an opioid drug, and that the person became addicted at least 1 year before admission for treatment. In addition, a program physician shall ensure that each patient voluntarily chooses maintenance treatment and that all relevant facts concerning the use of the opioid drug are clearly and adequately explained to the patient, and that each patient provides informed written consent to treatment.

2. **Maintenance treatment for persons under age 18**

A person under 18 years of age is required to have had two documented unsuccessful attempts at short-term withdrawal management or drug-free treatment within a 12-month period to be eligible for maintenance treatment. No person under 18 years of age may be admitted to maintenance treatment unless a parent, legal guardian, or responsible adult designated by the relevant state authority consents in writing to such treatment.

3. **Maintenance treatment admission exceptions**

If clinically appropriate, the program physician may waive the requirement of a 1-year history of addiction under part (e), paragraph (1), of 42 CFR 8.12, for patients released from penal institutions (within 6 months after release), for pregnant patients (program physician must certify pregnancy), and for previously treated patients (up to 2 years after discharge).

OTS 4

OPIOID TREATMENT PROGRAM
DIMENSIONAL ADMISSION CRITERIA (CONTINUED)

1

DIMENSION 1:
Acute Intoxication and/or
Withdrawal Potential

[42 CFR 8.2]

"Opioid addiction" is described in 42 CFR 8.2 as a cluster of cognitive, behavioral, and physiological symptoms in which the individual continues use of opioids despite significant opioid-induced problems. Opioid use disorder is characterized by repeated self-administration that usually results in opioid tolerance, withdrawal symptoms, and compulsive drug taking. Addiction involving the use of opioids is defined by ASAM through the ASAM Definition of Addiction.

Opioid use disorder as described in the *Diagnostic and Statistical Manual of Mental Disorders*, Fifth Edition (*DSM-5*) may occur with or without the physiological symptoms of tolerance and withdrawal.

The patient's current physiological dependence (in addition to a history of addiction) is confirmed by vital signs, early physical signs of narcotic withdrawal, a urine screen that is positive for opioids, the presence of old or fresh needle marks, and documented reports from medical professionals, the patient or family, treatment history, or (if necessary) a positive reaction to a naloxone test.

2

DIMENSION 2:
Biomedical Conditions and
Complications

In Dimension 2, the patient meets specifications in **one** of the following:
- a. The patient meets the biomedical criteria for opioid use disorder, with or without the complications of opioid addiction, and requires outpatient medical monitoring and skilled care;
  or
- b. The patient has a concurrent biomedical illness or pregnancy, which can be treated on an outpatient basis with minimal daily medical monitoring;
  or
- c. The patient has biomedical problems that can be managed on an outpatient basis, such as liver disease or problems with potential hepatic decomposition, pancreatitis, gastrointestinal problems, cardiovascular disorders, HIV and AIDS, sexually transmitted diseases, and tuberculosis.

3

DIMENSION 3:
Emotional, Behavioral, or
Cognitive Conditions and
Complications

In Dimension 3, the patient meets specifications in **one** of the following:
- a. The patient's emotional, behavioral, or cognitive problems, if present, are manageable in an outpatient structured environment;
  or
- b. The patient's substance-related abuse or neglect of his or her spouse, children, or significant others requires intensive outpatient treatment to reduce the risk of further deterioration;
  or
- c. The patient has a diagnosed and stable emotional, behavioral, or cognitive problem or thought disorder (such as stable borderline personality disorder or obsessive-compulsive disorder) that requires monitoring, management, or medication because of the risk that the problem(s) will distract the patient from his or her focus on treatment;
  or
- d. The patient poses a mild risk of harm to self or others, with or without a history of severe depression, suicidal or homicidal behavior, but can be managed safely in a structured outpatient environment;
  or
- e. The patient demonstrates emotional and behavioral stability but requires continued pharmacotherapy to prevent relapse to opioid use.

OPIOID TREATMENT PROGRAM
DIMENSIONAL ADMISSION CRITERIA (CONTINUED)

4

DIMENSION 4:
Readiness to Change

In Dimension 4, the patient meets specifications in **one** of the following:
a. The patient requires structured therapy, pharmacotherapy, and programmatic milieu to promote treatment progress and recovery;
or
b. The patient attributes his or her problems to persons or external events rather than to the substance-related disorder. He or she thus is unable to make behavioral changes in the absence of clinically directed and repeated structured motivational interventions. However, the patient's low interest in recovery does not render treatment ineffective.

5

DIMENSION 5:
Relapse, Continued Use, or
Continued Problem Potential

In Dimension 5, the patient meets specifications in **one** of the following:
a. The patient requires structured therapy, pharmacotherapy, and a programmatic milieu to promote treatment progress because he or she attributes continued relapse to physiologic craving or the need for opioids;
or
b. Despite active participation in other treatment interventions without provision for opioid pharmacotherapy, the patient is experiencing an intensification of addiction symptoms (such as difficulty in postponing immediate gratification and related drug-seeking behavior) or continued high-risk behaviors (such as shared needle use), and his or her level of functioning is deteriorating, despite revisions of the treatment plan;
or
c. The patient is at high risk of relapse to opioid use without opioid pharmacotherapy, close outpatient monitoring, and structured support (as indicated by his or her lack of awareness of relapse triggers, difficulty in postponing immediate gratification or ambivalence toward or low interest in treatment);
or
d. The patient is pregnant and requires continued opioid pharmacotherapy to avert repeated episodes of withdrawal by the fetus and ensure its continued health.

6

DIMENSION 6:
Recovery Environment

In Dimension 6, the patient meets specifications in **one** of the following:
a. The patient has a sufficiently supportive psychosocial environment to render opioid pharmacotherapy feasible. For example, significant others are supportive of recovery efforts, the patient's workplace is supportive, the patient is subject to legal coercion, the patient has adequate transportation to the program, and the like;
or
b. The patient's family members or significant others are supportive, but require professional intervention to improve the patient's likelihood of treatment success (such as assistance with limit-setting, communication skills, avoiding rescuing behaviors, education about opioid pharmacotherapy treatment and HIV-risk avoidance, and the like);
or
c. The patient does not have a positive social support system to assist with immediate recovery efforts, but he or she has demonstrated motivation to obtain such a support system or to pursue (with assistance) an appropriate alternative living environment;
or
d. The patient has experienced traumatic events in his or her recovery environment (such as physical, emotional, sexual, or domestic abuse) or has manifested the effects of emotional, behavioral, or cognitive problems in the environment (such as criminal activity), but these are manageable on an outpatient basis.

OTS **4**

Adult and Adolescent Continued Service and Transfer/Discharge Criteria

The notion that the duration of treatment varies with the severity of the individual's illness and his or her response to treatment is a foundational principle of the ASAM criteria. Thus, fixed length of stay (LOS) programs are not consistent with individualized, person-centered, and outcomes-driven treatment. Patients, especially those mandated to treatment in fixed LOS programs, often focus more on "doing time" rather than "doing treatment." They are more focused on their discharge date than on addressing the concerns that led them to treatment initially. The LOS and level of care is determined by the progress and outcomes of treatment, not on predetermined program lengths of stay.

The continued service and transfer/discharge criteria thus play a prominent role in guiding when a patient should continue in the current level of care, or when his or her progress and outcome in treatment warrants transfer or discharge to a different level and/or type of service. In the process of patient assessment, certain problems and priorities are identified, the treatment of which indicates admission to a particular level of care. The resolution of those problems and priorities determines when a patient can be transferred and treated at a different level of care, referred to a different type of treatment, or discharged from treatment. The appearance of new problems may require services that can be provided effectively at the same level of care, or they may require a more or less intensive level or type of care.

After the admission criteria for a given level of care have been met, the criteria for continued service, transfer, or discharge from that level of care are as follows.

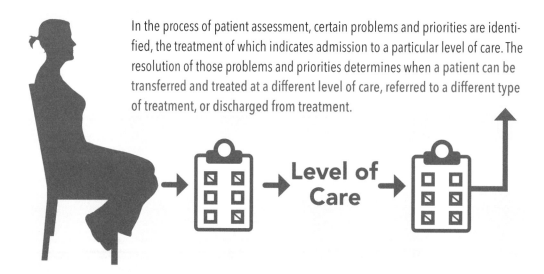

In the process of patient assessment, certain problems and priorities are identified, the treatment of which indicates admission to a particular level of care. The resolution of those problems and priorities determines when a patient can be transferred and treated at a different level of care, referred to a different type of treatment, or discharged from treatment.

CONT/TRANS/DISCHARGE

4

Continued Service Criteria

It is appropriate to retain the patient at the present level of care if:

Ⓐ The patient is making progress, but has not yet achieved the goals articulated in the individualized treatment plan. Continued treatment at the present level of care is assessed as necessary to permit the patient to continue to work toward his or her treatment goals;
or

Ⓑ The patient is not yet making progress, but has the capacity to resolve his or her problems. He or she is actively working toward the goals articulated in the individualized treatment plan. Continued treatment at the present level of care is assessed as necessary to permit the patient to continue to work toward his or her treatment goals;
and/or

Ⓒ New problems have been identified that are appropriately treated at the present level of care. The new problem or priority requires services, the frequency and intensity of which can only safely be delivered by continued stay in the current level of care. The level of care in which the patient is receiving treatment is therefore the least intensive level at which the patient's new problems can be addressed effectively.

To document and communicate the patient's readiness for discharge or need for transfer to another level of care, each of the six dimensions of the ASAM criteria should be reviewed. If the criteria apply to the patient's existing or new problem(s), the patient should continue in treatment at the present level of care. If not, refer to the Transfer/Discharge Criteria provided in this section.

For continued service, typical findings in each of the six dimensions follow for both adult and adolescent, with examples given.

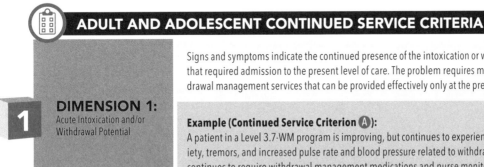

ADULT AND ADOLESCENT CONTINUED SERVICE CRITERIA

DIMENSION 1:
Acute Intoxication and/or Withdrawal Potential

Signs and symptoms indicate the continued presence of the intoxication or withdrawal problem that required admission to the present level of care. The problem requires monitoring or withdrawal management services that can be provided effectively only at the present level of care.

Example (Continued Service Criterion Ⓐ):
A patient in a Level 3.7-WM program is improving, but continues to experience withdrawal anxiety, tremors, and increased pulse rate and blood pressure related to withdrawal. The patient continues to require withdrawal management medications and nurse monitoring every 8 hours. Therefore, continued treatment can be provided effectively only in a Level 3.7-WM service.

ADULT AND ADOLESCENT CONTINUED SERVICE CRITERIA (CONTINUED)

2

DIMENSION 2:
Biomedical Conditions and Complications

The physical health problem that required admission to the present level of care, or a new problem, requires biomedical services that can be provided effectively only at the present level of care.

a **Adolescent Example (Continued Service Criterion Ⓑ):**
An adolescent patient in a Level 3.7 program who has experienced significant weight loss from a co-occurring disorder (anorexia nervosa) has not yet regained sufficient weight to allow safe transfer to a less intensive level of care. However, the adolescent is following through with the treatment plan. He or she needs further medical monitoring and 24-hour nurse management to monitor for insomnia, excessive exercise, or purging behavior, and to provide dietary structure. These services can be provided effectively only in a Level 3.7 program.

3

DIMENSION 3:
Emotional, Behavioral, or Cognitive Conditions and Complications

The emotional, behavioral, and/or cognitive problem that required admission to the present level of care continues, or a new problem has appeared. This problem requires interventions than can be provided effectively only at the present level of care.

Example (Continued Service Criterion Ⓑ):
A patient in a Level 2.5 program has substance-induced depressive symptoms and suicidal ideation persisting beyond the "crash" of cocaine withdrawal. The patient thus requires consistent monitoring of depression and suicidal ideation at a frequency that can be provided effectively in a co-occurring enhanced Level 2.5 program.

Example (Continued Service Criterion Ⓒ):
Following a methamphetamine binge, a patient in a Level 2.5 setting has cognitive and impulse control problems beyond what might be seen as self-limiting or substance-induced. The patient thus requires consistent behavioral interventions at a frequency that can be provided effectively only in a Level 2.5 program.

4

DIMENSION 4:
Readiness to Change

The patient continues to demonstrate a need for engagement and motivational enhancement that can be provided effectively only at the present level of care.

Example (Continued Service Criterion Ⓐ):
A patient in a Level 2.1 program is attending group sessions and has articulated increasing awareness that his marijuana and alcohol use have negatively affected his work or school performance and family relationships. However, the patient is not yet implementing recommended changes in his friends and recovery support groups. Further family work, employer involvement, peer confrontation, and education about addiction are thus required to increase the patient's readiness to change. The family and employer or school counselor sessions are to explore if there is leverage to increase incentives for the patient to embrace recovery. The peer confrontation and intensive groups can hold him accountable as he tries his own "strong willpower" and "I can just stop" methods to achieve abstinence. These motivational enhancement strategies are of such intensity that they can be provided effectively only in a Level 2.1 program.

CONT/TRANS/DISCHARGE

ADULT AND ADOLESCENT CONTINUED SERVICE CRITERIA (CONTINUED)

5 **DIMENSION 5:**
Relapse, Continued Use, or
Continued Problem Potential

The patient continues to demonstrate a problem, or has developed a new problem, that requires coping skills and strategies to prevent relapse, continued use, or continued problems. These strategies can be provided effectively only at the present level of care.

Example (Continued Service Criterion Ⓑ):
A patient in a Level 1 program continues to experience cravings to drink on a daily basis, but is willing to continue addressing her alcohol problem. She is attending group therapy twice a week and Alcoholics Anonymous meetings four days a week. Even though there was a brief "slip" during which the patient drank two glasses of wine, she talked about it in group and identified the relevant relapse triggers and situations. Moreover, she articulated plans to avoid the friends and the parties associated with the slip. Continued service is required and can be provided effectively at Level 1.

6 **DIMENSION 6:**
Recovery Environment

The patient continues to demonstrate a problem in his or her recovery environment, or has a new problem, that requires coping skills and support system interventions. These interventions can be provided effectively only at the present level of care.

a **Adolescent Example (Continued Service Criterion Ⓒ):**
In a Level 3.5 program, family work has uncovered the fact that an adolescent patient is a victim of incest. As the effects of her use of alcohol, cocaine, and marijuana have cleared, the patient has become increasingly distressed, and her father, who has an alcohol use disorder, has become unwilling to attend family sessions. The individual and group strategies to help the adolescent cope with her emotional distress, as well as her relationship with her father, without reverting to substance use, can be provided effectively only in a Level 3.5 program. In addition, the family work is sufficiently intense that continued treatment at Level 3.5 is necessary until staff and social services can clarify whether the adolescent will require placement outside the family home to permit full recovery.

CONT/TRANS/DISCHARGE ④

To document and communicate the patient's readiness for discharge or need for transfer to another level of care, each of the six dimensions of the ASAM criteria should be reviewed. If the criteria apply to the existing or new problem(s), the patient should be discharged or transferred, as appropriate. If not, refer to the continued service criteria provided in this section.

For transfer/discharge service, adult and adolescent findings in each of the six dimensions, as well as examples, follow.

Transfer/Discharge Criteria

It is appropriate to transfer or discharge the patient from the present level of care if he or she meets the following criteria:

(A) The patient has achieved the goals articulated in his or her individualized treatment plan, thus resolving the problem(s) that justified admission to the present level of care. Continuing the chronic disease management of the patient's condition at a less intensive level of care is indicated;

or

(B) The patient has been unable to resolve the problem(s) that justified admission to the present level of care, despite amendments to the treatment plan. The patient is determined to have achieved the maximum possible benefit from engagement in services at the current level of care. Treatment at another level of care (more or less intensive) in the same type of service, or discharge from treatment, is therefore indicated;

or

(C) The patient has demonstrated a lack of capacity due to diagnostic or co-occurring conditions that limit his or her ability to resolve his or her problem(s). Treatment at a qualitatively different level of care or type of service, or discharge from treatment, is therefore indicated;

or

(D) The patient has experienced an intensification of his or her problem(s), or has developed a new problem(s), and can be treated effectively only at a more intensive level of care.

CONT/TRANS/DISCHARGE

4

ADULT AND ADOLESCENT TRANSFER/DISCHARGE CRITERIA

DIMENSION 1:
Acute Intoxication and/or Withdrawal Potential

The patient's intoxication or withdrawal problem has improved sufficiently to allow monitoring or withdrawal management services to be provided at a less intensive level of care. Or the patient's condition has worsened to a point at which more intensive monitoring or withdrawal management services are required.

Example (Transfer/Discharge Criterion (A)):
A patient in a Level 3.7-WM program exhibits significant and stable improvement in her withdrawal anxiety, tremors, pulse rate, and blood pressure that nurse monitoring no longer is necessary. The patient's treatment can continue in a Level 2-WM program.

ADULT AND ADOLESCENT TRANSFER/DISCHARGE CRITERIA (CONTINUED)

2

DIMENSION 2:
Biomedical Conditions and
Complications

The patient's physical health has improved sufficiently to allow biomedical services to be provided effectively at a less intensive level of care. Or the patient's condition has worsened to a point at which more intensive biomedical services are necessary.

Example (Transfer/Discharge Criterion B):
A patient in a Level 3.7 program exhibits worsening breathing difficulties and is showing evidence of more frequent asthma attacks. Therefore, daily medical management, 24-hour nurse monitoring, and intravenous therapy in a Level 4 program are required.

3

DIMENSION 3:
Emotional, Behavioral, or
Cognitive Conditions and
Complications

The patient's functioning has improved sufficiently to allow interventions or services to be provided effectively at a less intensive level of care. Or the patient's condition has worsened to a point at which more intensive services are necessary.

Example (Transfer/Discharge Criterion C):
A patient in a Level 2.5 program has not been able to resolve her depression and suicidal ideation despite behavioral, individual, and group therapy. The patient now requires more specific and structured mental health interventions, in addition to the addiction treatment. The medical monitoring, 24-hour nurse monitoring, medication management, other mental health services, and environmental structure the patient needs can be provided effectively only in a psychiatrically oriented Level 3.7 co-occurring enhanced service. If such a service is unavailable, transfer to a Level 4 psychiatric service is indicated.

a **Adolescent Example (Transfer/Discharge Criteria B and C):**
An adolescent patient in a Level 3.7 program is chronically disruptive and overstimulated, and has not developed coping skills to resist the negative peer influences that provoked similar behavior and drug use prior to admission. The adolescent also is unable to integrate or make use of therapeutic activities, materials, and behavior management techniques utilized in the program. Further evaluation was completed once the adolescent had cleared more cognitively from her heavy drug use. It showed that the adolescent has baseline cognitive impairment in the moderate range of intellectual disability (intellectual developmental disorder in the *DSM-5*). If the Level 3.7 program cannot provide the specialty services and programming needed to treat this degree of cognitive impairment, the adolescent should be transferred to a program that offers such specialty treatment (for example, a specialized Level 3.7, or Level 3.5, program with high-intensity special education services, or a Level 2.5 specialty program with adequate home environment supports) (Criterion (b)).

If, after such specialty treatment is provided, the adolescent is assessed as incapable of developing the necessary coping skills (Criterion (c)) because of the cognitive impairment, then an appropriate placement would involve transfer to a program that can provide indefinite monitoring and supervision (such as a Level 3.1 group home).

Alternatively, the adolescent could be transferred to a program in which long-term vocational training and/or other habilitative services are provided as substitutes for the internalization of coping skills.

CONT/TRANS/DISCHARGE 4

ADULT AND ADOLESCENT TRANSFER/DISCHARGE CRITERIA (CONTINUED)

The patient's stage of readiness to change has improved sufficiently to allow interventions or strategies to be provided effectively at a less intensive level of care. Or the patient has demonstrated sustained lack of interest in changing; or a lack of progress to such a degree that further interventions at the present level of care will be ineffective and/or decrease the patient's willingness to engage in treatment. Transfer to another level of care will permit the use of different strategies to engage the patient in treatment and enhance his or her readiness to change.

DIMENSION 4:
Readiness to Change

Example (Transfer/Discharge Criterion **B**):

A patient in a Level 2.1 program demonstrates an increasingly fixed belief that he does not have a drinking problem, despite education about addiction, motivational strategies involving the family, and group treatment. The patient asserts that he has no thoughts of drinking, no urges to use, a good understanding of what alcohol can do to his life, and an awareness of his overuse in the past. However, the patient insists that these behaviors were associated with the pressures of starting a new job or school, thus exhibiting inaccurate symptom attribution. Despite his family's and the treatment team's concern that the patient has a more severe problem than he is able to acknowledge, the patient is convinced his problematic use was temporary and is now under control. The patient is not ready to engage in recovery treatment, but is willing to attend a weekly group session and to abstain from alcohol for three months to demonstrate to treatment professionals and family members that he does not have a drinking problem. His family is willing to continue in family therapy. These motivational services can be provided effectively in a Level 1 program. The patient thus can be transferred from Level 2.1.

Example (Transfer/Discharge Criterion **B**):

A patient in a Level 0.5 program has been sporadic with attendance at drinking and driving education classes. The patient's focus on his legal problems and his intense anger at being compared to his father, who has an alcohol use disorder, make it difficult for him to grasp that he has a problem and to listen attentively enough to commit to change. Transfer to a Level 1 outpatient program for further evaluation and motivational enhancement therapy therefore is indicated.

Example (Transfer/Discharge Criterion C):

A patient with a schizophrenic disorder who has smoked marijuana daily for almost 25 years is sporadically attending a Level 2.5 co-occurring enhanced program while residing in a Level 3.1 therapeutic group home. Despite a variety of interventions, including intensive case management, assertive community treatment, and motivational enhancement therapy, the patient is making no progress toward his recovery goals. He is convinced that marijuana relieves his chronic hallucinations (which have not responded to other treatment), despite clear evidence that the marijuana actually makes the hallucinations worse. The patient's chronic signs and symptoms prevent any meaningful engagement in recovery activities.

The patient's lack of capacity to resolve his delusions requires strategies that are designed for maintenance of basic functioning and self-care. The patient thus is appropriately transferred from the Level 2.5 co-occurring enhanced program to a Level 1 co-occurring enhanced service, where the focus will be on maximizing control of the symptoms of schizophrenia and limiting his access to drugs. For his living situation, he will be transferred from the Level 3.1 therapeutic group home to a more structured Level 3.1 service to focus on interventions such as simple behavioral contingencies and limiting the patient's access to marijuana through custodial supervision in a controlled and structured environment.

ADULT AND ADOLESCENT TRANSFER/DISCHARGE CRITERIA (CONTINUED)

5 **DIMENSION 5:**
Relapse, Continued Use, or
Continued Problem Potential

The patient's coping skills have improved sufficiently that strategies to prevent relapse or continued use can be provided effectively at a less intensive level of care. Or the patient has demonstrated a regression or lack of progress so significant that further interventions at the present level of care will not enhance his or her ability to prevent relapse or continued use, and/or will decrease the patient's willingness to engage in treatment. Transfer to another level of service will allow different strategies to be employed to engage the patient in treatment and enhance his or her ability to prevent relapse or continued use.

Example (Transfer/Discharge Criterion D):
A patient in a Level 2.5 program has experienced intense thoughts of alcohol and other drug use, cravings, and impulses to use for more than two weeks. Her ability to cope is deteriorating, despite more focused role-playing to enhance peer refusal skills, other behavioral techniques, attendance at AA meetings, and increased individual sessions. Because the patient becomes depressed and suicidal when drinking, and, over the past two days, has been drinking daily, she is appropriately transferred to a Level 3.5 program.

6 **DIMENSION 6:**
Recovery Environment

The patient's environment and/or ability to cope with it have improved sufficiently to allow interventions or services to be provided effectively at a less intensive level of care. Or the patient's recovery environment and/or ability to cope with it have worsened to such a degree that the patient requires transfer to another level of care, where different interventions or strategies can be provided.

a Adolescent Example (Transfer/Discharge Criterion C):
The physically and sexually abusive father of an adolescent patient in a Level 3.5 program continues to use alcohol and refuses attendance at family meetings. There is no foreseeable way of making the patient's home environment safe. She continues to have difficulty in coping with anxiety and stress reactions, but has accommodated to the need for an out-of-home placement. Transfer to a Level 3.1 safe living environment, with concurrent Level 2.5 services, is needed to strengthen her ability to cope with both her substance use problem and her safety issues with her father.

Application To Adult Special Populations

There have been concerns raised from some quarters that ASAM's criteria do not apply readily to certain populations of persons with substance-related and co-occurring disorders. Heretofore, there have not been specific criteria for the following special populations, who may be in need of care for a substance-related condition, where usual assessment and treatment variables may require modification.

    The following sections describe the applicability of ASAM's criteria to these populations.

SPECIAL POPULATION SECTIONS

Older Adults

Parents or Prospective Parents Receiving Addiction Treatment Concurrently with Their Children

Persons in Safety-Sensitive Occupations

Persons in Criminal Justice Settings

Older Adults

As the population of older adults continues to expand, there is an increasing need to both understand the specific issues in treating older adults as well as modify the application of the ASAM criteria. The specific issues are involved in both diagnostic admission criteria and in evaluating all six assessment dimensions.

SETTING

Older adults often have mobility problems of two types, which may affect setting:

1. Many older adults do not drive at all or not at night, when many Level 2.1 IOPs operate. Older adults might not have a consistent means to attend either professionally led outpatient treatment services or com-munity-based recovery support meetings, such as Alcoholics Anonymous (AA). Public transportation, if it exists, might be difficult to access (eg, with motorized wheelchairs or during nighttime hours), or it may even be dangerous. For outpatient treatment, consideration should be given to van pick-up or appropriate third party systems for transportation (eg, in some states, Medicaid will pay the transportation costs).

2. For structured outpatient programs such as Levels 2.1 and 2.5, and possibly more so for Level 3 and 4 residential and inpatient programs, some older adult patients will have physical difficulty with mobility, resulting in extra time needed to get from one activity

to another. In addition, because of possible extended time to clear from the effects of the use of psychoactive drugs, it is suggested that the newly admitted older adult patient be paired with a "senior buddy" to help him or her negotiate the schedule and move from room to room or building to building during the treatment day.

Another problem related to setting is that of reimbursement. Currently, Medicare, which most older adult patients use as their primary form of health insurance, will only reimburse for acute inpatient stabilization in a licensed acute care or psychiatric hospital, and will *not* reimburse treatment provided in a residential or subacute level of care or subacute inpatient treatment (Levels 3.1, 3.3, 3.5, and 3.7). Most Medicare supplement ("Medi-gap") private insurance plans will deny coverage for a service if it is not covered by the primary carrier, Medicare. Older adults with fixed or limited incomes find it infeasible to enroll in treatment services if self-pay is their only option. Level 2 programs (Intensive Outpatient and Partial Hospitalization) also face reimbursement challenges: if the program is affiliated with a general hospital, most local Medicare carriers will cover the costs of treatment, but freestanding Level 2 programs may be considered a non-covered service. In Level 1 treatment (general outpatient treatment, either individual or group therapy), many Medicare plans will only cover services if offered by a doctoral-level provider (physician or clinical psychologist) and will not cover the services of a certified or licensed addiction counselor if the addiction professional does not have a doctoral degree.

If it is determined that an older adult patient requires the structure and intensity of a residential or Level 3.7 inpatient level of care, consideration should be given to combining Level 2.1 or Level 2.5 (whichever is deemed to be most appropriate based on a comprehensive assessment) with a supporting housing option. But even this degree of creativity in treatment planning may not result in the older adult patient having access to third-party payment to cover the costs of their care.

SUPPORT SYSTEMS

By the nature of aging alone, it can be assumed that older adult patients will have more medical problems and more needs for general medical services. The reality of aging is further complicated by the impact of the substance use either in creating or exacerbating medical problems. It is suggested that the intake assessment contain a comprehensive older adult-focused history and physical examination (H & P), ideally provided by a geriatrician. Problems with chronic pain, the most common cause of which is arthritis (a Dimensions 2 issue) and with dementia and other cognitive impairments (a Dimension 3 issue) may also complicate treatment.

Most older adults are on multiple medications for multiple chronic conditions. These medications can interact with each other and produce or contribute to problems with cognition, alertness, mobility, or coordination (including driving skills). Medications can also interact with alcohol or prescription drugs taken outside of a prescribing physician's recommendations. They can also interact with medications prescribed to treat the older adult's addiction, or to manage the patient's acute alcohol or other drug withdrawal syndrome. One aspect of support that may be needed by the older adult receiving care for a substance-related or co-occurring condition may be home health care services or other supports to assist with the safe use of prescribed medications, or case management services for the patient's multiple chronic conditions.

A major problem with support for the older adult population has to do with social isolation. Many older adults live alone and may be best served by living in an assisted-living environment, but decline to leave their own residence and accept the assisted-living option. Many older adults do not have adult children or other relatives living nearby who can provide assistance or support.

Many older adults are still married but face the burdens of being the primary caregiver for a spouse who has greater needs than their own. It is not unusual for an older adult with a substance use disorder to be advised that they meet medical necessity criteria for inpatient or partial hospitalization care. Still-married older adults may decline to make the commitment to such intensive services for themselves because they believe they cannot realistically abandon their caregiver duties for their spouse during the time projected for them to be in Level 2, 3, or 4 addiction care.

Extra attention should be paid in the discharge planning process for older adults leaving intensive addiction services to include how the patient will be able to receive routine or follow-up medical care for chronic medical problems. Patients should be linked with aging services and other community-based wrap-around services, as well as mental health services as needed. Introduction and referral to recovery support groups are important not only as a means of supporting recovery but also as a potential solution to isolation and loneliness commonly found with older adults.

An older adult-specific Alcoholics Anonymous meeting can serve as a major vehicle for socialization for an older adult beginning his or her early recovery, or becoming re-engaged with recovery activities for the first time in many years after experiencing a relapse.

STAFF

In addressing the special population treatment needs of older adults, a major staff issue is not only the special training or skills the staff may have (or not have), but the general attitude of staff toward older adults. The best results occur when staff is experienced in dealing with the physical, psychological, social, and spiritual issues unique to older adults. "Ageism" on the part of staff can be destructive. This can take the form of excessive (and usually unconscious) "caretaking" of the patient by staff that "go easy" on the older adult patient; or "therapeutic pessimism" by which staff have inappropriately low expectations regarding the success or ability of the older adult to change.

Terms like "alcoholic" or "drug addict," even if correct, should be avoided, as they are perceived as judgmental and disparaging by older adults. Instead, staff should help patients connect their substance use with resultant problems. Staff should like working with older adults, be knowledgeable about and sensitive to older adults' issues, and be able to treat older adults with dignity and respect. Clinical supervisors should attend to the possibility of transference issues, whereby staff members' life experiences with their own parents or grandparents may inappropriately shape their attitudes and behaviors toward a patient under their care. The staff point of view should be a belief in the ability of older adults to recover with dignity from their alcohol and other drug problems and to live healthier, productive, and satisfying lives in recovery.

THERAPIES

Confrontational therapy should be avoided at all costs. For structured programs treating both older adults and younger adults, the optimum approach is for primary therapy groups to include the option of senior-specific groups. Research has demonstrated that age-specific treatment is associated with significantly improved outcomes over mixed-aged treatment. Treatment should be paced to the individual's physical and cognitive capabilities and limitations. The daily pace of program schedules and expectations, and the overall pace of change and time allotted for clinical improvement, should be realistically designed and not assumed to be the same for older adults as it is for other patients. Research indicates that cognitive-behavioral therapies are effective with older adults, particularly to address negative emotional states which pose significant risks for relapse. There should be an educational component specific to the needs of older adults (eg, coping strategies for avoiding being "scammed"). Because isolation is a common problem among older adults, skills to rebuild a social support network to overcome isolation and loneliness are required. Treatment should be adapted to any gender-specific needs (eg, widowed or single older adult males may have more difficulty with loneliness than older adult women who are more likely to survive their husbands).

OLDER ADULTS

Family counseling should address family of origin, family of choice, and family of pro-creation issues. Staff will find that the adult children of older adults with substance use prob-lems act much like the parents of adolescents with such problems; they may vacillate between denial, over-protectiveness, and enabling on one hand; and anger, resentment, and rejection on the other; and can sometimes be unwilling to participate in family counseling.

The stresses of adults from the "sandwich generation" who have needs to care for their own children and their geriatric-cohort parents simultaneously should be acknowledged by staff. Family member services should specifi-cally and thoughtfully provide education and support to the adult children of older adult patients receiving care for a substance-related or co-occurring disorder.

ASSESSMENT/TREATMENT PLAN REVIEW

A comprehensive assessment designed around the issues of older adults should be performed. Assessment of sensory limitations in hearing and vision should be included, as well as an assessment of activities of daily living. Assess-ment should include that for depression and anx-iety, which are common co-occurring problems with substance use problems in older adults.

One of the major confounding factors in attempting to assess an older adult for a sub-stance-related disorder is the issue of shame and guilt. Older adults may be even more prone to shame about their use because of their own judgmentalism regarding alcohol or other drug addiction. They may have strong religious beliefs, which can lead them to use a moralistic lens to evaluate their own drinking. They may view it as admitting to "sin" to admit to having a significant problem with drinking or gambling. Minimization is the rule during history-taking and interviewing to collect a patient's substance use or addictive behavior history.

As is detailed on the following pages, stan-dard diagnostic criteria may not be applicable to patients in the older adult population under-going clinical assessment. Altered metabolism and brain function may mean that the quantity and frequency of use in the older adult may seem very low, but may indeed be quite signifi-cant. Issues of impairment at work and in social activities may not be relevant for the patient who has long since left the workplace and may have given up social activities due to the process of aging and not due to their substance use *per se*. Heightened levels of shame and guilt among older adults, even more so than in other age cohorts, may lead older adults to have greater difficulty in accurately recognizing their pattern of use or the consequences of their engagement with a pathological source of reward or relief—be it pills, alcohol, or gambling.

DOCUMENTATION

This is consistent with documentation requirements in whatever level of care the patient is enrolled. The only cautionary word has to do with the countertransference (by defi-nition, subconscious) of the assessor: primary care physicians and others may be particularly hesitant to document anything in the medi-cal record about an alcohol or other drug use problem in an older adult, especially a long-term patient of theirs, feeling that such a diagnosis could "besmirch the reputation" of the patient.

DIAGNOSTIC ADMISSION CRITERIA

While the ASAM criteria requires meeting the diagnostic criteria for a substance use and addictive disorder, there are concerns about how well the DSM-5 captures the various severities of substance use disorders when applied to older adult patients.

Diagnostic Criteria for Substance Use Disorder from the *DSM-5*[1]

A problematic pattern of substance use leading to clinically significant impairment or distress, as manifested by at least two of the following occurring in a 12-month period:

1. **The substance is taken in larger amounts or over a longer period of time than was intended**

The "larger" and "longer" variables may be different in older adults. The absolute amount of the substance taken may seem small, when in reality it is a difference from the older adult's customary "baseline." Also, the amount of exposure required for substance use to be addictive in the older adult may be deceptively low.

2. **There is a persistent desire or unsuccessful attempts to cut down or control substance use**

In order for the individual to desire or actually try to cut down or control use, there has to be a necessary connection made between the use and resultant problems to cut down or control use, eg, medical problems resulting from use. (See Criterion 9.)

3. **A great deal of time is spent in activities necessary to obtain the substance, use the substance, or recover from the substance's effects**

Creative inquiry is useful when conducting a multidimensional assessment for an older adult. Questions may probe the unique ways an older adult keeps himself or herself supplied with alcohol or pills (who do they get to purchase for them and deliver to them at home?). It is common for patients, their loved ones, or even their caregivers to miss hangovers or withdrawal symptoms, attributing physical or cognitive signs to another etiology other than the true one—alcohol or other drug withdrawal.

4. **Craving or strong desire to use the substance**

Differences attributable to the nature of this population are more likely to be found in early-onset disorders because of the chronicity of the problem and physiological dependence.

5. **Recurrent substance use resulting in failure to fulfill major role obligations at work, school, or home (eg, repeated absences or poor work performance related to substance use; substance-related absence, suspensions, or expulsions from school; neglect of children or household)**

Meeting this criterion for older adults is less likely because they may not work (are retired), and are less likely to attend school where there are role obligations. While they might fail to meet role obligations at home, because so many live alone and are isolated, there is the question of whether anyone is aware of their home situation and how they may be falling short in self-care.

6. **Continued substance use despite having persistent or recurrent social or interpersonal problems caused or exacerbated by the effects of the substance (eg, arguments with spouse about consequences of intoxication; physical fights)**

The older adult, and the professional assessing them, must make the necessary connections between the substance use and potentially resultant problems. However, at times other people in the older adult's life, such as family members or physicians, attribute current problems (eg, falling or hypersomnolence during the day) to the individual's age rather than the substance use, leaving the individual ignorant of the actual cause-and-effect connection between substance use and subsequent problems.

DIAGNOSTIC ADMISSION CRITERIA (CONTINUED)

In the case of gambling, many persons will look at the older adult and rationalize gambling as being an appropriate social outlet and source of recreation (which it is for the vast majority of older adults who partake in casino visits), and may have difficulty identifying and accepting when gambling behaviors have become addictive for the older adult.

7. **Important social, occupational, or recreational activities are given up or reduced because of substance use**

Substance use cannot interfere with occupational activities for an individual who is retired and no longer works. Furthermore, it is common for clinicians not experienced with this age group, or for family members, to fail to recognize the role of substances in an older person's giving up or reducing their activities, believing that this atrophy is a natural process of aging and not a sign of a substance use disorder. On the other hand, for some older adults, substance use (eg, drinking in the afternoon at the retirement community) *becomes* their dominant social or recreational activity.

8. **Recurrent substance use in situations in which it is physically hazardous (driving an automobile or operating a machine when impaired by substance use)**

Many older adults, recognizing the limitations that come with aging, do not engage in any hazardous activities, and are therefore less likely to engage in these activities when using substances. Among the more common potentially hazardous activities is driving, and many older adults either do not drive at all, or if they do drive, they limit their driving to local trips or daylight hours.

9. **Substance use is continued despite knowledge of having persistent or recurrent physical or psychological problems that are likely to have been caused or exacerbated by the substance**

Once again, the problem for older adult populations is the lack of perception of a causal connection between substance use and resultant problems, a disconnect often reinforced by "helpful others" in the older adult's life. Furthermore, feelings of shame might leave the individual less forthcoming about their substance use. Substance-related physical or mental health problems may be presented as general physical problems to the older adult's primary care physician without awareness of any connection to the substance use.

10. **Tolerance, as defined by either of the following:**
    a. **A need for markedly increased amounts of the substance to achieve intoxication or the desired effect**
    b. **Markedly diminished effect with continued use of the same amount of the substance**

Because of the changes that occur in the bodies of older adults, which slow the absorption and metabolism of alcohol, and many other psychoactive substances (including increased body fat, decreased lean body mass, decreased body water, decreased action in the gastrointestinal tract, decreased liver function, and decreased kidney functioning with age), older adults actually use at lower levels (overall) than younger-age populations, and their tolerance is notably lower (not higher) than others who meet four or more diagnostic criteria.

11. **Withdrawal as manifested by either of the following:**
    a. **The characteristic withdrawal syndrome for the substance**
    b. **The same (or closely related) substance is taken to relieve or avoid withdrawal symptoms**

About one-third of older adults who develop a substance use disorder develop it later in life ("late-onset") in response to the stress of aging. A common "breakpoint" between the early- and late-onset subtypes is forty-five years of age. One of the characteristics of the late-onset population is that such people often do not develop physiological dependence.

4

OLDER ADULTS

DIAGNOSTIC ADMISSION CRITERIA (CONTINUED)

As can be determined from the review of the 11 diagnostic criteria for a substance use disorder, it is possible that an older adult may not meet 9 of the 11 criteria because of reasons other than the nature of their substance use. This results in the possibility that the patient may only be able to meet two of the criteria as a result of age-related factors, limiting the diagnostic severity to mild and making the substance use disorder appear less severe than it may be. Therefore, the criteria used to diagnose substance use disorder in younger populations might not apply to older populations.

Complicating the diagnostic process is the fact that many older adults have substance use problems that may not meet criteria for substance use disorders (2-3 criteria), but are still at risk with their use of alcohol or prescribed psychoactive medications. These situations are captured in the ICD-10 diagnostic criteria under harmful use, but not in the *DSM*. These high-risk situations may be the result of ignorance on the part of patients or those who are at an early stage in the development of a diagnosable substance use disorder. It may be possible for an agency operating in an area with a sufficient population density to offer Level 0.5 services for older adults who do not meet the diagnostic criteria for a substance use disorder, but who clearly are at risk for developing one based on their pattern of use.

The response to many of these situations is one of harm reduction rather than abstinence (eg, helping an older adult learn how to use their prescribed pain medication properly as opposed to having them stop taking it entirely). One way of conceptualizing the range of substance use problems and appropriate responses is as follows:

PROBLEM	INTERVENTION
High-risk use	Education
Harmful substance use	Education
Substance use disorder, no more than moderate severity	Abstinence or lower-risk use
Substance use disorder, severe	Abstinence

An evidence-based model for early detection of high-risk substance use, and intervention and referral is SBIRT (Screening, Brief Intervention, and Referral to Treatment). This allows treatment interventions to be tailored to the severity of the substance problem.

OLDER ADULTS DIMENSIONAL ADMISSION CRITERIA

DIMENSION 1:
Acute Intoxication and/or Withdrawal Potential

Because of the changes that take place in the aging body, more care must be exercised when assessing older adults in Dimension 1. Acute intoxication may mask a stroke or the existence of dementia. The length of time for older adults' withdrawal management is often extended because of the delayed metabolism of the substances and a longer time for the patient to regain full cognitive function.

Older adults with an early-onset alcohol use disorder (eg, diagnosable before age 45) often have a chronic and severe history of drinking, putting them more at risk for serious withdrawal problems. Also, for this subset of older alcohol-addicted individuals, this history makes it more likely that they have developed multiple medical problems as a result of their drinking, which can complicate withdrawal. Conversely, older adults with a late-onset alcohol use disorder may not have developed physiological dependence, and withdrawal management may not be a concern if they are not physiologically dependent.

For both early- and late-onset alcohol-addicted individuals, the development of medical problems associated with aging may make withdrawal management more complex. The need for daily transportation for ambulatory withdrawal management (Levels 1-WM and 2-WM) and isolation at home are often issues when considering this type of withdrawal management. For all of these reasons, ambulatory withdrawal management may be a less appropriate option for older adults.

An additional consideration is the potential for withdrawal management medications to increase the risk for falls in older adults being medicated for withdrawal–yet another factor making Levels 3-WM and 4-WM withdrawal management the safer alternative.

DIMENSION 2:
Biomedical Conditions and Complications

Simply as a function of aging, older adults are more likely to have chronic medical conditions (eg, hypertension and other coronary-related disorders, diabetes, chronic pain), which might create risk or interfere with treatment. In addition to specific diseases, there is usually a reduction in sensory perception, including vision and hearing, which may impact a patient's ability to derive maximum benefit from addiction treatment. There also may be possible limitations to mobility (eg, getting to outpatient treatment or recovery groups, even more of an issue for those individuals who do not drive at night) as well as stamina when participating in structured treatment programs (IOP, PHP, residential, and inpatient). The daily schedule in Level 3 or 4 programs often needs to be altered for older adults to build in specific times for rest or naps during the daytime. A program schedule starting at 7:00 am and extending through an after-dinner 12-step meeting, with no "downtime," is generally infeasible for an older adult in residential treatment.

OLDER ADULTS DIMENSIONAL ADMISSION CRITERIA (CONTINUED)

DIMENSION 3:
Emotional, Behavioral, or Cognitive Conditions and Complications

Depression is a common co-occurring problem in older adults with substance use disorders, and is associated with higher rates of suicide. Many older adults do not identify as being depressed, and instead see these symptoms as the result of advanced age. The potential for depression in older adults is exacerbated by bereavement, widowhood, job loss, retirement, chronic medical problems, isolation, and mobility limitations. Depression often is reported instead as physical problems.

The potential for suicide is a major concern with older adults. The group most at risk overall for suicide is white males over 65 years of age. Up to age 64, there is one completed suicide for every 20 to 200 attempts, while for individuals 65 and older, there is one completed suicide for every four attempts. Elder attempters may have higher completion rates since they have less chance of discovery because of greater social isolation, greater frailty, and the use of more lethal means of suicidal behavior.

The second most common co-occurring disorder with substance use disorders is anxiety. This is followed by dementia. Be aware that aging alone does not lead to cognitive impairment great enough to interfere with activities of daily living, and therefore the actual causes for any observed cognitive impairment must be evaluated. Dementia may complicate assessment and treatment.

As mentioned earlier, heightened levels of shame and guilt are commonly present among older adults being assessed for or enrolled in a program of professional treatment for a substance-related or co-occurring disorder. Special care and finesse are required to respond to the shame-based hesitancy of the older adult to discuss his or her substance use or addictive behavior. Confrontation is to be avoided. Motivational interviewing techniques can generate the most accurate database during an assessment.

DIMENSION 4:
Readiness to Change

Readiness to change is, to some extent, related to age of onset of the substance use disorder. Older adults with early-onset substance use disorders (before age 45) may have multiple, unsuccessful attempts at recovery and may have "given up." Older adults with late-onset substance use disorders may perceive their substance-related problems as the result of things other than their use of substances (eg, aging) and therefore see little if any need to modify their use.

Among younger patients, initial motivation for change may stem from such things as a desire to retain employment, retain or regain custody of children, avoid incarceration, or avoid terminating a significant other relationship. These are less often sources of motivation for change in older adults. For them, sources of motivation for change, in increasing order of importance, are financial security, physical health, and, most importantly, maintaining their independence to the highest degree possible.

OLDER ADULTS

OLDER ADULTS DIMENSIONAL ADMISSION CRITERIA (CONTINUED)

5 **DIMENSION 5:**
Relapse, Continued Use, or
Continued Problem Potential

The two most common reasons for relapse in older adults are negative mood states and social pressure (others drinking/using nearby).

Patients with early-onset substance use disorder in older adult populations present greater challenges in treatment because their long and chronic history of use has likely led to significant medical, psychiatric, cognitive, and recovery environment problems. They have a greater array of significant problems and less capacity to cope with them.

In contrast, patients with late-onset substance use disorder in older adult populations are usually less "damaged," have usually achieved successes in their lives before the onset of the substance use problems, including such things as completing high school, college, or postgraduate studies; have had a stable employment history or career; have married and raised families; and have general accomplishments which are associated with stable functioning and good coping skills. These same coping skills and capabilities, when applied to their efforts at recovery, are likely to increase their chances for a positive treatment outcome.

One other group of older adults who might present unique issues are those who relapse after long periods of sobriety achieved through previous participation in treatment and/or recovery support groups. For these people, embarrassment, shame, guilt, and the fear of failure if they attempt recovery again may serve to make it more difficult for them to "try again."

6 **DIMENSION 6:**
Recovery Environment

It is in this dimension that older adults will have the most needs. Mobility and transportation present problems for involvement with recovery support groups, which have the potential to provide not only support for sobriety, but a new "family" for many who are isolated and lonely. The dilemma is how to get to meetings, since many do not drive or at least do not drive at night, when most recovery support meetings occur. Older adults may be dependent on assistive devices such as motorized wheelchairs that make transportation in personal cars more difficult, if not impossible. As people age, they develop more medical problems, which may require frequent medical appointments, again raising transportation issues.

In addition, some peer-support groups may not be receptive to the participation of older adults. Short of overt ageism, 12-step group members may not appreciate the needs or unique presentations of older adults, or may excuse their behaviors or tend to "caretake" someone who reminds them of their own parent or grandparent. Older adult-specific 12-step groups have proven useful in many communities. These may be held on-site at neighborhood senior centers or may be sponsored by a local coalition on aging, or even by a local religious congregation or parish. Some senior centers or churches offer facilitators or parish nurses to attend senior-specific 12-step groups, to act not as professional group psychotherapists but to be welcoming and provide additional support to attendees.

Many older adults live on a fixed income, which might be so inadequate that it may cause them to have to choose between rent, food, and medicines. Nutritional problems may be caused by inadequate finances, but also because of ignorance about what constitutes good nutrition, or an unwillingness to "cook healthy" for themselves alone. A meal delivery system (eg, "Meals on Wheels") may be required.

Leisure time activities may be compromised by health problems, isolation, and ignorance of what might be available to them.

For all of these issues, linking the older adult with aging services such as with Area Agencies on Aging, which are federally mandated in all communities, may provide answers and resources not otherwise obtainable by the older adults. These services range from respite care for caregivers, to help in choosing Medicare supplement plans, to assistance with housekeeping.

Levels of Care

Whatever level of care is considered, the literature suggests that older adult-specific treatment results in better outcomes. For levels of care other than Level 1, outpatient, there are three basic models of older adult-specific treatment programs:

1. a specific older adult program in which all of the patients meet the admission age requirements of the program;

2. a track (an organized older adult program subset) integrated into a larger mainstream treatment program; and

3. a mainstream treatment program in which certain older adult elements are provided by staff as an overlay to other treatment. Older adult-specific ongoing care groups (Level 1) can also be useful.

It appears that late-onset addiction in older adults may have better treatment outcomes in less intensive levels of care, while early-onset addiction in older adults may require more intensive levels of care. This is because the early-onset subset constitutes persons who developed their addiction during their adolescence or young-adult years, have a more severe subtype of addiction, and have "survived" with their addiction into their golden years. In either case, patients may require specialized medical or psychiatric treatment to stabilize Dimension 1, 2, or 3 problems before continuing with their addiction treatment.

Special Considerations for Continued Service and Discharge Criteria

Continued Service Criteria

When assessing for continued service, it is possible that the patient is making progress but at a rate slower than would be expected for younger patients due to a variety of issues. If the patient is not yet making progress, an evaluation is appropriate to determine whether the patient has the capacity to make treatment progress.

Treatment may need to be of a longer duration and slower pace to respond to any current issues, such as cognitive impairment.

External utilization review determinations of how much chronic disease management contact is "enough" for the person with addiction should take into account that older adults—for the multiple reasons stated thoroughly throughout this section—may need a longer period of professional contact for the benefits of professional treatment to take effect.

Discharge/Transfer Criteria

When patients have been unable to resolve the problems that justified admission to the current level of care, the causes are commonly worsening or development of new Dimension 2 or 3 problems, or the possibility of cognitive limits to their ability to utilize treatment (eg, dementia). An assessment is used to determine whether transfer to another type and/or intensity of addiction treatment is in order, or whether consideration for some type of custodial care should be considered. Such custodial care is discussed in consultation with family members.

Intensification or development of new Dimension 2 problems may require a transfer to a general hospital or specialized unit of an acute care hospital (eg, cardiac care unit). If at all possible, after the current Dimension 2 crisis is resolved, consider plans to return the patient to the most appropriate level of addiction treatment.

OLDER ADULTS

Parents or Prospective Parents Receiving Addiction Treatment Concurrently with Their Children

Treatment has evolved, first in recognizing the value of including children with parents, and then, in moving beyond simple child care to assessing the parent-child relationship, the needs of the child, and providing age-appropriate treatment. Because of limited resources, it has been the unfortunate reality that many residential programs have had to place limits on the number of children, their ages, and their needs in making the decision to admit. In this section, it is assumed that the level of care will be individualized to the needs of the parent and child and that by using the full ASAM criteria continuum of care, children of all ages can be screened, assessed, and provided treatment with a parent at a level of care that most efficiently and effectively meets the needs of the parent and child.

While the ASAM criteria for the parenting adult and the prospective parent in addiction treatment are consistent with the descriptions of Level 3: Residential/Inpatient Services and Level 2: Intensive Outpatient/Partial Hospitalization Services in Chapter 7, Level of Care Placement, parenting individuals who have the primary responsibility of offering care and nurturing to a young child have needs beyond those of the general adult population, specific to their parenting status. Children present both incentives to recovery and obstacles to treatment engagement for a parent needing treatment for a substance use disorder (SUD). This section will describe some additional requirements for serving parents with children in treatment.

When there is the actual or potential involvement of child protective services (CPS) or family court, entering addiction treatment is often perceived by a parent or a prospective parent as a possible threat to maintaining custody of children. When possible, preserving the parent/child relationship can be essential to motivating a parent to engage with and remain in treatment. However, the difficulties of being a parent or prospective parent in need of treatment or a parent newly in recovery create challenges specific to this population. These challenges are recognized by ASAM and led to the adoption by ASAM of a public policy statement addressing these issues.[1]

Who constitutes this special population?

Parents with children and prospective parents include several subpopulations that require considerations beyond those described in *The ASAM Criteria* for any other adult. For example, while it is usual to think of parents with children in treatment as women, the parenting individual receiving addiction treatment along with their young children includes a growing number of men responsible for children, as well as couples who share children and are participating in treatment simultaneously but in separate facilities. In this section, it is understood that "parent" may be male or female accompanied by a child in treatment. It is also understood that where "child" is used, there may be more than one child with the parent.

For many individuals, parenting is at the core of their identity, being instrumental to their role and function in society. In addition to acquiring a positive self-perception of their ability to parent with the support of treatment, participating in the resolution of issues with their children that resulted from their SUD provides a sense of control and accomplishment.

Within this section we have defined five subsections of subpopulations in treatment that have requirements beyond those defined previously in the ASAM criteria:

SUBPOPULATIONS

1. Parents with young children or pregnant women in specially designed residential substance-related or co-occurring disorders treatment

2. Parents with young children or pregnant women in specially designed intensive outpatient or partial hospitalization services for substance-related or co-occurring disorders

3. Factors involved in serving the accompanying child

4. Unique needs of pregnant and postpartum women

5. Needs of a parent and child connected with the court for reunification

1) Parents with young children or pregnant women in specially designed residential substance-related or co-occurring disorders treatment

Overall, criteria for the parent in residential treatment who has a child residing with them in treatment are congruent with the descriptions for Level 3 services for adults in the ASAM criteria. In addition, the criteria allowing admission of a parent with a child into residential services must demonstrate that the parent-child combination is in imminent danger as defined in *The ASAM Criteria*, eg, the level of abuse or neglect may be significant so as to endanger the child through abuse or neglect and/or the parent through stress and potential harm to self if not in a 24-hour treatment setting. The following also includes additions or emphases to the criteria for admission and continuing stay.

SETTING
The addition of children to a residential setting brings a number of challenges to a treatment facility in creating a supportive environment for increasing parenting skills. While it is assumed that residential facilities in general are aware of the influence of the recovery environment they provide, it is critical that parents with children have an environment that is also conducive to parent/child routines. Sleeping arrangements, food preparation and mealtimes, bathrooms, and common rooms should encourage positive interaction among the patients and between the parents and children. (See description of the factors involved in serving the accompanying child in subsection 3).

Standards for a residential facility licensed to treat adults with a substance use disorder with children are more complex than the usual adult residential setting. This complexity is inherent in the physical environment, expectations for staff, procedures for accountability, and need for a multidisciplinary team with specialized roles and coordinating mechanisms to address the needs of the parents, children, the parent-child relationship, and other family members. A substantial commitment is needed by administration to implement and maintain the program since there are major fiscal, administrative, organizational, and structural implications for serving parents and children.[2]

A facility that accepts both parents and young children into the residential setting must meet state certification/licensure standards addressing both children and adults in the same facility. (See description of the factors involved in serving the accompanying child in subsection 3).

While this special population is generally

described in this section of *The ASAM Criteria* in a gender-neutral manner, the reality is that too few communities have specialized residential programs available to provide substance-related and co-occurring disorders care to pregnant women or women with young children, and even fewer to men with young children. Those residential programs that do admit young children along with their parent who has a substance use disorder, admit female adults only. There are some agencies who are indeed developing support services for single fathers who have a need for residential addiction treatment and have primary custody of their young children. They can thus take advantage of a specialized residential program where men reside concurrently with their young children while participating in addiction care.

SUPPORT SYSTEMS

Support systems for the parenting adult in residential treatment concurrently with their young children are consistent with those described in the ASAM criteria for Level 3 programs for adults, with the following additions. (See also additions described in subsections 3 and 4.)

The Dimension 6 needs of most parenting individuals in residential treatment concurrently with their young children are extensive. It is critical that connections with supportive resources, including any supportive family members, be made early in treatment, be provided throughout treatment, and be in place in preparation for transfer/discharge. Initially, concrete support such as emergency funds, food, and clothing may be necessary to help establish the safety of the parent and child. Connections with agencies such as Medicaid, Work Force Services, Vocational Rehabilitation, and Temporary Assistance for Needy Families (TANF) should be made early so that services are in place and extend beyond the residential stay. Failure to have ongoing services in place can artificially extend the length of stay in residential treatment or, more critically, affect the parent and child if they are discharged without such services.

Timely access to the ASAM criteria level of care assessed as appropriate to the parenting individual's ongoing progress or lack of progress continues to be an essential support. Put another way, the optimum clinically indicated and necessary level of addiction treatment should be available and accessible to the parent with a substance-related or co-occurring disorder. Such a treatment setting is arguably the most important system of support for the parent and child's individual needs.

STAFF

Staffing criteria for the parenting adult in residential treatment concurrently with their young children remains consistent with those described in the ASAM criteria for Level 3 programs for adults with the following additions:

1. All clinical staff is trained in child development and positive parenting, trauma-informed care, and gender-specific treatment, and are knowledgeable about the skills required to establish and maintain recovery while parenting.

2. Some members of the staff need training and skills in couples and family therapy to assist the person with addiction in their interactions with the other parent of the child and/or with their current life partner including non-custodial parents and any supportive family members.

3. To meet the needs of the child (see later subsections), some members of the staff need training and skills in providing trauma-informed parenting training.

4. The primary therapist needs skills in case management or to work with case managers if available.

THERAPIES

In addition to therapies as described in the ASAM criteria for Level 3 programs for adults, the parenting individual needs evidence-based therapies designed to acquire,

PARENTS/PROSPECTIVE PARENTS

4

improve, and implement the parenting skills needed to address the demands of being a parent in recovery. Good case management is essential.

While increasing parenting skills has been shown to promote the health and well-being of the child, it follows that increasing parenting and attachment skills for the parent will decrease the stresses associated with parenting and increase the potential for a parenting individual's successful recovery. Successful parenting has deep implications: for many it means being successful at the thing that they believe most defines their sense of self. Interventions are designed to develop and improve a basic understanding of child development and what to expect of children at various ages. Therapies that educate, enlist, and motivate the parent to provide nurturing care for the child are a priority.

Staff provide observation of the parent-child interaction in order to coach and encourage non-critical, consistent disciplinary techniques and increase positive interactions between the parent and the child. Throughout the entire treatment process, feedback and coaching are done in a patient-centered, non-judgmental manner. The treatment environment, treatment services, and treatment staff all model the skills they want the patient to develop.

Being trauma informed is necessary but not sufficient in these settings. At the same time that the substance use has stopped, the parents become present for their children. The children are often constant reminders of their past trauma. Staff needs to be able to provide interventions that, at a minimum, assist the patient in using coping skills taught during the treatment process. It is also likely that individuals in treatment with their child will re-experience traumatic memories from their own childhood. They will need help identifying and addressing their own experiences of being parented and understand how these early experiences impact their parenting, their substance use or co-occurring mental health disorder, and how their experience affects their recovery.

Therapies include a comprehensive array of evidence-based treatments for improv-

ing parenting and are individualized to the gender, age, race, ethnicity, culture, marital status, and reproductive history of the parent, and are delivered at the level of understanding of the individual parent. Parents are encouraged to engage in age-appropriate meaningful activities to strengthen the parent-child relationship.

The overall success of treatment has been shown to increase when the goals of the parenting individual are family centered.[3] Additional counseling for a parenting couple as well as for extended family members involved with the parent and child, including the non-custodial parent, is available on-site or through arrangement with other agencies.

To successfully meet the challenges of parenting, rehabilitative skills related to the daily demands of parenting are available on-site. A strong case management component to address Dimension 6 issues is essential.

ASSESSMENT/TREATMENT PLAN REVIEW

In addition to meeting the ASAM criteria for Level 3 criteria for admission and continued treatment, parenting skills, resources, and deficits are assessed in each dimension of the ASAM criteria to determine the extent to which the parent-child relationship has been affected by the individual's substance use and co-occurring disorder as well as how the stresses of parenting will affect the parent's recovery.

The treatment plan/treatment plan reviews also include an assessment in each dimension that reflects progress or lack of progress in each dimension toward achieving healthy parenting in recovery.

DOCUMENTATION

Documentation standards are consistent with all the ASAM criteria levels of care. However, while the parent and child may have similar or overlapping priorities, goals, and methods, the progress or lack of progress of the parent and child are individually documented. Therefore, separate clinical records are maintained.

DIAGNOSTIC ADMISSION CRITERIA

Admission criteria are as described in the ASAM adult admission criteria for Level 3 programs, with additional assessment of the parent-child combination. As a subpopulation, parents in residential substance-related or co-occurring disorder treatment concurrently with their young children also must meet the criteria for Level 3 residential care as a *parent-child combination*. An assessment concluding that the parent-child combination would be in imminent danger if not served at this level of care is helpful in making that case.

PARENTS WITH YOUNG CHILDREN OR PREGNANT WOMEN IN SPECIALLY DESIGNED RESIDENTIAL SUBSTANCE-RELATED OR CO-OCCURRING DISORDERS TREATMENT DIMENSIONAL ADMISSION CRITERIA

Assessment for admission to a residential level of care for a parenting individual entering treatment concurrently with their young child/children follows the ASAM criteria for Level 3 programs for adults with the addition of a further assessment of parenting skills (as described in the assessment/treatment plan review section). Each dimension of the ASAM criteria is assessed to determine the extent to which the existing or pending parent-child relationship has been affected by the individual's substance use or co-occurring mental health problems, including trauma, as well as how the stresses of parenting have affected or will affect the parent's recovery. Dimension 5 is evaluated for stresses of parenting and Dimension 6 emphasizes planning to provide connections to needed services, including other ASAM criteria levels of care or other types of services to ensure the safety and well-being of the parent and child after transfer or discharge from residential treatment.

DIMENSION 1:
Acute Intoxication and/or Withdrawal Potential

In addition to the ASAM adult residential dimensional admission criteria, assessing the risks of having a child whose primary caregiver is an individual who may be undergoing acute intoxication or withdrawal or the risk to an unborn child of experiencing acute abstinence in utero can be considered in Dimension 1. After the birth, women on medication assisted treatment need constant supervision with their infant prior to the significant drop in their medication doses (because, for example, they can fall asleep, jeopardizing the care of the infant).

DIMENSION 2:
Biomedical Conditions and Complications

See the ASAM adult residential dimensional admission criteria. In addition, a parent with a biomedical condition that does not preclude admission to residential services is evaluated for how this condition has had or will have an influence on the parent's ability to care for their child.

In addition to using the ASAM adult residential admission criteria, the effect of any co-occurring mental health issues on the individual's ability to parent is assessed. Additionally, the emotional readiness of the adult with a substance-related or co-occurring disorder to face the responsibilities of pregnancy or parenting is considered. Fear or ambivalence about being a parent (or having an additional child) may need to be addressed. Special attention should be given to the potential for postpartum depression, when the parent in treatment for a substance-related or co-occurring disorder is in the postpartum period.

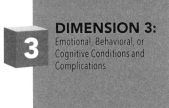

DIMENSION 3:
Emotional, Behavioral, or Cognitive Conditions and Complications

The parent's own experiences of being parented and experiences of trauma are assessed as to the effect of past poor parenting and how that will affect the child and the parent-child relationship.

If medications are involved, assess how they might have affected or will affect parenting.

4

PARENTS/PROSPECTIVE PARENTS

PARENTS WITH YOUNG CHILDREN OR PREGNANT WOMEN IN SPECIALLY DESIGNED RESIDENTIAL SUBSTANCE-RELATED OR CO-OCCURRING DISORDERS TREATMENT DIMENSIONAL ADMISSION CRITERIA (CONTINUED)

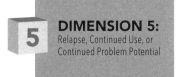

DIMENSION 4:
Readiness to Change

See ASAM adult residential dimensional admission criteria.

This is a critical assessment dimension in many cases. It may be determined that the parent-child combination is in sufficient imminent danger to require the parent to receive clinically necessary residential care. However, if such an admission requires the parent to leave children in the care of others (including, possibly, a temporary foster care placement), this may serve as an insurmountable barrier to accepting recommended treatment. Offering the possibility of bringing their young children with them into a safe, substance-free residential setting–away from substance-using partners or housemates, away from physically or emotionally or even sexually abusive partners, away from neighborhoods where pervasive availability of alcohol or other drugs would present major barriers to success at a non-residential level of care–may motivate the parent to actively pursue recovery by entering residential care. A good working relationship with the child welfare organization can also offer motivation as a successful treatment experience could mean the return of children.

As many children are conceived under the influence of alcohol or other drugs, parents are not always prepared or willing to accept the responsibilities of parenting. Therefore, the level of readiness and motivation to parent their children needs to be assessed. Additionally, the individual's readiness to parent is evaluated, taking into consideration their basic ability to function in the personal and parental tasks of daily living and what, in terms of direction and guidance, treatment will need to provide to help them become successful.

DIMENSION 5:
Relapse, Continued Use, or
Continued Problem Potential

See ASAM adult residential dimensional admission criteria.

Beyond the ASAM adult residential dimensional admission criteria, a Dimension 5 assessment will include how the individual copes with the demands of being a parent and how being a parent has influenced his/her patterns of use. Did the parent hide his/her use from the child? How involved was the parent/child in the culture of use? Examples of stressors that can lead to use include the lack of skills to perform tasks of daily living or the basic understanding of how to meet the child's needs. Also, taking too much responsibility and feeling overly remorseful for the difficulties their children experienced due to their use, if not sufficiently addressed, can become a powerful trigger to use. Demonstrating progress toward a better understanding between parent and child through improving parenting skills does much to ameliorate the effects of guilt and is essential to the recovery of the parent and child.

DIMENSION 6:
Recovery Environment

See ASAM adult residential dimensional admission criteria.

Often a parent with children who is assessed for residential placement does not want to enter this level of care for fear of losing housing. This becomes a barrier to seeking residential treatment. Treatment providers must make provisions for adequate housing as part of the continuum of care. When developing individual treatment plans for a parent with child, treatment agencies need to review the recovery environment to determine if housing options are safe, affordable, and drug free. Safe housing is an essential component for achieving sobriety for parents with children after transfer from residential treatment. The lack of adequate housing decreases the possibility of a successful outcome for both parent and child.

4

PARENTS/PROSPECTIVE
PARENTS

Level of Care

Assessment for admission to a residential level of care for a parenting individual follows the ASAM criteria for Level 3 programs for adults with an individualized assessment in all six dimensions of the ASAM criteria that demonstrates a high probability that substance use and any co-occurring mental health disorder behaviors present imminent danger to the parent-child combination. For the pregnant woman in need of addiction treatment, the person must meet admission criteria as described in the ASAM criteria for Level 3 programs for adults.

Special Considerations for Continued Service and Discharge Criteria

Continued Service Criteria

Continued service criteria are congruent with the ASAM criteria for Level 3 programs for adults with the addition of assessing all six ASAM criteria dimensions for progress, capacity for progress, and new problems connected with the parent's ability to parent in recovery. If the parenting individual or the soon-to-deliver pregnant woman is not making progress, an evaluation is appropriate to determine whether progress is likely to take place at this level of care or whether a more or less intensive level of care or different services (eg, mental health) will best serve the parent-child combination.

Continuing care must ensure that treatment is provided in an individualized, patient-cen-

NOTE

In some treatment agencies, the parent's TANF (Temporary Assistance for Needy Families) payments are used as payment/partial payment for services. As TANF funds are often limited, planning for discharge needs to ensure that the individual has sufficient funding remaining to support transition to independent living, such as safe and affordable housing.

tered, and supportive manner that accounts for the anticipated demands of parenting, employment, education, and participation in other healthy recovery activities.

Transfer/Discharge Criteria

The demand for residential services often exceeds availability. Issues around preparing for transition to less intensive levels of care and resources in the community in a timely fashion constitute a significant influence on the utilization of residential resources and outcomes. The goal of treatment and recovery services for a parent in residential treatment with a child, or for a pregnant woman in residential treatment, is stabilization of acute symptoms with timely access to ongoing recovery support in a less intensive level of care, combined when necessary with transitional/supportive housing and services in the community.

Identifying and addressing Dimension 6 needs early in residential treatment promotes progress toward independence, and self-sufficiency can help reduce long lengths of stay at more intensive levels of care when not clinically necessary. Reducing the length of stay at the acute level of care will shorten the time on waiting lists for those needing stabilization in residential treatment.

Throughout the community there are agencies and organizations designed to provide needed services such as housing, employment, education and training, legal advice, transportation, medical needs, and children's services, including child care. It is important that the treatment team actively develops collaborative relationships with community partners that help to meet the long-term recovery goals of the parenting individual or the individual soon to be a parent, as well as the health and safety needs of the child, the family, and the community.

Because navigating services can be overwhelming, parents will need the assistance of staff to connect with resources such as housing, employment, and child care that are essential to maintaining recovery after discharge.

PARENTS/PROSPECTIVE PARENTS

2) Parents with young children or pregnant women in specially designed intensive outpatient or partial hospitalization services for substance-related or co-occurring disorders

In determining a level of care, it is important that the full ASAM criteria continuum of care be utilized. Combining levels of care can be an excellent strategy for individualizing treatment to the needs of the parent and child. While the focus of this subsection is on the use of Level 2 services, Level 1 services could also be considered, both adjunctive to other levels of care, as well as, when housing is secure, in place of more intensive levels of service.

Overall, criteria for the parent in intensive outpatient or partial hospitalization treatment who attends treatment services concurrently with their young children, and for the pregnant woman in need of substance-related or co-occurring disorders care, are congruent with the descriptions for Level 2 services for adults in the ASAM criteria. In addition, the criteria allowing admission of a parent with child into concurrent Level 2 services must demonstrate that the parent-child combination would be adversely affected were they not treated concurrently, on site, in a Level 2.1 or 2.5 program. The following also includes additions or emphases to the criteria for admission and continuing stay for Level 2 services.

SETTING

The addition of children to a partial hospitalization program setting brings a number of challenges to a treatment facility in creating a supportive environment for increasing parenting skills and meeting the needs of the infant, toddler, or young child. Standards for a facility licensed to treat an adult population with substance use disorder with children may be more complex than the usual adult partial hospitalization treatment setting. This is because a facility that accepts both parents and young children into the treatment setting must meet state certification/licensure standards addressing both children and adults in the same facility (see description of the factors involved in

serving the accompanying child in subsection 3). Thus, the facility may need to be licensed to provide services to children for the hours that infants, toddlers, or young children are in the facility and not in the same room with their parent (usually, parents and offspring receive active treatment concurrently, in the same room, only when parenting training or family therapy services are being delivered).

While this special population is generally described in this chapter of *The ASAM Criteria* in a gender-neutral manner, the reality is that too few communities have specialized day treatment programs available to provide substance-related and co-occurring disorders care to men with young children. Those partial hospitalization and intensive outpatient programs that do admit young children along with their parent who has a substance use disorder tend to admit female adults only, but the need to provide support services for single fathers who have primary custody of their young children is great. The gender-specific needs of both men and women in addiction treatment, including histories of sexual abuse or domestic violence, would often preclude a design of mixed-gender groups. Both male and female parents of young children in addiction treatment benefit from parenting training or family or couples therapy. The setting for such services would be the Level 2 or even Level 1 program where the parent is receiving addiction care.

SUPPORT SYSTEMS

Support systems for the parenting adult in partial hospitalization or intensive outpatient treatment concurrently with their young children are consistent with those described in the ASAM criteria for Level 2 programs for adults, with the following additions. (See also additions described in subsections 3 and 4.)

The Dimension 6 needs of most parenting individuals in day treatment concurrently with their young children may be extensive. It is critical that connections with supportive resources be made early in treatment, provided throughout treatment, and are in place in preparation for transfer/discharge. Initially, concrete support such as emergency funds, food, and clothing may be necessary to help establish the safety of the parent and child. Connections with agencies such as Medicaid, Work Force Services, Vocational Rehabilitation, and Temporary Assistance for Needy Families (TANF) should be made early so that services are in place and extend beyond the Level 2 treatment stay. Failure to have ongoing services in place can artificially extend the length of stay in treatment or, more critically, affect the parent and child if they are discharged without such services.

Timely access to the ASAM criteria level of care assessed as appropriate to the parenting individual's ongoing progress or lack of progress continues to be an essential support. Put another way, the optimum clinically indicated and medically necessary level of addiction treatment should be available and accessible to the parent with a substance-related or co-occurring disorder. Such a treatment setting is arguably the most important system of support for the parent and child's individual needs.

STAFF

Staffing criteria for the pregnant or parenting adult in day treatment concurrently with their young children remains consistent with those described in the ASAM criteria for Level 2 programs for adults with the following additions:

1. All clinical staff is trained in child development and positive parenting, trauma-informed care, and gender-specific treatment, and are knowledgeable about the skills required to establish and maintain recovery while parenting.

2. Some members of the staff need training and skills in couples and family therapy to assist the person with addiction in their interactions with the other biological parent of the child and/or with their current life partner, including non-custodial parents and any supportive family members.

3. To meet the needs of the child (see subsection 3), some members of the staff need training and skills in providing parenting training.

4. The primary therapist needs skills in case management or to work with case managers if available.

THERAPIES

In addition to therapies as described in the ASAM criteria for Level 2 programs, the parenting individual needs evidence-based therapies designed to help them acquire, improve, and implement the parenting skills needed to address the demands of being a parent in recovery. Good case management is essential. Parents are encouraged to be engaged in age-appropriate, meaningful activities to strengthen the parent-child relationship.

While increasing parenting skills has been shown to promote the health and well-being of the child, it follows that increasing parenting and attachment skills for the parent will decrease the stresses associated with parenting and increase the potential for a parenting individual's successful recovery. Successful parenting has deep implications: for many it means being successful at the thing that they believe most defines their sense of self. Interventions are designed to develop and improve a basic understanding of child development and what to expect of children at various ages. Therapies that educate, enlist, and motivate the parent to provide nurturing care for the child are a priority.

Staff provide observation of the parent-child interaction in order to coach and encourage non-critical, consistent disciplinary techniques and increase positive interactions between the parent and the child. Throughout the entire treatment process, feedback and coaching are done in a person-centered, non-judgmental way. The treatment environment, treatment services, and staff all model the skills they want the parent to develop.

Being trauma informed is necessary but not sufficient in these settings. At the same time that the substance use has stopped, the parents become present for their children. The children are often constant reminders of their past trauma. Staff needs to be able to provide interventions that, at a minimum, assist the patient in using coping skills taught during the treatment process. It is also likely that individuals in treatment with their child will re-experience traumatic memories from their own childhood. They will need help identifying and addressing their own experiences of being parented and understand how these early experiences impact their parenting, their substance use or co-occurring mental health disorder, and how their experience affects their recovery.

Therapies include a comprehensive array of evidence-based treatments for improving parenting and are individualized to the gender, age, race, ethnicity, culture, marital status, and reproductive history of the parent, and are delivered at the level of understanding of the individual parent. Parents are engaged in age-appropriate meaningful activities to strengthen the parent-child relationship.

The overall success of treatment has been shown to increase when the goals of the parenting individual are family-centered.[3] Additional counseling for a parenting couple as well as for extended family members including a non-custodial parent involved with the child is available on-site or through arrangement with other agen-cies. To successfully meet the challenges of parenting, rehabilitative skills related to the daily living tasks of parenting are available on-site.

ASSESSMENT/TREATMENT PLAN REVIEW

In addition to meeting the ASAM criteria for Level 2 criteria for admission and continued treatment, parenting skills, resources, and deficits are assessed in each dimension of the ASAM criteria to determine the extent to which the parent-child relationship has been affected by the individual's substance use disorder and any co-occurring mental health problems as well as how the stresses of parenting will affect the parent's recovery.

The treatment plan/treatment plan reviews include an assessment in each dimension that reflects progress or lack of progress in each dimension toward achieving healthy parenting in recovery.

DOCUMENTATION

Documentation standards are consistent with all of the ASAM criteria levels of care. However, while the parent and child may have similar or overlapping priorities, goals, and methods, the progress or lack of progress of the parent and child are individually documented. Therefore, separate clinical records are maintained.

DIAGNOSTIC ADMISSION CRITERIA

Admission criteria are described in the ASAM adult admission criteria for Level 2 programs, with additional assessment of the parent-child combination. As a subpopulation, parents in partial hospitalization or intensive outpatient substance-related or co-occurring disorder treatment concurrently with their young children also must meet the criteria for Level 2 outpatient care as a parent-child combination. An assessment concluding that the parent-child combination is at risk if not served at this level of care is helpful in making that case.

PARENTS WITH YOUNG CHILDREN OR PREGNANT WOMEN IN SPECIALLY DESIGNED INTENSIVE OUTPATIENT OR PARTIAL HOSPITALIZATION SERVICES FOR SUBSTANCE-RELATED OR CO-OCCURRING DISORDERS DIMENSIONAL ADMISSION CRITERIA

Assessment for admission to a partial hospitalization or intensive outpatient level of care for a pregnant woman or a parenting individual entering treatment concurrently with their young child follows the ASAM criteria for Level 2 programs for adults with the inclusion of parenting skills (as described in the assessment/treatment plan review section). Each dimension of the ASAM criteria is assessed to determine the extent to which the existing or pending parent-child relationship has been affected by the individual's substance use and co-occurring disorder, as well as how the stresses of parenting have affected or will affect the parent's recovery. Dimension 5 is evaluated for stresses of parenting and Dimension 6 emphasizes planning to provide connections to needed services, including other ASAM levels of care and other services to ensure the safety and well-being of the parent and child after discharge.

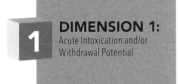

DIMENSION 1:
Acute Intoxication and/or Withdrawal Potential

See ASAM adult dimensional admission criteria for Level 2 services. However, at times considerations come into play regarding the risks of a young child having as their primary caregiver an individual who may be acutely intoxicated or undergoing withdrawal. After the birth, women on medication assisted treatment need constant supervision with their infant prior to the significant drop in their medication doses (because, for example, they can fall asleep, jeopardizing the care of the infant).

DIMENSION 2:
Biomedical Conditions and Complications

See ASAM adult dimensional admission criteria for Level 2 services. In addition, a parent with a biomedical condition that does not preclude admission to the Level 2 services is evaluated for how this condition has had or will have an influence on the parent's ability to care for their child.

DIMENSION 3:
Emotional, Behavioral, or Cognitive Conditions and Complications

In addition to using the ASAM adult Level 2 admission criteria, the effect of any co-occurring mental health issues on the individual's ability to parent is assessed. Additionally, a factor to be considered is the emotional readiness of the adult with a substance-related or co-occurring disorder to face the responsibilities of pregnancy or parenting. Fear or ambivalence about being a parent (or having an additional child) may need to be addressed. Special attention should be given to the potential for postpartum depression, when the parent in treatment is in the postpartum period.

The patient's own experiences of being parented and experiences of trauma are assessed as to what has been the effect of past poor parenting and how that will affect the child and the parent-child relationship. Also, if there are medications involved, assess how they might affect parenting.

DIMENSION 4:
Readiness to Change

See ASAM adult dimensional admission criteria for Level 2 services. Additionally, the individual's motivation and readiness to parent is evaluated.

An individual's functioning, motivation, and ability to care for their child while in treatment must be assessed and taken into consideration. While it is expected that individuals will have some impairment, assessing the readiness of an individual to parent is important in determining how to provide needed direction and guidance. The assessment needs to determine what's realistic and how much motivational support the parent may need.

4

PARENTS/PROSPECTIVE PARENTS

PARENTS WITH YOUNG CHILDREN OR PREGNANT WOMEN IN SPECIALLY DESIGNED INTENSIVE OUTPATIENT OR PARTIAL HOSPITALIZATION SERVICES FOR SUBSTANCE-RELATED OR CO-OCCURRING DISORDERS DIMENSIONAL ADMISSION CRITERIA (CONTINUED)

4

DIMENSION 4:
Readiness to Change

As many children are conceived under the influence of alcohol or other drugs, parents are not always prepared or willing to accept the responsibilities of parenting. Therefore, the level of readiness and motivation to parent their children needs to be assessed. Additionally, the individual's readiness to parent is evaluated, taking into consideration their basic ability to function in the personal and parental tasks of daily living and what, in terms of direction and guidance, treatment will need to provide to help them become successful.

If it is determined that the parent-child combination would be adversely affected were they not treated concurrently on-site in a Level 2.1 or 2.5 program, then medical necessity will dictate that admission for substance-related or co-occurring disorder care will be to a specialized partial hospitalization or intensive outpatient program designed for pregnant women or parents with young children, rather than to a less intensive level of care. When entering clinically necessary addiction care requires leaving young children in the care of others, this may serve as an insurmountable motivational barrier to the addicted parent's accepting recommended treatment. Offering the possibility of bringing their young children with them into a safe, substance-free day-treatment setting–away from substance-using partners or housemates, away from physically or emotionally or sexually abusive partners, even if only for several hours a day–may make the difference in the parent with young children being ready to actively pursue recovery by entering partial hospitalization or intensive outpatient care.

5

DIMENSION 5:
Relapse, Continued Use, or
Continued Problem Potential

See ASAM adult dimensional admission criteria for Level 2 services.

Beyond the ASAM adult intensive outpatient or partial hospitalization level of care admission criteria, a Dimension 5 assessment will include how the individual copes with the demands of being a parent and how being a parent has influenced his/her patterns of use. Did the parent hide his/her use from the child? How involved was the parent/child in the culture of use?

Examples of stressors that can lead to use include the lack of skills to perform tasks of daily living or the basic understanding of how to meet the child's needs. Also, taking too much responsibility and feeling overly remorseful for the difficulties their children experienced due to their use, if not sufficiently addressed, can become a powerful trigger to use. Demonstrating progress toward a better understanding between parent and child through improving skills does much to ameliorate the effects of guilt and is essential to the recovery of the parent and child.

6

DIMENSION 6:
Recovery Environment

See ASAM adult dimensional admission criteria for Level 2 services.

In many cases, Dimension 6 may be the most critical dimension in determining if Level 2 services fit the needs of the parent and child. Treatment providers must assure that the recovery environment is safe, affordable, and drug free as part of the criteria for admission to Level 2 services. Safe housing is an essential component for achieving sobriety for parents in treatment and can be provided through connection with Level 3.1 services or through other housing programs including shelter options. The lack of an adequate environment makes outpatient treatment a less viable treatment option for a parent in treatment with a child. When there isn't adequate housing available, parents with children are at risk of relapse, which also places their children at risk.

Level of Care

Assessment for admission to a Level 2 program for a parenting individual follows the ASAM criteria for Level 2 programs for adults with an individualized assessment in all six ASAM criteria dimensions that demonstrates a high probability that substance use and likely co-occurring mental health disorder behaviors present imminent risk to the parent-child combination. For the pregnant woman in need of addiction treatment, the person must meet admission criteria as described in the ASAM criteria for Level 2 programs for adults.

Special Considerations for Continued Service and Discharge Criteria

Continued Service Criteria

Continued service criteria are congruent with the ASAM criteria assessment for Level 2 programs for adults with the addition of a multidimensional assessment to determine progress, capacity for progress, and new problems connected with the parent's ability to parent in recovery. If the parenting individual or the soon-to-deliver pregnant individual is not making progress, an evaluation is appropriate to determine whether the progress is likely to take place at this level of care or whether a more or less intensive level of care or different services (eg, mental health) will best serve the parent-child combination.

Continuing care ensures that treatment is provided in an individualized, patient-centered,

NOTE

In some treatment agencies, the parent's TANF (Temporary Assistance for Needy Families) payments are used as payment/partial payment for services. As TANF funds are often limited, planning for discharge needs to ensure that the individual has sufficient funding remaining to support transition to independent living, such as safe and affordable housing.

and supportive manner that accounts for the anticipated demands of parenting, employment, education, and participation in other healthy recovery activities.

Transfer/Discharge Criteria

The demand for parent with children services often exceeds availability. Issues around preparing for transition to less intensive levels of care and resources in the community in a timely fashion remain a significant influence on the utilization of treatment resources and outcomes. The goal of treatment and recovery services for a parent in Level 2 treatment with a child, or for a pregnant woman in Level 2 treatment, is stabilization of symptoms with timely access to ongoing recovery support in a less intensive level of care, combined when necessary with transitional/supportive housing and services in the community.

Identifying and addressing early in treatment Dimension 6 needs that promote progress toward independence and self-sufficiency can help reduce long lengths of stay at more intensive levels of care when not clinically necessary. This can increase access to the treatment system for other parents with children and shorten the time on waiting lists for those needing stabilization in this level of care.

Throughout the community there are agencies and organizations designed to provide needed services such as housing, employment, education and training, legal advice, transportation, medical needs, and children's services, including child care. It is important that the treatment team actively develop collaborative relationships with community partners that help to meet the long-term recovery goals of the parenting individual or the individual soon to be a parent, as well as the health and safety needs of the child, the family, and the community.

Because navigating all of these services can be overwhelming, especially with the complexity of child care and transportation needs, parents will need close monitoring to facilitate meaningful use of these resources.

3) Factors involved in serving the accompanying child

The common factor among parents with children in treatment is the child. There is evidence to suggest that the lifetime risks to a child with a parent suffering a substance use or co-occurring disorder are high. However, with adequate parental addiction treatment, parenting support, and parenting training as indicated, and case supervision, a child may be better off residing with a parent who has a substance use disorder than being removed from the parent's custody.

Providing concurrent treatment to the parent and the child accompanying the parent into addiction treatment has been shown to increase the overall health and well-being of the child, leading to the child's improved behavioral and emotional functioning, enriched family relationships, and positive social networks that provide protective factors for children.[4]

Agencies admitting children with a parent to residential treatment or to partial hospitalization or intensive outpatient treatment in a specialized program designed for parents of young children, offer a range of child services. However, agencies offering simple day care or child care only may meet requirements for Level 1. They do not meet the requirements of the parent-child combination needing Level 3 or Level 2 substance use disorder service. While the child is 'adjunct' to the parent, he/she is an individual recipient of treatment services based on an assessment, treatment plan, and ongoing reviews.

SETTING

An addiction treatment setting that accommodates children differs significantly from the usual adult addiction treatment setting (licensing regulations will vary from state to state). Considerations for the welfare and safety of the children define the environment and include numerous amenities not found in a typical adult residential, partial hospitalization, or intensive outpatient program. Children in the treatment facility may differ widely in ages from newborn through elementary school.

The facility must be able to provide a physical environment suited to this wide range in ages, each with its own developmental requirements and do so on a flexible basis. Depending on the ages and physical needs of the children receiving treatment, accommodations for sleep, nutrition, toilet, play, schooling, and travel must be provided on an age-appropriate basis and may vary on a daily basis. Children will need proper facilities for their own individual, group, and play therapy: recall that offering "day care only services" to children is not sufficient for a program that professes to offer integrated services for a parent with a substance-related or co-occurring disorder and young children who have their own mental health needs or have been affected by the substance use history of their parent or other primary caregivers.

The culture of the environment is one that highly supports physical and emotional safety, with a focus on empathy not authority. It is relational, nurturing, and sees the parent-child relationship as extremely important in the treatment process.

SUPPORT SYSTEMS

Pediatric care is available 24/7, provided in-house, or through service agreements with appropriate outside agencies. Medical services for children who are medically compromised (asthma, diabetes, etc.), or who have special needs such as developmental delays, are also to be provided. Treatment providers will have service agreements with appropriate outside agencies to ensure that children be referred for needed medical, psychological, or other types of care.

As children are more susceptible to infections, and children mingling in a treatment setting are even more susceptible to communicable diseases, emergency planning for treatment facilities will include how to isolate and contain highly communicable diseases such as measles, chicken pox, streptococcal infections, methicillin-resistant staphylococcus aureus (MRSA), etc. The plan will clearly define how the facility will deal with infectious children who are in their care until the risk of their transmitting an air or fluid or food-borne illness has subsided.

Close coordination with schools that serve the educational needs of the school age child is developed and maintained during treatment. The ethical and legal aspects of confidentiality for the child must be considered.

Transportation is available to ensure that the child can connect with support systems and schooling if not provided on-site.

Case management for the child is essential to coordinating services.

STAFF

Staff is appropriately credentialed professionals familiar with infant and child development. Staff can identify the signs and symptoms of exposure to a variety of traumas and have training to provide a broad range of age-appropriate interventions to address identified vulnerabilities.

THERAPIES

Therapy begins with a safe, enriched environment. Using a developmental perspective, therapies are designed to reduce the negative impact of ineffective parenting, enhance resilience, and increase the ability to achieve developmental competence, achieve healthy social interaction, and cope with adversity.

Activities are planned to engage the child with the parent and promote healthy attachment, development, and mental health.

Early intervention programs are helpful for children who are developmentally delayed or have been diagnosed with failure to thrive. Treatment also develops services to encourage attachment and bonding and support parent-child relationships. It is the responsibility of treatment to facilitate reunification for children who are not able to be actively involved in treatment with their parent.

Therapies are individualized to the child's assessed needs and adapted to the child's developmental stage and ability to comprehend. Children are often receiving occupational and physical therapy, speech therapy, individual therapy, play therapy, family therapy, and multiple family therapy, as well as birth-to-three services.

To successfully meet the challenges of parenting, rehabilitative skills related to the daily living tasks of parenting are available on-site and can involve the child. Additional counseling for the child in relation to the parenting couple including a non-custodial parent, as well as extended family members connected with the child, is available on-site or through arrangements with other agencies.

ASSESSMENT/TREATMENT PLAN REVIEW

The child accompanying a parent into residential or outpatient treatment for a substance-related or co-occurring disorder is assessed as an individual using age-appropriate biopsychosocial assessment tools to determine medical/clinical necessity. Parent information about the child is vital to the assessment and is included in the child's assessment as collateral. The assessment is used to determine treatment needs and to create an individualized treatment/service plan for the child.

DOCUMENTATION

Documentation as described elsewhere in *The ASAM Criteria* pertains to the child. Note, however, that a separate health record is established and maintained for the child. It should contain the child's assessment, service plan, progress notes, releases, correspondence, and any documentation pertinent to the child.

DIAGNOSTIC ADMISSION CRITERIA

Young children accompanying parents into specially designed concurrent treatment programs will not meet the criteria for clinical necessity with a substance-related diagnosis, however, they most often meet medical/clinical necessity for treatment with diagnoses such as disorders of attachment, behavior, attention, development, learning, etc. Older children could be appropriate to participate in family programming for the adult receiving Level 3 or Level 2 substance-related or co-occurring disorders care, but such care would be described in the regular adult sections of *The ASAM Criteria*. Such clinical participation by older children is not the intended subject of this chapter.

For infants or young children whose presenting clinical history is inadequate to substantiate a formal diagnosis, information provided by collateral parties (such as family members or a legal guardian) can indicate a high probability of a clinically necessary diagnosis, subject to confirmation by further evaluation.

FACTORS INVOLVED IN SERVING THE ACCOMPANYING CHILD DIMENSIONAL ADMISSION CRITERIA

DIMENSION 1:
Acute Intoxication and/or Withdrawal Potential

This dimension as traditionally defined in the ASAM criteria would not apply to young children in treatment with a parent. However, effects on the child of a parent's Dimension 1 issues including in utero, could be noted here. Also, a physically dependent neonate at birth may undergo management of neonatal withdrawal syndrome in the nursery.

DIMENSION 2:
Biomedical Conditions and Complications

Children need to be assessed for current as well as historical medical issues, with emphasis on biological and genetic disease vulnerabilities and early development and immunizations including the effects of exposure to substances, including alcohol and tobacco in utero and second-hand smoke after birth. Fetal alcohol spectrum disorder (FASD) is clearly a consideration to be evaluated in some cases. Screening for tuberculosis and other communicable diseases is completed at intake.

DIMENSION 3:
Emotional, Behavioral, or Cognitive Conditions and Complications

Normal stages of a child's physical and psychological development can be disturbed by abuse and neglect, including exposure to violence, social isolation, separations, nutritional deficiencies, infections, and toxins related to living in a household where a parent is using substances. The effects of trauma, mental health problems, poor attachment to the parent, harmful patterns of behavior, and delay in achieving developmental milestones are expected to distract from healthy adaptation and require monitoring and intervention by clinical staff and other professionals specializing in child development. Consideration is given to special needs children, children with developmental delays, FASD, and other emotional, behavioral, or cognitive conditions requiring additional services.

DIMENSION 4:
Readiness to Change

A child's potential for change can be assessed using the measures of risk and protective factors current in prevention protocols. Measures of well-being can be assessed for positive adaptation despite adversity or risk and can indicate how best to target interventions to increase well-being. Children's readiness to change also involves issues related to their emotional and social development, eg, readiness to deal with trauma, difficulties with isolation or loneliness, etc.

PARENTS/PROSPECTIVE PARENTS

FACTORS INVOLVED IN SERVING THE ACCOMPANYING CHILD
DIMENSIONAL ADMISSION CRITERIA (CONTINUED)

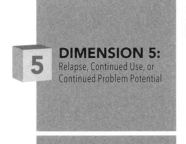

DIMENSION 5:
Relapse, Continued Use, or Continued Problem Potential

Assessment in Dimension 5 evaluates the risks of a child returning to the same or similar problems that include the risk that the parent may relapse, socioeconomic disadvantage, family dysfunction, parenting deficits, and other stressful life events. High level of risk in this dimension may rise to the level of imminent danger for a child. An assessment of how the child coped with past situations will include both positive and negative behaviors. The likelihood is that with appropriate supervision and stimulation the child can achieve success. Dimension 5 will include an age-appropriate safety plan addressing the need for supervision and stimulation for the child.

DIMENSION 6:
Recovery/Living Environment

Dimension 6 focuses on assessing current and future issues related to stable living that improve family support in the community with planning and connections to housing, child care, learning opportunities, and other assessed environmental and social needs and supports. Dimension 6 includes a safety plan. Unresolved issues in this dimension can rise to the level of imminent danger for a child.

Level of Care

Although it may appear that the child "follows" the parent into treatment, the needs of the child should be considered conjointly as well as separately from those of the parent. This requires the child to be assessed using an age-appropriate assessment to determine the level of care and to create a treatment/service plan individualized to the needs of the child. The child's level of care may differ from the parent's, requiring a clinical override to provide services at a particular level of care; or to provide treatment conjointly with the parent. It is possible that a child may need only attachment and bonding with a parent through the activities of daily living, while another child may need extensive therapy to address significant problems or developmental delays.

Special Considerations for Continued Service/Discharge Criteria

Continued Service Criteria

Based on an ongoing assessment of individual needs, the goal of treatment for a child is to provide stabilization and continuing care to address the assessed needs in all six ASAM criteria dimensions. Case management is an important link between levels of care and ongoing services in the community.

Transfer/Discharge Criteria

After participating in their parent's care in a specialized residential or Level 2 treatment setting, a child needs preparation and support in making a transition to other accommodations. Termination of important relationships needs to be facilitated in an individually tailored manner. A school-age child in residential treatment needs preparation and coordination in making a change to a new address, especially when a change of school is necessary.

Discharge without Dimension 6 services such as safe housing, good nutrition, child care, parental stability, and a safety plan in place can constitute a situation of imminent danger to the child. Unresolved problems in any dimension can raise the level of risk to that of imminent danger. In assessing for imminent danger, the possibility of terminating a parent's right to custody must be considered and be part of the child's safety plan. The safety plan should also include arrangements for appropriate supervision and stimulation for each child. Treatment providers should be skilled in assessing for imminent danger and in taking the necessary precautions to ensure the child's safety.

4) Unique needs of pregnant and postpartum women

There is evidence that targeted interventions to pregnant women with substance use disorders increase the incidence of prenatal visits, improve birth outcomes, and, overall, lower health care costs for mother and baby.[5] A pregnant woman may be reluctant to seek treatment if she believes she will lose custody of her baby, or be criminally charged with abuse or neglect. Ideally, the medical community at large has the ability and the obligation to be an understanding ally to a pregnant woman in assessing her addiction treatment needs and providing her with a connection to treatment options.[6] Toxicology screening of pregnant women is designed to help mother and child and should be done universally to avoid targeting racial minorities and economically disadvantaged women. When done punitively, addicted women have been shown to avoid prenatal care.

While many women want what's best for their babies and are therefore motivated to change their harmful behaviors when pregnant, others who are pregnant and addictively using illicit substances are reluctant to seek prenatal care due to the severity of their SUD. Fears of social services interventions, possible loss of custody of her baby and other children she might have, and, in some jurisdictions, even criminal charges are a valid concern and policies vary by locality. Providers of prenatal care should stress that treatment of her substance use disorder provides the best opportunity for a healthy baby and healthy mother who is able to parent with love and responsibility. Engaging in treatment is often the best way to retain child custody and the health care provider should act as her advocate as she is progressing in treatment.

Connecting with treatment services during pregnancy increases the chances that the baby will be born drug free, that the mother's ability to parent in recovery will be increased, and that child protective services (CPS) will not become involved or, if involved, will be supportive of her rights as a parent as she progresses in her recovery efforts.

SETTING

The setting for providing parent-with-children services to pregnant women is congruent with the descriptions in the ASAM adult residential and Level 2 criteria and the descriptions in subsections 1 and 2. Additionally, the setting has the ability to accommodate the physical stresses of pregnancy, such as difficulty climbing stairs or performing chores that are physically too demanding or when bed rest is medically determined.

SUPPORT SYSTEMS

Support systems for the pregnant woman in treatment are consistent with those described in the ASAM adult residential and Level 2 criteria and the additions to the support systems in subsections 1 and 2, with emphasis on health care needs. Pregnant women in residential treatment, in addition to primary medical services, receive prenatal, labor, and delivery medical care in a timely manner through on-site and/or connections in the community.

Access to medication assisted treatment for pregnant women who are opioid addicted is the accepted standard of care.[7]

Methadone treatment in particular, within the context of other components of comprehensive care, has been shown to be effective in reducing the use of illicit substances and related consequences during pregnancy.[8] Increasingly, combination buprenorphine and naloxone (Suboxone) treatment is also being used with pregnant women with opioid use disorder.

Medication assisted treatment stabilizes the woman, protects the fetus from repeated episodes of withdrawal, eliminates the risk of infection from contaminated needles, and creates a mandatory link to prenatal care.[9] When initiating medication assisted treatment, the woman is counseled regarding Neonatal Abstinence Syndrome and what to expect at delivery.

STAFF

Staffing criteria for serving a pregnant woman in parent-with-children treatment remains consistent with those described in the ASAM adult residential and Level 2 criteria and in subsections 1 and 2 with the following additions:

All staff members are trained in procedures for accessing medical services related to prenatal care, labor, and delivery. A healthy birth, as well as any complications connected with the birth, can have a profound impact on the birth mother, staff, and other patients. Staff members are aware of and trained in how to respond therapeutically to the numerous outcomes of a pregnancy.

Staff is trained in a multidimensional approach to assessing and delivering services individualized to the needs of the pregnant woman. It is especially important that staff be trained in techniques to contain and/or de-escalate situations which could become physically volatile.

THERAPIES

Therapies described in the ASAM adult residential and Level 2 criteria and in subsections 1 and 2, are consistent with the needs of pregnant women in residential treatment with the following emphases:

Treatment is interdisciplinary, comprehensive, evidence-based, and coordinated to address issues related to prenatal, perinatal, and postpartum mental and physical health concerns, as well as psychosocial and practical issues.[10] The benefits of choosing to reduce or eliminate the use of alcohol and other drugs at any time during pregnancy are emphasized. Services are provided in a non-judgmental, supportive environment in which the physical changes related to pregnancy and childbirth; concerns about the effects of alcohol, tobacco, and other drug use during pregnancy on the health the fetus; and the social stigma of using alcohol, tobacco, and other drugs while pregnant can be discussed openly and therapeutically.

While pregnant women, as a class, require a general array of services related to their pregnancy and delivery, as individuals, each woman has a set of circumstances unique to her situation. Staff is proficient in assessing her current situation and reproductive history: Is this a welcome pregnancy? Is this the patient's first pregnancy? How many children has the patient borne? How many are living? With whom are they living and does she have legal custody? What role does CPS play in her relationship to her children? What were the circumstances of her pregnancy? What is the anticipated role of the father in the pregnancy, delivery, and parenting? Other areas to be examined are whether she has parented previous children; if those children are living with others, the role she has played in parenting them; whether previous pregnancies have been substance exposed; whether she has received addiction treatment or used opioid agonist medication during previous pregnancies; whether she was using birth control when she became pregnant; and what her future child-bearing and contraceptive plans are. The impact of sexual abuse on prenatal care visits and delivery should also be examined and addressed.

While pregnancy may provide motivation to enter treatment, motivational therapies are essential to continuing engagement and recovery. Therapies that incorporate reproductive counseling, promote bonding with the expected child, and encourage commitment to health, wellness, and ongoing recovery are recommended.

Most treatment services usually continue for stabilization after delivery. Post-delivery treatment services include support for parenting a newborn, choices about breast feeding, integration with other children and family members, regaining physical health, coping with hormonal swings, and continuing to pursue recovery goals.

Other services include family planning and the importance of spacing future pregnancies; identifying relapse triggers that delivery introduces, such as no longer worrying about exposing the infant to substances; dealing with the stress of being a parent or having to take care of other children, if any, without proper support systems; and the importance of the postpartum environment and caregiving to the newborn's development. Case management to obtain the needed equipment, clothing, and food is also important.

ASSESSMENT/TREATMENT PLAN REVIEW

Assessment/treatment plan review criteria for serving a pregnant woman in residential and Level 2 treatment remain consistent with those described in the ASAM adult residential and Level 2 criteria and in subsections 1 and 2 with the following additions:

The assessment and treatment plan and reviews will highlight the physical needs related to the health and well-being of the woman and the fetus.

DOCUMENTATION

As described in the ASAM adult residential and Level 2 criteria.

DIAGNOSTIC ADMISSION CRITERIA

As described in the ASAM adult residential and Level 2 criteria.

UNIQUE NEEDS OF PREGNANT AND POSTPARTUM WOMEN DIMENSIONAL ADMISSION CRITERIA

Dimensional admission criteria are congruent with the ASAM adult residential and Level 2 criteria with the following cautions in each dimension:

DIMENSION 1: Acute Intoxication and/or Withdrawal Potential

There is assurance that a pregnant woman has been assessed for risk of hazardous consequences of withdrawal from alcohol or other drugs on herself and on the fetus. Withdrawal needs may be addressed with medication assisted treatment and managed within the treatment setting.

DIMENSION 2: Biomedical Conditions and Complications

While pregnancy and delivery are not considered a disorder, it is critical to assess for current and potential biomedical problems connected with prenatal, perinatal, and postpartum stages. Chronic health care issues such as hepatitis, HIV, and diabetes must be assessed and considered for safe delivery.

Information is also gathered regarding prior pregnancies and their outcomes and whether the patient is using any medications as prescribed.

DIMENSION 3: Emotional, Behavioral, or Cognitive Conditions and Complications

Assessment includes the degree of stress that the pregnancy has created, the potential for additional stresses of childbirth, and the presence of perinatal depression and the potential for postpartum episodes of depression. If the use of psychotropic medications during pregnancy is considered, a risk-benefit analysis should be discussed with the patient.

DIMENSION 4: Readiness to Change

Readiness to change is often enhanced by a woman's desire to have a healthy, substance-free baby, but her pregnancy and future parenting obligations may also be a source of stress. Assessing readiness to change includes an assessment of her ability to cope with stress and her potential for following through with treatment and parenting.

UNIQUE NEEDS OF PREGNANT AND POSTPARTUM WOMEN DIMENSIONAL ADMISSION CRITERIA (CONTINUED)

DIMENSION 5: Relapse, Continued Use, or Continued Problem Potential

As childbirth can be accompanied by physical problems necessitating the use of medications with relapse potential, risks for relapse are assessed and addressed realistically. Relapse prevention education that addresses postpartum triggers and planning for responding to those triggers without resorting to substances is provided.

DIMENSION 6: Recovery Environment

The need for a safe and stable environment is of critical concern during pregnancy, birth, and postpartum stages. It is expected that, while some environments might be acceptable in other circumstances, pregnancy demands, and the federal guidelines require, that a pregnant woman be given priority for the safety and support that treatment services offer.

Level of Care

While Federal Priority Guidelines for admission to treatment give preference to pregnant and female parenting injecting drug users and pregnant and female parents with addiction, they do not prescribe a particular level of care. Assessment for admission to a residential level of care for a pregnant woman follows the ASAM adult residential criteria with an individualized assessment in all six ASAM criteria dimensions that demonstrates a high probability that substance use behaviors present imminent danger to the woman and/or her fetus may lead to another level of care more appropriate to her situation.

Special Considerations for Continued Service and Discharge Criteria

Continued Service Criteria

Continued service criteria are congruent with the ASAM adult residential and Level 2 criteria and subsections 1 and 2 of this description. Treatment is not expected to end with delivery. Services usually continue for stabilization after delivery. An ASAM criteria multidimensional assessment of progress, capacity for progress, and new problems connected with the health of the woman, her ability to deliver a healthy baby,

and the health and safety of the mother and child postpartum determines medical necessity and continued stay in treatment.

Women are at increased risk of resuming use following delivery because they may be no longer worried about exposing the infant to substances. They may be experiencing postpartum depression, may have stopped or lowered their psychotropic medications, may experience enormous shame and guilt, and they may feel overwhelmed by the responsibility of having a child, which might lead to a return of the previous alcohol and other drug connected behaviors. At the same time, the first years of life for attachment and infants' brain development are critically important. While for optimal development, it may be best if the mother or a parenting adult can be fully available to care for their children during this time, there are many economic and personal reasons why this may not be possible. Treatment needs to be aware of these issues and have the ability to support the individual in their choices.

Discharge/Transfer Criteria

Discharge/transfer criteria are congruent with the ASAM adult residential and Level 2 criteria and subsections 1 and 2 of this description.

5) Needs of a parent and child connected with the court for reunification

Often a parent is made aware of the need for treatment through legal interventions on behalf of the child. Criteria for assessing, admitting, and providing treatment services to the parent in treatment who has court obligations related to the custody and/or welfare of their child are well covered in the ASAM adult residential and Level 2 criteria and subsections 1, 2, and 3. The distinguishing characteristic of this subpopulation is its unique connection with the courts and the responsibility that treatment bears in working collaboratively within multiple disciplines and systems with a variety of mandates, timelines, and protocols. Most of the children in such circumstances have a Guardian ad Litem appointed by the court to assure that the needs of the child, as an individual, are met. Regular communication with such parties is essential.

In order to regain or maintain custody of a child, a parenting individual with a substance use disorder is often mandated by the court to residential treatment where reunification can be safely guided. Child welfare concerns are multifaceted and often contradict the realities of addiction treatment and recovery.

The Center for Substance Abuse Treatment (CSAT) of the U.S. Department of Health and Human Services sets regulations for federally funded addiction care. CSAT holds the view that recovery from a substance use disorder is long-term and includes the possibility of relapse. Timelines for reunification set by federal law through the Adoption and Safe Families Act (ASFA) as well as time limits and policies of Temporary Assistance to Needy Families (TANF) (which often provide necessary support for a parent newly in recovery) are often in conflict with this view of substance use disorders.

When agreeing to provide treatment services to parents attempting reunification with a child, staff needs to be trained and knowledgeable about the laws and rules governing reunification. Many jurisdictions have developed specialized programs to bring child welfare, addiction, and court services together to support reunification within the time limits prescribed by law. It is critical that treatment providers be willing to participate in a collaborative process among agencies across multiple systems in order to facilitate the reunification process in a timely manner. Decisions related to progress or lack of progress in treatment need to be carefully considered, as delays can result in the removal and loss of custody of a child. Decisions that adversely determine the outcome of custody can rise to the level of imminent danger for the parent and/or child.

PARENTS/PROSPECTIVE PARENTS

Persons in Safety-Sensitive Occupations

Safety-sensitive workers with substance use disorders have four special qualities that lead to important and distinct treatment needs:

1. All safety-sensitive workers, by definition, have a responsibility to the public. The extent of the effect on the public comes from two factors:

   a. The size of the population safety-sensitive workers affect and the depth of the effect from potential impairment, and

   b. The amount of public trust that is implied in that worker's occupation.

   Both these factors place a burden on treatment, its efficacy, and the importance of that patient's recovery for overall public welfare. These two factors color decisions that are made regarding the type, intensity, and setting of treatment provided to this special population.

   It is important to note that aggressive treatment and continued monitoring does more than assure the safety of the public at large. The consistent and sustained care

SAFETY-SENSITIVE OCCUPATIONS

Safety-sensitive workers can come from many different occupations, including:

» Police officers

» Health care professionals

» Airline pilots

» Attorneys

Here, you will see the four qualities that lead to distinct treatment needs for this special population.

of one individual helps his or her entire cohort. For example, if a police officer suffers an addiction relapse that has the slightest possibility of an adverse effect on public safety, his peers, the leadership of the police force, officials in the government jurisdiction served by the police force, and public opinion may reactively punish subsequent officers who develop a substance use disorder. "Guilt by association" is not an altogether inappropriate term for such realities. In contrast, the compulsory and consistent management of a given individual's recovery status "pays forward" to others in his or her cohort; success of treatment and recovery for the one can have a positive "halo effect" for the many in that individual's occupational or professional cohort.

2. Safety-sensitive workers do best when offered cohort-specific treatment, which facilitates adequate self-disclosure and the subsequent repair of the damage produced by past substance-related behaviors. Once they develop a substance use disorder, many safety-sensitive workers compromise their job efficiency and (although less often than sensationalist journalism might suggest) at times create public harm. When it happens to someone in the general public, harm from substance misuse or addiction has a limited effect size. In the safety-sensitive worker, however, the depth and breadth of the potential damage to the public and the environment can be much larger. Addiction in a nuclear plant manager has an effect size that is greater than in a retail worker, for example. Most individuals in safety-sensitive positions take their oath of duty to heart; the breach of this commitment engenders shame. Safety-sensitive workers need to disclose, accept responsibility, normalize, and

SAFETY-SENSITIVE WORKERS' KEY QUALITIES

1. All safety-sensitive workers, by definition, have a responsibility to the public.

2. Safety-sensitive workers do best when offered cohort-specific treatment, which facilitates adequate self-disclosure and the subsequent repair of the damage produced by past substance-related behaviors.

3. Some safety-sensitive workers have direct access to addicting substances.

4. Health care professionals commonly have difficulty adopting the role of a patient.

learn to prevent any future breach without excessive self-castigation. Participation in group therapy and/or support groups by individuals who have similar work issues and who conduct themselves under the same professional codes for ethical behavior is essential for a return of a healthy self-concept, and for a decreased probability of relapse. Such needs often prolong the treatment encounter.

3. Some safety-sensitive workers have direct access to addicting substances. Health care workers (physicians, advanced practice registered nurses (APRNs), physician assistants, dentists and dental workers, veterinarians and animal workers, nurses, pharmacists, and drug manufacturers) commonly have ready access to addictive substances. Police officers, especially those in undercover drug operations, have easy access to gray and black market drugs. Attorneys who represent drug traffickers may also find an unfettered access to highly addictive drugs. The treatment of such individuals should include management of drug access, drug refusal skills, work environment modification to decrease drug access, and other occupation-specific interventions geared to decrease relapse. This too may require additional time in treatment to allow the patient to learn the complex skills necessary to remain abstinent in an environment that is "hostile," or at least

not "neutral," when it comes to providing support for abstinence and recovery.

4. Health care professionals commonly have difficulty adopting the role of a patient. The origins of this difficulty are beyond the scope of this document. However, one needs to become a patient before treatment can successfully commence; this is especially true for behavioral health care workers. The more responsibility an individual has in his or her day-to-day life, the more difficult it is to adopt the patient role—one that accepts suggestions and sets aside one's well-formed worldviews, which may have become distorted by substance use. For example, academic health care workers who serve as faculty in a health professionals' school, or who may be medical directors of hospitals or other treatment facilities, have the most difficulty in this regard. They have such special expertise and depth of technical knowledge that they overrely on those assets. They may have difficulty maintaining the patient role and accepting the recommendations of their own treating physician or other clinician.

SETTING
During the initial diagnostic portion of the treatment experience, safety sensitive workers should discontinue work. They should stay away from work until:

1. Public risk issues have been addressed and appropriately managed.

2. All work regulations, licensure, and legal issues have been addressed and permit a return to the workplace.

3. Work cues and triggers have been delineated, and a management plan is in effect.

4. The work environment has made appropriate alterations to maximally encourage sustained recovery. This is especially important for workers who have steady personal access to their previously addictive drugs.

5. Supervisory personnel have training to address profession-specific workplace issues for the recovering addicted worker.

Removing the worker from his or her work setting may involve Level 3 care, but, at the very least, the initial treatment setting should shield the patient, coworkers in the work environment, and members of the general public from the potential dangers created by addiction in the workplace. Specifically, when the patient in need of substance-related or co-occurring disorders care is a health professional, that individual should not return to practice and thus expose their own patients to the potential dangers posed by their own addiction. Abstinence and recovery should first be solidly established, and risks of relapse in the workplace should be fully identified with an initial management plan for those in place.

In addition, the setting of addiction treatment for safety-sensitive workers should reflect the reality that treatment is best executed for such persons in a milieu containing one's peers. This may necessitate travel to a specialized facility with expertise and a sufficient number of other patients with the same or similar professional training, licensure, and work environment as the safety-sensitive worker entering treatment. Once the patient (the worker with a substance use disorder) has accepted and internalized his or her need for addiction care, effective management of occupation-specific stressors is established, and triggers and recovery skills are addressed, safety-sensitive workers can usually continue their treatment in more generalized addiction care.

SUPPORT SYSTEMS

Safety-sensitive workers demonstrate similar medical and psychiatric comorbidities as the general population, except for a decrease in the probability of psychotic disorders (these tend to be screened out during professional training). An efficient and well-integrated continuum of care is the most important component of the support system. Management of medical issues may be especially challenging with health care workers, as they are prone to critique their personal medical care due to "insider bias" and the misguided belief that they are their own best doctor, nurse, pharmacist, counselor, etc.

Many subgroups of safety-sensitive workers have profession-specific recovery monitoring programs that improve outcomes and increase public safety. Most states in the U.S. have Physician Health Programs, for example. Many nurses, dentists, pharmacists, airline pilots, and attorneys in the U.S. have comparable programs. Similar programs exist in many countries, with varied degrees of sophistication. Treatment providers must learn about each of these support networks, learn how to interface with such programs, and how to refer to and support the continued development of these programs. Indeed, these monitoring programs are critical for the long-term success of the safety-sensitive worker. Such programs are best visualized as an integral part of the continuum of chronic care for the chronic disease of addiction.

It is the job of initial treatment providers to seek out any available monitoring program for a patient under their care, and to help the safety-sensitive worker understand that these monitoring programs are an integral part of their care. Such programs are critical in maintaining a good outcome, and are more than just an optional "support system." Monitoring programs that are independent of licensure and credentialing bodies provide a means of continuous support and advocacy for the patient whose career is a safety-sensitive occupation. Research has shown that such programs dramatically improve long-term prognoses as well. The combination of effective, managed initial treatment and long-term contingency contracting has been proposed as the gold standard for all addiction care in the United States.[1]

Beyond formal monitoring and case management programs such as Physician Health Programs (PHPs) and Lawyer Assistance Programs (LAPs), peer-led, cohort-specific support groups may also be available. Physicians have "Caduceus" groups, pilots have "Birds of a Feather" groups, and attorneys have attorney-specific Alcoholics Anonymous groups, for example. Unlike monitoring programs, these support groups use volunteers and mutual help to ensure the recovery of each member. These mutual help groups are at times integrated into a monitoring program; in other places they are distinct. Treatment providers should locate peer-specific support groups for a patient under their care and integrate them into treatment whenever and wherever possible. For example, a treatment program may provide information to patients about International Doctors in Alcoholics Anonymous (IDAA), and help its patients register for and attend IDAA conferences.

Cohort-specific treatment of safety-sensitive workers may require travel to another part of the country, or even to another country. Such programs often have decades of experience with the subtleties of treatment in a particular cohort. Especially since the wars in the Middle East of the past quarter century, and since the events of September 11, 2001, the need for trauma-informed care for members of the armed forces, local first responders, and public safety officers has led to the development of specialized treatment programs or treatment tracks tailored to the needs of persons in safety-sensitive occupations outside of health care. Specialized treatment cohorts are available for police and fire fighters to go through treatment with others who have comparable workplace experiences.

However, addiction is a chronic disease requiring chronic care. Therefore, the specialty programs located away from a patient's home should seek out practitioners in the worker's home locale that have demonstrated expertise in step-down care of safety-sensitive workers. Conversely, the local practitioner who focuses on a specific cohort should learn about the step-up facilities that have demonstrated expertise in their target population, and be willing to refer his or her patients to such facilities. These offer the patient a cohort of peers with whom they can relate regarding workplace, licensure, and return-to-work issues.

STAFF

Treatment staff that work with safety-sensitive workers need a variety of therapeutic skills. Every staff member in a multidisciplinary setting need not have all skills, but all of the following skills should be at hand to ensure a positive outcome. These staff skills are as follows:

1. The staff should be trained in the specifics of their patient's work environment (eg, staff who work with pilots should know about aviation training, changing shifts from day to night, aviation-ingrained thinking patterns, and concerns over aeromedical and FAA rules and regulations).

2. The staff needs supervision to avoid reactive judgment and negative confrontive interpretations (eg, "When you were working undercover, you arrested the same person who sold you drugs the previous day?"). Such insights are important in the process of discovery, shame, and commitment to recovery, but the staff must guide such insight, not demand it before the patient is ready.

3. The staff needs training to be able to manage the dynamic defenses of the particular cohort (eg, learning how to circumvent argumentation with attorneys who are patients under their care).

4. The staff needs to manage intellectualization in highly educated safety-sensitive workers, and be sensitive, empathic, skilled, and firm when working with a patient whose occupation requires him or her to assume great responsibilities. Such individuals may be in the position of making decisions that affect many employees or subordinates, but their personal recovery requires them to be open to the advice and even direction of their clinical caregivers.

5. The staff needs to understand the stresses and traumas that often accompany safety-sensitive positions. Staff with direct experience are helpful, even mandatory. One example might be having on staff a former fire fighter who has experienced the horrors of managing a conflagration of several city blocks.

6. The staff needs to understand the political context of addiction care in the patient's particular cohort. This is critical when giving advice to a safety-sensitive worker regarding self-disclosure after treatment and how best to reintegrate into his or her work environment.

7. The staff needs to understand, interface with, and work within the established continuum of care that may be present for a specific cohort, and know what will be expected at the next point of care, including reporting progress and raising concerns when appropriate.

8. The staff will have to know about specifics of drug testing in health care practitioners with substance use disorders, including the types of drugs typically used in that cohort and their effects on the brain and body.

9. The staff will have to develop confidence in addressing a patient's cognitive abilities, have access to neurocognitive testing, and understand when to take action to

delay or prohibit a physically or cognitively impaired safety-sensitive worker from returning to work. This limit-setting skill is both intellectually challenging and emotionally difficult, particularly when the treating clinician identifies with the professional who is a patient under his or her care.

THERAPIES

Profession-specific Group Therapy

Therapy skills of safety-sensitive workers vary according to their cohort. Put another way, not every patient who is a safety-sensitive worker has the same "psychological-mindedness" or is equally adept at being a constructive member of a therapy group or a therapeutic milieu. Many health professionals who are in treatment, for instance, slip into a role of "junior therapist" in groups or within the patient community. These tendencies need to be managed skillfully, without having patients feel ashamed when they realize how they have been conducting themselves.

All types of safety-sensitive workers should have a setting where they talk openly with peers and staff about their responsibility to the public, and how this was potentially or actually breached in the course of their addiction. This type of therapy is best performed in a group setting. A specific reparative sequence occurs, where the patient discloses fully, and subsequently takes responsibility for his or her past actions. The group then normalizes such events without minimizing them, and the patient learns to prevent any future breach without falling into nihilistic self-blame. Safety-sensitive workers who intellectualize (of course, this means virtually all of them early in treatment) tend to move from the disclosure to a false normalization stage of intellectual acceptance without proper emotional and dynamic internalization.

Profession-specific Support Groups

Profession-specific support groups are distinctly different from (and often confused with) profession-specific group therapy. Support groups may be in the format of 12-Step groups or a more informal discussion group. They may be led by a professional facilitator, but are more often organized and led by volunteers from the same cohort. The purpose of such support groups is to provide understanding about substance use disorders in that profession and normalize past behaviors (normalizing is different from absolving blame or responsibility). Members of the group who are further along in recovery provide mentorship, sponsorship, and hope for patients who have just entered the support group. The group addresses the nuts and bolts of how to work in a safety-sensitive occupation with a history of a substance use disorder, and how to interact with coworkers, supervisors, and those who rely on the patient's future integrity.

Job and Career Issues

Proper treatment of a substance use disorder in a safety-sensitive worker should address the pragmatic, logistical, and emotional problems that the worker will face in recovery. Such information and its processing may occur in profession-specific group therapy (discussed earlier), but commonly needs to be addressed in individual sessions as well. The therapist assigned to occupational reentry should understand the profession of the patient. The therapist often works with a supervisor, credentialing body, licensing board, and workplace peers to structure work reentry. Reentry should be staged and timed to ensure the best possible prognosis for the safety-sensitive worker, lest public opinion be swayed against the profession or, more dramatically, a member of the public is placed in harm's way.

Drug Safety and Drug Refusal Skills

Safety-sensitive workers who are in many health care fields may be required to handle, on a daily basis, the same drugs to which they are addicted (eg, an opioid-addicted anesthesiologist who handles her drug of choice every day during the course of a routine work day). Much of the success of their clinical recovery and reintegration into work comes from proper environmental controls (eg, ensuring narcotics accountability systems are in place in a veterinary practice)

combined with drug refusal skills. Health care professionals need a very different set of skills than the alcohol-addicted person who goes to dinner in an environment where alcohol is served. Cue exposure, role-playing, workbook activities, and experiential therapies should all be used in combination to ensure that the health care worker is prepared for returning to a high-risk environment.

Medication Management

Pharmacotherapies for addiction (such as the prescribing of an opioid receptor antagonist) may be useful components of a treatment plan and return-to-work agreement. Programs and physicians who treat commercial airline pilots have to be especially cautious about prescribing medications for addiction or co-occurring conditions, carefully balancing the pilot's need for medication with grave consequences to his or her career should a non-approved medication be prescribed. Physicians who treat commercial pilots should be familiar with Federal Aviation Regulations (FARs) 61.53, 67.113, 67.213, 67.313, and 91.17.

ASSESSMENT/TREATMENT PLAN REVIEW

The assessment and treatment planning process in the treatment of safety-sensitive workers is complicated by two factors:

1. The difficult line between an individual's privacy needs and the imperative for public safety. This is covered in the documentation section.

2. The need for more extensive cognitive testing in safety-sensitive workers.

The assessment process should, naturally, involve family members and peers at work as collateral sources of historical clinical data. Often, formerly high-functioning individuals will show a more intense deterioration at home while they try (and are successful for a time) to hold their career together. Those conducting the assessment should have the knowledge and experience to realize that the workplace is usually the last domain of a health professional's life to manifest signs of impairment, and that just because there have been no "workplace incidents" does not mean that the patient's addiction is not serious or even advanced.

A careful balance between the patient's need for privacy and the work environment's involvement exists here too. The work environment must be involved because the breadth and depth of the breach in public safety (if any) must be assessed. This often conflicts with the patient's need for privacy. A multidisciplinary team should work on this balance for each patient they assess.

Neurocognitive testing should be performed in almost every case. Such testing requires a seasoned neuropsychologist who can determine how the results of a substance use disorder impact the safety-sensitive worker's work. Neurocognitive testing should be covered by third party payers.

Assessment of comorbid psychiatric and medical disorders is crucial, as with any patient who suffers from a substance use disorder.

Treatment planning and its review for the safety-sensitive worker should include the following elements:

1. A commitment to a long-term, de-escalating treatment process with checks and balances that ensure the public's safety.

2. Structured, long-term schedules for body fluid or tissue analysis (collection of samples of urine, saliva, hair, etc., for drug testing), which ensures the best treatment prognosis and thus public safety.

3. Involvement of the patient's work environment, which provides input into treatment issues, managed and scaled work reentry, work environment safety (to prevent relapse), and management of certification and licensure issues.

4. Contingency planning that would come into effect should the individual discontinue treatment without a viable alternative (to prevent a surreptitious and premature reentry into the workforce).

5. The involvement of profession-specific group therapy (if available) and profession-specific support groups.

6. Neurocognitive testing and repeat neurocognitive testing, if indicated.

7. Other therapies noted in the therapies section.

DOCUMENTATION

Documentation in the treatment of safety-sensitive workers necessitates a balance between the needs of the patient and the needs of the public. Strict confidentiality with regard to the patient's record will engender trust. On the other hand, many safety-sensitive workers require letters or other forms of communication that attest to their overall condition. This type of reporting is commonly an ongoing process for a number of years, and may include updates as to the patient's status to licensing boards, superior officers, a state bar association, commanding officers, or regulatory bodies.

At times, these agencies demand more specific information than a simple **Safe/Unsafe** to work assertion. Disclosure of limited information in the medical record may be required before that individual is cleared for work. Thus, the medical record in facilities that care for safety-sensitive workers must be clearly delineated into "potential release information" and "strict privacy" sections. All treatment providers must be aware on a daily basis that their chart entries may result in a complete loss of their patient's professional career if careful attention is not paid to detail.

Every evaluation performed on the safety-sensitive worker patient must be carefully conducted with such information in mind. Some evaluators split their evaluations into two parts, one focused on the patient's ability to work and a second focused on internal treatment needs. Many consider such a process to constitute best practice in the medical records management of this population.

DIAGNOSTIC ADMISSION CRITERIA

The diagnostic admission criteria for safety-sensitive workers who have a substance use disorder do not differ in form from diagnostic admission criteria for patients from the general public. The final treatment placement, however, may need to be distinctly different for reasons described in this section.

One notable exception to the diagnostic admission criteria exists. In an effort to ensure all professional pilots are not underdiagnosed, and to ensure public safety, pilots in the United States are subject to 14 CFR 67.107.[2] In this section of the U.S. Code of Federal Regulations, both the *DSM-IV* diagnoses of substance abuse and substance dependence are treated in a similar fashion. Pilots who meet *DSM-IV* criteria for substance abuse are to be treated in a fashion similar to those diagnosed with substance dependence. This issue will change in a yet to be determined manner after the implementation of the *DSM-5*, which no longer distinguishes between "substance abuse" and "substance dependence."

Careful assessment is important with safety-sensitive workers, as they may derive intense secondary gain from underreporting symptoms of any substance use disorder. The final treatment disposition of a safety-sensitive worker with a substance use disorder should commence only after a thorough assessment is complete, including interviews with (usually more than one) a collateral source of information, such as a workplace superior, a coworker, and/or a spouse.

PERSONS IN SAFETY-SENSITIVE OCCUPATIONS
DIMENSIONAL ADMISSION CRITERIA

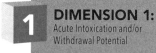

DIMENSION 1: Acute Intoxication and/or Withdrawal Potential

DIMENSION 2: Biomedical Conditions and Complications

In Dimension 1, withdrawal management can be provided at any level that is medically appropriate, provided that the individual is kept from his or her work if there are known or suspected concerns for public safety. In Dimension 2, biomedical problems may prove especially vexing in health care professionals who "know too much for their own good" and attempt to direct their personal care without input from their real medical team. Experience has shown that health care providers can develop a rigid but incorrect analysis of their own medical illnesses, often to their own detriment. Data shows that physicians with a substance use disorder often have no personal physician, and have not received usual, periodic physical examinations or preventive health care procedures. A firm hand combined with differential diagnosis acumen should be applied to all such patients.

DIMENSION 3: Emotional, Behavioral, or Cognitive Conditions and Complications

The emotional and behavioral needs of safety-sensitive workers are similar to those of the general public. Physicians, for instance, have rates of depression that are comparable to rates among the general public (though their rates of suicide are higher). As previously described, the safety-sensitive worker must have a more comprehensive assessment, and a more measured approach to intellectual deficits caused by substance use disorders, whether acute or chronic. The older adult patient may attempt to cover up cognitive slippage in an attempt to return to a demanding job that is central to his or her life meaning.

SAFETY-SENSITIVE OCCUPATIONS

PERSONS IN SAFETY-SENSITIVE OCCUPATIONS
DIMENSIONAL ADMISSION CRITERIA (CONTINUED)

4
DIMENSION 4:
Readiness to Change

This dimension is important in the care of safety-sensitive workers. Workers are often motivated and ready for action in order to keep their job more than they are interested in recovery and wellness. It is usual for them to be quite ambivalent about whether they have an addiction or not. Safety-sensitive workers may be very intelligent, have years of post-secondary education, and may learn the language of recovery quickly. They can repeat it back to the staff and combine their words with whatever sincerity they perceive will maximize their chances of quickly returning to their work or profession. As summarized in "walking the talk," assessment of a patient's stable progress in stages of change involves tracking outcomes in behavior, attitude, application of skills, and reports of improvement from collateral sources, not just in what a patient says.

For patients in non-safety-sensitive occupations, progress in the other five dimensions may be such that one would normally return the patient to a work setting. However, for patients in safety-sensitive occupations, the treatment team may need to hold ambivalent individuals away from the risky portions of their work, or keep them from their work completely, until Dimension 4 issues mend. Because risks to the public are so high, skilled individual and group therapists assess for measurable improvement in readiness to change to be sure that recovery is well underway before returning the worker to full work activity.

5
DIMENSION 5:
Relapse, Continued Use, or Continued Problem Potential

The most important issue in Dimension 5 comes from what is termed "relapse intolerance." Substance use disorders, including other addictive disorders are, by nature, potentially relapsing disorders. The normal course of care is to work with a patient over time, often through repeated recurrences of signs and symptoms, until the patient fully and consistently understands the total impact of the negative consequences of his or her continued substance use, and the mounting life problems associated with such use. Even after the illness is internalized, the patient may lapse into alcohol or other drug use from time to time. With safety-sensitive workers, there is not the luxury for the treating clinician to stand back and sagely watch while a series of lapses and relapses helps the patient internalize full acceptance of his or her addiction. For many safety-sensitive workers, there can be little or no tolerance for relapse. This intolerance comes from two places: (1) the potential for real public harm, and (2) the reprisal from licensing agencies, legal action, professional organizations, or command structures.

Careful attention must be paid to relapse prevention. All types of relapse prevention skills should be taught and effectively displayed back to the treatment team by the patient. Traditional lecture formats are of limited benefit in learning these skills. Skills in cognitive-behavioral therapy, de-escalation of harmful thoughts and emotions, drug refusal skills, and moving away from high-risk stimuli should be practiced prior to a return to work. All safety-sensitive workers should have a confidential individual, sponsor, or therapist ready at their fingertips when triggered to relapse, so that urges do not become drug use behaviors.

All safety-sensitive workers should participate in a random, observed drug-screening program of sufficient sophistication to detect surreptitious substance use or other addictive drug/alcohol use which was not identified in the original assessment. Such drug screening of body fluids and hair provides reassurance to the workplace system at risk were the individual to relapse to use. It also provides a comfort to the patient who has a substance use disorder. Treatment providers often hear: "I had a craving and began thinking about using, and then thoughts about those drug tests popped in my head. I realized that if I used, the test would show it, and that I couldn't hide it. I felt disappointed and safe at the same time."

4

SAFETY-SENSITIVE
OCCUPATIONS

PERSONS IN SAFETY-SENSITIVE OCCUPATIONS
DIMENSIONAL ADMISSION CRITERIA (CONTINUED)

6 | **DIMENSION 6:**
Recovery Environment

All patients who develop substance use disorders need to address their environment. In the case of many safety-sensitive workers who have drug exposure in their workplace, the work environment should be modified to accommodate the patient returning from treatment for a substance use disorder. Early in recovery, when their recovery is fragile, it may be necessary to limit drug exposure in this subgroup. All safety-sensitive workers should also have decreased exposure to alcohol.

Safety-sensitive workers are no different from others with substance use disorders in needing to address their living environment. Returning home to a using spouse, or to a spouse ignorant of or even hostile to recovery, is not a safe path to ongoing recovery. Moving from a highly structured treatment environment to living alone, in isolation, is never recommended. Some sort of extended residential care in a halfway house or sober house, especially one designed for professionals in safety-sensitive occupations, is preferable to living alone, especially during early recovery.

Levels of Care

With concerns for public safety in mind, treatment should be aggressive and definitive. Many safety-sensitive workers are given only one chance to attain recovery by licensing boards, professional organizations, command hierarchies, and civil agencies. With this in mind, the initial level of care that provides the best possible prognosis should be selected. Referral to the "least intensive level of care that is effective" or to the "least restrictive environment for care" is generally the norm for members of the general public who seek addiction treatment. But for those living under a "one strike and you're out" professional environment, where there is "zero-tolerance" of any lapse or relapse, the driving force behind the level of care chosen is the level that has the best chance of establishing stable recovery.

Containing the alcohol or other drug use and sequestering the patient away from work may mandate a more intensive level of initial care than with the general public. "Fail first" requirements for admission to a more intensive level of care are formulae for disaster when designing treatment plans for this special population of individuals with substance-related and co-occurring disorders. Many workers in the health professionals treatment field have seen suicides. Such experienced clinicians have also seen cases of the public being placed at risk by a safety-sensitive worker who was sent to a less intensive level of care because of misplaced notions based upon application of the ASAM criteria without taking into account the dangers attendant to the patient's occupation.

Transfer to a less intensive level of care should occur only if that level of care has exhibited past expertise in managing the multiple patient- and environment-related issues for the patient's professional cohort. The lack of expertise at a less intensive level of care may necessitate treatment away from the patient's geographical home, or remaining in a more intensive level of care for a longer period of time.

Persons in Criminal Justice Settings

This population includes individuals with a substance use disorder, gambling disorder, or related disorder who are incarcerated or under community-based supervision, such as those housed in correctional halfway houses or monitored in the community under the supervision of community corrections (probation or parole officers) or through court-ordered alternatives to incarceration (such as through participation in drug court programs). In each of these circumstances, the individual is accountable to comply with a criminal justice sanction. The contingency applied by the criminal justice system may involve a reduction in, or the absence of, criminal penalties should the individual successfully complete a plan of care to address his or her substance-related or addictive disorder.

SETTINGS

Settings can include:

» Jails (offenders who most often are sentenced to 2½ years or less, and non-sentenced offenders/detainees awaiting trial in a jail).

» Prisons (maximum, medium, or minimum security level).

» Pre-release, such as work-release centers.

» Other criminal justice mandated, supervised settings where movement is monitored and controlled.

» Community corrections-involved offenders on probation or parole. Many such offenders are given intermediate or alternative diversionary sanctions; intensive supervision (which may include electronic monitoring of their location or status); or are mandated to a community-based addiction treatment service stemming from a judge's order, a condition placed by a probation or parole officer, from an appearance before a specialty drug/mental health court, or as a step-down from a jail or prison.

Because of the various security levels, disposition of the courts, classification policies and procedures, differences in types of programming available, and staff capabilities and staffing patterns, the ASAM criteria may or may not have applicability. The challenge is in determining where and how the ASAM criteria are fitting and can be meaningfully applied.

Applicability Issues

The justice system's appropriate mission of applying penalties, such as fines or serving time under incarceration and placing the highest priority on assuring public safety, may at times appear to conflict with a treatment provider's mission of helping people change through collaboration on treatment goals and motivational enhancement. However, high rates of incarceration for drug use, high costs of incarceration, high rates of relapse and recidivism, and the effectiveness of mandated treatment have guided many criminal justice administrators and policymakers to embrace the habilitative/rehabilitative role of addiction treatment among criminal justice populations.

The objectives of public safety and desirable clinical outcomes can be, and most often are, complementary when the ASAM criteria are artfully and skillfully introduced and applied to persons with a diagnosable substance use or other addictive or co-occurring disorder who find themselves under the auspices and sanctions of the criminal justice system. Both clinicians and criminal justice professionals are likely to be focused on outcomes such as reduced substance use, reduced criminal recidivism, and improvements in functional areas of a person's life, such as education/employment and prosocial relationships. Rates of reoffending and reincarceration generally are lower when rates of relapse to addiction are lower, and when rates of relapse are lower, rates of readmission to withdrawal management services, addiction treatment services, emergency medical services, and hospitalizations are lower.

4

CRIMINAL JUSTICE

There are, however, five challenges and special considerations when using the ASAM criteria with this population:

1. The ASAM criteria assesses Dimension 4 (Readiness to Change) and applies individualized treatment using evidence-based practices (EBPs), which assess stages of change and apply motivational enhancement strategies with flexible lengths of stay (LOS). However, frequently there is an expectation in criminal justice systems that the individual should be in the action stage in order to manifest healthy, prosocial behaviors and remain in compliance with court orders. In addition, this is often mistakenly thought to be attainable in addiction treatment programs in criminal justice systems by designing a fixed length of stay and non-individualized program completion/graduation targets. The criminal justice system may have unrealistic assumptions about how soon a person can reach the action stage, and correctional services may involve a mandated length of stay in clinical care that is too brief to achieve reasonable clinical outcome goals, including goals for motivational enhancement interventions.

Judges, other court officials, and probation and parole officers often mandate specific levels of care (eg, residential treatment) and lengths of stay (eg, 1 year) versus focusing on mandating comprehensive assessment and ongoing treatment adherence. It is understood that judges, other court officials, and probation and parole officers often do what they do because they perceive it as being required of them, as is the case in the context of sentencing and supervision guidelines given to those in the criminal justice system by a legislature or an executive branch authority. It is the treatment community's role, and challenge, to assist the criminal justice system in interpreting the guidelines in a manner that offers the best match to the treatment options for this population.

2. Due to limited resources, community and institutional corrections most often make treatment and placement decisions based not on "offenders' needs" but on "what resources are available."

3. Criminal justice's emphasis on criminogenic risk, need, and responsivity (RNR) may place the need for addressing substance use disorders or co-occurring disorders as a secondary or tertiary focus, versus addressing these disorders concurrently. While recognizing substance use disorders as a criminogenic need, criminal justice may place higher priority and resource focus on other high-risk criminogenic factors such as antisocial values, criminal associates, and antisocial personality traits. The challenging question for the treatment community in linking the ASAM criteria to this population may be as follows: Is the behavioral health care provider adequately trained or equipped to address the RNR for the offender population? And if not, what should be done to improve this capability? However, the treatment of the other non-criminogenic disorders, while not the priority, are necessary for recovery and reducing criminogenic factors.

4. The individual's responsivity to a formal course of treatment and other recommended interventions at times may be in conflict with the criminal justice system's expectations of the participant. It is critical to involve all parties (eg, judges, probation and parole officers, other court officials) as well as the justice-involved individual in the decision-making process. It is also important to create learning opportunities for criminal justice personnel to understand more about substance-related and addictive disorders, and also co-occurring mental health conditions.

5. Most treatment programs in prisons and jails, drawing from clinical traditions employed in therapeutic communities, emphasize the group and community as primary change agents in contrast to individual, one-on-one counseling. Individual sessions are provided, but are secondary to the group structure and milieu interventions. This approach may be followed because of high caseloads and budgetary considerations, but it may also be based on the belief that criminogenic risks and needs are best addressed in a group context, and thus take priority over individual counseling and individualized treatment planning. This is not to say that individualized treatment does not occur for this special population; it does, but it needs to be contextualized to the limitations of the specific criminal justice setting.

SUPPORT SYSTEMS

In a community setting, it is particularly important for treatment providers to create a strong working relationship with probation and parole officers, judges, the court, and/or other legal entities involved in the participant's care. This working relationship entails establishing a good communication system where clear conflict resolution steps are in place and professional confidentiality codes are followed. Such a relationship may start with joining together in the common goal of improving individuals' self-directed functioning, which increases public safety, decreases legal recidivism, and enhances safety for children and families. From there, mutual discussion and cross-training can develop consensus on understanding the stages of change, motivational enhancement therapies, and how collaboration among all stakeholders promotes lasting accountable change for those involved in justice services.

If the participant is in an institutional or prison-based setting, treatment providers should place emphasis on community reintegration support and case management prior to release.

In cases where offenders in the community relapse, consideration of the substance use dis-

order needs to be taken into account. Conducting an updated multidimensional ASAM criteria assessment and intensifying the level of clinical services may be warranted in lieu of reincarceration. If, after assessment of the causes of a slip or relapse, it is clear to the patient (the justice-involved individual) and the treatment team what can be done to improve the outcome, and the patient is willing and able to adhere to a revised treatment plan, then progress is being made and treatment should continue without sanctions. However, if it is clear that certain behaviors need to change to improve the clinical outcome (eg, the justice-involved individual must stay away from drug-using friends or practice peer-refusal skills), but the patient is not interested in adhering to those strategies, then the patient has the right to refuse the revised treatment plan, even if this places him or her out of compliance with the order for treatment, and results in the application of criminal penalties or sanctions that would otherwise have applied to the individual.

At this point, or at any point when the patient is just "doing time," not engaging in therapeutic activities and not working actively on improving treatment outcomes, then graduated sanctions are useful in lieu of an all-or-nothing imposition of the full penalty or sanction possible. Graduated sanctions can raise the patient's awareness that he or she is not adhering to treatment and that this is out of compliance with mandated treatment. A sanction should occur whenever the patient demonstrates that he or she is not actively participating in treatment.

STAFF

It is critical that treatment staff working with criminal justice populations be versed in working with criminogenic risk, need, and responsivity (RNR) as well as substance use disorders and co-occurring disorders.

In institutional settings, clinical staff should be versed in working within a correctional setting and should be able to integrate treatment goals with the goals of the larger institution (eg, safety and security). Additional specialized training may include the following: behavior management techniques, correctional crisis intervention, suicide prevention, and management of hostage situations.

Clinical staff need to be well versed in trauma-informed care, should manifest the interpersonal skills that are related to positive outcomes (eg, empathy, respect, genuineness), utilize evidence-based practices (eg, cognitive-behavioral therapy, medication assisted treatment, 12-Step facilitation, contingency management, motivational interviewing, and modified therapeutic community treatment), and incorporate cultural and gender responsiveness.

THERAPIES

In general, approaches should parallel those used in any level of care with an individual with a substance use or co-occurring disorder who is not involved with the criminal justice system. These therapies should be based on a multidimensional assessment and specific participant needs. An additional emphasis may need to be placed on addressing Dimension 6 (Recovery Environment) areas in collaboration with criminal justice personnel for the purpose of community reintegration when the individual is transitioning from a 24-hour institution-based program such as a prison or jail setting. These include addressing safe housing, job preparation and employment, education, and health care needs in assisting the criminal justice participant to address the lifestyle changes necessary to manage their addiction and criminal lifestyle patterns.

Providers should be capable of using evidence-based practices designed to address substance-related, mental health, and criminogenic needs. Examples of these include but are not limited to:

» **Cognitive-behavioral therapy** addressing thinking that increases a person's risk, not only for continued use of substances (relapse), but also antisocial behaviors leading to criminal recidivism (reoffending).

» Skills in **motivational interviewing**, **motivational enhancement therapy**, and a sophisticated understanding of the **transtheoretical model of behavior change**.

» **Family and systemic therapies** addressing dysfunctional family and peer relationships.

» **Contingency management therapies** and the use of incentives and sanctions to maintain participant engagement.

» Understanding of **trauma-informed care** and how trauma affects individuals cognitively, emotionally, and behaviorally.

» An understanding of and skill at being a provider in a **modified therapeutic communities** setting.

ASSESSMENT/TREATMENT PLAN REVIEW

A comprehensive assessment designed around the issues of criminal justice-involved individuals is performed. Assessment of criminogenic risk, need, and responsivity (RNR) such as criminal identity, anger management, impulse control, values and behaviors, antisocial peer relationships (including gang involvement), family structure and functioning, criminal lifestyle (attitudes, beliefs, and values), locus of control, and low self-control should be integrated into the assessment data. Assessment should include that for a potential increased risk for suicide, traumatic brain injury, attention deficit hyperactivity disorder, developmental and cognitive disorders, mood and anxiety disorders, impulse control issues, as well as antisocial values and behaviors, even if not meeting criteria for antisocial personality disorder.

It is essential to collaborate with correctional staff on identified participant treatment goals to ensure that clinical goals are in alignment with correctional case planning, supervision planning, and/or release conditions.

DOCUMENTATION

Treatment documentation for criminal justice populations is consistent with documentation requirements for the level of care in which the patient is enrolled. It is structured to provide sufficient participant information to meet the decision-making needs of the courts while maintaining adherence to professional confidentiality codes. Paraprofessional correctional staff working with patients are often prohibited from reading medical records. Therefore, medical/ addiction/mental health providers working with correctional patients should provide case summaries and updates to keep correctional staff aware of participant progress.

DIAGNOSTIC ADMISSION CRITERIA

The ASAM Criteria primarily addresses treatment of substance use, co-occurring, and gambling disorders. If, upon assessment, a person who has drug-related charges and is mandated for treatment does not meet diagnostic criteria for a substance use disorder, then addiction treatment is not needed. For example, if a person is arrested for drug dealing not involving the individual's own substance use, and he or she does not meet criteria for a substance use disorder, then treatment should not be used as a means to achieve less time in jail or prison, or to avoid other legal consequences appropriate to the crime.

If treatment is recommended but the individual does not meet criteria for a substance use disorder, medical necessity for addiction treatment will not be met and services will not be funded. There may be possible criminal justice interventions, which, if done in collaboration, can increase positive outcomes for the individual and public safety. Education and risk advice as is done in Level 0.5, Early Intervention, is useful for such individuals.

Other mental and physical health concerns may also be an entrée into care. For example, criminogenic needs may be present in a criminal justice services-involved individual, but the individual may not meet diagnostic criteria for a clinical condition, and therefore medical necessity will not be present to justify clinical services. Criminogenic needs are dynamic factors which include antisocial values, beliefs, cognitive-emotional states, rage, anger, defiance, criminal identity, antisocial friends, isolation from prosocial others, substance use, lack of empathy, impulsive behavior, low levels of personal education, and family dysfunction (such as criminality, psychological problems, abuse, and neglect among family members).[1] Finding ways of addressing these needs may be challenging and require additional funding streams.

If, upon assessment, a person who has criminal charges that result in incarceration does meet diagnostic criteria for a substance use disorder, then addiction treatment should be provided, as needed, and not withheld from the individual (see ASAM Public Policy Statement[2]).

PERSONS IN CRIMINAL JUSTICE SETTINGS
DIMENSIONAL ADMISSION CRITERIA

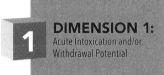

DIMENSION 1:
Acute Intoxication and/or Withdrawal Potential

In institutional, prison, and jail settings, up-front assessment and identification of potential acute intoxication and withdrawal potential needs to be done in a timely manner. This is especially important due to the fact that the individual is placed in a controlled environment where he or she will not have access to alcohol or other drugs that he or she might usually use in the outside community to self-manage a withdrawal episode. Persons facing incarceration in an institutional setting should be referred to medically necessary withdrawal management care prior to entering the criminal justice institution, or should have access to withdrawal management services within the institution. Persons who are incarcerated and who need withdrawal management services should not be deprived of receiving such services (see ASAM Public Policy Statement[3]).

Prison or jail inmates are not allowed to continue opioid treatment services such as agonist or partial agonist addiction medications like methadone or buprenorphine, and will need to receive appropriate withdrawal management services prior to or immediately upon reporting for incarceration. Treatment planning may call for safe discontinuation of such treatments under a physician's care prior to the scheduled date of incarceration.

4

CRIMINAL JUSTICE

PERSONS IN CRIMINAL JUSTICE SETTINGS
DIMENSIONAL ADMISSION CRITERIA (CONTINUED)

1

DIMENSION 1:
Acute Intoxication and/or Withdrawal Potential

Individuals recently released from a controlled environment may be at increased risk of acute intoxication and/or withdrawal complications due to the absence of tolerance following a period of forced abstinence during incarceration. Immediate referral (on the day of release from prison or jail) to an opioid treatment program may be indicated for some individuals.

2

DIMENSION 2:
Biomedical Conditions and Complications

Providers will want to gain access to correctional medical records to ensure medical and dental needs are identified and addressed (eg, treatment for HIV, hepatitis C, tuberculosis, or tobacco use disorder). Care transitions are important for the uninterrupted management of chronic medical conditions. Eligibility for Medicaid or pharmacy benefit plans may need to be re-established, medication supplies provided for the time span before the first appointment with a community-based general medical provider, and appointment times secured with private-sector clinics, public-sector clinicians, or community health centers.

3

DIMENSION 3:
Emotional, Behavioral, or Cognitive Conditions and Complications

Assessment of co-occurring conditions including criminogenic risk, need, and responsivity (RNR) factors such as criminal identity, values, and behaviors; antisocial peer relationships (including gang involvement); family structure and functioning; criminal lifestyle (attitudes, beliefs, and values); impaired judgment and anger management skills; and low self-control need to be incorporated in the assessment process. Additional attention needs to be placed on identifying any potential increased risk for suicide; traumatic brain injury; attention deficit hyperactivity disorder; posttraumatic stress disorder; mood, anxiety, and personality disorders; and impulse control issues, as well as antisocial values and behaviors, even if not meeting criteria for antisocial personality disorder.

4

DIMENSION 4:
Readiness to Change

Individuals may be at different stages of readiness to change as it relates to their substance-related disorder and criminogenic behaviors. Clinicians should identify strengths, resources, and abilities that may increase hope, motivation, and commitment to change, which may include family, children, self-sufficiency, self-efficacy, and meaning and purpose. For individuals in community settings, gather collateral data including probation, parole, or court terms. If the participant's main goal is to "get off paper," (finish probation or parole) connect this to the probation and parole plan and use motivational interviewing techniques to identify the steps the individual can and is willing to take to accomplish his or her goals.

5

DIMENSION 5:
Relapse, Continued Use, or Continued Problem Potential

For many criminal justice system-involved persons, it is important to place additional emphasis on impulsivity and coping skills in order to facilitate a slowing down of the decision-making process. Explore what the benefits of continued use are for the individual, how they experience incarceration, and whether or not they use while incarcerated. Identify what role alcohol and/or other drug use plays in their criminal activity. Work to develop agreements with criminal justice authorities for clinical steps that can be taken when the participant relapses, rather than automatically sanctioning the individual for violation of probation or parole. Contingencies should be applied for failure of the individual to participate in treatment planning, rather than basing sanctions solely on the appearance of a positive urine drug test result. Co-occurring conditions including antisocial personality disorder, trauma, fetal alcohol spectrum disorders, cognitive impairment, untreated learning disabilities, untreated mood disorders, criminal lifestyle, and criminal thinking all need to be addressed in the context of relapse, continued use, and continued problem potential. Locus of control should be assessed. Beliefs about power and influence are important to access and address in the treatment process.

4

CRIMINAL JUSTICE

PERSONS IN CRIMINAL JUSTICE SETTINGS
DIMENSIONAL ADMISSION CRITERIA (CONTINUED)

5 **DIMENSION 5:**
Relapse, Continued Use, or
Continued Problem Potential

While at the current time, addiction pharmacotherapies are not usually used to prevent relapse or continued use in criminal justice systems, more collaboration with criminal justice services is needed to identify ways for medication management to become a part of a relapse prevention plan, where clinically indicated.

6 **DIMENSION 6:**
Recovery Environment

Legal contingencies can be powerful and positive motivating factors in the treatment process. Employment difficulty is, statistically, one of the most important predictors of criminal recidivism and should be thoroughly assessed and addressed. Housing, finances, education (particularly obtaining a high school diploma or GED), and prosocial peer and family support are all key factors of success with this population.

Levels of Care

When the ASAM criteria are artfully and skillfully introduced and applied to the criminal justice system, the full continuum of care can be appropriately delivered in the context of the participant's current living circumstances, including when the individual is held in a controlled criminal justice system environment. Specific provision of services in an institutional, prison, or jail setting may require finding effective ways to increase timely access by individuals, and consideration should be made for placement of such participants in specialized yards, programs (Level 1 or 2), dormitories, or buildings (Level 3 services). When custody and security needs require the placement of a participant in a secure housing unit (lockup), policies and procedures may need to be addressed to allow the participant to receive appropriate treatment services even under these circumstances.

If a person is considered to have a substance-related or co-occurring condition affecting or explaining their criminogenic behavior—and if the court has offered treatment—then treatment should be given in a treatment setting with the level of care appropriate to the clinical assessment and progress of the participant. Thus, the setting should match severity of illness and functional level. The individual should not be placed in a residential setting solely for public safety reasons or as an extension of the correctional system if there is no actual multidimensional assessment of severity that requires a 24-hour setting.

Special Considerations of Continued Service and Discharge Criteria

Continued Service Criteria

Continued service should be based on clinical progress and function, not time- or program-based lengths of stay. Coordination is needed with the justice system in community settings. Basic needs of transportation, housing, employment, and educational support may be ongoing throughout treatment and recovery support services. Family, peer support services, continuing care, and peer support/self-help options can be important for sustained recovery and preventing reinvolvement in the criminal justice system.

Discharge/Transfer Criteria

An additional emphasis may need to be placed on addressing Dimension 6 (Recovery Environment) areas in collaboration with justice service personnel. Safe housing, job preparation and employment, education, and health care needs should be emphasized in assisting criminal justice participants in addressing the lifestyle changes that are necessary to make in managing their substance use disorder and criminogenic lifestyle.

4

CRIMINAL JUSTICE

Emerging Understandings of Addiction

Gambling Disorder

Gambling is a human behavior that is practiced around the world, in almost all cultures, at a frequency comparable to drinking alcoholic beverages or caffeine. Just as those behaviors are essentially ubiquitous and not in and of themselves pathological, gambling is in the vast majority of cases a social or recreational event. The *Diagnostic and Statistical Manual of Mental Disorders (DSM)*, published by the American Psychiatric Association, has recognized that gambling can be involved with a pathological state, and has named it Pathological Gambling in previous editions. The Fifth Edition of the manual (*DSM-5*, 2013) classifies this condition as "gambling disorder" and groups it with substance use disorders in a chapter titled "Substance-Related and Addictive Disorders."

For years, clinical experts have applied diagnostic and treatment methods used for the treatment of substance use disorders in the evaluation and management of cases of pathological gambling, even though this diagnosis appeared in a separate chapter of the *DSM* ("Impulse-Control Disorders Not Elsewhere Classified"). The definition of addiction adopted by the ASAM Board of Directors in April 2011 states that persons with addiction can be seen as "pathologically pursuing reward and/or relief by substance use and other behaviors." This definition does not state that alcohol addiction, opioid addiction, and gambling addiction are separate conditions. It states that addiction can be involved with various substances and behaviors. The qualitative difference between individuals who have addiction and those who do not is that persons with addiction manifest a pathological pursuit of reward or relief, and have a "disease of brain reward, motivation, memory, and related circuitry" which is "characterized by inability to consistently abstain, impairment in behavioral control, craving, diminished recognition of significant problems with one's behaviors and interpersonal relationships, and a dysfunctional emotional response."[1]

Under this definition, addiction can be associated with pathological engagement in gambling. Thus, addiction treatment can address the pathological pursuit of reward or relief via gambling, or what *DSM-5* calls "gambling disorder." This edition of *The ASAM Criteria* thus includes, appropriately, a discussion of treatment for gambling disorder. When approaching gambling disorder clinically, there is considerable applicability to the ASAM criteria's assessment dimensions and levels of care. Gambling disorder is widespread and often co-occurs with substance-related disorders as well as other mental disorders. Various estimates indicate that 1-2% of U.S. adults and 2-4% of U.S. adolescents are diagnosable with gambling disorder.

The following sections provide special considerations when applying the ASAM criteria to gambling disorder.

SETTING

One issue associated with the setting of treatment is that of reimbursement. In contrast with substance use disorders, it is currently uncommon for commercial or governmental health plans to offer payment for treatment in residential or inpatient levels of care unless there are co-occurring medical or psychiatric problems, which would, in and of themselves, justify reimbursement for such placements.

Even partial hospitalization or intensive outpatient treatment programs for gambling disorder have historically been considered a "non-covered benefit;" patients needed to meet criteria for a substance use disorder or a separate mental disorder in order for payment to be authorized when the treatment focus would otherwise be the person's pathological gambling. Patients with gambling disorder and with a co-occurring substance use disorder may be treated by a provider who can address both problems concurrently in an integrated way. Patients who are diagnosed with a gambling disorder but without a co-occurring substance use disorder and who are admitted to a gambling disorder treatment service should still be screened for a co-occurring substance use disorder. At the time of the development of this edition of *The ASAM Criteria*, it is unclear what impact, if any, the Mental Health Parity and Addiction Equity Act of 2008, or the Patient Protection and Affordable Care Act of 2010, will have on insurance payments for treatment of gambling disorder under Medicare, Medicaid, or commercial health insurance plans.

SUPPORT SYSTEMS

Refer to support systems for the particular level of care in the table provided on pages 365-366.

STAFF

Staff providing treatment to patients with gambling disorder should have a state-sponsored or -approved gambling counselor certification. Since not all states have such credentialing at the time of the writing of this edition of *The ASAM Criteria*, some states accept a national credential such as the National Certified Gambling Counselor (NCGC), provided by the National Council on Problem Gambling. State certification or licensure as an alcohol and drug, chemical dependency, or substance abuse counselor should not be considered a substitute for or equivalent to a gambling counselor certification. In the future, the evolution of professional training and professional certification, possibly being influenced by the 2011 ASAM definition of addiction, may mean that all addiction counselors will receive sufficient training in addiction associated with gambling, and thus separate certification will not be necessary. But at this time, there are relatively few well-trained and certified gambling treatment professionals, especially given the number of persons diagnosable with this condition and their need for informed, evidence-based, and compassionate care.

THERAPIES

Individual and group therapies should address the gambling disorder specifically. When the gambling disorder co-occurs with a substance use or other mental disorder(s), all should be treated in a concurrent and integrated manner.

ASSESSMENT/TREATMENT PLAN REVIEW

A comprehensive assessment designed around the issues of gambling and co-occurring conditions needs to be performed, with a particular focus on financial and legal problems and suicidality. Because gambling problems, which are assessed under Dimension 3 of the ASAM criteria, commonly co-occur with substance use disorders, and either the gambling or substance use may often act as a trigger for relapse to the other disorder, screening for gambling problems should be a routine part of assessment for patients' substance use disorders. This is clearly consistent with the 2011 ASAM definition of addiction, which considers addiction to be a health condition distinct from other mental disorders or general medical conditions, but also considers that addiction can involve the pathological pursuit of "reward and/or relief by substance use or other behaviors," which can include gambling.

Gambling disorder can be episodic or persistent, and the course of the disorder can vary by type of gambling as well as life circumstances.[2,3] For example, an individual who wagers problematically only on football games may have gambling disorder during football season and not wager at all, or not wager problematically, throughout the remainder of the year. Gambling disorder may also occur at one or more points in an individual's life but be absent during other periods. Alternately, some individuals experience chronic gambling disorder throughout all or most of their lives.

The term "addiction" is now used to characterize substance use and gambling disorders.

DOCUMENTATION

All documentation should be consistent with the highest standards of documentation requirements in whatever level of care the patient is admitted.

DIAGNOSTIC CRITERIA

DSM-5 Gambling Disorder

a. Persistent and recurrent problematic gambling behavior leading to clinically significant impairment or distress, as indicated by four (or more) of the following in a 12-month period.

1. Needs to gamble with increasing amounts of money in order to achieve the desired excitement.
2. Is restless or irritable when attempting to cut down or stop gambling.
3. Has made repeated unsuccessful efforts to control, cut back, or stop gambling.
4. Is often preoccupied with gambling (eg, having persistent thoughts of reliving past gambling experiences, handicapping or planning the next venture, thinking of ways to get money with which to gamble).
5. Often gambles when feeling distressed (eg, helpless, guilty, anxious, depressed).
6. After losing money gambling, often returns another day to get even ("chasing" one's losses).
7. Lies to conceal the extent of involvement with gambling.
8. Has jeopardized or lost a significant relationship, job, or educational or career opportunity because of gambling.
9. Relies on others to provide money to relieve desperate financial situations caused by gambling.

b. The gambling behavior is not better accounted for by a manic episode.

Course Specifiers
» Episodic
» Persistent
» In early remission
» In sustained remission

Current Severity
» Mild: 4-5 criteria met
» Moderate: 6-7 criteria met
» Severe: 8-9 criteria met

Addiction is characterized by:
1. Inability to consistently abstain
2. Impairment in behavioral control
3. Craving
4. Diminished recognition of significant problems with one's behaviors and interpersonal relationships, and

5. A dysfunctional emotional response.[1]

When comparing substance use disorders and gambling disorder, it becomes clear that there is a comparable gradation of behaviors and associated pathological states.

This table shows the gradation, from no problem, through subclinical states, to a pathological state meeting full diagnostic criteria, and is comparable for substance use disorder and for gambling disorder.

GRADATION OF SUBSTANCE USE & GAMBLING BEHAVIORS

SUBSTANCE USE BEHAVIORS	GAMBLING BEHAVIORS
No use of substances (eg, "total abstainer" or "teetotaler")	No gambling
Non-problem use (eg, "social use, social drinker")	Non-problem gambling (eg, "social gambling")
Mild severity or at-risk use – score of 2-3 of 11 criteria (diagnostic scale)	At-risk gambling
Moderate severity – score of 4-5 of 11 criteria (the former "Substance Abuse" diagnosis in the *DSM-IV*)	Problem gambling
Severe – score of 6 or more of 11 criteria (the former "Substance Dependence" diagnosis in the *DSM-IV*)	Gambling addiction (4 or more of the 9 criteria of the *DSM-5*)

SIMILARITIES & DIFFERENCES BETWEEN SUBSTANCE USE DISORDER & GAMBLING DISORDER

SIMILARITIES	DIFFERENCES
A state of euphoria resulting from engagement in the behavior. Thus, the behavior–at least early in the course of the chronic condition–is pleasurable (engagement in the behavior for purposes of reward);	No objective tests to determine problem gambling in contrast to laboratory tests which can detect for the presence of alcohol or other drugs (though not the presence of the condition of addiction);
Preoccupation when engaging in the activity;	Problem gambling can be easier to hide from others;
Loss of control at times when engaging in the behavior;	Overuse of alcohol or other drugs can be self-limiting, eg, if there is physical or mental "shut down" as when an individual passes out. Gambling is not self-limiting in the sense that a physical or mental state "shuts down" the gambling behavior;
Progression of problems and symptoms over time;	
Stage of change, readiness to change, and interest in changing issues, usually manifesting as diminished recognition of problems associated with addictive behavior;	

GAMBLING DISORDER
5

SIMILARITIES & DIFFERENCES BETWEEN SUBSTANCE USE DISORDER & GAMBLING DISORDER (CONTINUED)

SIMILARITIES	DIFFERENCES
The behavior is continued in spite of adverse consequences;	Suicide rates are higher among problem gamblers (20% attempted);
Tolerance develops with repeated engagement in the behavior;	Problem gamblers' financial situation is often more critical and must be addressed;
Urges and cravings develop regarding further engagement in the behavior;	Less public awareness and acceptance of gambling disorder;
There is enhanced cue responsiveness, which can trigger relapse to the behavior;	Fewer treatment resources (treatment programs, certified gambling counselors, support groups);
Withdrawal symptoms occur when the activity is unavailable;	More restricted third party reimbursement for treatment of gambling disorders.
Psychological drives of escape, self-medication, and avoidance exist (engagement in the behavior for purposes of relief);	
Committing illegal acts to fund ongoing engagement with the behavior (substance use or gambling) can be episodic, chronic, or in remission.	

NOTE: Use of different substances and engagement in different forms of gambling can have different "addictive potential," associated with the schedule of reinforcement of the behavior (gambling is most "addictive" when there is a variable schedule of reinforcement), and associated with the time of onset of the reward or relief after engagement in the behavior (the immediacy of physiological effect after intravenous drug use or after initiation of video poker play). This may result in different rates of addiction progression.

Screening and Assessment

The key component on which good treatment and positive outcome rests is screening and comprehensive assessment. There are over 27 instruments for identifying disordered gambling, though there is debate about them and what they measure. Since an appropriate instrument should be able to screen for gambling disorders in both the general population and a population of persons who have a substance use disorder, two screening tools are recommended.

The first is the two-item "Lie/Bet Screen." Its advantage is that it is only two questions, and is more likely to be used in community and clinical settings where clinicians feel overwhelmed with current assessment responsibilities and other paperwork. This is especially important given the extent of comorbidity between gambling disorders, substance use disorders, and other mental disorders (mood disorders, anxiety disorders, posttraumatic stress disorder, attention deficit hyperactivity

disorder, etc.), and personality disorders (antisocial, avoidant, narcissistic, or borderline personality disorders).

The "Lie/Bet" two item questionnaire is:

1. Have you ever had to lie to people important to you about how much you gambled?

2. Have you ever felt the need to bet more and more money?[4]

The second and better-known and researched screening instrument is the South Oaks Gambling Screen (SOGS), a 16-item scorable questionnaire, which is in the public domain and can be found on the Internet.[5]

The purpose of screening is to conduct a preliminary inquiry to rule an individual "in" or "out." If ruled "in," the next step is to perform a comprehensive diagnostic assessment using the *DSM-5* criteria for gambling disorder in the diagnostic criteria shown in this section.

Dimensional Issues

Once a gambling disorder diagnosis is established, the next question—answerable by use of the ASAM criteria—is: what is the severity of the disorder? Severity of illness guides the clinician to an intensity of service recommendation for the patient.

In the first column of the following chart there is a list of questions that would be asked in a multidimensional assessment of individuals

Fully articulated dimensional admission criteria are not provided in this chapter, as these emerging understandings of addiction require further study and clinical application and consensus. Therefore "dimensional issues" are discussed as a foundation to stimulate the development of more treatment services, levels of care, and payment and funding mechanisms.

APPLYING THE ASAM CRITERIA TO GAMBLING DISORDER: EXAMPLE QUESTIONS

SUBSTANCE USE DISORDER	GAMBLING DISORDER
DIMENSION 1: ACUTE INTOXICATION AND/OR WITHDRAWAL POTENTIAL	
Are there current signs of withdrawal?	Are there current signs of withdrawal (*restlessness or irritability when attempting to cut down or stop gambling*)?
Does the patient have supports to assist in ambulatory withdrawal management if medically safe?	Does the patient have supports in the community to *enable him/her to safely tolerate the restlessness or irritability when attempting to cut down or stop gambling*?
Has the patient been using multiple substances in the same drug class?	*What forms of gambling has the individual engaged in?* Has the patient also been using *psychoactive substances to the point where alcohol or other drug withdrawal management is necessary*?
If the withdrawal concern is about alcohol, what is the patient's CIWA-Ar score?	
DIMENSION 2: BIOMEDICAL CONDITIONS AND COMPLICATIONS	
Are there current physical illnesses, other than withdrawal, that need to be addressed or which complicate treatment?	Are there current physical illnesses, other than withdrawal, that need to be addressed or which complicate treatment? *Does the individual manifest any acute conditions associated with prolonged periods of gambling (eg, urinary tract infection)?*
Is there a need for medical services which might interfere with treatment (eg, chemotherapy or kidney dialysis)?	Is there a need for medical services which might interfere with treatment (eg, chemotherapy or kidney dialysis)?
Are there chronic illnesses, which might be exacerbated by withdrawal (eg, diabetes, hypertension)?	*Are there chronic medical conditions such as hypertension, peptic ulcer disease, or migraines that might be exacerbated by either cessation or continuation of the gambling behavior?*
Are there chronic conditions that might interfere with treatment (eg, chronic pain with narcotic analgesics)?	Are there chronic conditions that might interfere with treatment (eg, chronic pain)?
DIMENSION 3: EMOTIONAL, BEHAVIORAL, OR COGNITIVE CONDITIONS AND COMPLICATIONS	
Are there current psychiatric illnesses or psychological, behavioral, or emotional problems that need to be addressed or which complicate treatment?	Are there *other* current psychiatric illnesses or psychological, behavioral, or emotional problems *or a substance use disorder* that need to be addressed or which complicate treatment?
Are there chronic conditions that affect treatment?	Are there chronic conditions that affect treatment?
Do any emotional/behavioral problems appear to be an expected part of the addiction, or do they appear to be separate?	Do any emotional/behavioral problems appear to be an expected part *of the gambling disorder*, or do they appear to be separate?
Even if connected to addiction, are they severe enough to warrant specific mental health treatment?	Even if connected to the *gambling*, are they severe enough to warrant specific mental health treatment?
Is the patient suicidal, and if so, what is the lethality?	Is the patient suicidal, and if so, what is the lethality?
If the patient has been prescribed psychiatric medications, is he/she adherent?	If the patient has been prescribed psychiatric medications, is he/she adherent?
	Does the individual have distortions in thinking such as superstitions, overconfidence, or an inflated sense of power and control?

APPLYING THE ASAM CRITERIA TO GAMBLING DISORDER: EXAMPLE QUESTIONS

SUBSTANCE USE DISORDER	GAMBLING DISORDER

DIMENSION 4: READINESS TO CHANGE

Does the patient feel coerced into treatment or actively object to receiving treatment?	Does the patient feel coerced into treatment or actively object to receiving treatment?
How ready is the patient to change (stage of "readiness to change")?	How ready is the patient to change (stage of "readiness to change")?
If willing to accept treatment, how strongly does the patient disagree with others' perception that s/he has an addiction problem?	If willing to accept treatment, how strongly does the patient disagree with others' perception that s/he has a *gambling* problem?
Is the patient adherent to avoid a negative consequence (externally motivated) or internally distressed in a self-motivated way about his/her alcohol or other drug use problems?	Is the patient adherent to avoid a negative consequence (externally motivated) or internally distressed in a self-motivated way about his/her *gambling* problem?
Is there leverage available?	Is there leverage available?

DIMENSION 5: RELAPSE, CONTINUED USE, OR CONTINUED PROBLEM POTENTIAL

How aware is the patient of relapse triggers, ways to cope with cravings, and skills to control impulses to use?	How aware is the patient of relapse triggers, ways to cope with cravings, and skills to control impulses *to gamble*?
What is the patient's ability to remain abstinent or psychiatrically stable based on history?	What is the patient's ability to *stop gambling* or remain psychiatrically stable based on history?
What is the patient's level of current craving, and how successfully can s/he resist using?	What is the patient's level of current preoccupation with or craving to *gamble*, and how successfully can s/he resist *gambling behaviors*?
If the patient had another chronic disorder (eg, diabetes), what is the history of adherence with treatment for that disorder?	If the patient had another chronic disorder (eg, diabetes), what is the history of adherence with treatment for that disorder?
Is the patient in immediate danger of continued severe distress and drinking/drugging or other high-risk behavior due to co-occurring mental health problems?	Is the patient in immediate danger of continued severe distress and *gambling* or other high-risk behavior due to co-occurring mental health *or substance use* problems?
Does the patient have any recognition of and skills to cope with addiction and/or mental health problems and prevent relapse or continued use/continued problems?	Does the patient have any recognition of and skills to cope with *gambling* and/or *other* mental health problems *or substance use problems* and prevent relapse or continued *gambling*?
What severity of problems and further distress will potentially continue or reappear, if the patient is not successfully engaged into treatment at this time?	What severity of problems and further distress will potentially continue or reappear if the patient is not successfully engaged into treatment at this time?
If on psychiatric medications, is the patient adherent?	If on psychiatric medications, is the patient adherent?

DIMENSION 6: RECOVERY/LIVING ENVIRONMENT

Are there barriers to access to treatment, such as transportation or child care responsibilities?	Are there barriers to access to treatment, such as transportation or child care responsibilities?
Are there legal, vocational, social service agency, or criminal justice mandates that may enhance motivation for engagement into treatment?	Are there legal, vocational, social service agency, or criminal justice mandates that may enhance motivation for engagement into treatment?
Is the patient able to see value in recovery?	Is the patient able to see value in recovery?
Are there any dangerous family, significant others, living, school, or work situations threatening treatment engagement and success?	Are there any dangerous family, significant others, living, school, or work situations threatening treatment engagement and success?
Does the patient have supportive friendship, financial, or educational/vocational resources to improve the likelihood of successful treatment?	Does the patient have supportive friendship, financial, or educational/vocational resources to improve the likelihood of successful treatment?
	Are the patient's financial circumstances due to the gambling or associated legal problems an obstacle to receiving or a distraction from treatment, or a threat to personal safety (eg, loan sharks)?

5 GAMBLING DISORDER

with substance use disorder. The second column contains the questions as they would apply to individuals with gambling disorder with the *italics* identifying the differences. It is striking how there are such common characteristics between the two sets of disorders, with the least overlap being in Dimension 1: Acute Intoxication and/or Withdrawal Potential. The assessment questions of the other dimensions are generally a very close match.

Placement

The issue of level of care placement is more complicated than with substance use disorders because of the absence of adequate resources and reimbursement. With substance use disorder treatment, even while short of ideal, the resources available are much greater than those that exist for the treatment of gambling disorders. In urban areas, there might be dozens of addiction treatment programs at all levels of care, and hundreds of self-help meetings available each week; but at best only a handful of such professional and peer-support services exist that are prepared to treat persons with gambling disorders.

The situation is much more critical in rural areas—even though many casinos have been constructed in the last several decades in rural areas. One potential solution is to encourage and incentivize already-existing addiction treatment programs to develop gambling treatment services, a relatively easy shift given the similarities between the disorders. This would be completely consistent with the 2011 ASAM definition of addiction. Treatment professionals would be advised to fully assess and recommend an appropriate level of care and document that recommendation, along with the flexibility to fit the available treatment, length of time, and methods to address the gambling disorder appropriately.

With patients who are engaged in "at-risk" gambling, Level 0.5, Early Intervention, may be appropriate, as well as a Brief Intervention using the SBIRT (Screening, Brief Intervention, and Referral to Treatment). For "problem" gambling (gambling problems not severe enough to reach the diagnostic threshold for gambling addiction), one of the outpatient levels of care (1, 2.1, or 2.5) may be considered, depending on the results of the comprehensive multidimensional ASAM criteria assessment for both gambling and substance use disorders. For those diagnosable as gambling addicted (meeting 4 of the 9 criteria for a gambling disorder), it is likely that there will be co-occurring problems in Dimensions 1, 2, and/or 3 found in a multidimensional ASAM criteria assessment that might justify admission to an inpatient level of care. For those patients with co-occurring substance use and gambling disorders, admission to a residential level of care (Level 3.1, 3.3, or 3.5) for problems in Dimensions 5 and/or 6 may be justified.

Payment for treatment is the other obstacle. Most insurance companies that do not categorically exclude coverage for the treatment of gambling disorder have had benefits for the treatment of gambling disorders. But those benefits do not include payment for residential or inpatient treatment unless there is another, primary diagnosis such as major depressive disorder. It is the major depressive disorder that generates the reimbursement, not the gambling disorder. A state or local drug and alcohol authority could elect (and some do) to pay for the treatment of gambling disorder, regardless of level of care.

However, without the presence of a co-occurring physical, mental, or substance use disorder, it is hard to justify placement in the more intensive levels of care as indicated by the chart on pages 365-366. That is, clinical necessity for placement in more intensive levels of care may actually not be present in most cases.

COMPARING ADULT ASAM CRITERIA LEVELS OF CARE FROM SUBSTANCE USE DISORDERS WITH THOSE FOR GAMBLING DISORDERS

ASAM CRITERIA LEVELS OF CARE	LEVEL	DESCRIPTION	LEVELS OF CARE FOR GAMBLING DISORDERS
Early Intervention	0.5	Assessment and education for at-risk individuals who do not meet diagnostic criteria for a disorder	Prevention, screening, and intervention of high-risk persons
Outpatient Services	1	Less than 9 hours of service/week (adults); less than 6 hours/week (adolescents) for recovery or motivational enhancement therapies/strategies	Outpatient counselor or clinic
Intensive Outpatient (IOP)	2.1	9 or more hours of service/week (adults); 6 or more hours/week (adolescents) to treat multidimensional instability	Intensive Outpatient (IOP)
Partial Hospitalization (PHP)	2.5	20 or more hours of service/week for multidimensional instability not requiring 24-hour care	Day Program (Partial Hospitalization Program)
Clinically Managed Low-Intensity Residential	3.1	24-hour structure with available trained personnel; at least 5 hours of clinical service/week (eg, halfway house)	For those requiring transitional living
Clinically Managed Population-Specific High-Intensity Residential	3.3	24-hour care with trained counselors to stabilize multidimensional imminent danger. Less intense milieu and group treatment for those with cognitive or other impairments unable to use full active milieu or therapeutic community	Not applicable in the absence of co-occurring cognitive problems or substance use disorder requiring this intensity and type of service, or Dimension 4, 5, and 6 problems that require this type of 24-hour care
Clinically Managed High-Intensity Residential	3.5	24-hour care with trained counselors to stabilize multidimensional imminent danger and prepare for outpatient treatment. Able to tolerate and use full active milieu or therapeutic community	Not applicable in the absence of co-occurring medical, mental, or substance use disorders requiring this intensity of service, or Dimension 4, 5, and 6 problems that require 24-hour care. However, an individual with gambling disorder who is assessed to be unable to abstain from the pathological pursuit of reward or relief through gambling when in an ambulatory setting, even with the provision of Level 2.1 or 2.5 clinical services for gambling disorder, this level of care may be clinically necessary, if in imminent danger
Medically Monitored Intensive Inpatient	3.7	24-hour nursing care with physician availability for significant problems in Dimensions 1, 2, or 3. 16-hour/day counselor availability	Not applicable in the absence of co-occurring medical, mental, or substance use disorders requiring this intensity of service
Medically Managed Intensive Inpatient	4	24-hour nursing care and daily physician care for severe, unstable problems in Dimensions 1, 2, or 3. Counseling available to engage patient in treatment	Not applicable in the absence of co-occurring medical, mental, or substance use disorders requiring this intensity of service
Opioid Treatment Program (Level 1)	OTP	Daily or several times weekly opioid medication and counseling available to maintain multidimensional stability for those with severe opioid use disorder	Not applicable in the absence of a co-occurring opioid use disorder

COMPARING ADULT ASAM CRITERIA LEVELS OF CARE FROM SUBSTANCE USE DISORDERS WITH THOSE FOR GAMBLING DISORDERS

ASAM CRITERIA ADULT WITHDRAWAL MANAGEMENT SERVICES	LEVEL	DESCRIPTION	LEVELS OF CARE FOR "WITHDRAWAL MANAGEMENT" FOR GAMBLING DISORDERS
Ambulatory Withdrawal Management without Extended On-Site Monitoring	1-WM	Mild withdrawal, with daily or less than daily outpatient supervision; likely to "complete detox" and to continue treatment or recovery	Service through a primary care physician to manage anxiety, depression and mood swings
Ambulatory Withdrawal Management with Extended On-Site Monitoring	2-WM	Moderate withdrawal, with all-day withdrawal management support and supervision; at night, has supportive family or living situation; likely to "complete detox"	Same as above, if more structure is needed
Clinically Managed Residential Withdrawal Management	3.2-WM	Moderate withdrawal, but needs 24-hour support to "complete detox" and increase likelihood of continuing treatment or recovery	As above, with the addition of overnight accommodations
Medically Monitored Inpatient Withdrawal Management	3.7-WM	Severe withdrawal, and needs 24-hour nursing care and physician visits as necessary; unlikely to "complete detox" without medical, nursing monitoring	Not applicable in the absence of co-occurring disorders requiring this intensity of service
Medically Managed Inpatient Withdrawal Management	4-WM	Severe, unstable withdrawal, and needs 24-hour nursing care and daily physician visits to modify the withdrawal management regimen and manage medical instability	Not applicable in the absence of co-occurring disorders requiring this intensity of service

GAMBLING DISORDER ⑤

Tobacco Use Disorder

Why tobacco use disorder is given special attention in *The ASAM Criteria*

Tobacco use disorder is underdiagnosed and undertreated in primary and specialty care, and psychiatric and addiction treatment. Patients are rarely treated for this addiction during their health care visits and hospitalizations, despite the fact that the chance that a lifelong smoker will die prematurely from a complication of smoking is approximately 50 percent.[1] The health consequences of tobacco use, be it smoked or smokeless, are staggering. Globally, cigarette smoking claims more than 5 million lives annually.[2] More people suffer and die from tobacco-related causes than any other addiction.

Nicotine is the determinant of addiction to tobacco. As a psychoactive drug, nicotine fine-tunes mood and enables both increased alertness and relaxation. Nicotine is found in tobacco products. It is the combustion and absorption of tobacco, and the additives in these products, rather than the nicotine itself, that causes the majority of cancer, chronic lung disease, and cardiovascular morbidity and mortality, as well as numerous medical problems including osteoporosis, duodenal and gastric ulcers, diabetes, delayed wound healing, and intrauterine growth retardation, to name only a few.

Nicotine is both similar to and different from other addictive drugs. Although nicotine is mood-altering, its use is not associated with the same behavioral disruption and social and legal consequences as the other drugs. While nicotine is less intoxicating, its rapid onset of action, ability to hone behavior, and frequent dosing associated with environmental cues makes cessation and relapse prevention extremely challenging.

Growing public awareness that tobacco use is associated with illness and death, along with the increased cost of smoking and the denormalization of smoking behavior have led to a reduction in prevalence of smoking in North America. Currently, many of those who continue to use tobacco products have additional addiction and/or medical and/or psychiatric comorbidity. During 2009-2011, among the persons with acute mental illness in the United States, 36.1 percent were current smokers, compared with 21.4 percent among adults with no mental illness.[3] The prevalence of tobacco use amongst patients in substance use treatment programs ranges 65-97% with an increased percentage in opiate substitution programs.[4,5] In repeated surveys, a majority of chemically dependent persons would like to quit smoking. They would take part in a smoking cessation intervention if it were available.

Despite the advancements in treatment, interventions with tobacco use disorders have not generally been integrated into the currently existing treatments for addiction, psychiatry, medicine (including ob-gyn, pediatrics, oncology, otolaryngology, cardiac care, etc.), and dentistry. Primary care and specialist physicians, dentists, pharmacists, nurses, counselors, and all health care professionals need better skills to assess severity of nicotine dependence and intervene with their patients.

Since tobacco use causes less social and legal consequences as a result of intoxication, historically the levels of care for nicotine addiction have been less intensive. Self-help, computer-based counseling programs, telephone quitline support, individual and group outpatient counseling, and outpatient pharmacotherapies have been the mainstays of treatment. There are few intensive outpatient programs, residential treatments, and consultative services within health care institutions that

The purpose of this section is to further the recognition, diagnosis, assessment, and availability of different intensities of treatment for tobacco use disorders, and to increase the availability and reimbursement of these activities not only as a stand-alone service but also as integrated in medical, obstetric, addiction, and psychiatric care.

5

TOBACCO USE DISORDER

are dedicated to tobacco cessation. These additional levels of treatment need to be developed and reimbursed.

Our challenge is to develop a range of intensities within currently existing treatment settings so that individual patients' dimensional assessments can be matched to levels of care, treatment can be accessible, and therapeutic outcomes maximized.

Persons who continue to use tobacco products despite multiple attempts to quit with less intensive therapy need more intensive care and levels of care. Monitored medications are even more important with persons who have significant addiction, medical, and/or psychiatric comorbidity.

The mandate to improve access to and quality of treatment for tobacco use disorder

With the passage of the Affordable Care Act, enhanced coverage by the Centers for Medicare & Medicaid Services (CMS), and a new measure set by the Joint Commission (formerly the Joint Commission on Accreditation of Healthcare Organizations (JCAHO)), tobacco cessation has been elevated as a priority in the delivery of quality medical care. According to this performance measure set adopted by the Joint Commission in 2011, all patients over the age of 18 who are inpatients will be screened for tobacco use, provided cessation treatment (including counseling and medications) during the hospital stay and at discharge, and follow-up care for up to 30 days after discharge. The Joint Commission encourages hospitals to provide tobacco cessation interventions to patients younger than 18 (though these are not included in the measure set). It requires that all patients 13 years of age and older be screened for tobacco use, and that this information be documented in their electronic heath record. Although there is concern that this measure will be overlooked because it requires greater effort (intensive identification, treatment, and post-discharge follow-up of all tobacco users) and because accredited hospitals are required to report on only 4 of the 14 performance measures, it is an important step toward enabling consis-

tent delivery of tobacco use disorder treatment in health care settings.[6]

The American Society of Addiction Medicine agrees with the Surgeon General's 2010 statement[7] that there is no safe level of consumption of tobacco products by any age group or among any special population. Nonetheless, the addiction field as a whole has been very conflicted about diagnosing and treating tobacco use disorder.

While we recognize that nicotine is one of the most difficult types of addiction to overcome, addiction treatment professionals have not assumed a leadership role in the treatment of tobacco use disorder. Most addiction treatment programs do not even list nicotine addiction on the problem list or treatment plan, even though many, if not most, of their patients are actively consuming tobacco products. Common belief systems espouse, "you can only deal with one addiction at a time" or "you should wait at least a year before you attempt to stop smoking." Addiction professionals generally insist that their patients cease more than one psychoactive substance at a time (eg, alcohol, methamphetamine, opiates, and marijuana) as long as the additional substance is not nicotine. Some addiction and mental health providers rationalize that nicotine addiction treatment can be delayed because tobacco use disorders are less harmful than the immediate consequences of alcohol, illicit drug use, and/or other self-harm behaviors. However, the data does not support this practice.[8]

Mental health and addiction treatment settings have an ethical duty to intervene in patients' tobacco use and provide available evidence-based treatments. Addiction professionals should embrace the treatment of tobacco use disorder as a key condition under their treatment realm because:

1. Treatment of tobacco use disorder during addiction treatment enhances outcomes. Stopping all psychoactive drugs and obtaining treatment for all addiction simultaneously can result in an easier withdrawal process and increased possibility for recovery. In one study, among

REASONS TO TREAT TOBACCO USE DISORDER

ADDICTION PROFESSIONAL	MENTAL HEALTH PROFESSIONAL
» Treatment of tobacco use disorder during addiction treatment enhances outcomes.	» Treatment of tobacco use disorder improves mental health outcomes.
» Treatment of tobacco use disorder in persons with other substance addiction decreases morbidity and improves longevity.	» Treatment of tobacco use disorder allows more consistent dosing of psychiatric medication.
	» Treatment of tobacco use disorder in those who have mental illness improves quality and quantity of life.

patients receiving treatment for substance use disorders, smoking abstinence at the end of the first year of treatment was the most robust predictor of abstinence from illicit drug use at a 9-year follow-up.[9] A meta-analysis of 19 randomized controlled trials found that smoking cessation interventions were associated with a 25 percent increased likelihood of long-term

abstinence from alcohol and illicit drugs.[10] It is possible that learning non-drug ways to cope with feelings and deal with stress, as well as avoiding the same cue-induced triggers, supports this improved result.

2. Treatment of tobacco use disorder in persons with other substance addiction decreases morbidity and improves lon-

A NOTE ABOUT TERMINOLOGY

Terminology is confusing throughout addiction medicine and addiction psychiatry, but it is arguably no more complicated than when dealing with nicotine and tobacco use. Tobacco is not the only addictive drug that is smoked, but no other drug is dosed (puffed) 100-400 times per day (ie, the consumption of 10-40 cigarettes per day). Originally, psychologists and pulmonologists developed behavioral interventions under the rubric of "smoking cessation." However, most addiction professionals view "cessation" as a necessary but insufficient step in establishing a sustained state of remission and recovery. In 2011, ASAM adopted a revised definition of addiction, which describes addiction as a "primary disease…of brain reward, memory, motivation, and related circuitry."[18] Since similarities rather than differences among individual drug addiction are emphasized, "addiction associated with nicotine" is the wording most aligned with this concept. The longstanding terminology, "nicotine dependence" has been retired due to confusion with the more limited concept of withdrawal. The *DSM* remains the most widely accepted system for diagnosis, coding, and billing in American health care. The revised term in the *DSM-5* is "substance use disorder," and the specific condition associated with tobacco and nicotine is termed "tobacco use disorder." For the purposes of this section of *The ASAM Criteria*, the authors have deferred to the *DSM* term, while recognizing that addiction occurs when people use tobacco products compulsively, and return to use after periods of abstinence, even in the face of major health and other life problems deriving from such use. This is due to the addictive properties of nicotine itself.

gevity. Continued tobacco use is a leading cause of death in persons with alcohol and other drug addiction. In one study, 845 patients who were previously treated for alcoholism and/or other non-nicotine drug dependence were found to have an increased cumulative mortality that was 48.1 percent versus an expected 18.5 percent at 20 years. Of the 214 deaths, 50.9 percent had a tobacco-related underlying cause, and 34.1 percent had an alcohol-related underlying cause.[11] Persons with drug problems who also smoke tobacco are four times more likely to die prematurely relative to individuals with drug problems who do not use tobacco.[12] Tobacco use is the number one preventable cause of disease and death in persons with alcohol, nicotine, and drug addiction.

Similarly, mental health professionals should embrace the treatment of tobacco use disorder as a key condition under their treatment realm because:

1. Treatment of tobacco use disorder improves mental health outcomes. Tobacco cessation is associated with decreased (not increased) depressive symptoms and suicidal risk behavior.[13] Abstinence from tobacco is not associated with worsening of attention, verbal learning/memory, working memory, or executive function/inhibition, nor worsening of clinical symptoms in individuals with schizophrenia.[14]

2. Treatment of tobacco use disorder allows more consistent dosing of psychiatric medication. The polycyclic aromatic hydrocarbons in tobacco smoke induce the drug metabolism of many psychiatric medications, including clozapine, fluvoxamine, haloperidol, olanzapine, phenothiazines, propanolol, tertiary tricyclic amines such as amitryptiline, and thiothixene by CYP1A2, as well as drugs metabolized by CYP2A6, CYP2B6, and CYP2D6. Tobacco cessation results in less fluctuation of levels of psychiatric medications, and allows decreased dosages of these medications.

3. Treatment of tobacco use disorder in those who have mental illness improves quality and quantity of life. Tobacco use is estimated to account for 179,000 deaths annually, and is the leading preventable cause of death among individuals with mental illness.[15] Persons with serious mental illness die on average 25 years prematurely, with the leading cause of death being tobacco-related diseases.[16]

Becoming abstinent from tobacco has been shown to have substantial beneficial effects on health and longevity as well as reduce the risk of relapse to other substances and improve response to treatment for psychiatric illnesses. The time is now for us to address this dangerous addictive substance.

Description of Population

According the 2011 National Survey on Drug Use and Health, 68.2 million Americans aged 12 and older reported current use of tobacco products:

» 56.8 million (22.1% of the population) currently smoke cigarettes,

» 12.9 million (5%) smoke cigars,

» 8.2 million (3.2%) use smokeless tobacco,

» 2.1 million (0.8%) smoke pipes.[17]

There are several ways to look at this population, as seen in the chart on page 371.

TOBACCO USE DISORDER 5

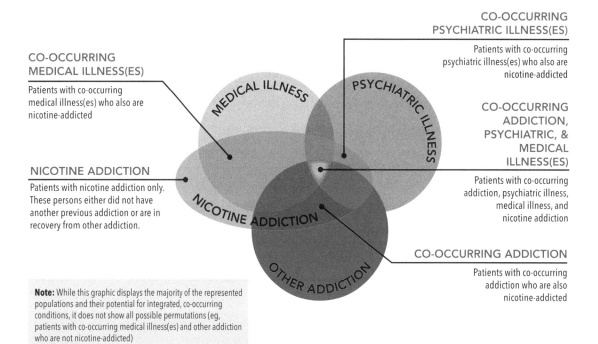

CO-OCCURRING MEDICAL ILLNESS(ES)

Patients with co-occurring medical illness(es) who also are nicotine-addicted

NICOTINE ADDICTION

Patients with nicotine addiction only. These persons either did not have another previous addiction or are in recovery from other addiction.

CO-OCCURRING PSYCHIATRIC ILLNESS(ES)

Patients with co-occurring psychiatric illness(es) who also are nicotine-addicted

CO-OCCURRING ADDICTION, PSYCHIATRIC, & MEDICAL ILLNESS(ES)

Patients with co-occurring addiction, psychiatric illness, medical illness, and nicotine addiction

CO-OCCURRING ADDICTION

Patients with co-occurring addiction who are also nicotine-addicted

Note: While this graphic displays the majority of the represented populations and their potential for integrated, co-occurring conditions, it does not show all possible permutations (eg, patients with co-occurring medical illness(es) and other addiction who are not nicotine-addicted)

Silos of Neglect

Currently, patients with tobacco use disorder are seen in a variety of health care settings, but the recognition, assessment, and treatment of the tobacco use disorder is often cursory or completely lacking. Treatment settings operate as independent silos, with professionals focused exclusively on their areas of expertise. If other co-occurring conditions are discovered, making referrals for assessment and treatment outside their "system" can be difficult.

Of the existing tobacco-only cessation programs, which may be funded by state resources or located in the community, many offer only a low intensity of care and do not provide treatment for other significant medical or psychiatric illness, or addiction. Appointments with outside physicians may be needed for pharmacologic therapy.

If screened for tobacco use, patients in medical care settings may have motivational interventions by their health care providers and be referred for tobacco cessation. Unfortunately, there are few consultative services for tobacco intervention in hospitals and outpatient medical settings. If tobacco cessation services are not integrated with medical care, patients may fail to follow through with these recommendations. Telephone quitlines are available for cessation support. The accessibility of these services is excellent. One limitation is that the counselors servicing quitlines do not have access to the patient's physician and medical record. They are ill-equipped to deal with significant medical, psychiatric, or addiction comorbidities. Because counselors cannot prescribe medications, there can be issues with initiating pharmacotherapy, encouraging adherence to pharmacotherapy over an appropriate duration of care, and any drug-drug interactions relevant to other medications they may be taking for co-occurring health conditions.

Addiction treatment programs, no matter the intensity of their care, often ignore tobacco use disorders. For example, survey studies administered across methadone and outpatient treatment settings have reported estimates of smoking cessation services being offered only in approximately 18% to 41% of programs that responded.[19,20]

Patients with serious mental illnesses are treated in community mental health centers and psychiatric hospitals. It is rare that tobacco cessation is routinely addressed in these venues.

The shortcomings of providing treatments in separate arenas are not speculative. A multicenter randomized trial of 943 smokers with military-related posttraumatic stress disorder (PTSD) in 10 Veterans Affairs medical centers demonstrated the feasibility and benefits of integrated care. The patients were randomized to smoking cessation treatment integrated within mental health care for PTSD or referral to a VA smoking cessation clinic. Medications were equally available in both treatment venues. The study's randomization controlled for sex, current alcohol abuse or dependence in partial remission, current major depressive disorder, prior smoking abstinence of greater than one year and heavy smoking of greater than 25 cigarettes daily. The subjects were followed with self-report and biochemical measures of smoking cessation, and standardized questionnaires to assess PTSD and depression for 18-48 months between November 2004 and July 2009.

At 6 months, the bio-verified 7-day point prevalence tobacco abstinence was 16.5% for integrated care versus 7.2% for those referred to the smoking cessation clinics. The difference remained significant at 18 months (18.2% versus 10.8%) and the rates of prolonged abstinence were 8.9% versus 4.5%. Patients did not as readily attend the separate smoking cessation clinics, and the number of counseling sessions received and days of cessation medication used explained 39.1% of the treatment effect. There were no appreciable adverse events caused by smoking cessation in patients with current PTSD, depression, or past histories of depression, which may be partially attributable to the ongoing psychiatric care. Between baseline and 18 months, posttraumatic stress disorder symptoms improved equally for the quitters and non-quitters. The researchers also reported that

the manualized treatment for smoking cessation within the integrated care was relatively easy to implement.[21]

Recent Trends

Some inroads are being made. New Jersey pioneered the importance of integrating nicotine treatment into its addiction programs. In 2008, New York legislated that its greater than 150 prevention and treatment programs overseen by the NY State Office of Alcoholism and Substance Abuse maintain a tobacco-free environment and integrate evidence-based nicotine dependence treatment into all levels of care. Significant progress is being made by other states including Massachusetts, Indiana, Colorado, and Wisconsin.

Certified tobacco treatment specialists are being trained to provide comprehensive tobacco cessation consultations and evidence-based treatment. While some tobacco treatment specialists have counseling backgrounds and act under the supervision of a prescribing physician, other physician assistants and nurse practitioners need less supervision and may have prescriptive authority. ATTUD is a growing organization of treatment providers in the U.S. and Global Bridges is addressing training for health care professionals across the globe. The Mayo Clinic has trained approximately 1,300 certified tobacco treatment specialists and other training programs now include the University of Mississippi, Rutgers Tobacco Dependence Program, University of Massachusetts, Ohio State, and the UK's national Centre for Smoking Cessation and Training. These midlevel providers have the capability of improving interventions and treatment across a wide range of disciplines, settings, and intensities.

Due to public health and governmental advocacy, tobacco assessment and treatment is now more readily available as a third-party reimbursed benefit.* Even so, as of December 2011, only nine states (Colorado, Illinois, Maryland, New Jersey, New Mexico, North Dakota, Oregon,

*An excellent guide which can facilitate coding for the treatment of tobacco use disorder can be found on the American College of Chest Physicians' website in their Tobacco Dependence Treatment Toolkit under the Clinical Background tab (http://tobaccodependence.chestnet.org/tk/correct-coding-principles-tobacco-dependence-treatment).

TOBACCO USE DISORDER ⑤

Rhode Island, and Vermont) mandated tobacco cessation coverage, and the services that were mandated varied widely.[22] Deductibles, copays, and limitations on coverage for pharmacologic and behavioral treatments continue to be problematic. Behavioral carve-outs that segregate billing codes and a lack of parity with other medical illnesses can stand in the way of patients accessing the medical, psychiatric, and addiction care for tobacco use disorder that they need.

SUPPORT SYSTEMS

Relapse to tobacco use can be triggered by environmental cues. Community support for smoke-free environments is needed at 12-Step meetings, halfway houses, shelters, group homes, indoor and outdoor workplaces, and recreational areas. Families and friends can support tobacco abstinence by not smoking, and not using other psychoactive drugs around their loved one.

PROGRAM DEVELOPMENT TO INITIATE SERVICE INTEGRATION

To facilitate the treatment of tobacco use disorder in the context of other addiction and/or mental illnesses, programs may integrate manualized smoking cessation treatment. Programmatically, they may also find it helpful to follow this step-by-step approach:

1. Recognize that tobacco use disorder can no longer be ignored during the prevention, diagnosis, and treatment of other addiction and mental illnesses.

2. Establish a leadership group or committee to secure the commitment of the organization.

3. Develop an approach to tobacco use disorder that fits the treatment philosophy of the program.

4. Develop a policy with clear goals and objectives.

5. Obtain administrative support.

6. Obtain staff support.

7. Provide recovery assistance for nicotine-addicted staff and develop a 100-percent tobacco-free staff.

8. Obtain support of accessory departments (housekeeping, maintenance, security, dietary, etc.).

9. Train staff in the diagnosis and treatment of tobacco use disorder, including the management of acute nicotine withdrawal.

10. Develop clear consequences for breaches of policy.

11. Establish ongoing communication with referral resources (persons and agencies that refer patients to the program and/or supply further support and treatment to patients after the program).

12. Obtain the support of self-help groups including Nicotine Anonymous, Alcoholics Anonymous, Narcotics Anonymous, Al-Anon, etc.

13. Communicate changes to patients.

14. Incorporate nicotine/tobacco education and treatment into the patient curriculum.

15. Document the diagnosis of tobacco use disorder in patients' problem list and integrate it into their treatment planning.

16. Maintain the approach to tobacco use disorder through active review and attention to policy and procedures.

17. Practice patience and perseverance.

(Hoffman AL, Slade J. Following the pioneers: addressing tobacco in chemical dependency treatment. *J Subst Abuse Treat.* 1993;10:153-160 and Hurt RD, Slade J, Karan LD, Eberman K. Treating nicotine addiction in patients with other addictive disorders. In: Slade J, Orleans CT, eds. *Nicotine Addiction: Principles and Management.* New York, NY: Oxford University Press; 1993:310-326.)

TREATMENT SETTING AND STAFF

Treatment settings and their surrounding grounds need be tobacco free. While "clean indoor air" laws and environmental health standards for addiction and psychiatric treatment facilities have resulted in tobacco use being forbidden inside facilities where inpatient and outpatient care is offered, only recently have a growing number of treatment programs not allowed tobacco use on their grounds. The definition of "tobacco free" varies greatly among treatment centers, from no smoking during group sessions all the way to no smoking or tobacco use on campus. It is this latter definition that ASAM endorses.

How programs operationalize "tobacco treatment" also varies greatly. "Tobacco treatment" ranges from 1) instructing patients that they cannot smoke during active programming, but allowing them to smoke on breaks, to 2) providing nicotine replacement therapy (NRT) during withdrawal management, but not offering support for quitting tobacco and managing cravings, to 3) prescribing pharmacotherapy and integrating nicotine addiction education and relapse prevention skills training in the treatment program. Enlightened programs assert that abstinence from all mood-altering substances is the goal. They address nicotine addiction as an integral part of their treatment plans for alcohol and other drug addiction, including giving chips for days of abstinence and rewarding NOT using tobacco with increased privileges. Those programs that fully integrate the treatment of nicotine addiction with other addictive disorders will intensify treatment and respond to tobacco relapse as they would respond to relapse with alcohol and other drugs.

All facility staff, including both clinical and non-clinical support staff, such as janitors and cafeteria workers, should not smell of tobacco. Patients readily detect a double message when they are told that they are not in recovery when they continue to use tobacco, but they detect this smell around them. Non-clinical staff may need training to understand the importance of treating tobacco

use disorder. There have been instances when these facility workers "feel sorry" for patients and sabotage treatment by providing patients with a source of underground tobacco.

One might argue that staff who are not addicted to tobacco do not need to become tobacco-free, just as staff without alcohol use disorder are able to have a sip of wine during the evening. However, because smoking is generally dosed much more frequently than alcohol, and because tobacco use is easily detectable by smell for many hours after its last use, it is difficult to assure that episodic off-hours tobacco use is not detected by the patients. Patients have an extremely difficult time succeeding in their efforts to quit using tobacco products when their therapist smells of tobacco. Research has shown that therapists who continue to use tobacco are reticent to diagnose and treat nicotine addiction in their patients compared to therapists who are non-smokers and/or in recovery from nicotine addiction.[23]

All staff who use tobacco and want to quit should have access to or support in receiving their own treatment. This should be provided with ample time before a treatment program goes "online" as a tobacco treatment center.

While the *DSM-5* strives for similar and consistent criteria amongst all substance use disorders, these criteria are of little help to qualify a patient's severity of nicotine addiction, or to predict a patient's ability for cessation or their likelihood to relapse. Patients who satisfy more of the *DSM-5* criteria (shown on page 375) are said to have more severe addiction, but some of the measures are context-specific, and there is no threshold to determine if a given criterion is met. Dose escalation and tolerance (criteria 1 and 10) is less of a factor with nicotine than with other drugs. Nicotine does not cause intoxication. Whereas individuals may give up parts of important social and recreational activities (criterion 7) because tobacco use is not allowed or is not socially acceptable, this is not the same as giving up these activities because of the behavioral disruption due to gross intoxication or having interpersonal problems caused by problems in judgment due to nicotine (crite-

TOBACCO USE DISORDER ❺

DIAGNOSTIC CRITERIA

Tobacco use disorder is defined by the following criteria in the *DSM-5*:

a. A problematic pattern of tobacco use leading to clinically significant impairment or distress.

A patient meets the *DSM-5* definition of tobacco use disorder if he or she meets two or more of the following criteria for tobacco use within a 12-month period:

1. Tobacco is often taken in larger amounts or over a longer period than was intended.

2. There is a persistent desire or unsuccessful efforts to cut down or control tobacco use.

3. A great deal of time is spent in activities necessary to obtain or use tobacco.

4. Craving, or a strong desire or urge to use tobacco.

5. Recurrent tobacco use resulting in a failure to fulfill major role obligations at work, school, or home (eg, interference with work).

6. Continued tobacco use despite having persistent or recurrent social or interpersonal problems caused or exacerbated by the effects of tobacco (eg, arguments with others about tobacco use).

7. Important social, occupational, or recreational activities are given up or reduced because of tobacco use.

8. Recurrent substance use in situations in which it is physically hazardous (eg, smoking in bed).

9. Tobacco use is continued despite knowledge of having a persistent or recurrent physical or psychological problem that is likely to have been caused or exacerbated by tobacco.

10. Tolerance, as defined by either of the following:

    a. A need for markedly increased amounts of tobacco to achieve the desired effect.

    b. A markedly diminished effect with continued use of the same amount of tobacco.

11. Withdrawal, as manifested by either of the following:

    a. The characteristic withdrawal syndrome for tobacco (refer to Criteria A and B of the criteria set for tobacco withdrawal).

    b. Tobacco (or a closely related substance, such as nicotine) is taken to relieve or avoid withdrawal symptoms.[24]

NOTE

Tobacco is not a drug; it is a set of toxic chemicals that serves as a flavorant and drug delivery system. Tobacco is not psychoactive and it does not cause dose escalation, tolerance, intoxication, or withdrawal. If tobacco is stripped of nicotine (and there are such products), there is no withdrawal, and none of the other properties. *DSM-5* criteria for tobacco use disorder have nevertheless been included since many clinicians use *DSM-5*, and when referring to *DSM* criteria, "tobacco" is used rather than the preferred and more accurate "nicotine."

---

rion 6). Similarly, persons may continue to use tobacco despite the medical problems it causes, but this is not the same as having a problem of recurrent nicotine use impairing physical dexterity (criterion 8). It is unusual for tobacco use to result in a failure of major role obligations at work, school, or home (criterion 5).

Tobacco use disorder, like other substance use disorders, is defined by continued use despite adverse consequences. Craving and

5

TOBACCO USE DISORDER

relapse are prominent characteristics of tobacco use disorder. In response to, "What is the wildest thing you ever did for a cigarette?" patients can often discuss elaborate efforts to procure cigarettes and other tobacco products. The price of cigarettes is high and can impinge on basic food budgets or other discretionary purchases. Smoking is not socially acceptable and can have an ostracizing effect. There are many medical illnesses caused and worsened by continued tobacco use. Both nicotine and other addictive drugs exert their effects by acting on central dopaminergic systems, are influenced by genotype, and share risks of heritability.

It has been proposed that developing criteria to assess the severity of a substance addiction for the purpose of determining a differential response to treatment might need to be specific to the drug (nicotine) and its method of administration (smoking, chewing tobacco, water pipe, etc.). The Heaviness of Smoking Index includes two questions: 1) the number of cigarettes per day, and 2) the time to the first cigarette after awakening. This index was helpful in predicting cessation outcome in 10 varenicline trials in persons who were asking for help to quit smoking.[25] There is evidence that craving ratings made during a normal smoking day can predict success of subsequent attempts to quit.[26] Quantifying withdrawal is conceptually important but methodologically difficult. There are differences in nicotine withdrawal measures over time, and with temporary abstinence versus long-term quitting.

ASSESSMENT AND TREATMENT OF TOBACCO USE DISORDERS

The U.S. Public Health Service (USPHS) Clinical Practice Guideline for Treating Tobacco Use and Dependence, 2008 Update[27] works from the framework of the 5 As: Ask, Advise, Assess, Assist, and Arrange. The recommendations put forth in the USPHS guideline are based upon a careful literature review of approximately 8,700 English-language peer-reviewed articles and abstracts published between 1975 and 2007, which formed the basis for more than 35 meta-analyses synthesized by a panel of 24 scientists and clinicians and reviewed externally by more than 90 experts.

The Tobacco Dependence Toolkit of the American College of Chest Physicians[28] employs a chronic disease model. This toolkit advocates: Assess, Recommend, Monitor, and Revise.

Both guidelines are helpful and have thorough references. The material that follows is compiled from a combination of these resources. The comprehensive listing of the assessment topics, questionnaires, and laboratories is included here as a compendium of available tools. These may be streamlined according to the clinic setting and available time.

The overarching goal of these recommendations is that clinicians strongly recommend the use of effective tobacco use disorder counseling and medication treatments to their patients who use tobacco, and that health care systems, insurers, and purchasers assist clinicians in making such effective treatments available.

1. **The U.S. Public Health Service recommends that all patients in all settings should be screened for tobacco use at each visit. They advocate that tobacco use should be noted as a "fifth vital sign."**

2. **Assessment**

   a. History: Taking a tobacco history is no different from taking any other drug history. Rather than merely quantitating the number of pack years (the number of years a patient smoked multiplied by the number of cigarette packs smoked per day during those years) to assess medical risk, the patient's age of onset, patterns of use, psychological effects desired, prior quit attempts, relapse triggers, stage of change, self-efficacy, and social support can all be queried. Other important aspects of the tobacco use history include:

      i. Medical illnesses caused and/or exacerbated by tobacco use. The

TOBACCO USE DISORDER

5

Borg Scale of physical activity and the St. George's Respiratory Questionnaire may be employed.

ii. Use of alcohol, other drugs, and/or gambling. The *DSM-5* contains diagnostic criteria. Many of the current assessment tools are being modified to include the new language. These should be available by early 2014.

iii. Depression, anxiety, suicidality, posttraumatic stress disorder, and other psychopathology, which may be unmasked by tobacco cessation. Potential measures include the Beck Depression Inventory-II (BDI-II), the Center for Epidemiologic Studies Depression Scale (CES-D), the Patient Health Questionnaire (PHQ-9), the Behavior and Symptom Identification Scale (BASIS-32), and/or the Profile of Moods State (POMS).

Ordering information on all questionnaires can be found on the web as part of the American College of Chest Physicians Tobacco Dependence Treatment Toolkit.[28]

b. Physical findings upon examination may include secondary stigmata due to tobacco use. There is no literature that demonstrates improved cessation outcome by remarking about these findings to the patient. However, engaging with the patient and physically examining him or her, and personalizing the message is an important aspect of being a physician that lends credibility to our work. Physical findings may include:

i. Skin: wrinkles, tobacco stains on fingers, clubbing of nails.

ii. Mouth: tobacco stains on teeth, mucosal lesions, tobacco smell on breath.

iii. Pulmonary: distant lung sounds, wheezes, rales.

iv. Cardiovascular: abnormal heart rhythm and sounds, carotid bruits.

v. Extremities: diminished peripheral pulses, poor wound healing.

c. The questionnaires that are most clinically useful to determine physical dependence are:

i. The Fagerström Test for Nicotine Dependence (FTND), (also can be modified for adolescents and the use of smokeless tobacco) or its two-question subset, the Heaviness of Smoking Index

ii. Withdrawal scales (The Minnesota Withdrawal Scale (7 items), the Wisconsin Withdrawal Scale (28 questions) or the Nicotine Withdrawal Symptom Scale, which is adopted from the Minnesota Withdrawal Scale and is on the American College of Chest Physicians' website).

d. Laboratory measures of tobacco use and tobacco use disorder:

i. Salivary and serum cotinine levels correlate with the Fagerström questions, and with physical withdrawal. Cotinine is a metabolite of nicotine that has a half-life of 18-20 hours and reflects nicotine exposure over a period of several days. When these measures are elevated, increased doses of nicotine replacement therapy and/or combination pharmacotherapies are needed to facilitate tobacco cessation.

ii. Carbon monoxide can be detected in expired air. This is easy to measure. Studies have not been able to correlate the use of carbon monoxide levels with improved smoking cessation outcomes, but many providers find this information motivational when shared with patients. Although levels of <10 ppm are used in studies, levels less than 5 ppm are more sensitive to confirm abstinence from smoking.

NOTE

Both cotinine and carbon monoxide can be used to biochemically confirm nicotine abstinence. Anabasine, a tobacco alkaloid, is a research tool that can differentiate between smoked tobacco and nicotine replacement.

e. Other diagnostics may be indicated for the patient's clinical care. However, this personalized information has *not* been shown to improve tobacco cessation results:[29]

   i. Complete blood count (hemoglobin may be elevated in smokers due to the effects of carbon monoxide on oxygen release in the tissues).

   ii. Pulmonary function testing, including spirometry (some clinicians use baseline and subsequent FeV1 values to demonstrate improvement in lung function to their patients).

   iii. Spiral CT is recommended by the American Cancer Society to screen for lung cancer in patients 55 to 74 years of age who have at least a 30 pack year history of smoking and who currently smoke or have quit within the past 15 years.[30]

   iv. EKG

f. Additional preventative care, including influenza vaccination, pneumovax,

and tuberculosis testing, may also be performed.

3. Advice

a. Recurring, brief, friendly, unambiguous physician advice to stop smoking increases long-term smoking cessation rates from 0.3 percent to 5.1 percent (a 17-fold increase).[31]

b. Motivational interviewing can be used to increase readiness for those not yet ready to quit.

4. Assist/Monitor

a. Work with the patient to set a target quit date.

b. Adding only one medication increases the effect of physician advice significantly.[32]

   i. Medications proven effective to date (2013): Nicotine gum, inhaler, lozenge, nasal spray and patch, varenicline and buproprion SR.

   ii. The USPHS guidelines recommend that all smokers trying to quit should be offered pharmacotherapy unless medically contraindicated or within specific populations where there is insufficient evidence of effectiveness (ie, pregnant women, smokeless tobacco users, light smokers, and adolescents).[27] This is the standard of care.

c. Monitor withdrawal symptoms and cravings that may predict relapse.

d. Individual, group, and telephone counseling, especially including problem solving, skills training, and social support, are effective. For instance, patients can identify specific triggers to use

TOBACCO USE DISORDER 5

tobacco, and develop an action plan for each trigger.

e. By increasing the intensity of pharmacotherapy and behavioral modalities, tobacco cessation outcomes are further improved.

5. Arrange continuing and supportive care

6. When following a patient's progress, revisions may be needed. Examples include:

a. Altering medication and increasing support if relapse is imminent.

b. Addressing relapse prevention issues, including coping with stress and weight gain.

c. Assessing anticipated threats to tobacco abstinence and investment in continuing to be tobacco free.

d. Tapering off pharmacotherapies when patient has been stable for some length of time.

e. If relapse occurs, initiating repeated intervention and cessation, learning from setback(s), and intensifying treatment as appropriate.

DOCUMENTATION
The diagnosis of tobacco use disorder should be noted on the patient's problem list, addressed as part of a comprehensive treatment plan, and integrated within other medical, addiction, and/or mental health services as applicable. Documentation standards include individualized progress notes in the patient's record that clearly reflect implementation of the treatment plan and the patient's response to therapeutic interventions for all disorders treated, as well as subsequent amendments to the plan.

Dimensional Issues

DIMENSION 1: NICOTINE INTOXICATION AND/OR WITHDRAWAL POTENTIAL

Intoxication:
Nicotine intoxication occurs with overdose and poisoning, and this is rare. Most reports of intoxication and poisoning are about tobacco farmhands who harvest the plants without protection and develop "green tobacco illness" due to transdermal absorption of nicotine.[33]

Like other substances, nicotine is mood-altering. However, it refines rather than acts as a sledgehammer. Nicotine fine-tunes alertness and can result in stimulation *and/or* relaxation. With usual doses of nicotine, the loss of consciousness and impairment of judgment that is characteristic of other drugs does not occur. For instance, it is highly unlikely that a patient would get arrested for driving under the influence of tobacco.

The *DSM-5* characterizes tobacco withdrawal[24]:
Acute withdrawal symptoms include:

» Irritability, frustration, or anger

» Anxiety

» Difficulty concentrating

» Increased appetite

» Restlessness

» Depressed mood

» Insomnia

Nicotine withdrawal symptoms are at their peak 24-72 hours after stopping smoking and decrease over the next four weeks, but tobacco cravings may last for much longer.

Generally, the more aggressively nicotine withdrawal is treated, the better the outcome. Medications, often in combination with each other, are effective in treating nicotine withdrawal. The medications include nicotine replacement (patch, gum, lozenge, nasal spray, and inhaler), buproprion, and varenicline. The severity rating in the chart on this page can be utilized to help determine if increased doses of nicotine replacement, combination pharmacotherapy, and/or aggressive use of nicotine rescue medications (in response to acute situational or cue-induced relapse triggers) are needed.

Modified American College of Chest Physicians' Severity of Nicotine Withdrawal Symptoms Use Scale:

The time to first cigarette is a critical measure of withdrawal, as this demonstrates the need to replace nicotine after levels fall during sleep. The serum cotinine level is proportional to the amount of nicotine consumed and is also genetically determined by the rate of nicotine metabolism. The Minnesota Withdrawal Scale, first developed by John Hughes and Dorothy Hatsukami, includes seven of the *DSM-IV* items which patients can self-report (thus not heart rate). These items are depression, insomnia, irritability/frustration/anger, anxiety, difficulty concentrating, restlessness, and increased appetite/weight gain. The Nicotine Withdrawal Scale

used by David Sachs and the American College of Chest Physicians includes those items in the Minnesota Scale as well as craving/desire to smoke a cigarette, constipation, tension, psychological need to smoke a cigarette, pimples, and mouth sores. The *DSM-5* includes all items in the nicotine withdrawal scale.

Nicotine withdrawal is uncomfortable and leads to relapse. Unlike alcohol withdrawal, nicotine withdrawal in itself is not life threatening although the behavioral disruption can be quite marked (eg, smoking in an airplane and causing an emergency landing; wheeling outside a hospital in inclement weather to smoke despite being admitted to hospital for a tobacco-associated disease, leaving addiction treatment AMA due to tobacco withdrawal).

2 DIMENSION 2: BIOMEDICAL CONDITIONS AND COMPLICATIONS

Tobacco use is the leading preventable cause of disease, disability, and death in the United States. According to the Centers for Disease Control (CDC), cigarette smoking results in more than 443,000 premature deaths in the United States each year; about 1 in every 5 U.S. deaths is caused by smoking, and an additional 8.6 million people suffer with serious illnesses caused by smoking. Thus, for every person who dies from smoking, 20 more suffer from at least one

MODIFIED AMERICAN COLLEGE OF CHEST PHYSICIANS' SEVERITY OF NICOTINE WITHDRAWAL SYMPTOMS USE SCALE

SEVERITY RATING	NUMBER OF CIGARETTES	TIME TO FIRST CIGARETTE	NICOTINE WITHDRAWAL SCALE	FAGERSTRÖM TEST FOR CIGARETTE DEPENDENCE	SERUM COTININE LEVEL
Very Severe	>40	0-5 min	>40	8-10	>400 ng/ml
Severe	20-40	6-30 min	31-40	6-7	251-400 ng/ml
Moderate	6-19	31-60 min	21-30	4-5	151-250 ng/ml
Mild	1-5	>60 min	11-20	2-3	51-150 ng/ml
None	Non-daily	>60 min	<10	0-1	<50 ng/ml

(http://tobaccodependence.chestnet.org/tk/stepwise-tobacco-dependence-treatment-guide-table-1)

TOBACCO USE DISORDER ⑤

serious tobacco-related illness. Each year, an estimated 126 million Americans are regularly exposed to secondhand smoke, and almost 50 thousand non-smokers die from diseases caused by secondhand smoke exposure.[34]

Cigarette smoking harms nearly every organ in the body. It accounts for one third of all cancer deaths, including lung cancer (90% of all lung cancers are related to smoking). Other smoking-linked cancers include cancers of the mouth, pharynx, larynx, esophagus, stomach, pancreas, cervix, kidney, bladder, and acute myeloid leukemia. Ninety percent of all deaths related to COPD are attributable to smoking. Smoking leads to atherosclerosis, heart disease, and stroke. Smoking during pregnancy lowers the amount of oxygen available to the fetus, causing intrauterine growth retardation as well as increased chance of miscarriage and stillbirth.

Cigarette smoking isn't the only dangerous use of tobacco. A growing number of patients have switched partially or completely to using smokeless tobacco, also known as chewing tobacco, oral tobacco, spit or spitting tobacco, dip, chew, and snuff. Most people chew or suck (dip) the tobacco in their mouth and spit out the tobacco juices that build up, although "spitless" smokeless tobacco has also been developed. Nicotine in the tobacco is absorbed through the lining of the mouth. People in many regions and countries, including North America, northern Europe, India, other Asian countries, and parts of Africa, have a long history of using smokeless tobacco products.[35]

There is no safe form of tobacco. At least 28 chemicals in smokeless tobacco have been found to cause cancer. The most harmful chemicals in smokeless tobacco are tobacco-specific nitrosamines, which are formed during the growing, curing, fermenting, and aging of tobacco. The level of tobacco-specific nitrosamines varies by product. Scientists have found that the nitrosamine level is directly related to the risk of cancer. In addition to a variety of nitrosamines, other cancer-causing substances in smokeless tobacco include polonium-210 (a radioactive element found in tobacco fertilizer) and polynuclear aromatic hydrocarbons (also known as

polycyclic aromatic hydrocarbons). Smokeless tobacco causes oral cancer, esophageal cancer, and pancreatic cancer. Using smokeless tobacco may also cause heart disease, gum disease, and oral lesions other than cancer, such as leukoplakia (precancerous white patches in the mouth).[36]

Hookah is tobacco use by a water pipe. Smoke, generated by the indirect heating of tobacco, often via charcoal, is passed through a chamber containing water before reaching the user via a hose. When researchers compared smoking an average of 3 hookah sessions with smoking 11 cigarettes per day, the water pipe use was associated with a significantly lower intake of nicotine, greater exposure to carbon monoxide, and greater exposure to benzene (associated with an increased leukemia risk), as well as high molecular weight polycyclic aromatic hydrocarbons.[37] Former cigarette smokers who adopt cigar or pipe use as a harm reduction strategy typically continue to inhale whereas primary cigar and pipe users generally do not inhale. Cigars differ in pH levels, which affects their delivery of nicotine. Cigar and pipe use are associated with cancers of the mouth, nose, and upper airway, while cigar use, but not pipe use, appears to be associated with pancreatic cancer.[38]

Electronic nicotine delivery systems work by vaporizing a solution containing nicotine dissolved with flavorants in a carrier medium (usually propylene glycol). Nicotine delivered by vapor with few known toxicants should be less risky when compared to cigarettes, but this has not yet been well studied for tobacco cessation or for its environmental impact. Significant concerns have been expressed about the purity of ingredients, as well as the lack of oversight in quality control, manufacturing, and marketing of electronic nicotine delivery systems.

When persons quit using tobacco, improvements in health occur immediately and accrue over time. After smoking cessation, heart rate and blood pressure drop within 20 minutes and carbon monoxide blood levels drop to normal within 12 hours after quitting. Coughing, shortness of breath, and pulmonary infections diminish as cilia, mucous clearance, and other lung functions recover 1-9 months after quitting.

The excess risk of coronary heart disease is half that of a continuing smoker's one year after quitting. The risk of cancer of the mouth, throat, esophagus, and bladder are cut in half 5 years after quitting. At this time, cervical cancer risk falls to that of a non-smoker. The risk of dying from lung cancer is about half that of a person who is still smoking 10 years after quitting, and the risk of coronary heart disease equals that of a non-smoker 15 years after quitting.[39]

DIMENSION 3: EMOTIONAL, BEHAVIORAL, OR COGNITIVE CONDITIONS AND COMPLICATIONS

People with severe mental illness (SMI) are two to three times more likely to be smokers than the general population. Smokers with a high level of psychological distress smoke a greater number of cigarettes per day.[40] People with serious mental illness die 25 years younger than the general population, largely from conditions caused or worsened by smoking, according to a 2007 report by the National Association of State Mental Health Program Directors (NASMHPD).[41(p6)]

Tobacco use disorder is the most common co-occurring disorder for the severely mentally ill population. Those smokers with a severe mental illness tend to be heavy smokers (more than 20 cigarettes per day), and people with schizophrenia tend to be more efficient smokers (they are able to achieve higher cotinine levels relative to smokers with no mental illness).[42]

Of particular concern for the SMI population is the fact that tobacco use not only causes medical illnesses, but also alters the rate at which many widely used psychiatric medications are metabolized. Due to enzyme induction and increased clearance, smokers can require increased medication when smoking, and dosage adjustments when they stop smoking.

In addition, nicotine and some of the other 7,000 chemicals in tobacco smoke such as the beta carbolines (harman and norharman MAO A and B inhibitors) have numerous and widespread effects on brain and neurotransmitter activity, and these effects can affect mental illness symptoms and neurobiological vulner-

abilities. These factors account for some of the reasons why this population continues to smoke at such high rates, and why it is necessary to identify the additional clinical issues that must be considered in helping this population quit smoking.[43]

DIMENSION 4: READINESS TO CHANGE

Nicotine does not have the gross intoxicant effects of other psychoactive substances. Tobacco use causes longer-term medical consequences, but less immediate overt disruption to an individual's occupation, family, or social functioning, and fewer and less severe legal consequences. Therefore, the source of motivation to stop tobacco use may be different from patients' motivation to stop other drugs, and patients may not experience the same "bottom" as those who enter addiction treatment to cease other addictive substances. Patients may differ in their understanding of the problems caused by tobacco use, how nicotine ties in with their other addiction, and their feelings of self-efficacy in their ability to quit tobacco. Some patients will want to quit tobacco, alcohol, and other drugs simultaneously, whereas others may want a more staged approach, and some may not see the need to quit tobacco at all.

Motivation for discontinuing the use of tobacco products may come from concerns about hygiene and physical attractiveness, desire to participate in competitive sports, awareness of the health consequences of using tobacco, pregnancy, diagnosis or worsening of a medical condition, worry about exposure of children/grandchildren to secondhand smoke, experiencing increasing restrictions at work or in the community regarding smoking, and/or increased expenses, including the costs of the cigarettes themselves and of health care and life insurance premiums as more companies are charging subscribers a higher price if they use tobacco.

Tailoring the intervention to the stage of change is clinically helpful. Persons in the precontemplation stage of change often benefit from education about how reliance upon nicotine to modulate alertness and mood is problematic, the negative consequences of tobacco use, and potential strategies for tobacco cessation. Persons in the contemplation stage can benefit from specific planning and ideas to increase self-efficacy when they decide to quit. Persons in the action stage can benefit from the creation of a treatment plan, including setting a quit date, building support around their quit attempt (including medication management), generating strategies to overcome anxiety and cravings, and reinforcing intrinsic rewards for their new behavior. (See Dimension 5 for those in the relapse prevention stage.)

5 DIMENSION 5: RELAPSE, CONTINUED USE, OR CONTINUED PROBLEM POTENTIAL

Use of tobacco is often believed to be more difficult to quit than other drugs. Approximately 70 percent of current smokers want to quit, 44 percent attempt to stop smoking each year, and only 4-7 percent are able to stop on their own.[27] Here are some of the reasons that tobacco is so reinforcing and has such a high rate of relapse:

1. If the patient's mother used tobacco during pregnancy, then the patient's first exposure to this drug was actually *in utero*. Animal models have shown that fetal exposure to nicotine and tobacco alters neuronal development and neuronal adaptation.

2. Tobacco is often the earliest drug used, and may begin in the preteen years. The earlier an individual begins to use tobacco, the more likely they will become addicted and have a difficult time quitting use.

3. Tobacco is used more frequently than other drugs. If one puff is a dose and a person smokes a pack per day (20 cigarettes is 1 pack per day in the U.S. and 25 cigarettes is 1 pack per day in Canada), then an individual is taking 200-250 doses per day. No other drug is consumed so frequently throughout the day and for so many years.

4. Cigarettes allow nicotine to be "freebased" directly to the brain due to the alkaline

nature of cigarette smoke and the addition of ammonia to cigarettes. Upon inhalation, nicotine is distributed from the lungs' large surface area directly to the arterial circulation and brain, bypassing the venous circulation. The seconds between self-administration and onset of drug effect is both very rapid and very reinforcing.

5. Nicotine finely modulates behavior without gross intoxication. Nicotine can be used to stimulate or relax, depending on the person and the situation. Individuals quickly learn to rely on nicotine to help them feel the way they would like, which occurs within seconds of taking the dose or puff.

6. Smokers can regulate their dose of nicotine by the way they inhale and puff on a cigarette to achieve their desired effect. (When "light" cigarettes are more deeply smoked (including putting one's fingers over the holes on the filter), an individual will inhale more tobacco combustion products, which in turn negates any health benefit for the "lighter" cigarette.)

7. Doses of nicotine become linked with mood states and environmental cues. Users of tobacco products rely on nicotine to wake up in the morning, complete a meal, relax, and deal with stressful situations. Triggers for craving may include having coffee, getting into one's car, and passing a certain area outside one's house or workplace. Olfactory triggers, including the smell of stale cigarette smoke, are some of the most primitive and powerful of the human brain. Such conditioned cues may be reinforced 100-400 times a day over many years.

8. Patients may also have difficulty with cessation due to the state-dependent learning that took place when they were smoking.

9. Tobacco is often the most continuous drug used, even during periods of abstinence

from other drugs. Some patients who do not quit tobacco simultaneously with other substances will increase their tobacco use, in part as a way of coping with stress.

When patients wish to quit tobacco, they need to combat the desired pharmacologic effects of nicotine and the conditioned cues that are delineated above.

Later, after successful cessation, prolonged craving, continued symptoms of nicotine withdrawal, the emergence of depressive symptoms, difficulty coping with stress, and the fear of weight gain may all contribute to relapse.

It is important to inquire about symptoms of prolonged nicotine withdrawal such as anxiety, irritability, and difficulty with sleep after tobacco cessation. Skill building is needed to delay and resist relapse triggers. Aggressive pharmacotherapy with rescue nicotine replacement can assist coping with cue-invoked craving. The principles of sleep hygiene (ie, avoiding daytime naps, going to sleep and waking at the same each day, daily exercise) can be helpful for persons with insomnia. The emergence of depressive symptoms after quitting tobacco may be an indication for buproprion, other pharmacotherapeutics, and/or counseling measures.

Weight gain can be problematic with smoking cessation. Persons who quit smoking gain an average of 4-10 pounds, with one out of 10 gaining as much as 25-30 pounds. Most weight tends to be gained in the first six months. This occurs due to a decreased metabolic rate without daily nicotine, increased preference for sugar and fatty foods, need to put something in one's mouth, using food to reward oneself, and/or eating to deal with stress, boredom, and/or to be social. In order to prevent relapse, smokers may need to accept a small amount of weight gain and emphasize that "not smoking" is the primary goal. Healthy eating and regular exercise are key to avoiding excessive weight gain.

As with other addiction, stress management is critical to help the patient decrease his or her vulnerability to relapse. Many smokers have been using tobacco to cope with stress and anxiety for their entire adult lives. Therefore,

they may not have fully developed other coping strategies. Being aware of relapse triggers/behaviors, environmental cues, and coupling this knowledge with an action plan are important to enable continued tobacco cessation.

6 DIMENSION 6: RECOVERY/LIVING ENVIRONMENT

Interpersonal skills and judgment are not affected by nicotine; therefore, patients are generally able to return to their homes. They do not require halfway or three-quarter-way houses, sober-living programs, or other similar programs. However, exposure to social settings and environments where others continue to smoke can trigger relapse.

Families, friends, and coworkers need to be invited to become a part of the recovery team, and support for their "sobriety" is critical for the patient's best chance of recovery from tobacco use disorder.

Addiction treatment service providers should make their facilities and grounds smoke-free environments for patients, staff, and visitors alike. Tobacco use is an addiction, and treatment programs can no longer support addiction by condoning smoking by patients or staff. If the staff is not 100% smoke free, then co-smoking between staff and patients of the program needs be specifically addressed. There must be an end to "smoking breaks" for patients in treatment, especially "smoking breaks" for adolescents, because of both the clinical and legal implications of use, such as laws prohibiting underage possession and use of tobacco products.

Second- and third-hand smoke poses risks to families, coworkers, and anyone in the vicinity of the smoker, according to the U.S. Surgeon General's report, *Health Consequences of Involuntary Exposure to Tobacco Smoke*:[44]

» Secondhand smoke exposure causes premature death and disease in children and adults who do not smoke.

» Children exposed to secondhand smoke are at risk for Sudden Infant Death Syndrome (SIDS), acute respiratory infections, asthma, respiratory symptoms, and impeded lung development. They are also at risk for chronic otitis media. There may be a link with prenatal and postnatal secondhand smoke exposure and childhood cancers, including leukemia, lymphomas, and brain tumors.

» There is NO risk-free level of exposure to secondhand smoke.

Addiction treatment programs and other treatment providers should become skilled in education and assessment of possible damage to family members from tobacco use in the home, and help the family generate rules about smoking exposure to loved ones as part of the family program. If family members and others in the home persist in using tobacco, then the treatment and discharge plan should include not using tobacco around the recovering individual, limiting any smoking to over 20 feet from any doors and windows, and making the home and car smoke free. Of course, it would be best if these persons could also be motivated to seek help and quit.

Level of Care Issues

Assessments ought be matched with intensity of care to maximize treatment outcome.

Because tobacco use causes fewer social and legal consequences as a result of intoxication than other drugs, historically the levels of care for tobacco use disorder have been less intensive. Treatment for tobacco cessation is currently available as follows:

Level 0.5/1: Print and online self-help education

Level 0.5/1: Over-the-counter nicotine replacement

Level 0.5/1: Online social support and problem solving

Level 0.5/1: Brief interventions: Physicians who ask (screen), advise, assess, assist, and arrange tobacco cessation

Level 0.5/1: Telephone quitline counseling

Level 0.5/1: Interactive online counseling programs

Level 1: Group face-to-face outpatient treatment programs (ie, SmokEnders, American

Cancer Association, and American Lung Association Tobacco Cessation programs)

Level 1: Tobacco treatment specialty consultation and follow-up (stand-alone, or in ambulatory health care settings)

Level 3.7: Medically Monitored Inpatient Treatment

The eight-day residential treatment program at the Mayo Clinic Nicotine Dependence Center in Minnesota provides 1) a secure, tobacco-free setting, 2) individual and group counseling, 3) pharmacotherapy, including both tailored dosing and medications trials, 4) physician-supervised care including medical, psychiatric, and addiction expertise, and 5) long-term follow-up to prevent relapse.

As of now, there are no known stand-alone Level 2 intensive outpatient/partial hospitalization treatment programs for tobacco cessation or addiction associated with nicotine use, and residential and inpatient treatment programs (Levels 3 and 4) are few in number. Specialty consultative services are difficult to find. Third-party reimbursement for intensive services under commercial and government-sponsored health insurance plans is typically non-existent.

As individuals with less severe addiction have quit using tobacco products, those who persist often have additional addiction, psychiatric, and/or medical comorbidity. Persons need a more intensive level of care when there is continued tobacco use despite multiple unsuccessful attempts to quit with less intensive therapy (including both pharmacotherapy and counseling modalities).

Treatment of patients with tobacco use disorder in combination with pregnancy, comorbid addiction, psychiatric, and/or medical illness(es) will be facilitated not only by the increased availability of different intensities of tobacco cessation treatment, but, more importantly, by the integration of such services into the currently existing addiction, obstetrics, general medicine, cardiology, pulmonology, oncology, psychiatric systems, and other systems of care. Strategies are needed to integrate tobacco cessation programming into other health care settings.

Despite evidence that more intensive interventions are more effective, they are rarely provided, except by clinicians who have special expertise in treating tobacco dependence.[45]

Treatment capacity for integrated and specialty care including careful assessment and the potential for aggressive pharmacotherapy needs to be expanded at levels of care of 1 and higher.

Tobacco Cases: Determining Level of Care

The examples on pages 387-392 demonstrate real-life challenges determining levels of care for tobacco cessation treatment. Tobacco use disorder does not exist in isolation. Patients experience these gaps in treatment when confounding problems occur. Collaboration, additional resources, and increased emphasis on preventive medicine are needed to advance management of tobacco use disorders, and to break down our current silos of care.

When integrated care is not available and/ or a patient continues to relapse, then specialty tobacco use disorder treatment is needed. There is a dose response for counseling interventions. Advanced pharmacotherapeutic management can improve treatment outcome.

While levels of care are specifically suggested in these examples, the actual treatment such patients might receive will depend upon their willingness for the care suggested, the availability of such care, and the funding for the services provided.

Summary

This section of *The ASAM Criteria* has discussed the importance of addressing and treating tobacco use disorders. Tobacco use is the number one preventable cause of illness and lost life, and if untreated, is especially harmful to those who have other alcohol and drug addiction and/ or severe mental illness.

Interventions for tobacco cessation should take place by all physicians when they identify patients with tobacco use disorder. Assessing the six ASAM criteria dimensions can help tailor appropriate treatment modalities and intensities of care to the patient's needs.

Tobacco cessation programs of lesser intensity have been developed because nicotine is not intoxicating and does not cause the same behavioral problems as alcohol and other drug addiction, even though it is one of the most difficult drugs to quit. The challenge is to develop increased intensities of tobacco use disorder treatment for those who have not yet been successful at less intensive levels of care. Integrating tobacco cessation treatments within obstetrics, medical, addiction, and psychiatric care is critical to improve treatment outcomes, and may require matching to the intensity of the patient's other problems.

TOBACCO CASE STUDIES

CASE 1

MP is a 28-year-old single mother of one who is currently 16 weeks pregnant. She has smoked 1 ½ packs per day for approximately 10 years. MP first started smoking at age 14, and was smoking daily by 16. She has made several attempts to quit, but her longest period of time without cigarettes was less than 36 hours. She tried to quit during her first pregnancy, but was unable to do so successfully. Her first child was born 3 weeks prematurely, had a low birth weight of 6 lbs., and has struggled with asthma and allergies. MP says she does not use alcohol or other drugs. She indicated that she has not had a history of depression, and she states that she has been healthy and active. MP is currently prescribed the nicotine patch and nicotine gum, of which she is only partially adherent. Her doctor has advised her to stop smoking for the health of her 4 year old and the unborn child. MP said she is motivated to stop, but she doesn't have transportation or child care to attend a local Freedom from Smoking Class. MP has frequent urges to smoke. She is constantly triggered by her home environment, where she and her cousins smoke most of the time.

To enable tobacco cessation and protect the unborn fetus, it would be best if this 28-year-old pregnant woman agreed voluntarily to a residential perinatal treatment program (Level 3.1-3.5) that included tobacco cessation (Level 2.1-2.5) and child care. She could also be observed in an ob-gyn ward with smoking cessation consultation (Level 3.7, Level 4) including skill building. Both treatment options provide MP a protective environment in light of her lack of transportation and her inability to cease tobacco use in her own home.

Although this sounds like expensive treatment, babies born to smoking mothers often have low birth weight and are at risk for cognitive impairment. The cost-effectiveness of smoking cessation in pregnant women is unparalleled. However, relapse prevention is critical, as these women often return to smoking after childbirth.

TOBACCO CASE STUDIES

CASE 2

WR is a 46-year-old married male executive with a large public relations firm. WR started smoking in college at age 19, and is currently smoking 1 pack per day. He smokes more on the weekends while playing golf. He also occasionally smokes cigars. WR is very frustrated by his workplace being smoke free. He has tried "cold turkey," but is only able to stop for 5 days or so. He has hypertension and elevated cholesterol, and he takes medication for both conditions. His wife is a smoker as well, and she has no interest in stopping. Both WR and his wife drink alcohol on a regular basis, but WR does not think they are alcoholics. Their children have tried for years to get their parents to stop smoking, but to no avail. WR has been caught smoking at work once already, and his boss is very unhappy with him. WR is on notice that his continued smoking will not be tolerated by the company, especially as an executive who is supposed to be setting an example for the rest of the company.

WR should be referred to an Employee Assistance Program for treatment of his tobacco use disorder, as well as for assessment of concomitant alcohol use disorder. An addiction treatment program would optimally address both issues. For tobacco cessation, WR could benefit from education about addiction, pharmacotherapy, and skill building. Assuming WR has a diagnosis of addiction involving alcohol, he may need additional motivational enhancement, and possibly assistance with alcohol withdrawal.

If available outpatient counseling (Level 1) does not enable tobacco and alcohol cessation, the intensity of treatment could be progressively increased (Level 2.1). WR should see his medical provider for follow-up and care of his hypertension and elevated cholesterol. WR should be encouraged to sign releases to allow communication between medical and addiction care providers. When in recovery from alcohol, WR should be monitored by his primary care physician to determine if he still needs antihypertensive therapy. Both WR and his wife would benefit from a program that has a family component. WR's wife may need to be assessed for alcohol use disorder and motivated for smoking cessation treatment of her own.

TOBACCO CASE STUDIES

CASE 3

BR is a 63-year-old Vietnam veteran who has been homeless for the past 6 years. He doesn't have Veterans' benefits because he was dishonorably discharged. BR's doctor is aware of his recovery from heroin addiction and praises him for this. BR has been diagnosed with chronic obstructive pulmonary disease (COPD) due to his smoking habit of 2 packs per day. His doctor at the free clinic, which BR rarely attends, has told him he must stop smoking immediately and has offered to help him with nicotine replacement medication. BR's posttraumatic stress disorder and paranoia developed after his second tour in Vietnam, and he has been poorly adherent with his medication and therapy. BR's anxiety and mistrust of the system makes it difficult for him to engage with his doctor. Smoking has gotten to be more and more expensive, so BR "wouldn't mind stopping," but he has a difficult time organizing himself enough to follow through with the recommendations.

BR will not be accepted for admission to the state hospital because he is not in imminent danger of harming himself or others. He is, however, appropriate for the community mental health center, which may also be able to assist him with shelter, transportation, food, and obtaining Medicaid and disability benefits. BR needs to be stabilized on psychotropic medication. This will facilitate BR's taking pharmacotherapy and learning skills for tobacco cessation. Quitting smoking will in turn enable more consistent blood levels of BR's psychotropic medication.

BR is appropriate for partial hospitalization with day treatment (Level 2.5). Tobacco cessation services should be integrated into BR's mental health treatment plan. BR should attend group therapy for tobacco cessation with others who have mental illnesses, as he will not fit in with groups run for a general population.

BR may be provided a more permanent medical home and primary care provider through the Affordable Care Act. BR should also have his smoking cessation and lung function monitored by a primary care physician. He may need tuberculosis testing, a pneumovax, and lung cancer screening by spiral CT.

As so often happens, individuals with the most severe problems and comorbidities need the most intensive treatments, but have the fewest resources. Community mental health facilities should have nicotine addiction treatment and medical treatment embedded or easily accessible in their services.

TOBACCO CASE STUDIES

CASE 4

George and Matilda come to your office because they are upset that their 17-year-old son, TJ, is smoking cigarettes and hanging around with the "wrong" group of friends. Recently, TJ's driving license was taken away for a Minor in Possession infraction. The police came to a party where there was underage drinking and "busted" him. TJ has been cutting some classes, but he will have no problem graduating high school this year. TJ has been experimenting with alcohol and marijuana, but his only clear regular usage is cigarettes. He is otherwise healthy and without concern. TJ doesn't want to stop smoking, and he feels that his parents are overreacting. TJ states his underage drinking was an isolated event and that it was his friends who got rowdy.

TJ will be attending alcohol education classes due to the charge of Minor in Possession. Given the considerable amount of overlap between teens who smoke cigarettes and drink alcohol, it would be preferable if these education classes (Level 0.5) covered both substances.

TJ's pediatrician (Level 0.5/1) can motivate him for tobacco cessation using personally relevant harms of tobacco use (ie, personal hygiene as well as financial and legal consequences) and the benefits of cessation. This physician may ask TJ about his family history of addictive disorders. The physician may educate TJ about nicotine and concomitant addiction. He may offer pharmacotherapy and treatment options should TJ not easily be able to quit on his own.

TOBACCO CASE STUDIES

CASE 5

SW is a 65-year-old retired carpenter who was hospitalized for pneumonia complicating COPD 6 months ago. At that time he was delirious and had a PO$_2$ of 65%. Now, SW has been out of the hospital for six months. His PO$_2$ is within normal limits without supplemental oxygen or respiratory therapy. SW walks slowly due to back and knee ailments, but he lives independently.

SW's family members and physicians tell him repeatedly to stop smoking. However, he gets very anxious at this thought and avoids the subject. SW chain-smokes. He has smoked 2-4 packs of cigarettes daily since age 16. SW smokes within seconds of awakening, and he leaves conversations to smoke, even when this is not socially acceptable. The only time SW did not smoke was for a few days when he was ill. SW has tried smoking cessation books, classes, and groups, as well as nicotine gum and the patch, to no avail.

SW would benefit from residential smoking cessation treatment. His nicotine addiction is severe and his continued tobacco use will shorten his life. SW needs motivational interviewing to get him to treatment and intensive counseling and pharmacotherapeutic intervention once he is there. Tailored treatment to combat withdrawal with aggressive pharmacotherapy will help ensure that SW does not leave care precipitously. In a premier nicotine dependence treatment center, addiction and behavioral counseling with continuing care and a strong relapse prevention plan gives SW a >50% chance of 1 year success of tobacco abstinence.

TOBACCO CASE STUDIES

CASE 6

TH is a 50-year-old addiction counselor who works at a residential addiction treatment center. The center has decided that they are going to begin treating tobacco addiction along with all other addiction. The staff is not going to be able to smoke at all at work, and will not be allowed to come to work smelling of tobacco smoke. TH is in recovery from addiction to alcohol and pain medications. He has been sober for 23 years and always felt that tobacco was not part of his disease. He feels that he has extra rapport with patients since he goes out smoking with them on breaks. TH has often advised patients who wanted to stop smoking that they should wait at least a year before they even consider stopping, because "it is too hard to quit more than one thing at a time." TH has been told by his doctor that his frequent bouts of bronchitis are directly related to his smoking, and that he needs to stop before he does permanent damage to his lungs. TH is about 40 lbs. overweight and fears that if he stops smoking, he will gain even more weight. He has never tried to quit, and is angry about his workplace forcing him to stop.

TH is in the precontemplation stage of change. He needs education about nicotine addiction and motivation for tobacco cessation. If TH will accept treatment, he may benefit from combination pharmacotherapy, taking into account his concern about weight gain. Outpatient counseling (Level 1) is the most appropriate place to begin, with additional online resources and quitline assistance. TH may find Nicotine Anonymous helpful, since he will be able to use the same philosophy and skills to quit tobacco that he used to enable recovery from alcohol and pain medications in the past. Group support at work will help motivate TH and enable his tobacco cessation attempts to be successful. TH's primary care physician should monitor his tobacco cessation and weight, and give positive feedback about improvements in his bronchitis and lung function.

TOBACCO CASE STUDIES

CASE 7

CK is a 63-year-old woman with alcohol use disorder who has been in recovery for 8 years but continues to smoke three-fourths of a pack per day (15 cigarettes per day). She cannot stop tobacco use despite the recent diagnosis of adenocarcinoma of the esophagus. She uses the nicotine replacement therapy prescribed for her, but she continues to smoke on top of this. CK is upset by her diagnosis and stressed with the possibility of facing her own mortality. CK tried SmokEnders several yeas ago but only quit smoking for 3 weeks. CK was depressed when her husband left her 10 years ago. However, she went to 12-Step meetings, became sober, and went back to work after outpatient counseling. CK never participated in formal addiction treatment, but she continues to attend 12-Step meetings 3 times per week. She has no other significant past medical history.

It would be optimal if CK could access tobacco cessation services amidst oncology treatment. Her surgery, chemotherapy, and radiation will leave her little time or energy for additional outside referrals and care.

CK requires aggressive pharmacotherapy. Support groups (Level 1) may integrate tobacco cessation with discussions about quality of life. Patients with continued tobacco use are more likely to have recurrent and more quickly growing cancers than those who quit smoking.

When the initial treatments for esophageal cancer have been completed, CK may benefit from intensive outpatient (Level 2.1), partial hospitalization (Level 2.5), and/or residential treatment (Levels 3.5, 3.7) if she still continues to smoke. Intensive treatment may especially be needed if CK fears alcohol relapse and/or if she has significant depression. Hospitalization (Level 4) may be needed if she has suicidal ideation.

Over time, CK's acceptance of illness, response to chemotherapy and radiation, threshold for experiencing stress, level of depression, and risk of relapse to alcohol and/or cigarettes may change. Levels of care are meant to be fluid.

A Look to the Future

Ideally, physicians would suggest the most salient questions, elements of the physical exam, laboratory, and radiologic assessments, and match these with corresponding components of treatment to maximize efficacy and outcome. As of yet, controlled studies have not proven how best to fine-tune treatment based upon specific assessment information. We do know that treatment is effective and that primary, secondary, and tertiary prevention of tobacco use disorder improves quality of life and longevity. Future editions of *The ASAM Criteria*, based upon such outcomes research, will continue to advance our capability to match assessment variables with modalities of treatment and levels of care.

Appendices

Appendix A
Withdrawal Management Instruments

CIWA-Ar[1]

This section of *The ASAM Criteria* includes the CIWA-Ar, with updated information about the correct use of the CIWA-Ar as follows:

The CIWA-Ar scale can be a useful tool, but it has only been validated for tracking the withdrawal management process – not for making level of care decisions. Because it does not take into account the influence of the other five ASAM criteria dimensions, it should only be used as part of the decision-making process, and not as a stand-alone determinant for level of care decisions. Studies have documented its misapplication in at least two scenarios[2,3,4]:

» When the elevated CIWA score is in fact due to a delirium with an etiology other than Alcohol Withdrawal Syndrome (AWS), resulting in the actual disorder going untreated.

APPENDIX A: INSTRUMENTS

Clinical Institute Withdrawal Assessment for Alcohol, Revised (CIWA-Ar)

Clinical Opiate Withdrawal Scale (COWS)

Fagerström Nicotine Dependence Test

The Clinical Institute Narcotic Assessment (CINA)

NOTE

While CIWA scores are widely used and may be somewhat helpful as an imprecise general guide to the overall severity of withdrawal symptoms, they should not be regarded as comprehensive (eg, they do not reflect vital signs, and do not take into account the relative weight of particular features of withdrawal, such as tremulousness, confusion, psychosis, etc.). The presence of particular clinical signs and symptoms (as outlined in this text) should be taken as "red flags" and used as a more important guide to treatment service and level of care decisions. CIWA scores are more useful as a monitoring tool to track the changing severity of withdrawal (up or down) for a particular patient over time (for example, in response to treatment).

ADDICTION RESEARCH FOUNDATION
CLINICAL INSTITUTE WITHDRAWAL ASSESSMENT FOR ALCOHOL, REVISED (CIWA-AR)

Patient: _____

Date: _____ Time: _____

Pulse or heart rate, taken for 1 minute: _____

Blood pressure: _____

Nausea and Vomiting: Ask, "Do you feel sick to your stomach? Have you vomited?" Observation:

0 No nausea and no vomiting

1 Mild nausea with no vomiting

2

3

4 Intermittent nausea with dry heaves

5

6

7 Constant nausea, frequent dry heaves and vomiting

Tremor: Arms extended and fingers spread apart. Observation:

0 No tremor

1 Not visible but can be felt fingertip to fingertip

2

3

4 Moderate, with patient's arm extended

5

6

7 Severe, even with arms not extended

Paroxysmal Sweats: Observation:

0 No sweat visible

1

2

3

4 Beads of sweat obvious on forehead

5

6

7 Drenching sweats

Tactile Disturbances: Ask, "Have you any itching, pins and needles sensations, any burning, any numbness, or do you feel bugs crawling under your skin?" Observation:

0 None

1 Very mild itching, pins and needles, burning or numbness

2 Mild itching, pins and needles, burning or numbness

3 Moderate itching, pins and needles, burning or numbness

4 Moderately severe hallucinations

5 Severe hallucinations

6 Extremely severe hallucinations

7 Continuous hallucinations

Auditory Disturbances: Ask, "Are you more aware of sounds around you? Are they harsh? Do they frighten you? Are you hearing anything that is disturbing to you? Are you hearing things you know are not there?" Observation:

0 Not present

1 Very mild harshness or ability to frighten

2 Mild harshness or ability to frighten

3 Moderate harshness or ability to frighten

4 Moderately severe hallucinations

5 Severe hallucinations

6 Extremely severe hallucinations

7 Continuous hallucinations

Visual Disturbances: Ask, "Does the light appear to be too bright? Is the color different? Does it hurt your eyes? Are you seeing anything that is disturbing to you? Are you seeing things you know are not there?" Observation:

0 Not present

1 Very mild sensitivity

2 Mild sensitivity

3 Moderate sensitivity

4 Moderately severe hallucinations

5 Severe hallucinations

6 Extremely severe hallucinations

7 Continuous hallucinations

» When the assumption is incorrectly made that a patient is being dishonest in denying recent drinking, resulting in unnecessary treatment for withdrawal management.

In addition, this section includes as resources the COWS, the Fagerström Test for Nicotine Dependence (FTND) (also can be modified for adolescents and smokeless tobacco) and the CINA.

ADDICTION RESEARCH FOUNDATION
CLINICAL INSTITUTE WITHDRAWAL ASSESSMENT FOR ALCOHOL, REVISED (CIWA-AR)

Patient: _____ Pulse or heart rate, taken for 1 minute: _____

Date: _____ Time: _____ Blood pressure: _____

Anxiety: Ask, "Do you feel nervous?" Observation:

0 No anxiety, at ease

1 Mildly anxious

2

3

4 Moderately anxious, or guarded, so anxiety is inferred

5

6

7 Equivalent to acute panic states, as seen in severe delirium or acute schizophrenic reactions

Agitation: Observation:

0 Normal activity

1 Somewhat more than normal activity

2

3

4 Moderately fidgety and restless

5

6

7 Paces back and forth during most of the interview, or constantly thrashes about

Headache, Fullness in Head: Ask, "Does your head feel different? Does it feel like there is a band around your head?" Do not rate dizziness or lightheadedness. Otherwise, rate severity.

0 Not present

1 Very mild

2 Mild

3 Moderate

4 Moderately severe

5 Severe

6 Very severe

7 Extremely severe

Orientation and Clouding of Sensorium: Ask, "What day is this? Where are you? Who am I?" Observation:

0 Oriented and can do serial additions

1 Cannot do serial additions or is uncertain about date

2 Disoriented for date by no more than 2 calendar days

3 Disoriented for date by more than 2 calendar days

4 Disoriented for place and/or person

Total CIWA-Ar Score: _____

(maximum possible score = 67)

Patients scoring less than 10 do not usually need additional medication for withdrawal. Rater's Initials: _____

Clinical Opiate Withdrawal Scale (COWS) Flow Sheet[5]

The following flow sheet can be used for measuring symptoms over a period of time during buprenorphine induction.

For each item, write in the number that best describes the patient's signs or symptoms. Give a rating only on the apparent relationship to opioid withdrawal. For example, if heart rate is increased because the patient was jogging just prior to assessment, the increased pulse rate would not add to the score.

CLINICAL OPIATE WITHDRAWAL SCALE (COWS) FLOW SHEET

Patient's Name: _____

Date: _____

Buprenorphine induction: _____

Enter scores at time zero, 30 minutes after first dose, 2 hours after first dose, etc.

Times:

_____ _____ _____ _____

Resting Pulse Rate: (record beats per minute) Measured after patient is sitting or lying for one minute

0: pulse rate 80 or below

1: pulse rate 81-100

2: pulse rate 101-120

4: pulse rate greater than 120

Sweating: Over past ½ hour, not accounted for by room temperature or patient activity

0: no report of chills or flushing

1: subjective report of chills or flushing

2: flushed or observable moistness on face

3: beads of sweat on brow or face

4: sweat streaming off face

Restlessness: Observation during assessment

0: able to sit still

1: reports difficulty sitting still, but is able to do so

3: frequent shifting or extraneous movements of legs/arms

5 unable to sit still for more than a few seconds

Pupil size:

0: pupils pinned or normal size for room light

1: pupils possibly larger than normal for room light

2: pupils moderately dilated

5: pupils so dilated that only the rim of the iris is visible

CLINICAL OPIATE WITHDRAWAL SCALE (COWS)
FLOW SHEET

Bone or joint aches:

If patient was having pain previously, only the additional component attributed to opiates withdrawal is scored

0: not present

1: mild diffuse discomfort

2: patient reports severe diffuse aching of joints/muscles

4: patient is rubbing joints or muscles and is unable to sit still because of discomfort

Runny nose or tearing: Not accounted for by cold symptoms or allergies

0: not present

1: nasal stuffiness or unusually moist eyes

2: nose running or tearing

4: nose constantly running or tears streaming down cheeks

GI Upset: Over last ½ hour

0: no GI symptoms

1: stomach cramps

2: nausea or loose stool

3: vomiting or diarrhea

5: multiple episodes of diarrhea or vomiting

Tremor: Observation of outstretched hands

0: no tremor

1: tremor can be felt, but not observed

2: slight tremor observable

4: gross tremor or muscle twitching

Yawning: Observation during assessment

0: no yawning

1: yawning once or twice during assessment

2: yawning three or more times during assessment

4: yawning several times/minute

Anxiety or Irritability:

0: none

1: patient reports increasing irritability or anxiousness

2: patient obviously irritable or anxious

4: patient so irritable or anxious that participation in the assessment is difficult

Gooseflesh skin:

0: skin is smooth

3: piloerection of skin can be felt or hairs standing up on arms

5: prominent piloerection

Total scores
with observer's initials

Score:

5-12 = mild	**25-36 = moderately severe**
13-24 = moderate	**more than 36 = severe withdrawal**

FAGERSTRÖM TEST FOR NICOTINE DEPENDENCE[6]

1. How soon after you wake up do you smoke your first cigarette?
   Within 5 minutes (3)
   6-30 minutes (2)
   31-60 minutes (1)
   After 60 minutes (0)

2. Do you find it difficult to refrain from smoking in places where it is forbidden?
   Yes (1)
   No (0)

3. Which cigarette would you hate most to give up?
   The first in the morning (1)
   Any other (0)

4. How many cigarettes per day do you smoke?
   10 or less (0)
   11-20 (1)
   21-30 (2)
   31 or more (3)

5. Do you smoke more frequently during the first hours after waking than during the rest of the day?
   Yes (1)
   No (0)

6. Do you smoke even if you are so ill that you are in bed most of the day?
   Yes (1)
   No (0)

Score:
0-2 = Very low dependence;
3-4 = Low dependence;
5 = Medium dependence;
6-7 = High dependence;
8-10 = Very high dependence

The Clinical Institute Narcotic Assessment (CINA) Scale for Withdrawal Symptoms[7]

The Clinical Institute Narcotic Assessment (CINA) Scale measures 11 signs and symptoms commonly seen in patients during narcotic withdrawal. This can help to gauge the severity of the symptoms and to monitor changes in the clinical status over time.

THE CLINICAL INSTITUTE NARCOTIC ASSESSMENT (CINA) SCALE FOR WITHDRAWAL SYMPTOMS		
PARAMETERS	FINDINGS	POINTS
Parameters based on Questions and Observation:		
(1) abdominal changes: Do you have any pains in your abdomen?	No abdominal complaints; normal bowel sounds	0
	Reports waves of crampy abdominal pain	1
	Crampy abdominal pain; diarrhea; active bowel sounds	2
(2) changes in temperature: Do you feel hot or cold?	None reported	0
	Reports feeling cold; hands cold and clammy to touch	1
	Uncontrolled shivering	2
(3) nausea and vomiting: Do you feel sick in your stomach? Have you vomited?	No nausea or vomiting	0
	Mild nausea; no retching or vomiting	2
	Intermittent nausea with dry heaves	4
	Constant nausea; frequent dry heaves and/or vomiting	6
(4) muscle aches: Do you have any muscle cramps?	No muscle aching reported; arm and neck muscles soft at rest	0
	Mild muscle pains	1
	Reports severe muscle pains; muscles in legs, arms or neck in constant state of contraction	3
Parameters based on Observation Alone:		
(5) goose flesh	None visible	0
	Occasional goose flesh but not elicited by touch; not permanent	1
	Prominent goose flesh in waves and elicited by touch	2
	Constant goose flesh over face and arms	3
(6) nasal congestion	No nasal congestion or sniffling	0
	Frequent sniffling	1
	Constant sniffling, watery discharge	2

THE CLINICAL INSTITUTE NARCOTIC ASSESSMENT (CINA) SCALE FOR WITHDRAWAL SYMPTOMS		
PARAMETERS	**FINDINGS**	**POINTS**
Parameters based on Observation Alone:		
(7) restlessness	Normal activity	0
	Somewhat more than normal activity; moves legs up and down; shifts position occasionally	1
	Moderately fidgety and restless; shifting position frequently	2
	Gross movement most of the time or constantly thrashes about	3
(8) tremor	None	0
	Not visible but can be felt fingertip to fingertip	1
	Moderate with patient's arm extended	2
	Severe even if arms not extended	3
(9) lacrimation	None	0
	Eyes watering; tears at corners of eyes	1
	Profuse tearing from eyes over face	2
(10) sweating	No sweat visible	0
	Barely perceptible sweating; palms moist	1
	Beads of sweat obvious on forehead	2
	Drenching sweat over face and chest	3
(11) yawning	None	0
	Frequent yawning	1
	Constant uncontrolled yawning	2
TOTAL SCORE	[Sum of points for all 11 parameters]	

Minimum score=0, Maximum score=31. The higher the score, the more severe the withdrawal syndrome. Percent of maximal withdrawal symptoms=((total score)/31) x 100%.

Appendix B
Special Considerations for Dimension 5 Criteria:
Relapse, Continued Use, or Continued Problem Potential

Relapse is quintessential in addiction treatment; however, assessing and treating relapse is not straightforward, and may even be controversial, particularly if meaningful placement, treatment planning, and staff response are lacking.[1] Furthermore, the term "relapse" sometimes carries with it negative judgments about the person who has relapsed. Thus, there are special considerations for Dimension 5 that this appendix will address. In assessing Dimension 5, Relapse, Continued Use, or Continued Problem Potential, it may be helpful to consider a conceptual organization that links biological, psychological, and clinical paradigms into a coherent process. This process is based on several sources: a review of the Dimension 5 constructs and criteria developed for earlier editions of *The ASAM Criteria*, field data from the Massachusetts General Hospital (MGH)/Harvard ASAM Criteria Validity Study, and a literature review of behavioral pharmacology, behavioral psychology, learning theory, and psychopathology. This appendix provides guidance for understanding, teaching, and implementing the Dimension 5 criteria, and serves as a background for understanding the decision logic and assessment procedures in *The ASAM Criteria Software*.

Dimension 5 Constructs and Criteria

The definition of Dimension 5 has been broadened to include continued use potential for patients who have not achieved any significant degree of abstinence beyond withdrawal, and thus cannot meet the definition of relapse. The key distinctions between Dimension 5 levels of care are described as follows:

Level 0.5 (Early Intervention)
Needs an understanding of the risks of current use patterns, or help in developing skills to change those risks.

Level 1 (Outpatient Services)
Able to control use or maintain abstinence with minimal support while pursuing recovery goals.

Level 2 (Intensive Outpatient/Partial Hospitalization Services)
Experiencing intensified addiction symptoms and functional deterioration, despite participating in treatment at a less intensive level of care, and despite efforts to revise the treatment plan. Level 2.5 (Partial Hospitalization) is reserved for the patient who has failed to progress toward recovery at Level 2.1, *or* who continues his/her drinking and/or other drug use, *or* is likely to have impending relapse, *and* for whom less intensive treatment is judged to be insufficient for stabilization.

Level 3 (Residential/Inpatient Services)
Impending relapse or continued use is associated with *imminent danger* in the absence of 24-hour structured support. This circumstance might result from an inability to cope with environmental access to substances, difficulty in postponing immediate gratification or—in the event of Level 3.3 (Clinically Managed Population-Specific High-Intensity Residential Services)—cognitive limitations, high chronicity, or intensity of substance use. In the less-structured but still residential Level 3.1 (Clinically Managed Low-Intensity Residential Services), the patient understands the nature of his/her problems, but is at risk because of an inability to apply recovery skills.

Opioid Treatment Services (OTS)

Addiction involving opioids in which relapse is attributed to: (1) physiological craving, *or* (2) intensification of addiction symptoms, *or* (3) continued high-risk behaviors accompanied by deteriorating function, despite treatments other than opioid agonist medication and efforts to adjust the treatment plan. Alternatively, OTS may be indicated for the patient who is at high risk of relapse because of lack of awareness of relapse triggers, difficulty in postponing immediate gratification, or low readiness to change.

Constructs for Understanding, Training for, and Implementing Dimension 5: Relapse, Continued Use, or Continued Problem Potential

In order to prepare for assessment of the patient's needs in Dimension 5, it is helpful to consider four discrete domains that cover the key clinical, biological, psychological, and behavioral constructs that contribute to relapse potential. Repeated exposure to addictive drugs induces behavioral sensitization, and following discontinuation, organisms can become exquisitely prone to relapse with only small, "priming" doses of the drug, conditioned cues, or stress.[2] Prospective studies indicate multiple clinical, biological, and neural factors that predict relapse risk, including subjective measures (eg, depressive symptoms, stress, and craving), biological measures (endocrine measures, eg, cortisol and the cortisol/corticotropin (ACTH) ratio measure of adrenal sensitivity, and serum brain-derived neurotrophic factor), and neural measures (eg, brain atrophy in the medial frontal regions and hyperreactivity of the anterior cingulate during withdrawal).[3] Repeated drug use and relapse induces direct Pavlovian reinforcement, but also causes the brain to form conditioned cue or instrumental drug-associated memories to previously neutral environmental stimuli, which become associated with drug highs (and/or withdrawal states), and subsequently maintain drug-taking behavior or trigger unconscious relapse.[4] These cues operate for all addictive substances and can be as diverse as odors, the time of day, and unemployment.[5] Such relevant cues are likely to operate also for a person with addiction involving addictive behaviors such as gambling.

These relapse factors must all be taken into account for effective selection of modalities of care and level of care placement. Long-held biases about preferred settings of care can no longer hold sway when resources and payment are managed aggressively and data actually exist. For example, while therapeutic community is associated with decreases in drug use, the majority of patients do not complete treatment (they actually complete only about one-third of the recommended length of stay), and after discharge, relapse is frequent.[6] Thus, it is paramount to consider individualized treatment needs and continuity of care. Another bias often held is that if a previously treated patient has relapsed, that is evidence that the previous level of care was of insufficient intensity and now the patient must be referred to a more intensive level of care rather than basing the level of care recommendation on a current, comprehensive assessment which incorporates information about the post-treatment relapse.

CONSTRUCTS FOR UNDERSTANDING, TRAINING FOR, AND IMPLEMENTING DIMENSION 5: RELAPSE, CONTINUED USE, OR CONTINUED PROBLEM POTENTIAL

A. Historical Pattern of Use

    1. Chronicity of problem use or behavior

    2. Treatment or change response

B. Pharmacologic Responsivity

    1. Positive reinforcement (pleasure, euphoria)

    2. Negative reinforcement (withdrawal discomfort, fear)

C. External Stimuli Responsivity

    1. Reactivity to acute cues

    2. Reactivity to chronic stress

D. Cognitive and Behavioral Measures of Strengths and Weaknesses

    1. Locus of control and self-efficacy

    2. Coping skills

    3. Impulsivity

    4. Passive and passive/aggressive behavior

There have also been long-held biases and policies about dealing with relapse or continued use, especially while a patient is in treatment. Such policies warrant re-examination in the context of understanding addiction as a chronic, potentially relapsing illness. Many clinicians and programs have traditionally adhered to policies of zero tolerance for any substance use while in treatment. Thus, if a person shows up to an outpatient group having had a drink, or having used some other drug, they may be assessed for immediate safety, but then may be required to leave until stable. Or, if a patient uses while in a residential level of care, immediate discharge or transfer to a withdrawal management setting is policy, even if a person has not used to the level of needing withdrawal management. Such policies are inconsistent with understanding addiction as a chronic, potentially relapsing illness. A mental health patient would not be suspended from treatment if presenting to a group or session with suicidal ideation, a recurrence of panic attacks, mania, or psychotic behavior. Cutting behavior would not be grounds for immediate discharge or transfer to a more intensive level of care.

Common concerns raised by treatment providers about allowing non-abstinent patients to remain in a group or residential program include the effect of a person under the influence on other patients, as a trigger to also use or relapse and/or to affect their motivation to continue treatment; and the effect on the clinician who may struggle to facilitate a group when one of the members is under the influence of alcohol or other drugs. (See the Example Policy and Procedure to Deal with Dimension 5 Recovery and Psychosocial Crises on page 407 for more on how to view and handle non-abstinent patients in group settings.)

In considering individualized treatment needs and continuity of care, it is vital to consider both biological and psychosocial needs, as they may be insufficient to address only biological risks, even with proven, effective pharmacologic treatments. A systematic review of the literature on methadone's impact on reducing opioid craving reported that of 16 articles, 7 found heroin craving reductions, 4 reported continued risk of heroin craving, 1 reported increased heroin craving, and 4 studies reported only neutral effects. This suggests that patients receiving opioid pharmacotherapy using methadone may still be at risk of cue-induced heroin cravings.[7] Similarly, a Cochrane review of eleven studies of opioid dependent participants (N=1,592) found that, compared to any pharmacological treatment alone, the combination of any psychosocial treatment with any pharmacotherapy was shown to significantly improve reductions in both treatment dropout and opioid use.[8]

The following four constructs, therefore, should be evaluated as an integrated set of considerations. They also offer a conceptually clear sequence of factors that contribute to relapse potential. The sequence involves the historical phenomenon of relapse, the current acute pharmacologic response to the substance(s), second-order behavioral responsivity that may mediate the preceding factors, and third-order personality or learned responses that may modify the preceding factors.

A. Historical Pattern of Use

1. Chronicity of problem use or behavior

    How long has the individual had problem use or addictive use or behavior, and at what level of severity?[9]

2. Treatment or change response

    Has the individual managed brief or extended abstinence or reduction of use or behavior in the past?

The clinical history should take into account the sequence of use, misuse, and addictive use or behavior, as well as prior episodes of cessation, withdrawal management, and treatment. A good number of studies show that demographic variables such as onset of alcohol or other drug problems by age 25, never having been married, lacking a high school education, and being unemployed predict continued use or relapse. Single variables such as these may combine, aggravating risk in Dimension 5. Clinical history variables, such as past treatment response, are good predictors of future resilience or risk. Even if the patient has not previously experienced treatment, any past change efforts to reduce or cease substance use behavior or history of adherence to management of other chronic diseases (eg, diabetes) are informative. This may apply to substances other than the one that is the current primary risk for the patient. For example, it may be helpful to know if the patient who must cease drinking has previously succeeded in quitting smoking.

B. Pharmacologic Responsivity

1. Positive reinforcement (pleasure, euphoria)

    What is the amount of pleasure or euphoria the individual obtains or expects from substance use or addictive behavior? Expectancies, which may be defined as the outcomes the individual anticipates from a particular behavior, have been shown to be related to substance use consumption and relapse.[10] To what extent does the patient obsess or ruminate about substance use?[11]

2. Negative reinforcement (withdrawal discomfort, fear)

How much discomfort from withdrawal can the patient objectively expect, and does the patient subjectively fear abstinence? Anticipatory fear of acute withdrawal and the post-acute withdrawal syndrome can be potent drivers of continued use and relapse.

Pharmacologic responsivity refers to internal stimuli at the neuronal and circuitry levels of the brain from reinforcing substances that produce either positive or negative reinforcement – or both. Note that negative reinforcement is not used here to represent the acute withdrawal symptoms themselves, as those are addressed in Dimension 1 (Acute Intoxication and/or Withdrawal Potential).

C. External Stimuli Responsivity

1. Reactivity to acute cues

   To what extent does the patient tend to react to trigger objects and situations that are reminiscent of substance use or addictive behavior? Take into account both the strength of the reaction and the frequency or likelihood that the patient will encounter these cues. These issues interact with the patient's recovery environment (Dimension 6); however, the extent to which the patient is likely to react to those cues is assessed in Dimension 5.

2. Reactivity to chronic stress

   What is the patient's tendency to react to chronic stress, particularly ongoing environmental stressors that are not specific to substance use or addictive behavior? Acute and chronic cues and stressors may include negative stressors such as social pressure or conflict, as well as ongoing environmental challenges such as homelessness, divorce, and financial problems. It is also import-

ant to remember that the provocation for continued use and relapse can occur in response to positive stressors as well, for example, resolving a court obligation, gaining a job promotion, restoring a relationship, etc.

D. Cognitive and Behavioral Measures of Strengths and Weaknesses

There are numerous theories of behavior that are specifically relevant to relapse risk and its treatment.[12] The constructs in this section differ from disease conditions in Dimension 3 (Emotional, Behavioral, or Cognitive Conditions and Complications). These constructs are behavioral traits that are specific to relapse risk, although they may not be pathological in other contexts. They are traits or coping characteristics that are more specific to substance use and other addictive disorders relapse and relapse prevention, which is why they are retained in Dimension 5. For example, the self-administration of daily medication has repeatedly been shown to be beyond the majority of patients,[13] which is a feature of substance use and other addictive disorders, not indicative of broader psychopathology. This distinguishes the problem from Dimension 3 constructs, which usually are psychiatric (*DSM*) diagnoses (eg, borderline personality disorder) that generalize to many behaviors and risk situations.

1. Locus of control and self-efficacy

   Is there an internal sense of self-determination and confidence that the patient can direct his or her own behavioral change?[14,15]

2. Coping skills

   These include stimulus control, affect management, and other cognitive strategies.[9,16,17]

3. Impulsivity

To what extent does the patient tend to pursue risk taking, thrill seeking or novelty seeking?[18]

4. Passive and passive/aggressive behavior

Does the individual demonstrate active initiative to sense, identify, anticipate, and cope with internal and external stressors, or is there a tendency to abdicate or blame others for responsibility? These are specific relapse risk traits (Dimension 5), rather than pathological conditions (Dimension 3) or cognitive perception problems needing motivational enhancement (Dimension 4).

Also, it is important to recognize that relapse risk is constantly changing. Therefore, the time frame for prediction is limited. In a given patient, each of the above constructs is highly variable; therefore, the patient requires frequent reassessment as withdrawal subsides, a new treatment response is established, coping strengths are learned and tested, character traits grow, and euphoric expectancies extinguish. This stresses the importance of assessment, service planning, and level of care decisions that are based on the particular needs of each individual, level of engagement, and the individual's response to treatment. How Dimension 5 issues are treated is based on person-centered care, not predetermined policies about suspension from treatment, discharge, or transfer to other settings or levels of care. A suggested policy on dealing with Dimension 5 issues outlines steps that are person-centered to promote recovery, rather than program-driven policies that inhibit engagement into recovery.

In the interview process, it can be difficult for patients to tease apart these various phenomena themselves, given the subjective nature of the relapse risk experience. Patients can, however, respond to prompting about the above constructs in a manner that is relevant and meaningful. The interviewer is prompted to do so in *The ASAM*

Criteria Software, with questions that put the above constructs into practice. A subset of these questions follows:

» History:

Have your addiction symptoms increased recently? How?

(Ask any not mentioned) Have you had more craving, risk behaviors, more frequent use, increased amounts of the substance(s), or have you used a more rapid route of administration?

» Craving:

How strong is your desire to use any drug right now?

» Cue Responsivity:

Rate how strong your urges are for alcohol and/or another drug when something in the environment reminds you of it.

» Control, Coping, and/or Impulsivity:

Imagine yourself in the environment in which you previously used alcohol and/or other drugs. If you were in this environment today, what is the likelihood that you would use?

Clinical, Policy, and Procedure Considerations for Dimension 5: Relapse, Continued Use, or Continued Problem Potential

It is not always apparent, and thus often goes unrecognized even by treating professionals working with a patient, exactly how to respond to relapse clinically. There is not universal consensus. Some parties view relapse as occurring when there is a return to any substance use after a period of abstinence. Researchers view relapse as occurring when an adequate number of diagnostic criteria for substance use disorder are present; thus, an individual can have resumed substance use, but if one or two criteria of substance use disorder were present, the case was considered one of "partial remission" (interestingly, never termed "partial relapse"), and only if three or more criteria of substance use disorder were present would a case of "active disease" (ie, no longer "in full remission") be identified.

Others view relapse as a complex biopsychosocial process, with its onset prior to the resumption of any substance use (ie, when cognitive structures have reverted to those in the active disease state, such as "telling oneself" that one is "cured" and that "I can avoid getting into trouble if 'I have just one' dose of alcohol, tobacco, or another drug.") Most would argue that the "potential for relapse" is ubiquitous in addiction and never fully gets back to zero.

Further, there is a range of responses to relapse: some clinicians view it as such an inevitability that, when it arises, they use it as "clinical material" and a basis to explore cognitions, feeling states, motivations, and cravings with a patient but to otherwise not change the treatment plan. Other clinicians may view relapse to any substance use as highly significant clinically: it can be used as a reason to discharge a patient from low-intensity residential care (such as a halfway house), or to discharge a patient from an Opioid Treatment Service.

In the treatment of persons who work in safety-sensitive occupations, any return to substance use at all can result in significant clinical contingencies as well as other contingencies (eg, continued ability to work, continued ability to have an unrestricted license to practice). In any event, relapse—be it cognitive or emotional, or the behavioral relapse in which actual return to "use" (the pathological pursuit of reward or relief through the use of substances or other addictive behaviors)— should gain the attention of the clinician, who then should thoughtfully consider what, if any, change is indicated in the patient's treatment plan (intensity or "dosage" of treatment). To fail to respond at all to relapse is generally considered substandard clinical practice. What

follows is one possible example of a policy and procedure for a Dimension 5 crisis.

Example Policy and Procedure to Deal with Dimension 5 Recovery and Psychosocial Crises

Recovery and psychosocial crises cover a variety of situations that can arise while a patient is in treatment. Examples include, but are not limited to, the following:

1. Slip/using alcohol or other drugs while in treatment.

2. Suicidal, and the individual is feeling impulsive or wanting to use alcohol or other drugs.

3. Loss or death, disrupting the person's recovery and precipitating cravings to use or other impulsive behavior.

4. Disagreements, anger, or frustration with fellow patients or therapist.

The following procedures provide steps to assist in implementing the principle of re-assessment and modification of the treatment plan:

1. Set up a face-to-face appointment as soon as possible. If not possible in a timely fashion, follow the next steps via telephone.

2. Convey an attitude of acceptance; listen and seek to understand the patient's point of view rather than lecture, enforce "program rules," or dismiss the patient's perspective.

3. Assess the patient's safety for intoxication/ withdrawal and imminent risk of impulsive behavior and harm to self, others, or property. Use the ASAM criteria assessment dimensions to screen for severe problems and identify new issues in all biopsychosocial areas.

The Six ASAM Criteria Assessment Dimensions
» Acute intoxication and/or withdrawal potential
» Biomedical conditions and complications
» Emotional, behavioral, or cognitive conditions and complications
» Readiness to change
» Relapse, continued use, or continued problem potential
» Recovery environment

4. If there are no immediate needs, discuss the circumstances surrounding the crisis, developing a sequence of events and precipitants leading up to the crisis. If the crisis is a slip, use the six ASAM criteria dimensions as a guide to assess causes. If the crisis appears to be willful, defiant, non-adherence with the treatment plan, explore the patient's understanding of the treatment plan, level of agreement on the strategies in the treatment plan, and reasons s/he did not follow through.

5. Modify the treatment plan with patient input to address any new or updated problems that arose from your multidimensional assessment in steps 3 and 4 above.

6. If there appears to be a lack of interest in developing a modified treatment plan in step 5 above, reassess the treatment contract and what the patient wants out of treatment. If it becomes clear that the patient is mandated and "doing time" rather than "doing treatment and change," explore what Dimension 4, Readiness to Change, motivational strategies may be effective in re-engaging the patient into treatment.

7. Determine if the modified strategies can be accomplished in the current level of care, or a more or less intensive level of care in the continuum of services or different services, such as co-occurring enhanced services. The level of care decision is based on the individualized treatment plan needs, not an automatic increase in the intensity of level of care.

8. If, on completion of step 6, the patient recognizes the problem/s, and understands the need to change the treatment plan to learn and apply new strategies to deal with the newly identified issues, but still chooses not to accept treatment, then discharge is appropriate, as he or she has chosen not to move his/her treatment in a positive direction. Such a patient may also demonstrate his/her lack of interest in treatment by bringing alcohol or other drugs into the treatment milieu and encouraging others to use or engage in gambling behavior while in treatment. If such behavior is a willful disruption to the treatment milieu and not overwhelming Dimension 5 issues to be assessed and treated, then discharge or criminal justice graduated sanctions are appropriate to promote a recovery environment.

9. If, however, the patient is invested in treatment as evidenced by collaboration to change his/her treatment plan in a positive direction, treatment should continue. To discharge or suspend a patient for an acute recurrence of signs and symptoms is to break continuity of care at precisely a crisis time when the patient needs support to continue treatment. For example, if the patient is not acutely intoxicated and has alcohol on his/her breath from a couple of beers, such an individual may come to group to explore what went wrong to cause a recurrence of use and to gain support and direction to change his/her treatment plan. Concerns about "triggering" others in the group are handled no differently from if a patient was sharing trauma issues, sobbing, and this triggered identification and tearfulness in other group members. Such a patient with posttraumatic stress disorder would not be excluded from group

or asked to leave for triggering others. Group members and/or other patients in a residential setting are best helped to deal with such "triggering" with the support of peers and a trained clinician. To protect fellow patients from exposure to relapse or recurrence of signs and symptoms excludes the opportunity to learn new coping skills. In addition, it jeopardizes the safety of the patient at the very time he or she needs more support and guidance in such a crisis, rather than rejection, discharge, or transfer.

10.   Document the crisis and modified treatment plan or discharge in the medical record.

Application to Clinical Vignettes

A recurrence of signs and symptoms of any illness, and in particular addiction, warrants an immediate reassessment of what went wrong, with a goal to improve the outcomes by changing the treatment plan in a positive direction. Once the assessment and new service plan are agreed upon with the patient, the next question is where can that plan be safely and efficiently delivered? The new plan may be provided in the current level, or may need a less intensive or more intensive level or different services. But the level of care decision is driven by the individualized treatment plan, not a predetermined policy to always move the person to a more intensive level of care. See examples on page 410.

Future Directions on Terminology

The term "relapse" has generally been assigned to the resumption of use once abstinent (See Glossary for the ASAM definition of relapse). It may no longer be appropriate for ASAM to use the term in this manner when we describe an illness that has symptoms that can be suppressed through the use of antiaddiction medicines. In addition, ASAM's understanding of addiction as a chronic illness recognizes that recurrences of symptoms are normal in chronic diseases, and managing those recurrences is what disease management is all about. When a person with hypertension or diabetes becomes unstable and exhibits signs and symptoms, they are not described as having relapsed.

However, if a person with addiction drinks or uses substances and exhibits signs and symptoms of addiction, there is often a pejorative and disapproving tone to say the patient has relapsed, and then a discharge or suspension of the patient from treatment at the very time of crisis when continuity of care is most needed. In addition, the very concept of relapse implies that there are only two possible states: clean and dirty, sober and relapsed. In this view, if the patient has used any substance, he or she has relapsed, is no longer in recovery, and his or her sobriety clock restarts again with a new sobriety date.

In attempts to soften the definition of relapse, some have talked of slips and lapses. However, how severe does a slip or lapse need to be before it becomes a relapse? How many days of drinking or drugging are required, or does one drink or drug experience suffice? How many days or weeks does a patient have to be abstinent before his or her next use qualifies as a relapse? Is being abstinent for six weeks or six months needed before any further use qualifies as a relapse?

Observing the terminology used with other chronic illnesses can be informative for addiction. Relapse is used rarely in other chronic illnesses, if at all. Possible terms that would be less value-laden and disapproving in tone could be:

» A recurrence of signs and symptoms

» An exacerbation of signs and symptoms

» A flare-up of the person's addiction

» Acute instability of the patient's addiction

The ASAM Criteria maintains the current terminology of relapse. But further consideration of this term is needed in the context of recurrences and remissions in other chronic illnesses.

EXAMPLE APPLICATION TO CLINICAL VIGNETTES

TRANSFER TO A LESS INTENSIVE LEVEL OF CARE

The patient used while in residential or intensive outpatient treatment because he now believes that after a period of abstinence, he is not really addicted. He is sure that recent substance use problems were caused by a lot of stress with family and work difficulties. It is his view that since he was able to be abstinent with little difficulty, he can safely return to social drinking, which is why he had a couple of beers when having dinner with friends on a recent transitional therapeutic pass or birthday party. While the clinical team is sure he has addiction, they agree to transfer him from residential to outpatient services, or from intensive outpatient to once-per-week outpatient sessions to do "discovery, dropout prevention" motivational strategies.

TRANSFER TO A MORE INTENSIVE LEVEL OF CARE

The patient has had increasing cravings to use, but was reluctant to process these cravings with her counselor and peers for fear of lengthening her treatment stay. As her urges to use became almost unbearable, she hoped she could secretly get her old drug dealer to drop off some heroin, which she could use to get some relief. She succeeded in smuggling some heroin into the residential setting and was found slumped over in the bathroom, having overdosed with the needle still in her arm. She was transferred to intensive care. The same transfer would occur if the patient was in outpatient treatment, overdosed, and was discovered by her roommate.

TRANSFER TO THE SAME LEVEL OR A DIFFERENT LEVEL OF CARE WHERE DIFFERENT SERVICES ARE AVAILABLE

The patient has been diagnosed with a major depression disorder and has been stable on her antidepressant medication. She has a significant re-emergence of her depressive symptoms and has suicidal ideation with moderate to high lethality. She has become intoxicated between her IOP sessions and believes that only drinking will relieve her depressive symptoms. This patient needs co-occurring enhanced services provided in the same level of care, if possible, or in a different level of care where theses services are available.

CONTINUE IN THE SAME LEVEL OF CARE

The patient again has had increasing cravings to use, and was reluctant to process these cravings with his counselor and peers. He arranges for some friends to bring him some oxycodone pain pills and some marijuana, which he uses while in residential treatment. Some of his peers notice the flare-up of his addiction and when confronted, the patient owns up to his return to substance use. He realizes as he processes this flare-up in group that he needs to sever all contact with his old drug-using friends and is willing to do it. His peers promise to support him as he role-plays with them what to say to end his relationship with old drug-using friends. This treatment plan is best continued in the current level of residential care where he has the support of peers who can also learn from his flare-up of addiction while being in a more protected environment.

In an outpatient setting, a patient with two weeks of abstinence off methamphetamine and narcotic analgesic pills is genuinely excited about his recovery process. He visits friends still using methamphetamine on the weekend to try to attract them into recovery. Overwhelmed, he ends up using. Thankfully, he talks about this use in group the next day. He realizes his mistake of visiting with using friends too early in his recovery and determines to stay away and instead go to more Narcotics Anonymous meetings. This treatment plan is best continued in the current level of care where his updated treatment plan can safely be provided. To transfer him to a more intensive level of care would be a waste of resources and break continuity of care.

If a patient is not invested in treatment and just wants a place to stay as a respite from homelessness, or to get out of jail sooner, and in that context brings alcohol or other drugs into the facility and even influences others to use with him or her, then discharge is reasonable. The treatment program is a treatment place, not a hotel, resort, or marketplace. But if a patient is trying to do treatment to the best of his or her ability, gets a craving to use, and resumes substance use, the procedure is to reassess and change the treatment plan accordingly, rather than automatically discharge or transfer to a more intensive level of care.

Appendix C
Glossary of Terms Used in *The ASAM Criteria*

A glossary of terms used in *The ASAM Criteria* is given here to help the reader interpret the criteria. Terms are defined as follows:

[NOTE: an asterisk denotes a definition that has been formally adopted by ASAM's Board of Directors.]

*Abstinence
Intentional and consistent restraint from the pathological pursuit of reward and/or relief that involves the use of substances and other behaviors. These behaviors may involve, but are not necessarily limited to, gambling, video gaming, spending, compulsive eating, compulsive exercise, or compulsive sexual behaviors.

Abuse
This term is not recommended for use in clinical or research contexts.
Harmful use of a specific psychoactive substance. When used to mean "substance abuse," this term also applies to one category of psychoactive substance-related disorders in previous editions of the *Diagnostic and Statistical Manual of Mental Disorders* of the American Psychiatric Association (*DSM*). While recognizing that "abuse" is part of past diagnostic terminology, ASAM recommends that an alternative term be found for this purpose because of the pejorative connotations of the word "abuse."

*Addiction
Addiction is a primary, chronic disease of brain reward, motivation, memory, and related circuitry. Dysfunction in these circuits leads to characteristic biological, psychological, social, and spiritual manifestations. This is reflected in an individual pathologically pursuing reward and/or relief by substance use and other behaviors.

Addiction is characterized by inability to consistently abstain, impairment in behavioral control, craving, diminished recognition of significant problems with one's behaviors and interpersonal relationships, and a dysfunctional emotional response. Like other chronic diseases, addiction often involves cycles of relapse and remission. Without treatment or engagement in recovery activities, addiction is progressive and can result in disability or premature death.[1]

Addiction-Credentialed Physician
A physician who has achieved professional recognition in the treatment of addiction by meeting a predetermined set of standards, such as certification.

Physicians can be certified for their expertise in addiction by one of three pathways. Any physician may either complete an addiction medicine fellowship or meet other eligibility criteria and then by examination, receive certification and diplomate status from the American Board of Addiction Medicine. A second pathway is exclusive to psychiatrists. A psychiatrist may complete a fellowship in addiction psychiatry, and then by examination become certified by the American Board of Psychiatry and Neurology, a member board of the American Board of Medical Specialties.

A third pathway is exclusive to osteopathic physicians. A doctor of osteopathy (DO) can receive certification in addiction medicine through examination by the American Osteopathic Association (AOA). Many physicians in the American Osteopathic Academy of Addiction Medicine, a membership organization, have obtained certification from the AOA.

In situations where a certified addiction physician is not available, physicians treating addiction should have had some specialty training and/or experience in addiction medicine or addiction psychiatry and if treating adolescents, experience with adolescent medicine.

Addiction-Only Services (AOS)

Services directly solely at the treatment of addictive disorders. Such services are not directed at co-occurring mental disorders: for example, an AOS program typically would not accept an individual who needs psychotropic medications, and mental health issues generally would not be addressed in treatment planning or content. Such AOS are not recommended by *The ASAM Criteria*.

Addiction Psychiatrist

A physician who specializes in addiction psychiatry and is board certified in this subspecialty by the American Board of Psychiatry and Neurology.

Addiction Specialist Physician

A physician who holds a board certification in addiction medicine from the American Board of Addiction Medicine, a subspecialty board certification in addiction psychiatry from the American Board of Psychiatry and Neurology, or a subspecialty board certification in addiction medicine from the American Osteopathic Association.

Addiction Treatment Services

Addiction treatment services are professional health care services, offered to a person diagnosed with addiction, or to that person's family, by an addiction professional. Addiction professionals providing addiction treatment services are licensed or certified to practice in their local jurisdiction and may be nationally certified by a professional certification body for their professional discipline.[2]

Addictionist

Also, "addictionologist." A physician who specializes in addiction medicine (usually someone certified by the American Board of Addiction Medicine, ABAM.

The preferred term is addictionist or addiction specialist physician rather than the older term addictionologist.

Addictive Conditions

Clinical presentations due to addictive behaviors such as gambling or Internet gaming that may or may not demonstrate sufficient signs or symptoms to substantiate a diagnosis of an addictive disorder. *The ASAM Criteria* requires sufficient assessment to establish a diagnosis to indicate treatment at any level of care, other than in Level 0.5, Early Intervention.

Addictive Disorder

Clinical presentations, such as gambling, that demonstrate signs or symptoms to substantiate a diagnosis of an addictive disorder in the *Diagnostic and Statistical Manual of Mental Disorders (DSM-5)* of the American Psychiatric Association; as well as other presentations in which the engagement in a behavior manifests a pathological pursuit of reward or relief as described in the ASAM definition of addiction. While substance use disorders are a part of the broader grouping of addictive disorders, the term addictive disorder often refers to those manifestations of addiction that do not involve pathological use of substances such as alcohol, tobacco, or other drugs. At this time, gambling disorder is the only addictive disorder considered in the *DSM-5* other than those involving substances, the substance-related disorders. With additional research, other non-substance addictive disorders may be specified.

Adherence

Adherence is a term that the health care field has been increasingly using to replace the term "compliance." Both terms have been used, sometimes interchangeably, to refer to how closely patients cooperate with, follow, and take personal responsibility for the implementation of their treatment plans. The terms are often used with the more narrow sense of how well patients accomplish the goal of persistently taking medications, but also refer more broadly to all components of treatment. Assessment of patients' efforts to accomplish the goals of a treatment plan is essential to treatment success. These efforts occur along a complex spectrum from independent proactive commitment, to mentored collaboration, to passive cooperation, to reluctant partial agreement, to active resistance, to full refusal. Attempts to understand factors that promote or inhibit adherence/compliance must take into account behaviors, attitudes, willingness, and varying degrees of capacity and autonomy. To "adhere" is "to cling, cleave (to be steadfast, hold fast), to stick fast" (*Webster's Dictionary*). The term "adherence" emphasizes the patient's collaboration and participation in treatment. It contributes to a greater focus on motivational enhancement approaches that engage and empower patients. "To comply" is "to act in accordance with another's wishes, or with rules and regulations" (*Webster's Dictionary*). The term "compliance" is falling into disuse because patient engagement and responsibility to change is a goal beyond passive compliance.[3(p25)]

Admission

That point in an individual's relationship with an organized treatment service when the intake process has been completed and the individual is eligible to receive the services and accepts these services.

Adolescent

As used in *The ASAM Criteria*, an individual aged 13 through 18. The term also frequently applies to young adults aged 18 to 21, who may be in need of adolescent-type services rather than adult-type services. (Many states classify individuals up to age 21 as adolescents.)

*Alcoholics Anonymous

"A fellowship of men and women who share their experience, strength and hope with each other that they may solve their common problem and help others recover from alcoholism. The only requirement for membership is a desire to stop drinking" (from the Alcoholics Anonymous Preamble).

Alcoholism

A general but not diagnostic term, usually used to describe alcohol use disorder, but sometimes used more broadly to describe a variety of problems related to the use of beverage alcohol.

Ambivalence

"Ambivalence is a state of mind in which an individual has concurrent but conflicting feelings about something. The person may be ambivalent about engaging in certain behavior (eating, drinking, smoking, gambling, etc.) or resisting it."[3p(179)]

Ambulatory Withdrawal Management

Withdrawal management that is medically monitored and managed but that does not require admission to an inpatient, medically or clinically monitored, or managed 24-hour treatment setting.

ASAM PPC-2R

ASAM Patient Placement Criteria for the Treatment of Substance-Related Disorders, Second Edition-Revised (*ASAM PPC-2R*). This edition was published in 2001.

Assertive Community Treatment (ACT)

Active outreach to persons, usually with serious and chronic mental illness, who need a support system that facilitates living and functioning adequately in the community. ACT involves comprehensive services designed to engage and retain patients in treatment and assist them in managing daily living, obtaining work, building and strengthening family and friendship networks, managing symptoms and crises, and preventing relapse.

Assessment

Those procedures by which a clinician evaluates an individual's strengths, resources, preferences, limitations, problems, and needs, and determines priorities so that an individualized treatment plan can be developed.

A credentialed counselor or clinician may gather diagnostic and multidimensional assessment data relevant to the six ASAM criteria dimensions. However, interpretation of such information must be within their scope of practice. Consultation with the interdisciplinary team is required whenever the assessor is outside of his/her scope of practice and expertise. For example, a counselor can gather a substance history of recent use and past history of withdrawal but would need nursing or medical consultation to determine the severity of withdrawal and the matched level of withdrawal management.

*At-risk Use
See **Hazardous Use**

*Binge or Binge Drinking
This term is not recommended for use in clinical or research contexts.
These terms can be useful in public health discourse because a "binge" is often understood to be a heavy drinking episode. The Centers for Disease Control and Prevention uses the term to mean a heavy drinking episode. However, because it is used variably with different meaning it is not generally preferred. Some who have heavy drinking episodes will consider "binge" to be pejorative.

"Heavy drinking episode" is simply descriptive and therefore preferred for that use. The *Journal of Studies on Alcohol and Drugs* proscribes use of the term "binge" because it has been used to mean many different things, from four standard drinks in a day for a woman, to a "bender" during which a person drinks continuously for several days in a row. The general public often uses the terms "binge" and "bender" interchangeably to describe a days-long episode of heavy drinking.

The National Institute on Alcohol Abuse and Alcoholism has a specific definition for a "binge": "A 'binge' is a pattern of drinking alcohol that brings blood alcohol concentration (BAC) to 0.08 gram percent or above. For the typical adult, this pattern corresponds to consuming 5 or more drinks (male), or 4 or more drinks (female), in about 2 hours. ...

"In the above definition, a "drink" refers to half an ounce of alcohol (eg, one 12oz. beer, one 5oz. glass of wine, or one 1.5oz. shot of distilled spirits). Binge drinking is distinct from "risky" drinking (reaching a peak BAC between .05 gram percent and .08 gram percent) and a "bender" (2 or more days of sustained heavy drinking). For some individuals (eg, older people or people taking other drugs or certain medications), the number of drinks needed to reach a binge-level BAC is lower than for the 'typical adult.'"[4]

The NIAAA definition can be useful for research purposes. But even in research, data definitions have not been used in various studies with consistency: "binge drinking" can mean drinking in a "binge" (a single heavy-drinking episode) once per week, twice per week, once per month, twice per month, etc. Similarly, some have used the term "frequent binge drinking" but there is no standardly accepted sense of how "frequently" an individual must "binge drink" to be described as a "frequent binge drinker."

Biomarker
A biomarker, or biological marker, is in general a substance that is objectively measured and evaluated as an indicator of normal biological processes, pathogenic processes, or pharmacologic responses to a therapeutic intervention. A biomarker can also be used to indicate exposure to various environmental substances in toxicology. In these cases, the biomarker may be the external substance itself, eg, alcohol or an opioid or a variant of the external substance processed by the body (a metabolite) (eg, THC metabolites from marijuana use).

Biomedical
Biological and physiological aspects of a patient's condition that require physical health assessment and services. In addiction treatment, biomedical problems may be the direct result of a substance use disorder or be independent of and interactive with them, thus affecting the total treatment plan and prognosis.

*Blackout
Acute anterograde amnesia with no formation of long-term memory, resulting from the ingestion of alcohol or other drugs; ie, a period of memory loss for which there is no recall of activities.

Bundling
An approach to treatment that ties or "bundles" several treatment services together, often

delivering them in a specific treatment setting. Because this approach often overlooks a patient's individual needs and can lead to inappropriately more intensive and unnecessary services, the current trend is toward "unbundled" services.

Case Management

Case management is a collaborative process which assesses, plans, implements, coordinates, monitors, and evaluates the options and services to meet an individual's health needs, using communication and available resources to promote quality, cost-effective outcomes.[5]

*Chemical Dependency

A generic term relating to psychological or physical dependency, or both, on one or more psychoactive substances.

Client

An individual who receives treatment for alcohol, tobacco, and/or other drug and addictive behavior problems. The terms "client" and "patient" sometimes are used interchangeably, although staff in medical settings more commonly use "patient," while staff of non-medical residential, outpatient, and publicly funded treatment settings refer to "clients."

Clinically Driven

Services received and the length of stay in a particular level of care are determined primarily by the individual's multidimensional assessment and treatment outcomes. Such programs have flexible lengths of stay where transfer to other levels of care depends on the patient's severity of illness, level of function, and progress in treatment.

Clinically Managed Services

Clinically managed services are directed by non-physician addiction specialists rather than medical and nursing personnel. They are appropriate for individuals whose primary problems involve emotional, behavioral, or cognitive concerns, readiness to change, relapse, or recovery environment, and whose problems in Dimension 1 (Acute Intoxication and/or Withdrawal Potential) and Dimension 2 (Biomedical Concerns or Complications), if any, are minimal or can be managed through separate arrangements for medical services.

Clinical Necessity

Synonymous with the intent of "medical necessity." Sometimes used to broaden inappropriately narrow definitions of medical necessity.

Clinician

A health professional, such as a physician, psychiatrist, psychologist, or nurse, involved in clinical practice, as distinguished from one specializing in research.

Coalition for National Clinical Criteria

A multidisciplinary group of individuals involved in addiction treatment, research, reimbursement, professional associations, and state and federal government. The Coalition formed in November 1992 to assess support for the adoption of national clinical and patient placement criteria and to determine methods of garnering the support of the treatment field for such criteria.

Complexity Capability

Individuals and families with multiple co-occurring needs have not only substance use, addictive behavior and mental health issues, they frequently have medical, legal, trauma, housing, parenting, educational, vocational, and cognitive/learning issues. In addition, these individuals and families are culturally and linguistically diverse. In short, they are characterized by "**complexity**," and tend to have poorer outcomes and higher costs of care.

There is a need for a process of organizing systems to focus on the complex needs of the people and families seeking help. Some systems have begun to use the terminology of "complexity capability" to reflect this broader perspective. Although *The ASAM Criteria* primarily uses the terminology "co-occurring capability," we anticipate that over time this term may well be replaced with "complexity capability."

Compliance
See also **Adherence**

Webster's dictionary defines "comply" as "to act in accordance with another's wishes, or with rules and regulations."[3(p25)] Given the importance of shared decision making to improve collaboration and outcomes, patients are empowered to actively participate in treatment decisions and take responsibility for their treatment, rather than passively follow medication prescriptions and treatment recommendations.

Continued Service Criteria

In the process of patient assessment, certain problems and priorities are identified as indicating admission to a particular level of care. Continued service criteria describe the degree of resolution of those problems and priorities and indicate the intensity of services needed. The level of function and clinical severity of a patient's status in each of the six assessment dimensions is considered in determining the need for continued service.

Continuing Care

The provision of a treatment plan and organizational structure that will ensure that a patient receives whatever kind of care he or she needs at the time, particularly at the point of discharge or transfer from the current level of care. The treatment program thus is flexible and tailored to the shifting needs of the patient and his or her level of readiness to change. (This term is preferred to "aftercare.")

Continuum of Care

An integrated network of treatment services and non-clinical modalities, designed so that an individual's changing needs will be met as that individual moves through the treatment and recovery process. Movement between providers is characterized by seamless transfer, congruence of treatment philosophy, and rapid clinical record transfer.

Co-Occurring Capable

Treatment programs that address co-occurring mental and substance use disorders in their policies and procedures, assessment, treatment planning, program content, and discharge planning are described as "co-occurring capable" (formerly "dual diagnosis capable" (DDC)). Such programs have arrangements in place for coordination and collaboration between addiction and mental health services. They also can provide medication monitoring and addiction and psychological assessment and consultation, either on-site or through coordinated consultation with off-site providers. Program staff are able to address the interaction between mental and substance use disorders and their effect on the patient's readiness to change—as well as relapse and recovery environment issues—through individual and group program content. The primary focus of co-occurring capable programs in addiction treatment settings is the treatment of substance use disorders. Within mental health settings, a co-occurring capable program's primary focus is the treatment of mental disorders.

Co-Occurring Conditions

Concurrent substance use, addictive behaviors, physical health, and mental health clinical presentations that may or may not demonstrate sufficient signs or symptoms to substantiate a diagnosis of an addictive, physical, and/or mental disorder. *The ASAM Criteria* requires sufficient assessment to establish a diagnosis to indicate treatment at any level of care.

Co-Occurring Disorders

Concurrent substance use and mental disorders. Other terms used to describe co-occurring disorders include "dual diagnosis," "dual disorders," "mentally ill chemically addicted" (MICA), "chemically addicted mentally ill" (CAMI), "mentally ill substance abusers" (MISA), "mentally ill chemically dependent" (MICD), "concurrent disorders," "coexisting disorders," "comorbid disorders," and "individuals with co-occurring psychiatric and substance symptomatology" (ICOPSS). Use of the term carries no implication as to which disorder is primary and which secondary, which disorder occurred first, or whether one disorder caused the other.

Co-Occurring Enhanced

Describes treatment programs that incorporate policies, procedures, assessments, treatment and discharge planning processes that accommodate patients who have both unstable co-occurring mental and substance use disorders (formerly "dual diagnosis enhanced" (DDE)). Mental health symptom management groups are incorporated into addiction treatment and vice versa. Motivational enhancement therapies specifically designed for those with co-occurring mental and substance use disorders are more likely to be available (particularly in outpatient settings), and, ideally, there is close collaboration or integration between addiction and mental health services that provides crisis backup services and access to addiction and mental health case management and continuing care. In contrast to co-occurring capable services, co-occurring enhanced services place their primary focus on the integration of services for mental and substance use disorders in their staffing, services, and program content such that both unstable addiction and mental health issues can be adequately addressed by the program.

Counselor

A person trained to give guidance on personal, social, or psychological problems. Clinical addiction and mental health counseling is a distinct profession with national standards for education, training, and clinical practice.

*Craving

A state of desire to use substances or engage in addictive behaviors, experienced as a physical or emotional need for reward and/or relief.

Craving generally refers to conscious craving, involving subjective awareness of preoccupations or even obsessional thoughts to impulsively or compulsively seek reward and/or relief through substance use and other behaviors. Some have also hypothesized the existence of unconscious craving, in which motivation and drive are increased as part of the neurobiology of addiction. Craving may perpetuate active addiction or lead to relapse in an individual who has been in remission.

*Cross-tolerance

Tolerance, induced by repeated administration of one psychoactive substance, that is manifested toward another substance to which the individual has not been recently exposed.

*Decriminalization

Removal of criminal penalties for the possession and use of illicit psychoactive substances.

Dependence

Used in three different ways: (1) physical dependence is a state of adaptation that is manifested by a drug class specific withdrawal syndrome that can be produced by abrupt cessation, rapid dose reduction, decreasing blood level of the drug, and/or administration of an antagonist; (2) psychological dependence is a subjective sense of need for a specific psychoactive substance, either for its positive effects or to avoid negative effects associated with its abstinence; and (3) one category of psychoactive substance use disorder in previous editions of the *Diagnostic and Statistical Manual of Mental Disorders*, but not in *DSM-5*, 2013.

Detoxification

Usually used to refer to a process of withdrawing a person from a specific psychoactive substance in a safe and effective manner. The term actually encompasses safe management of intoxication states (more literally, "detoxification") and of withdrawal states.

In this edition of *The ASAM Criteria*, this term has been replaced by the term withdrawal management.

Diagnostic Admission Criteria

To be eligible for admission to each level of care, a person must meet a required diagnosis as indicated by diagnostic criteria as defined in the current *Diagnostic and Statistical Manual of Mental Disorders* (*DSM*) of the American Psychiatric Association or other standardized and widely accepted criteria.

Diagnostic and Statistical Manual of Mental Disorder (DSM) terms

The *Diagnostic and Statistical Manual of Mental Disorders* (*DSM*) has been published by the American Psychiatric Association for decades and is the most commonly used manual of nosology for insurance coding and claims payment and for epidemiological research, at least in North America. This manual provides diagnostic criteria to identify and describe substance-related, addictive, and mental disorders.

The fourth edition of the *DSM* (*DSM-IV*) described two substance use disorder conditions: substance abuse and substance dependence. The fifth edition (*DSM-5*) includes a list of substance use disorders (from mild to moderate to severe) and abandons the use of the terms substance dependence and substance abuse. *DSM* terms are not particularly relevant to defining the spectrum of substance use that affects health. The same is true for the International Classification of Diseases (ICD). The reason is that unlike other medical conditions (ie, impaired glucose tolerance and diabetes, pre-hypertension, hypercholesterolemia, and heart disease), the bodies responsible for the development and publication of *DSM* and ICD have ignored the spectrum of relevance to health and have not addressed "sub-threshold" conditions or risk factors. They define "disorders" and not substance use states that fail to meet their own diagnostic criteria for a "disorder."

It is important to note that there is overlap between some terms for the spectrum of use as found herein, and the conditions, which constitute *DSM-5* substance use disorder and ICD 10 dependence. Some with hazardous or harmful use will meet criteria for a *DSM-5* substance use disorder (most likely "mild" or "moderate"). Harmful use, as described here, is essentially an ICD 10-defined condition (except that ICD 10 requires recurrence in a specific time frame).

Dimension

A term used in *The ASAM Criteria* to refer to one of six patient biopsychosocial areas that must be assessed in making a service and placement decision.

Dimensional Admission Criteria

To be eligible for admission to each level of care, a person must meet required specifications in an indicated number of the six assessment dimensions.

Discharge

"The point at which an individual's active involvement with a treatment service is terminated, and he or she no longer is carried on the service's records as a patient."[3(p182)]

Disease Management

A system of coordinated health care interventions and communications for populations with conditions in which patient self-care efforts are significant. It involves an organized effort to achieve desired health outcomes in populations with prevalent, often chronic diseases, for which care practices may be subject to considerable variation.

In *The ASAM Criteria*, disease management may require the personalized use of the whole continuum of care as a seamless array of services that produce effective outcomes and ongoing recovery.

*Drug Intoxication

Dysfunctional changes in physiological functioning, psychological functioning, mood state, cognitive process, or all of these, as a consequence of consumption of a psychoactive substance; usually disruptive, and often stemming from central nervous system impairment.

Dual Diagnosis

Refers to the patient who has signs and symptoms of concurrent substance-related and mental disorders. Other terms used to describe such co-occurring disorders include "co-occurring disorders," "dual disorders," "mentally ill chemically addicted" (MICA), "chemically addicted mentally ill" (CAMI), "mentally ill substance abusers" (MISA), "mentally ill chemically dependent" (MICD), "concurrent disorders," "coexisting disorders," "comorbid disorders," and "individuals with co-occurring psychiatric and substance symptomatology" (ICOPSS). In this edition of

The ASAM Criteria this term is replaced with "**Co-Occurring Disorders**."

Early Intervention

Services that explore and address any problems or risk factors that appear to be related to use of alcohol, tobacco, and/or other drugs and addictive behaviors and that help the individual to recognize the harmful consequences of high-risk use or behavior. Such individuals may not appear to meet the diagnostic criteria for a substance use or addictive disorder, but require early intervention for education and further assessment. This is a component of the evidence-based Screening, Brief Intervention, and Referral to Treatment (SBIRT) initiative.

*Enabling

Any action by another person or an institution that intentionally or unintentionally has the effect of facilitating the continuation of an individual's addictive process, ie, his or her engagement with pathological sources of reward or relief in a pattern consistent with the disease of addiction or a substance use or related disorder as described in the *DSM*.

Facility

The physical structure (building or portions thereof) in which treatment services are delivered.

Failure (as in treatment failure)

This term is not recommended for use in clinical or research contexts.
Lack of progress and/or regression at any given level of care. Such a situation warrants a reassessment of the treatment plan, with modification of the treatment approach. Such situations may require changes in the treatment plan at the same level of care or transfer to a different (more or less intensive) level of care to achieve a better therapeutic response and outcome. Sometimes used to describe relapse after a single treatment episode—an inappropriate construct in describing a chronic disease or disorder. The use of "treatment failure" is therefore not a recommended concept or term to be used.

Family and Couples Therapy

The effects of addiction are far-reaching and patients' family members and loved ones also are affected by the disorder. By including family members and partners in the treatment process, education about factors that are important to the patient's recovery (such as establishing a substance-free environment) as well as their own recovery can be conveyed. Family members and partners can provide social support to the patient, help motivate their loved one to remain in treatment, and receive help and support for their own family recovery as well.

*Family Intervention

A specific form of intervention, involving family members of an alcoholic/addict, designed to benefit the patient as well as the family constellation.

*Familial Alcoholism

A pattern of alcoholism occurring in more than one generation within a family, due to either genetic or environmental factors or both.

Habilitation

The development, for the first time in an individual's life, of an optimum state of health through medical, psychological, and social interventions (also see **Rehabilitation**).

*Harm Reduction

A treatment and prevention approach that encompasses individual and public health needs, aiming to decrease the health and socio-economic costs and consequences of addiction-related problems, especially medical complications and transmission of infectious diseases, without necessarily requiring abstinence.

Abstinence-based treatment approaches are themselves a part of comprehensive harm reduction strategies. A range of recovery activities may be included in every harm reduction strategy.

*Harmful Use

Harmful substance use is use with health consequences **in the absence of** addiction.

*Hazardous Use (Alternatively, At-Risk Use)
Use that increases the risk for health consequences.

Imminent Danger
Three components in combination for addiction can also constitute imminent danger: (a) a strong probability that certain behaviors (such as continued alcohol or drug use or relapse) will occur, (b) the likelihood that such behaviors will present a significant risk of serious adverse consequences to the individual and/or others (as in a consistent pattern of driving while intoxicated), and (c) the likelihood that such adverse events will occur in the very near future, within hours and days, not weeks or months. For example, a person who may drive drunk or continue substance use resulting in serious adverse consequences in some months in the future is not considered in imminent danger in this context.

On the one hand, the concept of imminent danger *does not* encompass the universe of possible adverse events that could happen at some distant point in the future, eg, intoxication with impulsive reckless driving under the influence, combative public intoxication behavior, loss of employment or legal problems from forging prescriptions, or embezzling money for drugs. Its evaluation should be restricted to the three factors listed above. On the other hand, the interpretation of imminent danger should not be restricted to just acute suicidality, homicidality, or medical or psychiatric problems that create an immediate, catastrophic risk. In *The ASAM Criteria*, patients in imminent danger need stabilization in a 24-hour treatment setting until no longer meeting the three components listed above.

*Impairment
A dysfunctional state resulting from use of psychoactive substances, or mental, emotional, or cognitive problems.

*Inappropriate Use
This term is not recommended for use in clinical or research contexts.
The definition of "inappropriate" is unclear and some may find it pejorative. Questions arise as to who determines if use is "inappropriate" and adjudged by what criteria.

Individualized Treatment
Treatment that is person-centered and collaborative designed to meet a particular patient's needs and preferences guided by services that are directly related to a specific, unique patient assessment.

Intensity of Service/"Dose" of Services
The number, type, and frequency of staff interventions and other services (such as consultation, referral, or support services) provided during treatment at a particular level of care.

Intensive Case Management
Intensive case management is a comprehensive community service that includes evaluation, outreach, and support services, usually provided on an outpatient basis. The case manager (or management team) advocates for the patient with community agencies and arranges services and supports. He or she also may teach community living and problem-solving skills, model productive behaviors, and teach the patient to become self-sufficient.[6]

Intensive Outpatient Treatment
An organized service delivered by addiction professionals or addiction-credentialed clinicians, which provides a planned regimen of treatment, consisting of regularly scheduled sessions within a structured program, for a minimum of 9 hours of treatment per week for adults and 6 hours of treatment per week for adolescents.

Interdisciplinary Team
A group of clinicians trained in different professions, disciplines, or service areas (such as physicians, counselors, psychologists, social workers, nurses, and certified addiction counselors), who function interactively and interdependently in conducting a patient's biopsychosocial assessment, treatment plan, and treatment services.

Inter-rater Reliability

The degree of agreement among raters. In the context of *The ASAM Criteria*, this refers to what degree two clinicians would assess a patient's severity of illness and level of function and reach the same or similar severity profile in the multidimensional assessment.

*Intervention

A planned interaction with an individual who may be dependent on one or more psychoactive substances, with the aim of making a full assessment, overcoming denial, interrupting drug-taking behavior, or inducing the individual to initiate treatment. The preferred technique is to present facts regarding psychoactive substance use in a caring, believable, and understandable manner.

*Intoxication

"A clinical state marked by dysfunctional changes in physiological functioning, psychological functioning, mood state, cognitive process, or all of these, as a consequence of consumption of a psychoactive substance."[3(p184)]

Intoxication Management

This refers to the services required for Dimension 1, Acute Intoxication and/or Withdrawal Potential, where the patient's level of intoxication is assessed and treated, eg, preventing drunk-driving by holding a person's car keys until he or she is abstinent or in safety with family members; managing acute alcohol poisoning in an adolescent experimenting with rapid intake. The patient may or may not proceed into a full withdrawal syndrome.

*Legalization

Removal of legal restrictions on the cultivation, manufacture, distribution, possession, and/or use of a psychoactive substance.

Length of Service

The number of days (for inpatient care) or units/visits (for outpatient care) of service provided to a patient, from admission to transfer/discharge, at a particular level of care.

Level of Care

As used in *The ASAM Criteria*, this term refers to a discrete intensity of clinical and environmental support services linked together and available in a variety of settings.

Level of Function

An individual's degree of health, wellness, and freedom from specific signs and symptoms of a mental or substance use or addictive disorder, which determines the individual's required treatment. The individual's strengths, skills, and resources are utilized in treatment.

Level of Service

As used in *The ASAM Criteria*, this term refers to broad categories of patient placement, which encompass a range of clinical services such as early intervention, withdrawal management, or opioid treatment services, and levels of care such as intensive outpatient treatment or clinically managed high-intensity residential treatment.

*Loss of Control

The inability to consistently limit the self-administration of a psychoactive substance.

*Low Risk Use (Alternatively, Lower Risk Use), Including No Use

Consumption of an amount of alcohol or other drug below the amount identified as hazardous, and use in circumstances not defined as hazardous.

Maintenance Treatments

Pharmacotherapy on a consistent schedule for persons with addiction, usually with an agonist or partial agonist, which mitigates against the pathological pursuit of reward and/or relief and allows for remission of overt addiction-related problems.

Maintenance treatments of addiction are associated with the development of a pharmacological steady-state in which receptors for addictive substances are occupied, resulting in relative or complete blockade of central nervous system receptors such that addictive substances are no longer sought for reward and/or relief. Maintenance treatments of addiction are also designed to mitigate against the risk of overdose. Depending on the circumstances of a given case, a care plan including maintenance treatments can be time-limited or can remain in place life-long. Integration of pharmacotherapy via maintenance treatments with psychosocial treatments generally is associated with the best clinical results. Maintenance treatments can be part of an individual's treatment plan in abstinence-based recovery activities or can be a part of harm reduction strategies.

Matching

A process of selecting treatment resources to conform to an individual patient's needs and preferences, based on careful assessment. Matching has been shown to increase treatment retention and thus to improve treatment outcome. It also improves resource allocation by directing patients to the most efficient and effective level of care and intensity of services.

Medical Necessity

Pertains to necessary care for biopsychosocial severity and is defined by the extent and severity of problems in all six multidimensional assessment areas of the patient. It should not be restricted to acute care and narrow medical concerns (such as severity of withdrawal risk as in Dimension 1); acuity of physical health needs (as in Dimension 2); or Dimension 3 psychiatric issues (such as imminent suicidality). Rather, "medical necessity" encompasses all six assessment dimensions so that a more holistic concept would be "**Clinical Necessity**," "necessity of care," or "clinical appropriateness."

Medically Managed Treatment

Services that involve daily medical care, where diagnostic and treatment services are directly provided and/or managed by an appropriately trained and licensed physician. Such services are provided in an acute care hospital or psychiatric hospital or treatment unit.

Medically Monitored Treatment

Services that are provided by an interdisciplinary staff of nurses, counselors, social workers, addiction specialists, and other health care professionals and technical personnel, under the direction of a licensed physician. Medical monitoring is provided through an appropriate mix of direct patient contact, review of records, team meetings, 24-hour coverage by a physician, and quality assurance programs.

*Medication Assisted Recovery (MAR)
*Medication Assisted Treatment (MAT)

Transitional terms to help the general public, recipients of health care services, and professional health care service providers understand that pharmacotherapy can be helpful in supporting recovery. The manifestations of addiction-related problems are addressed in their biological, psychological, social, and spiritual dimensions during addiction treatment, in treatment approaches that are abstinence-based, and in treatment approaches that are harm-reduction-based. MAR is one component of the treatment and recovery process.

Medication assisted treatment (MAT), another variation on the concept of MAR, may involve pharmacotherapy alone. It is essential that addiction treatment and recovery approaches address the various aspects of biological, psychological, social, and spiritual dimensions for optimum health and wellness. It is hoped that as the public and professionals recognize that recovery and treatment need to be holistic, appropriate pharmacotherapy would be well accepted as part of treatment and recovery, such that the terms MAR and MAT would be deemed unnecessary.

Misuse

This term is not recommended for use in clinical or research contexts.
Any use of a prescription drug that varies from accepted medical practice. This can also refer to unhealthy use of alcohol outside the context of addiction.

The WHO Lexicon defines misuse as use for a purpose not consistent with legal or medical guidelines.[7] It notes that the term "misuse" may be less pejorative than the term "abuse." In its screening efforts, the U.S. Department of Veterans Affairs describes misuse as the target of screening and intervention. The definition in that context has been the spectrum of use that increases consequences (similar to unhealthy use as defined here). A journal, *Substance Use and Misuse*, has been published in the United Kingdom since 1996. The main reason the term misuse is not preferred is because there is confusion about whether or not it includes addiction or substance use disorders. For example, the Department of Veterans Affairs uses "severe misuse" to mean dependence. But "misuse" is not an appropriate descriptor for "dependence" or "addiction" because it minimizes the seriousness of the disorder and suggests the disorder is due to choice (to "misuse" the substance). "Misuse" also seems to have value judgment at least potentially implied, as if it were an accident, mistake, or alternatively purposeful, neither of which would be appropriate for describing the varied states incorporated in "unhealthy use."

"Misuse" is often used to refer to hazardous or harmful prescription (or non-prescription but potentially addictive) drug use. However, for similar reasons as those described above, it is not a preferred term. "Misuse" of prescription or non-prescription over-the-counter drugs has been used to describe the spectrum of unhealthy use or to denote hazardous or harmful use but not addiction. In addition, "misuse" in this context is sometimes used to refer to non-adherence to (eg, non-psychoactive) medication (eg, missed doses of an antihypertensive medication). Therefore to avoid confusion and to clearly describe use of potentially addictive drugs in ways that risk or have caused consequences, ASAM recommends the preferred terminology framework of low or lower risk use and unhealthy use.

Modality

A specific type of treatment (technique, method, or procedure) that is used to relieve symptoms and promote recovery. Modalities of addiction treatment include, for example, withdrawal man-

agement or anti-craving, agonist, and antagonist medication; motivational interviewing; cognitive-behavioral therapy; individual, family, and group therapy; social skills training; vocational counseling; and self/mutual help groups.

Modalities Needed

Based on the assessed multidimensional severity and level of function profile of a patient, an individualized treatment plan contains specific treatment interventions (modalities), and patient tasks. These contribute to the intensity of services that matches a person's severity of illness and level of function.

*Moderate Drinking

This term is not recommended for use in clinical or research contexts.
Moderate drinking is not preferred as a term because it implies safety, restraint, avoidance of excess, and even health. Since alcohol is a carcinogen (and breast cancer risk increases at amounts lower than those generally defined as hazardous, and lower limit amounts harmful to the fetus are not well defined), better terms for amounts lower than at-risk amounts include "lower risk" or "low risk" amounts or simply the term "alcohol use."

Motivational Enhancement Therapy

A patient-centered counseling approach for initiating behavior change by helping patients to resolve ambivalence about engaging in treatment and stopping substance use or gambling. This approach employs strategies to evoke rapid and internally motivated change in the patient, rather than guiding the patient stepwise through the recovery process.[8]

Motivational Interviewing

Layperson's definition: Motivational interviewing is a collaborative conversation style for strengthening a person's own motivation and commitment to change.
Practitioner's definition: Motivational interviewing is a person-centered counseling style for addressing the common problem of ambivalence about change.

Technical definition: Motivational interviewing is a collaborative, goal-oriented style of communication with particular attention to the language of change. It is designed to strengthen personal motivation for and commitment to a specific goal by eliciting and exploring the person's own reasons for change within an atmosphere of acceptance and compassion.[9(p29)]

Multidimensional Family Therapy

Outpatient family-based addiction treatment for adolescents. Multidimensional family therapy views adolescent drug use in terms of a network of influences (individual, family, peer, community) and suggests that reducing unwanted behavior and increasing desirable behavior occur in multiple ways in different settings. Treatment includes individual and family sessions held in the clinic, in the home, or with family members at the family court, school, or other community locations.[8]

Multisystemic Therapy

Addresses factors associated with serious antisocial behavior in children and adolescents who have substance use disorders. Such factors include characteristics of the adolescent (such as favorable attitudes toward drug use), the family (involving poor discipline, family conflict, or parental drug use, for example), the school (such as early school-leaving or poor academic performance) and the neighborhood (a criminal subculture, for example). Multisystemic therapy emphasizes intensive treatment in natural environments (such as home, school, and neighborhood settings).[8]

Opioid Agonist Medication

Opioid agonist medications pharmacologically occupy opioid receptors in the body. They thereby relieve withdrawal symptoms and reduce or extinguish cravings for opioids.

Opioid Antagonist Medication

Opioid antagonist medications pharmacologically occupy opioid receptors in the body, but do not activate the receptors. This effectively blocks the receptor, preventing the brain from responding to opioids. The result is that further use of opioids does not produce reinforcing euphoria or intoxication.

Office-based Opioid Treatment (OBOT)

Physicians in private practices or a number of types of public sector clinics can be authorized to prescribe outpatient supplies of the partial opioid agonist buprenorphine (though OTPs can administer or dispense buprenorphine products as well). There is no regulation *per se* of the clinic sites where buprenorphine-prescribing physicians practice. It is the practice of the individual physician, which is regulated by federal regulations addressing office-based treatment.

Opioid Treatment Program (OTP)

Opioid treatment programs using methadone and/or buprenorphine are presented in *The ASAM Criteria* as a Level 1 outpatient service because opioid agonist medications are most commonly used for opioid use disorders and an outpatient setting is the context in which it is most commonly offered. Patients receiving Level 2 and 3 substance use and co-occurring disorders care can be referred to, or otherwise concurrently enrolled in, OTP services or OBOT services.

Previous terms for OTP are methadone maintenance treatment (MMT) or opioid maintenance therapy (OMT) as was used in the *ASAM PPC-2R*.

Opioid Treatment Services (OTS)

An umbrella term that encompasses a variety of pharmacological and non-pharmacological treatment modalities. This term broadens understanding of opioid treatments to include all medications used to treat opioid use disorders and the psychosocial services that are offered concurrently with these pharmacotherapies. Pharmacological agents include opioid agonist medications such as methadone and buprenorphine, and opioid antagonist medications such as naltrexone.

Outcome-informed

In the context of *The ASAM Criteria*, decisions

made about the patient's transfer to another level of care is partially based on outcomes data derived from measures of the patient's subjective experience of the therapeutic alliance and the person's multidimensional progress in treatment.

Outpatient Service

An organized nonresidential service, delivered in a variety of settings, in which addiction and mental health treatment personnel provide professionally directed evaluation and treatment for substance-related, addictive, and mental disorders. Basically synonymous with outpatient treatment.

Outpatient Treatment

An organized service, delivered in a variety of settings, in which treatment staff provide professionally directed evaluation and treatment of substance-related, addictive, and mental disorders. This also includes the services of an individual licensed practitioner. Basically synonymous with **Outpatient Service**.

Outpatient Withdrawal Management

See **Ambulatory Withdrawal Management**.

*Overdose

The inadvertent or deliberate consumption of a dose much larger than that either habitually used by the individual or ordinarily used for treatment of an illness, and likely to result in a serious toxic reaction or death.

Partial Hospitalization

A generic term encompassing day, night, evening, and weekend treatment programs that employ an integrated, comprehensive, and complementary schedule of recognized treatments. Commonly referred to as "day treatment." A partial hospitalization program does not need to be attached to a licensed hospital.

Participant-Directed

See **Shared Decision Making**.

Patient

As used in *The ASAM Criteria*, an individual

receiving alcohol, tobacco, and/or other drug or addictive disorder treatment. The terms "client" and "patient" sometimes are used interchangeably, although staff in non-medical settings more commonly refer to "clients."

Patient-Centered

Assessment that is collaborative and treatment that is tailored to the needs of the individual and guided by an individualized treatment plan. This plan is developed in consultation with the patient and is respectful of informed consent and the preferences of the patient. Patient-centered care establishes a therapeutic alliance with the individual and therefore contributes significantly to treatment outcomes.

Patient Centered Health Care Home

(also described as Patient Centered Medical Home) A model or philosophy of primary care that is patient-centered, comprehensive, team-based, coordinated, accessible, and focused on quality and safety.[10]

Patient Centered Health Care Neighborhood

(also described as Patient Centered Medical Neighborhood) A concept which connects primary care with other community-based health care providers to create a more efficient, coordinated health care delivery network that improves care at a lower cost; the primary care component can be a patient-centered medical home or a traditional primary care medical practice.[11]

Person-Centered

See **Patient-Centered**.

Physical Dependence

Physical dependence is a state of adaptation that is manifested by a drug class specific withdrawal syndrome that can be produced by abrupt cessation, rapid dose reduction, decreasing blood level of the drug, and/or administration of an antagonist.[3]

Placement

Selection of a clinically driven level of service,

based on assessment of a patient's individual needs and preferences.

Prevention

Social, economic, legal, medical, and/or psychological measures aimed at minimizing the use of potentially addicting substances, lowering the dependence risk in susceptible individuals, or minimizing other adverse consequences of psychoactive substance use. Primary prevention consists of attempts to reduce the incidence of addictive diseases and related problems in a general population. Secondary prevention aims to achieve early detection, diagnosis, and treatment of affected individuals. Tertiary prevention seeks to diminish the incidence of complications of addictive diseases.

"The Institute of Medicine defines three broad types of prevention interventions:

"1. Universal preventive interventions take the broadest approach, targeting 'the general public or a whole population that has not been identified on the basis of individual risk.'[12] Universal prevention interventions might target schools, whole communities, or workplaces.

"2. Selective preventive interventions target 'individuals or a population sub-group whose risk of developing mental disorders [or substance abuse disorders] is significantly higher than average,' prior to the diagnosis of a disorder.[12] Selective interventions target biological, psychological, or social risk factors that are more prominent among high-risk groups than among the wider population.

"3. Indicated preventive interventions target 'high-risk individuals who are identified as having minimal but detectable signs or symptoms foreshadowing mental, emotional, or behavioral disorder' prior to the diagnosis of a disorder.[12] Interventions focus on the immediate risk and protective factors present in the environments surrounding individuals."[13]

*Problem Drinking

This term is not recommended for use in clinical or research contexts.

An informal term describing a pattern of drinking associated with life problems prior to establishing a definitive diagnosis of alcoholism. Also, an umbrella term for any harmful use of alcohol, including alcoholism. ASAM recommends that the term not be used in the latter sense.

*Problem Use

This term is not recommended for use in clinical or research contexts.

The meaning of this term is the same as "harmful" use. The term is not preferred because when used with patients, it has connotations that are not helpful and can be seen as pejorative if the patient is viewed as being the problem or having a problem, as opposed to the substance being a problem.

Program

A generalized term for an organized system of services designed to address the treatment needs of patients.

Program-Driven

Services received and the anticipated length of stay are determined primarily by the philosophy, design and model of treatment rather than on the individual's multidimensional assessment and treatment outcomes. Such programs are often for a fixed length of stay from which a patient graduates and is said to then have completed treatment.

Psychotherapy

"Individual and/or group psychotherapy can help patients reduce the frequency of alcohol use and the amount of alcohol consumed. Individual therapy can be provided in many different types of treatment settings (inpatient, outpatient, or a criminal justice institution); affords privacy (which can help some patients disclose more freely); and allows for more one-on-one time than would be possible in a group setting. Group therapy is one of the most common non-pharmacologic interventions used to treat alcohol dependence. Group therapy's primary advantages are that it is economical and allows one health care provider to meet with multiple patients in a given session, it typically costs less than individual therapy, and it has the added bonus of peer support."[3(p187)]

Readiness to Change

An individual's emotional and cognitive awareness of and interest in the need to change, coupled with a commitment to change. When applied to addiction treatment and particularly assessment, Dimension 4, "Readiness to Change," describes the patient's degree of awareness of the relationship between his or her alcohol, tobacco, and/or other drug use, addictive behavior or mental health problems, and the adverse consequences of such use or behavior, as well as the presence of specific readiness to change personal patterns of alcohol, tobacco, and/or other drug use or addictive behavior.

Recognize, Understand, and Apply

The distinction in the criteria is made between an individual's ability to recognize an addiction problem, understand the implications of alcohol, tobacco, and/or other drug use or addictive behavior on the individual's life, and apply coping and other recovery skills in his/her life to limit or prevent further alcohol, tobacco, and/or other drug use or addictive behavior. The distinction is in the difference between an intellectual awareness and more superficial acknowledgment of a problem (recognition) and a more productive awareness of the ramifications of the problem for one's life (understanding); and the ability to achieve behavior change through the integration of coping and other relapse prevention skills (application).

Recovery

A process of sustained action that addresses the biological, psychological, social, and spiritual disturbances inherent in addiction. This effort is in the direction of a consistent pursuit of abstinence, addressing impairment in behavioral control, dealing with cravings, recognizing problems in one's behaviors and interpersonal relationships, and dealing more effectively with emotional responses. Recovery actions lead to reversal of negative, self-defeating internal processes and behaviors, allowing healing of relationships with self and others. The concepts of humility, acceptance, and surrender are useful in this process.

Note: ASAM continues to explore, as an evolving process, improved ways to define recovery.

Recovery Environment

As used in Dimension 6 of *The ASAM Criteria*, recovery environment encompasses the external supports for recovery. The quality and extent of services (such as child care, transportation, crisis, and transitional housing, and other "wrap around" services), all of which influence treatment outcome.

Recovery-Oriented

Interactions with, assessments and treatment of individuals that are designed to attract and enhance patients' interest in exploring and embracing recovery. (See **Recovery**.)

Recovery Support Services

Any services designed to initiate, support and enhance recovery. In *The ASAM Criteria*, such services are considered Dimension 6, Recovery Environment, such as transportation, child care, housing, financial assistance, vocational and school counseling, peer supports, legal services, etc.

*Rehabilitation

The restoration of an optimum state of health by medical, psychological, and social means, including peer group support, for an alcoholic or addict, a family member, or a significant other.

*Relapse

A process in which an individual who has established abstinence or sobriety experiences recurrence of signs and symptoms of active addiction, often including resumption of the pathological pursuit of reward and/or relief through the use of substances and other behaviors. When in relapse, there is often disengagement from recovery activities.

Relapse can be triggered by exposure to rewarding substances and behaviors, by exposure to environmental cues to use, and by exposure to emotional stressors that trigger heightened activity in brain stress circuits. The event of using or acting out is the latter part of the process, which can be prevented by early intervention.

Relapse, Continued Use, or Continued Problem Potential

As used in Dimension 5 of *The ASAM Criteria*, the patient's attitudes, knowledge, and coping skills, as well as the likelihood that the patient will relapse from a previously achieved and maintained recovery and/or stable and healthy mental health function. If an individual has not yet achieved recovery and/or stable and healthy mental health function, this dimension assesses the likelihood that the individual will continue to use alcohol, tobacco, and/or other drugs and/or continue to have addictive behavior or mental health problems.

*Remission

A state of wellness where there is an abatement of signs and symptoms that characterize active addiction. Many individuals in a state of remission remain actively engaged in the process of recovery. Reduction in signs or symptoms constitutes improvement in a disease state, but remission involves a return to a level of functioning that is free of active symptoms and/or is marked by stability in the chronic signs and symptoms that characterize active addiction.

Resistance

Resistance is often perceived as pathology within the person, rather than an interactive process; or even a phenomenon induced and produced by the clinician. Reluctance to embrace treatment and recovery and a lack of interest in recovery and relapse prevention indicate a person's readiness to change the use of a particular substance or addictive behavior (See **Stages of Change**). It is as much a knowledge,

skills, and attitudes "clinician" problem as it is a "patient" problem. A related definition is: "A term previously used in Motivational Interviewing, now deconstructed into its components: sustain talk and discord."[8(p412)]

*Risky Use
See **Hazardous Use**.

Role Induction
The process of preparing people for treatment by informing them about the rationale of treatment, the treatment process, and their part in therapy.

Setting
A general environment in which treatment is delivered. There may be a variety of facilities that are within a general setting. Settings for addiction treatment include hospitals, residential programs, opioid treatment programs, community mental health centers, and prisons or jails.

Severe and Chronic
These terms are used to describe the high disabling impact, non-acute clinical presentation, and long duration of a person's addiction and/or mental illness. These terms are more descriptive compared with a commonly used phrase of severe and persistent mental illness (SPMI), which is less hopeful and not recovery-oriented. SPMI connotes that the patient cannot recover and will persistently remain seriously ill. Using terminology as with other illnesses, "severe" and "chronic" are descriptive and non-value laden terms compared with SPMI.

Severity of Illness
Specific signs and symptoms for which a patient requires treatment, including the degree of impairment and the extent of a patient's support networks.

Shared Decision Making/Participant-Directed
Treatment adherence and outcomes are enhanced by patient collaboration. Shared decision making engages people in treatment and

recovery using informed consent that indicates that the adult, adolescent, legal guardian, and/or family member has been made aware of the proposed modalities of treatment, the risks and benefits of such treatment, appropriate alternative treatment modalities, and the risks of treatment versus no treatment. In this context, the patient collaborates on what services are provided and accepted in the patient-centered treatment plan.

Skilled Treatment Services/Types of Services

Such services may include individual and group counseling, medication management, family therapy, educational groups, occupational and recreational therapy, and other therapies. Attendance at self/mutual help meetings such as Alcoholics or Narcotics Anonymous; volunteer activities; or homework assignments involving watching videos, journaling, and workbooks do not represent "skilled treatment services" for the purpose of clinical service hours for each level of care.

*Sobriety

A state of sustained abstinence with a clear commitment to and active seeking of balance in the biological, psychological, social, and spiritual aspects of an individual's health and wellness that were previously compromised by active addiction.

Social Support System

The network of relationships that surround an individual. A health social support system—involving family members, friends, employers, members of mutual support groups, and others—tends to support an individual's recovery efforts and goals. What these individuals have in common is that their relationship with the individual is current and that the individual is comfortable contacting them in times of distress.

Spirituality

A personal experience of existence or consciousness that provides context, meaning, and purpose in an individual's life, and guides attitude, thinking, and behavior. It is characterized by an individual's connection with self, with others, and with the transcendent (referred to as "God" by many, the "Higher Power" by 12-step groups, or "higher consciousness" by others). It may take many forms and include nature, meditation, prayer, religious observance, music, art, or a community, which may be religious or secular.

Stages of Change

This refers principally to the work of Prochaska and DiClemente, who described how individuals progress and regress through various levels of awareness of a problem, as well as the degree of activity involved in a change in behavior. While their original work studied individuals who changed from smokers to nonsmokers, the concept of stages of change subsequently has been applied to a variety of substances and behaviors.

The stages of change in this model are precontemplation, contemplation, preparation, action, and maintenance. Relapse or recycling is a stage that is also possible when a patient returns to one of the stages of change and experiences a recurrence of addictive use or behavior.

Subdomain

A subdomain is an assessment subcategory within Dimension 3 (Emotional, Behavioral, or Cognitive Problems), as described below:

» Dangerousness/Lethality. This subdomain describes how impulsive an individual may be with regard to homicide, suicide, or other behaviors that pose a risk of harm to self or others and/or to property. The seriousness and immediacy of the individual's ideation, plans, and behavior—as well as his or her ability to act on such impulses—determine the patient's severity and the type and intensity of services needed.

» Interference with Addiction Recovery Efforts. This subdomain describes the degree to which a patient is distracted from addiction recovery efforts by emotional, behavioral and/or cognitive problems, and, conversely, the degree to which a patient is able to focus on addiction recovery. For co-occurring capable and enhanced mental health programs, a similar domain could be named Interference with Mental Health Recovery Efforts, describing the degree to which a patient is distracted from mental health recovery efforts by addiction problems.

» Social Functioning. This subdomain describes the degree to which an individual's relationships (that is, ability to cope with friends, significant others or family, or vocational or educational demands, or ability to meet personal responsibilities) are affected by his or her substance use and/or other emotional, behavioral, and cognitive problems.

» Ability for Self-Care. This subdomain describes the degree to which an individual's ability to perform activities of daily living (such as personal grooming and obtaining food and shelter) is affected by his or her substance use and/or other emotional, behavioral, or cognitive problems.

» Course of Illness. This subdomain employs the history of the patient's illness and response to past treatment to help interpret the patient's current signs, symptoms, and presentation and predict the patient's likely response to future treatment. Thus, the domain assesses the interaction between the chronicity and severity of the patient's current difficulties. A determination of high severity is warranted when the individual is assessed as at significant risk for dangerous consequences, either because of severe or acute symptoms and/or because a history of instability suggests that high-intensity services are needed to prevent dangerous consequences.

For example, a patient who recently discontinued antipsychotic medications may present with medication adherence problems. If such a patient has a history of rapidly decompensating into acute psychosis when medication

is stopped, he or she is assessed as at high severity. However, if in the past he or she slowly became isolated, without any rapid deterioration, when medication was stopped, the severity is assessed as lower.

The key lies in using the patient's past course of illness to predict his or her future course of illness. For example, a patient with medication adherence problems may present after having recently discontinued antidepressant medication. If the patient has a history of rapid decompensation with suicidal depression when medication is stopped, then his or her severity is high in the "course of illness" subdomain. However, if the patient has a history of gradual recurrence of mood disorder and social isolation when medication is stopped, then the "course of illness" severity is lower. Another example is a patient who presents with a recent lapse/relapse and who has a history of cycles of remission and relapse. If the patient has had grave difficulties in the past with a rapidly deteriorating pattern of addictive use, his or her severity would be much higher than if he or she has a history of a slower pattern of relapse.

Substance Abuse
This term is not recommended for use in clinical or research contexts.
See **Abuse**.

Substance Dependence
This term is not recommended for use in clinical or research contexts.
This term applies to one category of psycho-active substance-related disorders in previous editions of the *Diagnostic and Statistical Manual of Mental Disorders* of the American Psychiatric Association (*DSM*). It is generally aligned with moderate and severe substance use disorder in the fifth edition (*DSM-5*). While recognizing that "substance dependence" is a part of past diagnostic terminology, ASAM recommends that the current term, "substance use disorder" be used, especially because of the confusion between the term "substance dependence" and the term "physical dependence."

Substance Use Disorder

Substance use disorder is marked by a cluster of cognitive, behavioral, and physiological symptoms indicating that the individual continues to use alcohol, tobacco, and/or other drugs despite significant related problems. The cluster of symptoms can include tolerance; withdrawal or use of a substance in larger amounts or over a longer period of time than intended; persistent desire or unsuccessful efforts to cut down or control substance use; a great deal of time spent in activities related to obtaining or using substances or to recover from their effects; relinquishing important social, occupational or recreational activities because of substance use; and continuing alcohol, tobacco, and/or drug use despite knowledge of having a persistent or recurrent physical or psychological problem that is likely to have been caused or exacerbated by such use; craving or strong desire to use. Specific diagnostic criteria are given in the *Diagnostic and Statistical Manual of Mental Disorders*, Fifth Edition (*DSM-5*) of the American Psychiatric Association.

Substance use disorders is the new nomenclature for what previously included substance dependence and substance abuse (*Diagnostic and Statistical Manual of Mental Disorders*, Fourth Edition *(DSM-IV)*) of the American Psychiatric Association.

Substance-Induced Disorders

Substance-induced disorders include intoxication, withdrawal, and other substance/medication-induced mental disorders, eg, substance-induced psychotic disorder, substance-induced depressive disorder. Specific diagnostic criteria are given in the *Diagnostic and Statistical Manual of Mental Disorders*, Fifth Edition (*DSM-5*) of the American Psychiatric Association. In *The ASAM Criteria*, substance-induced disorder is part of the diagnostic criteria for admission for several of the levels of service.

Substance-Related Conditions

Clinical presentations due to substance use that may or may not demonstrate sufficient signs or symptoms to substantiate a diagnosis of substance use disorder. *The ASAM Criteria* requires sufficient assessment to establish a diagnosis to indicate treatment at any level of care. If the substance use is subdiagnostic (for example, it constitutes harmful use or hazardous/risky/at-risk use), the individual meets diagnostic criteria for Level 0.5, Early Intervention services. See **Harmful Use** and **Hazardous Use**.

Substance-Related Disorders

Substance-related disorders include disorders related to the taking of alcohol/tobacco or another addictive drug, to the side effects of a medication, and to toxin exposures. They include substance use disorders, substance-intoxication, substance withdrawal, and substance-induced disorders, as defined in the *Diagnostic and Statistical Manual of Mental Disorders*, Fifth Edition (*DSM-5*) of the American Psychiatric Association.

Support Services

Support services are those readily available to the program through affiliation, contract, or because of their availability to the community at large (for example, 911 emergency response services). They are used to provide services beyond the capacity of the staff of the program and which will not be needed by patients on a routine basis or to augment the services provided by staff.

Therapeutic Alliance

Three components comprise the alliance: a trusting mutually respectful working bond and relationship; agreement on treatment goals developed with the patient; and shared mutually negotiated methods and interventions to reach those goals. The therapeutic alliance contributes greatly to treatment outcomes.

*Tolerance

A state of adaptation in which exposure to a drug induces changes that result in diminution of one or more of the drug's effects over time.

Transfer

Movement of the patient from one level of service to another, within the continuum of care.

Transfer/Discharge Criteria

In the process of patient assessment, certain problems and priorities are identified as indicating treatment in a particular level of care. Transfer/discharge criteria describe the degree of resolution of those problems and priorities and thus are used to determine when a patient can be treated at a different level of care or discharged from treatment. Also, the appearance of new problems may require services that can be provided effectively only at a more or less intensive level of care. The level of function and clinical severity of a patient's status in each of the six assessment dimensions is considered in determining the need for discharge or transfer.

Trauma

Individual trauma results from an event, series of events, or set of circumstances that is experienced by an individual as physically or emotionally harmful or threatening and that has lasting adverse effects on the individual's functioning and physical, social, emotional, or spiritual well-being.[14] Trauma can be due to physical injury, or due to emotional injury. Physical abuse, sexual abuse, verbal abuse, and emotional abuse can lead to trauma, as can the emotionally traumatic experiences of someone (soldier or civilian) in a battlefield situation.

Trauma-Informed Care

A program, organization, or system that is trauma-informed realizes the widespread impact of trauma and understands potential paths for healing; recognizes the signs and symptoms of trauma in staff, clients, and others involved with the system; and responds by fully integrating knowledge about trauma into policies, procedures, practices, and settings.[14]

*Treatment

Application of planned procedures to identify and change patterns of behavior that are maladaptive, destructive, and/or injurious to health; or to restore appropriate levels of physical, psychological, and/or social functioning.

*Treatment of Addiction

The use of any planned, intentional intervention in the health, behavior, personal, and/or family life of an individual suffering from alcohol use disorder or from another drug addiction, and which is designed to facilitate the affected individual to achieve and maintain sobriety, physical, spiritual, and mental health, and a maximum functional ability.[2]

Treatment Plan

The individualized plan should be based on a comprehensive biopsychosocial assessment of the patient and, when possible, a comprehensive evaluation of the family as well.

Triage

As used in *The ASAM Criteria*, decision-making at the conclusion of an initial assessment process to determine the specific assignment of the patient to a level of care or service.

Twenty-Three Hour Observation Bed

Admission for no more than 23 hours for assessment and stabilization to determine the need for inpatient versus outpatient care. Such a "bed" may be located in an inpatient or an outpatient setting (such as a hospital emergency department).

Types of Services

See **Skilled Treatment Services**.

Withdrawal Management

This refers to the services required for Dimension 1, Acute Intoxication and/or Withdrawal Potential. Previously referred to as "detoxification services," *The ASAM Criteria* more accurately describes services to assist a patient's withdrawal. The liver detoxifies, but clinicians manage withdrawal. If the person is intoxicated and not yet in withdrawal, Dimension 1 services needed would be intoxication management.

*Withdrawal Syndrome

The onset of a predictable constellation of signs and symptoms following the abrupt discontinuation of, or rapid decrease in, dosage of a psychoactive substance.

Unbundling

An approach to treatment that seeks to provide the appropriate combination of specific services to match a patient's needs. The goal of unbundling is to provide an array of options for flexible individualized treatment, which can be delivered in a variety of settings. The intensity of clinical services are determined independently of the individual's need for supportive living arrangements and other environmental supports.

*Unhealthy Use

Unhealthy alcohol and other drug (substance) use is **any** use that increases the risk or likelihood for health consequences (hazardous use), or has already led to health consequences (harmful use).

42 CFR 8.12

The Code of Federal Regulations (CFR) for Title 42 pertaining to Public Health has close to 2,000 parts. Part 8 pertains to certification of opioid treatment programs. Sub-part .12 are the regulations that pertain to federal opioid treatment standards.

References

The ASAM Criteria: Then and Now

1. Institute of Medicine. *Broadening the Base of Treatment for Alcohol Problems.* Washington, DC: National Academy Press; 1990.

2. American Psychiatric Association. *Diagnostic and Statistical Manual of Mental Disorders.* 5th ed. Arlington, VA: American Psychiatric Association; 2013.

3. Definition of Addiction [public policy statement]. Chevy Chase, MD: American Society of Addiction Medicine; April 19, 2011. http://www.asam.org/for-the-public/definition-of-addiction.

4. Wampold BE, Mondin GW, Moody M, Stitch F, Benson K, Ahn H. A meta-analysis of outcome studies comparing bone fide psychotherapies: empirically, "all must have prizes." *Psychol Bull.* 1997;122(3):203-215.

5. Orlinsky DE, Grawe K, Parks BK. Process and outcome in psychotherapy—noch einmal. In: Bergin A, Garfield S, eds. *Handbook of Psychotherapy and Behavior Change: An Empirical Analysis.* 4th ed. New York, NY: Wiley; 1994:270-378.

6. Bachelor A, Horvath A. The therapeutic relationship. In: Hubble MA, Duncan BL, Miller SD, eds *The Heart and Soul of Change: What Works in Therapy.* Washington, DC: American Psychological Association; 1999:133-178.

7. Duncan B, Miller S, Sparks J. *The Heroic Client.* San Francisco, CA: Jossey-Bass; 2004.

8. Wampold BE. *The Great Psychotherapy Debate: Model, Methods, and Findings.* Mahwah, NJ: Lawrence Erlbaum Associates; 2001.

9. Mee-Lee D, McLellan AT, Miller SD. What works in substance abuse and dependence treatment. In: Duncan BL, Miller SD, Wampold BE, Hubble MA, eds. *The Heart and Soul of Change.* 2nd ed. Washington, DC: American Psychological Assocation; 2010:393-417.

Chapter 2

Applications

1. Substance Abuse Mental Health Services Administration. A Report to Congress on the Prevention and Treatment of Co-Occurring Substance Abuse Disorders and Mental Disorders. 2002. http://www.samhsa.gov/reports/congress2002/index.html.

2. McGovern MP, Matzkin AL, Giard J. Assessing the dual diagnosis capability of addiction treatment services: The Dual Diagnosis Capability in Addiction Treatment (DDCAT) Index. *J Dual Diagn.* 2007;3(2):111-123.

3. Cline C, Minkoff K. COMPASS-EZ: A Self-Assessment Tool for Behavioral Health Programs. San Rafael, CA: Ziapartners; 2009.

4. Minkoff K, Cline C. Changing the world: the design and implementation of comprehensive continuous integrated systems of care for individuals with co-occurring disorders. *Psychiatr Clin North Am.* 2004;27:727-743.

5. Minkoff K, Cline C. Developing welcoming systems for individuals with co-occurring disorders: the role of the Comprehensive Continuous Integrated System of Care model. *J Dual Diagn.* 2005;1:63-89.

6. Center for Substance Abuse Treatment. *Substance Abuse Treatment for Persons With Co-Occurring Disorders.* Treatment Improvement Protocol (TIP) Series 42. Rockville, MD: Substance Abuse and Mental Health Services Administration; 2005. DHHS Publication No. (SMA) 05-3992.

7. Minkoff K, Cline C. Dual diagnosis capability: moving from concept to implementation. *J Dual Diagn.* 2006;2(2):121-134.

8. Najavits LM. *Seeking Safety: A Treatment Manual for PTSD and Substance Abuse.* New York, NY: Guilford Press; 2002.

9. Mauer, BJ. Substance Use Disorders and the Person-Centered Healthcare Home. Washington, DC: National Council for Community Behavioral Healthcare; 2010.

10. McLellan AT, Luborsky L, Woody GE, O'Brien CP. An improved diagnostic evaluation instrument for substance abuse patients: the Addition Severity Index. *J Nerv Ment Dis.* 1980;168(1):26-33.

11. Center for Substance Abuse Treatment. *Definitions and Terms Relating to Co-Occurring Disorders.* COCE Overview Paper 1. Rockville, MD: Substance Abuse and Mental Health Services Administration, and Center for Mental Health Services; 2006. DHHS Publication No. (SMA) 06-4163.

12. Minkoff K. Dual diagnosis enhanced programs. *J Dual Diagn.* 2008;4(3):320-325.

13. Gastfriend DR, Mee-Lee D. The ASAM Patient Placement Criteria: context, concepts and continuing development. *J Addict Dis.* 2003;22(suppl 1):1-8.

14. Gastfriend DR, Lu SH, Sharon E. Placement matching: challenges and technical progress. *Subst Use Misuse.* 2001;35(12-14):2191-2213.

15. Hser YI, Polinsky ML, Maglione M, Anglin MD. Matching clients' needs with drug treatment services. *J Subst Abuse Treat.* 1999;16:299-305.

16. McKay JR, Cacciola JS, McLellan AT, Alterman AI, Wirtz PW. An initial evaluation of the psychosocial dimensions of the

American Society of Addiction Medicine criteria for inpatient vs. intensive outpatient substance abuse rehabilitation. *J Stud Alcohol.* 1997;58(5):239-252.

17. Gastfriend DR, McLellan AT. Treatment matching: theoretic basis and practical implications. *Med Clin North Am.* 1997;81(4):945-966.

18. Alterman AI, O'Brien CP, McLellen AT, et al. Effectiveness and costs of inpatient versus day hospital cocaine rehabilitation. *J Nerv Ment Dis.* 1994;182:157-163.

19. Annis H. Patient-treatment matching in the management of alcoholism. *NIDA Res Monogr.* 1988;90:152-161.

20. Hayashida M, Alterman AI, McLellan AT, et al. Comparative effectiveness and costs of inpatient and outpatient detoxification of patients with mild-to-moderate alcohol withdrawal syndrome. *N Engl J Med.* 1989;320:358-365.

21. Mechanic D, Schlesinger M, McAlpine DD, et al. Management of mental health and substance abuse services: state of the art and early results. *Milbank Q.* 1995;73:19-55.

22. Plough A, Shirley L, Zaremba N, Baker G, Schwartz M, Mulvey K. CSAT Target Cities Demonstration Final Evaluation Report. Boston, MA: Office for Treatment Improvement; 1996:1-25.

23. Morey L. Patient placement criteria: linking typologies to managed care. *Alcohol Health Res World.* 1996;20(1):36-44

24. Gregoire TK. Factors associated with level of care assignment in substance abuse treatment. *J Subst Abuse Treat.* 2000;18:241-248.

25. O'Toole TP, Freyder PJ, Gibbon JL, Hanusa BJ, Seltzer D, Fine MJ. ASAM Patient Placement Criteria treatment levels: do they correspond to

care actually received by homeless substance abusing adults? *J Addict Dis.* 2004;23(1):1-15.

26. Deck D, Gabriel R, Knudson J, et al. Impact of patient placement criteria on substance abuse treatment under the Oregon Health Plan. *J Addict Dis.* 2003;22(suppl 1):27-44.

27. Book J, Harbin H, Marques C, Silverman C, Lizanich-Aro S, Lazarus A. The ASAM and Green Spring alcohol and drug detoxification and rehabilitation criteria for utilization review. *Am J Addict.* 1995;4:187-197.

28. Gondolf E, Coleman K, Roman S. Clinical-based vs. insurance-based recommendations for substance abuse treatment level. *Subst Use Misuse.* 1996;318:1101-1116.

29. May WW. A field application of the ASAM Placement Criteria in a 12-step model of treatment for chemical dependency. *J Addict Dis* 1998;17(2):77-91.

30. Camilleri AC, Cacciola JS, Jenson MR. Comparison of two ASI-based standardized patient placement approaches. *J Addict Dis* 2012;31(2):118-129.

31. Turner WM, Turner KH, Reif S, Gutowski WE, Gastfriend DR. Feasibility of multidimensional substance abuse treatment matching: automating the ASAM Patient Placement Criteria. *Drug Alcohol Depend.* 1999;55:35-43.

32. Baker SL, Gastfriend DR. Reliability of multidimensional substance abuse treatment matching: implementing the ASAM Patient Placement Criteria. *J Addict Dis.* 2003;22(suppl 1):45-60.

33. Endicott J, Spitzer R, Fleiss JL, Cohen J. The Global Assessment Scale: a procedure for measuring overall severity of psychiatric diagnosis. *Arch Gen Psychiatry.* 1976;33:766-773.

34. Hall R. Global assessment of functioning: a modified scale. *Psychosomatics.* 1995;36:267-275.

35. Regier DA, Kaebler CT, Roper M, Rae DS, Sartorius N. The ICD-10 clinical field trial for mental and behavioral disorders: results in Canada and the United States. *Am J Psychiatry.* 1994;151:1340-1350.

36. Turner WM, Turner KH, Reif S, Gutowski WE, Gastfriend DR. Feasibility of multidimensional substance abuse treatment matching: automating the ASAM Patient Placement Criteria. *Drug Alcohol Depend.* 1999;55:35-43.

37. Kang SK, Sharon S, Pirard S, et al. Predictors for residential rehabilitation and treatment no-show in high frequency cocaine users: validation of the American Society of Addiction Medicine (ASAM) Criteria. Paper presented at: Annual Meeting and Symposium of the American Academy of Addiction Psychiatrists; December 15, 2002; Las Vegas, NV.

38. Angarita GA, Reif S, Pirard S, Lee S, Sharon E. No-show for treatment in substance abuse patients with comorbid symptomatology: validity results from a controlled trial of the ASAM Patient Placement Criteria. *J Addict Med.* 2007;1:79-87.

39. Magura S, Staines G, Kosanke N, Rosenblum A, Foote J, DeLuca A, Bali P. Predictive validity of the ASAM Patient Placement Criteria for naturalistically matched vs. mismatched alcoholism patients. *Am J Addict.* 2003;12(5):386-397.

40. Sharon E, Krebs C, Turner W, Desai N, Binus G, Penk W, Gastfriend DR. Predictive validity of the ASAM Patient Placement Criteria for hospital utilization. *J Addict Dis.* 2003;22(suppl 1):79-93.

41. U.S. Department of Health and Human Services, Center for Substance Abuse Treatment.

KAP KEYS Based on TIP 13: The Role and Current Status of Patient Placement Criteria in the Treatment of Substance Use Disorders. CSAT's Knowledge Application Program. Washington, DC; 2001. DHHS Publication No. (SMA) 01-3565.

42. Kolsky GD. Current State AOD Agency Practices Regarding the Use of Patient Placement Criteria (PPC) - An Update. Washington, DC: National Association of State Alcohol/Drug Abuse Directors; Nov. 1, 2006:1-17.

43. Willenbring ML, Kivlahan D, Kenny M, Grillo M, Hagedorn H, Postier A. Beliefs about evidence-based practices in addiction treatment: a survey of Veterans Administration program leaders. *J Subst Abuse Treat.* 2004;26:79-85.

44. Hoopfer S, Ryan M, Lucena A, Gastfriend E. ASAM PPC Assessment Software Business Plan. Harvard Business School Volunteer Consulting Organization; July 26, 2011:1-30.

45. McLellan AT, Carise D, Kleber HD. Can the national addiction treatment infrastructure support the public's demand for quality care? *J Subst Abuse Treat.* (2003)25:117-121.

46. Enos G. Treatment program profile: common-sense efforts improve access, revenues at Maine center. *Alcoholism and Drug Abuse Weekly.* 2011;23(30):1,6-7.

47. Chuang E, Wells R, Alexander JA, Friedmann PD, Lee IH. Factors associated with use of ASAM criteria and service provision in a national sample of outpatient substance abuse treatment units. *J Addict Med.* 2009;3:139-150.

48. Treatment Matching Interest Group (TMIG) study finds growing use of placement criteria and an association with program survival. *National Institute on Drug Abuse Clinical Trials Network Bulletin.* 2004;4-5:3.

Chapter 3

Intake and Assessment

1. Definition of Addiction [public policy statement]. Chevy Chase MD: American Society of Addiction Medicine; April 19, 2011. http://www.asam.org/for-the-public/definition-of-addiction.

2. Prochaska JO, DiClemente CC, Norcross JC. In search of how people change: applications to addictive behaviors. *Am Psychol.* 1992;47:1102-1114.

3. Prochaska JO, Norcross JC, DiClemente CC. *Changing for Good: A Revolutionary Six-Stage Program for Overcoming Bad Habits and Moving Your Life Positively Forward.* New York, NY: Avon Books; 1994.

4. The Joint Commission. *2013 Comprehensive Accreditation Manual for Behavioral Health Care (CAMBHC).* Joint Commission; 2012.

5. Fishman MJ, Shulman GD, Mee-Lee D, Kolodner G, Wilford BB. *ASAM Patient Placement Criteria: Supplement on Pharmacotherpaies for Alcohol Use Disorders.* Philadelphia, PA: Lippincott Williams & Wilkins; 2010.

Chapter 5

1. Boltaev AA, Bakhtiyor Samadov B, Gromov I, Lefebvre R, Gastfriend DR. ASAM PPC-2R vs. actual placements in mandatory substance abuse treatment in Uzbekistan. Presented at: the International Society of Addiction Medicine; June 2-5, 2004; Helsinki, Finland.

2. Reggers J, Ansseau M, Gustin F, Pirard S, Van Deun P, Seghers A, Earley P, Besson J, Gastfriend DR. Adaptation and validation of the ASAM PPC-2R Criteria in French and Dutch speaking Belgian drug addicts. Presented at: the College on Problems of Drug Dependence; 2003; Miami, FL.

3. National Institute on Drug Abuse. *Principles of drug addiction treatment: a research-based guide.* Rockville, MD: National Institute on Drug Abuse; 2009. NIH Publication No 09-4180.

Other References

Mee-Lee D, Shulman GD. The ASAM Placement Criteria and matching patients to treatment. In: Ries RK, Miller S, Fiellin DA, Saitz R, eds. *Principles of Addiction Medicine.* 4th ed. Philadelphia, PA: Lippincott Williams & Wilkins; 2009:387-399.

Chapter 6

Addressing Withdrawal Management and Intoxication Management

1. Feldman DJ, Pattison EM, Sobell LC, Graham T, Sobell MB. Outpatient alcohol detoxification. *Am J Psychiatry.* 1975;132:407-412.

2. Kolodner G. Ambulatory detoxification as an introduction to treatment. In: Seixas F, ed. *Currents in Alcoholism.* Vol 2. New York, NY:

Grune and Stratton; 1977:311-317.

3. Hayashida M, Alterman AI, McLellan AT, et al. Comparative effectiveness and costs of inpatient and outpatient detoxification of patients with mild-to-moderate alcohol withdrawal syndrome. *N Engl J Med.* 1989;320:358-365.

4. Soyka M, Horak M. Outpatient alcohol detoxification: implementation efficacy and outcome effectiveness of a model project. *Eur Addict Res.* 2004;10:180-187.

5. Fishman MJ, Shulman GD, Mee-Lee D, Kolodner G, Wilford BB. *ASAM Patient Placement Criteria: Supplement on Pharmacotherpaies for Alcohol Use Disorders.* Philadelphia, PA: Lippincott Williams & Wilkins; 2010.

6. Mayo-Smith MF. Management of Alcohol Intoxication and Withdrawal. In: Ries RK, Fiellin DA, Miller SC, Saitz R, eds. *Principles of Addiction Medicine.* 4th ed. Philadelphia, PA: Lippincott Williams & Wilkins; 2009:559-572.

7. Wetterling T, Weber B, Depfenhart M, Scheider B, Junghanns K. Development of a rating scale to predict the severity of alcohol withdrawal syndrome. *Alcohol Alcohol.* 2006;41(6):611-615.

8. Bostwick JM, Lapid MI. False positives on

the Clinical Institute Withdrawal Assessment for Alcohol – Revised: is this scale appropriate for use in the medically ill? *Psychosomatics.* 2004;45:256-261.

9. Hecksel KA, Bostwick JM, Jaeger TM, Cha SS. Inappropriate use of symptom-triggered therapy for alcohol withdrawal in the general hospital. *Mayo Clin Proc.* 2008;83(3):274-279.

10. Berge KH, Morse RM. Protocol-driven treatment of alcohol withdrawal in a general hospital: when theory meets practice. *Mayo Clin Proc.* 2008;83(3):270-271.

11. Dickinson WE, Eickelberg SJ. Management of sedative-hypnotic intoxication and withdrawal. In: Ries RK, Fiellin DA, Miller SC, Saitz R, eds. *Principles of Addiction Medicine.* 4th ed. Philadelphia, PA: Lippincott Williams & Wilkins; 2009:573-588.

12. Tetrault JM, O'Connor PG. Management of opioid intoxication and withdrawal. In: Ries RK, Fiellin DA, Miller SC, Saitz R, eds. *Principles of Addiction Medicine.* 4th ed. Philadelphia, PA: Lippincott Williams & Wilkins; 2009:589-606.

13. Budney AJ, Hughes JR. The cannabis withdrawal syndrome. *Curr Opin Psychiatry.* 2006;19:233-238.

Chapter 7

Level 0.5: Early Intervention

1. Kumpfer KL, Baxley GB, Drug Control Policy Group. *Drug Abuse Prevention: What Works.* National Institute on Drug Abuse Prevention Package. Washington, DC: Supt. of Docs., U.S. Government Printing Office; 1997. NIH Pub. No. 97-4110.

Opioid Treatment Services (OTS)

1. Part 8–Certification of Opioid Treatment Programs. *Fed Regist.* 2012;77(235):72752-72761. Codified at 42 CFR 8.

2. Center for Substance Abuse Treatment. *Clinical Guidelines for the Use of Buprenorphine in the Treatment of Opioid Addiction.* Treatment Improvement Protocol (TIP) Series 40.

Rockville, MD: Substance Abuse and Mental Health Services Administration; 2004. DHHS Publication No. (SMA) 04-3939.

3. Center for Substance Abuse Treatment. *Medication-Assisted Treatment for Opioid*

Addiction in Opioid Treatment Programs. Treatment Improvement Protocol (TIP) Series 43. Rockville, MD: Substance Abuse and Mental Health Services Administration; 2005. HHS Publication No. (SMA) 12-4214.

Chapter 8

Older Adults

1. Adapted from: American Psychiatric Association. *Diagnostic and Statistical Manual of Mental Disorders.* 5th ed. Arlington, VA: American Psychiatric Association; 2013.

Parents or Prospective Parents Receiving Addiction Treatment Concurrently with Their Children

1. Women, Alcohol and Other Drugs, and Pregnancy [public policy statement]. Chevy Chase MD: American Society of Addiction Medicine; July 11, 2011. http://www.asam.org/advocacy/find-a-policy-statement/view-policy-statement/public-policy-statements/2011/12/15/women-alcohol-and-other-drugs-and-pregnancy.

2. See: Reed BG. Developing women-sensitive drug dependence treatment services: why so difficult? *J Psychoactive Drugs.* 1987;19(2):151-164.

3. Kovalesky A. Women with substance abuse concerns. *Nurs Clin North Am.* 2004;39:205-217.

4. Clark W. Residential substance abuse treatment for pregnant and postpartum women and their children: treatment and policy implications. *Child Welfare.* 2001;80:2.

5. Sweeney PJ, Schwartz RM, Mattis NG, Vohr B. The effect of integrating substance abuse treatment with prenatal care on birth outcome. *Perinatol.* 2000;20(4):219-24.

6. Wong S, Ordean A, Kahan M, et al. Substance use in pregnancy. *J Obstet Gynaecol Can.*

2011;33(4):367-384.

7. Center for Substance Abuse Treatment. *Clinical Guidelines for the Use of Buprenorphine in the Treatment of Opioid Addiction.* Rockville, MD: Substance Abuse and Mental Health Services Administration; 2004. Treatment Improvement Protocol (TIP) Series 40. DHHS Publication No. (SMA) 04-3939.

8. United Nations Office on Drugs and Crime. *Substance Abuse and Care for Women: Case Studies and Lessons Learned.* Vienna, Austria: United Nations; 2004:69-71. Drug Abuse Treatment Toolkit.

9. Center for Substance Abuse Treatment. *Substance Abuse Treatment: Addressing the Specific Needs of Women.* Rockville, MD: Substance Abuse and Mental Health Services Administration; 2009. Treatment Improvement Protocol (TIP) Series 51. HHS Publication No. (SMA) 09-4426.

10. Daley M, Argeriou M, McCarty D. Substance abuse treatment for pregnant women: a window of opportunity? *Addict Behav.* 1998;23(2):239-249.

Persons in Safety-Sensitive Occupations

1. DuPont RL, McLellan AT, White WL, Merlo LJ, Gold MS. Setting the standard for recovery: Physicians' Health Programs. *J Subst Abuse Treat.* 2009;36(2):159-171.

2. Part 67.107–Medical Standards and Certification, Mental. *Fed Regist.* 2006;71:35764. Codified at 14 CFR 67.107.

Persons in Criminal Justice Settings

1. Latessa EJ, Cullen FT, Gendreau P. Beyond Correctional quackery – professionalism and the possibility of effective treatment. *Federal Probation* 2002;66(2):43-49.

2. Treatment for Prisoners with Addiction to Alcohol or Other Drugs [public policy statement]. Chevy Chase MD: American Society of Addiction Medicine; December 1, 2000. http://asam.org/advocacy/find-a-policy-statement/view-policy-statement/public-policy-statements/2011/12/16/treatment-for-prisoners-with-addiction-to-alcohol-or-other-drugs.

3. Access to Appropriate Detoxification Services for Persons Incarcerated in Prisons and Jails [public policy statement]. Chevy Chase MD: American Society of Addiction Medicine; July 1, 2002. http://asam.org/advocacy/find-a-policy-statement/view-policy-statement/public-policy-statements/2011/12/16/access-to-appropriate-detoxification-services-for-persons-incarcerated-in-prisons-and-jails.

Other References

Taxman FS, Shepardson ES, Byrne JM. *Tools of the Trade: A Guide to Incorporating Science into Practice.* National Institute of Corrections, US Department of Justice and Maryland Department of Public Safety and Correctional Services; 2004.

National Institute on Drug Abuse. *Principles of Drug Abuse Treatment for Criminal Justice Populations – A Research-based Guide.* NIH Publication No. 11-5316. National Institutes of Health, NIDA; 2012.

Chapter 9

Gambling Disorder

1. Definition of Addiction [public policy statement]. Chevy Chase MD: American Society of Addiction Medicine; April 19, 2011. http://www.asam.org/for-the-public/definition-of-addiction.

2. Hodgins DC, el-Guebaly N. Retrospective and prospective reports of precipitants to relapse in pathological gambling. *J Consult Clin Psychol.* 2004;72(1):72-80.

3. Slutske WS. Natural recovery and treatment-seeking in pathological gambling: results of two US national surveys. *Am J Psychiatry.* 2006;163:297-302.

4. Johnson EE, Hammer R, Nora RM, Tan B, Eistenstein N, Englehart C. The lie/bet questionnaire for screening pathological gamblers. *Psychol Rep.* 1997;80:83-88.

5. Lesieur HR, Blume SB. The South Oaks Gambling Screen (SOGS): A new instrument for the identification of pathological gamblers. *Am J Psychiatry.* 1987;144(9):1184-1188.

Tobacco Use Disorder

1. Doll R, Peto R, Boreham J, Sutherland I. Mortality in relation to smoking: 50 years' observations on male British doctors. *BMJ*. 2004;328(7455):1519.

2. World Health Organization (WHO). WHO Global Report: Mortality Attributable to Tobacco. Geneva, Switzerland: WHO; 2012.

3. Centers for Disease Control and Prevention (CDC). Vital signs: current cigarette smoking among adults aged ≥18 years with mental illness-United States, 2009-2011. *MMWR Morb Mortal Wkly Rep*. 2013;62:81-7.

4. Guydish J, Passalacqua E, Tajima B, Chan M, Chun J, Bostrom A. Smoking prevalence in addiction treatment: a review. *Nicotine Tob Res*. 2011;13(6):401-411. doi: 10.1093/ntr/ntr048.

5. Pajusco B, Chiamulera C, Quaglio G, Moro L, Casari R, Amen G, Lugononi F. Tobacco addiction and smoking status in heroin addicts under methadone vs. buprenorphine therapy. *Int J Environ Res Public Health*. 2012;9(3):932-942. doi:103390/ijerph9030932

6. Fiore MD, Goplerud E, Schroeder S. The Joint Commission's new tobacco-cessation measures-will hospitals do the right thing? *N Engl J Med*. 2012;366(13):1172-1174.

7. U.S. Department of Health and Human Services. *How Tobacco Smoke Causes Disease: The Biology and Behavioral Basis for Smoking-Attributable Disease: A Report of the Surgeon General*. Atlanta, GA: U.S. Department of Health and Human Services, Centers for Disease Control and Prevention, National Center for Chronic Disease Prevention and Health Promotion, Office on Smoking and Health; 2010.

8. Prochaska JJ. Failure to treat tobacco use in mental health and addiction treatment settings: a form of harm reduction? *Drug Alcohol Depend*. 2010;110:177-182.

9. Tsoh JY, Chi FW, Mertens JR, Weisner CM. Stopping smoking during first year of substance use treatment predicted 9-year alcohol and drug treatment outcomes. *Drug Alcohol Depend*. 2011;114:2-3,110-118. doi: 10.1016/j.drugalcdep.2010.09.008.

10. Prochaska JJ, Delucchi K, Hall SM. A meta-analysis of smoking cessation interventions with individuals in substance abuse treatment or recovery. *J Consult Clin Psychol*. 2004;72(6):1144-1156.

11. Hurt RD, Offord KP, Croghan IT, Gomez-Dahl L, Kottke TE, Morse RM, Melton LJ 3rd. Mortality following inpatient addictions treatment: role of tobacco use in a community-based cohort. *JAMA*. 1996;275:1097-1103.

12. Hser YI, McCarthy WJ, Anglin MD. Tobacco use as a distal predictor of morality among long-term narcotics addicts. *Prev Med*. 1994;23:61-69.

13. Prochaska JJ. Ten critical reasons for treating tobacco dependence in inpatient psychiatry. *J Am Psychiatr Nurses Assoc*. 2009;15(6):404-409.

14. Evins AE, Deckersbach T, Cather C, Freudenreich O, Culhane MA, Henderson DC, et al. Independent effects of tobacco abstinence and buproprion on cognitive function in schizophrenia. *J Clin Psychiatry*. 2005;66(9):1184-1190.

15. Lasser K, Boyd JW, Woolhandler S, Himmelstein DU, McCormick D, Bor DH. Smoking and mental illness: a population-based prevalence study. *JAMA*. 2000;284(20):2606-2610.

16. Colton CW, Manderscheid RW. Congruencies in increased mortality rates, years of potential life lost, and causes of death among public mental health clients in eight states. *Prev Chronic Dis*. 2006;3(2):A42.

17. Substance Abuse and Mental Health Services Administration. *Results from the 2011 National Survey on Drug Use and Health: Summary of National Findings.* Rockville, MD: Substance Abuse and Mental Health Services Administration; 2012. NSDUH Series H-44. HHS Publication No. (SMA) 12-4713.

18. Definition of Addiction [public policy statement]. Chevy Chase MD: American Society of Addiction Medicine; April 19, 2011. http://www.asam.org/for-the-public/definition-of-addiction.

19. Richter KP, Choi WS, McCool RM, Harris KJ, Ahluwalia JS. Smoking cessation services in US methadone maintenance facilities. *Psychiatr Serv.* 2004;55(11):1258-1264. doi: 10.1176/appi.ps.55.11.1258.

20. Friedmann PD, Jiang L, Richter KP. Cigarette smoking cessation services in outpatient substance abuse treatment programs in the United States. *J Subst Abuse Treat.* 2008;34(2):165-172. doi: 10.1016/j.jsat.2007.02.006.

21. McFall M, Saxon AJ, Malte CA, et al. Integrating tobacco cessation into mental health care for posttraumatic stress disorder: a randomized controlled trial. *JAMA.* 2010;304(22):2485-2493.

22. American Lung Association. All Insurance Plans Should Cover Tobacco Cessation Treatments. December 1, 2011. http://www.lung.org/assets/documents/tobacco-control-advocacy/tobacco-cessation-treatments-insurance.pdf.

23. Bobo JK, Davis CM. Recovering Staff and Smoking in Chemical Dependency Programs in Rural Nebraska. *J Subst Abuse Treat.* 1993;10:221-227.

24. American Psychiatric Association. *Diagnostic and Statistical Manual of Mental Disorders.* 5th ed. Arlington, VA: American Psychiatric Association; 2013.

25. Fagerström K, Russ C, Yu CR, Foulds J. The Fagerström Test for Nicotine Dependence as a predictor of smoking abstinence: a pooled analysis of Varenicline clinical trial data. *Nicotine Tob Res.* 2012;14(12):1467-1473.

26. Fidler JA, Shabab I, West R. Strength of urges to smoke as a measure of severity of cigarette dependence: comparison with the Fagerström Test for Cigarette Dependence and its components. *Addiction.* 2011;106:631-638.

27. Fiore MC, Jaén CR, Baker TB, et al. *Treating Tobacco Use and Dependence: 2008 Update.* Clinical Practice Guideline. Rockville, MD: U.S. Department of Health and Human Services, Public Health Service; 2008.

28. Sachs DPL, Leone FT, Farber HJ, et al. American College of Chest Physicians Tobacco-Dependence Treatment ToolKit. 3rd ed. Northbrook, IL: American College of Chest Physicians; 2009. http://tobaccodependence.chestnet.org.

29. Bize R, Burnand B, Mueller Y, Rege-Walther M, Camain JY, Cornuz J. Biomedical risk assessment as an aid for smoking cessation. *Cochrane Database Syst Rev.* 2012;12:CD004705.

30. Brawley OW. Weighing the benefits and risks of lung cancer screening. American Cancer Society. Jan 11, 2013.

31. Russell MA, Wilson C, Taylor C, Baker CD. Effect of general practitioner's advice against smoking. *Br Med J.* 1979;2:231-235.

32. Russell MA, Merriman R, Stapleton J, Taylor W. Effect of nicotine chewing gum as an adjunct to general practitioner's advice against smoking. *Br Med J (Clin Res Ed).* 1983;287:1782-1785.

33. Arcury TA, Quandt SA, Preisser JS, Bernert JT, Norton D, Wang J. High levels of transdermal nicotine exposure produce green tobacco sickness in Latino farmworkers. *Nicotine Tob Res.* 2003;5:315–321.

34. Centers for Disease Control and Prevention (CDC). Smoking-attributable mortality, years

of potential life lost, and productivity losses—United States, 2000–2004. *MMWR Morb Mortal Wkly Rep.* 2008;57(45):1226-1228.

35. National Cancer Institute. *Smokeless Tobacco or Health: An International Perspective.* Bethesda, MD: National Cancer Institute; 1992. Smoking and Tobacco Control Monograph 2.

36. International Agency for Research on Cancer. *Smokeless Tobacco and Some Tobacco-Specific N-Nitrosamines.* Lyon, France: World Health Organization International Agency for Research on Cancer; 2007. IARC Monographs on the Evaluation of Carcinogenic Risks to Humans Volume 89.

37. Jacob P 3rd, Abu Raddaha AH, Dempsey D, Havel C, Peng M, Yu L, Benowitz NL. Comparison of nicotine and carcinogen exposure with water pipe and cigarette smoking. *Cancer Epidemiol Biomarkers Prev.* 2013;22(5):765-772. doi: 10.1158/1055-9965.

38. O'Connor RJ. Non-cigarette tobacco products: what have we learnt and where are we headed? *Tob Control.* 2012;21:181-190. doi: 10.1136/tobaccocontrol-2011-050281.

39. American Cancer Society. 2012. Guide to Quitting Smoking. http://www.cancer.org/healthy/stayawayfromtobacco/guidetoquittingsmoking/guide-to-quitting-smoking-benefits.

40. Lawrence D, Mitrou F, Zubrick S. Smoking and mental illness: results from population surveys in Australia and the United States. *BMC Public Health.* 2009;9:285. doi: 10.1186/1471-2458-9-285.

41. National Association of State Mental Health Program Directors (NASMHPD). *Tobacco-free Living in Psychiatric Settings: A best practices toolkit promoting wellness and recovery.* Alexandria, VA: NASMHPD; 2007, updated 2010.

42. Williams JM, Ziedonis DM, Abanyie F, Steinberg ML, Foulds J, Benowitz NL. Increased

nicotine and cotinine levels in smokers with schizophrenia and schizoaffective disorder is not a metabolic effect. *Schizophr Res.* 2005;79(2-3):323-335.

43. Ziedonis D, Williams JM, Smelson D. Serious mental illness and tobacco addiction: a model program to address this common but neglected issue. *Am J Med Sci.* 2003;326(4):223-30.

44. U.S. Department of Health and Human Services. *The Health Consequences of Involuntary Exposure to Tobacco Smoke: A Report of the Surgeon General.* Atlanta, GA: U.S. Department of Health and Human Services, Centers for Disease Control and Prevention, Coordinating Center for Health Promotion, National Center for Chronic Disease Prevention and Health Promotion, Office on Smoking and Health; 2006.

45. Hurt RD, Ebbert JO, Hays JT, McFadden DD. Treating Tobacco Dependence in a Medical Setting. *CA Cancer J Clin.* 2009;59:314-326. doi: 10.3322/caac.20031.

Other References

Ries RK, Miller S, Fiellin DA, Saitz R, eds. *Principles of Addiction Medicine.* 4th ed. Philadelphia, PA: Lippincott Williams & Wilkins; 2009.

Resources for Clinicians

American College of Chest Physicians
http://tobaccodependence.chestnet.org/

Association for the Treatment of Tobacco Use and Dependence
http://www.attud.org

Global Bridges: Healthcare Alliance for Tobacco Dependence Treatment
www.globalbridges.org

Hurt RD, Ebbert JO, Hays JT, McFadden DD. Treating tobacco dependence in a medical setting. *CA Cancer J Clin*. 2009;59(3):314-326. http://www.ncbi.nlm.nih.gov/pubmed/19706827

Joint Commission Partnership for Prevention's ActionToQuit Initiative http://www.prevent.org/data/files/resourcedocs/hpq,%20full,%20final,%2010-31-11.pdf

National Association of State Mental Health Program Directors, Tobacco-Free Living in Psychiatric Settings: A Best Practices Tool Kit for Promoting Wellness and Recovery http://smokingcessationleadership.ucsf.edu/Downloads/nasmhpd_toolkit_2010.pdf

New York University, Tobacco Resources for Providers http://pophealth.med.nyu.edu/divisions/mtcp/health-care-providers?CSRT=8383444176073162525

Rutgers, Tobacco Dependence Program www.tobaccoprogram.org

University of California, San Francisco, Clinician-Assisted Tobacco Cessation: Rx for Change http://rxforchange.ucsf.edu

University of Wisconsin Center for Tobacco Research and Intervention http://www.ctri.wisc.edu

U.S. Department of Health and Human Services, Public Health Service's Clinical Practice Guidelines http://www.ahrq.gov/clinic/tobacco/treating_tobacco_use08.pdf

Resources for Patients and Families

American Cancer Society
1-800-ACS-2345
www.cancer.org

American Heart Association
1-800-242-1893
www.heart.org

American Lung Association
1-800-586-4872
www.lung.org

Nicotine Anonymous
1-877-TRY-NICA
www.nicotine-anonymous.org

Smokefree.gov (includes links to state services)
1-800-QUIT-NOW
smokefree.gov

text2quit
www.text2quit.com

Tobacco-free Workplace Resources

Americans for Nonsmokers' Rights
www.no-smoke.org

Centers for Disease Control and Prevention. Save Lives, Save Money: Make Your Business Smoke-Free
http://www.cdc.gov/tobacco/basic_information/secondhand_smoke/guides/business/pdfs/save_lives_save_money.pdf

The Health Consequences of Involuntary Exposure to Tobacco Smoke: A Report of the Surgeon General
http://www.surgeongeneral.gov/library/reports/secondhandsmoke/report-index.html

Appendices

Appendix A: Withdrawal Management Instruments

1. The CIWA-Ar is not copyrighted and may be used freely. Source: Sullivan JT, Sykora K, Schneiderman J, Naranjo CA, Sellers EM. Assessment of alcohol withdrawal: The revised Clinical Institute Withdrawal Instrument for Alcohol Scale (CIWA-Ar). *Br J Addict.* 1989;84:1353-1357.

2. Bostwick JM, Lapid MI. False positives on the Clinical Institute Withdrawal Assessment for Alcohol – Revised: is this scale appropriate for use in the medically ill? *Psychosomatics.* 2004;45:256-261.

3. Hecksel KA, Bostwick JM, Jaeger TM, Cha SS. Inappropriate use of symptom-triggered therapy for alcohol withdrawal in the general hospital. *Mayo Clin Proc.* 2008;83(3):274-279.

4. Berge KH, Morse RM. Protocol-driven treatment of alcohol withdrawal in a general hospital: when theory meets practice. *Mayo Clin Proc.* 2008;83(3):270-271.

5. Wesson DR, Ling W. The Clinical Opiate Withdrawal Scale (COWS). *J Psychoactive Drugs.* 2003;35(2):253-259. Reprinted by permission of the publisher (Taylor & Francis Ltd, http://www.tandf.co.uk/journals).

6. Heatherton TF, Kozlowski LT, Frecker RC, Fagerström KO. The Fagerström Test for Nicotine Dependence: a revision of the Fagerström Tolerance Questionnaire. *Br J Addict.* 1991;86(9):1119-1127. Reprinted by permission of Karl Fagerström.

7. Adapted from Peachey, JE, Lei, H. Assessment of opioid dependence with naloxone. *Br J Addict.* 1998;83(2):193–201. Reprinted by permission of Wiley.

Appendix B: Special Considerations for Dimension 5 Criteria: Relapse, Continued Use, or Continued Problem Potential

1. Condon TP, Jacobs P, Tai B, Pintello D, Miner L, Elcano JC. Patient relapse in the context of drug abuse treatment. *J Addict Med.* 2011;5(3):157-62.

2. Steketee JD, Kalivas PW. Drug wanting: behavioral sensitization and relapse to drug-seeking behavior. *Pharmacol Rev.* 2011;63(2):348-65.

3. Sinha R. New findings on biological factors predicting addiction relapse vulnerability. *Curr Psychiatry Rep.* 2011;13(5):398-405.

4. Milton AL, Everitt BJ. The persistence of maladaptive memory: addiction, drug memories and anti-relapse treatments. *Neurosci Biobehav Rev.* 2012;36(4):1119-39.

5. Henkel D. Unemployment and substance use: a review of the literature (1990-2010). *Curr Drug Abuse Rev.* 2011;4(1):4-27.

6. Malivert M, Fatséas M, Denis C, Langlois E, Auriacombe M. Effectiveness of therapeutic communities: a systematic review. *Eur Addict Res.* 2012;18(1):1-11.

7. Fareed A, Vayalapalli S, Stout S, Casarella J, Drexler K, Bailey SP. Effect of methadone maintenance treatment on heroin craving, a literature review. *J Addict Dis.* 2011;30(1):27-38.

8. Amato L, Minozzi S, Davoli M, Vecchi S.

Psychosocial and pharmacological treatments versus pharmacological treatments for opioid detoxification. *Cochrane Database Syst Rev.* 2011;(9):CD005031.

9. Finney JW, Moos RH. Research report - entering treatment for alcohol abuse: a stress and coping model. *Addiction.* 1995;90:1223-1240.

10. Brown SA, Christiansen BA, Goldman MS. The Alcohol Expectancy Questionnaire: an instrument for the assessment of adolescent and adult alcohol expectancies. *J Stud Alcohol.* 1987;48:483-491.

11. Roberts JS, Anton RF, Latham PK, Moak DH. Factor structure and predictive validity of the Obsessive Compulsive Drinking Scale. *Alcohol: Clin Exp Res.* 1999;23:1484-1491.

12. Webb TL, Sniehotta FF, Michie S. Using theories of behaviour change to inform interventions for addictive behaviours. *Addiction.* 2010;105(11):1879-92.

13. Willette RE, Barnett G. *Narcotic Antagonists: Naltrexone Pharmacochemistry and Sustained-Release Preparations.* Supt. of Docs., U.S. Government Printing Office. Washington, DC: 1-5; 1981. National Institute on Drug Abuse

Research Monograph 28. DHEW Pub. No. (ADM) 81-902.

14. Bunch JM, Schneider HG. Smoking-specific locus of control. *Psychol Rep.* 1991;69:1075-1081.

15. DiClemente CC, Carbonari JP, Montgomery RPG, Hughes SO. The Alcohol Abstinence Self-Efficacy Scale. *J Stud Alcohol.* 1994;55:141-148.

16. Litman GK, Stapleton J, Oppenheim AN, Peleg M, Jackson P. The relationship between coping behaviors, their effectiveness and alcoholism relapse and survival. *Br J Addict.* 1984;79:283-291.

17. Myers, MG, Brown, SA, Mott MA. Coping as a predictor of adolescent substance abuse treatment outcome. *J Subst Abuse.* 1993;5:15–29.

18. Cloninger CR, Svrakic DM, Przybeck TR. A psychobiological model of temperament and character. *Arch Gen Psychiatry.* 1993;50:975-990.

Other References

American Psychiatric Association. *Diagnostic and Statistical Manual of Mental Disorders.* 5th ed. Arlington, VA: American Psychiatric Association; 2013.

Appendix C: Glossary

1. Definition of Addiction [public policy statement]. Chevy Chase, MD: American Society of Addiction Medicine; April 19, 2011. http://www.asam.org/for-the-public/definition-of-addiction.

2. Treatment for Alcohol and Other Drug Addiction [public policy statement]. Chevy Chase, MD: American Society of Addiction Medicine; May 1, 1980. http://www.asam.org/advocacy/find-a-policy-statement/view-policy-statement/public-policy-statements/2011/12/15/treatment-for-alcohol-and-other-drug-addiction.

3. Fishman MJ, Shulman GD, Mee-Lee D, Kolodner G, Wilford BB. *ASAM Patient Placement Criteria: Supplement on Pharmacotherpaies for Alcohol Use Disorders.* Philadelphia, PA: Lippincott Williams & Wilkins; 2010.

4. National Institute on Alcohol Abuse and Alcoholism. NIAAA Council approves definition of binge drinking. *NIAAA Newsletter.* 2004;3:3.

5. Commission for Case Manager Certification. Certification Guide to the CCM® Examination. Commission for Case Manager Certification; 2013.

6. Moss S. *Contracting for Managed Substance Abuse and Mental Health services: A Guide for Public Purchasers.* Center for Substance Abuse Treatment. Rockville, MD: 217-237; 1998. Technical Assistance Publication Series No. 22.

7. Babor T, Campbell R, Room R, Saunders J, compilers. *Lexicon of Alcohol and Drug Terms.* Geneva, Switzerland: World Health Organization; 1994. Available at http://whqlibdoc.who.int/publications/9241544686.pdf.

8. Adapted from National Institute on Drug Abuse. *Principles of drug addiction treatment: a research-based guide.* Rockville, MD: National Institute on Drug Abuse; 2009. NIH Publication No 09-4180.

9. Miller WR, Rollnick S. *Motivational Interviewing: Helping People Change.* 3rd ed. New York, NY: Guilford Press; 2013.

10. Patient-Centered Primary Care Collaborative. Defining the medical home: a patient-centered philosophy that drives primary care excellence. 2013. http://www.pcpcc.org/about/medical-home.

11. Adapted from TransforMed. TransforMed: transforming medical practices. 2013. http://www.transformed.com/PDF/Transformed-brochure-July2013.pdf.

12. O'Connell ME, Boat T, Warner KE, eds. *Preventing mental, emotional, and behavioral disorders among young people: Progress and possibilities.* National Research Council and Institute of Medicine of the National Academies. Washington, DC: The National Academies Press; 2009.

13. Substance Abuse and Mental Health Services Administration. Levels of Risk, Levels of Intervention: Universal, Selective, & Indicated Prevention. http://captus.samhsa.gov/prevention-practice/prevention-and-behavioral-health/levels-risk-levels-intervention/2.

14. Substance Abuse and Mental Health Services Administration. Trauma Definition; December 10, 2012. http://www.samhsa.gov/traumajustice/traumadefinition/.

Key Concepts and Definitions

The following terms represent some of the key concepts and definitions used throughout *The ASAM Criteria*, and corresponding page numbers where more information can be found. This list is not comprehensive, and the referenced pages are not the only place in the text where these concepts are used. For additional definitions, see the Glossary in Appendix C.

Contributors

Additional information on contributors, steering committee members, and field reviewers is available in the web-based version of *The ASAM Criteria*.

Susan Blank, MD, FAPA
Tobacco Use Disorder – Lead Author
President and Chief Medical Officer
Atlanta Healing Center, LLC
Atlanta, GA

Michael V. Burke, EdD
Tobacco Use Disorder – Workgroup Member
Program Coordinator
Mayo Clinic Nicotine Dependence Center
Rochester, MN

Ray Daugherty, BA
Level 0.5 – Lead Author; Level 3 – Workgroup Member
President
Prevention Research Institute
Lexington, KY

Paul H. Earley, MD, FASAM
Persons in Safety Sensitive Occupations – Lead Author
Earley Consultancy, LLC
Medical Director, Georgia Professionals Program, Inc.
Atlanta, GA

Marc J. Fishman, MD, FASAM
Deputy Editor; Adolescent Criteria – Lead Author
Medical Director
Maryland Treatment Centers
Assistant Professor
Department of Psychiatry, Johns Hopkins University School of Medicine
Baltimore, MD

Karen Garrett, MA, CPLP, CAP, CPP, CMHP
Level 3 – Workgroup Member
Associate Vice President, River Region Human Services, Inc.
Jacksonville, FL

David R. Gastfriend, MD
Deputy Editor; The ASAM Criteria Software – Lead Author
President & CEO, RecoverySearch, Inc.
Newton, MA
Vice President, Scientific Communication
Alkermes, Inc.
Waltham, MA

Manuel Guantez, PsyD, LCADC
Level 3 – Workgroup Member
Chief Executive Officer
Turning Point
Paterson, NJ

Robert M. Hooper, PhD, LGSW
Persons in Criminal Justice Settings – Workgroup Member
Director of Recovery Services
Eastern Shore Psychological Services
Salisbury, MD

Richard D. Hurt, MD
Tobacco Use Disorder – Workgroup Member
Professor of Medicine, College of Medicine
Director, Nicotine Dependence Center
Mayo Clinic
Rochester, MN

Contributors

Carleen Jimenez, MA, CMHC, ASUDC
Parents or Prospective Parents Receiving Addiction Treatment Concurrently with their Children – Lead Author
Mental Health Contract Compliance Specialist
Salt Lake County Behavioral Health Services
Salt Lake City, UT

Lori D. Karan, MD, FACP, FASAM
Tobacco Use Disorder – Lead Author
Medical Director
Department of Public Safety, Hawaii
Professor of Psychiatry
John A. Burns School of Medicine, Hawaii
Associate Clinical Professor of Medicine
University of California, San Francisco
Publications Chair and Treasurer
American Society of Addiction Medicine
Honolulu, HI

George Kolodner, MD
Withdrawal Management and Intoxication Management – Lead Author
Medical Director, Kolmac Clinic
Clinical Professor of Psychiatry
Georgetown University School of Medicine and
    University of Maryland School of Medicine
Burtonsville, MD

Margaret Kotz, DO, FASAM
Withdrawal Management and Intoxication Management – Workgroup Member
Professor of Psychiatry and Anesthesiology
Case Western Reserve University School of
    Medicine
Director, Addiction Recovery Services
Case Medical Center
University Hospitals of Cleveland
Cleveland, OH

Frankie D. Lemus, MA, LMFT
Level 0.5 – Lead Author; Persons in Criminal Justice Settings – Lead Author
Senior Vice President
The Change Companies®
Carson City, NV

Kevin Lowe, PhD
Persons in Criminal Justice Settings – Workgroup Member
Vice President of Training
The Change Companies®
Carson City, NV

David Mee-Lee, MD
Chief Editor;
Level 4 – Lead Author; Co-Occurring Disorders – Lead Author
Senior Vice President
The Change Companies®
Davis, CA

Joel L. Millard, DSW, LCSW
Opioid Treatment Services – Lead Author

Michael M. Miller, MD, FASAM
Managing Editor;
Tobacco Use Disorder – Workgroup Member
Medical Director, Herrington Recovery Center,
    Rogers Memorial Hospital – Oconomowoc, WI
Clinical Adjunct Associate Professor, University
    of Wisconsin School of Medicine and Public
    Health
Clinical Assistant Professor, Medical College of
    Wisconsin
Past President, American Society of Addiction
    Medicine
Madison, WI

Kenneth Minkoff, MD
Co-Occurring Disorders – Workgroup Member
Senior System Consultant, ZiaPartners, Inc.
San Rafael, CA
Clinical Asst Professor of Psychiatry
Harvard Medical School

Contributors

Patrice Muchowski, ScD, CADAC
Level 3 – Workgroup Member
Vice President, Clinical Services
AdCare Hospital of Worcester, Inc.
Worcester, MA

David M. Ockert, PhD
Withdrawal Management and Intoxication Management – Workgroup Member
Executive Director
Parallax Center, Inc.
Adjunct Senior Research Scientist
Columbia University School of Social Work
New York, NY

Judith Prochaska, PhD, MPH
Tobacco Use Disorder – Workgroup Member
Associate Professor of Medicine
Stanford University
Stanford, CA

Scott M. Provence, MA, MFA
Publication Editor
Vice President of Product Development
The Change Companies®
Carson City, NV

David Sachs, MD
Tobacco Use Disorder – Workgroup Member

Edwin A. Salsitz, MD, FASAM
Opioid Treatment Services – Workgroup Member
Medical Director Out-Patient Opioid Therapy
Beth Israel Medical Center
New York, NY

Peter Selby, MBBS, CCFP, FCFP, FASAM
Tobacco Use Disorder – Workgroup Member
Chief, Addictions
Centre for Addiction and Mental Health/University of Toronto
Toronto, ON

Gerald D. Shulman, MA, FACATA
Deputy Editor; Levels 1, 2, and 3 – Lead Author; Special Populations – Chair; Older Adults – Lead Author; Parents or Prospective Parents Receiving Addiction Treatment Concurrently with their Children – Workgroup Member; Gambling Disorder – Lead Author
Shulman & Associates, Training and Consulting in Behavioral Health
Jacksonville, FL

Glenda J. Spencer, MS, LAC
Level 3 – Workgroup Member
CEO
Center for Solutions
Devils Lake, ND

George E. Stavros, MD
Opioid Treatment Services – Workgroup Member
CEO
Community Medical Services LLC
Vice President, AATOD
Phoenix, AZ

Michael Steinberg, MD, MPH
Tobacco Use Disorder – Workgroup Member
Associate Professor
Rutgers – Robert Wood Johnson Medical School
New Brunswick, NJ

Stephen K. Valle, ScD, MBA, LADC I, CADAC
Persons in Criminal Justice Settings – Workgroup Member
President & CEO
AdCare Criminal Justice Services, Inc.
Worcester, MA

Ken Wassum
Tobacco Use Disorder – Workgroup Member
Director, Clinical and Quality Support
Alere Wellbeing
Seattle, WA

Vicky Westmoreland, LSAC, APC
Persons in Criminal Justice Settings – Workgroup Member

Jill M. Williams, MD
Tobacco Use Disorder – Workgroup Member
Professor of Psychiatry
Robert Wood Johnson Medical School
New Brunswick, NJ

ASAM Coalition for National Clinical Criteria Steering Committee

Paul H. Earley, MD, FASAM
Earley Consultancy, LLC
Medical Director, Georgia Professionals Program, Inc.
Atlanta, GA

Marc J. Fishman, MD, FASAM
Medical Director
Maryland Treatment Centers
Assistant Professor
Department of Psychiatry, Johns Hopkins University School of Medicine
Baltimore, MD

David R. Gastfriend, MD
President & CEO
RecoverySearch, Inc.
Newton, MA
Vice President, Scientific Communication
Alkermes, Inc.
Waltham, MA

John M. Golden, CAPT, USPHS, PhD, ABPP
Deputy Director of Clinical Programs
Deployment Health Clinical Center
Walter Reed National Military Medical Center
Bethesda, MD

Daniel R. Kivlahan, PhD
National Mental Health Program Director, Addictive Disorders
Mental Health Services
Veterans Health Administration
Seattle, WA

George Kolodner, MD
Medical Director, Kolmac Clinic
Clinical Professor of Psychiatry,
Georgetown University School of Medicine and University of Maryland School of Medicine
Burtonsville, MD

Margaret Kotz, DO, FASAM
Professor of Psychiatry and Anesthesiology
Case Western Reserve University School of Medicine
Director, Addiction Recovery Services
Case Medical Center
University Hospitals of Cleveland
Cleveland, OH

Robert J. Lindsey, MEd, CEAP
President and CEO
National Council on Alcoholism and Drug Dependence, Inc. (NCADD)
New York, NY

Barbara A. Marin, PhD
Chief, Department of Addiction Treatment Services
Directorate of Behavioral Health
Walter Reed National Military Medical Center
Bethesda, MD

Brendan McEntee
Publications Manager and Managing Editor
American Society of Addiction Medicine
Chevy Chase, MD

ASAM Coalition for National Clinical Criteria Steering Committee

David Mee-Lee, MD (Chair)
Senior Vice President
The Change Companies®
Davis, CA

Penny Mills
Executive Vice President and CEO
American Society of Addiction Medicine
Chevy Chase, MD

Cynthia Moreno Tuohy
Executive Director
NAADAC, the Association for Addiction
  Professionals
Alexandria, VA

Rob Morrison
Executive Director
National Association of State Alcohol and Drug
  Abuse Directors (NASADAD)
Washington, DC

Patrice Muchowski, ScD, CADAC
Vice President, Clinical Services
AdCare Hospital of Worcester, Inc.
Worcester, MA

Robert Richards, MA, CADCIII, NCACII
NAADAC President
Alexandria, VA
Executive Director
Willamette Family Inc.
Eugene, OR

Richard Ries, MD
Director, Division of Addictions
University of Washington
Harborview Medical Center 359911
Seattle, WA

Gerald Shulman, MA, FACATA
Shulman & Associates, Training and Consulting
  in Behavioral Health
Jacksonville, FL

R. James Thatcher, MD
Medical Director
Massachusetts Behavioral Health Partnership
Boston, MA

Field Reviewers

Emil Affsa III, LPC, LCADC
Statewide TASC Coordinator
State of New Jersey Judiciary TASC
Trenton, NJ

J. Craig Allen, MD
Chief Medical Officer
Rushford Center
Meriden, CT

Armando L. Andujar, BS, CADC
Substance Abuse Evaluator
State of New Jersey Judiciary TASC
Camden, NJ

Daniel H. Angres, MD
Medical Director
Resurrection Addiction Services
Chicago, IL

Randolph Atkins, PhD
Social Science Researcher
National Highway Traffic Safety
  Administration
Washington, DC

Louis E. Baxter, MD, FASAM
Executive Medical Director
Professional Assistance Program of
  New Jersey
Consulting Medical Director
Behavioral Health of the Palm Beaches
Princeton, NJ

Edwin R. Bergen, PhD
Professor/Coordinator, Human Services
  Program
San Antonio College
San Antonio, TX

Field Reviewers

Michelle R. Berthon, MA, LPC, MHSP
Utilization Manager
UnitedHealthcare
Brentwood, TN

Claudia A. Blackburn, MS, PsyD
Content Expert Director
CDM
Bethesda, MD

Carlos Blanco, MD, PhD
Professor of Psychiatry
Columbia University
New York, NY

Sara A. Bower, MSW
Portland, OR

Randy T. Brown, MD, PhD, FASAM
Assistant Professor, Department of
    Family Medicine
Director, Center for Addictive Disorders,
    UW Hospitals & Clinics
Director, UW-VA Addiction Medicine
    Fellowship Program
University of Wisconsin School of Medi-
    cine and Public Health
Madison, WI

Ann Bruner, MD
Staff Physician
Maryland Treatment Centers
Baltimore, MD

Michael V. Burke, EdD
Program Coordinator
Mayo Clinic Nicotine Dependence
    Center
Rochester, MN

Gary D. Carr, MD, FAAFP, FASAM
Physician
Southern Neuro and Spine Institute
Hattiesburg, MS

Janet M. Carter, MEd
Executive Director
Regional Alcohol and Drug Abuse
    Training Program (RADACT)
Anchorage, AK

Jayne S. Cavanaugh, MA, LCADC
Statewide TASC Coordinator
State of New Jersey Judiciary, TASC
Trenton, NJ

**Stacy R. Chamberlain, MA, Licensed
    Addiction Counselor**
State Methadone Authority/SUD Clinical
    Services Coordinator
Kansas Department of Aging and Dis-
    ability Services/Behavioral Health
    Services
Topeka, KS

Darwyn Chern, MD
Chief Psychiatrist
Partners in Recovery
Mesa, AZ

Michael Cunningham, MA
Acting Director
California Department of Alcohol and
    Drug Programs
Sacramento, CA

Ray Daugherty
President
Prevention Research Institute
Lexington, KY

Christopher M. Davidson, MD
Assistant Professor
Sanford School of Medicine, University
    of South Dakota
Sioux Falls, SD

Christina M. Delos Reyes, MD
Associate Professor, Department of
    Psychiatry
University Hospitals Case Medical Center
Cleveland, OH

Paul A. Donaher, MD
Medical Director - Substance Abuse
    Treatment Unit
Coatesville Veterans Affairs Medical
    Center
Coatesville, PA

Kay Doughty, MA, CAP, CPP
Vice President of Family and Commu-
    nity Services
Operation PAR, Inc.
Pinellas Park, FL

Paul H. Earley, MD, FASAM
Earley Consultancy, LLC
Medical Director, Georgia Professionals
    Program, Inc.
Atlanta, GA

Seth G. Eisenberg, MD
ACT Psychiatrist
Gateway BHS
Saint Simons Island, GA

John Femino, MD, FASAM, MRO
Medical Director and President
Meadows Edge Recovery Center
North Kingston, RI

Dawn B. Fitzgerald, LCSW, LCADC
Substance Abuse Evaluator
State of New Jersey Judiciary TASC
Hackensack, NJ

Susan E. Foster, MSW
V.P. & Director, Division of Policy
    Research and Analysis
CASAColumbia
New York, NY

Richard A. Foster, PhD
Executive Vice President of Treatment
    Programs
Gateway Rehab
Moon Township, PA

Michael L. Fox, DO, FASAM
Medical Director, Chemical Dependency
    Unit
St. Mary Mercy, Department of Behav-
    ioral Medicine
Livonia, MI

**Kenneth I. Freedman, MD, MS, MBA,
    FACP, FASAM, AGAF**
Chief Medical Officer
Lemuel Shattuck Hospital
Boston, MA

**Peter D. Friedmann, MD, MPH,
    FASAM, FACP**
Director, HSR&D Research Enhance-
    ment Award Program
Providence VA Medical Center
Providence, RI

Stuart Gitlow, MD, MPH, MBA
Executive Director
Annenberg Physician Training Program
    in Addictive Disease
Woonsocket, RI

Eric Goplerud, PhD
Senior Vice President
NORC at the University of Chicago
Bethesda, MD

Field Reviewers

Jon E. Grant, JD, MD, MPH
Professor of Psychiatry
University of Chicago
Chicago, IL

Jeanie Griffin, DD, LPC, MFT, LCDC
Senior Clinical Advisor
Origins Recovery Centers LLC
Grapevine, TX

Raymond A. Griffin, PhD, LADC,
Diplomate & Fellow ABMP
The Greenwich Center For Addiction
    Medicine
Greenwich, CT

Manuel Guantez, PsyD, LCADC
Chief Executive Officer
Turning Point
Paterson, NJ

Lynda A. Guerrero
Utilization Review Coordinator
Austin Recovery
Austin, TX

Joan Hartman, MEd
Central Regional Manager
Chestnut Health Systems
Bloomington, IL

Philip Herschman, PhD
Chief Clinical Officer
CRC Health Group, Inc
Carlsbad, CA

Arnold J. Hill, MD, MSc, FASAM
Associate
Dept. Psychiatry, UMass. Medical
    School Associate
Moose Factory, ON

Colin Hodgen, MA, LADC-S, CPGC-S,
NCGC-II
Clinical Director
RENEGADE Counseling
Reno, NV

Robert M. Hooper, PhD, LGSW
Director of Recovery Services
Eastern Shore Psychological Services
Salisbury, MD

Elizabeth F. Howell, MD, FASAM
Associate Professor of Psychiatry (Clinical)
University of Utah Neuropsychiatric
    Institute
Salt Lake City, UT

Brian Hurley, MD, MBA
Fellow in Addiction Psychiatry
New York University - Bellevue Hospital
    / NY Veteran's Administration
New York, NY

Mikala Iris, RN
Portland, OR

Edward Lawrence James, III, MSW,
ACSW, LMSW
RSC Clinical Trainer
Magellan Health Services
Phoenix, AZ

Shivkumar Jha, MD
Richardson, TX

Carleen Jimenez, MA, CMHC, ASUDC
Mental Health Contract Compliance
    Specialist
Salt Lake County Behavioral Health
    Services
Salt Lake City, UT

Kristen A. Jiorle, MBA
Associate Director of Treatment and
    Recovery Services
Maine Department of Health and
    Human Services, Office of Substance
    Abuse and Mental Health Services
Augusta, ME

Lori D. Karan, MD, FACP, FASAM
Medical Director, Department of Public
    Safety, Hawaii
Professor of Psychiatry, John A. Burns
    School of Medicine, Hawaii
Associate Clinical Professor of Medi-
    cine, University of California, San
    Francisco
Publications Chair and Treasurer, Amer-
    ican Society of Addiction Medicine
Honolulu, HI

Richard A. Kates, MA, CADC
Substance Abuse Evaluator
State of New Jersey Judiciary TASC
Cape May, NJ

Murray B. Kelly, PhD Cand.
Director
Patient Support International
Woodlawn, ON

Michelle R. Kilgore, MA, CADC
Adolescent Substance Abuse Statewide
    Youth Coordinator
Kentucky Department for Behavioral
    Health, Intellectual and Develop-
    mental Disabilities
Frankfort, KY

John D. King, BA, MDiv
Lead Trainer
Personal Performance
Mary Esther, FL

Jack L. Kline, MS, LPC, LPCS, LCAS,
CCS
Executive Director
Four Circles Recovery Center
Horse Shoe, NC

Suzanne M. Kossman, LCSW, LCADC
Substance Abuse Evaluator
State of New Jersey Judiciary TASC
Toms River, NJ

Margaret Kotz, DO, FASAM
Professor of Psychiatry and
    Anesthesiology
Case Western Reserve University School
    of Medicine
Director, Addiction Recovery Services
Case Medical Center
University Hospitals of Cleveland
Cleveland, OH

Dean D. Krahn, MD, MS
Professor (CHS), Psychiatry, University
    of Wisconsin School of Medicine and
    Public Health
Director, Addiction Psychiatry
    Fellowship
Chief, Mental Health Service Line,
    VA-Madison
Madison, WI

Ashok B. Krishnamurthy, MD, CM,
CFFP
Consultant Physician and Co-Director
AAPRICOT
Toronto, ON

Alejandro Dario Kudisch, MD, DFAPA
CEO
Recovery Medical Group, PA
McAllen, TX

Heidi E. Kunzli, MS, LADC
Owner/Executive Director
Privé-Swiss
Essex, CT

Field Reviewers

Martha Kurgans, LCSW
Program Specialist/Women's Services Coordinator
Department of Behavioral Health and Developmental Services
Richmond, VA

Roland C. Lamb, BA, MA
Director, Office of Addiction Services
Department of Behavioral Health Intellectual disAbility Services
Philadelphia, PA

Richard D. Lane, BArts (Hons), BComm (Hons)
Executive Assistant to the Assistant Deputy Minister
Retired Federal Civil Servant
Kanata, ON

Rasha Lawrence, MD
Medical Director
The Watershed Treatment Program
Delray Beach, FL

Kenneth Lawrence, CADC, CSW
Substance Abuse Evaluator
State of New Jersey Judiciary TASC
Newark, NJ

Frankie D. Lemus, MA, LMFT
Senior Vice President
The Change Companies®
Carson City, NV

Benjamin A. Levenson
CEO
Origins Recovery Centers
South Padre Island, TX

Petros Levounis, MD, MA, FASAM
Chair, Department of Psychiatry, Rutgers New Jersey Medical School
Chief of Service, Department of Psychiatry, University Hospital
Newark, NJ

Ryan Ley, MD, MBA, MS
Chief of Staff
West Hills Hospital
Reno, NV

Joseph G. Liberto, MD
Associate Chief of Staff for Education and Academic Affairs
VA Maryland Health Care System
Associate Professor
Department of Psychiatry
University of Maryland School of Medicine
Baltimore, MD

Mark R. Loes, MBA, CDP
Director of Quality Assurance
Sundown M Ranch
Yakima, WA

Kevin Lowe, PhD
Vice President of Training
The Change Companies®
Carson City, NV

Robert Lubran, MS, MPA
Director, Division of Pharmacologic Therapies
SAMHSA
Rockville, MD

Jennifer A. Luyster, MA, LCADC, CCS, DRCC
Freehold, NJ

Bob Lynn, EdD
Clinical Consultant
Origins Recovery Centers, C4 Recovery Solutions, Counseling Group and Family Institute, Navajo Nation - Project K'e
Bostic, NC

Nayyera B. Malik, MD, MSC
New York, NY

Elisabeth Malone Bergeron, LPC, ICAADC, ICCDP-D
Executive Director
Chemical Addictions Program, Inc.
Montgomery, AL

Todd Mandell, MD
Chief Medical Officer
Community Substance Abuse Centers, Inc.
Westfield, MA

Darrin R. Mangiacarne, DO
Medical Director
Virginia Premier Health Plan, Inc.
Roanoke, VA

Tami Mark, PhD
Vice President
Truven Health Analytics
Bethesda, MD

J. Paul Martin, MD, FABFM, FABAM, FASAM
Chief Medical Officer
Crescent Health Solutions
Asheville, NC

Jennifer M. McConniel, CCDCII
South Dakota Methamphetamine Corrections Director
Keystone Treatment Center
Sioux Falls , SD

Denise W.L. McGaughey, BA, CDP
Program Supervisor
Kitsap Adolescent Recovery Services/ Kitsap County Juvenile Department
Port Orchard, WA

Patrick M. McGinn, MS, MA
Director of Clinical Operations
Harbor Hall, Inc
Petoskey, MI

John A. McGuffey, LPC, LMFT
Senior Supervisor, Behavioral Health Utilization Management
Health Care Service Corporation
Richardson, TX

Stephen S. McLaughlin, MS, LADC
Treatment Team Supervisor, Health Program Specialist II
State of Nevada Substance Abuse Prevention and Treatment Agency
Las Vegas, NV

Shannon Miller, MD, FASAM, DFAPA, CTTS
Program Director, Addiction Medicine Research Fellowship; Medical Director, Dual Diagnosis
VA Medical Center
Co-Program Director, Addiction Psychiatry Fellowship
Professor of Clinical Psychiatry, Affiliated
Department of Psychiatry & Behavioral Neuroscience
University of Cincinnati College of Medicine
Cincinnati, OH

Karen Miotto, MD
Director, Addiction Medicine Service
UCLA
Los Angeles, CA

Pamela M. Mizzi, MS, CASAC, LMHC
Director, Prevention Resource Center
Prevention Resource Center @ South Oaks Hospital
Amityville, NY

Field Reviewers

Ivan Montoya, MD, MPH
Deputy Director
Division of Pharmacotherapies and
    Medical Consequences of Drug
    Abuse
NIDA at NIH
Bethesda, MD

Maria L. Morris-Groves, MSEd
Project Director NY-SAINT/Coordinator
    of Adolescent, Women and Chil-
    dren's Services
NYS Office of Alcoholism and Substance
    Abuse Services
Albany, NY

Patrice M. Muchowski, ScD, CADAC
Vice President, Clinical Services
AdCare Hospital of Worcester, Inc.
Worcester, MA

Tim Naugher
Executive Director
The Bridge Addiction Treatment Centers
Gadsden, AL

Michael Newberry, MD
Director of Addiction Medicine
Boise VA Medical Center
Boise, ID

David M. Ockert, PhD
Executive Director
Parallax Center, Inc.
Adjunct Senior Research Scientist
Columbia University School of Social
    Work
New York, NY

Miguel Oquendo, MA, LCADC
Substance Abuse Evaluator
State of New Jersey Judiciary TASC
Freehold, NJ

Emilio A. Orozco, NP
Nurse Practitioner/Program Manager
City and County of San Francisco, Dept
    of Public Health, CBHS, Behavioral
    Health Access Center, Treatment
    Access Program
San Francisco, CA

Theodore Parran, MD, FACP
Professor and Chair in Medical
    Education
CWRU School of Medicine
Cleveland, OH

**Ana Patricia Ackermann-Blanco, MA,
    LCADC, CSW**
Vice President of Clinical Services
CURA, Inc.
Newark, NJ

**Laura L. Post, MD, FABPN, FAB-
    PN-Addiction Psychiatry, PAB-
    PN-Forensic Psychiatry, PhD, JD,
    CCHP-A, CCSOTS**
Medical Director
Marianas Psychiatric Services
Tamuning, GU

Marc N. Potenza, MD, PhD
Professor of Psychiatry, Child Study and
    Neurobiology
Yale School of Medicine
New Haven, CT

Judith Prochaska, PhD, MPH
Associate Professor of Medicine
Stanford University
Stanford, CA

**Denise F. Quirk, MA, MFT, LCADC,
    BACC-NCGC-II, CPGC-S**
CEO and Clinical Director
Reno Problem Gambling Center
Reno, NV

Jared Ray, BA, LADC, SAP
Director of Substance Abuse
First Step Recovery Inc.
Lincoln, NE

**Donna L. Richardson, LCSW, LCADC,
    CTTS**
Tobacco Dependence Program
Rutgers, The State University of New
    Jersey
New Brunswick, NJ

Linda Richter, PhD
Associate Director, Division of Policy
    Research and Analysis
CASAColumbia
New York, NY

Rhonda J. Robinson Beale, MD
Chief Medical Officer, External Affairs
Optum Behavioral Solutions
Glendale, CA

**Peter Rogers, MD, MPH, FAAP,
    FASAM**
Clinical Professor of Pediatrics
Ohio State University
Westerville, OH

**Brenda Rohren, MA, MFS, LIMHP,
    LADC, MAC**
President
Behavioral Health Resources, LLC
Lincoln, NE

**A. Kenison Roy, III, MD, FASAM,
    DFAPA**
Medical Director
Addiction Recovery Resources
Metairie, LA

Edwin A. Salsitz, MD, FASAM
Medical Director Out-Patient Opioid
    Therapy
Beth Israel Medical Center
New York, NY

Mario F. San Bartolome, MD, MBA
President & CEO
Ventana Health & Medical Center
Pismo Beach, CA

William Santoro, MD
Addictionist
The Reading Hospital Medical Group
Laureldale, PA

Christine K. Scalise, LPC, LCADC
Manager & Women's Services
    Coordinator
NJ Division of Mental Health and Addic-
    tion Services
Trenton, NJ

Philip J. Scherer
Administrative Director
Illinois Institute for Addiction Recovery
    - Proctor Hospital
Peoria, IL

**Jeffrey H. Schiffman, MD, Board Cer-
    tified in General Psychiatry, ASAM
    certified**
Addiction Psychiatrist
William S. Middleton VA Hospital
Madison, WI

Mark Schwartz, MD FAAFP, FASAM
Medical Director
Inpatient Detox Services
Princeton House Behavioral Health
Princeton, NJ

Field Reviewers

Starleen Scott Robbins, MSW, LCSW
State Women's Services Coordinator/
Mental Health Program Manager
NC Division of Mental Health, Developmental Disabilities and Substance Abuse Services
Raleigh, NC

Randy M. Seewald, MBBS
Medical Director MMTP
Beth Israel Medical Center
New York, NY

Peter Selby, MBBS, CCFP, FCFP, FASAM
Chief, Addictions
Centre for Addiction and Mental Health/
University of Toronto
Toronto, ON

Blaine Shaffer, MD, DLFAPA
Chief Clinical Officer
Nebraska Department of Health and Human Services, Division of Behavioral Health
Lincoln, NE

Howard Shaffer, PhD
Director, Division on Addiction, Cambridge Health Alliance
Teaching Affiliate of Harvard Medical School
Cambridge, MA

Rosemary H. Shannon, MEd
Clinical Services Administrator
New Hampshire Bureau of Drug and Alcohol Services
Concord, NH

Richard R. Silbert, MD
Senior Medical Director
Community Care Behavioral Healthcare Organization
Moosic, PA

Samuel Silverman, MD, FAPA
Medical Director Addiction Services
Rushford Center
West Hartford, CT

Richard G. Soper, MD, JD, MS, FASAM
Chief Medical Officer
Center for Behavioral Wellness
Nashville, TN

Jacquelyn Starer, MD, FACOG, FASAM
Director of Women's Addiction Services
CleanSlate Centers
Northampton, MA

George E. Stavros, MD
CEO
Community Medical Services LLC
Vice President, AATOD
Phoenix, AZ

Michael Steinberg, MD, MPH
Associate Professor
Rutgers – Robert Wood Johnson Medical School
New Brunswick, NJ

Katrina D. Stokes, MA, LPC, ICAADC, PLC
Behavioral Health Services
Harper Woods, MI

Trusandra E. Taylor, MD, FASAM, MPH
Act2 - Medical Director
JEVS Human Services
Philadelphia, PA

Blaise E. Tomczak, BS, CCDC III
Program Coordinator
Our Home, Inc. Rediscovery
Huron, SD

David R. Turpin, MA, LCAS, CCS
President/CEO
Clinical Services of North Carolina, Inc
Raleigh, NC

Steve K. Valle, ScD, MBA, LADC I, CADAC
President & CEO
AdCare Criminal Justice Services, Inc.
Worcester, MA

James W. Van Hook, MD
Professor and Director- Division of Maternal Fetal Medicine
Dept. OB-GYN., University of Cincinnati College of Medicine
Cincinnati, OH

Frank J. Vocci, PhD
President
Friends Research Institute
Baltimore, MD

Alan A. Wartenberg, MD, FACP, FASAM
President
Massachusetts Chapter, ASAM
Attleboro, MA

Donald F. Weinbaum, MBA, LCADC, CCJP
Executive Director
The Council on Compulsive Gambling of New Jersey, Inc.
Hamilton, NJ

Katie M. Wells, MPA, LAC
Manager, Adolescent Substance Use Disorder Programs
Colorado Department of Human Services, Division of Behavioral Health
Denver, CO

Christopher Welsh, MD
Associate Professor
University of Maryland School of Medicine
Baltimore, MD

Howard Wetsman, MD, FASAM
Chief Medical Officer
Townsend
New Orleans, LA

Norman Wetterau, MD, FAAFP, FASAM
Physician
Tricounty Family Medicine
Dansville, NY

Jill M. Williams, MD
Professor of Psychiatry
Robert Wood Johnson Medical School
New Brunswick, NJ

Andrea Winston, MS, LPC
Clinical Director
New Horizons Community Service Board
Columbus, GA